GW00468881

Blackstone's

Police Operational Handbook

Blackstone's
Police
Operational
Handbook

Second Edition

Police National Legal Database

Editor: Ian Bridges

Consultant Editor: Fraser Sampson

OXFORD
UNIVERSITY PRESS

OXFORD

UNIVERSITY PRESS

Great Clarendon Street, Oxford OX2 6DP

Oxford University Press is a department of the University of Oxford.
It furthers the University's objective of excellence in research, scholarship,
and education by publishing worldwide in

Oxford New York

Auckland Cape Town Dar es Salaam Hong Kong Karachi
Kuala Lumpur Madrid Melbourne Mexico City Nairobi
New Delhi Shanghai Taipei Toronto

With offices in

Argentina Austria Brazil Chile Czech Republic France Greece
Guatemala Hungary Italy Japan Poland Portugal Singapore
South Korea Switzerland Thailand Turkey Ukraine Vietnam

Oxford is a registered trademark of Oxford University Press
in the UK and in certain other countries

Published in the United States
by Oxford University Press Inc., New York

© West Yorkshire Police Authority 2007

The moral rights of the authors have been asserted

Database right Oxford University Press (maker)

Crown copyright material is reproduced under Class Licence
Number C01P0000148 with the permission of OPSI
and the Queen's Printer for Scotland

First published 2006
Second edition published 2007

British Library Cataloguing in Publication Data

Data available

Library of Congress Cataloging in Publication Data

Blackstone's police operational handbook : police national legal
database / editor, Ian Bridges ; consultant editor, Fraser Sampson.—
2nd ed.
    p. cm.
  Includes index.
  ISBN 978-0-19-922928-4 (flexicover: alk. paper)
  1. Criminal law—England. 2. Police—England—Handbooks,
manuals, etc. I. Bridges, Ian. II. Sampson, Fraser.
    KD7869.3.B55 2007
    344.4205′23—dc22

                                                    2007030684

Typeset by Laserwords Private Limited, Chennai, India
Printed and bound in Italy
on acid-free paper by
Rotolito Lombarda SpA

ISBN 978-0-19-922928-4

10 9 8 7 6 5 4 3 2 1

Preface

This is the second edition of the *Blackstone's Police Operational Handbook*, which has been specifically designed to meet the needs of the operational police officer, community support officer, special constable, or other practitioner who has to interpret and apply the criminal law within our community.

Due to the phenomenal success of the first edition and the positive comments that we have received it is apparent that the format and contents of the handbook are meeting the needs of our readers and proving to be an invaluable addition to the police officer's 'tool kit'.

Formulated and written by staff from the Police National Legal Database (PNLD) <http://www.pnld.co.uk>, the book covers a wide range of offences and clearly explains and interprets the relevant legislation. It follows the style of the database by providing the wording of the offences, points to prove, meanings, explanatory notes, relevant cases, and practical considerations. In order to assist the officer further, the law/guidance notes are all presented in a 'bullet point', easy-to-understand format; thus at a glance, a quick and informed decision can be made in a host of everyday policing situations.

Although every effort has been made to include as many 'commonly dealt with offences' as possible, the size of the handbook dictates how many offences can be included. However, the number and variety of offences given within the areas of crime, assaults, drugs, sexual offences, public disorder, firearms, road traffic, licensing, and PACE powers and procedures; together with the guidance chapters and useful appendices, should be more than sufficient to cover most eventualities.

The handbook is fully up to date as of 1 June 2007 and includes all recent legislative developments and changes in the law, such as the Fraud Act 2006, Animal Welfare Act 2006, Emergency Workers (Obstruction) Act 2006, Violent Crime Reduction Act 2006, Road Safety Act 2006, Police and Justice Act 2006 and updates to PACE Codes of Practice.

As a result of the Serious Organized Crime and Police Act 2005, officers are now expected to know what offences are indictable or either way—the mode of trial icons (within each offence) provided in the book give this important information.

Whilst every care has been taken to ensure that the contents of this handbook are accurate, neither the publisher nor the authors can accept any responsibility for any action taken, or not taken, on the basis of the information contained within this handbook.

Please email <police.uk@oup.com> with any comments or queries.

Ian Bridges
Editor
April 2007

Acknowledgements

The Police National Legal Database (PNLD) (www.pnld.co.uk), is an ACPO managed (not-for-profit) organization, which is subscribed to and well known by all police forces in England and Wales, the Crown Prosecution Service, and other recognized organizations from within the criminal justice system.

The handbook, which is a natural development from our premier electronic database, would not have been created without the foresight and determination of Heather Croft (Business Director), the hard work of Ian Bridges (Legal Adviser), and the support and guidance from staff at the Oxford University Press and Fraser Sampson (Consultant Editor).

Thanks are also extended to the PNLD legal advisers and writers who have contributed to the production of the first edition of the *Blackstone's Police Operational Handbook*.

Contents—Summary

Contents—Detailed

Contents—Detailed

Contents—Detailed

Contents—Detailed

Contents—Detailed

Table of Cases

Table of Cases

Table of Cases

Table of Cases

Table of Cases

European Court of Human Rights

Table of Statutes

Table of Statutes

Table of Statutes

Table of Statutes

Table of Statutes

Table of Statutes

Table of Statutes

Table of Statutes

Home Office Circulars

Table of Conventions

Icons List

SSS   **Stop, search, and seize powers** under the Police and Criminal Evidence Act 1984, s 1 or stop, search, and seize powers under a statutory authority given within that chapter.

E&S   **Entry and search powers** under the Police and Criminal Evidence Act 1984, ss 17, 18, and 32.

PND   **Penalty Notices for Disorder offences** under the Criminal Justice and Police Act 2001, s 1.

TFPN   **Traffic Fixed Penalty Notices** under the Road Traffic Offenders Act 1988.

RRA   **Racially or Religiously Aggravated offences** under the Crime and Disorder Act 1998 ss 28–32.

CHAR   **Offences where evidence of bad character can be introduced** under the Criminal Justice Act 2003, s 103.

TRIG   **Trigger offences**—when police can test (request to take samples) for presence of Class A drugs, under the Criminal Justice and Court Services Act 2000, Sch 6

CSO   **Instances/offences when CSO can use their powers** (if Chief Constable of the force concerned has designated the power(s) in question to CSO), under the Police Reform Act 2002.

Mode of trial
Indictable, either way, or summary.

Penalty
Sentence (maximum) allowed by law.

Prosecution time limit
The time limit allowed for submission of the file (laying of the information).

Chapter 1

Introduction

1.1 **Human Rights**

Since its introduction the Human Rights Act 1998 has greatly affected not just operational policing issues, but legislation and court decisions as well.

The Human Rights Act 1998 guarantees and encompasses the fundamental rights and freedoms contained in the European Convention. The following summarized sections relate to the police and criminal justice system:

Section 2

Requires a court to take account of the opinions and decisions of the European Court of Human Rights; the Commission and Committee of Ministers when determining a question relating to a **Convention right**.

Section 3

Demands that all United Kingdom legislation must be construed and given effect in such a way as to be compatible with Convention rights.

Section 4

Permits the High Court or Court of Appeal to make a declaration of non-compatibility on any question of United Kingdom law.

Section 6

Makes it unlawful for a **public authority** to act in a way incompatible with a Convention right. This includes a failure to act.

Section 7

Provides for an aggrieved party to take proceedings where a public authority has breached (or proposes to breach) s 6, but only if that person is (or would be) a victim of the unlawful act.

Section 8

Empowers a court to grant such remedy or **relief** within its powers as it considers just and appropriate.

Section 11

Preserves any other right or freedom enjoyed under United Kingdom law.

Meanings

Convention Right

Means the following rights and freedoms given in **Schedule 1**:

- Articles 2 to 12 and 14 of the **Convention**;
- Articles 1 to 3 of the First Protocol;
- Article 1 of the Thirteenth Protocol.

Public authority

This includes:

- a court or tribunal;
- any person (eg a police officer) certain of whose functions are functions of a public nature.

Relief

Includes an award of damages or payment of compensation which can be given through the civil courts, such as the county court or the High Court.

Convention

Means the Convention for the Protection of Human Rights and Fundamental Freedoms, agreed by the Council of Europe at Rome on 4 November 1950 as it has effect for the time being in relation to the United Kingdom

Schedule 1—Articles

Article 2—Right to life

This right shall be protected by law. No one shall be deprived of life intentionally.

Deprivation of life shall not be regarded as being in contravention of this Article if force is used, being no more than absolutely necessary, in order to:

- defend from unlawful violence;
- effect a lawful arrest;
- prevent the escape of a person lawfully detained;
- quell a riot or insurrection.

Article 3—Prohibition of torture

No one shall be subjected to torture or to inhuman or degrading treatment or punishment.

Article 4—Prohibition of slavery and forced labour

No one shall be held in slavery or servitude or be required to perform forced or compulsory labour.

Article 5—Right to liberty and security

No one shall be deprived of these rights save in the following cases and in accordance with a procedure prescribed by law:

- lawful detention (after conviction) by a competent court;
- lawful arrest or detention for failing to comply with the lawful order of a court or in order to secure the fulfilment of any obligation prescribed by law;

- lawful arrest or detention for the purpose of bringing the person before the competent legal authority on reasonable suspicion of having committed an offence or when it is reasonably considered necessary to prevent his committing an offence or fleeing after having done so;
- detention of a minor by lawful order for the purpose of educational supervision or his lawful detention for the purpose of bringing him before the competent legal authority;
- lawful detention for the prevention of the spreading of infectious diseases, of persons of unsound mind, alcoholics or drug addicts, or vagrants;
- lawful arrest or detention to prevent unauthorized entry into the country or with a view to deportation or extradition.

This Article also deals with:
- promptly being informed as to the reason for arrest/charge;
- entitlement to trial within a reasonable time or release pending trial;
- entitlement to take proceedings for unlawful detention and the right to compensation in these instances.

Article 6—Right to a fair trial

Everyone is entitled to a fair and public hearing within a reasonable time by an independent and impartial tribunal established by law. Protection shall be given against publicity (for all or part of the trial) in the interests of: morals, public order, national security, juveniles, the private lives of the parties, or if it would prejudice the interests of justice.

Furthermore, everyone charged with a criminal offence shall:
- be presumed innocent until proved guilty according to law;
- be informed promptly, in a language which they understand, of the detail, nature, and cause of the accusation against them;
- have adequate time and facilities for the preparation of their defence;
- be allowed to defend themselves in person or through legal assistance of their choosing or be provided with free legal assistance (if insufficient funds) when the interests of justice so require;
- be allowed to produce/examine witnesses for/against him;
- have the free assistance of an interpreter if he cannot understand or speak the language used in court.

Article 7—No punishment without law

No one shall be found guilty of a criminal offence arising out of actions which at the time were not criminal, neither shall a heavier penalty be imposed.

Article 8—Right to respect private/family life

Everyone has the right to respect for their private and family life, home, and correspondence, except where a public authority acts in accordance with the law **and** it is necessary in a democratic society in the interests of national security, public safety or the economic well-being of the country, for the prevention of disorder or crime, for the protection of health or morals, or for the protection of the rights and freedoms of others.

1.1 Human Rights

Article 9—Freedom of thought, conscience, and religion

Everyone has this right, including the freedom to change their religion or belief. These rights can be limited in certain circumstances.

Article 10—Freedom of expression

Everyone has the right to hold opinions and express their views either on their own or in a group without interference by a public authority.

These rights can only be restricted in specified circumstances.

Article 11—Freedom of assembly and association

Everyone has the right to assemble with other people in a peaceful way, to associate with other people, including the right to form and join trade unions for the protection of their interests.

These rights may be restricted, but only in specified circumstances.

Article 12—Right to marry

Men and women of marriageable age have the right to marry and to found a family, according to the national laws governing the exercise of this right.

Article 14—Prohibition of discrimination

The enjoyment of the rights and freedoms set forth in this Convention shall be secured without discrimination on any ground such as sex, race, colour, language, religion, political or other opinion, national or social origin, association with a national minority, property, birth, or other status.

1st Protocol—Article 1 Protection of property, entitled to peaceful enjoyment of possessions

1st Protocol—Article 2 Right to education

1st Protocol—Article 3 Right to free elections

13th Protocol—Article 1 relates to abolition of the death penalty

Explanatory notes

- Examples of public authorities include: central and local government, the police, immigration officers, prisons, courts and tribunals, and the core activities of private utilities companies that were once publicly owned.
- Section 7(8) stipulates that nothing in the Act creates a criminal offence.
- A criminal trial judge does not have the power to award damages for an alleged breach of a Convention right.
- Infringement of an individual's human rights will be open to examination in every criminal trial, civil or care proceedings, and tribunals.

Practical considerations

- Police officers should take particular note of s 6, which makes it unlawful for them to act in a way which is incompatible with a Convention right. In order to ensure compliance with this requirement, officers should make themselves familiar with these 'rights' which have been incorporated into this legislation.

- The proportionality and necessity test asks 'were the measures taken **necessary** in a democratic society and in **proportion** to the ultimate objective?' This test should always be borne in mind by a police officer when dealing with an incident, members of the public, or an individual (eg is the force using proportionate and necessary to prevent disorder, protect life/property, or deal with offenders).
- This test is reflected in the new powers of arrest (see **12.2**)—unless an officer can show that arrest was **necessary** (eg there was no alternative) then the arrest power cannot be used.
- Before using their powers a police officer should consider this test in their decision making process and ask themselves:
  - ✦ What is the objective to be achieved?
  - ✦ Is it urgent or (if desirable) could it be delayed?
  - ✦ If action is needed now what are the alternative means of dealing with this incident/individual?
  - ✦ Is the proposed action proportionate to the intended aim and the means to be used?
  - ✦ Can the least intrusive means be deployed?
  - ✦ If not, does a lawful power exist?
- The use of force must always be justified and reasonable otherwise an assault will be committed and any action taken could be rendered unlawful (see **1.2.1**).
- Where excessive force is used there is the possibility of a breach of Art 3 (inhuman or degrading treatment).
- If force is used disproportionately, this may amount to a breach of Art 8, as this Article guarantees not just the right to privacy, but also the right to physical integrity—the right not to be hurt in an arbitrary or unjustifiable way.
- There must be some objective justification for the decision or action taken.
- An important point, often overlooked, is the need to strike a proper balance between the interests and rights of the community at large as well as considering the rights of the individual.
- Lawful interference with an individual's human rights, especially depriving them of these rights must be necessary and proportionate to the aim required to be achieved (eg lawful arrest/detention of a suspect meets the legitimate aim for the prevention and detection of crime).
- Always consider whether the aim can be met with minimal impact on the rights of the suspect and any other person likely to be affected.
- Article 15 allows governments to 'derogate' from the Convention in time of war or other public emergency threatening the life of the nation.

Links to alternative subjects and offences

1.2 Use of Force Resolution

If a police officer uses force, this must be justified and reasonable and be based on a lawful authority—otherwise it will be an assault and would therefore become an unlawful act.

1.2.1 Lawful authorities for using force

Statute, case law, and human rights set out the circumstances in which the use of force will be lawful, but each case will be decided upon its own peculiar facts.

Statute

Criminal Law Act 1967

The starting point for the use of force in relation to crime applies to any person:

A person may use such force as is **reasonable** in the circumstances in the prevention of **crime**, or in effecting or assisting in the lawful arrest of offenders or suspected offenders or of persons unlawfully at large.

Criminal Law Act 1967, s 3(1)

Meanings

Crime

This refers to crimes committed against domestic law or statute, it does not cover crimes recognised as international law and not given effect in domestic law either by statute or judicial decision (*R v Jones; R v Milling; R v Olditch; R v Pritchard; R v Richards; Ayliffe & others v DPP; Swain v DPP* [2006] UKHL 16).

Reasonable

Whether the force used in: self defence, preventing crime, or in making an arrest is reasonable or excessive will be determined by the court; taking into account all the circumstances. It is important to consider the words of Lord Morris in *Palmer v R* [1971] AC 814, HL which emphasize the difficulties often facing someone confronted by an intruder or defending himself/herself against attack:

'*If there has been an attack so that defence is reasonably necessary, it will be recognised that a person defending himself cannot weigh to a nicety the exact measure of his defensive action. If the jury thought that in a moment of unexpected anguish a person attacked had only done what he honestly and instinctively thought necessary, that would be the most potent evidence that only reasonable defensive action had been taken.*'

> **Police and Criminal Evidence Act 1984**
>
> The next statutory authority for the use of force concerns that of a police officer:
>
> Where any provision of this Act—
> (a) confers a power on a constable; and
> (b) does not provide that the power may only be exercised with the consent of some person, other than a police officer, the officer may use **reasonable** force, if necessary, in the exercise of the power.
>
> Police and Criminal Evidence Act 1984, s 117

Self-defence under Common Law may also be a consideration (see **2.1.2**).

Human rights

- In addition, under the provisions of the European Convention on Human Rights (see **1.1**), a further dimension in respect of the necessity and proportionality must be considered alongside the common law or statutory powers.
- Apart from using no more force than is absolutely necessary, the further consideration of proportionality will bring other factors into the equation, such as whether the force used is:
  - ♦ proportionate to the wrong that it seeks to avoid or the harm it seeks to prevent;
  - ♦ the least intrusive or damaging option available at the time.
- Striking a fair balance between the rights of the individual and the interests, rights of the community at large must be carefully considered.
- Any limited breaching of an individual's human rights must be both necessary and proportionate to the legitimate aim to be pursued (eg the lawful arrest or detention of that person is to pursue the legitimate aim of the prevention and detection of crime). Note, however, that certain Articles such as Art 3 cannot be lawfully breached.
- Therefore, any use of powers to cause inhuman or degrading treatment may amount to a breach—and even words alone can constitute such treatment.
- If force is not used proportionately, then this may amount to a breach of various Articles of the European Convention on Human Rights (see **1.1** for details):
  - ♦ Article 2: Use of lethal force, unless the level of force used was strictly proportionate to the lawful aim pursued;
  - ♦ Article 3: If excessive force is used—inhuman or degrading treatment;
  - ♦ Article 8: Guarantees not only the right to privacy/family life, but also the right not to be hurt in an arbitrary or unjustifiable way.

1.2.2 **Evidential considerations**

Police officers should choose the most reasonable, proportionate option available to them after taking the person's behaviour, circumstances and other factors into account.

Whenever force has been used by an officer at an incident this must be justified. Here are some points to consider when preparing your evidence:

Upon arrival

- In uniform or plain clothes?
- Officers at scene/en route?
- Type of vehicle used?
- Observations and perceptions?
- Type of incident?

Upon approach

- Observations and perceptions now?
- Any communications made?
- *Threat assessment* (see **1.2.3**).
- Potential to escalate?

Attitude of individual(s)/group

- Reaction to police instructions?
- Any threats made?

Response of police

- Means used (or attempted) to control situation?
  - ◆ presence, stance taken;
  - ◆ communication skills;
  - ◆ physical control skills:
    - ▪ offensive or defensive.
- Resulting injuries (if any)—all parties?

If the evidence is prepared thoroughly, applying this format, then apart from giving evidence at court more professionally, complaints and civil litigation against the force or individual officers should also be reduced.

1.2.3 **Resolution tactics**

Gathering information

Obtain as much information and intelligence as possible, this may come from:

- what an officer:
  - ◆ sees;
  - ◆ hears;
  - ◆ is aware of;
  - ◆ feels;
  - ◆ is told by a third person;

1.2.3 Resolution Tactics

- local or force systems;
- communications staff;
- experience from previous encounters with suspect.

A police officer's feelings are important and relevant, it is quite acceptable to feel frightened and have reservations. If this is admitted it may help the court or other person(s) to understand why the officer(s) reacted as they did.

Threat assessment

After gathering sufficient information/intelligence, the officer will be able to make a more affective assessment of the threat they face.

These threats to the officer(s) are most likely to emanate from the behaviour of the person(s) they are dealing with. Some issues to consider are:

Person(s) reactions

- Compliant.
- Threats—verbal or by body language.
- Resistant being either:
  - ✦ passive;
  - ✦ reactive;
  - ✦ aggressive;
  - ✦ assaults;
  - ✦ weapons used.

Factors to consider

Person(s)

- Number of person(s) involved.
- Sex, age, size.
- Potential strength and skill threat.
- Injuries (if any)/physical state.
- Whether consumed alcohol or taken drugs.
- Mental state—aggression or making threats.
- Their perception, reactions to situation.

Environmental

- Objects/weapons—available or possessed.
- Vehicles at scene.
- Locus features:
  - ✦ shelters;
  - ✦ concealed/hidden areas;
  - ✦ alleys/side roads;
  - ✦ properties—licensed premises, schools, private;
  - ✦ potential to escalate with other persons in the area;
  - ✦ other dangers not mentioned.

Police officer(s)

- Number of officers at scene.
- Number of officers available to assist—distance away/warned.
- Sex, age, size.
- Strength and skill level.
- Physical state—exhaustion level or injured.

- Experience and specialist knowledge.
- Morale, confidence to deal with incident.
- Overall perception to threats, danger, situation.

Once all these factors have been established the threat assessment can be categorized. In order to avoid complacency or complications by grading the incident, it is best to rate if as being either a high or unknown risk.

Use of force options

It is impossible to give all the different combination of options available to deal with conflict. However, each of the techniques described represents a tactical option. You should always consider the consequences of your actions, including the risk of causing long term and/or significant injury. An option that carries a high risk of serious injury to the person(s), is less likely to be justified where the threat posed carries a limited risk to others.

The tactical option chosen must always be proportionate to the threat faced in all the circumstances.

Response options available

- Mere presence and/or containment.
- Use of communication skills.
- Primary control—empty hand tactics, pressure points, use of handcuffs and baton.
- Secondary control—incapacitants.
- Defensive and offensive—escalation in use of unarmed skills and restraints.
- Deadly force—likely to cause serious injury or even death.

Having considered all the above aspects, you are more likely to make the right decision in relation to the action you take.

These tactics can also be applied to a non-conflict policing situation in order to avoid danger or conflict.

The need to constantly reassess the situation, because if anything changes, any original intended action may no longer be appropriate.

Links to alternative subjects and offences

1.3 **Managing Crime Scenes**

These guidelines have been adopted as a result of accepted 'best practice' although police officers must always be familiar with force policy and procedures and ensure that these are complied with.

Anybody asked to protect/guard a crime scene must ensure that they are fully briefed about the circumstances of the offence being investigated.

A person chosen to perform this duty must never underestimate the responsibility of this role and its importance to the enquiry, and be aware that at a future date they may be called upon to give evidence at court.

The primary role (and responsibility) of managing a crime scene is to:
- protect the scene from contamination by others; and
- preserve the integrity of everything which could be used as evidence.

Protecting the crime scene

The extent of the scene:
- needs to be established;
- the perimeter clearly marked with tape—denoting that it is a crime scene (remembering that is always easier to reduce the size than expand it later);
- the area needs to be secure and effectively cordoned off;
- if the scene is insecure and problems arise in trying to maintain a sterile scene, then assistance should be provided from the enquiry team.

Explanatory notes

Cordon off a crime scene

- When investigating crime, the police do not have a right to restrict movement on private land. However, in the circumstances (wounding in a private shopping mall), the police were entitled to assume consent to cordon off a crime scene (*DPP v Morrison* [2003] EWHC 683, HC).
- Sections 34–36 of the Terrorism Act 2000 give the police a power to cordon off an area for a terrorist investigation—for example to carry out a meticulous search for evidence in the wake of a bomb blast.

Maintaining a scene log

An accurate log must be contemporaneously recorded providing:
- a chronological report of any matters of note;
- full details of all authorized people attending, including time/date entering or leaving the scene;
- details/description of any person taking an unusual interest in the area of the crime (together with any vehicle used);
- any suspicious activities in or around the scene should be brought to the attention of the enquiry team as soon as possible.

Managing the scene

A person performing this role must be briefed as to:
- preventing any unauthorized access;
- preventing access to people who are not wearing protective suits;
- updating the SIO or scene manager with any significant matters or developments;
- what can and cannot be said to people.

Dealing with the media

Person(s) protecting the scene of a crime must:
- be mindful of their appearance as they may be filmed or photographed by the media;
- avoid joking with colleagues, which although innocent, may cause offence;
- avoid being seen smoking or chewing gum;
- prevent journalists from breaching the cordon;
- avoid restricting journalists from taking pictures of the scene or talking to members of the public who may be present as long they remain outside the cordon (the editor will be responsible for determining which pictures are used and details included);
- not offer opinions or views to members of the press. Any enquiries should be directed to the press office.

Preserving the integrity of exhibits

Preservation of a crime scene is of paramount importance in order to ensure that evidence is recovered and its integrity maintained.

Consideration should always be given to:
- weather conditions;
- type of surface;
- visible evidence (eg fingerprints, blood, shoe marks, property);
- other matters (eg Have repairs been carried out? Will the forensic evidence be of any value?).

Any evidential prints/marks or objects, which are found outside, must be covered in order to protect them from the elements.

Make sure a contact telephone number for the victim is included with the details for the 'scenes of crime officer'.

Fingerprints

- Smooth, clean, and dry surfaces provide the best opportunity of finding and recovering fingerprints. Ensure such items/areas are preserved for examination by the 'scenes of crime officer'.
- Recover removable items found outside and place them against an internal wall to dry. Wet items should not be placed against radiators.
- Any pieces of paper, envelopes, or bin liners left by the offender(s) are often a good source of fingerprints.
- Fingerprints from scenes of crime can now be searched nationally on the National Automated Fingerprint Identification System (NAFIS).
- Details of any genuine suspects should be given to either the attending 'scenes of crime officer' or to the Fingerprint Bureau (eg suspect's name, date of birth, and CRO details, if known).

DNA

- DNA can be present in bloodstains and in saliva. Consequently police officers should be mindful that this can be present in discarded: chewing gum, drink cans or bottles, and cigarette ends.
- DNA can also be recovered from saliva, hair, and skin (dandruff) left in masks or balaclavas, or from the handles of tools. Also, semen or other body fluids in sexual offences.
- The national DNA Database is maintained by the Forensic Science Service which collates two profile types of DNA:
  - ◆ that left at the scene of the crime by the offender—'Scene Samples';
  - ◆ that of people arrested and charged or cautioned with a recordable offence—'Criminal Justice (CJ) Samples'.
- Ensure that a DNA CJ sample is obtained from all people who are arrested for a 'recordable offence'.

Shoes

- Shoe marks found at the scene should be preserved (they must show some pattern detail to be of any evidential value). In this regard consider shoes worn by all burglary suspects.
- Surfaces where footwear marks might be present, but not immediately obvious (eg windowsills, linoleum, work surfaces), the mark may be revealed by techniques used by 'scenes of crime officers'.
- Some forces maintain a computerized database of shoes marks and offenders' shoe impressions.

Glass

- Glass can rarely be of strong evidential value, but can be corroborative.
- Consider calling a 'scenes of crime officer' to serious crime scenes where a suspect is in custody, before glass is cleared away.
- Consider also combing a suspect's hair and retaining clothing and shoes for traces of glass as soon as they arrive in custody.

Other items

- Fibres, paint, tool, and glove mark evidence can also connect an individual to a scene.

Forensic procedure

- Evidential items should be placed in brown paper bags, sealed, labelled, and continuity maintained.
- Remember special packaging requirements apply to certain categories of exhibits (eg bladed weapons and fire accelerants) for which specific advice may be obtained from your 'scenes of crime officers'.
- Further details regarding preserving the integrity of evidence in relation to accelerants can be found in arson (see **4.5.2**).

Prisoner handling

- In appropriate cases clothing should be taken from detainees at the earliest opportunity.

- Beware of contamination. Prisoners should be treated as a crime scene and dealt with by officers who have not been to the scene of the offence.
- If more than one prisoner arrested, ensure they are transported in different vehicles.

Vehicle crime

- Stolen vehicles and vehicles used in crime invariably yield forensic evidence which may be linked to other crimes and provide a valuable source of intelligence.
- Depending on force procedure, where practicable, all stolen vehicles, or those used in crime, should be recovered to a suitable location where there is good lighting and the vehicle can be dried before examination.

Mobile phones

- If the mobile phone is switched on, record what is on the display.
- Do not push buttons other than to turn it off.
- Turn the mobile off.
- Seal in tamper-proof box, making sure buttons cannot be pressed.
- Submit to appropriate forensic supplier, with full details.
- Be aware that fingerprint powder can damage electronic equipment (seek advice).

Continuity

- Unfortunately, many cases are lost because police officers have failed to maintain evidential continuity of exhibits.
- You should be able to account for the exhibit's movements at every stage (point in time), between seizure and production in evidence.
- Ensure that this is maintained and reflected in the Criminal Justice Act witness statements, exhibit logs and labels.
- Major investigations will have a trained exhibits officer appointed.

Links to alternative subjects and offences

1.3 Managing Crime Scenes

1.4 **Identification Issues**

The area of law dealing with physical identification is quite involved and cannot be dealt with in sufficient detail in this book. Therefore, only a brief overview of the subject can be given and the details provided are only meant to be a rough guide.

PACE Code of Practice D

Part 3 of this code deals with identification by witnesses: making a record of first description and then detailing the various identification procedures where the suspect is known/not known.

Record of first description

- A record shall be made of the suspect's description as first given by a potential witness.
- This record of first description must:
  + be made and kept in a form which enables details of that description to be accurately produced from it, in a visible and legible form, which can be given to the suspect or the suspect's solicitor in accordance with this Code; and
  + unless otherwise specified, be made before the witness takes part in any identification procedures.
- A copy of the record shall where practicable, be given to the suspect or their solicitor before any identification procedures are carried out.

Identity of suspect not known

- In these cases, a witness may be taken to a particular area to see whether they can identify the person they saw.
- Although the number, age, sex, race, general description, and style of clothing of other people present at the location (and the way in which any identification is made) cannot be controlled, the formal procedure principles shall be followed as far as practicable.
- A witness must not be shown photographs, computerized or artist's composite likenesses or similar likenesses or pictures (including 'E-fit' images) if the identity of the suspect is known to the police and the suspect is available to take part in a video identification, an identification parade, or a group identification.

Identity of suspect known and available

If the suspect's identity is **known** to the police and they are **available**, the following identification procedures may be used:
- video identification;
- identification parade;
- group identification.

1.4 Identification Issues

Video identification

This is when the witness is shown moving images of a known suspect, together with similar images of others who resemble the suspect. In certain circumstances still images may be used.

Identification parade

This is when the witness sees the suspect in a line of others who resemble the suspect.

Group identification

This is when the witness sees the suspect in an informal group of people.

Arranging identification procedures

- The arrangements for, and conduct of, the above identification procedures and circumstances in which an identification procedure must be held shall be the responsibility of an officer not below inspector rank who is not involved with the investigation, 'the identification officer'.
- Generally, another officer or police support staff, can make arrangements for, and conduct, any of these identification procedures. Although the identification officer must be available to supervise effectively, intervene, or give advice.
- Officials involved with the investigation, cannot take any part in these procedures or act as the identification officer (except that required by these procedures).
- This does not preclude the identification officer from consulting with the officer in charge of the investigation to determine what procedure to use.
- When an identification procedure is required, in the interest of fairness to suspects and witnesses, it must be held as soon as practicable.

When an identification procedure must be held

- This is whenever:
  - ♦ a witness has identified a suspect or purported to have identified them prior to any of the above identification procedures having been held; or
  - ♦ there is a witness available, who expresses an ability to identify the suspect, or where there is a reasonable chance of the witness being able to do so, and they have not been given an opportunity to identify the suspect in any of the above procedures, and the suspect disputes being the person the witness claims to have seen.
- An identification procedure shall then be held unless it is not practicable or it would serve no useful purpose in proving or disproving whether the suspect was involved in committing the offence (eg when it is not disputed that the suspect is already well known to the witness claiming to have seen them commit the crime).
- Similarly an identification procedure may be held if the officer in charge of the investigation considers it would be useful.

Selecting the type of identification procedure

- If an identification procedure is to be held, the suspect shall initially be offered a video identification unless:
  - ♦ a video identification is not practicable; or
  - ♦ an identification parade is both practicable and more suitable than a video identification; or
  - ♦ a group identification is the more appropriate method.
- A group identification may initially be offered if the officer in charge of the investigation considers it is more suitable than a video identification or an identification parade and the identification officer considers it practicable to arrange.
- The identification officer and the officer in charge of the investigation shall consult with each other to determine which option is to be offered.
- An identification parade may not be practicable because of factors relating to the witnesses: their number, state of health, availability, and travelling requirements.
- A video identification would normally be more suitable if it could be arranged and completed sooner than an identification parade.
- A suspect who refuses the identification procedure first offered shall be asked to state their reason for refusing and may get advice from their solicitor and/or if present, their appropriate adult.
- The suspect, solicitor, and/or appropriate adult can make representations about why another procedure should be used.
- A record should be made of the reasons for refusal and representations made.
- After considering any reasons given, and representations made, the identification officer shall, if appropriate, arrange for the suspect to be offered an alternative which the officer considers suitable and practicable.
- If the officer decides it is not suitable and practicable to offer an alternative identification procedure, the reasons for that decision shall be recorded.

Notice to suspect

Prior to identification procedures being arranged, the following shall be explained to the suspect :
- the purposes of the identification procedures;
- their entitlement to free legal advice;
- the procedures for holding it, including their right to have a solicitor or friend present;
- that they do not have to consent to or cooperate in these identification procedures;
- if they do not consent to or co-operate in these identification procedures, their refusal may be given in evidence and police may proceed covertly without their consent or make other arrangements to test whether a witness can identify them,
- if appropriate, special arrangements for juveniles; mentally disordered or mentally vulnerable people;

- if they significantly alter their appearance between being offered and any attempt to hold an identification procedure, this may be given in evidence and other forms of identification may be considered;
- a moving image or photograph may be taken of them when they attend any identification procedure;
- if, before their identity became known, the witness was shown photographs, a computerised or artist's composite likeness or similar likeness or image by the police;
- if they change their appearance before an identification parade, it may not be practicable to arrange another one and, alternative methods of identification maybe considered;
- that they or their solicitor will be provided with details of the first description of the suspect given by any witnesses who are to attend identification procedures.

This information must be in a written notice handed to the suspect, who should then be asked to sign a second copy and indicate if they are willing to take part or co-operate with the identification procedure.

Identity of suspect known but not available

- When the **known** suspect is not **available** or has ceased to be available, the identification officer may make arrangements for a video identification.
- If necessary, the identification officer may follow the video identification procedures but using still images.
- Any suitable moving or still images may be used and these may be obtained covertly if necessary. Alternatively, the identification officer may make arrangements for a group identification.
- The identification officer may arrange for the suspect to be **confronted** by the witness if none of the options referred to above are practicable.
- A confrontation does not require the suspect's consent.
- Requirements for information to be given to, or sought from, a suspect or for the suspect to be given an opportunity to view images before they are shown to a witness, do not apply if the suspect's lack of cooperation prevents this action.

Meanings

Known

Where there is sufficient information known to the police to justify the arrest of a particular person for suspected involvement in the offence.

Available

A suspect being immediately available or will be within a reasonably short time and willing to take an effective part in at least one of the identification procedures which is practicable to arrange.

Confrontation

This is when the suspect is directly confronted by the witness.

Related cases

R v Turnbull (1976) 63 Cr App R 132, HL This case set out guidelines for when dealing with a case involving disputed identification. The jury must examine the circumstances in which the identification was made, in particular:

A—Amount of time under observation.

D—Distance between witness and suspect.

V—Visibility at all times (in what light).

O—Observation impeded/obstructed in any way (traffic, objects or people).

K—Known or seen before, how often, and in what circumstances.

A—Any reason to remember the suspect, if only seen occasionally and not well known.

T—Time lapse between observation and subsequent identification to police.

E—Error or material discrepancy between description given to police and actual appearance.

In every case where a witness describes a suspect, it is essential to consider these points, all of which should be included in any written statement.

R v Forbes The Times 19 December, 2000, HL When identification is disputed by the suspect, an identification parade shall be held (if the suspect consents) unless—unusual appearance, refusal, or other practical alternatives apply. A parade may also be held if the officer in charge of the investigation considers that it would be useful, and the suspect consents. Otherwise there will be a breach of Code of Practice D.

Practical considerations

• Where practicable, the 'first description' from the witness should be recorded in the police officer's pocket note book, which should be made before asking the witness to make any identification.

• Do not assume that the description has been recorded elsewhere.

• Avoid using 'closed' questions (those which only need a 'yes' or 'no' answer) when obtaining description details.

• Care must be taken not to direct the witness's attention to any individual.

• However, this does not prevent a witness being asked to look in a particular direction, if this is necessary to:
  ♦ make sure that the witness does not overlook a possible suspect simply because the witness is looking in the opposite direction; and
  ♦ to enable the witness to make comparisons between any suspect and others who are in the area.

• Where there is more than one witness, every effort should be made to keep them separate.

• A written record should be made of any identification including:
  ♦ date, time, and place when the witness saw the suspect;
  ♦ whether any identification was made;
  ♦ if so, how it was made and the conditions at the time;

+ if the witness's attention was drawn to the suspect (reason for this); and
+ anything said by the witness or the suspect about the identification or the conduct of the procedure.

• It is best practice, for any officer who recognizes a suspect from either a 'still' photograph or CCTV image, to avoid being involved in the arrest of that individual, thereby ensuring they are available to take part in any forthcoming identification procedure, should the identification be disputed.

Links to alternative subjects and offences

Chapter 2

Assaults and Violence

2.1 Assault (Common/Actual Bodily Harm)

What is often thought of (and referred to) as a common assault under s 39 of the Criminal Justice Act 1988 is in fact two separate matters: an assault and/or a battery. This area of law and the meaning of assault are dealt with first, before covering the more serious assault occasioning actual bodily harm under the Offences Against the Person Act 1861. Any defences which may be available (to all assaults) are then discussed.

2.1.1 Common assault—battery

Offence

It is an offence for any person to unlawfully **assault** or beat any other person.   Criminal Justice Act 1988, s 39

Points to prove
- ✓ date and location
- ✓ unlawfully
- ✓ assaulted
- ✓ another person

Battery
- ✓ all points above
- ✓ the application of unlawful force (eg by beating)

Meanings

Assault

Any act, which **intentionally** or **recklessly**, causes another person to apprehend immediate and **unlawful** personal violence (*Fagan v Metropolitan Police Commissioner* [1968] 3 All ER 442, QBD).

Intent (see 4.1)

Reckless (see 2.3.1)

Unlawful (see 2.3.1)

Explanatory notes

- There are two offences created by this legislation; 'assault' and 'assault by beating' (battery).
- There is also a civil wrong of assault/battery.
- An 'assault' does not have to involve an actual application of force: it may involve a threat alone, although if violence is threatened, there must be the ability to carry out the threat at the time. Words alone will never amount to an assault. A mere omission to act cannot be an assault.
- A 'battery' is an act by which a person intentionally or recklessly applies force to the complainant.
- In both offences there has to be either an intentional causing of apprehension of immediate unlawful violence or subjective recklessness as to that apprehension.

Defences (see 2.1.2)

Related cases

Haystead v Chief Constable of Derbyshire [2000] 3 All ER 890, QBD A mother was punched by her boyfriend and as a result dropped and injured the baby she was carrying. The defendant was convicted of assault by battery directly on the mother, and indirectly on the baby.

Mepstead v DPP [1996] Crim LR 111, QBD Touching someone to draw their attention may be lawful.

Fagan v Metropolitan Police Commissioner [1968] 3 All ER 442, QBD It is irrelevant whether the battery is inflicted directly by the body of the offender or with a weapon or instrument such as a car.

Practical considerations

- If racially or religiously aggravated, the more serious racially/religiously aggravated offence should be considered (see **7.10**).
- An individual should be charged with either 'assault' or 'battery'—the inclusion of both in the same charge is bad for duplicity and could result in the charge being dismissed (*DPP v Taylor* [1992] QB 645, QBD and *DPP v Little* (1994) 95 Cr App R 28, CA).
- Ensure that visible injuries are photographed.
- Include in your CJA witness statement evidence as to intent or recklessness.
- Ascertain whether any of the defences could apply.

Assault

- Unless extenuating circumstances apply the police/CPS will invariably invite the aggrieved party to take their own action either by criminal prosecution or by civil action.

- Note that where a court decides that the assault or battery has not been proved or that it was justified, or so trifling as not to merit any punishment, they must dismiss the complaint and forthwith make out a certificate of dismissal. This certificate releases the defendant from any further proceedings in this case (civil or criminal) (Offences Against the Person Act 1861, s 44).
- The conduct may take the form of threatening acts, words, gestures, or a combination of these, in which case consider alternative offences under the Public Order Act 1986, breach of the peace or harassment (see **7.8**).

Battery

- Ascertain the degree/severity of injury before charging.
- CPS guidelines specify the following injuries should normally be charged as battery: grazes; scratches; abrasions; minor bruising; swellings; reddening of the skin; superficial cuts; and a 'black eye'.
- Consider ss 47, 20, or 18 of the Offences Against the Person Act 1861 for more serious injuries.

 Summary   6 months

 6 months' imprisonment and/or a fine not exceeding level 5 on the standard scale.

2.1.2 Assault occasioning actual bodily harm (AOABH)/defences to assaults

Offence

Whosoever shall be convicted upon an indictment of any assault **occasioning actual bodily harm** shall be guilty of an offence.

Offences Against the Person Act 1861, s 47

Points to prove

✓ date and location
✓ unlawfully
✓ assaulted
✓ another person
✓ occasioning him/her
✓ actual bodily harm

Meaning of actual bodily harm

Actual bodily harm has been defined as 'any hurt which interferes with health or comfort but not to a considerable degree'.

Explanatory notes

- CPS guidance states that this offence is committed when a person assaults another, thereby causing actual bodily harm to that other person.
- Bodily harm has its ordinary meaning and is that which is calculated to interfere with the health or comfort of the victim, but must be more than transient or trifling.
- Examples of 'actual bodily harm' physical/mental injuries are given in **Practical considerations**.
- A conviction can be obtained if actual bodily harm is caused to the victim by some action which is the natural and reasonably foreseeable result of what the defendant said or did.

Defences

Accident (as long as malice is not present)

Consent

- This can be expressly given to an application of force (such as tattooing or an operation), providing the activity is not illegal itself (injection of illegal drugs); it can also be implied (by getting into a crowded train where contact is unavoidable).
- A belief by the defendant that consent had been given (or would have been given—emergency surgery to save life) can be a defence, even based on unreasonable grounds, provided that the belief is honestly held.
- Submitting to an assault is not the same as consent. Similarly, consent is negated if given due to duress or fraud (a trick), but the burden of proof is on the prosecution to prove that this was how consent was obtained.
- Consent cannot be given by a child or young person if they fail to understand the true nature of the act (what is involved).
- Consent cannot be given to an assault that inflicts bodily harm of a substantial nature, such as in sado-masochism (*R v Brown & others* [1994] 1 AC 212, HL).
- However, some body mutilation in limited and non-aggressive circumstances may be acceptable (*R v Wilson* [1996] 2 Cr App R 241, CA).

Lawful sport

- Properly conducted lawful sports are considered to be for the public good and injuries received during the course of an event kept within the rules are generally accepted.
- Players are taken to have consented to any injuries which they might reasonably expect to suffer during the course of the match or contest.
- However, any injury caused by a player acting outside the rules of the sport will be an assault, and criminal proceedings may be brought.

Lawful correction

The Children Act 2004, s 58 ensures that parents no longer have the right to use force in the course of reasonable chastisement of their child.

Self-defence

In cases of self-defence—'A jury must decide whether a defendant honestly believed that the circumstances were such as required him to use force to defend himself from an attack or threatened attack; the jury has then to decide whether the force used was reasonable in the circumstances' (*R v Owino* [1996] 2 Cr App R 128, CA and *DPP v Armstrong-Braun* (1999) 163 JP 271, CA).

Statutory use of reasonable force   (see 1.2.1)

Related cases

R v Savage [1992] 1 AC 699, HL and DPP v Parmenter [1991] 3 WLR 914, HL No intent to cause injury is needed for assault occasioning actual bodily harm.

DPP v Smith [2006] 1 WLR 1571, QBD Cutting hair, or 'injuring' it by, for example, putting paint on it or some unpleasant substance that marked or damaged it without causing injury elsewhere, was capable of being assault causing actual bodily harm.

R v Donovan (1934) 25 Cr App R 1, CA Consent to excessive violence cannot normally be given.

R v Brown & others [1994] 1 AC 212, HL Similarly sadomasochists engaged in torture with each other cannot give consent, even though the 'victims' were all willing participants.

Actual Bodily Harm can include causing:

- a psychiatric illness (*R v Ireland* [1998] AC 147, HL);
- mental 'injury' or hurt (which need not be permanent, but must be more than a passing fear) (*R v Chan-Fook* [1994] 2 All ER 552, CA);
- shock (*R v Miller* (1953) 118 JP 340, Assize Court).

Practical considerations

- If racially or religiously aggravated, the more serious racially/religiously aggravated offence should be considered (see **7.10**).
- Ensure that visible injuries are photographed.
- Include in your CJA witness statement details of the injuries, circumstances of the incident, include any evidence as to intent or recklessness.
- Obtain medical evidence (hospital or doctor).
- Could any of the defences apply or be relied upon by the defendant later?
- CPS charging standards and guidance give examples of injuries which could amount to 'actual bodily harm':
  - ◆ loss or breaking of a tooth or teeth;
  - ◆ temporary loss of sensory functions (includes loss of consciousness);
  - ◆ extensive or multiple bruising;

- ◆ displaced broken nose;
- ◆ minor fractures;
- ◆ minor cuts (not superficial), may require stitches (medical treatment);
- ◆ psychiatric injury (proved by appropriate expert evidence) which is more than fear, distress or panic.
- Consider ss 20 or 18 of the Offences Against the Person Act 1861 for more serious injuries.

 Either way   ⏱ None

 Summary: 6 months' imprisonment and/or a fine not exceeding the statutory maximum.
Indictment: 5 years' imprisonment.

Links to alternative subjects and offences

SSS Stop, search and seize powers   **RRA** Racially or religiously aggravated offence

2.2 Assault/Resist Arrest and Obstruct—Police/Designated/ Accredited Person/Emergency Workers

This area addresses offences involving assault with intent to resist or prevent lawful arrest; assault or resist or wilfully obstruct either a police constable, designated or accredited person while in the execution of their duty.

2.2.1 Assault with intent to resist or prevent lawful arrest

Section 38 of the Offences Against the Person Act 1861 creates the offence of 'assault with intent to resist or prevent lawful arrest'.

> **Offence**
>
> Whosoever shall **assault** any person with **intent** to resist or prevent the lawful apprehension or detainer of himself or of any other person for any offence shall be guilty of an offence.
>
> Offences Against the Person Act 1861, s 38

> **Points to prove**
> - ✓ date and location
> - ✓ assaulted
> - ✓ with intent to resist/prevent
> - ✓ the lawful apprehension/detention of
> - ✓ self/some other person (including the defendant)
> - ✓ for the offence or other relevant reason

Meanings

Assault (see 2.1.1)

Intent (see 4.1)

Resist or prevent

These terms are not legally defined. The Oxford English Dictionary offers the following meanings:
- *resist*—'to strive against, oppose, try to impede or refuse to comply with';

2.2.1 Assault with Intent to Resist or Prevent Lawful Arrest

- *prevent*—'stop from happening or doing something; hinder; make impossible'.

Explanatory notes

- The assault itself need not be any more serious than a common assault (which could be considered as an alternative charge).
- The intention to resist the lawful arrest (either of themselves or another person) must be proved.
- Prevent means to 'stop or render impossible'.

Defences to assault (see 2.1.2)

Related cases

R v Self (1992) 95 Cr App R 42, CA The resisted arrest/detention must have been a lawful one. This is particularly problematic where so-called 'citizen's arrests' are involved and the arresting person did not have any lawful power to arrest/detain.

R v Lee (2000) 150 NLJ 1491, CA It is not a defence to this offence to hold an honest belief that a mistake is being made by the arresting/detaining officers.

Practical considerations

- It must be proved that:
  - ♦ the arrest/detention was lawful, and
  - ♦ the person concerned knew that an arrest was being made on himself or another.
- Intention (at the time of commission of the offence) can be proved by:
  - ♦ interviewing defendant—admissions made and explanations as to his/her state of mind, actions, and intentions, and/or
  - ♦ inferences drawn from the circumstances of the offence, evidence from witnesses, property found on defendant or in his/her control and any other incriminating evidence.
- If this offence is committed by the person initially being arrested, the power of arrest comes from the original offence. Otherwise consider assaulting a police officer in the execution of his/her duty, or breach of the peace.
- Could any of the general assault defences apply?
- Consideration must be given to CPS guidelines on charging standards and the specific guidance for assault with intent to resist arrest.

Either way   None

 Summary: 6 months' imprisonment and/or a fine not exceeding the statutory maximum.
Indictment: 2 years' imprisonment.

2.2.2 Assault a constable in the execution of his/her duty

The Police Act 1996 consolidates certain legislation relating to the police. Section 89(1) provides the offence of assaulting a constable or person assisting a constable acting in the execution of his/her duty.

Offence

Any person who **assaults** a constable in the execution of his duty, or a person assisting a constable in the **execution of** his **duty**, commits an offence.   **Police Act 1996, s 89(1)**

Points to prove

✓ date and location
✓ assaulted a constable (**or** assaulted a person assisting constable)
✓ in the execution of his/her duty

Meanings

Assault (see 2.1.1)

Execution of duty

The officer must be acting lawfully and in the execution of his/her duty (see related cases).

Explanatory notes

- The duties of a constable have not been defined by any statute (see related cases).
- This offence also applies to police officers from Scotland or Northern Ireland (while in England or Wales) who are acting within statutory powers or executing a warrant.
- Section 30 of the Police Act 1996 defines the jurisdiction of a constable as being throughout England and Wales and the adjacent UK waters. Special constables have the same jurisdiction, powers and privileges of a constable.

Defences to assault (see 2.1.2)

Related cases

DPP v Hawkins [1988] 1 WLR 1166, QBD Arrest rendered unlawful by a failure to provide reason for arrest as soon as practicable after initial lawful arrest. The reason could not be given retrospectively.

Robson v Hallett [1967] 2 All ER 407, QBD An officer may be a trespasser (and therefore not acting in the execution of his/her duty) if permission to enter or remain on property is withdrawn, but reasonable time must be given to leave property.

R v Basher [1993] COD 372, DC, CA A decision to release without charge or charge with other offences will not make initial arrest unlawful.

Mepstead v DPP [1996] Crim LR 111, QBD Touching someone to draw their attention may be lawful.

DPP v L [1999] Crim LR 752, QBD An unlawful arrest does not mean that the custody staff subsequently act unlawfully in detaining the person.

Practical considerations

- It is vital to prove that the officer was acting lawfully in the execution of his/her duty at the time of the assault.
- Officers should ensure they are acting within their powers and following relevant requirement or procedures, otherwise they may no longer be acting within the execution of their duty.
- In general, it will be for the defence to show, on the balance of probabilities, that the constable was not acting in the execution of his/her duty.
- The offence does not require proof that the defendant knew or ought to have known that the victim was a constable or that he/she was acting in the execution of their duty.
- A plain clothes officer should identify him/herself, as a failure to do so could mean that the officer was acting outside the execution of their duty.
- Officers should comply with s 28 of the Police and Criminal Evidence Act 1984—information to be given on arrest (see **12.2.2**).
- Do any of the general assault defences apply?
- Consideration must be given to CPS guidelines and the specific guidance for this offence relating to injuries received amounting to:
  - ♦ grazes; scratches; abrasions; minor bruising; swellings; reddening of the skin; superficial cuts and a 'black eye'.
- If the injuries justify a s 47 charge (see **2.1.2**) for a member of the public, then this will also be the appropriate charge for a constable.

Summary   6 months

6 months' imprisonment and/or a fine not exceeding level 5 on the standard scale.

2.2.3 Resist/obstruct a constable in the execution of his/her duty

The Police Act 1996 consolidates legislation relating to the police and deals with the offence of resisting or wilfully obstructing a constable in the execution of his/her duty.

Offence

Any person who **resists** or **wilfully obstructs** a constable in the **execution** of his duty, or a person assisting a constable in the execution of his duty, commits an offence.   **Police Act 1996, s 89(2)**

Points to prove

✓ date and location
✓ resisted/wilfully obstructed a constable (OR person assisting a constable)
✓ in the execution of constable's duty

Meanings

Resists (see 2.2.1)

Wilful obstruction

In this context it has to be deliberate obstruction.

Execution of duty (see 2.2.2)

Explanatory notes

- Resists does not imply that any assault has taken place and where a person in the process of being lawfully arrested, tears himself away from the constable or person assisting, this will constitute resistance.
- The obstruction must be some form of positive act which prevents or impedes the officer in carrying out his/her duty.
- For the constable's duty and jurisdiction see **2.2.2**.
- It must be proved that the officer was acting in the execution of his/her duty.

Related cases

Moss & others v McLachlan (1985) 149 JP 167, QBD A constable is under a general duty to prevent a breach of the peace occurring.

Lewis v Cox [1984] Crim LR 756, QBD A wilful act has to be deliberate and prevent the constable from carrying out his/her duty. It is sufficient for defendant to be aware that his/her actions cause this.

Rice v Connolly [1966] 2 All ER 649, QBD A citizen is entitled to refuse to answer questions or assist/accompany a police officer, where no lawful reason exists and therefore this conduct does not automatically amount to resistance/obstruction.

Sekfali and others v DPP [2006] EWHC 894, QBD Citizens have no legal duty to assist the police, but most would accept that it is a moral and social one; however running away and fleeing can amount to an obstruction.

Smith v DPP (2001) 165 JP 432, QBD An officer can take someone aside to aid entry to premises even if there is no obstruction being caused.

Practical considerations (see 2.2.2)

  Summary   6 months

  1 month imprisonment and/or a fine not exceeding level 3 on the standard scale.

2.2.4 Assault or resist/wilfully obstruct a designated/accredited person in the execution of their duty

Section 46 of the Police Reform Act 2002 refers to offences in respect of suitably designated and accredited people and is as follows:

Offence

(1) Any person who assaults—
   (a) a designated person in the execution of his duty,
   (b) an accredited person in the execution of his duty, or
   (c) a person assisting a designated or accredited person in the execution of his duty, is guilty of an offence.
(2) Any person who resists or wilfully obstructs—
   (a) a designated person in the execution of his duty,
   (b) an accredited person in the execution of his duty, or

(c) a person assisting a designated or accredited person in the execution
   of his duty, is guilty of an offence.

Police Reform Act 2002, s 46(1), (2)

Points to prove
✓ date and location
✓ assaulted **or** resist/wilfully obstruct
✓ a designated/accredited person or person assisting them
✓ while in the execution of his/her duty

Explanatory notes
- References to the execution of their duties relate to exercising any power or performing any duty by virtue of their designation or accreditation.
- A designated person means community support officer, investigating officer, detention officer, escort officer, or employees of companies contracted to provide detention and escort services.
- An accredited person relates to community safety accreditation schemes set up by chief officers for their police area under ss 40 and 41 of the Police Reform Act 2002 **or** a person contracted out under pt 4 of the Police Reform Act 2002 (with powers defined under sch 5 to that Act).

Defences to assault (see 2.1.2)

Related cases (see also 2.2.2 and 2.2.3)
R v Forbes and Webb (1865) 10 Cox CC 362 It is not necessary that the offender knows the person is a designated or accredited person.

Practical considerations (see also 2.2.2 and 2.2.3)
- Given the extensive and detailed restrictions on the powers of these individuals, the precise activities that were involved at the time will be closely scrutinized by a court. It will be critical to establish that the person was acting within the lawful limits of their powers at the time.

 SSS RRA

 Summary   6 months

 Assaulted/assaulted a person assisting
6 months' imprisonment and/or a fine not exceeding level 5 on the standard scale, or to both.

Resist/wilfully obstruct or resisted/obstructed a person assisting
1 month imprisonment and/or a fine not exceeding level 3 on the standard scale.

2.2.5 Obstruct/hinder certain emergency workers and persons assisting

The Emergency Workers (Obstruction) Act 2006 creates two offences of: obstructing/hindering certain emergency workers responding to an emergency, and obstructing/hindering persons who are assisting emergency workers.

Offences against emergency workers

A person who without reasonable excuse obstructs or hinders another while that other person is, in a **capacity** mentioned in subsection (2) below, responding to **emergency circumstances**, commits an offence.

Emergency Workers (Obstruction) Act 2006, s 1(1)

Points to prove
✓ without reasonable excuse
✓ obstructed or hindered
✓ emergency worker as described in s 1(2) who is
✓ attending/dealing/preparing to deal
✓ with emergency circumstances as given in s 1(3) and 1(4)

Meanings

Capacity (of emergency worker)

The capacity referred to in subsection (1) above is—
(a) that of a person employed by a fire and rescue authority in England and Wales;
(b) in relation to England and Wales, that of a person (other than a person falling within paragraph (a)) whose duties as an employee or as a servant of the Crown involve—
   (i) extinguishing fires; or
   (ii) protecting life and property in the event of a fire;
(c) that of a person employed by a relevant NHS body in the provision of ambulance services (including air ambulance services), or of a person providing such services pursuant to arrangements made by, or at the request of, a relevant NHS body;
(d) that of a person providing services for the transport of organs, blood, equipment or personnel pursuant to arrangements made by, or at the request of, a relevant NHS body;
(e) that of a member of Her Majesty's Coastguard;
(f) that of a member of the crew of a vessel operated by—
   (i) the Royal National Lifeboat Institution, or
   (ii) any other person or organisation operating a vessel for the purpose of providing a rescue service,

or a person who musters the crew of such a vessel or attends to its launch or recovery.

Emergency Workers (Obstruction) Act 2006, s 1(2)

Emergency circumstances

(3) For the purposes of this section and section 2 of this Act, a person is responding to emergency circumstances if the person—

    (a) is going anywhere for the purpose of dealing with emergency circumstances occurring there; or

    (b) is dealing with emergency circumstances or preparing to do so.

(4) For the purposes of this Act, circumstances are 'emergency' circumstances if they are present or imminent and—

    (a) are causing or are likely to cause—

        (i) serious injury to or the serious illness (including mental illness) of a person;

        (ii) serious harm to the environment (including the life and health of plants and animals);

        (iii) serious harm to any building or other property; or

        (iv) a worsening of any such injury, illness or harm; or

    (b) are likely to cause the death of a person.

Emergency Workers (Obstruction) Act 2006, s 1(3), (4)

Offences against person assisting

(1) A person who without reasonable excuse obstructs or hinders another in the circumstances described in subsection (2) below commits an offence.

(2) Those circumstances are where the person being obstructed or hindered is assisting another while that other person is, in a capacity mentioned in section 1(2) of this Act, responding to emergency circumstances.

Emergency Workers (Obstruction) Act 2006, s 2(1), (2)

Points to prove

✓ without reasonable excuse
✓ obstructed or hindered
✓ a person who was assisting
✓ an emergency worker as described in s 1(2) who was
✓ attending/dealing/preparing to deal
✓ with emergency circumstances as given in s 1(3) and 1(4)

Explanatory notes

- In s 1(2) a 'relevant NHS body' is a NHS foundation trust, National Health Service trust, Special Health Authority, Primary Care Trust or Local Health Board.
- A person may be convicted of the offence under s 1 or s 2 of this Act notwithstanding that it is effected by: means other than physical means; or action directed only at any vehicle, vessel, apparatus,

equipment or other thing or any animal used or to be used by a person referred to in that section.

- For the purposes of s 1 and s 2, circumstances to which a person is responding are to be taken to be emergency circumstances if the person believes and has reasonable grounds for believing they are or may be emergency circumstances.
- Further details on this 2006 Act are dealt with in HOC 3/2007.
- The 2006 Act does not include police or prison officers because obstruction of a police constable is an offence under the Police Act 1996 (see **2.2.3**). This 1996 Act also covers prison officers by virtue of the Prisons Act 1952 which stipulates that prison officers, whilst acting as such, enjoy the same protections and privileges as a constable.
- See **2.2.4** for assault or resist/wilfully obstruct a suitable designated or accredited person.

 Summary   6 months

Fine not exceeding level 5 on the standard scale.

Links to alternative subjects and offences

2.3 Wounding/Grievous Bodily Harm

The offences of 'wounding or inflicting grievous bodily harm' and the more serious 'wounding or causing grievous bodily harm with intent' (under ss 18 and 20 (respectively) of the Offences Against the Person Act 1861) are dealt with in the subject/offence area.

2.3.1 Wounding or inflicting grievous bodily harm

Section 20 of the Offences Against the Person Act 1861 provides the offence of 'wounding or inflicting grievous bodily harm'.

Offence

Whosoever shall **unlawfully** and **maliciously wound** or **inflict** any **grievous bodily harm** upon any other person, either with or without any weapon or instrument shall be guilty of an offence.

Offences Against the Person Act 1861, s 20

Points to prove

✓ date and location
✓ unlawfully
✓ maliciously
✓ wounded **or** inflicted grievous bodily harm
✓ upon another person

Meanings

The meanings given here have invariably been derived from case law.

Unlawfully

Means without excuse or justification at law.

Maliciously

- Means malice (ill-will or an evil motive) must be present.
- 'Maliciously requires either an actual intention to do the particular kind of harm that was done or **recklessness** whether any such harm should occur or not; it is neither limited to, nor does it require, any ill-will towards the person injured' (*R v Cunningham* [1957] 2 All ER 412, CA).

2.3.1 Wounding or Inflicting Grievous Bodily Harm

Recklessness

Is one element of the term 'Maliciously', in *R v Cunningham* [1957] 2 All ER 412, CA it was held that the prosecution have to prove that the defendant was aware of the existence of the risk but nonetheless had gone on and taken it.

Wound

Means any break in the continuity of the whole skin.

Inflict

- Inflict does not have as wide a meaning as 'cause'— grievous bodily harm can be inflicted without there being an assault.
- 'Grievous bodily harm may be inflicted either by: directly and violently assaulting the victim; **or** something intentionally done which although in itself is not a direct application of force to the body of the victim, does directly result in force being applied to the body of the victim so that he suffers grievous bodily harm' (*R v Wilson and Jenkins* [1983] 3 All ER 448, HL).

Grievous bodily harm

- Means 'serious or really serious harm' (*R v Saunders* [1985] Crim LR 230, CA).
- Bodily harm can include inflicting/causing a psychiatric harm/illness (silent/heavy breathing/menacing telephone calls— *R v Ireland* [1998] AC 147, HL).
- It could include psychiatric injury, in serious cases, as well as physical injury (stalking victim— *R v Burstow* [1997] 4 All ER 225, HL).

Explanatory notes

- If it is possible that the target of the attack was not the actual victim, then the 'doctrine of transferred malice' provides that if a person mistakenly causes injury to a person other than the person who he intended to attack, he/she will commit the same offence as if he/she had injured the intended victim. The doctrine only applies if the crime remains the same and the harm done must be of the same kind as the harm intended (*R v Latimer* (1886) 17 QBD 359, QBD).
- As wounding and grievous bodily harm are both different, the distinction as to which offence is appropriate should be made.

Defences

A general defence may be available to a s 20 offence (see *2.1.2*).

Related cases

R v Wilson & Jenkins [1983] 3 All ER 448, HL Frightened by the defendant the victim jumps through a window and breaks a leg. Grievous bodily harm has been 'inflicted' by the offender by inducing substantial fear, even though there is no direct application of force

R v Martin [1881–85] All ER 699, CA The defendant came out of a theatre, extinguished the lights, and placed a bar across the doorway. Panic was intended to be the natural consequences of his actions but, if in the ensuing panic, people suffered serious injuries the defendant will have 'inflicted GBH' on those people.

Attorney-General's Reference (No 3 of 1994) [1997] Crim LR 829, HL The doctrine of transferred malice was accepted where the defendant stabbed his girlfriend knowing she was pregnant and the knife penetrated the foetus.

R v Cunningham [1957] 2 All ER 412, CA Meaning of 'maliciously' and recklessness test (above).

R v Savage [1992] 1 AC 699, HL and DPP v Parmenter [1991] 3 WLR 914, HL In s 20 wounding/GBH cases:
- A s 47 assault (AOABH) can be an alternative verdict if it includes implications of assault occasioning actual bodily harm.
- 'Cunningham malice' will suffice. It is enough that the defendant should have foreseen that some physical harm might result— of whatever character.

R v Brown & others [1994] 1 AC 212, HL Consent cannot be given to an assault that inflicts bodily harm of a substantial nature such as in sado-masochism.

R v Wilson [1996] 2 Cr App R 241, CA However, some body mutilation in limited and non-aggressive circumstances may be acceptable.

R v Dica [2005] EWCA Crim 2304, CA Inflicting grievous bodily harm by infecting the victim with HIV through unprotected consensual sexual intercourse.

R v Konzani [2005] EWCA Crim 706, CA For a valid defence, there has to be a willing and informed consent to the specific risk of contracting HIV—this cannot be inferred from consent to unprotected sexual intercourse.

Practical considerations

- Consider the more serious racially/religiously aggravated offence (see **7.10**).
- In cases of 'transferred malice' the charge must specify at whom the intent was aimed (eg 'A wounded C with intent to cause GBH to B').
- It is not strictly necessary to describe any weapon or instrument used in the actual charge, but it is good practice to do so, particularly if the article has been recovered and is to be produced at court.
- The distinction between 'wound' and 'GBH' must be identified and considered, as they do not have the same meaning.
- Where both a wound and grievous bodily harm have been inflicted, choose which part of s 20 reflects the true nature of the offence (*R v McCready* [1978] 1 WLR 1376, CA).
- The prosecution must prove under s 20 that either the defendant intended, or actually foresaw, that the act would cause harm.
- The prosecution has to prove that the defendant was aware of the existence of the risk but nonetheless went on to take it. It is not

2.3.1 **Wounding or Inflicting Grievous Bodily Harm**

necessary to prove these elements in relation to the extent of the specific injuries received.

- The s 18 offence requires intent while s 20 is 'unlawfully and maliciously'.
- A s 47 assault can be an alternative verdict to s 20 if it includes implications of assault occasioning actual bodily harm.
- Consideration must be given to **CPS advice** and the specific guidance for unlawful wounding/inflicting GBH which is as follows:
  - ◆ The distinction between charges under s 18 and s 20 is one of **intent**. The gravity of the injury resulting is not the determining factor, although it may provide some evidence of intent.
  - ◆ Wounding means the breaking of the continuity of the whole of the outer skin, or the inner skin within the cheek or lip. It does not include the rupturing of internal blood vessels.
  - ◆ Wounds within this definition are sometimes minor, such as a small cut or laceration. Such minor injuries should more appropriately be charged under s 47. Section 20 should be reserved for those wounds considered to be serious (thus equating the offences with the infliction of grievous, or serious, bodily harm under the other part of the section).
  - ◆ Grievous bodily harm means serious bodily harm. Examples of this are:
    - injury resulting in permanent disability or permanent loss of sensory function; injury which results in more than minor permanent, visible disfigurement;
    - broken or displaced limbs or bones, including fractured skull, compound fractures, broken cheekbone, jaw, ribs, etc;
    - injuries which cause substantial loss of blood, usually necessitating a transfusion; injuries resulting in lengthy treatment or incapacity;
    - psychiatric injury. As with assault occasioning actual bodily harm expert evidence is essential to prove the injury.
- Obtain medical evidence to prove extent of injury.
- Obtain photographs of victim's injuries.

Either way   None

Summary: 6 months' imprisonment and/or a fine not exceeding the statutory maximum.
Indictment: 5 years' imprisonment.

2.3.2 **Wounding or grievous bodily harm—with intent**

Section 18 of the Offences Against the Person Act 1861, creates the offences of 'wounding or causing grievous bodily harm with intent'.

Offence

Whosoever shall **unlawfully** and **maliciously** by **any means whatsoever wound** or **cause grievous bodily harm** to any person with **intent** to do some grievous bodily harm to any person or with intent to **resist or prevent** the lawful apprehension or detainer of any person, shall be guilty of an offence.   Offences Against the Person Act 1861, s 18

Points to prove

✓ date and location
✓ unlawfully and maliciously
✓ cause grievous bodily harm **or** wounded a person
✓ with intent to
✓ do grievous bodily harm **or** resist/prevent lawful apprehension/detention of self/another

---

Meanings

The meanings given here have invariably been derived from case law.

Unlawfully (see 2.3.1)

Maliciously (see 2.3.1)

Any means whatsoever

This is given its literal meaning. The only thing that must be proved is a connection between the means used and the harm caused.

Wound (see 2.3.1)

Cause

This has been defined as 'anything that produces a result or effect'.

Grievous bodily harm (see 2.3.1)

Intent (see 4.1)

Resist or prevent (see 2.2.1)

Explanatory notes

• Cause has a wider meaning than 'inflict'. All that needs to be proved is some connection between the action (the means used) and the injury (sometimes called the chain of causation). There does not need to be a direct application of force.
• The issue of causation is separate from the test for intent.

2.3.2 Wounding or Grievous Bodily Harm—with Intent

- An example would be where the defendant intends to assault a person and kicks down a door, making the victim jump out of the window to escape thereby suffering harm/injuries. There is clearly a causal link between the actions of the defendant and the victim's injuries and the chain of causation is unbroken.
- Intent must be proved either from verbal admissions on interview and/or other and incriminating evidence (eg subsequent actions).
- The statutory test under s 8 of the Criminal Justice Act 1967 must be considered (see **4.1**).
- In relation to the offence of wounding or causing GBH with intent to resist or prevent the lawful arrest/detention of any person the following points must be proved:
  - ✦ the arrest/detention must be lawful;
  - ✦ the person concerned must know that an arrest is being made on him/her or another person.

Defences (see 2.1.2)

Related cases

R v Belfon [1976] 3 All ER 46, CA For the offence of wounding with intent the prosecution must prove that the defendant:
- wounded the victim;
- the wounding was deliberate and unjustified;
- with intent to cause really serious bodily harm;
- and the test of intent is subjective.

R v Roberts (1972) 56 Cr App R 95, CA A victim of an ongoing sexual assault jumped out of a car to escape and was seriously injured in doing so. The court considered the actions of a victim which could affect the 'chain of causation' and applied a 'causation test' to determine whether the harm/injury was the natural result of what the assailant had said or done:
- If victim's actions are reasonable ones which could be foreseen and were acceptable under the circumstances, then the defendant will be liable for injuries resulting from them.
- If the harm/injury to the victim is really brought by a voluntary act on the part of the victim which could not reasonably be foreseen, then the chain of causation between the defendant's actions and the harm/injury received will be broken and the defendant will not be liable for them.

Practical considerations (see also 2.3.1)

- Section 18 does not come under racially or religiously aggravated assaults (see **7.10.2**). However, the courts must consider such matters when determining sentence.
- The essential ingredient here is **intent**: either a specific intent to cause grievous bodily harm or intent to resist arrest.

- Proof is required that the defendant specifically intended to cause grievous bodily harm. Knowledge that grievous bodily harm was a virtually certain consequence of his/her action will not amount to an intention, but it *will* be good evidence from which a court can infer such an intention.
- Other factors which may indicate the specific intent include:
  - ✦ a repeated or planned attack;
  - ✦ deliberate selection of a weapon or adaptation of an article to cause injury, such as breaking a glass before an attack;
  - ✦ making prior threats;
  - ✦ using an offensive weapon against, or kicking, the victim's head.
- Proof is required that the wound/GBH was inflicted maliciously. This means that the defendant must have foreseen some harm—although not necessarily the specific type or gravity of injury suffered or inflicted.
- Generally an assault under this section may take one of four different forms:
  - ✦ wounding with intent to do grievous bodily harm;
  - ✦ causing grievous bodily harm, with intent to do grievous bodily harm;
  - ✦ wounding with intent to resist or prevent the lawful arrest/detention of self/any person;
  - ✦ maliciously causing grievous bodily harm with intent to resist or prevent the lawful arrest of self/any person.
- Where evidence of intent is absent, but a wound or grievous bodily harm is still caused, then both s 18 and s 20 should be included on the indictment.
- Consideration must be given to **CPS advice** and the specific guidance for wounding/causing GBH with intent:
  - ✦ The distinction between charges under s 18 and s 20 is one of **intent**. The gravity of the injury resulting is not the determining factor, although it may provide some evidence of intent.
- In cases involving grievous bodily harm, remember that s 20 requires the infliction of harm, whereas s 18 requires the causing of harm, although this distinction has been greatly reduced by the decisions in *R v Ireland* [1998] AC 147, HL and *R v Burstow* [1997] 4 All ER 225, HL (see **2.3.1**).
- A s 18 offence includes wounding or causing grievous bodily harm with intent to resist or prevent the lawful detention of any person. This part of s 18 is of assistance in more serious assaults upon police officers, where the evidence of an intention to prevent arrest is clear, but the evidence of intent to cause grievous bodily harm is in doubt.
- Section 6(3) of the Criminal Law Act 1967 permits a conviction of s 20: inflicting grievous bodily harm in respect of a count for s 18 causing grievous bodily harm with intent as 'cause' includes 'inflict' (*R v Wilson and Jenkins* [1983] 3 All ER 448, HL)
- Obtain medical evidence to prove extent of injury.
- Obtain photographs of victim's injuries.

2.3.2 Wounding or Grievous Bodily Harm—with Intent

 SSS E&S

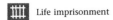 Indictable only None

Life imprisonment

Links to alternative subjects and offences

2.4 Child Cruelty and Taking a Child into Police Protection

The Children and Young Persons Act 1933 was introduced to prevent any child or young person being exposed to moral or physical danger. Section 1 of the Act creates offences relating to the treatment of children below the age of 16 years by persons with responsibility for them.

This topic area deals with child cruelty and taking a child into police protection.

2.4.1 Child cruelty

Offence

If a person who has attained the age of 16 years and has **responsibility** for a **child** or **young person** under that age wilfully assaults, ill-treats, neglects, abandons, or exposes him, or causes or procures him to be assaulted, ill-treated, **neglected**, abandoned, or exposed, **in a manner likely to cause** him unnecessary suffering or **injury to health** (including injury to or loss of sight, hearing, limb, or organ of the body, and any mental derangement), that person is guilty of an offence. **Children and Young Persons Act 1933, s 1(1)**

Points to prove

✓ date and location
✓ being a person
✓ 16 years or over
✓ having responsibility
✓ for a child/young person
✓ wilfully
✓ assaulted/ill-treated/neglected/abandoned/exposed the child/young person **or** caused/procured/the child/young person to be assaulted/ill-treated
✓ in manner likely
✓ to cause unnecessary suffering/injury to health

Meanings

Responsibility (s17)

• The following will be presumed to have responsibility for a child or young person:
 (a) any person who:
  (i) has **parental responsibility** for the child/young person; or

(ii) is otherwise legally liable to maintain the child/young
person; and
(b) any person who has care of the child/young person
- A person who is presumed to be responsible for a child or young
person by virtue of (a) will not be taken to have ceased to be
responsible for him by reason only that he does not have care of him.

Parental responsibility

In this Act parental responsibility means all the rights, duties, powers,
responsibilities, and authority which by law a parent of a child has in
relation to that child and his property.

Child

Means a person under 14 years of age.

Young person

Means a person who has attained the age of 14 but is under the age of
17 years.

Neglect in a manner likely to cause injury to health

- A parent or other person legally liable to maintain a child or young
person, or the **legal guardian** of such a person, is deemed to have
neglected in a manner likely to cause injury to health if they have
failed to provide adequate food, clothing, medical aid, or lodging, or
if, having been unable to do so, they have failed to take steps to
procure it to be provided under relevant enactments.
- A person may be convicted of this offence:
  - even though actual suffering or injury to health, or the likelihood
  of it, was prevented by the action of another person;
  - notwithstanding the death of the child or young person in
  question.

Legal guardian

In relation to a child or young person, means a **guardian** of a child as
defined in the Children Act 1989.

Guardian

In relation to a child or young person, includes any person who, in
the opinion of the court having cognizance of any case in relation to
the child or young person or in which the child or young person is
concerned, has for the time being the care of the child or young person.

Explanatory notes

- The term 'ill-treated' is not specifically defined, but will include
bullying, frightening, or any conduct causing unnecessary suffering
or injury to physical or mental health.
- Under s 58 of the Children Act 2004, battery of a child cannot be
justified on the ground that it constituted reasonable punishment.

Practical considerations

- The circumstances that satisfy this offence may justify a more serious charge, such as manslaughter (see **2.7.2**), or causing/allowing the death of a child or vulnerable adult (see **2.7.3**).
- Section 548 of the Education Act 1996 prevents teachers in any school from giving corporal punishment.
- The prosecution must prove a deliberate or reckless act or failure to act. The test is **subjective**, not based on the notion of a reasonable parent or person in charge.
- If a child has been ill-treated by one or both parents, but there is no evidence to suggest which one, it may be possible to consider them jointly responsible.
- Consideration should be given to taking the child/young person into police protection (see **2.4.2**).

E&S

 Either way   None

Summary: 6 months' imprisonment and/or a fine not exceeding the statutory maximum.
Indictment: 10 years' imprisonment and/or a fine.

2.4.2 Taking a child at risk into police protection

The Children Act 1989 comprehensively reformed the law in relation to child welfare. Section 46 of the Act provides for the removal and accommodation of children by police in cases of emergency. The following relates to police powers to take children under 18 years old who are at risk of significant harm into police protection.

Powers

(1) Where a constable has reasonable cause to believe that a child would otherwise be likely to suffer significant harm, he may:
   (a) remove him to suitable accommodation and keep him there; or
   (b) take all reasonable steps to ensure that his removal from a hospital, or other place, in which he is being accommodated is prevented.
(2) For the purposes of this Act, a child with respect to whom a constable has exercised his powers under this section is referred to as having been taken into police protection.

(3) As soon as reasonably practicable after taking a child into police protection the constable concerned must:

(a) inform the local authority within whose area the child was found of the steps that have been, and are proposed to be, taken concerning him under this section and the reasons for taking them;

(b) give details to the authority within whose area the child is ordinarily resident ('the appropriate authority') of the place where he is being accommodated;

(c) inform the child (if he appears capable of understanding) of:

(i) the steps taken with respect to him under this section and of the reasons for taking them; and

(ii) the further steps that may be taken with respect to him under this section;

(d) take such steps as are reasonably practicable to discover the wishes and feelings of the child;

(e) secure that the case is inquired into by an officer designated for the purposes of this section by the chief officer of the police area concerned; and

(f) where the child was taken into police protection by being removed to accommodation which is not provided:

(i) by or on behalf of a local authority; or

(ii) as a refuge, in compliance with the requirements of section 51, secure that he is moved to such accommodation.

(4) As soon as is reasonably practicable after taking a child into police protection the constable concerned must take all reasonably practicable steps to inform:

(a) the child's parents;

(b) every person who is not a parent but has parental responsibility for him; and

(c) any other person with whom he was living immediately before being taken into police protection, of the steps that he has taken under this section with respect to the child, the reasons for taking them and the further steps that may be taken with respect to him under this section.

Children Act 1989, s 46(1)–(4)

Meaning of hospital

Any health service hospital within the meaning of the National Health Service Act 1977; **and** any accommodation provided by a local authority and used as a hospital by or on behalf of the Secretary of State under that Act, but not where high security psychiatric services are provided.

Explanatory notes

• The spirit of the legislation is that all the parties including the parents, the child, and the local authority are to be kept informed and given reasons for any actions. The child's wishes must be listened to but do not have to be acted upon.

- The term **'police protection'** is not defined in the Act, but means that the police will protect the child until more formal arrangements can be made. It would be possible to take children into police protection without physically moving them from their present location. For example, if a child is in hospital having been battered, s/he may be taken into police protection while leaving the child in the hospital.
- This power is appropriate for detaining and returning children missing from homes against their will, so long as they are at risk from significant harm.

Related cases

Langley and others v Liverpool City Council [2006] 1 WLR 375, CA
Section 46 gives the police power to remove and accommodate children in cases of emergency. If practicable the removal of a child should be authorized by an emergency protection court order under s 44 and carried out by the local authority. If the police are aware that such an order is in force, they should not exercise their s 46 powers, unless there are compelling reasons for doing so.

Practical considerations

- Home Office Circular 44/2003 provides guidance as follows:
  - The designated officer will usually be an officer of the rank of Inspector.
  - These powers should only be used when the child would be likely to suffer significant harm.
  - Except in exceptional circumstances (eg imminent threat to a child's welfare), no child is to be taken into police protection until the investigating officer has seen the child and assessed his/her circumstances.
  - An Emergency Protection Order cannot be obtained prior to the birth of a child, even if it is believed that it will be at risk of significant harm after it is born.
  - No specific power of entry is provided for the exercise of police protection powers under s 46(1).
  - A police station is not suitable accommodation for these purposes, but may be used as a temporary or emergency measure until suitable accommodation is identified.
  - If it is necessary for a child to be brought to a police station every effort should be made to ensure his physical safety, comfort, access to food and drink, and access to toilet and washroom facilities.
- Section 46 of the Children Act 1989 also defines the **duties** of the **designated officer** in respect of a child in police protection:
  - On completing any enquiry under s 46(3)(e), the officer conducting it must release the child from police protection unless he considers that there is still reasonable cause for believing that the child would be likely to suffer significant harm if released (s 46(5)).
  - No child may be kept in police protection for more than 72 hours (s 46(6)).
  - While a child is being kept in police protection, the designated officer may apply on behalf of the appropriate authority for an

emergency protection order to be made under s 44 with respect to the child (s 46(7)).

♦ An application may be made under subsection (7) whether or not the authority know of it or agree to its being made (s 46(8)).

♦ While the child is being kept in police protection:
   (a) neither the constable concerned nor the designated officer will have parental responsibility for him; but
   (b) the designated officer must do what is reasonable in the circumstances for safeguarding or promoting the child's welfare (considering in particular the length of time that the child will be so protected) (s 46(9)).

♦ Where the child has been taken into police protection, the designated officer must allow:
   (a) his parents;
   (b) a person who is not a parent but has parental responsibility for him;
   (c) a person with whom the child was living immediately before he was taken into police protection;
   (d) a person in whose favour a contact order is in force concerning the child;
   (e) a person who is allowed to have contact with the child under an order under s 34; and
   (f) any person acting on behalf of any of those persons,
   to have such contact with the child as, in the opinion of the designated officer, is both reasonable and in the child's best interests (s 46(10)).

• The Children Act 2004 introduced measures to safeguard and promote the welfare of children. The Act obliges a range of parties providing children's services, including the police, to cooperate to improve the well-being of children. This involves the establishment of a Local Safeguarding Children Board for each area, to which the police are a Board partner, and an information database whereby information can be shared between all partners.

♦ For further advice on instances involving child abuse see **13.2**.

Links to alternative subjects and offences

2.5 **Threats to Kill**

The offence of 'threats to kill' is a serious offence, particularly in its effect on the victim. Practically speaking, the threats are often made during a heated argument or a moment of aggression and it is not unusual for the case to fail to reach the courts owing to lack of proof of the required intent.

Section 16 of the Offences against the Person Act 1861 provides the offence of threats to kill. It states:

Offence

A person who, without lawful excuse makes to another a threat **intending** that the other would fear it would be carried out, to kill that other or a third person shall be guilty of an offence.

Offences Against the Person Act 1861, s 16

Points to prove
✓ date and location
✓ without lawful excuse
✓ made threat to kill
✓ intending to cause fear threat would be carried out

Meaning of Intending (see **4.1**)

Explanatory notes
- There is no need to show that the defendant intended to kill anyone. The relevant intent has to be that the person receiving the threat would fear the threat (to kill them or a third person) would be carried out.
- An unborn child (foetus in utero) is not a 'third person' for this purpose. Therefore, a threat to a pregnant woman to kill her unborn baby is not an offence under this section.

Defences
- The specific statutory defence to this offence is having a lawful excuse. Such excuse could arise from a number of sources, including the prevention of crime or self-defence.
- The defence will only apply if it was reasonable in all the circumstances to make the threat.

Related cases

R v Cousins [1982] 2 All ER 115, CA A lawful excuse can exist if a threat to kill is made for the prevention of crime or for self defence, provided that it is reasonable in the circumstances to make such a threat.

R v Tait [1990] 1 QB 290, CA An unborn child is not a third person as it is not distinct from its mother. Therefore, a threat to kill the child in the womb or cause a miscarriage will not commit this offence. However, a threat to kill the baby at birth will be an offence under this section.

Practical considerations

- The onus is on the prosecution to prove that there was no lawful excuse for making a threat. The jury should be directed to any facts that could give rise to a defence of lawful excuse which was reasonable. It is for the jury to decide what is reasonable and what amounts to a threat.
- Proof of the *mens rea* ('guilty mind'), as to the intention that the other person would fear the threat would be carried out to kill that person or a third person is required.
- Evidence of previous history between the parties is admissible as tending to prove that the defendant intended his words to be taken seriously.
- Detail in your file and CJA witness statements the following points:
  ♦ nature of the threats made—exact words used and in what context, include any previous threats made.
  ♦ the fact that the threat was **understood** by the person to whom it was made and that the person feared the threat would be carried out.
  ♦ describe the full circumstances of the incident, antecedent history details of the relationship between the defendant and complainant.
- Does the defendant have a lawful excuse (defence) for making the threat?
- Consider whether or not there are any 'aggravating' circumstances such as racial or religious motivation or terrorism.

SSS   **E&S**

 Either way   None

Summary: 6 months' imprisonment and/or a fine not exceeding the statutory maximum.
Indictment: 10 years' imprisonment.

Links to alternative subjects and offences

2.6 False Imprisonment, Kidnapping and Child Abduction

Contained within this topic area are the common law offences of kidnapping and false imprisonment and child abduction under the Child Abduction Act 1984. Although officers rarely deal with these incidents they should still be aware of the law in case they have to deal with any violent domestic incidents, sexual offences, or other cases where people are taken against their will.

2.6.1 False imprisonment

False imprisonment is an offence at common law. The ingredients are:

Offence
The unlawful and total restraint of the personal liberty of another, whether by constraining them or compelling them to go to a particular place or by confining them in a prison or police station or private place or by detaining them against their will in a public place.

Points to prove
✓ date and location
✓ imprisoned, detained, or arrested
✓ another person
✓ against his/her will
✓ unlawfully

Explanatory notes
- The wrongful act ('*actus reus*') of false imprisonment is the act of placing an unlawful restriction on the victim's freedom in the absence of any legal right to do so.
- There must also have been an element of intent ('*mens rea*') to restrain, either deliberately or recklessly.
- There is no offence if the victim is not physically restrained, unless the offender detains/intends to detain them by use of fear/threats.

2.6.1 False Imprisonment

Defences
That the taking or detaining was in the course of a lawful arrest or detention under the Police and Criminal Evidence Act 1984 (see **12.2**) or acting under another statutory or common law power.

Related cases

Bird v Jones (1845) 7 QB 742, QBD Preventing a person from proceeding along a particular way is not false imprisonment.

R v James (Anthony David) The Times, 2 October 1997, CA The victim's fear that she was being restrained had to arise from the defendant's intentional or reckless act to frighten her into staying where she was. If the victim's lack of will to escape was simply a by-product of an assault then the offence of false imprisonment is not committed.

R v Rahman (1985) 81 Cr App R 349, CA False imprisonment consists of the unlawful or reckless restraint of a person's freedom of movement from a particular place. 'Unlawful' is not restricted to the contravention of a court order.

Austin and Saxby v Commissioner of Police of the Metropolis [2005] EWHC 480, QBD Detaining thousands of people in a police cordoned area for several hours had been a deprivation of their liberty (in breach of Article 5—see **1.1**) and also amounted to false imprisonment. However, it was justified as there had been a conditional intention to arrest and was necessary for the protection of everyone to detain the crowd until dispersal could be arranged safely.

Practical considerations

- A parent has no right to imprison their own child, although a parent is allowed to detain a child for purposes of reasonable parental discipline. Whether it is reasonable in all the circumstances is for a jury to decide.
- A victim could bring civil action for damages (something which invariably happens after unlawful arrest by the police).

 Indictable   None

 Life imprisonment and/or unlimited fine

2.6.2 **Kidnapping**

Kidnapping is another offence at common law. The ingredients are:

> **Offence**
> The taking or carrying away of one person by another, by force or **fraud**, without the consent of the person so taken or carried away, and without lawful excuse.

Points to prove

✓ date and location
✓ without lawful excuse
✓ by force/fraud
✓ took/carried away
✓ another person
✓ without their consent

Meaning of fraud

Means deceit/guile/trick. It should not be confused with the narrower meaning given to it for the purposes of consent in sexual offences.

Explanatory notes

- The important points to prove are the deprivation of liberty and carrying away even where a short distance is involved—and the absence of consent.
- In the case of a child it is the child's consent that should be considered (rather than the parent/guardian) and in the case of a very young child, absence of consent may be inferred.

> **Defences**
> Consent or lawful excuse.

Related cases

R v Wellard [1978] 3 All ER 161, CA The defendant purported to be a police officer and escorted/placed a female victim into his car a short distance away. Held that the ingredients of the offence of kidnapping are :

- that the victim was deprived of their liberty; and
- carried away from the place where they wanted to be without lawful excuse.

R v Cort [2003] 3 WLR 1300, CA The defendant went to bus stops telling lone women that the bus they were waiting for had broken down and offering/providing lifts in his vehicle. The fact that the defendant had lied about the absence of the buses meant that, although they had got into the car voluntarily, the women had not given true consent to the journey and the offences of kidnap (and attempts) were complete.

R v Reid [1972] 2 All ER 1350, CA A husband has no right to kidnap his wife. It is immaterial whether the wife was living with her husband at the time of the offence.

R v D (1984) 79 Cr App R 313, HL A parent has no right to kidnap own child. Whether the child has consented, it will be a matter of the fact for the jury to decide. In the case of a very young child, absence of consent can be inferred (see Child abduction **2.6.3**).

Practical considerations

- A man or woman may be guilty of this offence in relation to their spouse or partner.
- Under s 5 of the Child Abduction Act 1984 (see **2.6.3**), except by or with the consent of the Director of Public Prosecutions no prosecution shall be instituted for an offence of kidnapping if it was committed:
  - ◆ against a child under the age of sixteen;
  - ◆ by a person connected with the child.
- In all other cases the consent of the Director of Public Prosecutions is not required.

 Indictable   None

Life imprisonment and/or unlimited fine

2.6.3 **Child abduction**

The Child Abduction Act 1984 amends the law in relation to the abduction of children. There are two different offences—one for a person connected with that child (parent/guardian) (s 1) the other committed by other persons (s 2).

Person connected with child

Offence

Subject to subsection 1(5) and 1(8), a **person connected** with a child under the age of 16 commits an offence if he **takes** or **sends** the child out of the United Kingdom without the **appropriate consent**.

Child Abduction Act 1984, s 1(1)

> **Points to prove**
> ✓ date and location
> ✓ being a parent/person connected with
> ✓ a child under 16 years of age
> ✓ took/sent that child
> ✓ out of the United Kingdom
> ✓ without the appropriate consent

Meanings

Person connected (s 1(2))

A **person connected** with a child for the purposes of this section is:

(a) a parent of the child; or
(b) in the case of a child whose parents were not married to each other at the time of his birth, there are reasonable grounds for believing that he is the father of the child; or
(c) the guardian of the child; or
(d) a person in whose favour a residence order is in force with respect to the child; or
(e) has custody of the child.

Takes

A person is regarded as **taking** a child if s/he causes or induces the child to accompany him/her or any other person or causes the child to be taken.

Sends

A person is regarded as **sending** a child if s/he causes the child to be sent.

Appropriate consent (s 1(3))

This means:

(a) the consent of each person:
    (i) who is parent or guardian of the child; or
    (ii) to whom custody of the child has been awarded (whether solely or jointly with any other person) by an order of a court in England or Wales; or
(b) if the child is the subject of a custody order, the leave of the court which made the order (including any magistrates' court acting for the same petty sessions area); or
(c) the leave of the court granted on an application for a direction.

Explanatory notes

The offence is committed subject to:

- a statutory defence of consent (s 1(5)—below).
- a child being in the care of a local authority or voluntary organisation or place of safety whilst subject to adoption proceedings (s 1(8)).

Defence

(5) A person does not commit an offence under this section by doing anything without the consent of another person whose consent is required under the forgoing provisions if:

(a) he does it in the belief that the other person:
  (i) has consented; or
  (ii) would consent if he was aware of all the relevant circumstances; or
(b) he has taken all reasonable steps to communicate with the other person but has been unable to communicate with him; or
(c) the other person has unreasonably refused to consent

(5A) Section 1(5)(c) above does not apply if:

(a) the person who refused consent is a person:
  (i) in whose favour there is a residence order with respect to the child; or
  (ii) who has custody of the child; or
(b) the person taking or sending the child out of the United Kingdom is, by so acting, in breach of an order made by a court in the United Kingdom.   Child Abduction Act 1984, s 1(5) & (5A)

Abduction of child by other persons

An offence in relation to the taking or detaining a child where the offender is not connected with that child states:

Offence

Subject to subsection 2(3), a person other than one mentioned in subsection 2(2) below, commits an offence if, without lawful authority or reasonable excuse, he *takes* or *detains* a child under the age of 16—

(a) so as to remove him from the lawful control of any person having lawful control of the child; or
(b) so as to keep him out of the lawful control of any person entitled to lawful control of the child.   Child Abduction Act 1984, s 2(1)

Points to prove

✓ date and location
✓ without lawful authority/reasonable excuse
✓ detained **or** took
✓ a child under 16 years of age
✓ so as to remove him/her
✓ from/out of the lawful control
✓ of a person having/entitled to lawful control
✓ of that child

Meanings

Takes

A person is regarded as taking a child if s/he causes or induces the child to accompany him/her or any other person or causes the child to be taken.

Detains

A person is regarded as detaining a child if s/he causes the child to be detained or induces the child to remain with him/her or any other person.

Explanatory notes

- The offence is committed subject to a statutory defence of consent (s 2(3)—below).
- This offence does not apply to the persons listed in s 2(2) namely:
  - ♦ the child's father and mother—where the father and mother of the child in question were married to each other at the time of his/her birth;
  - ♦ the child's mother—where the father and mother of the child in question were not married to each other at the time of his/her birth
  - ♦ any other person mentioned in s 1(2)(c), s 1(2)(d), or s 1(2)(e) above.
- **Remove from lawful control** can be satisfied if the child is induced to take some action that they would not normally have done.

Defences

It shall be a defence for that person to prove:
(a) where the father and mother of the child in question were not married at the time of his birth:
  (i) that he is the child's father
  (ii) that, at the time of the alleged offence, he believed, on reasonable grounds, that he was the child's father, or
(b) that, at the time of the alleged offence, he believed that the child had attained the age of 16 years.   Child Abduction Act 1984, s 2(3)

Related cases

R v Leather [1993] Crim LR 516, CA Children playing in the park were induced by the defendant to go to another part of the park to look for a stolen bike (which did not exist). No force was used and no attempt was made to restrain them. Held that the children had, without any lawful authority or excuse, been deflected from what they would otherwise have been doing into some activity induced by the accused. Therefore, the children had been taken—removed from lawful control.

R v A (Child Abduction) [2000] 2 All ER 177, CA The jury has to be satisfied that the defendant caused the child to accompany him/her. However, he/she does not have to be the sole or even the main cause for

2.6.3 Child Abduction

the child going with him/her (though the actions must be more than a peripheral or inconsequential cause).

Foster and another v DPP [2005] 1 WLR 1400, QBD   Section 2 has two separate offences and alternative charges cannot be made. The *mens rea* of s 2 is an intentional or reckless taking or detention. It is immaterial that the child consents to removal from lawful control, but the s 2(3)(b) defence is available if it is believed that the child was 16 or over.

Practical considerations

- Consider the more serious offence of kidnapping (see **2.6.2**).
- In relation to the s 1 offence (person connected with child): it can only be committed by those people listed **and** they must take or send that child out of the UK; the prosecution must rebut the defence of consent and the consent of the DPP is required before proceedings may be commenced.
- A Convention agreement exists between the UK and other countries regarding liaison between the different civil jurisdictions in those countries in order to recover the abducted child.
- Section 2 (other people not connected with the child) will cover the situation where an agent snatches a child for an estranged parent. The parent in such a case may commit the offence of aiding and abetting or the principal offence.

 Either way   None

Summary: 6 months, imprisonment and/or a fine not exceeding the statutory maximum.
Indictment: 7 years' imprisonment.

Links to alternative subjects and offences

2.7 Suspicious Deaths

When police officers investigate sudden/suspicious deaths they should have a basic knowledge of the relevant law and their powers. Apart from informing supervision, following Force policies/procedures and requesting the assistance of scenes of crime officers, be mindful of scene preservation and the obtaining of forensic evidence (see **1.3**).

The following topics: murder; manslaughter; causing or allowing the death of a child/vulnerable adult; 'over-laying' of an infant; infanticide; child destruction; and concealment of birth, will now be dealt with.

2.7.1 Murder

The offence of murder comes under the common law and is defined as:

> **Offence (at common law)**
>
> Where a person of **sound mind and discretion** unlawfully kills any **reasonable creature in being** and under the **Queen's peace**, with intent to kill or **cause grievous bodily harm**.

> **Points to prove**
> ✓ date and location
> ✓ unlawfully killed a human being
> ✓ with intent to kill or cause grievous bodily harm

Meanings

Sound mind and discretion

Every person of the age of discretion is presumed to be sane and accountable for his actions, unless the contrary is proved. This means anyone who is not insane or under 10 years old.

Unlawfully

Means without lawful authority, legal justification, or excuse.

Kills

This is 'the act' ('*actus reus*') which is the substantial cause of death (stabbed, shot, strangled, suffocated, poisoned, etc).

Reasonable creature in being

Any human being, including a baby born alive having an independent existence from its mother.

Under the Queen's peace

This is meant to exclude killing in the course of war. A British subject takes the Queen's peace with them everywhere in the world.

Intent

An intention to kill or to cause grievous bodily harm is the '*mens rea*' of murder (see **4.1**).

Cause/causation

If there is an 'intervening factor' between the defendant's actions and the death of the victim, the jury will consider whether the defendant's act **contributed significantly** to the death.

Grievous bodily harm   (see **2.3**)

Explanatory notes

- Children under 10 years of age are presumed incapable of forming the necessary intent to commit a crime (Children and Young Persons Act 1933, s 50).
- If a defendant wishes to plead insanity, they will be judged on McNaughten's Rules from *McNaughten's Case* (1843) 10 Cl & F 200. This states that, at the time of the commission of the offence, the person was 'labouring under such defect of reason from disease of the mind that either: (a) the defendant did not know what he/she was doing, **or** (b) s/he did know what s/he was doing but did not know it was wrong.'
- The onus is on the prosecution to prove that the killing was unlawful.
- If a person intentionally causes grievous bodily harm and the victim subsequently dies as a result, the defendant is guilty of murder.
- Traditionally it required 'malice aforethought', but practically it is the relevant intent that will determine whether an unlawful killing is murder or manslaughter.
- The jury will consider whether the defendant's act **contributed significantly** to the death by applying the 'substantial test' as set out in the case *R v Smith* [1959] 2 All ER 193, Court Martial CA.
- Whether the defendant intended or foresaw the results of his/her actions will be determined by a number of factors including the statutory test under the Criminal Justice Act 1967, s 8 (see **4.1**).

Defences

Insanity

See the meaning of 'sound mind and discretion' and explanatory notes as to 'insanity'.

Lawful killing

Means with lawful authority; legal justification or excuse (see **1.2.1**). Self defence.

At war

This is self explanatory, not being under the 'Queen's peace' (see meaning).

Specific defences

Provocation

Where on a charge of murder there is evidence on which the jury can find that the person charged was provoked (whether by things done or by things said or by both together) to lose his self-control, the question whether the provocation was enough to make a reasonable man do as he did shall be left to be determined by the jury; and in determining that question the jury shall take into account everything both done and said according to the effect which, in their opinion, it would have on a reasonable man.

Homicide Act 1957, s 3

Diminished responsibility

Where a person kills or is party to the killing of another, he shall not be convicted of murder if he was suffering from such abnormality of mind (whether arising from a condition of arrested or retarded development of mind or any inherent causes or induced by disease or injury) as substantially impaired his mental responsibility for his acts and omissions in doing or being party to the killing.

Homicide Act 1957, s 2(1)

Suicide pact

Means a common agreement between two or more persons having for its object the death of all of them, whether or not each is to take his own life, but nothing done by a person who enters into a suicide pact shall be treated as done by him in pursuance of the pact unless it is done while he has the settled intention of dying in pursuance of the pact.

Homicide Act 1957, s 4(1)

Related cases

R v Hatton [2005] EWCA Crim 2951, CA Self defence—not possible if mistake induced by intoxication.

R v Byrne [1960] 3 All ER 1, CA An abnormality of mind (diminished responsibility defence) is a 'state of mind so different from that of ordinary, reasonable human beings that they would call it abnormal'.

R v Cheshire [1991] 1 WLR 844, CA Even though medical negligence was the primary cause of death, the shooting had been a major contributory factor in death and the wounds inflicted were a significant cause of death.

R v Smith [1959] 2 All ER 193, Court Martial CA Only if the second cause is so overwhelming as to make the original wound merely part of the history can it be said that the death does not flow from the wound.

R v Malcherek & R v Steel (1981) 73 Cr App R 173, CA A defendant (who causes injury) necessitating medical treatment could not argue that the sole cause of death was the doctor's action in switching the life support system off.

R v Moloney [1985] 1 All ER 1025, HL The jury has to decide whether the defendant **intended** to kill or cause grievous bodily harm.

R v Smith [2001] 1 AC 146, HL Provocation requires some act by the victim, which causes the defendant a sudden temporary loss of self-control. The considerations for the jury in such cases are technically complex and require a consideration of both subjective and objective elements.

Practical considerations

- The defendant's act must be the substantial cause of death.
- The killing must be causally related to the acts of the defendant and not through an intervening factor which breaks the chain of causation.
- If there is doubt whether death was caused by some supervening event (such as medical negligence when treated), the prosecution do not have to prove that the supervening event was not a significant cause of death.
- Intention—*mens rea* ('guilty mind')—has to be proved (see **4.1**).
- The date of the offence is the actual date of death.
- Consent of the Attorney-General is required where:
  + the injury was sustained more than three years before death; **or**
  + the accused has been previously convicted of the offence alleged to be connected with the death.
- If a person is suffering from a terminal disease and receives a wound that hastens their death, this killing would (with the required intent) be murder or manslaughter.
- A murder or manslaughter committed by a British citizen outside the UK may be tried in this country as if it had been committed here (Offences Against the Person Act 1861, s 9, and the British Nationality Act 1948, s 3).
- Motivation will form a key part of any prosecution and will also be relevant in considering the availability of special or general defences.
- Motivation, such as revenge, would mean that a person has had time to think/reflect so negating the defence of provocation (no sudden and temporary loss of self-control) and increasing the likelihood that the defendant foresaw the consequences of their actions and therefore that they intended them to happen.
- Note that the only *mens rea* that will suffice for attempted murder is an intent to kill and the defence of diminished responsibility cannot be used in answer to such a charge.
- Section 2(1) of the Suicide Act 1961 creates the **offence** of aiding and abetting a suicide: 'A person who aids, abets, counsels or procures the suicide of another, or an attempt by another, shall be liable on conviction on indictment to imprisonment for a term not exceeding 14 years.'

♿ Indictable   🕔 None

▦ Life imprisonment

2.7.2 **Manslaughter**

> **Offence**
> Manslaughter is the **unlawful killing** of another human being which can either be a **voluntary** or **involuntary** manslaughter offence.
>
> Common Law

Points to prove
- ✓ date and location
- ✓ unlawful act **or** gross negligence
- ✓ killed a human being

Meanings

Unlawful killing (see 2.7.1)

Voluntary manslaughter

This occurs when a murder charge is reduced to voluntary manslaughter by reason of one of the specific defences to murder (see **2.7.1**).

Involuntary manslaughter

Is an unlawful killing without an intention to kill or cause grievous bodily harm. Apart from the required intent, the elements of the offence are the same as for murder (see **2.7.1**). Manslaughter can be caused by:
- **unlawful act** (not omission): The unlawful act must be unlawful in itself (eg another criminal offence such as an assault or a threat to kill) and must involve a risk that someone would be harmed by it;
- **gross negligence** (involving breach of duty): Gross negligence manslaughter requires a breach of a duty of care owed by the defendant to the victim under circumstances where the defendant's conduct was serious enough to amount to a crime.

Related cases

Attorney-General's Reference (No 3 of 1994) [1997] Crim LR 829, HL A baby was born prematurely after an intentional stabbing which penetrated and damaged the foetus. The baby only lived for 120 days.

The doctrine of 'transferred malice' was not wide enough to encompass murder, but was sufficient for manslaughter.

R v Roberts, Day (I) and Day (M) [2001] Crim LR 984, CA An intent to cause GBH is murder but an intention only to do some lesser harm is manslaughter.

R v Adomako Sulman & others [1993] 4 All ER 935, HL Manslaughter by gross negligence requires:
* that the defendant owed a duty of care to the victim;
* a breach of that duty;
* which caused the victim's death; and
* in circumstances where the defendant's conduct was so bad as to amount to a criminal act.

R v Misra and Srivastava [2004] All ER (D) 150, CA Grossly negligent medical treatment, which exposes the patient to the risk of death and causes the death of the victim would be manslaughter.

Practical considerations
* The previous convictions or past behaviour of the defendant in homicide cases may well be relevant, both to the issue of *mens rea*/intent and also to sentence.
* The burden of proof in relation to claiming diminished responsibility or acting in pursuance of a suicide pact lies with the defendant.
* Acts having fatal consequences for another person can arise in a number of forms—from workplace accidents to calculated acts of violence.
* Motivation will form a key part of any prosecution and will also be relevant in considering the availability of special or general defences.
* Motivation such as revenge would mean that a person has had time to think/reflect so negating the defence of provocation (no sudden and temporary loss of self-control) and increasing the likelihood that the defendant foresaw the consequences of their actions and therefore that they intended them to happen.
* Note that the only *mens rea* that will suffice for attempted murder is an intent to kill and the defence of diminished responsibility cannot be used in answer to such a charge.
* Section 2(1) of the Suicide Act 1961 creates the **offence** of aiding and abetting a suicide (see **2.7.1**).

 SSS E&S

 Indictable   🕐 None

 Life imprisonment

2.7.3 **Death of a child or vulnerable adult**

Section 5 of the Domestic Violence, Crime and Victims Act 2004 creates an offence of causing or allowing the death of a child or a vulnerable adult by means of an unlawful act.

Offence

A person ('D') is guilty of an offence if—
(a) a child or vulnerable adult ('V') dies as result of the unlawful act of a person who;
  (i) was a member of the same household as V, and
  (ii) had frequent contact with him,
(b) D was such a person at the time of that act,
(c) at that time there was a significant risk of serious physical harm being caused to V by the unlawful act of such a person, and
(d) either D was the person whose act caused V's death or
  (i) D was, or ought to have been, aware of the risk mentioned in paragraph (c),
  (ii) D failed to take such steps as he could reasonably have been expected to take to protect V from the risk, and
  (iii) the act occurred in circumstances of the kind that D foresaw or ought to have foreseen.   Domestic Violence, Crime and Victims Act 2004, s 5

Points to prove

✓ date and location
✓ being a member of the same household and having had frequent contact with a person who was at that time a child/vulnerable adult
✓ caused that person's death **or**
✓ was, or ought to have been, aware that there was a significant risk of serious physical harm being caused to that person
✓ by the unlawful act of a member of his/her household
✓ which occurred in circumstances of the kind that the defendant foresaw or ought to have foreseen and
✓ the defendant failed to take such steps as he/she could reasonably have been expected to take to protect him/her from that risk

Meanings

Child

Means a person under the age of 16 years.

Vulnerable adult

Means a person aged 16 or over whose ability to protect him/herself from violence, abuse or neglect is significantly impaired through physical or mental disability or illness, through old age or otherwise.

Unlawful act (see 2.7.2)

Act

This includes a course of conduct and also includes omission.

Member of the same household

This includes people who do not live in that household, providing they visit often and for such periods of time that they are regarded as a member of it.

Serious physical harm

Means grievous bodily harm (see **2.3**).

Explanatory notes

The meaning of a vulnerable adult also includes a temporary vulnerability as well as one which is permanent.

Practical considerations

- If the defendant was not the mother or father of the deceased then they may not be charged with this offence if they were under the age of 16 at the time of the act that caused the death. Similarly, they could not have been expected to take any such preventative steps to protect the victim before attaining that age.
- Charges can be brought against all members of a household who had responsibility for the death of a child or vulnerable adult.
- Despite this 'catch all' offence the death should still be thoroughly investigated to establish whether the person is responsible for murder or manslaughter.
- The offence is limited to an unlawful act, so it will not apply to accidental or cot deaths. Similarly the offence only applies to household members who had frequent contact with the victim, but is not restricted to family members or carers. It also imposes a duty to protect the victim from harm. However, the question of who is a household member will lie with the courts.

 Indictable   None

 14 years' imprisonment and/or a fine

2.7.4 **Over-laying/suffocation of infant under 3 in a bed**

The Children and Young Persons Act 1933 makes specific provision for circumstances where a child has been suffocated while sharing a bed with an adult.

2.7.5 Infanticide

Points to prove

✓ date and location
✓ being a person 16 years or over
✓ caused the death of an infant under
✓ years of age
✓ by suffocation
✓ while the infant was in bed with that person
✓ person under the influence of drink
✓ when he/she went to bed

Explanatory notes

The circumstances that satisfy this offence might justify a more serious charge, such as manslaughter and causing/allowing the death of a child (see **2.7.2**).

 E&S

 Either way   None

 Summary: 6 months' imprisonment and/or a fine not exceeding the statutory maximum.
Indictment: 10 years' imprisonment and/or a fine.

2.7.5 **Infanticide**

This offence is committed by the mother of a child (under 12 months old), who by any wilful act or omission, causes the death of her child whilst mentally unbalanced (such as post-natal depression) due to childbirth or lactation.

omission the balance of her mind was disturbed by reason of her not having fully recovered from the effect of giving birth to the child or by reason of the effect of lactation consequent upon the birth of the child, then, notwithstanding that the circumstances were such that but for this Act the offence would have amounted to murder, shall be guilty of a felony, that of infanticide, and may for such offence be dealt with and punished as if she had been guilty of the offence of manslaughter of the child.

Infanticide Act 1938, s 1(1)

Points to prove

✓ date and location
✓ a woman
✓ caused the death of her own child (being under 12 months of age)
✓ by wilful act/omission
✓ whilst balance of her mind disturbed.

Practical considerations

- On a count of infanticide, the accused may be convicted of an offence of child destruction under the Infant Life (Preservation) Act 1929 (see **2.7.6**).
- The date of offence will be the date death occurs.
- This offence is only appropriate to reduce what would otherwise be an act of murder to a lesser offence where the killing is done by a mother at a time when responsibility for her actions may have been reduced by the disturbance of her mind caused by childbirth.

 Indictable None

Life imprisonment

2.7.6 **Child destruction**

This is committed by any person, by any wilful act, intentionally destroying a child capable of being born alive, either at or before birth.

Offence

Any person who, with intent to destroy the life of a child capable of being born alive, by any wilful act causes a child to die before it has an existence independent of its mother, shall be guilty of an offence

Infant Life (Preservation) Act 1929, s 1(1)

Points to prove

✓ date and location
✓ with intent to destroy the life of a child capable of being born alive
✓ by a wilful act (specify)
✓ caused the child to die
✓ before it had existence independent of mother

Explanatory notes

Capable of being born alive

Evidence that a woman had at any material time been pregnant for a period of 28 weeks or more shall be prima facie proof that she was at that time pregnant of a child capable of being born alive.

Related case

Rance v Mid-Downs Health Authority [1991] 1 QB 587, QBD An abortion carried out when the baby was capable of being born alive at that stage of the pregnancy would have been unlawful.

Practical considerations

- It has been held that a foetus of between 18 and 21 weeks is not 'capable of being born alive' since it would be incapable of breathing even with the aid of a ventilator, and a termination of a pregnancy of that length is not an offence under this Act.
- No person shall be found guilty of this offence if it is proved that the act was done in good faith for saving the life of the mother.
- No offence under this Act is committed by a registered medical practitioner who terminates a pregnancy in accordance with the provisions of s 5(1) of the Abortion Act 1967.
- This Act and s 58 of the Offences Against the Person Act 1861 overlap. Section 58 (which relates to administering drugs or using instruments to procure abortion) prohibits attempts to procure a miscarriage at any time between conception and the birth of the child alive, while this Act prohibits the killing of any child capable of being born alive.

Indictable None

 Life imprisonment

2.7.7 **Concealment of birth**

Although this is not an offence of unlawful killing it is related to topics already discussed and concerns the offence of concealing the birth of a child, by secretly disposing of or hiding the body.

Offence

If any woman shall be delivered of a child, every person who shall, by any secret disposition of the dead body of the said child, whether such child died before, at, or after its birth, endeavour to conceal the birth thereof, shall be guilty of a misdemeanour, and being convicted thereof shall be liable, at the discretion of the court, to be imprisoned.

Offences Against the Person Act 1861, s 60

Points to prove

✓ date and location
✓ endeavoured to conceal the birth of a child
✓ by secret disposition of the dead body of the child

Related cases

R v Brown (1870) LR 1 CCR 244 'If the body were placed in the middle of a moor in winter, or on the top of a mountain, or in any other secluded place, where the body would not likely to be found', it would amount to a secret disposition.

R v Berriman (1854) 6 Cox 388 Concealment of a foetus only a few months old would not be an offence—'the child must have arrived at that stage of maturity at the time of birth that it might have been a living child'.

Practical considerations

• The offence is specific in that it must be a 'secret disposition'; the test being whether there is a likelihood that the body would be found.
• Where the body is put in a secluded place, even though it is not actually concealed from view, it may nevertheless be a secret disposition.

2.7.7 Concealment of Birth

- However, where a body was left in an area which is used regularly this would not be a secret disposition. Similarly, the same would apply to leaving a body in a dustbin awaiting collection.
- The defendant must be shown to have done some act of disposition **after** the child has died. If the living body of a child is concealed and then it dies where it is concealed, clearly a more serious offence of homicide should be considered.

 Either way   None

Summary: 6 months' imprisonment and/or a fine not exceeding the statutory maximum.
Indictment: 2 years' imprisonment.

Links to alternative subjects and offences

Chapter 3
Crime: Dishonesty

3.1 **Theft**

The Theft Act 1968 provides for the offence of theft and several other key offences of which theft is a constituent part. All references are to the 1968 Act unless otherwise stated.

Section 1 of the Act provides for the offence of theft, while s 11 covers the offence of removing articles from places open to the public and s 23 concerns advertising rewards for the return of stolen or lost goods.

3.1.1 **Theft**

Theft is defined by s 1 of the Act, while ss 2–6 explain the elements contained within that definition.

> **Offence**
>
> A person is guilty of theft if he dishonestly appropriates property belonging to another with the intention of permanently depriving the other of it; and 'thief' and 'steal' shall be construed accordingly.
>
> Theft Act 1968, s 1(1)

Points to prove
- ✓ dishonestly
- ✓ appropriates
- ✓ property
- ✓ belonging to another
- ✓ intention to permanently deprive the other of it.

Meanings

Dishonestly

Section 2 defines what will not be considered as 'dishonest'.

3.1.1 Theft

- It is not considered dishonest if a person takes possession of property belonging to another, whether for him/herself or a third person, believing that s/he has a legal right to deprive the other of it.
- It is not considered dishonest to take property belonging to another believing that, if the other had known about it and the circumstances, s/he would have consented.
- It will not be dishonest if, not being a trustee or personal representative, a person takes possession of property believing that, by taking reasonable steps, the owner could not be discovered.
- It is for the court to decide if a person acted dishonestly.
- Taking property belonging to another may be dishonest even if the perpetrator is willing to pay for it.

Appropriates

'Appropriates' is defined in s 3.

- If a person assumes the rights of an owner over property s/he is deemed to have appropriated it. This includes where s/he obtains the property without stealing and later assumes such rights by keeping or dealing with it as the owner.
- Where property (or a right or interest in it) is transferred to a person for its true value, any later assumption by the acquirer as to the rights of ownership will not amount to theft simply because the transferor had no right to transfer it.

Property

'Property' is defined by s 4.

- It includes money and all other property (real or personal) including 'things in action' and other intangible property.
- Land, or things forming part of it, and taken from it by a person or on his/her instructions, can only be stolen if:
  - ♦ the person is a trustee or personal representative, or is authorized by power of attorney, as a company liquidator, or in some other way, to sell or dispose of land belonging to somebody else, and s/he appropriates it or anything forming part of it, by dealing with it in breach of the confidence entrusted in him/her, or
  - ♦ when the person is not in possession of the land, s/he appropriates anything forming part of it by severing it, causing it to be severed or after it has been severed, or
  - ♦ when, being in possession of the land under a tenancy, s/he appropriates all or part of a fixture or structure let for use with that land.
- Mushrooms (and other fungus), flowers, plants (including shrubs and trees), and fruit or foliage from a plant are all capable of being 'property' for the purposes of theft. Picking mushrooms, flowers, fruit, or foliage **growing wild** on land is not theft unless it is done for reward, sale, or other commercial purpose.
- Wild creatures, tamed or untamed, are regarded as property. However, a wild creature which is not tamed or normally kept in captivity (or the carcass of such animal) cannot be stolen unless it has been taken into possession by or on behalf of another, and such possession has

not been lost or given up, or it is in the process of being taken into possession.

Belonging to another

'Belonging to another' is defined by s 5.

- Property belongs to any person having possession or control of it, or having a proprietary right or interest in it (such interest not being valid only because of an agreement to transfer or grant it).
- Where property is subject to a trust, ownership includes the right to enforce that trust, and any intention to break it is regarded as intending to deprive a person having such right.
- When a person obtains property because of another's mistake, and s/he is obliged to repay all or part of it, its proceeds or value then, to the extent of that obligation, the property or proceeds are regarded as belonging to the person entitled to restoration, and any intent not to repay it is an intention to deprive him/her of it.

Intention to permanently deprive

'Intention to permanently deprive' is defined by s 6.

- Appropriation of property belonging to another without meaning him/her permanently to lose it still has the intention of 'permanently depriving' him/her of it, if the appropriator intends to treat it as his/her own to dispose of regardless of the other's rights.
- Borrowing or lending the property may amount to treating it as his/her own if it is for a period and in circumstances equating to an outright taking or disposal.
- Where a person has possession or control of another's property, for his/her own purposes and without the other's permission, loans it to a third person with unachievable conditions for its return, s/he treats it as his own to dispose of regardless of the other's rights (eg pawning property belonging to another when not able to redeem it).

Explanatory notes

- It is immaterial whether the appropriation is made with a view to gain, or is made for the thief's own benefit.
- 'Things in action' include a cheque drawn to a payee, giving him/her an action (demand for payment), which s/he may enforce against the payer. It is, therefore, the property of the payee.
- 'Intangible property' includes patents, applications for patents, copyrights.
- 'Tenancy' means a tenancy for any period and includes a tenancy agreement, but a person who, when a tenancy ends, remains in possession as statutory tenant or otherwise will be treated as having possession under the tenancy.
- Possession, in general terms, means having the right to use property as your own without having any legal title to it (eg hiring a car—you have possession while legal ownership remains with the hire company).
- Possession may be 'actual' (an item in your hand or pocket) or 'constructive' (an item at your home while you are elsewhere).

- Control means having the power to use or manage items without having legal title to them (eg a delivery service having control of letters and packages for delivery—it does not actually own any of them and may not even have 'possession' at all times).
- Proprietary right or interest means ownership or having legal title of property or similar rights.
- An obligation to make restoration of property belonging to another must be a legal obligation, not a moral or social one.
- Simple and genuine borrowing of property is insufficient to constitute theft because the necessary *mens rea* is missing, unless the person intends to return the property in such a state that it loses its value or goodness (eg exam papers borrowed for copying would not be 'stolen' as they had not lessened in their intrinsic value).
- The theft or attempted theft of mail bags or postal packages, or their contents, whilst in transit between British postal areas is, even if it happens outside England and Wales, triable in England and Wales.

Related cases

R v Ghosh [1982] 2 All ER 689, QBD To determine dishonesty, the court must decide what is dishonest according to the ordinary standards of reasonable and honest people, **and** whether that person realized that what s/he was doing was dishonest by those standards.

R v Hinks [2000] 4 All ER 833, HL H influenced, coerced or encouraged the complainant who was naive, gullible and of limited intelligence to hand over sums of money, amounting to £60,000. The receipt of a valid gift is appropriation, and, if it is combined with circumstances where the acceptance of the property would be considered dishonest (by a reasonable person), then that conduct becomes theft.

R v Skivington [1967] 1 All ER 483, CA It is not considered dishonest if a person believes s/he has the **legal** (as opposed to moral) right to deprive the other of the property.

Lawrence v Metropolitan Police [1972] 2 All ER 1253, HL It is not necessary for the prosecution to prove that the property was taken without the consent of the owner. If consent is shown it does not mean that there is no dishonesty if the consent was obtained without full knowledge of the circumstances.

R v McPherson [1973] Crim LR 191, CA It is an appropriation if, at the time the property is taken, there is an intent to steal.

DPP v Gomez (1993) 96 Cr App R 359, HL Goods taken with the consent of someone empowered to give it can nevertheless be an 'appropriation'. Consent to the removal of items that are obtained by fraud, deception, or false representation amounts to the dishonest appropriation of goods.

R v Ngan [1998] 1 Cr App R 331, CA The appropriation must take place in England and Wales.

R v Arnold [1997] 4 All ER 1, CA Where property is received from, or on account of, another and the recipient is under an obligation to retain and deal with it (or its proceeds) in a particular manner, the property (or proceeds) are regarded as belonging to the other.

R v Fernandes [1996] 1 Cr App R 175, CA A person in possession or control of another's property, who dishonestly and for his/her own purpose, deals with it in a manner which s/he knows is risking its loss may be regarded as having the intention to permanently deprive.

National Employers MGIA Ltd v Jones [1987] 3 All ER 385, CA For a buyer to gain 'good title' to property that s/he buys, the seller must have a lawful right to it in the first place. Therefore someone who innocently buys goods that turn out to have been stolen does not become the lawful owner.

Practical considerations

- All five of the elements contained within the theft definition must be proved to obtain a conviction.
- In the absence of a reliable admission of dishonesty, this evidence will have to be proved by other evidence. Such things might include: Where was the property found? Had it been hidden? What were the subsequent actions of the defendant?
- Other matters that should be addressed include:
  - ♦ Evidence of who owns the property and/or that the defendant does not.
  - ♦ Does the offender have any claim on the property?
  - ♦ Does the offender own any similar property/have the means to have paid for it?
  - ♦ Any attempts to alter the property or change its appearance.
  - ♦ Proof that only some of the property was stolen is sufficient for a conviction.
  - ♦ The current location of the property.
  - ♦ The value of the property stolen/recovered.
- The fact that a man and woman are married or are civil partners, does not preclude one from stealing property belonging to the other.
  - ♦ A person is not exempt from answering questions in recovery proceedings on the grounds that to do so would incriminate him/her or his/her spouse or civil partner.
  - ♦ However, a statement or confession made in recovery proceedings is not admissible in proceedings for an offence under this Act as evidence against him/her or his/her spouse or civil partner.
- Penalty Notices for Disorder (PND) may be used for retail/commercial thefts under £200 (see **7.1**).
- Consider additional evidence (eg security video, CCTV footage).

SSS	E&S	PND	CHAR	TRIG

 Either way   None

SSS	Stop, search and seize powers	**E&S**	Entry and search powers	**PND**	Penalty notice for disorder offences	**83**
CHAR	Offences where bad character can be introduced	**TRIG**	Trigger offences			

Summary: 6 months' imprisonment and/or a fine not exceeding the statutory maximum.
Indictment: 7 years' imprisonment and/or a fine.

3.1.2 Removal of articles from places open to the public

Section 11 of the Theft Act 1968 covers the offence of removing articles from places open to the public.

Offence

Subject to subsections (2) and (3) below, where the public have access to a building in order to view the building or part of it, or a collection or part of a collection housed in it, any person who without lawful authority removes from the building or its grounds the whole or part of any article displayed or kept for display to the public in the building or that part of it or in its grounds shall be guilty of an offence. **Theft Act 1968, s 11**

Points to prove

✓ date and location
✓ without lawful authority
✓ removed from building/grounds of building
✓ to which public have access
✓ to view building/collection/part thereof
✓ the whole/part of article displayed/kept for display to public

Meaning of collection

This includes a collection got together for a temporary purpose, but references in this section to a collection do not apply to a collection made or exhibited for the purpose of effecting sales or other commercial dealings.

Explanatory notes

- Access to grounds alone is insufficient. The public must have access to a building to view it, part of it or a collection or part of it housed therein.
- Payment for the privilege of viewing the collection is irrelevant, as is whether such payment merely covers expenses or makes a profit.
- Articles displayed are not confined to works of art, the test being that the article, which may be priceless or valueless, is displayed or kept for public display.
- Note that this offence does not require any intent to permanently deprive the owner of the article taken.

Defence

A person does not commit an offence under this section if he believes that he has lawful authority for the removal of the thing in question or that he would have it if the person entitled to give it knew of the removal and the circumstances of it.   Theft Act 1968, s 11(3)

Defence notes

The burden is on the prosecution to prove the absence of genuine belief on the part of the defendant.

Practical considerations

- The dates on which the building/articles is/are on display.
- Public access to a building for other purposes (eg a shopping mall) when a collection is displayed as an incidental to the main purpose of access (shopping) is unlikely to fall into this section.
    - ✦ However, if the collection was displayed in a separate part of the building with access given purely to view it, it would fall into this section.
- Removal need not be during the times the public have access, it can occur even when the buildings/grounds are closed. However, per subsection (2), if the display is temporary, removal must take place on a day when the public have access to the buildings/grounds in order to view.
- Does the defendant have any claim on the property?
- Current location of the article(s).
- Value of property taken/recovered.
- Obtain CJA witness statements.
- Consider additional evidence (eg security video, CCTV footage).

 Either way   None

 Summary: 6 months' imprisonment and/or a fine not exceeding the statutory maximum.
Indictment: 5 years' imprisonment and/or a fine.

3.1.3 Advertising rewards for the return of stolen/lost goods

Section 23 of the Theft Act 1968 deals with the offence of advertising rewards for the return of stolen or lost goods.

3.1.3 Advertising Rewards for the Return of Stolen/Lost Goods

---

Offence

Where any public advertisement of a reward for the return of any goods which have been stolen or lost uses any words to the effect that no questions will be asked, or that the person producing the goods will be safe from apprehension or inquiry, or that any money paid for the purchase of the goods or advanced by way of loan on them will be repaid, the person advertising the reward and any person who prints or publishes the advertisement shall be guilty of an offence.   **Theft Act 1968, s 23**

Points to prove

✓ advertiser/printer/publisher
✓ publicly advertised
✓ offer of reward for return of lost/stolen goods
✓ used words implying
✓ no questions asked/producer safe from apprehension/inquiry or any money paid will be repaid/loan repaid

---

Explanatory notes

- This is an offence of strict liability and does not require any specific *mens rea*.
- The offence applies not just to the person advertising the reward, but the person who prints or publishes the advertisements is also liable.
- A charge under this section may consist of any one or more of the elements contained in the section.

Practical considerations

- What inducement was included in the advertisement?
- Obtain a copy of the advertisement.
- Obtain evidence of origin of advertisement (eg invoice from printer).
- Any evidence of who placed the advert?
- Obtain CJA witness statement.

 Summary   6 months

 A fine not exceeding level 3 on the standard scale.

Links to alternative subjects and offences

3.2 **Robbery**

The Theft Act 1968 provides for the offence of theft and several other offences of which theft is a constituent part. All references are to the 1968 Act unless otherwise stated. Section 8 provides for the offences of robbery and assault with intent to rob, whilst s 21 concerns the offence of blackmail.

3.2.1 **Robbery**

Offence

A person is guilty of robbery if he **steals**, and immediately before or at the time of doing so, and in order to do so, he uses **force** on any person or puts or seeks to put any person in fear of being then and there subjected to force.   Theft Act 1968, s 8(1)

Points to prove
✓ stole property
✓ immediately before/at the time of doing so
✓ and in order to do so
✓ used force on a person or put/sought to put person in fear of immediate force

Meanings

Steals (see **3.1.1**)

Force

Means the ordinary meaning and whether force has been used is a matter for the court to decide (*R v Dawson & James* (1976) 64 Cr App R 170, CA).

Explanatory notes
- The offence of theft must be proved before robbery can be substantiated.
- Section 8(2) deems that a person guilty of robbery is guilty of an offence.
- Force or the threat of force must be used immediately before or at the time of the theft.
- A threat to use force has to be made with the intention that something should happen immediately.
- The purpose of the use of force is to facilitate the theft; using force to escape is not robbery.
- If the offence is carried out by a number of assailants, but only one uses violence towards the victim, the others cannot be held

responsible for the violence unless a prior agreement between them to use that degree of violence in order to achieve their objective is shown.

- In order to seek to put somebody in fear, the state of mind of the offender is what is important (rather than that of the victim).
- If a person, while stealing or attempting to steal mail bags or postal packages, or their contents, whilst in transit between British postal areas, commits robbery or attempted robbery, the offence is triable in England and Wales, even if it is committed outside England and Wales.

Defence

An honest belief that a legal claim of right to the property exists is a defence to robbery (R v Skivington [1967] 1 All ER 483, CA).

Related cases

R v Hale (1979) 68 Cr App R 415, CA Appropriation is a continuing act and a defendant who takes items from a shop or a housekeeper and uses violence on the proprietor/owner during the course of the appropriation (eg when approached by the owner) may be guilty of robbery.

R v Clouden [1987] Crim LR 56, CA Very little force is required and a push or nudge to put the victim off balance to enable a theft to take place can be sufficient.

Smith v Desmond & Hall [1965] 1 All ER 976, HL The threat or use of force can be on any person, in order to make a set of circumstances arise, so that the theft can take place (eg threatening a signalman making him stop a train further down the track so that its contents can be stolen).

Corcoran v Anderton (1980) 71 Cr App R 104, CA Use of force applied indirectly (eg pulling at a handbag held by the victim) can under some circumstances amount to robbery as force is transferred to the person.

Practical considerations

- Is there evidence of a theft?
- Ownership of any property stolen.
- Value of property stolen/recovered.
- The fear of being subjected to force must be genuine and can be proved in the victim's statement (although it is the defendant's **intention** to cause fear that is the key element).
- Specific words used by the defendant will be critical.
- It is not necessary to prove that somebody was actually put in fear, only that the accused sought to put somebody in fear of force.
- The force used must be to enable the theft to take place.
- The use of force after the theft is complete is not robbery.
- A threat of force can also be implied, as long as the victim believes that force will be used against him/her and therefore allows the theft to take place.

- An assault committed as an afterthought following a theft is not robbery, but it is assault and theft.
- Obtain CJA witness statements.
- Consider blackmail (see **3.2.3**) when the threats are for force to be used on a future occasion.
- Any additional evidence (eg security video, CCTV footage).

 Indictment None

 Life imprisonment

3.2.2 **Assault with intent to rob**

Offence

A person guilty of robbery, or of an assault with intent to rob, is guilty of an offence.   Theft Act 1968, s 8(2)

Points to prove

✓ assault
✓ intended to rob

Meanings

Robbery (see **3.2.1**)

Intent (see **4.1**)

Explanatory notes

- This offence is committed if a victim is assaulted in order to rob him/her, but the robbery is not completed because of interference or resistance, or it could not be completed because the assailant demanded property which the victim did not have.
- If a person, whilst stealing or attempting to steal mail bags or postal packages, or their contents, whilst in transit between British postal areas, commits assault with intent to rob, the offence is triable in England and Wales, even if it is committed outside England and Wales.

Defence (see **3.2.1**)

Practical considerations

- What was the purpose of the assault?
- Was there an unsuccessful attempt to steal property from the victim?
- There is no need for actual violence, as an assault does not require it. However, where no force is actually used immediately before or at the time of the unsuccessful attempt to rob, consider a charge of attempted robbery under s 1 of the Criminal Attempts Act 1981 (see **4.1**).
- If the assault occurs when the assailant has a firearm in his/her possession consider charging with an offence under the Firearms Act 1968 (see **8.3**).
- The degree of violence used towards the victim.
- Obtain CJA witness statements.
- Consider any additional evidence (eg security video, CCTV footage).
- If the defence to robbery is available to the accused, consider the assault in isolation.

 Indictment   None

 Life imprisonment

3.2.3 Blackmail

Section 21 of the Theft Act 1968 deals with the offence of blackmail.

> **Offence**
>
> A person is guilty of blackmail if, with a view to gain for himself or another or with intent to cause loss to another, he makes any unwarranted demand with menaces, and for this purpose a demand with menaces is unwarranted unless the person making it does so in the belief:
> (a) that he has reasonable grounds for making the demands; and
> (b) that the use of the menaces is a proper means of reinforcing the demands.
> **Theft Act 1968, s 21(1)**

> **Points to prove**
>
> ✓ with view to gain for self/another or intent to cause loss to another
> ✓ made unwarranted demand with menaces.

SSS Stop, search and seize powers   **E&S** Entry and search powers   **CHAR** Offences where bad character can be introduced   **91**

TRIG Trigger offences

3.2.3 Blackmail

Meanings

Intent (see **4.1**)

Menaces

The ordinary English meaning of menaces applies (eg threats).

Explanatory notes

- The nature of the act or omission demanded is immaterial.
- It is also immaterial whether the menaces relate to action to be taken by the person making the demand or a third party.
- The posting, making or receipt of the threat must occur in this country.

> **Defences**
>
> In the belief:
>
> - that s/he has reasonable grounds for making the demands; and
> - that the use of the menaces is a proper means of reinforcing the demands.

Defence notes

The onus is on the defendant to prove the belief, but the prosecution must cover this defence in interview or by other means to negate it.

Related cases

R v Clear (1968) 52 Cr App R 58, CA The person threatened need not be frightened, but the menaces must be enough to unsettle the mind of an ordinary person when the threat and demand are made.

Treacy v DPP [1971] 1 All ER 110, HL A letter containing a demand with menaces posted in England and delivered abroad is sufficient for this offence.

R v Bevans [1988] Crim LR 237, CA Gain is not restricted to money; merely obtaining something s/he did not previously have will suffice.

R v Harvey [1981] Crim LR 104, CA Conduct including threats cannot be proper means of reinforcing a demand.

Practical considerations

- The menaces do not need to relate to action to be taken by the person making the demand.
- Cover the defence in interview or other means in order to negate it.
- Obtain CJA witness statement.
- If the evidence for 'gain' or 'loss' is vague, consider s 1 of the Malicious Communications Act 1988 (see **7.12**).
- Identify any evidence of contact/threats made to the complainant by the defendant (eg notes, letters, telephone calls).

Indictment None

14 years' imprisonment

Links to alternative subjects and offences

3.3 **Burglary**

The Theft Act 1968 provides for the offence of theft and several other offences of which theft is a constituent part.

Section 9 of that Act creates the offence of burglary.

Offence

(1) A person is guilty of burglary if:
  (a) he enters any building or part of a building as a trespasser and with intent to commit any such offence as is mentioned in subsection (2) below; or
  (b) having entered any building or part of a building as a trespasser he steals or attempts to steal anything in the building or that part of it or inflicts or attempts to inflict on any person therein any grievous bodily harm.

(2) The offences referred to in subsection (1)(a) above are offences of stealing anything in the building or part of a building in question, of inflicting on any person therein any grievous bodily harm or of doing unlawful damage to the building or anything therein.   Theft Act 1968, s 9(1), (2)

Points to prove

✓ entered a building/part of a building
✓ as a trespasser
✓ with intent
✓ to steal property therein/inflict grievous bodily harm on person therein/do unlawful damage to the building or anything therein

or

✓ having entered a building/part of a building
✓ as a trespasser
✓ stole or attempted to steal anything therein/inflicted or attempted to inflict grievous bodily harm on any person therein

---

Meanings

Building

'Building' includes an outhouse, a shed, an inhabited vehicle, or a vessel irrespective of whether the resident is there or not.

Intent (see **4.1**)

Explanatory notes

- There does not have to be a forced entry into the building, merely proof that the person has entered as a trespasser.
- Entry into a building may be an actual physical entry, by use of an instrument (eg a hook on a stick through an open window) or by an innocent agent (eg a child under 10 years old).

- The offence does not differentiate between different types of building—but the punishment does (see below).
- A person who has entered one part of a building legally and then enters into another part of the same building as a trespasser falls within this section.
- In sub-s (1)(a) the original intention need not be completed—it is sufficient that the intention existed at the time of entry.
- In sub-s (1)(b) no specific intention is required at the time of entry as the intruder commits one of the acts having entered as a trespasser.

Related cases

R v Brown [1985] Crim LR 212, CA The least degree of entry is sufficient to constitute this element of the offence, eg putting a hand through an open window would be enough.

B & S v Leathley [1979] Crim LR 314, CC A freezer container may be a building under this section.

R v Walkington [1979] 2 All ER 716, CA A person who enters a building as a trespasser with the intention of committing a relevant offence therein and then gets caught before s/he manages to commit that offence, still commits this offence.

R v Wilson & Jenkins [1983] 3 All ER 448, HL If force is applied either directly or indirectly then harm is inflicted, eg a victim who is so intimidated by an intruder that s/he jumps from a window thereby causing injury then harm has been caused although no actual force is used.

Practical considerations

- Ensure a degree of entry into the building can be proved, otherwise consider other offences relevant to the circumstances.
- If satisfied the offender entered the building gather evidence as to right to be there—CJA witness statements.
- A building may include structures made of wood, steel or plastic, but it would not include a tent (inhabited or not), an open-sided bus shelter or a carport.
- An inhabited caravan would be a building under this legislation.
- A static caravan permanently connected to mains water, sewers, and gas/electricity would probably be a building even when it was not occupied.
- A touring caravan parked in the driveway of a house is a vehicle. However, if it was no longer used for touring, and instead used for storage as a garden shed, it may well then be a building.
- A person who enters a shop legally and then goes into a store room may be a trespasser.
- A person who has legally entered premises and later becomes a trespasser because of hostilities by him/her does not become a trespasser under this legislation. S/he must have been a trespasser at the time of entry into that part of the building.
- The damage intended must be sufficient to substantiate an offence under the Criminal Damage Act 1971 (see **4.4**).
- A person acting as a lookout should be treated as a principal.

3.3 Burglary

- Is there any other evidence available (eg security video, CCTV)?
- Is there any evidence of the intent for an offence under s 9(1)(a)? For theft this may be easy to prove (eg the possession of burgling tools), but it may be more difficult for grievous bodily harm, or damage.
- The type of building may affect the sentence.
- Burglary dwelling—if any person in the dwelling was subjected to violence or the threat of violence then the case is triable on indictment only.
- If the defendant had a firearm/imitation firearm with them, then consider also s 17(2) of the Firearms Act 1968 (see **8.3.5**).

| SSS | E&S | CHAR | TRIG |

 Either way   None

Summary: 6 months' imprisonment and/or a fine not exceeding the statutory maximum.
Indictment: 10 years' imprisonment (dwelling 14 years' imprisonment).

Links to alternative subjects and offences

SSS Stop, search and seize powers   E&S Entry and search powers   CHAR Offences where bad character can be introduced
TRIG Trigger offences

3.4 Aggravated Burglary

The Theft Act 1968 provides for the offence of theft and several other offences of which theft is a constituent part. All references are to the 1968 Act unless otherwise stated.

Section 10 creates the offence of aggravated burglary, where the trespasser has with him/her, at the time of committing the burglary, one or more of the specified weapons.

Offence

A person is guilty of aggravated burglary if he commits any burglary and at the time has with him any firearm or imitation firearm, any weapon of offence, or any explosive.
Theft Act 1968, s 10

Points to prove
✓ committed burglary
✓ had with him/her
✓ firearm/imitation firearm/weapon of offence/explosive

Meanings

Has with him

This phrase has a narrower meaning than 'possession' (see **8.3.6**).

Firearm (see **8.1.1**)

Includes an airgun or air pistol.

Imitation firearm (see **8.1.4**)

Means anything which has the appearance of being a firearm, whether capable of being discharged or not.

Weapon of offence

Means any article made or adapted for use for causing injury to or incapacitating a person, or intended by the person having it with him for such use.

Explosive

Means any article manufactured for the purpose of producing a practical effect by explosion, or intended by the person having it with him for that purpose.

Related cases

R v Daubney (2000) 164 JP 519, CA The accused must know that they had the article with them.

R v Kelly (1993) 97 Cr App R 245, CA A burglar who used a screwdriver to break into premises then, when challenged by the occupants, used that same screwdriver to threaten them, was held to have a weapon of offence with him at the time.

R v O'Leary (1986) 82 Cr App R 341, CA In a s 9(1)(a) burglary (enters with intent), if the burglar has with him/her an article (listed above), the offence is committed at the time of entry. However, under s 9(1)(b) (having entered), the point at which aggravated burglary is committed is when s/he commits the theft or grievous bodily harm with the article—not at the time of entry.

R v Klass [1998] 1 Cr App R 453, CA Entry into a building with a weapon is an essential element of this offence. Therefore, if there is only one weapon and it is with an accomplice who remains outside the building, neither of the offenders would commit aggravated burglary.

R v Stones [1989] 1 WLR 156, CA A burglar in possession of a knife for self-protection while carrying out a burglary may be tempted to use it if challenged and would therefore commit this offence.

Practical considerations

- Was the burglary committed under s 9(1)(a) or (b)? This affects the point in time at which the offence occurred.
- If there is more than one offender, is there evidence that somebody actually entered the building with the weapon? If not, charge with burglary or the relevant offence.
- What reason did the offender have for possessing the article?
- Where it is unclear whether the offender had the article with them at the relevant time, charge him/her with burglary and charge possession of the article separately.
- The offence may be committed where the offender takes possession of an article in one part of a building and then enters another part of the building with it.
- Obtain evidence of ownership and right of entry into building.
- Obtain CJA witness statements.
- Is there any other evidence (eg security video, CCTV footage)?

 Indictable   None

 Life imprisonment

Links to alternative subjects and offences

SSS Stop, search and seize powers   **E&S** Entry and search powers   **CHAR** Offences where bad character can be introduced   **TRIG** Trigger offences

3.5 Dishonestly—Abstract Electricity/Retain a Wrongful Credit

A further offence provided for by the Theft Act 1968 of which theft is a constituent part is abstracting electricity. All references are to the 1968 Act unless otherwise stated.

Section 13 deals with the offence of dishonestly abstracting electricity and section 24A the offence of dishonestly retaining a wrongful credit.

3.5.1 Dishonestly abstracting electricity

Offence

A person who dishonestly uses without due authority, or dishonestly causes to be wasted or diverted, any electricity commits an offence.

Theft Act 1968, s 13

Points to prove

✓ dishonestly
✓ used without due authority or caused to be wasted/diverted
✓ electricity

Meanings

Dishonestly

Means a state of mind as opposed to the defendant's conduct (although the conduct will often be a feature from which dishonesty can and will be inferred) (*Boggeln v Williams* [1978] 2 All ER 1061, QBD).

Uses

Implies a consumption of electricity that would not have occurred without an action of the accused.

Without due authority

Means without the proper authorization.

Explanatory notes

• This section is made necessary by the fact that electricity does not fit into the definition of property under s 4 and, therefore, it cannot be stolen. This also means that entering a building and abstracting electricity (or intending to) will not be burglary.

- A tramp who warms himself by an electric fire, which is already switched on, would not commit this offence, but if he switched the fire on he would commit the offence.
- Employees using their employer's electrically powered machinery for their own use would commit an offence under this section.
- It is not necessary for anybody to benefit from the wasted or diverted electricity. A person who, out of spite, switches on an electrical appliance before leaving a building would commit this offence.

Related cases

R v McCreadie & Tume [1992] Crim LR 872, CA It is sufficient for the prosecution to show that electricity was used without the authority of the electricity authority and that there was no intention to pay for it (eg squatters).

Boggeln v Williams [1978] 2 All ER 1061, QBD A householder who bypasses his electric meter after his supply has been disconnected dishonestly causes the electricity to be diverted.

Practical considerations

- Obtain evidence of dishonest use, waste, or diversion of electricity (eg note the state of the meter, cash box missing).
- The person using the electricity does not have to be the person who reconnects the supply (eg a person using electricity with no intention to pay for it after a disconnected supply has been unlawfully reconnected by a third person would commit this offence).
- Check for sign of break into the premises, which may negate or support the story of the householder.
- Utilities bill may assist to prove diversion to bypass the meter.
- There is no requirement for the electricity to be supplied through the mains (eg it may be supplied in a battery in a torch, car).
- Obtain CJA witness statement from electricity supplier.

 Either way   None

 Summary: 6 months' imprisonment and/or a fine not exceeding the statutory maximum.
Indictment: 5 years' imprisonment.

3.5.2 **Dishonestly retaining a wrongful credit**

Offence

A person is guilty of an offence if:

(a) a **wrongful credit** has been made to an account kept by him or in respect of which he has any right or interest;

(b) he knows or believes that the credit is wrongful; and

(c) he dishonestly fails to take such steps as are reasonable in the circumstances to secure that the credit is cancelled.

Theft Act 1968, s 24A(1)

Points to prove

✓ knowing/believing

✓ wrongful credit made to account

✓ kept by him/her in which s/he had right or interest

✓ dishonestly

✓ failed to take reasonable steps in the circumstances to cancel the credit

Meanings

Wrongful credit

A credit to an account is wrongful to the extent that it derives from:

• theft;

• blackmail;

• fraud (contrary to s 1 of the Fraud Act 2006; or

• stolen goods.

Credit

Means a credit of an amount of money.

Explanatory notes

• In determining whether a credit to an account is wrongful, it is immaterial (in particular) whether the account is overdrawn before or after the credit is made.

• Any money dishonestly withdrawn from an account to which a wrongful credit has been made may be regarded as stolen goods.

Practical considerations

• Where did the credit originate?

• Obtain supplementary evidence (eg bank statements, cheque book).

• What steps could/have been taken to cancel the credit.

• Obtain CJA witness statement.

Either way   None

 Summary: 6 months' imprisonment and/or a fine not exceeding the statutory maximum.
Indictment: 10 years' imprisonment.

Links to alternative subjects and offences

3.6 **Handling Stolen Goods**

Section 22 of the Theft Act 1968 creates various combinations of offences of handling stolen goods knowing or believing them to be stolen.

All references are to the 1968 Act unless otherwise stated.

Offence

A person handles stolen **goods** if (otherwise than in the course of the stealing) **knowing** or **believing** them to be stolen goods he **dishonestly receives** the goods, or dishonestly **undertakes** or assists in their **retention**, removal, disposal or **realisation** by or for the benefit of another person, or he **arranges to do so**.   Theft Act 1968, s 22(1)

Points to prove

✓ otherwise than in the course of stealing
✓ knowing/believing goods to be stolen
✓ dishonestly received them
or
✓ dishonestly undertook/assisted
✓ in the retention/removal/disposal/realization of them
✓ or arranged to do so
✓ by/for the benefit of another

Meaning

Goods

Includes money and every other description of property except land, and includes things severed from the land by stealing.

Knowing

Means actually having been told by somebody having first hand knowledge (eg the thief or burglar) that the goods had been stolen (*R v Hall* (1985) 81 Cr App R 260, CA).

Believing

Means the state of mind of a person who cannot be certain that goods are stolen, but where the circumstances indicate no other reasonable conclusion (*R v Elizabeth Forsyth* [1997] 2 Cr App R 299, CA).

Dishonestly

A court must decide what is dishonest according to the ordinary standards of reasonable and honest people, **and** whether that person knew that what s/he was doing was dishonest by those standards (*R v Ghosh* [1982] 2 All ER 689, QBD).

Receives

Means gaining **possession** or control of the goods.

Possession

Means either actual physical possession or constructive possession (storing the goods in premises belonging to him/her).

Undertakes

Includes where the person agrees to perform the act(s) that constitute the offence.

Retention

Means keeping possession of, not losing, continuing to have (*R v Pitchley* [1972] Crim LR 705, CA).

Realization

Means the conversion of the goods, invariably into money (*R v Deakin* [1972] Crim LR 781, CA).

Arranges to do so

Includes the contact who makes arrangements regarding the goods but never actually has anything to do with them.

Explanatory notes

- Either 'knowing' or 'believing' is sufficient in this case.
- Where a person is being proceeded against for handling stolen goods only, s 27(3)(a) provides for '**special evidence**' (eg his/her previous dealings with stolen goods within the 12 months prior to the current incident) to be introduced into the proceedings. No charge or conviction regarding the previous incident is necessary.
- Similarly, s 27(3)(b) allows the introduction of evidence of a previous conviction for theft or handling within 5 years of the present incident. In this case a notice must be served on the defence 7 days prior to use of the evidence in court.
- Any benefit to the receiver is irrelevant.
- The receiver must have knowledge or belief that the goods are stolen at the time of receipt—later knowledge would not substantiate this offence.
- Actions taken for the benefit of another are only relevant in the offence of handling stolen goods—they have no significance to the receiving of such goods.

Related cases

R v Duffus (1994) 158 JP 224, CA The 'special evidence' under s 27(3)(a) or (b) can only be introduced to assist in proving that the accused knew or believed that the goods were stolen.

R v Ghosh [1982] 2 All ER 689, QBD This case set out a two-stage test (see dishonestly meaning—above).

National Employers Mutual Ltd v Jones [1987] 3 All ER 385, CA Paying value for goods that subsequently turn out to be stolen does not transfer good title to the buyer.

R v Nicklin [1977] 2 All ER 444, CA The section creates only one offence, but where a particular form of handling is specified in the charge the defendant cannot then be found guilty of another form with which s/he has not been charged.

R v Brown [1969] 3 All ER 198, CA 'Assists' includes permitting the storage of stolen goods in premises and denying knowledge of their whereabouts.

R v Figures [1976] Crim LR 744, CC Handling of goods stolen abroad is only an offence in this country if the handling takes place here. If the handling is complete before coming here there is no offence under this section.

R v Bloxham (1982) 74 Cr App R 279, HL A person who innocently buys goods for value and later discovers they were, in fact, stolen goods cannot commit the offence of assisting in their disposal by selling them as he benefited from their *purchase* not their sale.

Practical considerations

- Ownership of the stolen goods.
- The goods must have been stolen.
- Check for any evidence of previous dealings with stolen goods within previous 12 months.
- Check previous convictions for theft or handling within previous 5 years.
- Consider need for 7 days' notice of intent to use previous convictions.
- Check for communications between the handler, the thief or any potential buyers/distributors.
- Check for evidence of removal or alteration of identifying features.
- Obtain evidence of the true value of the goods.
- If the facts fit both theft and handling stolen goods, use the relevant alternate charges and let the court decide which offence, if any, is committed.
- Goods are not regarded as still being stolen goods after they have been returned to a person having lawful possession or custody, or after the person having a claim to them ceases to have a right to restitution regarding the theft.
- Several people may be charged on one indictment, concerning the same theft, with handling all or some of the goods at the same or various times, and all such persons may be tried together. This does not apply to a summary trial.

 Either way   None

 Summary: 6 months' imprisonment and/or a fine not exceeding the statutory maximum.
Indictment: 14 years' imprisonment.

Links to alternative subjects and offences

3.7 **Going Equipped**

The Theft Act 1968 provides for several other key offences of which theft is a constituent part. All references are to the 1968 Act unless otherwise stated.

Section 25 creates the offence of going equipped for any burglary or theft.

Offence

A person shall be guilty of an offence if, when not at his **place of abode**, he **has with him** any **article** for use in the course of or in connection with any burglary or theft.   Theft Act 1968, s 25(1)

Points to prove

✓ not at place of abode
✓ had with him/her
✓ article(s) for use in course of/in connection with
✓ a burglary/theft

Meanings

Place of abode

This normally means the place or site where someone lives. Using its natural meaning it normally includes the garage and garden of a house, but it is ultimately a matter for the court or jury to decide.

Has with him

This phrase has a narrower meaning than 'possession' (see **8.3.6**).

Article

This has a wide meaning. It may include a whole range of items and substances, from treacle and paper to assist in breaking a window quietly, a car jack for spreading bars, or pieces of spark plug ceramic for breaking car windows.

Theft

This will include taking a conveyance without the owner's consent (see **4.3.1**).

Explanatory notes

- A direct connection between the article and a specific act of burglary or theft does not need to be proved.
- You do not need to prove that the person found with the article intended to use it themselves—intended use by another will suffice.

Related cases

R v Bundy [1977] 2 All ER 382, CA A 'place of abode' includes a person living rough in a car when on a site with the intention of abiding there. However, that same person in the same car would not be at his/her place of abode when travelling from one site to another.

R v Tosti & White [1997] Crim LR 746, CA A person charged with going equipped, when the offence of burglary or theft has not been completed, may also be charged with that offence or with attempting to commit it.

National Employers Mutual Ltd v Jones [1987] 3 All ER 385, CA For a buyer to gain a good title to property the person selling the property must have a lawful right to the property in the first instance. No such right could ever exist if the goods were originally stolen. In this case the insurance company was the true owner and entitled to the car.

Practical considerations

- What articles were with or available to the defendant?
- Where were the articles?
- What were their possible/intended uses?
- Did the defendant have a lawful purpose for having the article(s) in his/her possession at that particular time/place?
- Has the defendant used such articles in committing offence previously?
- Obtain CJA witness statements.
- This offence caters for some preparatory acts prior to the commission of one or more of the specified acts.
- This offence can only be committed before the intended burglary or theft, not afterwards.
- Possession of the article(s) after arrest is not sufficient for this offence.
- When two or more people are acting in concert the possession of housebreaking implements by one of them would be deemed to be possession by all of them.
- A person who has a relevant article with him/her, but has not yet made up his/her mind whether to use it if the opportunity presents itself, does not have the necessary intent to commit an offence under this section.
- Taking a conveyance without the owner's consent is, for the purposes of this section, to be treated as theft.
- Once it has been proved that the defendant had a relevant article with him/her, the defendant will need to prove that the article was in his/her possession for a purpose other than burglary or theft.

  SSS E&S CHAR TRIG

 Either way

 None

SSS Stop, search and seize powers   E&S Entry and search powers   CHAR Offences where bad character can be introduced   **109**

TRIG Trigger offences

Summary: 6 months' imprisonment and/or a fine not
exceeding the statutory maximum.
Indictment: 3 years' imprisonment.

Links to alternative subjects and offences

3.8 Making off without Payment

The Theft Act 1978 creates specific offences relating to fraudulent conduct. All references are to the 1978 Act unless otherwise stated.

Section 3 creates the offence of making off without payment (also known as 'bilking') when on-the-spot payment is required or expected for goods or a service and the perpetrator intends to avoid payment.

Offence

Subject to subs. (3) below, a person who, knowing that **payment on the spot** for any **goods** supplied or service done is required or expected from him, **dishonestly** makes off without having paid as required or expected and with **intent** to avoid payment of the amount due shall be guilty of an offence.

Theft Act 1978, s 3

Points to prove

✓ knowing immediate payment is required/expected
✓ for goods supplied/services done
✓ dishonestly
✓ made off
✓ without having paid as required/expected
✓ with intent to avoid payment of amount due

Meanings

Payment on the spot

This includes payment at the time of collecting goods on which work has been done or in respect of which service has been provided.

Goods

This includes money and every other description of property except land, and includes things severed from the land by stealing.

Dishonestly (see 3.6)

Intent (see 4.1)

Explanatory notes

- The term 'goods supplied or services done' will include making off without payment for fuel at a self-service petrol station, meals at restaurants or hotel accommodation/services where the charge is levied after supplying the goods/service.
- If a motorist forgets to pay for petrol and drives off, but later remembers that s/he has not paid, and then returns to the filling station to pay, s/he may not commit the offence due to lacking the necessary intent.

- Where there is an agreement to defer payment, any such agreement would normally eliminate the expectation of payment on the spot.

Defence

Subsection (1) above does not apply where the supply of the goods or the doing of the service is contrary to law, or where the service done is such that payment is not legally enforceable. **Theft Act 1978, s 3(3)**

Defence notes

Examples of a payment not being legally enforceable may be where the service provider breaks a contract (eg a taxi driver who fails to complete a journey) or where the contract cannot be enforced through the courts (eg betting).

Related cases

R v Brooks & Brooks (1983) 76 Cr App R 66, CA 'Making off' involves leaving the place or passing the point where payment is expected or required.

R v Vincent [2001] Crim LR 488, CA If an agreement to defer payment is obtained dishonestly it would not reinstate the expectation for payment on the spot.

Practical considerations

- What goods or services have been provided?
- The goods or services provided must be specified in the charge.
- It is important to prove that the person knew that 'payment on the spot' was required.
- Did the accused have money or means with which to pay the bill?
- Is the payment legally enforceable?
- There must be an intention to avoid payment completely and not merely intent to defer or delay it.
- Obtain CJA witness statement.
- Is there any further evidence (eg CCTV footage)?

 Either way None

 Summary: 6 months' imprisonment and/or a fine not exceeding the statutory maximum.
Indictment: 2 years' imprisonment.

Links to alternative subjects and offences

3.9 **Fraud Offences**

The Fraud Act 2006 provides for the offence of fraud and other fraudulent offences of which dishonesty is a constituent part. All references are to the 2006 Act unless otherwise stated.

Sections 1 to 4 detail the three different ways of committing fraud, s 12 the liability of company officers and s 13 evidential matters in relation to fraud.

3.9.1 **Fraud offence**

Section 1 creates the general offence of fraud, and ss 2 to 4 detail three different ways of committing fraud by false representation; failing to disclose information; or by abuse of position.

Offences

(1) A person is guilty of fraud if he is in breach of any of the sections listed in subsection (2) (which provide for different ways of committing the offence).

(2) The sections are—
   (a) section 2 (fraud by false representation),
   (b) section 3 (fraud by failing to disclose information), and
   (c) section 4 (fraud by abuse of position).   Fraud Act 2006, s 1(1)-(2)

Points to prove

False representation

✓ date and location
✓ dishonestly made a false representation
✓ intending to make a gain for yourself/another OR
✓ intending to cause loss to another/expose another to a risk of loss

Failing to disclose information

✓ date and location
✓ dishonestly failed to disclose to another
✓ information which you were under a legal duty to disclose
✓ intending, by that failure
✓ to make a gain for yourself/another OR
✓ to cause loss to another/expose another to a risk of loss

> ***Fraud by abuse of position***
> ✓ date and location
> ✓ occupying a position in which you were expected
> ✓ to safeguard, or not to act against, the financial interests of another person
> ✓ dishonestly abused that position
> ✓ intending to make a gain for yourself/another OR
> ✓ intending to cause loss to another/expose another to a risk of loss

Meanings

Fraud by false representation (see **3.9.2**)

Fraud by failing to disclose information (see **3.9.3**)

Fraud by abuse of position (see **3.9.4**)

Gain and loss

(1) The references to gain and loss in sections 2 to 4 are to be read in accordance with this section.
(2) 'Gain' and 'loss'—
    (a) extend only to gain or loss in money or other property;
    (b) include any such gain or loss whether temporary or permanent; and 'property' means any property whether real or personal (including things in action and other intangible property).
(3) 'Gain' includes a gain by keeping what one has, as well as a gain by getting what one does not have.
(4) 'Loss' includes a loss by not getting what one might get, as well as a loss by parting with what one has.   Fraud Act 2006, s 5(1)–(4)

Dishonestly (see **3.6**)

Intention (see **4.1**)

Explanatory notes

- Section 1 creates the general offence of fraud, and ss 2 to 4 detail three different ways of committing the fraud offence.
- All three fraud offences require an intention to make a gain for oneself or another OR cause loss to another/expose another to a risk of loss.
- Similarly in all of these fraud offences intention must be proved (see **4.1**).
- Property covers all forms of property, including intellectual property, although in practice this is rarely 'gained' or 'lost'.
- If any offences are committed by a company, the company officers may also be liable under s 12 (see **3.9.5**).
- Section 13 deals with evidential matters under this Act, conspiracy to defraud or any other offences involving any form of fraudulent conduct or purpose (see **3.9.6**).

3.9.2 **Meaning of fraud by false representation**

Meanings

Fraud by false representation

(1) A person is in breach of this section if he—
  (a) dishonestly makes a false representation, and
  (b) intends, by making the representation—
    (i) to make a gain for himself or another, or
    (ii) to cause loss to another or to expose another to a risk of loss.

(2) A representation is false if—
  (a) it is untrue or misleading, and
  (b) the person making it knows that it is, or might be, untrue or misleading.

(3) 'Representation' means any representation as to fact or law, including a representation as to the state of mind of—
  (a) the person making the representation, or
  (b) any other person.

(4) A representation may be express or implied.

(5) For the purposes of this section a representation may be regarded as made if it (or anything implying it) is submitted in any form to any system or device designed to receive, convey or respond to communications (with or without human intervention).

Fraud Act 2006, s 2(1)-(5)

Gain and loss (see **3.9.1**)

Dishonestly (see **3.6**)

Intention (see **4.1**)

Explanatory notes

- The offence of fraud by false representation comes under fraud s 1 (see **3.9.1**) and **not** s 2.
- The gain or loss does not actually have to take place.
- There is no restriction on the way in which the representation may be expressed. It can be spoken, written (hardcopy or electronically) or communicated by conduct.
- An example of a representation by conduct is where a person dishonestly uses a credit card to pay for goods. By tendering the card, they are falsely representing that they have the authority to use it for that transaction. It is immaterial whether the retailer accepting the card is deceived by this representation.
- The practice of 'phishing' (eg sending an email purporting to come from a legitimate financial institution in order to obtain credit card and bank account details, so that the 'phisher' can access and fraudulently use those accounts) is another example of false representation.

- Subsection (5) is given in broad terms because it may be difficult to distinguish situations involving modern technology and/or human involvement. It could well be that the only recipient of the false statement is a machine or a piece of software, where a false statement is submitted to a system for dealing with electronic communications and not to a human being (eg postal or messenger systems). Another example of fraud by electronic means can be entering a number into a 'chip and pin' machine.

3.9.3 Meaning of fraud by failing to disclose information

Meanings

Fraud by failing to disclose information

A person is in breach of this section if he—

(a) dishonestly fails to disclose to another person information which he is under a legal duty to disclose, and

(b) intends, by failing to disclose the information—

    (i) to make a gain for himself or another, or

    (ii) to cause loss to another or to expose another to a risk of loss.

Fraud Act 2006, s 3

Gain and loss (see 3.9.1)

Dishonestly (see 3.6)

Intention (see 4.1)

Explanatory notes

- The offence of fraud by failing to disclose information comes under fraud s 1 (see **3.9.1**) and **not** s 3.
- A legal duty to disclose information may include duties under both oral and/or written contracts.
- The concept of 'legal duty' may derive from statute, a transaction that requires good faith (eg contract of insurance), express or implied terms of a contract, custom of a particular trade/market, or a fiduciary relationship between the parties (eg between agent and principal).
- This legal duty to disclose information may be where the defendant's failure to disclose gives the victim a cause of action for damages, or the law gives the victim a right to set aside any change in his/her legal position to which s/he may consent as a result of the non-disclosure. An example of an offence under this section could be where a person intentionally failed to disclose information relating to their physical condition when making an application for life insurance.

3.9.4 **Meaning of fraud by abuse of position**

Meanings

Fraud by abuse of position

(1) A person is in breach of this section if he—
  (a) occupies a position in which he is expected to safeguard, or not to act against, the financial interests of another person,
  (b) dishonestly abuses that position, and
  (c) intends, by means of the abuse of that position—
    (i) to make a gain for himself or another, or
    (ii) to cause loss to another or to expose another to a risk of loss.
(2) A person may be regarded as having abused his position even though his conduct consisted of an omission rather than an act.

Fraud Act 2006, s 4(1)–(2)

Gain and loss (see 3.9.1)

Dishonestly (see 3.6)

Intention (see 4.1)

Explanatory notes

- The offence of fraud by abuse of position comes under fraud s 1 (see 3.9.1) and **not** s 4.
- The offence of committing fraud by dishonestly abusing their position applies in situations where s/he is in a privileged position, and by virtue of this position is expected to safeguard another's financial interests or not act against those interests.
- The necessary relationship could be between trustee and beneficiary, director and company, professional person and client, agent and principal, employee and employer, or even between partners. Generally this relationship will be recognized by the civil law as importing fiduciary duties. This relationship and existence of his/her duty can be ruled upon by the judge or be subject of directions to the jury.
- The term 'abuse' is not defined because it is intended to cover a wide range of conduct. Furthermore, the offence can be committed by omission as well as by positive action.
- Examples of offences under this section are—
  - ♦ Purposely failing to take up the chance of a crucial contract in order that an associate or rival company can take it up instead to the loss of his/her employer.
  - ♦ A software company employee uses his/her position to clone software products with the intention of selling the products to others.
  - ♦ Where a carer for an elderly or disabled person has access to that person's bank account and abuses their position by transferring funds for their own gain.

3.9.5 **Liability of company officers for offence by company**

Liability

(1) Subsection (2) applies if an offence under this Act is committed by a body corporate.

(2) If the offence is proved to have been committed with the consent or connivance of—

    (a) a director, manager, secretary or other similar officer of the body corporate, or

    (b) a person who was purporting to act in any such capacity,

    he (as well as the body corporate) is guilty of the offence and liable to be proceeded against and punished accordingly.

(3) If the affairs of a body corporate are managed by its members, subsection (2) applies in relation to the acts and defaults of a member in connection with his functions of management as if he were a director of the body corporate.

Fraud Act 2006, s 12(1)–(3)

Explanatory notes

- This section provides that if people who have a specified corporate role are party to the commission of an offence under the Act by their body corporate, they will be liable to be charged for the offence as well as the corporation.
- Liability for this offence applies to directors, managers, company secretaries and other similar officers of companies and other bodies corporate.
- Furthermore, if the body corporate is charged with an offence and the company is managed by its members, the members involved in management can be prosecuted too.

3.9.6 **Admissible evidence**

Evidence

(1) A person is not to be excused from—

    (a) answering any question put to him in proceedings relating to property, or

    (b) complying with any order made in proceedings relating to property,

    on the ground that doing so may incriminate him or his spouse or civil partner of an offence under this Act or a related offence.

(2) But, in proceedings for an offence under this Act or a related offence, a statement or admission made by the person in—

    (a) answering such a question, or

    (b) complying with such an order,

is not admissible in evidence against him or (unless they married or became civil partners after the making of the statement or admission) his spouse or civil partner.

(3) 'Proceedings relating to property' means any proceedings for—
    (a) the recovery or administration of any property,
    (b) the execution of a trust, or
    (c) an account of any property or dealings with property,
    and 'property' means money or other property whether real or personal (including things in action and other intangible property).

(4) 'Related offence' means—
    (a) conspiracy to defraud;
    (b) any other offence involving any form of fraudulent conduct or purpose.

Fraud Act 2006, s 13(1)–(4)

Explanatory notes

- This means that during any proceedings for—
  - ✦ the recovery or administration of any property,
  - ✦ the execution of a trust, or
  - ✦ an account of any property or dealings with property,
  a person cannot be excused from answering any question or refuse to comply with any order made in those proceedings on the grounds of incrimination under this Act; conspiracy to defraud; or an offence involving any form of fraudulent conduct or purpose.
- However, any statement or admission made in answering such a question, or complying with such an order, is not admissible in evidence against him/her or his/her spouse or civil partner (unless they married or became civil partners after the making of such a statement or admission).
- Although this section is similar to s 31(1) of the Theft Act 1968 where a person/spouse/civil partner is protected from incrimination, while nonetheless being obliged to co-operate with certain civil proceedings relating to property. It goes beyond that section by removing privilege in relation to this Act, conspiracy to defraud and any other offence involving any form or fraudulent conduct or purpose.
- A civil partnership is a relationship between two people of the same sex ('civil partners') registered as civil partners under the Civil Partnerships Act 2004 and ends only on death, dissolution or annulment.

Related cases

R v Ghosh [1982] 2 All ER 689, QBD The court/jury must decide whether, according to the standards of reasonable and honest people, what was done was dishonest. If it was dishonest by those standards they must then decide whether s/he realized that what s/he was doing was, by those standards, dishonest.

DPP v Gomez (1993) 96 Cr App R 359, HL If consent to take property is obtained by fraud then the property is obtained dishonestly and may fall into this offence or theft.

Practical considerations

- The words used may be spoken or written. Alternatively, there may be **nothing** done or said in circumstances where a reasonable and honest person would have expected something to be said/done (eg to correct a mistake).
- The fraud may be proved by admissions, the defendant's actions or a combination of both.
- Acts may be dishonest even if the perpetrator genuinely believed them to be morally justified.
- Schedule 2 of the Act concerns transitional provisions and any deception offences committed before the Act commenced (15th January 2007) should be dealt with under the repealed ss 15, 15A, 16, and 20(2) of the Theft Act 1968 and ss 1 and 2 of the Theft Act 1978.
- If committed by a body corporate with the consent or connivance of one of its officers s/he, as well as the body corporate, is liable to be proceeded against (see **3.9.5**).

 Either way   None

 Summary: 12 months' imprisonment and/or a fine not exceeding the statutory maximum.
Indictment: 10 years' imprisonment and/or a fine.

Links to alternative subjects and offences

3.10 Articles for use in Fraud

The Fraud Act 2006 provides for the offence of fraud and other fraudulent offences of which dishonesty is a constituent part. All references are to the 2006 Act unless otherwise stated.

3.10.1 Possess or control article for use in fraud

Sections 6 deals with the offence of having in their possession or under their control an article for use in fraud.

Offences

A person is guilty of an offence if he has in his possession or under his control any article for use in the course of or in connection with any fraud.

Fraud Act 2006, s 6(1)

Points to prove

✓ date and location
✓ had in your possession/under your control
✓ an article
✓ for use in the course of/in connection with a fraud

Meanings

Possession (see **8.1.1**)

Article

Means an article
- made or adapted for use in the course of or in connection with an offence of fraud; or
- intended by the person having it with them for such use by them or by some other person.

It also includes any program or data held in electronic form.

Fraud (see **3.9.1**)

Intention (see **4.1**)

Explanatory notes

- Having the article after the commission of the fraud is not sufficient for this offence.
- The prosecution must prove that the defendant was in possession of the article, and intended the article to be used in the course of or in

connection with some future fraud. It is not necessary to prove that s/he intended it to be used in the course of or in connection with any specific fraud; it is enough to prove a general intention to use it for fraud.

- Similarly it will be sufficient to prove that s/he had it with him/her with the intention that it should be used by someone else.
- Examples of electronic programs or data which could be used in fraud are: a computer program that can generate credit card numbers; computer templates that can be used for producing blank utility bills; computer files containing lists of other peoples' credit card details or draft letters in connection with 'advance fee' frauds.

SSS   **E&S**   **TRIG**

 Either way   None

Summary: 12 months' imprisonment and/or a fine not exceeding the statutory maximum.
Indictment: 5 years' imprisonment and/or a fine.

3.10.2 Making or supplying article for use in fraud

Sections 7 deals with the offences of making or supplying an article for use in fraud.

Offences

A person is guilty of an offence if he makes, adapts, supplies or offers to supply any article—
(a) knowing that it is designed or adapted for use in the course of or in connection with fraud, or
(b) intending it to be used to commit, or assist in the commission of, fraud.

Fraud Act 2006, s 7(1)

Points to prove

✓ date and location
✓ made/adapted/supplied/offered to supply
✓ an article
✓ knowing that it was designed/adapted for use in the course of/in connection with fraud OR
✓ intending it to be used to commit/assist in the commission of fraud.

3.10.2 Making or Supplying Article for Use in Fraud

Meanings

Article (see 3.10.1)

Fraud (see 3.9.1)

Intention (see 4.1)

Explanatory notes

- The offence is to make, adapt, supply or offer to supply any article, knowing that it is designed or adapted for use in the course of or in connection with fraud, or intending it to be used to commit or facilitate fraud.
- Such an example would be where a person makes devices which when attached to electricity meters cause the meter to malfunction. The actual amount of electricity used is concealed from the provider, who thus suffers a loss.

Practical considerations

- A general intention to commit fraud will suffice rather than a specific offence in specific circumstances (eg. credit card skimming equipment may provide evidence of such an intention).
- Proof is required that the defendant had the article for the purpose of or with the intention that it be used in the course of or in connection with fraud, and that a general intention to commit fraud will suffice.

  Either way   None

  Summary: 12 months' imprisonment and/or a fine not exceeding the statutory maximum.
Indictment: 10 years' imprisonment and/or a fine.

Links to alternative subjects and offences

3.11 **Obtaining Services Dishonestly**

The Fraud Act 2006 provides for the offence of fraud and other fraudulent offences of which dishonesty is a constituent part. All references are to the 2006 Act unless otherwise stated.

Section 11 makes it an offence for any person, by any dishonest act, to obtain services for which payment is required, with intent to avoid payment.

Offences

(1) A person is guilty of an offence under this section if he obtains services for himself or another—
  (a) by a **dishonest act**, and
  (b) in breach of subsection (2).
(2) A person obtains services in breach of this subsection if—
  (a) they are made available on the basis that payment has been, is being or will be made for or in respect of them,
  (b) he obtains them without any payment having been made for or in respect of them or without payment having been made in full, and
  (c) when he obtains them, he knows—
    (i) that they are being made available on the basis described in paragraph (a), or
    (ii) that they might be,
  but intends that payment will not be made, or will not be made in full.

Fraud Act 2006, s 11(1)— (2)

Points to prove

✓ date and location
✓ obtained services for yourself/another by a dishonest act
✓ services were made available on the basis that payment made for/in respect of them
✓ you obtained them without any payment/in full
✓ when you obtained them you knew that they were being/might be made available on the basis described above
✓ but you intended that payment would not be made/made in full

---

Meanings

Dishonest act   (see 3.6)

Intention   (see 4.1)

Explanatory notes

• This section makes it an offence for any person, by any dishonest act, to obtain services for which payment is required, with intent to avoid payment.

3.11 Obtaining Services Dishonestly

- This offence replaces the offence of obtaining services by deception in s 1 of the Theft Act 1978, although the new offence contains no deception element.
- It is not possible to commit the offence by omission alone and it can be committed only where the dishonest act was done with the intent not to pay for the services as expected.

Practical considerations

- The person must know that the services are made available on the basis that they are chargeable, or that they might be.
- There must be some action or communication by the defendant rather than an error wholly initiated by the supplier of the service which is unaffected by behaviour on the part of the defendant.
- The offence is not inchoate, it requires the actual obtaining of the service, for example data or software that is only available on the Internet once you have paid for access rights to that service.
- Examples of this offence would be where a person—
  - ◆ dishonestly uses false credit card details or other false personal information to obtain the service;
  - ◆ climbs over a wall and watches a football match without paying the entrance fee—such a person is not deceiving the provider of the service directly, but is obtaining a service which is provided on the basis that people will pay for it;
  - ◆ attaching a decoder to a television set in order to view/have access to cable/satellite channels for which s/he has no intention of paying.

 E&S

 Either way   None

Summary: 12 months' imprisonment and/or a fine not exceeding the statutory maximum.
Indictment: 5 years' imprisonment and/or a fine.

Links to alternative subjects and offences

Chapter 4

Crime: General

4.1 Criminal Attempts

There are certain circumstances where an offence is not actually committed but the **attempt** to do so is enough to be an offence in itself. This well-established common law principle became embodied in legislation when the Criminal Attempts Act 1981 created an offence of 'attempting' to commit certain crimes.

Offence

(1) If, with **intent** to commit an **offence to which this section applies**, a person does an act which is more than merely preparatory to the commission of the offence, he is guilty of attempting to commit the offence.

(2) A person may be guilty of attempting to commit an offence to which this section applies even though the facts are such that the commission of the offence is impossible.

(3) In any case where:

    (a) apart from this subsection a person's intention would not be regarded as having amounted to an intent to commit an offence; but

    (b) if the facts of the case had been as he believed them to be, his intention would be so regarded

    then, for the purposes of subsection (1) above, he shall be regarded as having had an intent to commit that offence.

Criminal Attempts Act 1981, s 1(1)– (3)

Points to prove

✓ date and location
✓ with intent
✓ attempted
✓ **(wording of the offence attempted)**

Meanings

Intent

The *mens rea*, which is Latin for 'guilty mind', has to be proved—more so in 'attempts' than in any other offence.

Offence to which this section applies

Section 1(4) of the Criminal Attempts Act 1981 stipulates that:

- This section applies to any offence which if it were completed, would be triable as an indictable offence, **other than**:
  - conspiracy (at common law or under s 1 of the Criminal Law Act 1977 or any other enactment);
  - aiding, abetting, counselling, procuring, or suborning the commission of an offence;
  - offences under s 4(1) (assisting offenders) or s 5(1) (accepting or agreeing to accept consideration for not disclosing information about a relevant offence) of the Criminal Law Act 1967.
- Therefore, a person may attempt an offence that is either indictable or triable either way. However, summary only offences are not included, together with the above specific exclusions.

Explanatory notes

Intent can be proved by drawing on various sources of information:

- admissions made by the defendant in interview which reveals their state of mind at the time of commission of the offence;
- answers given by the defendant to questions regarding their actions and intentions at the time of the offence;
- by inference from the circumstances of the offence;
- evidence from witnesses;
- the defendant's actions and property found on him/her or in their control (such as a vehicle for transporting property).

To prove intent, you need to take all this into account. However, the important thing is that you have to **prove** the defendant's **state of mind** at the time.

Statutory test

A jury/magistrates' court must consider the circumstances and decide whether the defendant would have intended or foreseen the results which occurred by way of a **subjective test**.

'A court or jury in determining whether a person has committed an offence—

(a) shall not be bound by law to infer that he intended or foresaw a result of his actions by reason only of its being a natural and probable consequence of those actions; **but**

(b) shall decide whether he did intend or foresee that result by reference to all the evidence, drawing such inferences from the evidence as appear proper in the circumstances'.

Criminal Justice Act 1967, s 8

Subjective test

The difference between 'objective' and 'subjective' tests are important here. *Blacks Law Dictionary* defines the terms as:

- *Objective*: 'Of, relating to, or based on externally verifiable phenomena, as opposed to an individual's perceptions, feelings, or intentions.' This is sometimes used in the context of the 'reasonable person' test—what would a reasonable man or woman perceive to be the rights or wrongs of the matter in question or the likely outcome?

- *Subjective*: 'Based on an individual's perceptions, feelings, or intentions, as opposed to externally verifiable phenomena.' In a legal context this is more or less the opposite of objective. Instead of the hypothetical reasonable person, subjectivity requires a court to establish whether the offender was in fact conscious of a risk or other factor.

Strict liability

However, for some offences, what is known as 'strict liability' will be enough. The liability for committing this type of offence does not depend on an intent (such as causing harm) or even recklessness, but is based on the breach of an absolute duty.

More than merely preparatory

- Whether an act is more than merely preparatory to the commission of an offence is ultimately for the jury/court to decide. However, two tests have been set out over the years and have been accepted by the higher courts. These are:
  - ♦ The test set out *in R v Eagleton* (1855) Dears CC 515: whether there was any further act on the defendant's part remaining to be done before the completion of the intended crime.
  - ♦ The decision in *Davey v Lee* (1967) 51 Cr App R 303: the offence of attempt is complete if the defendant does an act which is a step towards the commission of the specific crime, which is immediately (and not just remotely) connected with the commission of it, the doing of which cannot reasonably be regarded as having any other purpose than the commission of the specific crime.
- Remember—a criminal attempt is not the same as having the intent to commit the offence. If an act is only preparatory (eg obtaining an insurance claim form to make a false claim), then it is not an attempt. There would have to be some other act such as actually filling the form out and posting it. Mere intent is not enough.
- A typical example is *R v Geddes* [1996] Crim LR 894. Here G had hidden materials on school premises, which could be used for kidnapping a child. There was no evidence he had started to carry out his intended action. The Court of Appeal determined that his actions were merely preparatory to the offence and did not go far enough to amount to an attempt. Compare this case with *R v Tosti and White* [1997] Crim LR 746 in which examining a padlock was considered to be more than a preparatory act.
- Attempting the impossible can be sufficient for a criminal attempt, as illustrated in the case of *R v Shivpuri* [1986] 2 All ER 334:
  - ♦ S was arrested by customs officers in possession of a suitcase in which S believed he had hidden heroin. The 'drugs' turned out to be harmless powder. Held that by receiving and hiding the powder in the suitcase, S had done an act that was more than merely preparatory to the commission of the import heroin offence (even though it was harmless powder). By virtue of s 1(2) of the Criminal

Attempts Act 1981, he was guilty of attempting to import heroin—by attempting the impossible.

Related cases

R v Ilyas (1984) 78 Cr App R 17, CA When a criminal attempt begins, an act has to be more than merely preparatory.

Davey & others v Lee (1967) 51 Cr App R 303, CA What constitutes an attempt—see above.

R v Shivpuri [1986] 2 All ER 334, HL Attempting the impossible can still be a criminal attempt.

Attorney-General's Reference (No 1 of 1992) [1993] 2 All ER 190, CA
Attempted penetration not necessary for attempted rape.

R v Williams (Kevin John) (1990) 92 Cr App R 158, CA No attempt needed for perverting the course of justice charge.

Practical considerations

- Criminal attempt offences can only occur where the principal offence is either an indictable offence or one that is triable either way.
- Attempts to commit summary offences are not recognized in criminal law.
- Even though damage under £5,000 can be dealt with at magistrates' court, a suspect can still be charged with attempting to damage property under £5,000, because the attempt damage offence is still an 'either way' offence. It is not a purely summary offence in the normal sense (*R v Bristol Justices ex parte Edgar* [1998] 3 All ER 798).
- In circumstances where a person commits the full offence of aiding and abetting, the offender should be charged as principal to the main offence where the offence is indictable or either way.
- When investigating attempted murder consideration must be given to the CPS advice offered in the assault charging standards (see assault **2.1** and murder **2.7**).
- Powers of arrest, search, mode of trial, penalty, and time limits are the same as those relating to the principal offence.

E&S

CHAR (where substantive theft/sexual offences apply)

TRIG **Only** in relation to attempt of following Theft Act 1968 offences:
- Theft s 1 (see **3.1**)
- Robbery s 8 (see **3.2**)
- Burglary s 9 (see **3.3**)
- Obtain property by deception s 15 (see **3.9**)
- Handling stolen goods s 22 (see **3.6**)

Either way

 None

 Summary: 6 months' imprisonment and/or a fine not exceeding the statutory maximum.
Indictment: 5 years' imprisonment.

Links to alternative subjects and offences

4.2 Vehicle Interference and Tampering with a Motor Vehicle

The Criminal Attempts Act 1981 and the Road Traffic Act 1988 created offences designed to protect motor vehicles from the actions of others namely vehicle interference and tampering with motor vehicles. Although the defendant may be trying to take the vehicle without the owner's consent, the law does not allow 'criminal attempts' for purely summary offences.

4.2.1 Vehicle interference

Offence

(1) A person is guilty of the offence of vehicle interference if he interferes with a **motor vehicle** or **trailer** or with anything carried in or on a motor vehicle or trailer with the **intention** that an offence specified in subsection (2) below shall be committed by himself or some other person.

(2) The offences mentioned in subsection (1) above are—
   (a) theft of the motor vehicle or part of it;
   (b) theft of anything carried in or on the motor vehicle or trailer; and
   (c) an offence under section 12(1) of the Theft Act 1968 (taking a conveyance)

and if it is shown that a person accused of an offence under this section intended that one of those offences should be committed, it is immaterial that it cannot be shown which it was.   Criminal Attempts Act 1981, s 9

Points to prove

✓ date and location
✓ interfere with a
✓ motor vehicle/trailer/part of/anything carried in/on it
✓ with intent that an offence of
✓ theft/taking and drive away without consent
✓ should be committed

Meanings

Motor vehicle

Means a mechanically propelled vehicle intended or adapted for use on a road (see **10.1**).

Trailer

Means a vehicle drawn by a motor vehicle (see **10.1**).

Intention (see **4.1**)

Explanatory notes

This offence 'fits' between the offence of going equipped (an offence which may be committed prior to any contact with a 'conveyance') and the offence of taking a conveyance without the owner's consent or theft (which is dependent on whether or not an intention to permanently deprive can be established).

Practical considerations

- Has the suspect possession of any implements for use in the offence that would not necessarily complete the offence of going equipped?
- Is there any CCTV evidence available?
- Check on the availability of witness evidence for CJA statements.

 Summary 6 months, but if endanger road user: none.

 3 months' imprisonment and/or a fine not exceeding level 4 on the standard scale.

4.2.2 **Tampering with motor vehicles**

> ### Offence
>
> If while a motor vehicle is on a road or on a parking place provided by a local authority, a person
> (a) gets onto the vehicle, or
> (b) tampers with the brake or other part of its mechanism without lawful authority or reasonable cause he is guilty of an offence.
>
> **Road Traffic Act 1988, s 25(1)**

Points to prove

✓ date and location
✓ without lawful authority or reasonable cause
✓ got on to/tampered with
✓ the brakes/other part of the mechanism of a motor vehicle
✓ on a road/parking place provided by a local authority

Meanings

Tamper

Given its normal meaning namely: 'improperly interfering with something'.

Other part of its mechanism

Means any mechanical part and not just those of a similar type to the brake.

Explanatory notes

- The motor vehicle must be on a road and/or on a parking place provided by the local authority (see **10.1**).
- It is for the prosecution to prove the above and that the accused got onto or tampered with the motor vehicle without lawful authority or reasonable cause.

Defences

People with lawful authority and reasonable cause will have a defence. Lawful authority might take the form of a police officer or firefighter releasing the brake of a vehicle to move it in an emergency.

Practical considerations

- Has the suspect possession of any implements for use in the offence that would not necessarily complete the offence of going equipped?
- Is there any CCTV evidence available?
- Check on the availability of witness evidence for CJA statements.

 Summary   6 months

 Fine not exceeding level 3 on the standard scale.

Links to alternative subjects and offences

4.3 Taking a Conveyance Without Owner's Consent

The following topic covers three aspects: taking a conveyance without the owner's consent (TWOC), aggravated vehicle taking, and the taking of pedal cycles. TWOC can also be known as unlawful taking of a motor vehicle (UTMV) and taking and driving away (TDA).

4.3.1 Taking a conveyance without owner's consent

Offence

Subject to subsections 12(5) and 12(6) below, a person shall be guilty of an offence if, without having the consent of the **owner** or other lawful authority, he **takes** any **conveyance** for his own or another's use or, knowing that any conveyance has been taken without such authority, drives it or allows himself to be carried in or on it.   **Theft Act 1968, s 12(1)**

Points to prove

There are several sets of circumstances to consider depending on the role the person took in the committing of the offence. The following relates to the initial taker only.

✓ date and location
✓ without the consent
✓ of the owner/other lawful authority
✓ took a conveyance
✓ for your own/another's use

Meanings

Owner

If the conveyance is subject to a hiring or hire purchase agreement means the person in possession of the conveyance under that agreement.

Takes

Means that some movement of the conveyance is essential (*R v Bogacki* [1973] 2 All ER 864).

Conveyance

Means any conveyance constructed or adapted for the carriage of a person or persons whether by land, water, or air, **except** that it **does not include** a conveyance constructed or adapted for use only under the control of a person not carried in or on it.

Explanatory notes

- An important point is that the conveyance must be capable of carrying a person. A machine such as a small domestic lawn mower is not a conveyance, but one upon which the operator sits would be.
- A horse is an animal and therefore not 'constructed or adapted', so it is not a 'conveyance'.
- Pedal cycles are catered for in s 12(5) (see **4.3.3**) and sub-s 12(6) relates to defences.
- You must prove the use or intended use as a means of transport. If the conveyance is not used in this way (eg pushing a car away from a drive entrance to remove an obstruction), then there is no 'taking'.
- If it is used to ride on while being pushed then there may be a taking (*R v Bow* [1977] Crim LR 176).
- A dinghy on a trailer that is to be used as a dinghy at some future time is still 'taken' for the taker's/another's own use. Use has been held to mean 'use as a conveyance' and future intended use is sufficient (*R v Marchant and McAllister* (1985) 80 Cr App R 361).
- The term 'carried in or on' requires some movement of the conveyance. In *R v Miller* [1976] Crim LR 147, a man found sitting in a boat that had been moored was found not guilty of the offence. The normal movement of the waves was deemed insufficient for the ingredients of the offence. However, the vertical movement of a hovercraft would be sufficient, because that is not a 'natural' movement taking place independently of the use of the conveyance.
- The term 'consent of the owner' does not arise simply on occasions where specific permission has been given. Problems tend to arise where the owner has given some form of conditional consent, case law suggests that if the borrower of a car, for instance, makes a reasonable detour to his/her journey, then that detour will still be made 'with the consent of the owner'. However, using the conveyance for a wholly or substantially different purpose than that given by the owner may well be an offence. This element is also relevant to one of the statutory defences (below).
- To prove the term 'allows himself', it is necessary to show that the defendant knew that the conveyance had been taken without the consent of the owner or other lawful authority. The person may not know that when they get into the conveyance, but if they find out subsequently, they are expected to make some attempt to leave.
- The essential difference between this offence and the offence of theft contrary to s 1 of the Theft Act 1968 is that in this offence there is an absence of any intention to permanently deprive the owner of their property.

Defence

A person does not commit an offence under this section by anything done in the belief that he has lawful authority to do it or that he would have the owner's consent if the owner knew of his doing it and the circumstances of it.   Theft Act 1968, s 12(6)

4.3.1 Taking a Conveyance without Owner's Consent

Defence notes

- The prosecution must prove that the defendant did not believe that he had lawful authority (such as a police or local authority power of removal, or repossession by a finance company).
- Apart from the belief that the owner would have consented if s/he had known of the using of the conveyance; it must also be shown that s/he believed that the owner would have consented had they known of the circumstances of the taking and the using of it.

Related cases

R v Bogacki [1973] 2 All ER 864, CA 'Taking' must involve movement.

R v Pearce [1973] Crim LR 321, CA 'Taking' should be given its ordinary meaning.

R v Wibberley [1965] 3 All ER 718, CA Use of company vehicle outside working hours.

McKnight v Davies [1974] Crim LR 62, CA The taking is complete when consent is exceeded.

Whittaker v Campbell [1983] 3 All ER 582, QBD Consent of owner is valid even if obtained by fraud.

R v Peart [1970] 2 All ER 823, CA Misrepresentation must be fundamental to void consent.

R v Marchant and McAllister (1985) 80 Cr App R 361, CA Intended use sufficient.

Sturrock v DPP The Times, 9 February 1995, QBD Proof of ownership. No consent without an owner.

Practical considerations

- An alternative verdict to theft under s 1 of the Theft Act 1968 might be applicable: 'If on the trial of an indictment for theft, the jury are not satisfied that the accused committed theft, they may find him guilty of an offence under s 12(1)' (Theft Act 1968, s 12(4)).
- As the offence is only summary, there is no such thing as an 'attempted taking of a conveyance'.
- Consider the more serious offence of aggravated vehicle taking (see **4.3.2**).
- In the interview, the situation where the person becomes aware that the conveyance has been taken after s/he has entered it should be covered along with any subsequent efforts to leave the conveyance.
- The Act allows for the extension of **prosecution time limits**, where proceedings shall not be commenced after the end of the period of 3 years beginning with the day on which the offence was committed; but subject to that, may be commenced at any time within the period of 6 months beginning with the **relevant day**.
- The 'relevant day' means the day on which sufficient evidence to justify the proceedings came to the knowledge of any person responsible for deciding whether to commence any such prosecution.

Summary

Complex—see **prosecution time limits** above

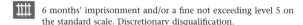

6 months' imprisonment and/or a fine not exceeding level 5 on the standard scale. Discretionary disqualification.

4.3.2 **Aggravated vehicle-taking**

The Aggravated Vehicle-Taking Act 1992 inserted s 12A into the Theft Act 1968 thereby creating the offence of 'aggravated vehicle-taking'.

Offence

(1) Subject to subsection 12A(3) *(defence)* a person is guilty of aggravated taking of a vehicle if—

(a) he commits an offence under section 12(1) (taking a conveyance without consent) (in this section referred to as the 'basic offence') in relation to a mechanically propelled vehicle, and

(b) is proved that, at any time after the vehicle was unlawfully taken (whether by him or another) and before it was recovered, the vehicle was driven or injury or damage was caused, in one or more of the circumstances set out in paragraphs (a) to (d) of subsection 12A(2).

(2) The circumstances referred to in subsection (1)(b) are—

(a) that the vehicle was driven dangerously on a road or other public place;

(b) that, owing to the driving of the vehicle, an accident occurred by which injury was caused to any person;

(c) that, owing to the driving of the vehicle, an accident occurred by which damage was caused to any property, other than the vehicle;

(d) that damage was caused to the vehicle.   **Theft Act 1968, s 12A(1), (2)**

Points to prove

Again, there are several sets of circumstances to consider depending on the role the defendant played in the commission of the offence.

✓ date and location

✓ without the consent

✓ of the owner/other lawful authority

✓ took (being the initial taker)

✓ a mechanically propelled vehicle for

✓ your own/another's use.

(The 'basic offence')

And after it was taken and before it was recovered, one of the following occurred—

✓ the vehicle was driven dangerously on a road/public place **or**

✓ owing to driving the vehicle an accident occurred by which injury was caused to person(s) **or**

✓ owing to driving the vehicle an accident occurred by which damage was caused to any property, other than the vehicle **or**

✓ damage was caused to the vehicle

Meanings

Dangerously

A vehicle is driven dangerously if:

* it is driven in a way which falls far below what would be expected of a competent and careful driver; **and**
* it would be obvious to a competent and careful driver that driving the vehicle in that way would be dangerous.

Accident

Means 'any unintended occurrence which has an adverse physical result' and the legislation does not specify that it has to occur on a road or even in a public place.

Damage

Means any damage not just criminal damage.

Explanatory notes

* 'Owner' has the same meaning as s 12(1) (see **4.3.1**).
* Consider the offence of dangerous driving (see **10.7**).
* A vehicle is recovered when it is restored to its owner or to other lawful possession or custody.
* It would appear that a vehicle has been recovered once the police, owner, or some other person with the authority of the owner, takes responsibility for the vehicle. However, where a member of the public has telephoned the police and informed them of the location of a taken vehicle, it has yet to be decided whether that vehicle is 'recovered' from the time of the call until the time the police arrive at the scene and take physical control.
* This offence only applies to mechanically propelled vehicles and not to all conveyances.

Defences

A person is not guilty of an offence under this section if he proves that, as regards any such proven driving, injury or damage as is referred to in subsection (1)(b) (aggravating factors) above, either—

(a) the driving, accident or damage referred to above occurred before he committed the basic offence; or

(b) he was neither in, nor on, nor in the immediate vicinity of, the vehicle when that driving, accident or damage occurred. **Theft Act 1968, s 12A(3)**

Related cases

Dawes v DPP [1995] 1 Cr App R 65, QBD   Injury to a person or damage to property owing to driving or damage caused to the taken vehicle (whether by driving or not) needs to be proved.

Practical considerations

- The fact that the person who originally took the vehicle is not the person who caused the accident resulting in personal injury is irrelevant—the initial taker can still be prosecuted for the aggravated offence. Nor is there any requirement that the driver of the 'taken vehicle' has to be at fault when a personal injury accident occurs (*R v Marsh* [1996] 8 CL 54).
- Always bear in mind the above defences when interviewing.
- The aggravated offence never becomes statute barred as it is an either way offence. Even if the damage caused is under £5,000 and the offence is triable only summarily, it is still an either way offence and so does not become statute barred.
- By virtue of s 12A(5), a person who is found not guilty of this offence can still be found guilty of taking a vehicle without consent as an alternative.

 Either way   None

Summary: 6 months' imprisonment and/or a fine not exceeding the statutory maximum.
Indictment: 2 years' imprisonment, **but** where a person dies as a result of an accident involving the offence, 14 years' imprisonment.

4.3.3 **Pedal cycles**

Taking or riding a pedal cycle without the consent of the owner or other lawful authority is an offence.

SSS Stop, search and seize powers   **E&S** Entry and search powers   **CHAR** Offences where bad character can be introduced   **141**

TRIG Trigger offences

4.3.3 Pedal Cycles

Offence

Taking a conveyance shall not apply in relation to pedal cycles; but, subject to subsection (6) below *(defences)*, a person who, without having the consent of the owner or other lawful authority takes a pedal cycle for his own or another's use, or rides a pedal cycle knowing it to have been taken without such authority, shall be guilty of an offence. **Theft Act 1968, s 12(5)**

Points to prove

✓ date and location
✓ consent of the owner
✓ takes/rides
✓ pedal cycle
✓ for own or other's use.

Explanatory notes

- A pedal cycle is neither propelled by mechanical power nor is it electrically assisted.
- There are many types of 'hybrid' vehicles, such as motorized scooters that may qualify as mechanically propelled vehicles or conveyances. Ultimately this is a question of fact for the court to decide.

Defences (see 4.3.1)

Practical considerations

- The prosecution must prove that the accused did not have lawful authority, such as a police or local authority power of removal, or repossession by a finance company.
- As this is a summary offence, there is no offence of 'attempting to take a pedal cycle'.

 Summary   6 months

 Fine not exceeding level 3 on the standard scale.

Links to alternative subjects and offences

4.4 **Criminal Damage**

The offence of criminal damage addressed in this chapter is designed to protect people's property from the unlawful actions of others. Section 1 of the Criminal Damage Act 1971 creates the offence of simple 'criminal damage'.

Offence

A person who without lawful excuse **destroys** or **damages** any **property belonging to another intending** to destroy or damage any such property or being **reckless** as to whether any such property would be destroyed or damaged shall be guilty of an offence.   Criminal Damage Act 1971, s 1(1)

Points to prove
- ✓ date and location
- ✓ without lawful excuse
- ✓ destroyed/damaged
- ✓ property to value of
- ✓ intending to
- ✓ destroy/damage such property **or**
- ✓ being reckless whether it was destroyed/damaged.

Meanings

Destroyed

Means property which is incapable of being repaired and can only be replaced.

Damaged

Means property that has suffered some physical harm, impairment, or deterioration.

Property (s10.1)

Means property of a tangible nature, whether real or personal, including money and:

(a) including wild creatures which have been tamed or are ordinarily kept in captivity, and any other wild creatures or their carcasses if, but only if, they have been reduced into possession which has not been lost or abandoned or are in the course of being reduced into possession; but

(b) not including mushrooms growing wild on any land or flowers, fruit or foliage of a plant growing wild on any land.

Belonging to another

This is property that belongs to another person who has custody or control of it, or who has a right or an interest in it, or has a charge over it.

Intending (see **4.1**).

Reckless

The test set out in *R v G and R* [2003] UKHL 50 applies, which states that a person acts 'recklessly' for the purposes of s 1 with respect to:

- circumstances where that person is aware of a risk that exists or will exist;
- a result when s/he is aware of a risk that it will occur;

and it is, in the circumstances known to him/her, unreasonable to take the risk.

The **first part** provides for those existing or future circumstances known to the defendant which, in the circumstances as known to him/her, made it unreasonable to take the risk they took. An example would be a tramp taking shelter in a barn full of dry hay, aware of the risk s/he lights a fire to boil water for a cup of tea, and sets the barn alight.

The **second part** of the test applies if the person is aware that the result of their actions are a risk and, in the circumstances as known to him/her, it would be unreasonable to take that risk. An example would be an adult who lets off a large rocket and ignores instructions which state that the firework should be launched from a tube embedded in the ground and instead launches it from a bottle standing upright on the pavement. As a result the rocket goes through the window of a house opposite and causes a fire.

The case of *G and R* involved two children aged 11 and 12 who set fire to a shop when lighting newspapers in a yard at the back. It was argued in their defence that, although the act might have been an obvious risk to the average person, it might not be obvious to such young children. The House of Lords agreed and overturned the previous 'objective' test in the case of *R v Caldwell* [1981] 1 All ER 961.

Explanatory notes

The important thing to prove or disprove (in addition to the damage itself) is the state of mind (intent) or that s/he was reckless in their actions, in destroying/damaging the property.

Defences

Lawful excuse

(1) This section applies to any offence under section 1(1) and any offence under section 2 or 3 other than one involving a threat by the person charged to destroy or damage property in a way which he knows is likely to endanger the life of another or involving an intent by the person charged to use or cause or permit the use of something in his custody or under his control so to destroy or damage property.

(2) A person charged with an offence to which this section applies shall, whether or not he would be treated for the purposes of this Act as having a lawful excuse apart from this subsection, be treated for those purposes as having a lawful excuse:

(a) if at the time of the act or acts alleged to constitute the offence he believed that the person or persons whom he believed to be entitled to consent to the destruction of or damage to the property in question had so consented, or would have so consented to it if he or they had known of the destruction or damage and its circumstances; or

(b) if he destroyed or damaged or threatened to destroy or damage the property in question or, in the case of a charge of an offence under section 3, intended to use or cause or permit the use of something to destroy or damage it, in order to protect property belonging to himself or another or a right or interest in property which was or which he believed to be vested in himself or another, and at the time of the act or acts alleged to constitute the offence he believed—

(i) that the property, right or interest was in immediate need of protection; and

(ii) that the means of protection adopted or proposed to be adopted were or would be reasonable having regard to all the circumstances.

(3) For the purposes of this section it is immaterial whether a belief is justified or not if it is honestly held.

Protect life or property

(4) For the purposes of subsection (2) above a right or interest in property includes any right or privilege in or over land, whether created by grant, licence or otherwise.

(5) This section shall not be construed as casting doubt on any defence recognized by law as a defence to criminal charges.

Criminal Damage Act 1971, s 5(1)– (5)

Defence notes

The courts have accepted that damage caused to protect life, prevent injury, or stop unlawful imprisonment of a person is also a valid defence (*R v Baker & another The Times*, 26 November 1996).

Related cases

Johnson v DPP [1994] Crim LR 673, QBD When lawful excuse is the defence, two questions need to be asked. The first is an objective question (eg whether the act of damage was done in order to protect property); and second, a subjective question (whether the defendant believed that the property was in immediate need of protection and the means of protection used were reasonable).

Chamberlain v Lindon The Times, 6 April 1998 The requirement of immediacy (under s 5(2)(b)(i) above) will still be satisfied if the threat to property (or rights in property) is already taking place. Here, the defendant was charged with criminal damage after destroying a wall erected by his neighbour which obstructed a right of access to his property. The court held that the defendant had a lawful excuse for his action because the obstruction to his rights had already happened and he believed that his rights would be further prejudiced if the wall remained in place.

Drake v DPP [1994] Crim LR 855, QBD   Damage must affect the integrity of the object damaged.

'A' (a Juvenile) v R [1978] Crim LR 689, CC   Spitting on a police uniform did not constitute damage.

Hardman & others v Chief Constable of Avon & Somerset [1986] Crim LR 330, CC   The cost of cleaning (here a pavement artist's water-soluble drawing on a street) may still amount to be 'damage'.

Practical considerations

- If property has been destroyed, the value specified in the charge should reflect the full replacement cost.
- Charging that property was both 'destroyed' and 'damaged' is an unnecessary duplication, so wherever possible a choice should be made.
- Consider applying for a warrant (under s 6) to search and seize for anything in custody or control of suspect on his/her premises. Having reasonable cause to believe, has been used **or is intended for use** without lawful excuse to either: destroy or damage property—belonging to another or in a way likely to endanger the life of another.
- If the destruction or damage has been caused by fire, an offence of arson under s 1(3) should be charged (see **4.5.2**).
- Consider the more serious offence of racially or religiously aggravated criminal damage (see **7.10**).
- Where the value of the damage is below £5,000, the offence would normally be tried at a magistrates' court.
- If the full offence is not committed consider attempt criminal damage (see **4.1**).
- The same incident may involve separate activities, some causing ordinary damage and some damage by fire (for example, protestors break into a laboratory building, smash laboratory equipment and set fire to some files). In such circumstances they are separate offences and best charged as such.
- There is a special offence of criminal damage to an ancient monument under the Ancient Monuments and Archaeological Areas Act 1979, s 28. The advantage of using this offence is that where the owner is responsible for damaging the protected monument which they own.
- Consider the offences of having an article with intent to commit damage (see **4.7**) or made threats to cause damage (see **4.6**).
- Section 48 of the Anti-social Behaviour Act 2003 enables certain local authorities to serve a 'graffiti removal notice' on the owners of street furniture, buildings, structures, apparatus, plant, or other objects in or

on any street, statutory undertakers, and educational institutions whose property is defaced with graffiti that is either detrimental to the local amenity of the area or deemed to be offensive. The notice will require the owners to remove the graffiti within a specified period of time (minimum 28 days).

 SSS **E&S**

PND (police only)

 RRA **CSO**

♿ Either way 🕑 None

▥ **Summary:** *Value below £5000:* 3 months imprisonment and/or a fine not exceeding level 4 on the standard scale. *Value of or exceeding £5000:* 6 months' imprisonment and/or a fine not exceeding the statutory maximum.
Indictment: 10 years' imprisonment.

Links to alternative subjects and offences

SSS	Stop, search and seize powers	**E&S**	Entry and search powers	**PND**	Penalty notice for disorder offences
RRA	Racially or religiously aggravated offence	**CSO**	Offences where CSO can use their powers		

4.5 Damage with Intent to Endanger Life and Arson

The offence of damage with intent to endanger life is also known as aggravated damage. This and arson are serious offences because of their potential to have disastrous effects on other people's lives and the wider community.

This section is presented in two parts: damage with intent to endanger life and then arson.

4.5.1 Damage with intent to endanger life

Section 1(2) of the Criminal Damage Act 1971 creates the serious offence of destroying or damaging property intending that, or being reckless as to whether life would be endangered.

Offence

A person who without lawful excuse, **destroys** or **damages** any **property**, whether **belonging to** himself or **another**

(a) **intending** to destroy or damage any property or being **reckless** as to whether any property would be destroyed or damaged; and

(b) intending by the destruction or damage to endanger the life of another or being reckless as to whether the life of another would be thereby endangered;

shall be guilty of an offence.   Criminal Damage Act 1971, s 1(2)

Points to prove

✓ date and location
✓ without lawful excuse
✓ destroy/damage
✓ property
✓ whether belonging to self or another
✓ with intent destroy/damage or reckless destroy/damage AND
✓ intending by destruction/damage to endanger life of another **or**
✓ being reckless as to whether such life would thereby be endangered.

4.5.1 Damage with Intent to Endanger Life

Meanings

Lawful excuse (see **Defence** (below))

Intent (see **4.1**)

Destroy (see **4.4**)

Damage (see **4.4**)

Property (see **4.4**)

Belonging to another (see **4.4**)

Endanger life

This does not require an attempt to kill nor for any actual injury to occur. It is sufficient that life was endangered.

Reckless (see **4.4**)

Explanatory notes

- Consider attempt murder or manslaughter (see **4.1** and **2.7**).
- No actual injury need occur; all that is required is evidence that life was endangered. For example, if a jealous person cuts the brake pipe of his rival's car, no harm may actually come to the intended victim, but the potential for harm exists. Either intention to endanger the life of another or recklessness in that regard must be proved and the potential for harm to someone other than the defendant must be proved.
- The actual damage caused must also be the cause of the danger. For example, shooting at a person in a room (through a window) both endangers life and damages the window, but it is not the damage that endangers the life.

Defence

- An example of having a lawful excuse could be attempting to effect a rescue in order to save life, but in doing so it could endanger life.
- The statutory lawful excuse defence for damage given in s 5 (see **4.4**) specifically precludes damage with intent to endanger life and arson.

Related cases

R v Webster & others [1995] 2 All ER 168, CA Intent to damage causing injury/endangerment to life. Two similar cases related to the offence of 'damage with intent to endanger life'. In the first case, the defendants pushed a coping stone from a bridge onto a moving railway carriage. No one was injured. The court decided that the principal intention of the defendants was for the stone to directly injure the passengers, therefore the offence of 'damage intending to endanger life' had not been committed. However, the court substituted a conviction for the offence of 'recklessness causing damage which could endanger life', (eg the debris that flew around the carriage following the incident). In the second case, the defendants threw bricks at a police car from a stolen car, aiming for its windscreen. The windscreen broke and injured one of the officers. In that case, the victim's resultant loss of vision would be sufficient for a conviction for the offence of causing damage with intent to endanger life. Establishing intention is important, so therefore ask in interview what the offender's intentions were or what he perceived the outcome of his actions would be.

R v Merrick [1995] Crim LR 802, CA Reckless if known risk is not avoided but remedied after. In this case, M cut an electric mains and left live cabling exposed for 6 minutes. M was convicted of damaging property and being reckless as to whether life was endangered. On appeal, M argued that he had weighed up the work and decided there was no significant risk, therefore he was not 'reckless'. However, the conviction was upheld on the reasoning that if M wanted to make sure that he was outside the definition of 'reckless', then he had to take remedies to eliminate any risk **before** starting the work. It was too late to take action once the risk had been created.

R v Hardie [1984] 3 All ER 848, CA Recklessness after defendant taken drugs insufficient as defendant could not form the necessary *mens rea*.

R v Steer [1988] 2 All ER 833, HL The actual damage caused must give rise to the danger to life, not just the act of causing the damage.

Practical considerations

- The same incident may involve separate activities, some causing ordinary damage and some damage by fire (for example, protestors break into a laboratory building, smash laboratory equipment, and set fire to some files). In such circumstances they are separate offences and best charged as such.
- Damage by fire is arson (see **4.5.2**).

 Indictable   None

 Life imprisonment

4.5.2 Arson

Section 1(3) of the Criminal Damage Act 1971 creates the offence of 'arson'.

Offence

An offence committed under this section by destroying or damaging property by fire shall be charged as arson. **Criminal Damage Act 1971, s 1(3)**

SSS Stop, search and seize powers   **E&S** Entry and search powers   **RRA** Racially or religiously aggravated offence   **151**

CSO Offences where CSO can use their powers

Points to prove

Arson

✓ date and location
✓ without lawful excuse
✓ destroy/damage
✓ by fire
✓ property with intent to destroy/damage it
✓ or being reckless as to whether such property was destroyed/damaged

Arson—endanger life

✓ all points to prove for arson (above) **and**
✓ intending by that destruction/damage to endanger life of another
   or
✓ being reckless as to whether life of another would thereby be
   endangered

Meanings

Destroy (see 4.4)

Damage (see 4.4)

Property (see 4.4)

Explanatory notes

For the offence to be complete, some of the damage must be by fire; this does not include smoke damage. It is enough, however, that wood is charred (*R v Parker* [1839] 9 C&P 45).

Defences

There is no specific defence for arson.

Practical considerations

• Intention or recklessness must be proved. A burglar who accidentally dropped a lighted match used for illumination could be reckless.
• The same incident may involve separate activities, some causing ordinary damage and some damage by fire. These are separate offences and should be so charged.
• Most arsons involve the use of 'accelerants' such as petrol or lighter fuel to start the fire. If it is suspected that accelerants might have been used, special procedures need to be implemented in order to obtain forensic samples.
• An accelerant is used to increase the speed of a chemical reaction. For police purposes, this usually means something to speed up the spread of a fire during an arson attack. Accelerants (such as petrol) are volatile and will evaporate if left in the open air. Do not confuse accelerants with oils and greases, which demand different treatment.

- Procedures for the careful preservation and packaging which must be carried out to enable the detection of accelerants can be divided into three basic areas:
  - ✦ clothing,
  - ✦ at the scene,
  - ✦ fragile items.
- Submit the control sample of the suspected accelerant in a **clean** metal container with a well fitting cap, sealed inside a **nylon bag**. If no metal can is available, use a clean glass container but protect any rubber insert in the cap with a nylon film. For this purpose cut up part of one of the nylon bags, and use the rest as a control—see below. Isolate from all other samples.
- Control sample of nylon bag used to seal any sample: in a case where a nylon bag has been employed to seal a sample, a control nylon bag from the same batch as the one used to contain the samples should be submitted. This should be sealed but should only contain air.
- Important—never dry out items suspected of containing fire accelerants before packaging. Never store or transport items for examination for the presence of fire accelerant materials, in close proximity to a control sample of fire accelerant or anything taken from the defendant. Even a suspicion of contamination will destroy the evidential value of the samples.

Either way

 None

 Summary: 6 months' imprisonment and/or a fine not exceeding level 5 on the standard scale.
Indictment: Life imprisonment.

Links to alternative subjects and offences

4.6 Threats to Destroy or Damage Property

Section sec2 of the Criminal Damage Act 1971 creates specific offences relating to threats to destroy or damage property.

> **Offence**
>
> A person who without **lawful excuse** makes to another a threat, **intending** that the other would fear it would be carried out—
> (a) to **destroy** or **damage** any **property** belonging to that other or a third person; or
> (b) to destroy or damage his own property in way which he knows is likely to **endanger** the **life** of that other or a third person
>
> Criminal Damage Act 1971, s 2

Points to prove

✓ date and location
✓ without lawful excuse
✓ threatened to destroy/damage property of a person
✓ intending
✓ a person would fear that the threat would be carried out

Threaten damage own property to endanger life

✓ date and location
✓ without lawful excuse
✓ threatened to destroy/damage
✓ your own property
✓ in a way you knew
✓ was likely to endanger life of another
✓ intending a person would fear threat would be carried out.

Meanings

Lawful excuse (see defences **4.4**)

Intending (see **4.1**)

Destroy (see **4.4**)

Damage (see **4.4**)

Property (see **4.4**)

Endanger life (see **4.5.1**)

Explanatory notes

- It is not necessary to show the other person is actually in fear that the threat will be carried out; what has to be proved is that the defendant intended the other to fear it will be carried out.
- It does not matter that the defendant may not actually intend to carry out the threats and/or the victim may not even believe them. The offender's intention to create such a fear is sufficient—and necessary—to complete the offence.
- The test for whether the action amounts to a threat is objective ie 'would the reasonable person conclude that a threat had been made?' *(R v Cakmak and others, The Times,* 28 March 2002). Only intention will do; unlike s 1 there is no mention of reckless in this section.
- The threat must be to another person, and can relate to a third party—such as 'I will smash up your son's car if you don't do what I say'—the threat is to one person about their or a third person's property.
- In s 2(b) above, the offender can threaten to damage his own property in a way that is likely to endanger the life of another, such as a landlord threatening to burn down a house he owns if a tenant will not leave.
- In relation to the meaning of 'threats in criminal damage', two points must be considered:
  - ✦ the type of conduct threatened; and
  - ✦ the threat itself.
- There is no specific requirement for the threatened act to be immediate and a threat to do damage to a property at some time in the future may well suffice; each case will depend on the circumstances surrounding it.

Defence

Having a lawful excuse will be a defence under s 5 (see **4.4**).

 SSS   E&S

 Either way   None

 Summary: 6 months' imprisonment and/or a fine not exceeding the statutory maximum.
Indictment: 10 years' imprisonment.

Links to alternative subjects and offences

4.7 Custody/control of Articles with Intent to Damage and Sale of Paint Aerosols to Persons Under 16

Even when criminal damage has not been committed or threatened, there may still have been an offence arising out of the possession of articles where there is an intention to cause damage. An offence of selling paint aerosols to children, is designed to address the increasing problem of criminal damage to property by way of graffiti.

4.7.1 Custody/control of articles with intent to damage

Section 3 of the Criminal Damage Act 1971 creates the offence of 'going equipped' intending to destroy or damage property.

Offence

A person who has **anything** in his **custody** or under his **control intending** without **lawful excuse** to use it or **cause** or **permit** another to use it—
(a) to **destroy** or **damage** any **property belonging to** some **other person** or
(b) to destroy or damage his own or the user's property in a way which he knows is likely to **endanger** the **life** of some other person;
shall be guilty of an offence.   Criminal Damage Act 1971, s 3

Points to prove
- ✓ date and location
- ✓ had in custody/control
- ✓ an article/object/substance/anything at all
- ✓ intending
- ✓ without lawful excuse
- ✓ to destroy/damage **or** to cause/permit another to use the article etc.
- ✓ property belonging to another/own or user's property where s/he knows life of another is likely to be endangered thereby

4.7.1 Custody/control of Articles with Intent to Damage

Meaning

Anything

Means its natural/everyday meaning and can range from explosives to a box of matches or a hammer.

Custody or control

It must be proved that the defendant had custody or control of the article in question. This is a wider term than possession and could cover occasions where the defendant does not have the article with him/her.

Intent (see 4.1)

Lawful excuse (see 4.4)

Cause

Means some degree of dominance or control, or some express or positive authorization, from the person who 'causes'.

Permit

Requires general or particular permission, as distinguished from authorization, and the permission may be express (eg verbal/written) or implied (eg the person's actions). A person cannot permit unless s/he is in a position to forbid and no one can permit what s/he cannot control.

Destroy (see 4.4)

Damage (see 4.4)

Property (see 4.4)

Belonging to another (see 4.4)

Endanger life (see 4.5.1)

Explanatory notes

- The offence is split into two parts, but certain elements are common to both. Intent to use/cause/permit must be proved in all cases, as must the element of having anything in the defendant's custody/control and the absence of lawful excuse.
- The act intended does not have to be immediate; it can be at some time in the future (eg someone storing bomb-making materials for future use).
- The only difference between s 3(a) and s 3(b) offences is that, in (b) there is an element of knowledge of the likelihood of endangering the life of someone else and the offender's own property can be the object of the intended damage (eg a person carrying a can of petrol to set fire to his/her own house with his/her partner inside it).

Defences

Having a lawful excuse (see 4.4).

Related cases

R v Fancy [1980] Crim LR 171, HL The intention must be to commit some specific damage.

R v Buckingham (1976) 63 Cr App R 159, CC Intention for an 'immediate use' is not necessary; an intention to use some time in the future will suffice.

 Either way   None

 Summary: 6 months' imprisonment and/or a fine not exceeding the statutory maximum.
Indictment: 10 years' imprisonment.

4.7.2 **Sale of aerosol paints to children**

Section 54 of the Anti-Social Behaviour Act 2003 makes it an offence to sell aerosol spray paints to persons aged under 16. The objective is to reduce the incidence of graffiti criminal damage, caused by young persons using cans of aerosol spray paint.

Offence

A person commits an offence if he sells an aerosol paint container to a person under the age of sixteen.   Anti-Social Behaviour Act 2003, s 54(1)

Points to prove
✓ date and location
✓ sale
✓ an aerosol paint container
✓ to a person who was, at the time, under the age of 16

Meaning of aerosol paint container

Means a device which contains paint stored under pressure, and is designed to permit the release of the paint as a spray.

Defences

(4) It is a defence for a person charged with an offence under this section in respect of a sale to prove that—

4.7.2 Sale of Aerosol Paints to Children

> (a) he took all reasonable steps to determine the purchaser's age, and
> (b) he reasonably believed that the purchaser was not under the age of sixteen.
>
> (5) It is a defence for a person charged with an offence under this section in respect of a sale effected by another person to prove that he (the defendant) took all reasonable steps to avoid the commission of an offence under this section.   Anti-Social Behaviour Act 2003, s 54(4) and (5)

Practical considerations

- You will need to show that the sale was concluded, rather than simply the advertising or negotiating.
- There is no need to prove any intention by the purchaser or any specific knowledge/suspicion of intended knowledge on the part of the seller.
- Age to be proved by a birth certificate and testimony that it belongs to the person producing it.

 Summary   6 months

A fine not exceeding level 4 on the standard scale.

Links to alternative subjects and offences

4.8 Intimidation of a Witness/Juror and Perverting the Course of Justice

Witnesses and/or jurors involved in the investigation or trial of criminal offences are protected from intimidation and/or threat, by s 51 of the Criminal Justice and Public Order Act 1994. This area of law is presented in two parts: intimidation of a witness/juror, and perverting the course of justice.

4.8.1 Intimidation of a witness/juror

Offences

Intimidation

A person commits an offence if—
(a) he does an **act** which intimidates, and is intended to intimidate, another person ('the victim'),
(b) he does the act knowing or believing that the victim is assisting in the **investigation of an offence** or is a witness or **potential** witness or a juror or potential juror in proceedings for an offence; and
(c) he does it **intending** thereby to cause the investigation or the course of justice to be obstructed, perverted or interfered with.

Criminal Justice and Public Order Act 1994, s 51(1)

Threats

A person commits an offence if—
(a) he does an act which harms, and is intended to harm, another person or, intending to cause another person to fear harm, he threatens to do an act which would harm that other person,
(b) he does or threatens to do the act knowing or believing that the person harmed or threatened to be harmed ('the victim'), or some other person, has assisted in an investigation into an offence or has given evidence or particular evidence in proceedings for an offence, or has acted as a juror or concurred in a particular verdict in proceedings for an offence; and
(c) he does or threatens to do it because of that knowledge or belief.

Criminal Justice and Public Order Act 1994, s 51(2)

Points to prove

Intimidate a witness/juror

✓ date and location
✓ knew/believed person was
✓ assisting investigation of offence or a witness/potential witness or juror/potential juror
✓ in proceedings for offence
✓ did an act which
✓ intimidated that person and was intended to intimidate that person
✓ intending to cause investigation/course of justice to be obstructed or perverted or interfered with.

Harm/threaten a witness/juror

✓ date and location
✓ knew/believed person or another had assisted in investigation/given evidence in proceedings/given particular evidence in proceedings/acted as juror/concurred in particular verdict
✓ because of that knowledge/belief
✓ threatened/did an act which
✓ harmed/was intended to harm/would have harmed person

Meanings

Investigation into an offence

Means such an investigation by the police or other person charged with the duty of investigating offences or charging offenders.

Offence

Includes an alleged or suspected offence.

Potential

In relation to a juror, means a person who has been summonsed for jury service at the court at which proceedings for the offence are pending.

Intending

Intimidation offence

If, in proceedings against a person for an offence under subsection (1), it is proved that he did an act falling within paragraph (a) with the knowledge or belief required by paragraph (b), he shall be presumed, unless the contrary is proved, to have done the act with the intention required by paragraph (c) of that subsection.

Criminal Justice and Public Order Act 1994, s 51(7)

Threatened/harmed offence (see 4.1)

Act

In proceedings against a person for an offence under subsection (2) (**threats**) if it can be proved by the prosecution that within the **relevant period** he did or threatened to do an act described by (a) above with the knowledge or belief of (b) above, then he shall be

---

presumed, unless the contrary is proved, to have done the act (or threatened to do the act) with the motive required by (c) above.

Criminal Justice and Public Order Act 1994, s 51(8)

The relevant period

In this section 'the relevant period'—

(a) in relation to a witness or juror in any proceedings for an offence, means the period beginning with the **institution of the proceedings** and ending with the first anniversary of the conclusion of the trial or, if there is an appeal or reference under s 9 or 11 of the Criminal Appeal Act 1995, of the conclusion of the appeal;

(b) in relation to a person who has, or is believed by the accused to have, assisted in an investigation into an offence, but was not also a witness in proceedings for an offence, means the period of one year beginning with any act of his, or any act believed by the accused to be an act of his, assisting in the investigation; and

(c) in relation to a person who both has, or is believed by the accused to have, assisted in the investigation into an offence and was a witness in proceedings for the offence, means the period beginning with any act of his, or any act believed by the accused to be an act of his, assisting in the investigation and ending with the anniversary mentioned in paragraph (a) above.

Criminal Justice and Public Order Act 1994, s 51(9)

Institution of proceedings

For the purposes of the definition of the relevant period in subsection (9) above—

(a) proceedings for an offence are instituted at the earliest of the following times:
   (i) when a justice of the peace issues a summons or warrant under s 1 of the Magistrates' Courts Act 1980 in respect of the offence;
   (ii) when a person is charged with the offence after being taken into custody without a warrant;
   (iii) when a bill of indictment is preferred by virtue of s 2(2)(b) of the Administration of Justice (Miscellaneous Provisions) Act 1933;

(b) proceedings at a trial of an offence are concluded with the occurrence of any of the following, the discontinuance of the prosecution, the discharge of the jury without a finding, the acquittal of the accused or the sentencing of or other dealing with the accused for the offence of which he was convicted; and

(c) proceedings on an appeal are concluded on the determination or abandonment of the appeal.

Criminal Justice and Public Order Act 1994, s 51(10)

Explanatory notes

- For equivalent offences in some civil proceedings see s 39 and s 40 of the Criminal Justice and Police Act 2001.
- In respect of the relevant period, this subsection means that the statutory presumption can only be used during the relevant period. It is still possible to bring a prosecution for this offence many years

after that period, but the prosecution will not have the advantage of being able to use this presumption.

- Section 51(3) states that, in relation to both offences, it will be immaterial whether or not the act is (or would be) done, or that the threat is made—
  (a) otherwise than in the presence of the victim, or
  (b) to a person other than the victim.
- Two cases regarding the above provision have determined the following—
  ♦ Relating to both offences, the person making the threats still commits an offence if s/he uses a third party to convey them to the witness/juror. The 'messenger', could be an innocent agent (eg a victim's relative), who simply passes on a message without understanding its meaning or effect (*Attorney-General's Reference (No 1 of 1999) The Times*, 6 July 1999).
  ♦ The threats can be made by telephone, letter, or by other means. It is not necessary for the offender and victim to be in the same place at the same time (*DPP v Mills* [1996] 3 WLR 1093).
- Section 51(4) provides that the harm done or threatened may be financial as well as physical (whether to the person or a person's property) and the same applies with regard to any intimidatory act that consists of threats.
- Section 51(11) states that this offence is in addition to, and does not necessarily replace any offence which currently exists at common law (eg perversion of the course of justice, which is usually charged as an attempt, conspiracy, or incitement).

Related cases

R v Normanton [1998] Crim LR 220 Spitting, although a common assault, is not harm for the purposes of this legislation unless it causes some physical or mental injury, such as an infection.

R v Waters [1997] Crim LR 823 Sudden 'loss of memory' during testimony due to fear.

R v Singh (b), Singh (c) and Singh (I) [1999] Crim LR 681 There must be evidence that the investigation had started at the time of the intimidation.

 Either way

 None

 Summary: 6 months' imprisonment and/or a fine not exceeding the statutory maximum.
Indictment: 5 years' imprisonment and/or a fine.

4.8.2 **Perverting the course of justice**

Offence

This is a common law offence. It is committed where a person or persons—
• acts or embarks upon a course of conduct
• which has a tendency to, and
• is intended to pervert,
• the course of public justice.

Points to prove

✓ date and location
✓ with intent to pervert
✓ the course of public justice
✓ do an act/series of acts
✓ tending to pervert course of public justice

Explanatory notes

• Listed below are some examples where conduct is capable of
amounting to this offence:
  ♦ making false allegations;
  ♦ perjury;
  ♦ concealing offences;
  ♦ obstructing the police;
  ♦ assisting others to evade arrest;
  ♦ failing to prosecute;
  ♦ procuring and indemnifying sureties;
  ♦ interference with witnesses, evidence, and jurors;
  ♦ publication of matters calculated to prejudice a fair trial.
• A positive act is required (eg failing to respond to a summons was
insufficient to warrant a charge of perverting the course of justice).
• Any act or course of conduct that tends or is intended to interfere
with the course of public justice can amount to an offence. In order
to get a conviction, it is not sufficient to prove that the conduct
actually did, or had a tendency to pervert the course of justice. The
evidence must prove that the offender intended that it would do so.
• It is not necessary for the offender's motives to be the procurement
of a false verdict or the defeat of the ends of justice. Trying to
introduce genuine evidence by unlawful means is perverting the
course of justice (eg a witness takes incriminating photos but refuses
to give evidence). Steps are then taken by the investigator to get
another witness to introduce them as evidence (*Attorney-General's
Reference (No 1 of 2002)* [2002] Crim LR 410).

Related cases

R v Headley The Times, 15 February 1995, CA Deliberate inaction is
not perverting the course of justice. H was the brother of a man who

was stopped by police and asked to produce driving documents. The man gave H's details. H was subsequently summonsed, convicted, and fined in his absence. When the truth was discovered, H was convicted of perverting the course of justice. His appeal was upheld as he had done nothing to pervert the course of justice.

R v Kiffin [1994] Crim LR 449, CA   It is possible to pervert course of justice even if no offence could be shown to have been committed. In this case, removing account books/records subject of PACE warrant application out of jurisdiction.

R v Toney (1992) JP 899, CA   Perverting the course of justice need not be by improper means. T attempted to persuade a witness to alter his evidence at T's trial. There was no evidence of improper means, but T was still convicted of perverting the course of justice.

Practical considerations

- This offence is sometimes referred to as 'attempting to pervert the course of justice', but the word 'attempting' in a common law indictment was misleading (*R v K J Williams* (1991) 92 Cr App R 158). A better expression would be 'endeavouring to pervert the course of justice'.
- Perverting the course of justice, is usually charged as an attempt, conspiracy, or incitement.
- There has been comment by the courts where this offence has been used for relatively minor attempts to pervert the course of justice and it is charged alongside an offence that is serious enough to permit the offenders conduct to be taken into account when sentencing for the main offence. In *R v Sookoo* [2002] EWCA Crim 800, a shoplifter had attempted to hide his identity and inevitably failed, the prosecutors should not include a specific count of perverting the course of justice. Such conduct may serve to aggravate the original offence and the judge may increase the sentence as a result.

  A more appropriate use will be where a great deal of police time and resources are involved in putting the matter right, or there may be cases where innocent members of the public have their names given and they have been the subject of questioning and even detention.

E&S

  Indictment   None

Life Imprisonment

Links to alternative subjects and offences

Chapter 5

Drugs

5.1 Produce/Supply a Controlled Drug and Supply of Articles

The Misuse of Drugs Act 1971 was designed and intended to regulate the flow and use of controlled drugs. The Act designates which drugs are controlled and assigns them to certain categories (A, B or C). If the drug is a controlled drug it will then be unlawful, with exceptions, to import, export, produce, supply, or possess the drug in question. The first topic in this chapter deals with two aspects of production and supply: producing/supplying a controlled drug and supplying/offering articles for the purpose of administering or preparing controlled drugs.

5.1.1 Produce/supply a controlled drug

Section 4 of the Misuse of Drugs Act 1971 relates to the production and supply of controlled drugs. Section 4(1) provides a prohibition on the production, supply and the offering to supply controlled drugs. Offences that result from a contravention of this prohibition are set out in s 4(2) and (3).

Offence

(1) Subject to any **regulations** under s 7 of this Act for the time being in force, it shall not be lawful for a person—
   (a) to **produce** a **controlled drug**; or
   (b) to supply or offer to **supply** a controlled drug to another.
(2) Subject to s 28 (defence of lack of knowledge) of this Act, it is an offence for a person—
   (a) to produce a controlled drug in contravention of subsection (1) above; or
   (b) to be concerned in the production of such a drug in contravention of that subsection by another.
(3) Subject to s 28 of this Act, it is an offence for a person—

(a) to supply or offer to supply a controlled drug to another in contravention of subsection (1) above; or
(b) to be concerned in the **supplying** of such a drug to another in contravention of that subsection; or
(c) to be concerned in the making to another in contravention of that subsection of an offer to supply such a drug.

Misuse of Drugs Act 1971, s 4(1)–(3)

Points to prove

s 4(2)(a) offence

✓ date and location
✓ produced a controlled drug
✓ of class A/B/C

s 4(2)(b) offence

✓ date and location
✓ concerned in the production
✓ by another of
✓ a controlled drug
✓ of class A/B/C

s 4(3)(a) offence

✓ date and location
✓ supply or offered to supply (type of drug)
✓ a controlled drug
✓ of class A/B/C

s 4(3)(b) offence

✓ date and location
✓ was concerned in
✓ supplying (type of drug)
✓ a controlled drug
✓ of class A/B/C.

s 4(3)(c) offence

✓ date and location
✓ was concerned in making an offer
✓ to supply (type of drug)
✓ a controlled drug
✓ of class A/B/C

Meanings

Regulations

Currently this is the Misuse of Drugs Regulations 2001.

Produce

Means producing it by manufacture, cultivation, or any other method, and 'production' has a corresponding meaning. Stripping a cannabis plant of its leaves comes within the term 'any other method' for the purposes of production (*R v Harris & Cox* [1996] Crim LR 36).

Controlled drug

Drugs are classified as Class A, Class B, or Class C in Sch 2 to the Act. Essentially the classification affects the punishment. The PNLD website at www.pnld.co.uk lists the classes of drugs according to the chemical names and/or the 'trade name', and also the 'street' or 'slang' names by which most officers and defendants will know the drugs.

Supplying

The Act brings 'distributing' within the meaning of 'supplying' (s 37).

Supply

Has been held to mean 'furnishing or providing a person with something that that person wants or requires for that person's purposes'. It includes circumstances where an offender is looking after drugs whether voluntarily or involuntarily if s/he intends returning them to the person for whom they were being 'minded' or even anyone else. (*R v Maginnis* [1987] 1 All ER 907 (voluntary minding) and *R v Panton The Times*, 27 March 2001 (involuntary minding, for example after threats have been made against him/her)).

Explanatory notes

- The offence of offering to supply a controlled drug is complete when the offer is made—it does not matter whether the defendant intended ever to follow the offer through (see *R v Goddard* [1992] Crim LR 588).
- The purpose of the Misuse of Drugs Regulations 2001 is to control the lawful use, possession and type of drugs used for medicinal, research and other legitimate reasons—see **Defences** below.
- In *R v Hunt* [1987] 1 All ER 1, HL it was made clear that the onus is on the prosecution to prove all elements, including the fact that the drug could not be lawfully possessed by the defendant in the circumstances, or that it was not in a lawful form (some classified drugs are chemically mixed into a form which can be bought over the counter as a remedy for simple ailments).
- *R v Maginnis* [1987] 1 All ER 907, HL involved possession of a packet of cannabis which was being kept for a friend (a drug trafficker). The return of the drugs to the trafficker was deemed to be **supply**.
- Undercover or 'test purchase' officers may find themselves in circumstances where they are offered or are asked to mind controlled drugs. Such officers are trained to a National Standard and comply with ACPO guidelines. Where appropriate, authority is obtained under pt II of the Regulation of Investigatory Powers Act 2000, before surveillance takes place.

Defences

- A general defence is afforded by s 28 of the Misuse of Drugs Act 1971 if the defendant—
  - proves that s/he neither believed nor suspected nor had reason to suspect that the substance or product in question was a controlled drug; or
  - proves that s/he believed the substance or product in question to be a controlled drug or a controlled drug of a description such that, if it had been that controlled drug or a controlled drug of that description, s/he would not at the material time have been committing any offence to which this section applies.
- Regulation 6 of the Misuse of Drugs Regulations 2001 provides authority to possess/supply drugs in the following circumstances:
  - any person who is lawfully in possession of a controlled drug may supply that drug to the person from whom he obtained it;
  - any person who has in his/her possession a drug specified in Sch 2, 3, 4, or 5 which has been supplied by or on the prescription of a practitioner, an extended formulary nurse prescriber, a registered nurse, a supplementary prescriber, or a person specified in Sch 8 for the treatment of that person, or of a person whom he/she represents, may supply that drug to any doctor, dentist or pharmacist for the purpose of destruction;
  - any person who is lawfully in possession of a drug specified in Sch 2, 3, 4, or 5 which has been supplied by or on the prescription of a veterinary practitioner or veterinary surgeon for the treatment of animals may supply that drug to any veterinary practitioner, veterinary surgeon or pharmacist for the purpose of destruction;
  - a constable when acting in the course of his/her duty as such;
  - a person engaged in the business of a carrier when acting in the course of that business;
  - a person engaged in the business of a postal operator (within meaning of the Postal Services Act 2000) when acting in the course of that business;
  - an officer of customs and excise when acting in the course of his/her duty as such;
  - a person engaged in the work of any laboratory to which the drug has been sent for forensic examination when acting in the course of his/her duty as a person so engaged;
  - a person engaged in conveying the drug to a person who may lawfully have that drug in his/her possession.

Related cases

R v Prior [2004] EWCA Crim 1147, CA An offer to supply can be related to an immediate or future supply no matter how unspecified the offer itself may be. It is immaterial who took the initiative (whether it is the offeror or offeree).

5.1.1 Produce/Supply a Controlled Drug

R v Hodgson [2001] EWCA Crim 2697, CA Evidence of the number of visitors, for short periods, to a property may be evidence from which drug dealing may be inferred.

R v Shivpuri [1986] 2 All ER 334, HL Attempting to supply something that in fact was not a controlled drug can nevertheless be a criminal attempt.

R v Russell [1992] Crim LR 362, CA Making crack from cocaine is 'producing'.

R v Gill (Simon Imran) (1993) 97 Cr App Rep 2, CA An 'offer to supply' fake drugs is an offence.

R v Hunt [1987] 1 All ER 1 HL The prosecution must prove all elements of unlawful possession under the Misuse of Drugs Regulations.

Practical considerations

- Consider s 23 of the Offences Against The Person Act 1861 for the following offence: Whoever unlawfully and maliciously administers to, or causes to be administered to, or taken by, any other person any poison or other destructive or noxious thing, so as to endanger the life of that person, or so as to inflict grievous bodily harm upon that person is guilty of an offence (Mode of trial/penalty—Indictment/10 years' imprisonment).
- Section 4A of the Misuse of Drugs Act 1971 aggravates the offence of supplying a controlled drug where the offender (drug dealer) uses a courier (under 18) in the vicinity of school premises (including school land).
- Home Office Circular 82/1980 recommends that cultivation of cannabis (see **5.4.1**) be charged under this section instead of s 6 of the Misuse of Drugs Act 1971 in view of s 37(1) of this Act which provides a definition of 'produce'. The term has a much wider meaning than just chemically making a drug.
- Section 110 of the Powers of Criminal Courts (Sentencing) Act 2000 provides for a minimum sentence of seven years' imprisonment for a third successive conviction for an offence of trafficking in a class 'A' drug. Trafficking includes an offence under s 4(2) or (3) (production and supply of controlled drugs).
- Producing/cultivating magic mushrooms, being a class A drug (see **5.4.2** for further details).

 Either way   None

Class A drug
Summary: 6 months' imprisonment and/or the statutory maximum fine.
Indictment: Life imprisonment and/or a fine.

Class B drug
Summary: 6 months' imprisonment and/or the statutory maximum fine.
Indictment: Imprisonment for a term not exceeding 14 years and/or a fine.

Class C drug
Summary: 3 months' imprisonment and/or £2,500.
Indictment: Imprisonment for a term not exceeding 14 years and/or a fine.

5.1.2 Supply/offer articles to administer or prepare drugs

Section 9A of the Misuse of Drugs Act 1971 creates a prohibition on the supply or offering to supply articles for administering or preparing a controlled drug.

Offence

(1) A person who **supplies** or **offers** to supply any article which may be used or adapted to be used (whether by itself or in combination with another article or other articles) in the **administration** by any person of a **controlled drug** to himself or another, believing that the article (or the article as adapted) is to be so used in circumstances where the administration is unlawful, is guilty of an offence.

...

(3) A person who supplies or offers to supply any article which may be used to prepare a controlled drug for administration by any person to himself or another believing that the article is to be used in circumstances where the administration is unlawful is guilty of an offence.

Misuse of Drugs Act 1971, s 9A(1) and (3)

Points to prove
✓ date and location
✓ supplied/offered to supply article(s)
✓ which might be used/adapted
✓ for administration of a controlled drug

5.1.2 Supply/Offer Articles to Administer or Prepare Drugs

> ✓ to self/another
> ✓ believing article(s)
> ✓ was/were to be used
> ✓ in circumstances where administration unlawful.

Meanings

Supplies (see **5.1.1**)

Offers (see 'Related cases' **5.1.1**)

Controlled drug (see **5.1.1**)

Administration

Includes a reference to administering it to him/herself with the assistance of another.

Explanatory notes

The Misuse of Drugs Act 1971 generally penalizes the possession or supply of a drug, rather than the administration. However, the administration of a drug will be unlawful for the purpose of this section when its possession is unlawful.

Defences

(2) It is not an offence under subsection (1) above to supply or offer to supply a hypodermic syringe, or any part of one.

. . .

(4) For the purposes of this section, any administration of a controlled drug is unlawful except
   (a) the administration by any person of a controlled drug to another in circumstances where the administration of the drug is not unlawful under section 4(1) of this Act, or
   (b) the administration by any person of a controlled drug to himself in circumstances where having the controlled drug in his possession is not unlawful under section 5(1)

Misuse of Drugs Act 1971, s 9A(2) and (4)

Practical considerations

- The scope of the 'article(s)' is wide and includes, for example plastic bottles which are intended to be used or adapted for smoking controlled drugs.
- There are certain healthcare professionals specifically exempted from the effects of this section by reg 6A of the Misuse of Drugs Regulations 2001.
- It is not an offence to supply or offer to supply a hypodermic syringe, or any part of one.

- Consider s 23 of the Offences Against The Person Act 1861 for the offence of unlawfully and maliciously administering any poison or other noxious thing (see **5.1.1**).
- Section 9 of the Misuse of Drugs Act 1971 deals with Opium, and subject to s 28 (lack of knowledge defence) provides the following offences: smoke or use prepared opium; frequent a place used for opium smoking; have in his/her possession any pipes or other utensils made or adapted for use in connection with the smoking or preparation for smoking of opium, which have been used by him/her or with his/her knowledge and permission in that connection or which s/he intends to use or permit others to use in that connection.

 Summary   6 months

6 months' imprisonment and/or a fine not exceeding £5000

Links to alternative subjects and offences

SSS Stop, search and
     seize powers

5.2 Possessing and Possessing with Intent to Supply a Controlled Drug

The Misuse of Drugs Act 1971 makes a distinction between people who are lawfully allowed to possess controlled drugs and people who are **unlawfully** in possession of drugs. Possession (unless exempt) of a controlled drug is unlawful, as is possession of controlled drugs with intent to supply them to others. The following deals with both of these issues separately.

5.2.1 Possessing a controlled drug

Offence

(1) Subject to any **regulations** under s 7 of this Act for the time being in force, it shall not be lawful for a person to have a **controlled drug** in his **possession**.

(2) Subject to section 28 of this Act and to subsection 5(4), it is an offence for a person to have a controlled drug in his possession in contravention of subsection 5(1) above.

Misuse of Drugs Act 1971, s 5(1), (2)

Points to prove

✓ date and location
✓ possess [name of drug]
✓ a controlled drug of class A/B/C.

Meanings

Regulations   (see **5.1.1**)

Controlled drug   (see **5.1.1**)

Possession

Proof of unlawful possession requires the following three elements:
• the drug must be in the custody or control (actual or constructive) of the defendant;
• the defendant must know or suspect the existence of the drug in question;
• the drug must be a controlled drug within the meaning of the Act.

Explanatory notes

Constructive possession is when the defendant does not have immediate physical possession of the drugs but has almost as much control over them. An example would be a person who leaves drugs in a railway 'left luggage' locker and retains the keys. Although no longer having 'actual' custody of the drugs, s/he has a high degree of control over them which amounts to possession. If the defendant handed the keys to an innocent agent who holds them as a favour, the defendant still has constructive possession. However, if that other person knows that drugs are in the locker then, by keeping the keys, s/he is also in constructive possession of the drugs.

Defences

- Section 28 (lack of knowledge defence) (see **5.1.1**).
- In any proceedings for an offence under subsection 5(2) above in which it is proved that the accused had a controlled drug in his possession, it shall be a defence for him to prove.

  (a) that, knowing or suspecting it to be a controlled drug, he took possession of it for the purpose of preventing another from committing or continuing to commit an offence in connection with that drug and that as soon as possible after taking possession of it he took all such steps as were reasonably open to him to destroy the drug or to deliver it into the custody of a person lawfully entitled to take custody of it; or

  (b) that, knowing or suspecting it to be a controlled drug, he took possession of it for the purpose of delivering it into the custody of a person lawfully entitled to take custody of it and that as soon as possible after taking possession of it he took all such steps as were reasonably open to him to deliver it into the custody of such a person.

Misuse of Drugs Act 1971, s 5(4)

Defence notes

- The Misuse of Drugs Act 1971 makes a distinction between people who are lawfully allowed to possess controlled drugs (even though their use may be restricted) such as doctors, dentists, or police officers and people who are **unlawfully** in possession of drugs.
- The defence under s 5(4) is to cater for situations such as:
  - ♦ a parent discovers his child has a controlled drug in his bedroom, takes possession of it, and flushes it down the lavatory;
  - ♦ a passer-by discovers heroin lying on the pavement, takes possession of it and then gives it to the police.

Related cases

R v Hunt [1987] 1 All ER 1, HL Prosecution must prove all elements of unlawful possession under Misuse of Drugs Regulations.

R v Prior [2004] EWCA Crim 1147, CA An offer to supply a controlled drug does not have to be genuine in order to constitute an offence.

R v Leeson [2000] 1 Cr App R 233, CA It matters not whether a person thinks that they are dealing in amphetamines, when in fact it was cocaine. The fact is that they are still dealing in a controlled drug. The wording of the offence was such that the type did not matter.

Practical considerations

- For produce/supply a controlled drug (see **5.1.1**).
- The Misuse of Drugs Regulations 2001 allow some drugs to be in the possession of an individual for certain legitimate reasons (eg medicinal, research) (see **5.1.1**).
- The drug should be tested in the first instance to prove that it is in fact a controlled drug and what class of drug it is.
- Home Office Circular 40 of 1998 makes it clear that most drugs should be sent off for testing with certain exceptions.
- Provided a controlled drug is involved, it does not matter that a dealer thought s/he was supplying another controlled drug.
- Possessing magic mushrooms, is a class A drug (see **5.4.2** for further details).

 Either way   None

 Class A
Summary: 6 months' imprisonment and/or a fine not exceeding the statutory maximum.
Indictment: 7 years' imprisonment and/or a fine.

Class B
Summary: 3 months' imprisonment and/or a fine not exceeding level 4 on the standard scale.
Indictment: Imprisonment for a term not exceeding 5 years and/or a fine.

Class C
Summary: 3 months' imprisonment and/or a fine not exceeding level 3 on the standard scale.
Indictment: 2 years' imprisonment and/or a fine.

5.2.2 **Possession with intent to supply**

The Misuse of Drugs Act 1971 creates a specific offence of possessing a controlled drug with intent to supply it.

Offence

Subject to s 28 of this Act, it is an offence for a person to have a **controlled drug** in his **possession**, whether lawfully or not, with **intent** to **supply** it to another in contravention of s 4(1) of this Act. **Misuse of Drugs Act 1971, s 5(3)**

Points to prove

✓ date and location
✓ possess
✓ [name of drug]/an unspecified controlled drug of class A/B/C
✓ with intent to supply

Meanings

Controlled drug (see **5.1.1**)

Possession (see **5.2.1**)

Intent (see **4.1**)

Supply (see **5.1.1**)

Contravention of s 4(1) (see **5.1.1**)

Defence (see **5.1.1**)

Related cases (see also **5.1.1** and **5.2.1** cases)

R v Batt [1994] Crim LR 592, CA Cash found with drugs not evidence of intent to supply.

R v Kearley [1992] 2 All ER 345, HL Hearsay evidence alone will not prove intent.

R v Gordon [1995] Crim LR 142, CA Evidence must be relevant to the specific offence charged.

R v Maginnis [1987] 1 All ER 907, HL Giving drugs back to the owner can be 'supplying'.

R v Scott [1996] Crim LR 653, CA Lifestyle may prove possession, but not intent to supply.

R v Lambert [2001] UKHL 37 A judge must treat this defence as an evidential burden on the defendant rather than a legal requirement to be proved on the balance of probabilities. This makes life easier for the defence, it may be sufficient for the defendant to simply give evidence stating that he/she was ignorant of the nature of the substance. Officers should do all they can find evidence which will help refute any such claim.

Practical considerations (see also **5.1.1** and **5.2.1**)

• What is and what is not admissible evidence of 'possession' and 'intent to supply' is the subject of numerous cases. For example, in *R v Griffiths* [1998] Crim LR 567, the defendant was charged with 'possession with intent to supply' a huge amount of drugs which were found in his home. The defence conceded that whoever 'possessed' the drugs must be a dealer and therefore intending to supply. Possession was really the only disputed issue. The court accepted that evidence of large sums of cash in the defendant's house along with the drugs may be used as part of the prosecution case to show that the defendant was, indeed, the person in possession of those drugs.

- It would appear that lifestyle/paraphernalia can sometimes be used to help prove the 'possession' element but not the 'intent to supply' element where dealers are being prosecuted.

 Either way

 None

Class A
Summary: 6 months' imprisonment and/or a fine not exceeding the statutory maximum.
Indictment: Life imprisonment and/or a fine.

Class B
Summary: 6 months' imprisonment and/or a fine not exceeding the statutory maximum.
Indictment: Imprisonment for a term not exceeding 14 years and/or a fine.

Class C
Summary: 3 months' imprisonment and/or a fine not exceeding level 4 on the standard scale.
Indictment: Imprisonment for a term not exceeding 14 years and/or a fine.

Links to alternative subjects and offences

SSS Stop, search and seize powers

E&S Entry and search powers

TRIG Trigger offences

CSO Offences where CSO can use their powers

5.3 Occupier or Manager Permitting Premises to be used for Drugs and Closure Notices/Orders

It is illegal for occupiers and managers of premises to permit certain activities relating to drugs to take place on those premises.

5.3.1 Occupier/manager permit drug use on premises

Offence

A person commits an offence if, being the **occupier** or concerned in the **management** of any premises, he knowingly permits or suffers any of the following activities to take place on those premises, that is to say—

(a) **producing** or attempting to produce a **controlled drug** in contravention of s 4(1) of this Act;

(b) **supplying** or attempting to supply a controlled drug to another in contravention of s 4(1) of this Act, or offering to supply a controlled drug to another in contravention of s 4(1);

(c) preparing opium for smoking;

(d) smoking cannabis, cannabis resin or prepared opium.

Misuse of Drugs Act 1971, s 8

Points to prove

✓ date and location
✓ being the occupier/concerned in managing of premises
✓ knowingly
✓ permitted/suffered to take place
✓ on premises
✓ the production/attempted production **or**
✓ supplying/attempted to supply/offering to supply
✓ to another
✓ class A/B/C drug namely [name of drug if known] **or**
✓ the preparing of opium for smoking **or**
✓ the smoking of cannabis, cannabis resin, or prepared opium

Meanings

Occupier

The question of whether a person is in **lawful** occupation of premises has created some difficulty. In *R v Tao* [1976] 3 All ER 65, a college student who paid rent for a room on the campus was deemed to be the occupier of that room; Lord Justice Roskill commented that it would be 'somewhat astonishing' if a squatter could not be an 'occupier' under the Act. Similarly there may be different occupiers at different times or an occupier who only had that status for certain periods. The question was always one of fact (*R v Coid* [1998] Crim LR 199, CA).

Management

This implies a degree of control over the running of the affairs of the venture or business. If a person controls premises by running, planning, or organizing them s/he will be managing. Sharing or assisting in the running of premises is sufficient for the purposes of 'being concerned in the management'.

Produce (see **5.1.1**)

Controlled drug (see **5.1.1**)

Supply (see **5.1.1**)

Explanatory notes

- As long as the defendant is aware that the premises are being used to supply controlled drugs, it does not matter for the purposes of establishing guilt, which type of drug is involved (*R v Bett* [1998] 1 All ER 600). However, there is a difference so far as the penalty is concerned. Therefore, it is desirable, if possible, to identify the class of drugs and name them in the charge (of course, in the majority of cases the drugs will have been seized and this issue will not cause any difficulty).
- This offence is limited to the activities specified at (a) to (d). It is not committed, for example, by a landlord who knows that one of his tenants is in his room injecting himself with amphetamines. He may commit the offence if, for example:
  ♦ a drug is being supplied to others on the premises;
  ♦ a controlled drug is being produced on the premises;
  ♦ the occupants are smoking cannabis.
- The Misuse of Drugs Regulations 2001 allows some drugs to be in the possession of an individual for certain legitimate reasons (eg medicinal, research) (see **5.1.1**).

Related cases

R v Bett [1999] 1 All ER 600 The type of drug is immaterial to prove guilt but the defendant must be aware that the premises are being used to supply controlled drugs.

Practical considerations

- Whenever the decision to search premises can be planned in advance, a warrant should be obtained (Misuse of Drugs Act 1971, s 23(3)—see **12.4**).
- A key power for the police when dealing with Class A drug offences on premises is the closure procedure. There are two practical aspects to consider: closure notices and closure orders (see **5.3.2**)

Either way None

 Class A/B
Summary: 6 months' imprisonment and/or the statutory maximum fine.
Indictment: 14 years' imprisonment and/or a fine.

Class C
Summary: 3 months' imprisonment and/or a fine of £2,500 maximum.
Indictment: 14 years' imprisonment and/or a fine.

5.3.2 **Premises closure notices/orders**

Section 4 of the Anti-social Behaviour Act 2003 creates offences of remaining in or entering property subject to a closure notice or order without reasonable excuse and of obstructing a constable or authorized person carrying out certain functions under the provisions.

Offences

(1) A person commits an offence if he remains on or enters **premises** in contravention of a **closure notice**.
(2) A person commits an offence if—
   (a) he obstructs a constable or an **authorised person** acting under section 1(6) or 3(2),
   (b) he remains on premises in respect of which a **closure order** has been made, or
   (c) he enters the premises.   Anti-social Behaviour Act 2003, s 4(1), (2)

Points to prove

Obstruction

✓ date and location
✓ obstructed
✓ a constable/an authorized person
✓ acting under
✓ s 1(6) (service)/s 3(2) (closure order enforcement)

Closure notice

✓ date and location
✓ remained on/entered premises

> ✓ in contravention of a closure notice
> ✓ under s 1 of the Act
> ✓ issued by a constable/authorized person.
>
> ***Closure order***
>
> ✓ date and location
> ✓ entered/remained on premises
> ✓ in respect of which a closure order
> ✓ under s 2 of the Act
> ✓ made by magistrates on a date

Meanings

Premises

This includes:
- any land or other place (whether enclosed or not);
- any outbuildings which are or are used as part of the premises.

Closure notice   (see procedure—below)

Closure order   (see procedure—below)

Authorized person

Means a person authorized by the chief officer of police for the area in which the premises are situated.

Closure notice procedure

Grounds

(1) This section applies to premises if a police officer not below the rank of superintendent (the authorising officer) has reasonable grounds for believing—
  (a) that at any time during the relevant period the premises have been used in connection with the unlawful use, **production** or **supply** of a **Class A controlled drug**, and
  (b) that the use of the premises is associated with the occurrence of disorder or serious nuisance to members of the public.

Authorization

(2) The authorising officer may authorise the issue of a closure notice in respect of premises to which this section applies if he is satisfied—
  (a) that the local authority for the area in which the premises are situated has been consulted;
  (b) that reasonable steps have been taken to establish the identity of any person who lives on the premises or who has control of or responsibility for or an interest in the premises.

(3) An authorisation under subsection (2) may be given orally or in writing, but if it is given orally the authorising officer must confirm it in writing as soon as it is practicable.

Requirements

(4) A closure notice must—

   (a) give notice that an application will be made under section 2 for the closure of the premises;

   (b) state that access to the premises by any person other than a person who habitually resides in the premises or the owner of the premises is prohibited;

   (c) specify the date and time when and the place at which the application will be heard;

   (d) explain the effects of an order made in pursuance of section 2;

   (e) state that failure to comply with the notice amounts to an offence;

   (f) give information about **relevant advice providers**.

Service

(5) The closure notice must be served by a constable.

(6) Service is effected by—

   (a) fixing a copy of the notice to at least one prominent place on the premises,

   (b) fixing a copy of the notice to each normal means of access to the premises,

   (c) fixing a copy of the notice to any outbuildings which appear to the constable to be used with or as part of the premises,

   (d) giving a copy of the notice to at least one person who appears to the constable to have control of or responsibility for the premises, and

   (e) giving a copy of the notice to the persons identified in pursuance of subsection (2)(b) and to any other person appearing to the constable to be a person of a description mentioned in that subsection.

(7) The closure notice must also be served on any person who occupies any other part of the building or other structure in which the premises are situated if the constable reasonably believes at the time of serving the notice under subsection (6) that the person's access to the other part of the building or structure will be impeded if a closure order is made under section 2.

Anti-social Behaviour Act 2003, s 1(1)–(7)

Meanings

Produce (see **5.1.1**)

Supply (see **5.1.1**)

Class A controlled drug (see **5.1.1**)

Relevant advice providers

Relates to information about the names of and means of contacting persons and organizations in the area that provide advice about housing and legal matters.

Explanatory notes

- Section 1(1) sets out the relevant grounds before an officer of at least the rank of superintendent can authorize the issue of a closure notice.
- For the purpose of sub-s (6)(a) a constable may enter any premises to which this section applies, using reasonable force if necessary.
- It is immaterial whether any person has been convicted of an offence relating to the use, production, or supply of a controlled drug.
- Section 1 of the Anti-social Behaviour Act 2003 relates to closure notices. The police have power to close down premises, sometimes called 'crack houses', from being used for the supply, use or production of Class A drugs where there is associated serious nuisance or disorder.
- Various steps and consultations must be made before the police can apply to the magistrates' court for a closure order under s 2 (which must be heard by the magistrates within 48 hours of the closure notice being served).
- No drug-specific criminal offence has to be proved (at least, not beyond the level of reasonable suspicion) before a closure notice can be served or a closure order made. But if evidence is found that an occupier or manager knowingly permitted the premises to be used for drugs offences, then charges might be considered under s 8 of the Misuse of Drugs Act 1971 (see **5.3.1**).
- The local authority for the area in which the premises are situated must be consulted before a closure notice is served.

Practical considerations

Reasonable steps must be taken to establish the identity of any person who lives on the premises or who has control of or responsibility for or an interest in the premises.

Closure orders procedure

Sections 2 to 4 of the Anti-social Behaviour Act 2003 relates to closure orders.

Court procedure

(1) If a closure notice has been issued under section 1 a constable must apply under this section to a magistrates' court for the making of a closure order.
(2) The application must be heard by the magistrates' court not later than 48 hours after the notice was served in pursuance of section 1(6)(a).
(3) The magistrates' court may make a closure order if and only if it is satisfied that each of the following paragraphs applies—
  (a) the premises in respect of which the closure notice was issued have been used in connection with the unlawful use, production or supply of a Class A controlled drug;
  (b) the use of the premises is associated with the occurrence of disorder or serious nuisance to members of the public;

(c) the making of the order is necessary to prevent the occurrence of such disorder or serious nuisance for the period specified in the order. *Anti-social Behaviour Act 2003, s 2(1)–(3)*

Enforcement

(1) This section applies if a magistrates' court makes an order under s 2.
(2) A constable or an **authorised person** may—
  (a) enter the premises in respect of which the order is made;
  (b) do anything reasonably necessary to secure the premises against entry by any person.
(3) A person acting under subsection (2) may use reasonable force.
(4) But a constable or authorised person seeking to enter the premises for the purposes of subsection (2) must, if required to do so by or on behalf of the owner, occupier or other person in charge of the premises, produce evidence of his identity and authority before entering the premises.
(5) A constable or authorised person may also enter the premises at any time while the order has effect for the purpose of carrying out essential maintenance of or repairs to the premises.
Anti-social Behaviour Act 2003, s 3(1)–(5)

Meaning of authorized person

This is a person authorized by the chief officer of police for the area in which the premises are situated.

Explanatory notes

- The police can apply for a closure order once a s 1 closure notice has been served.
- The court must hear the application within 48 hours of the closure notice being posted on the property.
- The court must be satisfied that not only have the premises been used for the unlawful supply, use, or production of Class A drugs but also that closure will prevent future disorder or serious nuisance.
- The premises can be closed for up to 3 months and the order applies to all people, including owners and residents.

Defence

A person does not commit an offence under subsection 4(1) or subsection 4(2)(b) or (c) if he has a reasonable excuse for entering or being on the premises (as the case may be). *Anti-social Behaviour Act 2003, s 4(4)*

 CSO

 Summary 6 months

 6 months' imprisonment and/or a fine not exceeding level 5 on the standard scale

Links to alternative subjects and offences

5.4 Cultivating Cannabis and 'Magic Mushrooms'

This entry is in two parts: the first part deals with the offence of cultivating cannabis (class C drug) and the second part highlights recent changes in the law concerning 'magic mushrooms' (class A drug).

5.4.1 Cultivating cannabis

Section 6 of the Misuse of Drugs Act 1971 makes it an offence to cultivate cannabis plants.

> **Offence**
>
> (1) Subject to any **regulations** under s 7 of this Act for the time being in force, it shall not be lawful for a person to cultivate any plant of the genus **cannabis**.
> (2) Subject to s 28 of this Act, it is an offence to cultivate any such plant in contravention of subsection (1) above.
>
> Misuse of Drugs Act 1971, s 6(1), (2)

Points to prove

✓ date and location
✓ cultivation of cannabis plant(s) a class C drug

Meanings

Regulations (see 5.1.1)

Cannabis

This includes the whole plant.

Explanatory notes

- The mere growing of the cannabis plant is regarded as an act of 'production'.
- It is necessary to prove that the defendant gave some attention to the plant in order to show 'cultivation'—watering, heating, and lighting would be common examples.

Defences

- Section 28 (lack of knowledge) (see **5.1.1**).
- Regulation 5 of the Misuse of Drugs Regulations 2001 allows the Secretary of State to issue licences to anyone wishing to produce, supply, offer to supply or possess any controlled drugs. Regulation 12 has similar provisions in relation to cannabis.

Defence notes

- Acting without a valid licence or failing to comply with its conditions is an offence under s 18 of the Misuse of Drugs Act 1971 (although other more serious offences may also have been committed).
- Certain people can lawfully possess/supply a controlled drug and/or can be licensed to do so (see **5.1**).
- Note that there is no general defence of medical necessity to the offence of production/possession/supply of cannabis (*R v Quayle and others: Attorney-General's Reference (No 2 of 2004)* [2005] EWCA Crim 1415, CA).

Practical considerations

- Home Office Circular 82/1980 recommends that the cultivation of cannabis be charged under 'producing cannabis' or being 'concerned in the production of cannabis' (see **5.1**) (produce/supply a controlled drug), because the definition of 'produce' means: by manufacture, cultivation or any other method. Stripping a cannabis plant of its leaves comes within the term 'any other method' for the purposes of production (*R v Harris and Cox* [1996] Crim LR 36).
- Take photographs. Seize the 'growing equipment' for evidence and eventual disposal.

E&S

 Either way None

 Summary: 6 months' imprisonment and/or a fine not exceeding the statutory maximum.
Indictment: 14 years' imprisonment and/or a fine.

5.4.2 'Magic mushrooms'

Part 1 of Sch 2 to the Misuse of Drugs Act 1971 specifies drugs that are classified as Class 'A' drugs. Section 21 of the Drugs Act 2005 added fungus (of any kind) that contains psilocin or an ester of psilocin, commonly known as 'magic mushrooms'.

Offences

Possess

Possess a Class A controlled drug (see **5.2.1** for full wording)

Misuse of Drugs Act 1971, s 5 (2)

Produce

Produce a Class A controlled drug (see **5.1.1** for full wording)

Misuse of Drugs Act 1971, s 4(2)(a)

Points to prove

Possess

✓ date and location
✓ possess a fungus (of any kind) that contains psilocin or an ester of psilocin (namely magic mushrooms)
✓ being a Class A controlled drug

Produce

✓ date and location
✓ produce a fungus (of any kind) that contains psilocin or an ester of psilocin (namely magic mushrooms)
✓ being a Class A controlled drug

Meanings

Possess (see **5.2.1**)

Controlled drug (see **5.1.1**)

Produce (see **5.1.1**)

Explanatory notes

- Section 21 of the Drugs Act 2005 has made 'magic mushrooms' a Class A drug.
- Regulation 4A of the Misuse of Drugs Regulations 2001 (details given in defence—below) provides four circumstances where a person could possess 'magic mushrooms' and so would not be liable for committing a s 5(1) possession of a Class A controlled drug offence.

Defence

- The Misuse of Drugs Act, s 5(1) defences (see **5.2.1**).
- (1) Section 5(1) of the Act (which prohibits the possession of controlled drugs) shall not have effect in relation to a fungus (of any kind) which contains psilocin or an ester of psilocin where the fungus—
  - (a) is growing uncultivated;
  - (b) is picked by a person already in lawful possession of it for the purpose of delivering it as soon as is reasonably practicable into the

---

5.4.2 'Magic Mushrooms'

> custody of a person lawfully entitled to take custody of it and it
> remains in that person's possession for and in accordance with that
> purpose;
>
> (c) is picked for either of the purposes specified in paragraph (2) and is
> held for and in accordance with the purpose specified in paragraph
> (2)(b), either by the person who picked it or by another person; or
>
> (d) is picked for the purpose specified in paragraph (2)(b) and is held
> for and in accordance with the purpose in paragraph (2)(a), either
> by the person who picked it or by another person.
>
> (2) The purposes specified for the purposes of this paragraph are:
>
> (a) the purpose of delivering the fungus as soon as is reasonably
> practicable into the custody of a person lawfully entitled to take
> custody of it; and
>
> (b) the purpose of destroying the fungus as soon as is reasonably
> practicable   Misuse of Drugs Regulations 2001, reg 4A(1)–(2)

Practical considerations

- Section 110 of the Powers of Criminal Courts (Sentencing) Act 2000
  provides for a minimum sentence of 7 years' imprisonment for a
  third successive conviction (i.e. convictions on more than one
  occasion) for an offence of trafficking in a class 'A' drug committed
  after 30 September 1997. Trafficking includes an offence under s 4(2)
  or (3) (production and supply of controlled drugs).
- Simple possession of magic mushroom spores is not illegal, owing to
  the fact that they do not contain psilocin (the 'controlled drug') until
  they are actually cultivated.

SSS   **E&S**   **TRIG**   **CSO**

Either way   None

Possess—s 5(2) offence
Summary: 6 months' imprisonment and/or a fine not
exceeding the statutory maximum.
Indictment: 7 years' imprisonment and/or fine.

Produce—s 4(2)(a) offence

Either way   None

Summary: 6 months' imprisonment and/or a fine not
exceeding the statutory maximum.
Indictment: Life imprisonment and/or a fine.

192   **SSS** Stop, search and   **E&S** Entry and search   **TRIG** Trigger offences
      seize powers   powers
   CSO Offences where CSO
      can use their powers

Links to alternative subjects and offences

5.5 **Drug-Related Search Powers**

The police can exercise specific search powers under s 23 of the Misuse of Drugs Act 1971 which confers powers on a constable to stop, detain, and search a person, vehicle, or vessel for controlled drugs and various offences for failing to comply.

Offence

A person commits an offence if he:

(a) **intentionally obstructs** a person in the exercise of his powers under this section; or

(b) **conceals** from a person acting in the exercise of his powers under subsection (1) any such books, documents, stocks or drugs as are mentioned in that subsection; or

(c) without **reasonable excuse** (proof of which shall lie on him) fails to produce any such books or documents as are so mentioned where their production is demanded by a person in the exercise of his powers under that subsection. **Misuse of Drugs Act 1971, s 23(4)**

Points to prove

✓ date and location
✓ concealed from constable/authorized person acting in exercise of powers **or**
✓ without reasonable excuse
✓ failed to produce books/documents
✓ relating to dealings in production/supply
✓ of controlled drugs
✓ when so demanded by a
✓ constable/authorized person in exercise of powers **or**
✓ intentionally obstructed a person in the exercise of powers under this section

---

Meanings

Intentionally obstructs

Where a person deliberately does an act which, though not necessarily aimed at or hostile to the police, in fact makes it more difficult for him to carry out his duty and s/he knows that his/her conduct will have that effect (*Lewis v Cox* [1985] QB 509).

Conceals

No statutory meaning given. *The Oxford English Dictionary* defines 'conceals' as to hide, keep secret from, or refrain from disclosing or divulging.

Reasonable excuse

No statutory meaning given. *The Oxford English Dictionary* defines this term as likely or appropriate justification for an action.

Explanatory notes

Section 23(4)(b)–(c) refers to statutory powers under s 23(1) to inspect chemists and other similar suppliers of controlled drugs.

Power to search, detain, and seize drugs

If a constable has **reasonable grounds** to suspect that any person is in possession of a **controlled drug** in contravention of this Act or of any regulations made thereunder, the constable may—

(a) search that person, and detain him for the purpose of searching him;

(b) search any vehicle or vessel in which the constable suspects that the drug may be found, and for the purpose require the person in control of the vehicle or vessel to stop it;

(c) seize and detain, for the purposes of proceedings under this Act, anything found in the course of the search, which appears to the constable to be evidence of an offence under this Act.

Misuse of Drugs Act 1971, s 23(2)

Meanings

Reasonable grounds (see **12.1**)

Controlled drug (see **5.1.1**)

Explanatory notes

- This power is exercisable *anywhere*.
- The power to stop and search people and vehicles under s 23(2) must be conducted in accordance with the related Codes of Practice and the Police and Criminal Evidence Act 1984 (see **12.1**).

Practical considerations

Personal safety

- Contact with the blood or saliva of drug abusers (particularly those users who inject) carries a risk of infection with serious diseases such as Aids, HIV, and Hepatitis.
- Every effort should be made to avoid such fluids entering your own body through cuts, eyes, or the mouth. Should such contact occur, the possibility of infection is minimized by the contact area being thoroughly washed immediately and medical advice sought as soon as practicable.

Searching of suspects

- Care should always be taken to avoid unguarded needles piercing the skin, if such an event does occur seek medical advice as soon as practicable.
- When conducting a search initially request the suspect/prisoner to turn out their own pockets, then pat the outside of pockets to detect the presence of a syringe.
- Drug abusers will go to extreme lengths to conceal drugs on or in their bodies. Drugs are commonly found in body orifices. Certain

circumstances must prevail before an intimate search may be conducted.

- Search a person minutely, small amounts of drugs can be concealed, for example, in the lining of clothing, under elastoplasts supposedly covering an abrasion, or stuck to the skull under the hairline.
- Searching inside a person's mouth does not now constitute an intimate search.

Handling of drugs

- Certain types of drugs may be absorbed through the skin, it is therefore always advisable to wear gloves when handling drugs.
- **Never under any circumstances taste the drugs**.
- There will be occasions when the name of the drug seized is unknown and doubt as to whether it is controlled. Always seek advice and assistance from a supervisory officer or the drug squad.

Drug abusers equipment

- Abusers use a wide range of paraphernalia to prepare and administer their drugs, the following (which is not exhaustive) may provide evidence of that activity where premises are searched:
  - ✦ syringes and needles; scorched tinfoil and spoons; small mirrors, razors and straws; tubes of tinfoil; ligatures; lemon juice or citric acid; cigarette papers and home-made cigarettes; bloodstained swabs; square folds of paper which may contain powder; cling film; small self-sealing bags; weighing scales; hookah pipes.

General

- Section 23(3) of the Misuse of Drugs Act 1971 allows a justice of the peace (subject to conditions) to issue a warrant authorizing any constable for the police area in which the premises are situated to search the premises for evidence of offences relating to controlled drugs (see **12.4**).
- Grounds for carrying out a search must always be capable of justification. The mere appearance of a person is not sufficient—there must be something about their manner, deportment, conversations, and the surrounding circumstances that reasonably gives rise to that suspicion. See PACE powers generally (see **12.1**).
- Section 23(2) expressly authorizes detention of a suspect for the purpose of searching. It does not give the officer a general right to question the suspect, however, he/she may ask questions incidental to the exercise of that power.
- Section 23(2)(b) does not give an officer the right to stop a vehicle or to search it simply because s/he suspects the vehicle (not the occupants) has been used in connection with a drug offence on a previous occasion (*R v Littleford* [1978] CLR 48).
- Consider road traffic legislation as a means of causing a stop (see **10.2**).
- Compliance with PACE and the Codes of Practice are required with regard to the grounds for searching of people, the conduct of the search and completion of a search record (see **12.1**).

- Reasonable force may be used to detain and carry out a search (PACE s 117) (see **1.2**).

 Either way None

 Summary: 6 months' imprisonment and/or a fine not exceeding the statutory maximum.
Indictment: 2 years' imprisonment and/or a fine.

Links to alternative subjects and offences

Chapter 6

Sexual Offences and Assaults

6.1 **Rape**

Rape and other sexual offences have been consolidated by the Sexual Offences Act 2003.

6.1.1 **Rape**

The offence of rape is covered by ss 1 (rape) and 5 (rape of a child under 13) of the Sexual Offences Act 2003.

Offence

A person (A) commits an offence if—
(a) he **intentionally penetrates** the **vagina, anus or mouth** of another person (B) with his penis,
(b) B does not **consent** to penetration, and
(c) A does not **reasonably believe** that B consents.

Sexual Offences Act 2003, s 1

Points to prove
✓ date and location
✓ intentionally
✓ without consent
✓ penetrated
✓ the anus/vagina/mouth
✓ of another person
✓ with the defendant's penis
✓ not reasonably believing that s/he had consented

Meanings

Intention   (see **4.1**)

This is the defendant's aim or purpose in pursuing a particular course of action. If the defendant intended to penetrate but was physically unable to do so or he admitted that it was his intent then the law states that he had the necessary intent.

Penetration

Means a continuing act from entry to withdrawal (s 79(2)).

Vagina

Includes vulva.

Consent   (see **Defences** below)

Reasonable belief

Whether a belief is reasonable is to be determined having regard to all the circumstances, including any steps A has taken to ascertain whether B consents.

Explanatory notes

- As the definition of vagina includes vulva, then full penetration is not essential to commit rape.
- The offence of rape now includes not only penile penetration of the vagina and anus but also of the mouth as this act could be just as traumatizing and damaging for the victim.
- As penetration can be proved by reference to scientific evidence (sperm, semen, bruising, etc), consent often becomes the major, if not only, issue.
- The offence of rape is gender specific in that only a male (over the age of 10) can commit the offence; the gender of the complainant is irrelevant. This section and s 5 (see **6.1.2**) are the only offences throughout the whole Act that are gender specific because they refer to penile penetration.

Defences

A critical issue in rape cases is consent and s 74 to s 76 of the Sexual Offences Act 2003 deals specifically with these issues.

Consent

A person consents if he **agrees** by choice, and has the **freedom** and **capacity** to make that choice (s 74).

Evidential presumptions about consent

(1) If in proceedings for an offence to which this section applies it is proved—
  (a) that the defendant did the **relevant act**,
  (b) that any of the circumstances specified in subsection (2) existed, and
  (c) that the defendant knew that those circumstances existed,
  the complainant is to be taken not to have consented to the relevant act unless sufficient evidence is adduced to raise an issue as to whether he consented, and the defendant is to be taken not to have reasonably

believed that the complainant consented unless sufficient
evidence is adduced to raise an issue as to whether he reasonably
believed it.

(2) The circumstances are that:

(a) any person was, at the time of the relevant act or immediately before
it began, using violence against the complainant or causing the
complainant to fear that immediate violence would be used against
him;

(b) any person was, at the time of the relevant act or immediately before
it began, causing the complainant to fear that violence was being
used, or that immediate violence would be used, against another
person;

(c) the complainant was, and the defendant was not, unlawfully detained
at the time of the relevant act;

(d) the complainant was asleep or otherwise unconscious at the time of
the relevant act;

(e) because of the complainant's physical disability, the complainant
would not have been able at the time of the relevant act to
communicate to the defendant whether the complainant
consented;

(f) any person had administered to or caused to be taken by the
complainant, without the complainant's consent, a substance which,
having regard to when it was administered or taken, was capable of
causing or enabling the complainant to be stupefied or overpowered
at the time of the relevant act.

(3) In subsections (2)(a) and (b), the reference to the time immediately before
the **relevant act** began is, in the case of an act, which is one of a
continuous series of sexual activities, a reference to the time immediately
before the first sexual activity began.   **Sexual Offences Act 2003, s 75**

Conclusive presumptions about consent

(1) If in proceedings for an offence to which this section applies it is proved
that the defendant did the relevant act and that any of the circumstances
specified in subsection (2) existed, it is to be conclusively presumed—

(a) that the complainant did not consent to the relevant act, and

(b) that the defendant did not believe that the complainant consented to
the relevant act.

(2) The circumstances are that—

(a) the defendant intentionally deceived the complainant as to the nature
or purpose of the relevant act;

(b) the defendant intentionally induced the complainant to consent to
the relevant act by impersonating a person known personally to the
complainant.   **Sexual Offences Act 2003, s 76**

Defence notes

Meaning of 'relevant act' (s 77)

References to the term 'relevant act' in s 75 and s 76 varies according to the offence committed and are where the defendant intentionally:

- Penetrates, with his penis, the vagina, anus or mouth of another person ('the complainant') [Rape (s 1)].
- Penetrates, with a part of his body or anything else, the vagina or anus of another person ('the complainant'), where the penetration is sexual [Assault by penetration (s 2)].
- Touches another person ('the complainant'), where the touching is sexual [Sexual assault (s 3)].
- Causes another person ('the complainant') to engage in an activity, where the activity is sexual [Causing a person to engage in sexual activity without consent (s 4)].

Consent (s 74)

The **freedom** to **agree** is intended to stress that a lack of protest, injury or consent by the victim does not necessarily signify consent.

- Freedom is not defined in the Act so it must be a matter of fact as to whether the victim was free to agree or whether pressure or threats ruled out an agreement.
- A person might not have sufficient **capacity** if s/he suffers from a mental disorder or due to his/her age.
- Capacity is not defined: the matter will be one for the court to decide from all the available evidence.

Evidential presumptions about consent (s 75)

- The term 'substance' in s 75(2)(f) is not defined, so anything capable of stupefying or overpowering would be covered; this would include substances such as alcohol, GHB, or Rohypnol.
- Section 75(3) covers the situation where there have been a number of sexual acts, of which penetration is the culmination, and the defendant is being prosecuted for them and the threats occurred immediately before the first sexual act. In that case the presumption still applies.
- Where the prosecution proves that the defendant did a **relevant act** (in this case rape) and the situations described in s 75(2) existed and the defendant knew they existed, then the complainant will be presumed to have not consented and the defendant will be presumed not to have reasonably believed the complainant consented.

Conclusive presumptions about consent (s 76)

- Where the prosecution prove that the defendant did a relevant act and any of the circumstances described above existed then it is conclusively presumed that the complainant did not consent and the defendant did not believe that the complainant consented to the relevant act. The defendant will therefore be convicted and evidence as to the existence of the intentional deception will be critical.
- Deceiving the complainant as to the nature or purpose of the act could be where the complainant is told that digital penetration of her

vagina is necessary for medical reasons when in fact it is only for sexual gratification of the defendant.

- Impersonation would cover circumstances where the defendant deceives the complainant into believing that he is her partner causing the complainant to consent to the sexual act.

General

- If none of the situations described in ss 75 and 76 apply, then the prosecution must show that the circumstances of the offence were such that the defendant could not have reasonably believed that the complainant consented.

- If the defendant states that he did reasonably believe that the complainant consented then it would be a matter for the jury to decide as to whether a reasonable person would come to the same belief having regard to all the circumstances.

- The circumstances will include the personal characteristics of the defendant. The defendant's age; general sexual experience; sexual experience with this complainant; learning disability; and any other factors that could have affected his ability to understand the nature and consequences of his actions which may be relevant depending on the circumstances of the particular case.

- The Act makes it clear there is an onus on parties involved in a relevant sexual activity to ensure that they have the true consent of the other person(s) and that they took reasonable steps to make sure true consent has been freely given prior to any sexual act taking place.

Related cases

R v McAllister [1997] Crim LR 233 'The circumstances of a possibly reluctant consent may be infinitely varied, and on each occasion the jury has to decide whether an alleged agreement to a sexual act may properly be seen as a real consent or whether it should be regarded as a submission founded on improper pressure which this particular complainant could not reasonably withstand from this particular defendant.'

Practical considerations

- The Sexual Offences Act 2003 now takes into account surgically reconstructed genitalia.
- For example a male-to-female transsexual could be raped under s 1 and a female-to-male transsexual could commit rape.
- The Gender Recognition Act 2004 is now in force and in time only a medical examination would reveal that the person has undergone reconstructive surgery, as transsexuals can now legally have their birth certificate changed to reflect their new gender.
- Although there is no express reference to reconstructed genitalia in s 1, it can be found in s 79(3) of the Act.
- Ejaculation does not have to occur for the offence of rape to be committed.
- All reports of rape must be treated as genuine and the victims treated with sensitivity.

- The crime scene should be identified and preserved, ensuring that cross contamination does not occur (see **1.3**).
- Evidence of the offence should be seized and this includes clothing, and any articles used, such as condoms.
- Obtain evidence of first complaint if appropriate and available.
- Advise the victim not to shower, bathe, drink, or smoke and to retain the clothing they were wearing at the time of the attack.
- Consider CCTV and other potential evidence from independent witnesses.

 Indictable None

Life imprisonment

6.1.2 **Rape of a child under 13**

This is covered by s 5 of the Sexual Offences Act 2003.

Offence

A person commits an offence if—
(a) he **intentionally penetrates** the **vagina**, anus or mouth of another person with his penis, and
(b) the other person is under 13.   Sexual Offences Act 2003, s 5(1)

Points to prove

✓ date and location
✓ intentionally
✓ penetrated
✓ the anus/vagina/mouth
✓ of a person under 13
✓ with the defendant's penis.

Meanings

Intention (see **6.1.1**)

Penetration (see **6.1.1**)

Vagina (see **6.1.1**)

6.1.2 Rape of a Child Under 13

Explanatory notes

- There is no issue of consent under this section. Whether the child consented or not it is irrelevant making this almost an offence of 'strict liability'.
- This section also includes not only penetration of the vagina and anus but also penile penetration of the mouth as s 1.
- This section replaces the offence of unlawful sexual intercourse with a girl under 13 (Sexual Offences Act 1956, s 5).

Related cases

R v G [2006] 1 WLR 2052, CA G, aged 15, had sex with a girl of 12 years old in his room with her full consent and at the time he had believed her to be aged 15. Held that reasonable belief as to consent or age were irrelevant as the offence was absolute and imposed strict liability. Although a non-custodial sentence may be appropriate if consent is given and the defendant is very young.

Practical considerations

- Full penetration does not have to occur and it is not necessary to prove any additional consequences (eg that the hymen was broken).
- Once it can be proved that penetration occurred, it will be very hard to show that it was anything other than intentional but it is still a necessary ingredient of the offence.
- **Age of child**—the prosecution will normally use the child's birth certificate (although other documentation could be used) and testimony of a person who can state that the complainant is the person who the birth certificate relates to.
- Given the nature of this offence, only a suitably trained or qualified person should interview and obtain evidence from the victim.
- The Children Act 2004 makes specific provisions for the police and other agencies to protect the welfare and safety of children (see **2.4**).
- The CPS will always make charging decisions where a person under the age of 18 is investigated for a sexual offence and will be made in accordance with the principles set out in the Code for Crown Prosecutors.
- Consider all the evidential responsibilities highlighted as with the s 1 offence of rape above.

 Indictable None

 Life imprisonment

  Stop, search and seize powers   **E&S** Entry and search powers   **CHAR** Offences where bad character can be introduced

Links to alternative subjects and offences

6.2 Trespass with Intent to Commit a Sexual Offence

This offence is covered by s 63 of the Sexual Offences Act 2003 and replaces the part of s 9(1)(a) Theft Act 1968 that related to burglary with intent to rape.

Offence

A person commits an offence if—

(a) he is a **trespasser** on any **premises**,
(b) he **intends** to commit a **relevant sexual offence** on the premises, and
(c) he knows that, or is **reckless** as to whether, he is a trespasser.

Sexual Offences Act 2003, s 63

Points to prove

✓ date and location
✓ knowingly/recklessly
✓ trespassed on premises **and**
✓ with intent to
✓ commit a relevant sexual offence
✓ on those premises

Meanings

Trespasser

Is a person who is on any premises without the owner or occupier's consent or without lawful excuse.

Premises

Include a structure or part of a structure. This would include premises, yard, garden, vehicle, tent, vessel, or other temporary or moveable structure (eg caravans).

Intent (see **4.1**)

Relevant sexual offence

Means all the sexual offences included within pt 1 of the Act (ss 1 to 79 inclusive), including an offence of aiding, abetting, counselling or procuring such an offence.

Reckless

In these circumstances means that s/he was aware of the risk that they might be trespassing, but ignored that risk and continued with the course of action they were pursuing.

Explanatory notes

- A person could enter premises without being a trespasser but became one later. For example, a person enters a shop but then goes into the stock room; that person then becomes a trespasser because as a potential customer you have the owner's implied permission to enter the shop and browse but you do not have the right to go into the stock room.
- The old concept of burglary with intent to rape was a limited one and only covered buildings and rape. This offence now caters for a wider interpretation of premises and sexual offences.

Related cases

R v Cunningham [1957] 2 All ER 412 The test for 'subjective reckless-ness'. It is not sufficient to show that if the defendant had stopped to think, it would have been obvious to him/her that there was a risk. The prosecution had to prove that s/he was aware of the existence of the risk but nonetheless had gone on and taken it.

Practical considerations

- The offence is not gender specific, so can be committed by a male on a female or vice versa; equally the victim and defendant could be of the same sex.
- The defendant does not have to commit the relevant sexual offence for this offence to be committed, it is sufficient to have the intent to commit a relevant sexual offence at any time whilst a trespasser.
- Ensure evidence of trespass is obtained.
- Obtain CCTV evidence if available.
- Consider other offences (eg false imprisonment) if insufficient evidence available to prove this offence.

 Either way   None

 Summary: 6 months' imprisonment and/or a fine not exceeding the statutory maximum.
Indictment: 10 years' imprisonment.

Links to alternative subjects and offences

6.3 Sexual Assault by Penetration

These offences are covered by s 2 and s 6 (child under 13) of the Sexual Offences Act 2003.

6.3.1 Assault by penetration of a person aged 13 or over

Offence

A person (A) commits an offence if—
(a) he **intentionally penetrates** the **vagina** or **anus** of another person (B) with a part of his body or **anything else**,
(b) the penetration is **sexual**,
(c) B does not **consent** to the penetration, and
(d) A does not **reasonably believe** that B consents.

Sexual Offences Act 2003, s 2

Points to prove
✓ date and location
✓ intentionally
✓ sexually penetrated
✓ the anus/vagina of another person aged 13 or over
✓ with a part of the body and/or a thing
✓ without consent **and**
✓ not reasonably believing that s/he had consented

Meanings

Intentional (see 6.1.1)

Penetration (see 6.1.1)

Vagina (see 6.1.1)

Anything else

This term has not been defined but it is an extremely wide category and will cover anything that can be used to penetrate the body of another.

Sexual

For the purposes of this Part (except section 71), penetration, touching or any other activity is sexual if a reasonable person would consider that—
(a) whatever its circumstances or any person's purpose in relation to it, it is because of its nature sexual, or

(b) because of its nature it may be sexual and because of its circumstances or the purpose of any person in relation to it (or both) it is sexual.   Sexual Offences Act 2003, s 78

Touching (s79(8))

This includes touching—

(a) with any part of the body,

(b) with anything else,

(c) through anything,

and in particular includes touching amounting to penetration.

Consent (see **6.1.1**)

Reasonable belief (see **6.1.1**)

Explanatory notes

- Once penetration has been proved, it will be difficult for the defendant to show that it was not his/her intention to do so. However, as partial penetration will suffice, there may be occasions (such as during a sporting or gymnastic contact) where the defendant claims inadvertent partial penetration by, say, a finger. It would then be for the prosecution to prove otherwise.

- If the defendant states that s/he did reasonably believe that the complainant consented then it will be a matter for the jury to decide as to whether a reasonable person would come to the same belief having regard to all the circumstances.

- The circumstances include the personal characteristics of the defendant. The defendant's age; general sexual experience; sexual experience with this complainant; learning disability; and any other factor that could have affected his/her ability to understand the nature and consequences of his/her actions may be relevant depending on the circumstances of the particular case.

- The reasonableness test does not oblige the defendant to have taken any specific steps to ascertain consent, but any taken will be highly pertinent to the case.

- Parties to relevant sexual activity must ensure that they have the true consent of the other person(s) and that they took reasonable steps to make sure **true** consent has been freely given prior to any sexual act taking place.

- This offence was created in order to reflect the seriousness of assault by penetration, previously being indecent assault, but was perceived not to carry the appropriate penalties for such a serious offence. It carries the same penalty as rape (life imprisonment), thus reflecting its gravity.

- Section 78 which defines 'sexual' is a mixed test consisting of an objective test based on what a reasonable person would consider to be sexual and the purpose of the person involved—
  - subsection (a) where there is no doubt that the activity is sexual, such as oral sex or penetration by vibrator, and
  - subsection (b) where the activity could also have some other purpose, apart from a sexual one and also where the defendant's

act was not sexually motivated. This would cover situations where the defendant penetrates his victim with an object with the sole intent of committing a violent act not a sexual one (for example, penetration by gun barrel or screwdriver for the purpose of humiliating the victim and the defendant asserting his power over the victim).

- The defendant may not have intended the act to be sexual but from a reasonable person's point of view and because of its nature, a reasonable person would consider that it might be sexual.
- Medical examinations or intimate searches by the relevant authorities (such as police and customs) or such other treatment where penetration is involved but is not sexual (eg in colonic irrigation) will not normally be deemed sexual.
- Unlike rape, this offence can be committed by digital penetration and also penetration by any other part of the body, such as a fist, tongue, and toes.
- Full penetration is not essential to commit the offence.
- Items included in the term 'anything else' can be such objects as bottles, vibrators, and screwdrivers along with other objects and substances.

Practical considerations

- Any reports of serious sexual assault must be treated as genuine and the victims with sensitivity.
- Evidence of the offence should be seized and this includes clothing, condoms, and articles that were used.
- Ensure cross-contamination does not occur.
- Obtain evidence of first complaint if appropriate and available.
- Advise the victim not to shower, bathe, drink, or smoke and to retain the clothing they were wearing at the time of the attack.
- Consider CCTV and other potential evidence from independent witnesses.

 Indictable None

 Life imprisonment

6.3.2 Assault by penetration of a child under 13

This offence is the same as s 2 above, except the complainant is under 13 and there is no issue of consent.

Offence

A person commits an offence if—
(a) he **intentionally penetrates** the **vagina** or **anus** of another person with a part of his body or **anything else,**
(b) the penetration is **sexual,** and
(c) the other person is under 13.   Sexual Offences Act 2003, s 6

Points to prove

✓ date and location
✓ intentionally
✓ sexually penetrated
✓ the anus/vagina of a girl aged under 13
✓ the anus of a boy aged under 13
✓ with a part of the body and/or a thing

Meanings

Intentional   (see **6.1.1**)

Penetration   (see **6.1.1**)

Vagina   (see **6.1.1**)

Anything else   (see **6.3.1**)

Sexual   (see **6.3.1**)

Explanatory notes   (see **6.3.1** notes)

Practical considerations   (also see **6.3.1** considerations)

- This is an offence of strict liability (see **6.1.2**).
- It is not necessary for the victim to know or explain, what they were penetrated with.
- The offence can be used in cases where the child does not possess the knowledge to identify the nature of what s/he has been penetrated with.
- Age of the child to be ascertained by means of birth certificate or similar documentation and the testimony of a person who can confirm the birth certificate relates to the victim.
- Only a suitably trained and qualified person should be used to obtain evidence from a victim of this offence.
- The Children Act 2004 (see **2.4**) makes specific provisions for the police and other agencies to protect the welfare and safety of children.

Indictable None

 Life imprisonment

Links to alternative subjects and offences

6.4 Sexual Assault by Touching

6.4.1 Sexual assault by touching a person aged 13 or over

This offence is covered by s 3 of the Sexual Offences Act 2003.

Offence

A person (A) commits an offence if—
(a) he **intentionally touches** another person (B),
(b) the touching is **sexual,**
(c) B does not **consent** to the touching, and
(d) A does not reasonably believe that B consents.

Sexual Offences Act 2003, s 3

Points to prove

✓ date and location
✓ intentionally touched
✓ another person aged 13 or over
✓ by touching her/his body
✓ that touching was sexual
✓ not reasonably believing that s/he was consenting

Meanings

Intentional (see **6.1.1**)

Touching (see **6.3.1**)

Sexual (see **6.3.1**)

Consent (see **6.1.1**)

Explanatory notes

- This section covers non-penetration sexual assaults of another person aged 13 or over. This section will cover a wide spectrum of behaviour that would include the defendant rubbing up against the complainant's private parts through the person's clothes for his sexual gratification.
- Touching includes touching through clothes, touching with anything and touching that amounts to penetration. The touching does not necessarily have to involve using of the hands and can involve any part of the body being used or touched or even an object such as a sex toy.
- The offence does not require that the defendant intended that the touching be sexual, only that the touching itself was intentional. The sexual aspect of the touching is a separate element.

- Whilst there could not be many examples of 'accidental' or inadvertent penetration, accidental touching occurs all the time. Jostling in a crowded street, travelling on a busy train or bus, and attending sports events can all lead to some form of contact with others. Although in most cases of sexual touching it will be obvious that the defendant intentionally touched the victim (because of the part of the body touched or used, or because of accompanying circumstances) there will still be far more room for a defence of lack of intent than in penetration offences.
- In most cases of sexual assault the sexual element will be non-contentious. For example, where a man gropes a female's genitals, it would be hard to imagine a set of circumstances where this would not be sexual and in those cases s 78(a) will be relied on.
- If with regard to all the circumstances and the purpose and the nature of the touching, a reasonable person would consider it sexual then it will be covered by s 78(b). However, it is not certain if the more obscure sexual fantasies would be covered at all by s 78. Would a reasonable person consider the removal of a shoe as sexual, looking at the purpose and nature of it? If not then this would not constitute 'sexual' touching even if the offender received sexual gratification from doing it. This reflects the former common law position with regard to such offences (see **Explanatory notes** under **6.3.1** for further details on 'sexual' and s 78).
- Whether a belief is reasonable is to be determined having regard to all the circumstances, including any steps A has taken to ascertain whether B consents.

Defence (see 6.1.1)

Related cases

R v H [2005] 1 WLR 2005, CA A female (V) was approached by a man who said to her 'Do you fancy a shag?' and then grabbed at her tracksuit bottoms, attempting to pull her towards him. It was held that in the circumstances surrounding this offence, by applying s 78(b) the touching of the clothing was sexual and amounted to 'sexual assault by touching' for the purposes of s 3.

Practical considerations

- Any reports of serious sexual assault must be treated as genuine and the victims treated with sensitivity.
- As with all serious sexual offences identify any scene, preserve it and seize any articles or associated items relevant to the offence for which the offender has been arrested.
- Prevent any potential for cross contamination.
- Keep the offender and victim separate.
- Consider medical and forensic examination for victim and offender.

Either way None

Summary: 6 months' imprisonment and/or a fine not exceeding the statutory maximum.
Indictment: 10 years' imprisonment.

6.4.2 Sexual assault by touching a child under 13

This offence is covered by s 7 of the Sexual Offences Act 2003 and is the same as s 3 but there is no need to prove lack of consent by the child; any such consent is irrelevant.

Offence
A person commits an offence if—
(a) he **intentionally touches** another person,
(b) the touching is **sexual**, and
(c) the other person is under 13.   Sexual Offences Act 2003, s 7

Points to prove
✓ date and location
✓ intentionally touched
✓ a girl/boy under 13
✓ and the touching was sexual

Meanings

Intentional (see **6.1.1**)

Touching (see **6.4.1**)

Sexual (see **6.3.1**)

Explanatory notes
• Consent is not an issue in this offence, which means that the defendant cannot claim that the child understood and agreed to the sexual touching. This is an offence of strict liability (see **6.1.2**).
• Points raised in **6.4.1** relating to the touching and its sexual nature are still relevant to this offence.

Related cases

R v Weir [2005] EWCA Crim 2866, CA W was on trial for sexual assault by touching a 10–year-old girl. Despite it not being of the same offence category, a previous caution for taking an indecent photograph of a child was disclosed at court under s 103(2)(b) of the Criminal Justice Act 2003. This was allowed as it showed that W may have a propensity to commit the s 7 offence.

Practical considerations

- Age of child will be proved by use of the birth certificate or other similar documentation and testimony of a person who can state that the victim is the person who the birth certificate relates to.
- Only a suitably trained or qualified person should be used to take a statement or obtain evidence from the victim.
- The Children Act 2004 (see **2.4**) makes specific provisions for the police and other agencies to protect the welfare and safety of children.
- Remember if possible to identify and preserve a scene and seize any articles suspected of being used in the offence. Always consider the potential for cross-contamination (see **1.3**).

 E&S   CHAR

 Either way   None

 Summary: 6 months' imprisonment and/or a fine not exceeding the statutory maximum.
Indictment: 10 years' imprisonment.

Links to alternative subjects and offences

E&S Entry and search powers **CHAR** Offences where bad character can be introduced **217**

6.5 **Sexual Activity with a Child**

This offence is covered by s 9 of the Sexual Offences Act 2003.

Offence

(1) A person aged 18 or over (A) commits an offence if—
   (a) he intentionally touches another person (B),
   (b) the **touching** is **sexual**, and
   (c) either—
      (i) B is under 16 and A does not **reasonably believe** that B is 16 or over, or
      (ii) B is under 13.
(2) A person is guilty of an offence under this section, if the touching involved—
   (a) penetration of B's **anus or vagina** with a part of A's body or anything else,
   (b) penetration of B's **mouth** with A's penis,
   (c) penetration of A's **anus or vagina** with a part of B's body, or
   (d) penetration of A's **mouth** with B's penis.

Sexual Offences Act 2003, s 9(1), (2)

Points to prove

Non-penetrative under 13

✓ date and location
✓ offender aged 18 or over
✓ intentionally
✓ engaged in sexual activity
✓ with a girl/boy under 13 **or**
✓ by touching a part of her/his body

Penetrative under 13

✓ date and location
✓ intentionally
✓ engaged in sexual activity namely the penetration of:
   ◆ complainant's anus/vagina with part of D's body or thing **or**
   ◆ complainant's mouth with D's penis **or**
   ◆ D's mouth with his penis
✓ with a person under 13

Penetrative between 13 and 15

✓ per first three points of 'Penetrative under 13'
✓ with a girl/boy aged 13/14/15
✓ not reasonable believing that s/he was 16 or over

> *Non-penetrative aged between 13 and 15*
> ✓ date and location
> ✓ offender aged under 18 years of age
> ✓ intentionally touched a girl/boy aged 13/14/15
> ✓ not reasonably believing s/he was 16 or over
> ✓ the touching was sexual

Meanings

Touching (see **6.4.1**)

Sexual (see **6.3.1**)

Reasonable belief (see **Defence**)

Explanatory notes

This offence replicates s 3 and s 7 (see **6.4**) but the touching involved is specified in terms of what was used on/in what part of the body. In addition consent is irrelevant.

Defence

- The offence will not be complete if the defendant had a reasonable belief that the child was 16 or over at the time.
- This aspect is only relevant when the victim is aged between 13 and 15.

Defence notes

- If the victim is aged between 13 and 15 the prosecution must provide evidence that the defendant's belief was not reasonable. For example, that the defendant knew that a girl attended school and had not yet taken her GCSE examinations.
- However, if the defendant and the complainant met for the first time over the Internet, the complainant provided photographs of her in which she looked much older that she in fact was and if she told the defendant that she was 18 and she did look older, then his belief may be said to be reasonable.
- If the prosecution can provide such evidence it is open to the defendant to rebut it, if he can show on the balance of probabilities his belief was reasonably held.

Practical considerations

- This offence is gender neutral.
- Consent is not an issue.
- Identify and preserve any scene.
- Prevent cross-contamination.
- Seize any articles/clothing or associated equipment which is felt to be relevant.

6.5 Sexual Activity with a Child

- Decisions about whether to charge someone with this offence will be made in accordance with the principles set out in the Code for Crown Prosecutors.
- In deciding whether it is in the public interest to prosecute this offence, where there is enough evidence to provide a realistic prospect of conviction, prosecutors may take into consideration factors which include the age and emotional maturity of the parties, whether they entered into the sexual relationship willingly, any coercion or corruption by a person, the relationship between the parties and whether there was any existence of a duty of care or breach of trust.
- The discretion of the CPS not to charge where it is not in the public interest would be partially relevant where the two parties were close in age, for instance an 18-year-old and a 15-year-old, and had engaged in mutually agreed sexual activity.

E&S **CHAR**

s 9(1) offence

 Either way   None

Summary: 6 months' imprisonment and/or a fine not exceeding the statutory maximum.
Indictment: 14 years' imprisonment.

s 9(2) offence

 Indictment   None

14 years' imprisonment.

Links to alternative subjects and offences

6.6 Cause/Incite Child to Engage in Sexual Activity

These offences are covered by s 10 (child aged 13–15) and s 8 (child under 13) of the Sexual Offences Act 2003 to cause/incite the child to engage in sexual activity.

6.6.1 Cause/incite child aged 13–15 to engage in sexual activity

Offence

(1) A person aged 18 or over (A) commits an offence if—
  (a) he **intentionally causes** or **incites** another person (B) to engage in an activity,
  (b) the activity is **sexual**, and
  (c) either—
    (i) B is under 16 and A does not **reasonably believe** that B is 16 or over, or
    (ii) B is under 13.
(2) A person is guilty of an offence under this section, if the activity caused or incited involved—
  (a) penetration of B's anus or vagina,
  (b) penetration of B's mouth with a person's penis,
  (c) penetration of a person's anus or vagina with a part of B's body or by B with anything else, or
  (d) penetration of a person's mouth with B's penis.

Sexual Offences Act 2003, s 10(1), (2)

Points to prove

Non-penetration

✓ date and location
✓ offender aged 18 years of age or over
✓ intentionally
✓ caused/incited
✓ a girl or boy 13/14/15, not reasonably believing s/he was 16 or over **or**
✓ under 13
✓ to engage in sexual activity
✓ of a non-penetrative nature

Penetration

✓ per first seven points of 'Non-penetration'
✓ involving the penetration of
✓ her/his anus/vagina **or**
✓ her/his mouth with another person's penis **or**
✓ a person's anus/vagina with a part of her/his body or anything else **or**
✓ a person's mouth with the defendant's penis

Meanings

Intention (see **6.1.1**)

The defendant's aim or purpose in pursuing a particular course of action.

Cause

Defined by the *Concise Oxford Dictionary* as 'be the cause of, make happen'. This infers that the defendant must take some positive action rather than an omission to act. Examples could be the use of force, threats, deception, or intimidation.

Incite

Defined by the *Concise Oxford Dictionary* as 'encourage, stir up, urge or persuade'. Examples could be bribery, threats, or pressure.

Sexual (see **6.3.1**)

Reasonable belief

- If the defendant states that s/he did reasonably believe that the complainant consented then it will be a matter for the jury to decide as to whether a reasonable person would have come to the same belief having regard to all the circumstances.
- Those circumstances include the personal characteristics of the defendant; the defendant's age; general sexual experience; sexual experience with this complainant; learning disability; and any other factor that could have affected his/her ability to understand the nature and consequences of his/her actions may be relevant depending on the circumstances of the particular case.

Explanatory notes

- The sexual activity that is caused or incited may be activity with the victim (for example, where the defendant causes or incites the child to have sexual intercourse with him).
- It may be on the child himself (for example, where the defendant causes or incites the child to strip for the defendant's sexual gratification).
- It may be with a third person (for example, where the defendant causes or incites the child to have sexual intercourse with the victim's friend).
- The incitement itself is an offence so the sexual activity does not have to take place for the offence to be committed.

6.6.1 Cause/Incite Child Aged 13–15 to Engage in Sexual Activity

- Section 10(2) replicates some of the other offences covered in the Act, such as rape, assault by penetration. This duplication is intended to cover every possible scenario that could be envisaged ensuring that offenders do not escape prosecution as a result of a loophole in the law.
- Examples of an adult causing or inciting a child to engage in sexual activity could be promising a reward, persuading the child that it is perfectly acceptable behaviour that other children engage in all the time and s/he would be abnormal not to agree, or saying that the activity was necessary to check the child's body for bruises, lice etc, or to try on clothes.
- Where the child is under 13, the adult should be charged with the s 8 offence (see **6.6.2**). However, very rarely the s 10 offence might be used where the child is under 13. An example could be where a person was charged with this offence, and it only became known during trial that the child was actually under 13. The extension of s 10 to under-13s now means that the trial could continue with the original charge where necessary, thus closing a potential loophole in the law.

Practical considerations

- The age of the child will normally be proved by the production of a birth certificate or other similar and suitable documentation and the testimony of a person who can state that the complainant is the person who the birth certificate relates to.
- It is not intended to cover health professionals, or anyone providing sex education, advice, or contraception to children.
- This offence could be considered where the offender and victim are very close in age (for example, an offender of 18 and a victim of 15) and are in a relationship and both have entered into a sexual relationship willingly.
- Where the child is aged 13 or over, but under 16, the prosecution must prove that the defendant did not reasonably believe that s/he was 16 or over.
- If possible identify and preserve crime scene, seize any articles and documentation that is relevant to the offence.
- The obtaining of evidence from a child should be by suitably trained persons.

 E&S **CHAR**

s 10(1) offence

 Either way   ⏱ None

🏛 **Summary:** 6 months' imprisonment and or a fine not exceeding the statutory maximum.
Indictment: 14 years' imprisonment.

 E&S Entry and search powers   **CHAR** Offences where bad character can be introduced

s 10(2) offence

 Indictment None

 14 years' imprisonment

6.6.2 **Cause/incite child under 13 to engage in sexual activity**

This offence is covered by s 8 of the Sexual Offences Act 2003.

Offence

(1) A person commits an offence if—
   (a) he **intentionally causes** or **incites** another person (B) to engage in an activity,
   (b) the activity is **sexual**, and
   (c) B is under 13.
(2) A person is guilty of an offence under this section, if the activity caused or incited involved—
   (a) penetration of B's anus or vagina,
   (b) penetration of B's mouth with a person's penis,
   (c) penetration of a person's anus or vagina with a part of B's body or by B with anything else, or
   (d) penetration of a person's mouth with B's penis.

Sexual Offences Act 2003, s 8(1), (2)

Points to prove

Non-penetration

✓ date and location
✓ intentionally caused/incited
✓ a boy/girl under 13
✓ to engage in sexual activity
✓ of a non-penetrative nature

Penetration

✓ per first four points of 'Non-penetration'
✓ involving the penetration of
✓ her/his anus/vagina **or**
✓ her/his mouth with another person's penis **or**
✓ a person's anus/vagina with a part of her/his body or anything else **or**
✓ a person's mouth with the defendant's penis

6.6.2 Cause/Incite Child Under 13 to Engage in Sexual Activity

Meanings

Intention (see **6.6.1**)

Cause (see **6.6.1**)

Incite (see **6.6.1**)

Sexual (see **6.3.1**)

Explanatory notes

- This offence is the same as the s 10 offence save for the requirement that the victim must be under 13. Again this offence is intended to cover every possible scenario.
- In relation to sexual activity caused or incited, the offence covers the same situations as does the offence under s 4 except that, for this offence, consent is irrelevant.
- Provided incitement takes place there is no need to show the sexual activity itself took place.

Practical considerations

- The age of the child will normally be proved by the production of a birth certificate or other similar and suitable documentation and the testimony of a person who can state that the complainant is the person who the birth certificate relates to.
- If possible, identify and preserve crime scene, seize any articles and documentation that is relevant to the offence.
- The obtaining of evidence from a child should be by suitably trained persons.

s 8(1) offence

 Either way

 None

 Summary: 6 months' imprisonment and/or a fine not exceeding the statutory maximum.
Indictment: 14 years' imprisonment.

s 8(2) offence

 Indictment

 None

 Life imprisonment.

E&S Entry and search powers   **CHAR** Offences where bad character can be introduced

Links to alternative subjects and offences

6.7 Arranging/Facilitating Commission of a Child Sex Offence and Meeting a Child Following Sexual Grooming

6.7.1 Arranging/facilitating commission of a child sex offence

This offence is covered by s 14 of the Sexual Offences Act 2003.

Offence

A person commits an offence if—

(a) he **intentionally arranges** or facilitates something that he intends to do, intends another person to do, or believes that another person will do, in any part of the world, and

(b) doing it will involve the commission of an offence under any of sections 9 to 13.

Sexual Offences Act 2003, s 14(1)

Points to prove

✓ date and location
✓ intentionally
✓ arranged/facilitated
✓ an act which the defendant
✓ intended to do **or**
✓ intended/believed another person would do
✓ in any part of the world
✓ and doing it will involve the commission of an offence under
✓ ss 9/10/11/12/13 of the Sexual Offences Act 2003

Meanings

Intention   (see **6.6.1**)

Arranges

Defined by the *Concise Oxford Dictionary* as 'organize or plan' and 'reach agreement about an action or event in advance'.

Explanatory notes

• The defendant does not have to be the one who will commit the sexual offence; it will be enough if s/he intended/believed that s/he or another person will commit the relevant offence in any part of the world.

- The offence covers a situation where the defendant takes a person to a place where there is a child in the belief that the person is likely to engage in sexual activity with that child.
- It also caters for situations whereby the defendant arranges for self or another the procurement of a child with whom s/he proposes to engage in sexual activity with. For example, the defendant is going on holiday and plans to engage in sexual activity with children whilst there and so arranges through an agency to meet children.
- The sexual activity does not have to occur for the offence to be committed.
- The relevant offences are:
  - ◆ s 9 Sexual activity with a child
  - ◆ s 10 Causing or inciting a child to engage in sexual activity
  - ◆ s 11 Engaging in sexual activity in the presence of a child
  - ◆ s 12 Causing a child to watch a sexual act
  - ◆ s 13 Child sex offences committed by children or young persons.

Defence

(2) A person does not commit an offence under this section if—
  (a) he arranges or facilitates something that he believes another person will do, but that he does not intend to do or intend another person to do, and
  (b) any offence within subs (1)(b) would be an offence against a child for whose *protection* he acts.
(3) For the purposes of subsection (2), a person acts for the protection of a child if he acts for the purposes of:
  (a) protecting the child from sexually transmitted infection,
  (b) protecting the physical safety of the child,
  (c) preventing the child from becoming pregnant, or
  (d) promoting the child's emotional well-being by the giving of advice, and **not** for the purpose of obtaining sexual gratification **or** for the purpose of causing or encouraging the activity constituting the offence within subs (1)(b) **or** the child's participation in it.

Sexual Offences Act 2003, s 14(2), (3)

Defence notes

This is intended to protect those people such as health care workers who are aware that a person is having sex with a child under 16 and gives them condoms as s/he believes that if they do not the child will have unprotected sex. It appears as if the health care worker must warn the person that what they are doing is illegal but is allowed to give the condoms without committing an offence under this section.

Practical considerations

- The specified offence (under ss 9–13) does not have to take place. If it does occur or would have occurred if it were not for there being facts which made the commission of the offence impossible, then it may be easier to prove the above offence.

- Obtain any evidence which proves the links (eg advertisement, emails, bookings for hotels).
- Seize mobile phone and computer and any other physical evidence relevant to the offence.

 Either way   None

 Summary: 6 months' imprisonment and/or a fine not exceeding the statutory maximum.
Indictment: 14 years' imprisonment.

6.7.2 **Meeting a child following sexual grooming**

This offence is covered by s 15 of the Sexual Offences Act 2003.

Offence

A person aged 18 or over (A) commits an offence if—
(a) having met or communicated with another person (B) on at least two earlier occasions, he—
   (i) **intentionally** meets B, or
   (ii) travels with the intention of meeting B in any part of the world,
(b) at the time, he intends to do anything to or in respect of B, during or after the meeting and in any part of the world, which if done will involve the commission by A of a **relevant** offence,
(c) B is under 16, and
(d) A does not **reasonably believe** that B is 16 or over.

Sexual Offences Act 2003, s 15(1)

Points to prove

✓ date and location
✓ being a person 18 or over
✓ having on at least two earlier occasions met/communicated
✓ with a person under 16 at the time of the meeting
✓ and who the defendant did not reasonably believe was 16 or over
✓ intentionally met/travelled with the intention of meeting that person
✓ and at the time intended to do anything to/in respect of her/him

---

E&S Entry and search powers   **CHAR** Offences where bad character can be introduced

> ✓ during/after the meeting and in any part of the world
> ✓ which if done would have involved the commission by the defendant
> ✓ of a relevant offence

Meanings

Intention   (see 6.6.1)

Relevant offence   (see 6.2)

Reasonable belief   (see defence—below)

Explanatory notes

- A person must have at least communicated on two earlier occasions or had two prior meetings with the person. The communication could be by telephone, text messaging, or email. These communications do not have to contain sexually explicit language or pornography but could, for example, be something as seemingly innocuous as the offender giving the victim swimming lessons or meeting him/her incidentally through a friend.
- The defendant must intentionally meet or travel with the intention of meeting the victim. The meeting can take place anywhere in the world as long as some part of the journey took place in England, Wales, or Northern Ireland.
- The meeting itself does not have to take place, and the wording of the offence allows for the defendant being apprehended on the way to the meeting.
- This offence is intended to deal with those predators who groom young children by gaining their trust, lying about their age, and then arranging to meet them in order to sexually abuse them. This offence is preventative, in that the relevant sexual offence does not have to occur in order for the offence to be committed.

Defences

If the offender **reasonably believes** that the victim is 16 or over. This belief must be reasonable, not simply honest or genuine. Therefore, the issue has an objective element and it will not be enough for the defendant to rely on an unreasonable though honestly held belief.

Related cases

R v Mohammed [2006] EWCA Crim 1107, CA M worked as a security guard on a building site where school girls often hung out. He befriended a vulnerable 13 year old girl, who lived in a foster home, with severe learning difficulties and behavioural problems. They were found together 8 miles from her home and he was arrested. Their mobile phones were analysed which showed that M had sent intimate messages. M confirmed that she had visited his home; but the abduction was short lived, the girl was willing and initiated contact, and no sexual act had taken place. Held that his motivation was sexual and he had blatantly taken her from the control of carers. Convicted of child abduction and meeting a child following sexual grooming contrary to s 15(1).

R v Mansfield [2005] EWCA Crim 927, CA 'The law is there to protect young girls against their own immature sexual experimentation and to punish older men who take advantage of them'.

Practical considerations

- The victim must be under 16 and the prosecution would normally use the child's birth certificate (although other documentation could be used) and testimony of a person who can state that the complainant is the person who the birth certificate relates to.
- Any articles in the defendant's possession such as condoms, pornography, rope, and lubricant could help to prove this intention.
- Only a suitably trained or qualified person should be used to take statements or obtain evidence from the victims with this type of offence.
- The Children Act 2004 (see **2.4**) makes specific provision for the police and other agencies to protect the welfare and safety of children.
- This offence applies to all offences in pt 1 of the Act (s 1 to s 79)
- All evidence in relation to the grooming should be seized (eg any communications, bookings, or other documents which link the defendant and victim).
- Consider CCTV evidence.
- Seize any computer and mobile phone that could have been used.

E&S

 Either way   None

Summary: 6 months' imprisonment and/or a fine not exceeding the statutory maximum.
Indictment: 10 years' imprisonment.

Links to alternative subjects and offences

6.8 Indecent Photographs Under 18

6.8.1 Indecent photographs under 18

This offence is covered by s 1 of the Protection of Children Act 1978.

Offences

Subject to sections 1A and 1B *[defences]*, it is an offence for a person—

(a) to take, or permit to be taken, or to **make**, any **indecent photograph** or **pseudo-photograph** of a **child**; or

(b) to **distribute** or show such indecent photographs or pseudo-photographs; or

(c) to have in his possession such indecent photographs or pseudo-photographs, with a view to their being distributed or **shown by himself** and others; or

(d) to publish or cause to be published any advertisement likely to be understood as conveying that the advertiser distributes or shows such indecent photographs or pseudo-photographs or intends to do so.

Protection of Children Act 1978, s 1(1)

Points to prove

s 1(1)(a), (b)

✓ date and location
✓ made/permitted to be taken/took/showed/distributed
✓ indecent photograph(s)/pseudo-photograph(s)
✓ of a child/children

s 1(1)(c)

✓ date and location
✓ possessed
✓ indecent photograph(s)/pseudo-photograph(s)
✓ of child/children
✓ with a view to it/them being
✓ distributed/shown to another

s 1(1)(d)

✓ date and location
✓ published/caused to be published an advertisement
✓ likely to be understood as conveying
✓ that the advertiser
✓ distributes/shows or intend to distribute/show
✓ indecent photograph(s)/pseudo-photograph(s)
✓ of child/children

Meanings

Make

Includes downloading images from the Internet and storing or printing them (*R v Bowden* [2000] 1 WLR 1427).

Photographs

If they show children that are indecent they will be treated as indecent photographs of children; the same applies in respect of pseudo-photographs. It also includes: photographs in a film (not yet developed); the negative as well as the positive version; and data stored on a computer disc or by other electronic means which is capable of conversion into a photograph.

Indecent photograph

Includes indecent film, a copy of an indecent photograph or **film**, and an indecent photograph comprised in a film (s 7(2)).

Film

This includes any form of video recording (s 7(5)).

Pseudo-photograph

An image, whether made by computer graphics or otherwise howsoever, which appears to be a photograph (s 7).

Child

A person under the age of 18 (s 7(6)).

Distribute

A person is to be regarded as distributing an indecent photograph or pseudo-photograph if he parts with possession of it to, or exposes or offers it for acquisition by, another person (s 1(2)).

Shown by himself

Means shown by the defendant to other people.

Explanatory notes

- The image does not have to be stored in a way that allows it to be retrieved. However, the image must be made deliberately. Innocently opening a file from the Internet is not an offence (see below).
- The attendant circumstances of the way in which the images have been downloaded, stored, labelled, and filed will be important in demonstrating the extent to which the defendant was or should have been aware of their indecent nature. Other correspondence (by email or otherwise) with the defendant will also be useful here, as will any evidence of a general interest in paedophilia (*R v Mould* [2001] 2 Crim App R (S) 8).

Defences

1(4) Where a person is charged with an offence under subsection 1(b) or (c), it shall be a defence for him to prove—

(a) that he had a legitimate reason for distributing or showing the photographs or pseudo-photographs or (as the case may be) having them in his possession; or

(b) that he had not himself seen the photographs or pseudo-photographs and did not know, nor had any cause to suspect, them to be indecent.

1A(1) This section applies where, in proceedings for an offence under s 1(1)(a) of taking or making an indecent photograph of a child, or for an offence under s 1(1)(b) or (c) relating to an indecent photograph of a child, the defendant proves that the photograph was of the child aged 16 or over, and that at the time of the offence charged the child and he—

(a) were married, or

(b) lived together as partners in an enduring family relationship.

1A(2) Subsections (5) and (6) also apply where, in proceedings for an offence under s 1(1)(b) or (c) relating to an indecent photograph of a child, the defendant proves that the photograph was of the child aged 16 or over, and that at the time when he obtained it the child and he—

(a) were married, or

(b) lived together as partners in an enduring family relationship.

1A(3) This section applies whether the photograph showed the child alone or with the defendant, but not if it showed any other person.

1A(4) In the case of an offence under s 1(1)(a), if sufficient evidence is adduced to raise an issue as to whether the child consented to the photograph being taken or made, or as to whether the defendant reasonably believed that the child so consented, the defendant is not guilty of the offence unless it is proved that the child did not so consent and that the defendant did not reasonably believe that the child so consented.

1A(5) In the case of an offence under s 1(1)(b), the defendant is not guilty of the offence unless it is proved that the showing or distributing was to a person other than the child.

1A(6) In the case of an offence under s 1(1)(c), if sufficient evidence is adduced to raise an issue both—

(a) as to whether the child consented to the photograph being in the defendant's possession, or as to whether the defendant reasonably believed that the child so consented, and

(b) as to whether the defendant had the photograph in his possession with a view to its being distributed or shown to anyone other than the child,

the defendant is not guilty of the offence unless it is proved either that the child did not so consent and that the defendant did not reasonably believe that the child so consented, or that the defendant had the photograph in his possession with a view to its being distributed or shown to a person other than the child.

1B(1) In proceedings for an offence under s 1(1)(a) of making an indecent photograph or pseudo-photograph of a child, the defendant is not guilty of the offence if he proves that—

(a) it was necessary for him to make the photograph or pseudo-photograph for the purposes of the prevention, detection or investigation of crime, or for the purposes of criminal proceedings, in any part of the world,

(b) at the time of the offence charged he was a member of the Security Service, and it was necessary for him to make the photograph or pseudo-photograph for the exercise of any of the functions of the Service, or

(c) at the time of the offence charged he was a member of GCHQ, and it was necessary for him to make the photograph or pseudo-photograph for the exercise of any of the functions of GCHQ.
        Protection of Children Act 1978, s 1(4)–1B(1)

Defence notes

- The conditions in relation to an offence under s 1(1)(a) (taking or making indecent photographs) are listed under s 1A(1), 1A(3) and 1A(4). If any of these conditions are not satisfied, the prosecution need only prove the offence as set out in s 1(1)(a) of the Act. But if the three conditions are satisfied, the defendant is not guilty of the offence unless the prosecution also prove that the child did not consent and that the defendant did not reasonably believe that the child consented.

- The conditions in relation to an offence under s 1(1)(b) (distributing or showing indecent photographs) are listed under s 1A(1), (2), and 1A(3). If either of these conditions are not satisfied, the prosecution need only prove the offence as set out in s 1(1)(b). But if both the conditions are satisfied, the defendant is not guilty of the offence unless the prosecution proves that the showing or distribution was to a person other than the child.

- The conditions in relation to an offence under s 1(1)(c) (being in possession of indecent photographs with a view to their being distributed or shown) are listed in s 1A(2), 1A(3), and 1A(6). If any of these conditions are not satisfied, the prosecution need only prove the offence as set out in s 1(1)(c). But if the three conditions are satisfied, the defendant is not guilty of the offence unless the prosecution also prove either that the child did not so consent and that the defendant did not reasonably believe that the child so consented, or that the defendant had the photograph in his possession with a view to its being distributed to a person other than a child.

  ♦ For example, an email attachment was opened innocently and not subsequently deleted owing to a genuine lack of IT skill (deleting an email in 'Outlook' may only move it to a 'deleted' directory, much like the 'recycle bin', this directory needs to be emptied and there may be other 'temporary' directories where it could be held). In such circumstances the statutory defence would apply.

✦ Similarly, if an image was innocently downloaded from the web and immediately deleted without the defendant realizing that the computer has stored a back-up copy in a temporary Internet directory, the defence would apply.

• In a Crown Court case the 'Trojan Horse' virus defence was successful. In short, expert evidence confirmed the likelihood of this virus being responsible for 14 depraved images saved on the defendant's personal computer. It was accepted that these could have been sent remotely, without the defendant's knowledge. Although the case is not binding on any other court, and each case will be determined according to its own particular facts, officers should be aware of the possibility should such a defence be raised.

Related cases

R v Dooley [2005] EWCA Crim 3093, CA Where material downloaded was accessible to all club members then it is downloaded with a view to its distribution or showing to others.

R v T (1999) 163 JP 349, CA Courts will **not** accept an intention by the offender to show photographs to himself as sufficient to prove the offence under s 1(1)(c).

R v Smith and Jayson [2002] 1 Cr App R 13, CA Deliberately opening an indecent computer email attachment or downloading an indecent image from the Internet, so it can be viewed on a screen, is making a photograph.

R v Bowden [2001] 1 WLR 1427, CA Downloading would come within s 1 'to make' as a file is created when the photograph is downloaded.

Practical considerations

• It is not an offence under this legislation to possess photographs to show to oneself, this is dealt with by s 160 of the Criminal Justice Act 1988 (see **6.8.2**).

• Proceedings for an offence under this Act shall not be instituted except by or with the consent of the Director of Public Prosecutions.

• Seize all computer equipment as evidence.

• There are some authoritative factors in deciding whether or not a defence may apply, depending on whether the person(s):

✦ acted reasonably in all the circumstances;

✦ reported the photographs or pseudo-photographs as soon as was practicable and to the appropriate authority;

✦ stored the photographs or pseudo-photographs in a secure and safe manner;

✦ copied or distributed the photographs or pseudo-photographs unnecessarily;

• Ascertain how the photographs or pseudo-photographs were made or discovered.

Either way None

 Summary: 6 months' imprisonment and/or a fine not exceeding the statutory maximum.
Indictment: 10 years' imprisonment.

6.8.2 Possession of indecent photograph(s) of a child

Section 160 of the Criminal Justice Act 1988 concerns the offence of simple possession of indecent photographs or pseudo photographs of a child.

Offence

Subject to **subsection (1A)** it is an offence for a person to have any **indecent photograph** or **pseudo-photograph** of a **child** in his possession.

Criminal Justice Act 1988, s 160(1)

Points to prove
✓ date and location
✓ possessed
✓ indecent photo(s)/pseudo-photograph(s)
✓ of a child/children

Meanings

Subsection (IA)

Normally an introductory 'subject to' infers subject to a defence, but the legislators have so far failed to provide a sub-s (1A). In this instance the defences are sub-s (2) and s 160A, both of these are given under **Defences** (below).

Photographs (see **6.8.1**)

Indecent photograph (see **6.8.1**)

Pseudo-photograph (see **6.8.1**)

Child (see **6.8.1**)

Explanatory notes

Where there is no evidence of intent to distribute or show s 160 of the Criminal Justice Act 1988 should be used for simple possession.

Defences

160(2) Where a person is charged with an offence under subsection
   (1) above it shall be a defence for him to prove—
   (a) that he had a legitimate reason for having the photograph or
       pseudo-photograph in his possession; or
   (b) that he had not himself seen the photograph or
       pseudo-photograph and did not know, nor had any cause to
       suspect, it to be indecent; or
   (c) that the photograph or pseudo-photograph was sent to him
       without any prior request made by him or on his behalf and that
       he did not keep it for an unreasonable time.

160A(1) This section applies where, in proceedings for an offence under
   section 160 relating to an indecent photograph of a child, the
   defendant proves that the photograph was of the child aged 16 or
   over, and that at the time of the offence charged the child and
   he—
   (a) were married, or
   (b) lived together as partners in an enduring family relationship.

160A(2) This section also applies where, in proceedings for an offence under
   section 160 relating to an indecent photograph of a child, the
   defendant proves that the photograph was of the child aged 16 or
   over, and that at the time when he obtained it the child and he—
   (a) were married, or
   (b) lived together as partners in an enduring family relationship.

160A(3) This section applies whether the photograph showed the child alone
   or with the defendant, but not if it showed any other person.

160A(4) If sufficient evidence is adduced to raise an issue as to whether the
   child consented to the photograph being in the defendant's
   possession, or as to whether the defendant reasonably believed that
   the child so consented, the defendant is not guilty of the offence
   unless it is proved that the child did not so consent and that the
   defendant did not reasonably believe that the child so consented.

   Criminal Justice Act 1988, ss 160(2) and 160A(1)-(4)

Defence notes

The conditions for the defence are listed under s 160A(1)–(4). If any of
these conditions is not satisfied, the prosecution need only prove the
offence as set out in s 160. But if the three conditions are satisfied, the
defendant is not guilty of the offence unless the prosecution proves that
the child did not consent and that the defendant did not reasonably
believe that the child consented.

Related cases

R v Porter [2006] EWCA Crim 560, CA The computer hard drives of
P were found to contain deleted images which could only be retrieved
using specialist software, which P did not have. If a person cannot access
deleted images on a computer then he was no longer in custody, control
or possession of those images. The jury must decide on this issue having

regard to all the relevant circumstances and the defendant's knowledge at the time.

R v Matrix [1997] Crim LR 901 A shop assistant may possess indecent photographs as well as the shop owner.

Atkins v DPP and Goodland v DPP [2000] 2 All ER 425, QBD Atkins: Images stored in a temporary directory unbeknown to the defendant did not amount to possession, knowledge was required. Goodland: A montage of legal photographs made to look indecent did not come within the definition of pseudo-photograph (might have if the image was photocopied).

Practical considerations

- Remember to seize the photos or pseudo-photographs.
- Seize the computer or storage mechanism.
- Check on the audit chain for the photos and documents relating to them to ensure possession is the only suitable charge.
- Consent of the Director of Public Prosecutions required.

E&S

 Either way   None

 Summary: 6 months' imprisonment and/or a fine not exceeding the statutory maximum.
Indictment: 5 years' imprisonment.

Links to alternative subjects and offences

6.9 Exposure and Outraging Public Decency

6.9.1 Exposure

This offence is covered by s 66 of the Sexual Offences Act 2003.

> **Offence**
> A person commits an offence if—
> (a) he **intentionally** exposes his **genitals**, and
> (b) he intends that someone will see them and be caused alarm or distress.
>
> Sexual Offences Act 2003, s 66(1)

Points to prove
- ✓ date and location
- ✓ intentionally
- ✓ exposed genitals
- ✓ intending
- ✓ someone would see them
- ✓ and be caused alarm/distress

Meanings

Intention   (see **6.6.1**)

Genitals

Means male or female sexual organs.

Explanatory notes

- This offence would generally exclude naturists and streakers whose intention is not to cause alarm or distress.
- Exposure of the genitals must be intentional and not accidental.
- The offence applies to either sex and is not restricted (as with the previous legislation) to the male penis. However, genitals do not include a female's breasts or the buttocks of either sex, so a female flashing her breasts or someone mooning (exposing their buttocks) will not be caught within this offence.
- The offence can be committed anywhere and is not restricted to public places.

Practical considerations

- It is not necessary for a person to have actually seen the genitals or for anyone to be distressed or alarmed. For example, a male exposes his genitals to a female passing by. If his intent was for her to see them and be alarmed or distressed then even if she does not see them and whether or not she is distressed then he still commits the offence.

- Proof of the relevant intent (both as to the genitals being seen and alarm or distress being caused thereby) will be critical to a successful prosecution.
- The precise location and the time of day will be important in showing a likely intention by the defendant.
- The accompanying words/conduct of the defendant will be relevant here, along with any preparatory or subsequent actions.
- Is this offence isolated or one of a series?

E&S

 Either way   None

Summary: 6 months' imprisonment and/or a fine not exceeding the statutory maximum.
Indictment: 2 years' imprisonment.

6.9.2 **Outraging public decency**

This is an offence at common law.

> **Offence**
> It is an offence to commit an act of a **lewd, obscene,** and **disgusting** nature, which is capable of outraging public decency, in a **public place** where at least two members of the public could have witnessed it.
>
> Common Law

Points to prove
- ✓ date and location
- ✓ in a public place
- ✓ committed an act
- ✓ outraging public decency
- ✓ by behaving in indecent manner

Meanings

Lewd

Means 'lustful or indecent'.

Obscene

Means 'morally repugnant or depraved'.

6.9.2 Outraging Public Decency

Disgusting

Means 'repugnant or loathsome'.

Public place

Means a place to which the public have access or a place which is visible to the public.

Explanatory notes

- There are other offences which may be more suitable in the majority of cases. For example, offences under the Sexual Offences Act 2003, Public Order Act 1986, and the Obscene Publications Act 1959.
- Such conduct can also be an offence of public nuisance at common law (see **7.13.3**).

Related cases

Rose v DPP [2006] EWHC 852 (Admin), QBD A couple had oral sex in ATM area of bank captured on CCTV, foyer was well lit and passers by could have seen the act. Determined that more than one person must see the act for outraging public decency offence.

R v Walker [1996] 1 Cr App R 111, CA The defendant exposed himself and masturbated in front of two young girls in the living room of his home. The Court of Appeal quashed the conviction, on the basis that the public had not been able to observe what took place in his living room.

Smith v Hughes [1960] 1 WLR 830 It was held that the balcony of a private house that was visible to the public was a sufficiently public place for this offence.

R v Gibson [1990] 2 QB 619 The 'act' does not have to be a 'live' activity, nor does it have to be of a sexual nature. It may be the act of putting a disgusting object on public display, such as displaying a sculpted head with a real human foetus dangling from it in a public art gallery.

Practical considerations

- More than one person must have been able to witness the lewd act (see above related cases).
- In order to outrage public decency, the conduct must grossly cross the boundaries of decency and be likely to seriously offend the reasonable person (rather than simply upsetting or even shocking).
- In sexual offences, this offence is reserved for offences where masturbation or sexual intercourse occurs (as with the current fad of 'dogging'). There is no requirement to prove that those persons who witnessed the act were actually disgusted or outraged by it—the test is an objective one based on whether a reasonable person would be disgusted.
- Where the circumstances are appropriate, positive evidence of disgust can be given by a police officer.

Either way None

 Summary: 6 months' imprisonment and/or a fine not exceeding the statutory maximum.
Indictment: Imprisonment and/or a fine.

Links to alternative subjects and offences

6.10 **Voyeurism**

This offence is created by s 67 of the Sexual Offences Act 2003.

Offences

(1) A person commits an offence if—
   (a) for the purpose of obtaining sexual gratification, he observes another person doing a **private act**, and
   (b) he knows that the other person does not **consent** to being observed for his **sexual gratification**.

(2) A person commits an offence if—
   (a) he operates equipment with the intention of enabling another person to observe, for the purpose of obtaining **sexual gratification**, a third person (B) doing a private act, and
   (b) he knows that B does not **consent** to his operating equipment with that intention.

(3) A person commits an offence if—
   (a) he records another person (B) doing a **private act**,
   (b) he does so with the intention that he or a third person will, for the purpose of obtaining **sexual gratification**, look at an image of B doing the act, and
   (c) he knows that B does not consent to his recording the act with that intention.

(4) A person commits an offence if he installs equipment, or constructs or adapts a structure or part of a structure, with the intention of enabling himself or another person to commit an offence under subsection (1).

Sexual Offences Act 2003, s 67(1)–(4)

Points to prove

Observing s 67(1)

✓ date and location
✓ for the purpose of obtaining sexual gratification
✓ observed another person
✓ doing a private act
✓ knowing that the person
✓ does not consent to being observed
✓ for sexual gratification

Operating equipment to observe s 67(2)

✓ date and location
✓ operated equipment
✓ with the intention of enabling another person
✓ for the purpose of obtaining sexual gratification
✓ to observe a third person doing a private act

✓ knowing that person does not consent
✓ to the defendant operating that equipment with that intention

Recording a private act s 67(3)

✓ date and location
✓ recorded another person doing a private act
✓ with the intention that
✓ the defendant/a third person
✓ would for the purpose of obtaining sexual gratification
✓ look at an image of that other person doing the act
✓ knowing that the other person does not consent
✓ to the defendant recording the act with that intention

Install equipment/construct/adapt a structure s 67(4)

✓ date and location
✓ installed equipment **or**
✓ constructed/adapted a structure/part of a structure
✓ with intent
✓ enable the defendant/third person
✓ for the purpose of defendant/third person to observe and commit
  s 61 offence

Meanings

Private act

A person is doing a private act if they are in a place where they could reasonably expect privacy and their genitals, breasts, or buttocks are exposed or covered with underwear, they are using the toilet, or they are doing a sexual act that is not normally done in public (s 68).

Consent

The defendant must **know** that the person does not consent to being observed for *sexual gratification*. They may have consented to being observed for some other reason.

Sexual gratification

It is only in s 67(1) that the sexual gratification must be on the part of the defendant.

For the other subsections it could be for a third party's sexual gratification.

Explanatory notes

• Previously it was not an offence to watch someone for sexual gratification. This will cater for such situations involving 'peeping toms'.

• For s 67(2)–(4), it is irrelevant whether or not any third parties knew that the person did not consent.

• Section 67(2) is aimed at those who install web-cams or other recording equipment for their own gratification or for that of others. An image is defined as 'a moving or still image and includes an image produced by any means and, where the context permits, a three-dimensional image'.

- Section 67(4) would cover a person who installed a two-way mirror or a spy-hole in a hotel room. The offender would commit the offence even if the peephole or mirror was discovered before it was ever used.

Practical considerations

- Any equipment used requires seizing.
- CCTV footage may be of use.
- A search for films previously made would be beneficial.
- Evidence of equipment hire could be advantageous.
- Video tape(s) or DVD(s) can be seized for examination and evidence.

E&S

 Either way None

Summary: 6 months' imprisonment and/or a fine not exceeding the statutory maximum.
Indictment: 2 years' imprisonment.

Links to alternative subjects and offences

6.11 Sexual Activity in a Public Lavatory

This offence is covered by s 71 of the Sexual Offences Act 2003.

Offence

A person commits an offence if—
(a) he is in a lavatory to which the public or a section of the public has or is permitted to have access, whether on payment or otherwise,
(b) he **intentionally** engages in an activity, and,
(c) the **activity** is **sexual**.   Sexual Offences Act 2003, s 71(1)

Points to prove

✓ date and location
✓ being in a lavatory
✓ to which the public/a section of the public
✓ had/was permitted to have access
✓ whether on payment/otherwise
✓ intentionally
✓ engaged in a sexual activity

Meanings

Intention   (see 6.6.1)

Activity

The word activity can cover a whole range of recreational pursuits, including sexual intercourse, oral sex, and masturbation. It is irrelevant if the defendant did not consider the activity to be sexual if a reasonable person would (for example, kissing).

Sexual

An activity is sexual if a reasonable person would, in all the circumstances but regardless of any person's purpose, consider it to be sexual (s 71(2)).

Explanatory notes

- The offence covers lavatories where the public, or a section of the public, have access to, whether or not payment is involved. This would include staff toilets in large/small premises.
- The actual sexual activity itself does not have to be specified, it would be enough to record the details of what was seen or heard.
- There is no requirement to prove that anyone was alarmed or distressed by the activity.

6.11 Sexual Activity in a Public Lavatory

• This offence is intended to replace the former offence that became known as 'cottaging'.

Practical considerations

• The definition of sexual in this section is different from the one used throughout the Act in that it is what a reasonable person would consider sexual, regardless of the person's purpose.
• The offence is gender neutral.
• Independent evidence in the form of a CJA statement would be advantageous.

 Summary   6 months

 6 months' imprisonment and/or a fine not exceeding level 5 on the standard scale.

Links to alternative subjects and offences

6.12 Administering Substance with Intent and Committing an Offence with Intent to Commit Sexual Offence

6.12.1 Administering a substance with intent to commit a sexual offence

This offence is covered by s 61 of the Sexual Offences Act 2003.

Offence

A person commits an offence if he **intentionally administers** a substance to, or **causes** a substance **to be taken** by, another person (B)—
(a) knowing that B does not consent, and
(b) with the intention of stupefying or overpowering B, so as to enable any person to engage in a **sexual activity** that involves B.

Sexual Offences Act 2003, s 61(1)

Points to prove

✓ date and location
✓ intentionally
✓ administered a substance to **or**
✓ caused a substance to be taken by
✓ another person
✓ knowing s/he did not consent and
✓ with the intention of stupefying/overpowering him/her
✓ so as to enable any person
✓ to engage in a sexual activity involving him/her

Meanings

Intention (see 6.6.1)

Administer

In *R v Gillard* (1988) 87 Cr App Rep 189 it was held to include conduct that brings a substance into contact with the victim's body, directly or indirectly. For example, by injection or by holding a cloth soaked in the substance to the victim's face.

6.12.1 Administering Substance/Intent to Commit Sexual Offence

Causes to be taken

This would cover such conduct as slipping a date rape drug directly into a drink or deceiving the victim as to the nature of the substance (eg telling the victim it is a pain killer when in fact it is a sedative).

Sexual (see 6.3.1)

Activity (see 6.11)

Explanatory notes

- This offence replaces s 4 of the Sexual Offences Act 1956 but it has a much wider remit as it is gender neutral (the old offence could only be committed by a male on a female) and includes sexual activity not just sexual intercourse.
- This offence is intended to cover situations where so-called 'date rape' drugs (such as Rohypnol or GHB (gamma-hydroxybutrate)) are given to a person in order to allow the defendant or someone else to have sexual activity with them. It also covers the spiking of a person's drink with alcohol when they believed they were drinking a soft drink.
- It does not matter how the substance is administered (eg by drink, injection). The offence has a very wide ambit in that it allows for one person to administer the substance or cause the substance to be taken and another to engage in the sexual activity (although no sexual activity need actually take place).
- The required consent refers to the taking/administering of the substance as opposed to the intended sexual activity. However, under s 75 there is a presumption that the victim does not consent to the sexual activity where a substance which would stupefy or overpower has been administered.

Practical considerations

- The offence is committed whether or not there is any sexual activity as long as the substance was administered and there was the relevant intention. However, if there was no sexual activity, it may be hard for the prosecution to prove this offence.
- If there were sexual activity then the offender would obviously be charged with any substantive offence as well as this one.
- Consider taking samples and medical examinations where appropriate.
- Gather evidence by seizing any appropriate documentation.
- Seize mobile phones where there is evidence of link between defendants and victims at the relevant time.
- Consider CCTV footage.

Either way   None

 Summary: 6 months' imprisonment and/or a fine not
exceeding the statutory maximum.
Indictment: 10 years' imprisonment.

6.12.2 Commit an offence with intent to commit sexual offence

This offence is covered by s 62 of the Sexual Offences Act 2003.

Offence

A person commits an offence under this section if he commits any offence
with the **intention** of committing a **relevant sexual offence**.

Sexual Offences Act 2003, s 62(1)

Points to prove

✓ date and location
✓ committed any offence
✓ with the intention of committing
✓ a relevant sexual offence

Meanings

Intention   (see **6.6.1**)

Relevant sexual offence   (see **6.2**)

Explanatory notes

• This offence involves the commission of **any** criminal offence, with
  the relevant intention of the defendant carrying out a relevant sexual
  offence.
• *Any* offence will be covered: theft, assault, kidnap, criminal damage,
  and even road traffic offences.
• This offence is intended to cater for such situations where the victim
  is kidnapped, assaulted, poisoned or blackmailed in order that the
  defendant can thereby rape them or carry out some other sexual act
  that the victim would not otherwise consent to.
• The offence is committed whether or not the relevant sexual offence
  actually takes place, for example, if the police find the kidnap victim
  prior to their being raped, the offence would be committed.

6.12.2 Commit an Offence with Intent to Commit Sexual Offence

- This offence differs from the previous one in that the defendant must intend to carry out the ulterior sexual offence himself/herself; if the intention is that someone else carry out the ulterior sexual offence, this offence will not be appropriate.

Practical considerations

- The first offence does not necessarily have to involve the intended victim of the ulterior sexual offence. For example, where the defendant steals a car from one person in order to drive to the house of another person and rape them.
- If the sexual offence did take place then the defendant would be charged with the substantive offence as well as this one.
- Obtain forensic evidence by identifying and preserving crime scene.
- Ensure there is no cross-contamination.
- Seize any evidence of defendant's knowledge of victim through previous text messages and emails, and if necessary seize phones and computers.

 Either way   None

 Summary: 6 months' imprisonment and/or a fine not exceeding the statutory maximum.
Indictment: 10 years' imprisonment.
Note: If kidnapping or false imprisonment—Life imprisonment.

Links to alternative subjects and offences

6.13 Prostitution: Soliciting, Kerb Crawling, and Placing of Adverts

6.13.1 Prostitute soliciting in the street/public place

This offence is contrary to s 1 Street Offences Act 1959.

> **Offence**
>
> It shall be an offence for a **common prostitute** (whether male or female) to **loiter** or **solicit** in a **street** or **public place** for the purpose of prostitution.
>
> Street Offences Act 1959, s 1(1)

> **Points to prove**
> - ✓ date and location
> - ✓ common prostitute
> - ✓ loitered **or** solicited
> - ✓ in street/public place
> - ✓ for purpose of prostitution

Meanings

Common

Means that the prostitute has either been previously convicted of this offence or cautioned for such conduct.

Prostitute

Means 'any person who offers sexual services for reward' and includes a person acting as a 'clipper'—a person who offers a sexual service, but does not provide it themselves.

Loiter

Means 'dawdle or linger idly about a place, proceeding with frequent pauses' (see **Related cases**).

Solicit

Means to accost and offer oneself.

Street

It includes any bridge, road, lane, footway, subway, square, or passage, whether a thoroughfare or not, which is for the time being open to the public; and the doorways and entrances of premises abutting on a street, and any ground adjoining and open to a street.

6.13.1 Prostitute Soliciting in the Street/Public Place

Public place

This is not defined, but for the purposes of the Public Order Act 1986 and the Crime and Disorder Act 1998 means 'any highway and any place to which at the material time the public has access, on payment or otherwise, as of right or by virtue of express or implied permission'.

Explanatory notes

- Cautioned in this context means when someone who has not previously been convicted of loitering or soliciting for the purpose of prostitution is seen loitering or soliciting in a street or public place for that purpose, and receives a warning. The officer seeing them should obtain the assistance of a second officer as a witness.
- Men or women can be prostitutes.

Related cases

Williamson v Wright [1924] SC(J) 570 'Implying the idea of lingering, slowing down on one particular occasion does not amount to loitering'.

Horton v Mead [1913] All ER 954 'An action unaccompanied by words and need not reach the mind of the person intended to be solicited'.

Smith v Hughes [1960] 2 All ER 859 A prostitute soliciting from a balcony or window of a house adjoining a street is treated as being in the street for the purposes of this offence.

Behrendt v Burridge [1976] 3 All ER 285 A prostitute sitting on a stool in a window under a light is soliciting.

Weisz v Monahan [1962] 1 All ER 664 The placing of notices in windows offering the services of a prostitute has been held not to be soliciting.

Practical considerations

- When both officers, after having kept them under observation, are satisfied by their demeanour and conduct that the person(s) are in fact loitering or soliciting for the purpose of prostitution the officers will tell them what they have seen and caution the person(s). Details of the caution should subsequently be recorded at the police station.
- There are official guidelines for dealing with prostitution and the key element is for all the agencies to work in partnership. An important role for these agencies is to ensure that individuals do not become involved in prostitution in the first place. For those who are involved in prostitution it is essential to create opportunities for them to leave prostitution.
- Prosecution should only be used where there is evidence that the person has been offered exit opportunities and they have been ignored and that person has persistently and voluntarily returned to prostitution. This would include when two cautions as described above have been issued and where exit opportunities and support have been offered and ignored.
- CCTV to be seized.

Summary 6 months

 A fine not exceeding level 2 on the standard scale (after a previous conviction: level 3).

6.13.2 **Kerb crawling (involving motor vehicle)**

This offence is covered by s 1 of the Sexual Offences Act 1985.

Offence

A person commits an offence if he **solicits** another person (or different persons) for the purpose of **prostitution**—

(a) from a motor vehicle while it is in a **street** or **public place**; or

(b) in a street or public place while in the immediate vicinity of a motor vehicle that he has just got out of or off, persistently, in such a manner or in such circumstances as to be likely to cause annoyance to the person (or any of the persons) solicited, or nuisance to other persons in the neighbourhood.   **Sexual Offences Act 1985, s 1(1)**

Points to prove

✓ date and location
✓ solicited
✓ another person
✓ for purpose of prostitution
✓ from a motor vehicle **or**
✓ while in the vicinity of a motor vehicle
✓ in a street/public place
✓ persistently/in circumstances likely to cause annoyance
✓ to the other person
✓ solicited or
✓ nuisance to others in neighbourhood

Meanings

Solicit (see **6.13.1**)

Prostitution (see **6.13.1**)

Street (see **6.13.1**)

Public place (see **6.13.1**)

6.13.3 Kerb Crawling (no Motor Vehicle)

Explanatory notes

It is not necessary that the offender is in the motor vehicle but s/he must be in the immediate vicinity and must have just got out of the vehicle.

Practical considerations

Make a record of registration marks of vehicles suspected to be involved in kerb crawling and a description of the driver.

 Summary   6 months

 A fine not exceeding level 3 on the standard scale.

6.13.3 **Kerb crawling (no motor vehicle)**

Section 2 of the Sexual Offences Act 1985 can be used as an alternative offence where a motor vehicle is not used.

Offence

A person commits an offence if in a **street** or **public place** he persistently **solicits** another person (or different persons) for the purposes of prostitution.

Sexual Offences Act 1985, s 2(1)

Points to prove

✓ date and location
✓ being in a street/public place
✓ persistently solicited another person/different people for purpose of prostitution

---

Meanings

Street (see **6.13.1**)

Public place (see **6.13.1**)

Solicit (see **6.13.1**)

Prostitution (see **6.13.1**)

Practical considerations

• Obtain a description of any persons suspected of kerb crawling.
• Consider CCTV evidence.
• As persistent conduct is required, consider the offence of harassment (see **7.11.1**).

Summary 6 months

 A fine not exceeding level 3 on the standard scale.

6.13.4 Prostitution—placing of adverts in telephone boxes

This offence is covered by s 46 of the Criminal Justice and Police Act 2001.

Offence

A person commits an offence if—
(a) he places on, or in the immediate vicinity of, **a public telephone** an **advertisement** relating to **prostitution**, and
(b) he does so with the intention that the advertisement should come to the attention of any other person or persons.

Criminal Justice and Police Act 2001, s 46(1)

Points to prove
✓ date and location
✓ placed
✓ on/in immediate vicinity
✓ of public telephone
✓ an advertisement
✓ relating to prostitution
✓ with intent
✓ that advert should come to the attention
✓ of another person/persons.

Meanings

Public telephone

This is defined in s 46(5) as:

(a) any telephone which is located in a **public place** and made available for use by the public, or a section of the public, and
(b) where such a telephone is located in or on, or attached to, a kiosk, booth, acoustic hood, shelter or other structure, that structure.

6.13.4 Prostitution—Placing of Adverts in Telephone Boxes

Public place

This is defined in s 46(5) as:

Any place to which the public have or are permitted to have access, whether on payment or otherwise, other than—

(a) any place to which children under the age of 16 years are not permitted to have access, whether by law or otherwise, and

(b) any premises which are wholly or mainly used for residential purposes.

Advertisement

This is defined in s 46(2) as an advertisement which:

(a) is for the services of a prostitute, whether male or female; or

(b) indicates that premises are premises at which such services are offered.

Prostitution   (see 6.13.1)

Explanatory notes

- Section 46(3) states that an advertisement will be considered to be an advertisement for prostitution if a reasonable person would consider it one. However, this is a rebuttable presumption and the defendant may show that it was not such an advertisement.
- If there is evidence to satisfy the other points to prove (eg it is an advertisement for prostitution and it is in public telephone in public place), then the purpose of the advertisement will require little if any further proof; as the very nature of an advertisement is to bring goods or services to the attention of others and it has been placed where it undoubtedly will be seen by others.

Practical considerations

- Seize any advertisement used to commit the offence.
- Many public telephones are situated on privately owned land, such as railway station concourses or shopping centres. These **will** usually be covered by the legislation as the public have access. However, a telephone situated in a nightclub (eg where children under 16 are not permitted) or 'halls of residence' (eg where the general public do not have access) would not fall within the definition.

 Summary   6 months

 6 months' imprisonment and/or a fine not exceeding level 5 on the standard scale.

Links to alternative subjects and offences

Chapter 7

Public Disorder/Nuisance

7.1 Penalty Notices for Disorder

Penalty Notices for Disorder (PNDs) were established by s 1 of the Criminal Justice and Police Act 2001. The number of offences for which a PND can be issued has more than doubled since s 1 first came into force on 12 August 2002. This increase in offences for which PNDs can be issued is likely to continue.

7.1.1 Penalty notices for disorder offences

The offences for which a PND can be issued and the current penalties are as follows:

Being drunk in a highway, other public place or licensed premises

Licensing Act 1872, s 12
£50 penalty fine (see **7.2**)

Throwing fireworks in a thoroughfare

Explosives Act 1875, s 80
£80 penalty fine (see **8.8**)

Trespassing on a railway

British Transport Commission Act 1949, s 55
£50 penalty fine

Throwing stones at trains or other things on railways

British Transport Commission Act 1949, s 56
£50 penalty fine

Sale of alcohol to a person under 18

Licensing Act 2003, s 146(1) and s 146(3)
£80 penalty fine (see **9.1**)

Buying or attempting to buy alcohol by or for a person under 18

Licensing Act 2003, s 149
£80 penalty fine (see **9.1**)

Consumption of alcohol by a person under 18 or allowing such consumption in licensed premises

Licensing Act 2003, s 150

£50 penalty fine (see **9.1**)

Delivery of alcohol to a person under 18 or allowing such delivery

Licensing Act 2003, s 151

£80 penalty fine (see **9.1**)

Selling alcohol to a drunken person

Licensing Act 2003, s 141

£80 penalty fine (see **9.2**)

Disorderly behaviour while drunk in a public place

Criminal Justice Act 1967, s 91

£80 penalty fine (see **7.2**)

Wasting police time or giving false report

Criminal Law Act 1967, s 5(2)

£80 penalty fine (see **11.4**)

Theft

Theft Act 1968, s 1–7

£80 penalty fine (see **3.1**)

Note: The penalty notice for theft can only be issued by a police officer (see **7.1.2 Theft and criminal damage** as to further restrictions).

Destroying or damaging property

Criminal Damage Act 1971, s 1(1)

£80 penalty fine (see **4.4**)

Note: The penalty notice for damage can only be issued by police and designated community support officers (see **7.1.2 Theft and criminal damage** as to further restrictions).

Behaviour likely to cause harassment, alarm, or distress

Public Order Act 1986, s 5

£80 penalty fine (see **7.8**)

Depositing and leaving litter

Environmental Protection Act 1990, s 87

£50 penalty fine (see **7.16**)

Note: Designated community support officers *cannot* issue a penalty notice for litter, although they can issue a fixed penalty notice for litter (see **11.1.1 community support officers** for details).

Consumption of alcohol in designated public place

Criminal Justice and Police Act 2001, s 12

£50 penalty fine (see **9.4**)

Send offensive/false messages on public communications network

Communications Act 2003, s 127(2)

£80 penalty fine (see **7.12**)

Contravene a prohibition imposed by the Fireworks Regulations 2004

Fireworks Act 2003, s 11
£80 penalty fine (see **8.8**)

Knowingly giving a false alarm of fire

Fire and Rescue Services Act 2004, s 49
£80 penalty fine

7.1.2 **Police operational guidance for issuing PNDs**

The Home Office issued operational guidance to police officers for PNDs in March 2005. Edited extracts are shown below and have been updated where appropriate.

- The power to issue a penalty notice is additional to existing methods of disposal. The power to arrest should be exercised in the normal way with reporting for process remaining an option for offences where an arrest is considered unnecessary. No one has a right to demand a penalty notice; similarly, no one should be forced to accept one. The notice must be issued to, and received by, the offender. The use of police bail should never be ruled out where further enquiries are needed to inform proper case disposal decisions.
- Officers **may** issue a penalty notice for wasting police time without DPP consent. Where the offender requests a hearing, a summons will be raised in the normal way and the CPS will give delegated DPP consent.
- A constable, including a special constable who has reason to believe that a person aged 16 years of age or over has committed a penalty offence may give that person a penalty notice for that offence.
- The notice may be issued either on the spot (but it does not have to be issued exactly at the time of the offence) by an officer in uniform, or at a police station by an authorized officer. (An authorized officer is any officer authorized to issue penalty notices by the Chief Officer for the area in which he or she operates.)
- Paying a penalty notice discharges liability to conviction for the offence.
- On issue the recipient may elect to pay the penalty or request a court hearing. They must do one or the other within 21 days of the date of issue.
- Failure to do either may result in the registration of a fine of one and a half times the penalty amount or proceedings against them for the penalty offence.

Pre-conditions for issuing a penalty notice

Officers may issue a penalty notice **only** where:

- they have reason to believe a person has committed a penalty offence and they have sufficient evidence to support a successful prosecution (interviews and questioning must be consistent with the practice and procedures established by PACE 1984, Code C);

- the offence is not too serious and is of a nature suitable for being dealt with by a penalty notice;
- the suspect is suitable, compliant, and able to understand what is going on;
- a second or subsequent offence, which is known, does not overlap with the penalty notice offence (but see **Explanatory notes** below);
- the offence(s) involve(s) no one below the age of 16 (except in pilot areas for 10–15 year olds);
- sufficient evidence as to the suspect's age, identity, and place of residence exists.

Explanatory notes

- Officers might consider it appropriate to issue a penalty notice in association with any other offence, including where a warning, formal caution, or summons is issued, police bail set, or a charge brought or refused for the second or subsequent offence. This is provided that the subsequent or non-penalty offence can clearly be said not to 'overlap with' or be 'associated with' the first penalty offence. This may occur where a person is suspected of being drunk and disorderly or committing an offence under s 5 of the POA and they are found, upon arrest, to be in possession of a small quantity of cannabis or stolen credit cards for which, respectively, a caution and charge are deemed appropriate.

- Officers might consider it appropriate to issue a penalty notice in addition to dealing with a suspect for a second or subsequent offence in another way. However, discretion should be exercised to ensure that a penalty notice is not issued in addition to dealing with a very serious offence.

- Where a penalty notice is issued for a penalty offence and it subsequently comes to light after the incident that a more serious or non-penalty offence was committed on the same occasion, officers may bring a charge for the subsequent offence. Payment of a penalty discharges the recipient's liability to conviction only for the offence for which the penalty notice was issued. Ultimately, it will be for the CPS to determine, based on the facts of the case, whether a prosecution may be brought, in respect of the subsequent offence, and for the courts to decide whether or not to allow such a prosecution.

Offences for which a PND will not be appropriate

Issuing a penalty notice **will not** be appropriate where -

- there has been any injury to any person or any realistic threat or risk of injury to any person (officers may seek the views of any potential victim before making a decision on the most appropriate course of action);
- there has been a substantial financial/material loss to the private property of an individual;

- a penalty offence is committed in association with another penalty notice offence;
- there are grounds for believing that the terms of the Protection from Harassment Act 1997 might apply;
- the behaviour constitutes part of a pattern of intimidation;
- the offence relates to domestic violence;
- it is a football-related offence and it may be appropriate for a court to consider imposing a Football Banning Order;
- the victim is not compliant;
- the licensee has committed an offence (but may be appropriate for bar staff when taking action against premises found or known to be serving alcohol to under age drinkers).

Offenders for which a PND will not be appropriate

- A penalty notice *may not* be issued to a person below 16 years of age (except in the pilot scheme for 10–15 year olds).
- A penalty notice **will not** be appropriate where the suspect is unable to understand what is being offered to them, for example, those with a mental handicap or mental disorder, or where the suspect is drunk or under the influence of drugs. If a suspect is impaired by the influence of drugs or alcohol, and the officer is satisfied as to his/her identity and place of residence, it may be appropriate to consider issuing a PND at a later time (eg the next day). The officer should be satisfied that the suspect's offending behaviour has ceased, or take steps to ensure that this is the case. Officers should consider whether a suspect might have a substance addiction problem. In such circumstances a penalty notice may not be an appropriate response and another form of disposal should be considered and where possible, a referral made to an appropriate local scheme. For example, a drug treatment scheme.
- Similarly a penalty notice **will not** be appropriate where the suspect is—
  - ◆ uncooperative;
  - ◆ unable to provide a satisfactory address for enforcement purposes;
  - ◆ known to be already subject to-
    - ▪ a custodial sentence, including Home Detention Curfew;
    - ▪ a community penalty other than a fine, including Anti-Social Behaviour Orders (which may constitute a breach).

Theft and criminal damage

- PND disposal may only be used for thefts (retail/commercial only) under £200 and criminal damage under £500. (Thefts involving property over the value of £100 would not normally be suitable for PND disposal and explanation as well as the agreement of the victim/retailer would be required.)
- It is expected that in most cases of theft suitable for PND disposal the property will have been recovered, although the value of the property will be relevant in assessing seriousness.

- PND disposal for criminal damage over £300 would be exceptional (except for public property) and require explanation as well as the agreement of the victim/retailer.
- The PND for theft can only be issued by a police officer. Whereas a PND for damage can only be issued by police and designated community support officers.

Jointly committed offences

An officer may issue a penalty notice **only** where:
- the offence(s) involve(s) no one below the age of 16 years (except Pilot Areas for 10–15 year olds);
- where a juvenile, aged under 16, and an individual aged 16 years or over are jointly responsible for a penalty offence, a penalty notice will not be appropriate for the offender aged over 16 and existing forms of disposal should be considered. This should avoid any allegations of unfairness resulting from the older offender being able to discharge their liability to conviction.

Identification

An officer may issue a penalty notice **only** where:
- sufficient evidence as to age, identity, and place of residence exists. Age, identity, and address checks must be rigorous. Where doubt as to identity exists officers should exercise the powers under s 24 PACE 1984. Where possible, documentary evidence as to age, identity, and place of residence should be sought in preference to non-physical sources, eg electoral register or PNC checks;
- if fingerprints are taken this will support identification for any PND issued for a penalty offence;
- DNA and fingerprints may be taken with consent for a recordable offence where the suspect is not arrested. If DNA or fingerprints are taken with consent, officers should ensure that the appropriate consent forms are completed.

PNC entry

- Suspects issued with penalty notices will not receive a criminal record, but this does not preclude the retention of information as police intelligence.
- A facility is available on PNC, which allows an entry to be recorded that does not constitute a criminal record but is accessible for police information. This entry will not constitute a criminal record, but will enable DNA, fingerprints, and a photograph to be logged against the entry when appropriate.
- Issue of a PND may be used as evidence of bad character under s 101 of the Criminal Justice Act 2003.

PNDs and a criminal record check

In an Enhanced Disclosure issued by the CRB, a PND could be referred to, if the details of the behaviour leading to the PND were relevant to the matter at hand (eg the applicant's suitability to work with children).

However, the mere fact that a PND had been issued would not make it relevant.

PNDs and ASBOs

- Acceptance of a PND, and subsequent payment of the penalty, discharges all liability for that offence. However, this does not preclude the information being used in the civil context of seeking an ASBO.
- The fact that a PND has been issued can be disclosed in an ASBO hearing as this goes towards establishing a pattern of behaviour.

Links to alternative subjects and offences

7.2 Drunk and Disorderly in Public Places

Section 91 of the Criminal Justice Act 1967 and s 12 of the Licensing Act 1872 deal with offences to do with drunkenness in public places. This subject will cover two aspects: namely that of being drunk and disorderly and of being drunk in a highway.

7.2.1 Drunk and disorderly

Offence

It is an offence to behave in a disorderly manner in a public place whilst being drunk.   Criminal Justice Act 1967, s 91(1)

Points to prove

✓ date and location
✓ while in a public place
✓ whilst drunk
✓ guilty of disorderly behaviour

Meanings

Disorderly manner

Is defined by *The Oxford English Dictionary* as 'unruly or offensive behaviour'.

Public place

Includes any highway and other premises or place to which at the material time the public have or are permitted to have access, whether on payment or otherwise.

Drunk

Means the everyday meaning of 'drunk'. Defined by the *Collins* and *Oxford English Dictionaries* as: 'intoxicated with alcohol to the extent of losing control over normal physical and mental functions' and 'having drunk intoxicating liquor to an extent which affects steady self control' (*R v Tagg* [2001] EWCA Crim 1230, CA).

Explanatory notes

• It does not apply to a person who is disorderly as a result of **sniffing glue** or **using drugs**. The common meaning of 'drunk' does not cater for such conduct, as confirmed by *Neale v RMJE (a minor)* (1985) 80 Cr App R 20.

- If the offender has taken liquor and drugs, the court must be satisfied that the loss of self-control was due to the liquor and not the drugs.
- Whether or not someone was in a state of drunkenness was a matter of fact for the court/jury to decide.
- A landing in a block of flats, to which access was gained by way of key, security code, tenant's intercom, or caretaker, has been held **not** to be a public place because only those admitted by or with the implied consent of the occupiers had access.

Related cases

Williams (Richard) v DPP [1993] 3 All ER 365, QBD The landing in a block of flats, with access gained by a key code lock, was held not to have been a 'public place' because entry was restricted to residents, people admitted by residents, and trades people with knowledge of the code.

R (on the application of H) v CPS [2005] EWHC (Admin) 2459, QBD Conduct must be disorderly whilst drunk to satisfy the offence. Suspect must be both drunk and disorderly at the time of the arrest.

Practical considerations

- This offence can be dealt with by means of a penalty notice for disorder (PND)(see **7.1.1**).
- Police Operational Guidance issued by the Home Office gives examples of when it would be inappropriate to issue a PND (see **7.1.2**).
- Consideration must be given to the CPS advice given in the public order charging standards; see the general principles of public order and the specific guidance for drunk and disorderly.

 Summary   6 months

A fine not exceeding level 3 on the standard scale.

7.2.2 **Drunk on a highway**

Section 12 of the Licensing Act 1872 creates one of the most commonly used offences: that of being 'drunk and **incapable**'. In addition, the section also includes other less used offences relating to being drunk on a highway, public place, or licensed premises, with a loaded firearm and in charge of various means of conveyance and animals.

Offence

Every person found drunk on any highway or other public place, whether a building or not, or on any licensed premises, shall be liable to a penalty. Every person who is drunk while in charge on any highway or other public place of any carriage, horse, cattle, or steam engine, or who is drunk when in possession of any loaded firearms, shall be liable to a penalty.

Licensing Act 1872, s 12

Points to prove

Drunk and incapable

✓ date and location
✓ drunk
✓ incapable
✓ highway/public place/licensed premises

Other drunk offences

✓ drunk
✓ whilst in charge of
✓ pedal cycle/carriage/horse/cattle/steam engine **or** when in possession of a loaded firearm
✓ on/in a highway/public place

Meanings

Drunk (see **7.2.1**)

Public place (see **7.2.1**)

Incapable

Means 'incapable of looking after oneself and getting home safely'.

Carriage

Includes vehicles such as trailers and bicycles (whether being ridden or pushed).

Cattle

Includes sheep and pigs.

Firearm (see **8.1.1**)

Explanatory notes

- A motor vehicle is a 'carriage'. However, it may be more appropriate to consider the offence of driving or being in charge while over the prescribed limit under s 4 of the Road Traffic Act 1988 (see **10.10**).
- Case law suggests that residents in licensed premises cannot be convicted of this offence outside the permitted hours when the premises are closed to the public. However, the duty of the licensee to prevent drunkenness on the premises is unaffected.
- See also the related offences of drunk and disorderly in a public place (see **7.2.1**).

7.2.2 Drunk on a Highway

- Section 2 of the Licensing Act 1902 also makes it an offence to be drunk in charge of a child who appears to be under the age of 7 years.

Practical considerations

- This offence can be dealt with by means of a penalty notice for disorder (PND) (see **7.1.1**).
- Officers should frequently assess the condition of drunks which can sometimes be life threatening (eg inhalation of vomit).
- Be aware that other medical conditions could give the impression that somebody is drunk (eg diabetic coma). It is best to convey the person to hospital if there are any doubts.
- Section 34 of the Criminal Justice Act 1972 provides a police constable with a power to take a drunken offender to a 'detoxification' or alcohol treatment centre. While a person is being so taken s/he shall be deemed to be in lawful custody.

 Summary   6 months

 Drunk and incapable
A fine not exceeding level 1 on the standard scale.

Drunk in charge of firearm/carriage/horse/steam engine
1 month imprisonment or a fine not exceeding level 1 on the standard scale.

Links to alternative subjects and offences

7.3 **Breach of the Peace**

'Breach of the peace' provides a number of powers: one of which is to arrest and another is to intervene and/or detain by force, in order to prevent any action likely to result in a breach of the peace in both public and private places.

It is not a criminal offence, but a 'complaint' is laid before the court with an application made for the individual to be bound over to keep the peace.

Complaint

Breach of the peace

Used to mean 'any interruption of the peace and good order which ought to prevail in a civilised society'.

However, it was redefined in *R v Howell* [1982] QB 416, QBD and the following is the current test that must be applied: 'a breach of the peace may occur where harm is done or is likely to be done to a person, or to his property in his presence, or he is in fear of being harmed through assault, affray, riot or other disturbance'.

Points to prove
- ✓ behave in a manner
- ✓ whereby breach of the peace
- ✓ was occasioned/likely to be occasioned

Court powers

- Section 115 of the Magistrates' Courts Act 1980 provides magistrates' courts with the power to order a person to be 'bound over' to keep the peace and/or be of good behaviour towards a particular person (often a neighbour or partner who has complained about their behaviour). Any failure to comply with the conditions of an order is similar to committing an offence.
- The power of a magistrates' court on the complaint of any person to adjudge any other person to enter into a recognizance, with or without sureties, to keep the peace or to be of good behaviour towards the complainant shall be exercised by order on complaint.
- If any person ordered by a magistrates' court (above) to enter into a recognizance, with or without sureties, to keep the peace or to be of good behaviour fails to comply with the order, the court may commit him to custody for a period not exceeding 6 months or until he sooner complies with the order.

Explanatory notes

- The law and practice for dealing with bind-overs may require re-examination in the light of the adverse decision of the European

Court of Human Rights in *Hashman and Harrup v United Kingdom* (2000) 30 EHRR 241 where the notion of 'good behaviour' was found to breach the European Convention on Human Rights because it was too vague and uncertain. Any future orders made on this basis alone might be subject to challenge.

• In the case of *Steel v United Kingdom* (1998) 28 EHRR 603 it was held that the concept of breach of the peace had been clarified by the courts to the extent that it was sufficiently established that a breach of the peace was committed only when a person caused harm, or appeared likely to cause harm, to persons or property or acted in a manner the natural consequence of which was to provoke others to violence. It was a procedure that came within the ambit of the Human Rights Convention and is lawful so long as the action taken is proportionate to the nature of the disturbance and also having regard to the values of freedom of expression and assembly.

• Notwithstanding that for some purposes proceedings under s 115 are treated as criminal proceedings, since the procedure is by way of complaint it is primarily a civil process. The jurisdiction of the justices does not depend on a summons being issued, nor does the absence of a complaint in the form prescribed invalidate the procedure.

Related cases

Hashman and Harrup v United Kingdom [2000] Crim LR 185, ECHR Although they had disturbed a hunt by blowing a horn and shouting at the hounds, the defendants had not acted violently or threatened violence. The court stated that they had behaved *contra bonos mores* (behaviour seen as 'wrong rather than right in the judgement of the majority of contemporary fellow citizens') and should be bound over to be of good behaviour for a year. The ECHR stated that the expression 'to be of good behaviour' was imprecise and did not give sufficiently clear guidance for their future behaviour. Held that Art 10 (freedom of expression) had been violated, binding over for *contra bonos mores* behaviour was incompatible with the Convention and rights such as freedom of expression or assembly.

R (on the application of Hawkes) v DPP [2005] EWHC 3046 (Admin), QBD Verbal abuse not enough to commit breach of the peace.

R (on the application of Laporte) v Chief Constable of Gloucester-shire [2006] UKHL 55, HL Three coaches stopped and searched under a s 60 authority on intelligence that occupants would cause disorder at RAF base and returned back to London. QBD determined that police actions were a reasonable and honest belief in preventing an apprehended breach of the peace. However, the HL ruled that the police had acted unlawfully because a breach of the peace was not 'imminent' at the time the coaches were stopped; thus interfering with the protesters' rights under Art 10 and Art 11 and was disproportionate.

McGrogan v Chief Constable of Cleveland Police [2002] EWCA Civ 86, CA This test should be used where a person was to be detained in connection with an actual or threatened breach of the peace.

Continued detention is limited to circumstances where there was a real, rather than a fanciful fear, based on all the circumstances, that if released the detained person would commit/renew a breach of the peace within a relatively short time. It cannot be justified on the ground that sooner or later the prisoner, if released, is likely to breach the peace. The officer making the decision had to have an honest belief, based on objectively reasonable grounds, that further detention was necessary to prevent such a breach of the peace.

It is good practice if the police treat any person detained for a breach of the peace under the PACE COP (see **12.2.1**).

Practical considerations

* Because a breach of the peace is not an offence, a person cannot be granted bail in connection with it.
* A breach of the peace can occur on private premises. If the police have genuine grounds to apprehend such a breach, they have a right to enter private premises to make an arrest or ensure that one does not occur. The right of entry is not absolute, but must be weighed against the degree of disturbance that is threatened.
* An officer must not remain on private premises once a breach has finished (assuming it is not likely to re-occur), but so long as the officer is lawfully on the premises in the first instance, they are entitled to be given the opportunity to withdraw.
* There are, of course, other powers of entry for protecting life or property (the principal one being s 17 of PACE) that may be of assistance. On some occasions one of the parties involved may have called the police and lawfully invited an officer onto the premises for his/her assistance (albeit a breach has not occurred).
* Officers attending private premises with officials such as bailiffs may have to enter them to prevent a breach of the peace while a Court Order of some type is being enforced.
* If an individual has been arrested to prevent a breach of the peace, it is not always necessary to take him/her before a court. There is no power to continue the person's detention beyond the time where a recurrence or renewal of the breach of the peace is likely. If there is such a danger then s/he should be detained for court (see *McGrogan v Chief Constable of Cleveland Police* [2002] EWCA Civ 86, CA case above).
* Release may occur at any stage, not only after the offender has arrived at the police station, but also while the officer is detaining him/her at the scene or after s/he has taken the offender from the scene.

 Summary   6 months

 Complaint to be laid to be bound over to keep the peace. Breach of the order may result in up to 6 months' imprisonment.

Links to alternative subjects and offences

7.4 Riot and Violent Disorder

The Public Order Act 1986 provides the three statutory offences of riot, violent disorder, and affray. They descend in order of their gravity. In this subject, the first two offences, riot and violent disorder will be covered.

7.4.1 Riot

Offence
Where twelve or more persons who are present together use or threaten unlawful violence for a common purpose and the conduct of them (taken together) is such as would cause a person of reasonable firmness present at the scene to fear for his personal safety, each of the persons using unlawful violence for the common purpose is guilty of riot.

Public Order Act 1986, s 1(1)

Points to prove
✓ date and location
✓ 12 or more persons present together used/threatened unlawful violence for common purpose
✓ and conduct would cause fear for personal safety
✓ to a person of reasonable firmness

Meanings

Present together
Means that all the people concerned were actually present at the scene of the incident aiming for a common purpose.

Common purpose
The common purpose may be inferred from conduct (s 1(3)).

Violence
It includes violent conduct towards property as well as violent conduct towards persons. It is not restricted to conduct causing, or intended to cause, injury or damage, but includes any other violent conduct (eg throwing at or towards a person a missile of a kind capable of causing injury, which does not hit or falls short).

The person of reasonable firmness
This test is an objective one by which the court can judge the seriousness of the disturbance using a fixed standard—namely whether or not a person of reasonable firmness would be put in fear by the conduct.

Explanatory notes

- It is immaterial whether or not the 12 or more use or threaten unlawful violence simultaneously (s 1(2)).
- No **person of reasonable firmness** need actually be, or likely to be, present at the scene (s 1(4)).
- A court will not consider this hypothetical person (of reasonable firmness) to be someone who is the target for the people who are involved in the disturbance, but someone who is a bystander to the incident (*R v Sanchez The Times*, 6 March 1996).
- Riot may be committed in private as well as in public places (s 1(5)).
- The common purpose can be either lawful or unlawful, and must be proved either by admission or as above by inference from conduct.

Defences

Intention

(1) A person is guilty of riot only if he intends to use violence or is aware that his conduct may be violent.

(2) A person is guilty of violent disorder or affray only if he intends to use or threatens violence or is aware that his conduct may be violent or threaten violence.

...

(7) Subsection 6(2) does not affect the determination for the purposes of riot or violent disorder of the number of persons who use or threaten violence. Public Order Act 1986, s 6(1), 6(2), 6(7)

Effect of drunkenness or intoxication

(5) For the purposes of this section a person whose awareness is impaired by intoxication shall be taken to be aware of that of which he would be aware if not intoxicated, unless he shows either that his intoxication was not self induced or that it was caused solely by the taking or administration of a substance in the course of medical treatment.

Public Order Act 1986, s 6(5)

Defence notes

- Intent or awareness must be proved. Even if intent can only be proved against two people but they were part of a group of, say, 13 who can be shown to have used unlawful violence, the two can still be convicted of riot.
- Intoxication means any intoxication, whether caused by drink, drugs or other means, or by a combination of means.
- The intoxication provision applies to the mental elements of the following public order offences:
  - ◆ s 1 riot—unlawful violence,
  - ◆ s 2 violent disorder—unlawful violence,
  - ◆ s 3 affray—unlawful violence,
  - ◆ s 4 threatening words or behaviour, and
  - ◆ s 5 harassment, alarm, or distress.

Practical considerations

- Please refer to **8.11** for details of powers to stop and search when it is anticipated that serious violence may take place, and to remove masks.
- The consent of the Director of Public Prosecutions is required.
- Crown Prosecution Service advice: when investigating this offence consideration must be given to the advice offered in the public order charging standards.
- Court evidence: a person who was feeling threatened does not actually have to be a 'person of reasonable firmness', but his/her evidence may support other evidence that will satisfy the court that a 'person of reasonable firmness' would have been in fear of his personal safety had he been present. Such evidence could be provided by:
  - ♦ witnesses including police officers and bystanders (who may or may not be of reasonable firmness);
  - ♦ the types of injuries sustained;
  - ♦ damage to property;
  - ♦ security cameras;
  - ♦ news photographs or film footage.

 Indictable only   None

 10 years' imprisonment.

7.4.2 **Violent disorder**

Offence

Where three or more persons who are present together use or threaten unlawful violence and the conduct of them (taken together) is such as would cause a person of reasonable firmness present at the scene to fear for his personal safety, each of the persons using or threatening unlawful violence is guilty of violent disorder.   Public Order Act 1986, s 2(1)

Points to prove

✓ date and location
✓ used/threatened unlawful violence
✓ 3 persons present together

> ✓ who use/threaten unlawful violence and their conduct (taken together)
> ✓ would cause a person of reasonable firmness present at the scene
> ✓ to fear for his/her personal safety

Meanings

Present together (see **7.4.1**)

Person of reasonable firmness (see **7.4.1**)

Violence (see **7.4.1**)

Explanatory notes

- It is immaterial whether or not the three or more use or threaten unlawful violence simultaneously (s 2(2)).
- No person of reasonable firmness need actually be, or likely to be, present at the scene (s 2(3)).
- Violent disorder may be committed in private as well as in public places (s 2(4)).
- Three or more persons means that as long as 3 or more people can be proved to have been present together and using violence, even if intent can only be proved against one person, then that person can be convicted—it is not necessary that 'three or more persons' be charged with the offence. Following *R v Mahroof* [1988] Crim LR 72, CA it is good practice to specify 'others' in the charge, even if their identity is not known and they were not arrested.

Defences

Intention (see s 6(2) and s 6(7) 7.4.1)

Effect of drunkenness or intoxication (see 7.4.1)

Defence notes

Intent

To use or threaten violence must, therefore, be proved for each individual. This means that even if only one person has the intent they can still be charged if it can be proved that at least two others were using or threatening violence and they were present together. Words alone may suffice for the threats.

Intoxication (see **Defence notes** in **7.4.1**)

Related cases

R v Mahroof [1988] Crim LR 72, CA There must be 3 people involved in the violence or threatened violence. Two of the 3 charged were acquitted. There had been others who had not been mentioned in the charge. If they had, M could have been convicted. In the absence of three people M's appeal was allowed.

R v Fleming and Robinson The Times, 13 February 1989, CA This case followed *Mahroof*. There was no evidence of 3 or more people being involved so the appeal was allowed.

Practical considerations

- Please refer to **8.11** for details of powers to stop and search when it is anticipated that serious violence may take place, and powers to remove masks.
- Crown Prosecution Service advice: when investigating this offence consideration must be given to the advice offered in the public order charging standards and the specific guidance for violent disorder.

 Either way 🕐 None

🏛 **Summary**: 6 months' imprisonment and/or a fine not exceeding the statutory maximum.
Indictment: 5 years' imprisonment and/or a fine.

Links to alternative subjects and offences

SSS Stop, search and seize powers **E&S** Entry and search powers

7.5 **Affray**

The purpose of the offence of affray is to prevent incidents of public disorder and the fear of it. For the offence of affray to be committed, the threat of violence needs to be capable of affecting others. The primary objective of the offence is to protect the general public, not the participants in the violence.

Offence

A person is guilty of affray if he uses or threatens unlawful violence towards another and his conduct is such as would cause a person of reasonable firmness present at the scene to fear for his personal safety.

Public Order Act 1986, s 3(1)

Points to prove
- ✓ date and location
- ✓ used/threatened
- ✓ unlawful violence
- ✓ towards another
- ✓ and his/her conduct
- ✓ was such as would cause
- ✓ a person of reasonable firmness
- ✓ to fear for personal safety.

Meanings

Threatens

For the purposes of this section a threat cannot be made by the use of words alone (s 3(3)).

Violence

Section 8 of the Act provides a definition: it means any violent conduct, but unlike the related offences of riot and violent disorder (see **7.4**), in the case of affray the definition does not include violent conduct towards property.

Conduct

Where two or more persons use or threaten the unlawful violence, it is the conduct of them taken together that must be considered for the purposes of sub-s 3(1) (s 3(2)).

Reasonable firmness

- No person of reasonable firmness need actually be, or be likely to be, present at the scene (s 3(4)).
- The concept of the person of reasonable firmness meets the same criteria as riot (see **7.4.1**)

Explanatory notes

- Affray may be committed in private as well as in public places (s 3(5)).
- Notionally there are at least three parties involved in an affray:
  - ◆ the individual making threats;
  - ◆ the person subject of the threats;
  - ◆ the bystander of reasonable firmness who does not need to be physically present as long as evidence is available to prove that such a person would be affected.

Defences

Intent (see s 6(2) **7.4.1**)

Effects of drunkenness or intoxication (see Defence **7.4.1**)

Defence notes (see Defence notes 7.4.2)

Related cases

R v Plavecz [2002] Crim LR 837 A doorman pushed a female customer out of a nightclub doorway and she fell over. He was charged with assault and affray. The court stated that where the incident was basically one-on-one it was inappropriate to use the public order offence of affray.

I v DPP, M v DPP, H v DPP The Times, 9 March 2001, HL About 40 young people were 'hanging around' doing nothing in particular and some were carrying petrol bombs. None of them lit or threw a petrol bomb about in a threatening way and there was no actual disturbance. On the arrival of the police the gang scattered and the three defendants threw away their petrol bombs as they ran off. The House of Lords held that the mere possession of a weapon, without the threatening situation, would not be enough to constitute a threat of unlawful violence. The wording of affray states that the offender must be 'using/threatening unlawful violence towards another', what amounted to such a threat was a question of fact in each case, but in this instance, there were no threats made and no violence was used.

Practical considerations

- Unlike the other related offences (riot and violent disorder), affray can be committed by one person acting alone. However, where two or more people are involved in the violence or threatened violence, it is the conduct of them taken together that will be used to determine whether or not the offence is made out.
- Please refer to **8.11** for details of powers to stop and search when it is anticipated that serious violence may take place and to remove masks.
- When investigating this offence consideration must be given to the CPS public order charging standards for affray.
- See **8.11** for powers to stop and search for knives and offensive weapons.

7.5 Affray

- A person who was feeling threatened does not actually have to be a 'person of reasonable firmness', but his/her evidence may support other evidence that will satisfy the court that a 'person of reasonable firmness' would have been in fear of his personal safety had he been present. Such evidence could be provided by:
  - witnesses including police officers and bystanders (who may or may not be of reasonable firmness);
  - the types of injuries sustained;
  - damage to property (for affray, the violence must be directed at a person, although accompanying damage may have occurred);
  - security cameras;
  - news photographs or film footage.

 Either way   None

Summary: 6 months' imprisonment and/or a fine not exceeding the statutory maximum.
Indictment: 3 years' imprisonment.

Links to alternative subjects and offences

7.6 Fear or Provocation of Violence

The Public Order Act 1986 deals with offences and powers relating to the preservation of public order. Section 4 creates the offence of causing fear or provocation of violence, often known as 'threatening behaviour'.

Offence

A person is guilty of an offence if he—
(a) uses towards another person threatening, abusive or insulting words or behaviour, or
(b) distributes or displays to another person any writing, sign or other visible representation which is threatening, abusive or insulting,
with intent to cause that person to believe that immediate unlawful violence will be used against him or another by any person, or to provoke the immediate use of unlawful violence by that person or another, or whereby that person is likely to believe that such violence will be used or it is likely that such violence will be provoked.   Public Order Act 1986, s 4(1)

Points to prove

s 4(1)(a) offence

✓ date and location
✓ use towards another person
✓ threatening/abusive/insulting words or behaviour
✓ with intent to **either**
✓ cause that person to believe
✓ that immediate unlawful violence
✓ would be used against him/her/another
✓ by any person **or**
✓ provoke the immediate use of unlawful violence
✓ by that person/another **or**
✓ that person was likely to believe
✓ that such violence would be used or
✓ likely that such violence would be provoked

s 4(1)(b) offence

✓ date and location
✓ distribute/display
✓ to another
✓ a writing/sign/visible representation
✓ which was threatening/abusive/insulting
✓ with intent to **either**
✓ (continue from this point in above offence—to end)

Meanings

Threatening

Includes verbal and physical threats, and also violent conduct.

Abusive

Means using degrading or reviling language.

Insulting

Has been held to mean scorning, especially if insolent or contemptuous.

Intent   (see **4.1**)

Distribute

Means spread or disperse.

Display

Means a visual presentation.

Explanatory notes

- Limited circumstances apply for an offence in private: An offence under this section may be committed in a public or a private place, except that no offence is committed where the words or behaviour are used, or the writing, sign or other visible representation is distributed or displayed, by a person inside a dwelling and the other person is also inside that or another dwelling (s 4(2)).
- No offence will be committed if the display is inside a dwelling, if it is displayed only to people also inside, although if it is displayed from inside to people outside the dwelling, then an offence under s 4 may be committed.
- Insulting does not mean behaviour that might give rise to irritation or resentment (eg running onto a tennis court at Wimbledon blowing a whistle and stopping the game—*Brutus v Cozens* [1972] 2 All ER 1297, HL). However, each of these will be a question of fact to be decided by the relevant court in the light of all the circumstances.

Defences

Intent

A person is guilty of an offence under s 4 only if he intends his words or behaviour, or the writing, sign or other visible representation, to be threatening, abusive or insulting.   Public Order Act 1986, s 6(3)

Intoxication   (see intoxication defence in **7.4.1**)

Related cases

DPP v Ramos [2000] Crim LR 768, QBD If the victim believes that the threatened violence will occur at any moment, this will be sufficient for the 'immediacy' requirement. Also see *R v Horseferry Road Stipendiary ex parte Siadatan* [1991] 1 QB 260.

Swanston v DPP (1996) 161 JP 203, QBD A witness/officer present when the offence took place can give evidence to prove the threatening behaviour and intent, even if the victim does not give evidence.

Atkin v DPP [1989] Crim LR 581, QBD The person threatened should be present. The threatening words must be addressed directly to another person who is present and either within earshot or aimed at someone thought to be in earshot.

Simcock v Rhodes [1977] Crim LR 751, QBD Conduct can be threatening or abusive or insulting.

R v Ambrose (1973) 57 Crim App R 538, CA Words that are rude or offensive may not necessarily amount to abusive or insulting behaviour.

Brutus v Cozens [1972] 2 All ER 1297, HL Whether behaviour is insulting or not is a question of fact for justices to decide.

Practical considerations

- If this offence is **racially or religiously aggravated** the more serious offence under s 31(1)(a) of the Crime and Disorder Act 1998 should be considered (see **7.10.4**). Also be aware that ss 17 to 23 of the Public Order Act 1986 relate to racial hatred offences (see **7.9**).
- It is not duplicitous if the three alternatives 'threatening, abusive or insulting', are charged, though all three need not be present.
- When investigating this offence consideration must be given to the CPS advice given in the public order charging standards.

RRA

 Summary   6 months

 6 months' imprisonment and/or a fine not exceeding level 5 on the standard scale.

Links to alternative subjects and offences

7.7 Intentional Harassment, Alarm, or Distress

Section 4A of the Public Order Act 1986 creates the offence of using threatening, abusive or insulting words or behaviour or disorderly behaviour, or displaying any writing, sign, or other representation that is threatening, abusive, or insulting. All references are to the Public Order Act 1986 unless otherwise stated.

Offence

A person is guilty of an offence if, with intent to cause a person harassment, alarm or distress, he:

(a) uses threatening, abusive or insulting words or behaviour, or disorderly behaviour, or

(b) displays any writing, sign or other visible representation which is threatening, abusive or insulting,

thereby causing that or another person harassment, alarm or distress.

Public Order Act 1986, s 4A(1)

Points to prove

s 4A(1)(a) offence

✓ used threatening/abusive/insulting words/behaviour **or** used disorderly behaviour

✓ towards another person

✓ with intent to cause harassment/alarm/distress

✓ and caused that/another person

✓ harassment/alarm/distress

s 4A(1)(b) offence

✓ displayed threatening/abusive/insulting writing/sign/other visible representation

✓ with intent to cause a person harassment/alarm/distress

✓ and caused that/another person

✓ harassment/alarm/distress

Meanings

Harassment

Means to subject someone to constant and repeated physical and/or verbal persecution.

Alarm

Means a frightened anticipation of danger.

7.7 Intentional Harassment, Alarm, or Distress

Distress
Means to cause trouble, pain, anguish, or hardship.

Intent (see **4.1**)

Threatening (see **7.6**)

Abusive (see **7.6**)

Insulting (see **7.6**)

Explanatory notes

- This offence is very similar to the offence under s 5 (see **7.8**), but this offence requires proof of i**ntent** to cause alarm, harassment, or distress.
- An offence under this section may be committed in a public or private place, but no offence is committed if the words or behaviour are used, or the writing, sign, or other visible representation is displayed, inside a dwelling and the person who it affects is also inside that or another dwelling.
- Although this offence can be committed on private premises there is no specific power of entry.

Defences

It is a defence for the accused to prove:
(a) that he was inside a dwelling and had no reason to believe that the words or behaviour used, or the writing, sign or other visible representation displayed, would be heard or seen by a person outside that or any other dwelling, OR
(b) that his conduct was reasonable.   Public Order Act 1986, s 4A(3)

Related cases

Lodge v DPP The Times, 26 October 1988, QBD It is not necessary that the person alarmed was concerned about physical danger to himself, it could be alarm about an unconnected third party.

DPP v Orum [1988] 3 All ER 449, QBD A police officer can be subjected to harassment, alarm, or distress, but only where the words or behaviour amounted to more than what s/he would regularly see or hear in the normal cause of his/her duty.

Practical considerations

- There must be evidence of intent to cause harassment, alarm, or distress.
- Harassment, alarm, or distress must be caused.
- Where there is no evidence of the intent or that harassment, alarm, or distress was caused consider s 5 (see **7.8**).
- Where the extent of the behaviour results in the fear or realization of violence consider s 4(1) (see **7.6**) or assault charges (see **2.1,2.2** or **2.3**).

- If there is repeated harassment of individuals consider s 1 of the Protection from Harassment Act 1997 (see **7.11.1**).
- If a power of entry is required consider breach of the peace or whether the offence is serious enough to require action under s 4 (see **7.6**).
- Consider the behaviour in the context of the circumstances—behaviour that causes distress to an elderly woman may not be distressful to a young man.
- If other people, besides the police officer and the defendant, are present include that fact in your evidence.
- If this offence is racially and/or religiously aggravated consider the more serious offence under s 31 of the Crime and Disorder Act 1998 (see **7.10.4**). Also be aware that ss 17 to 23 of the Public Order Act 1986 relate to racial hatred offences (see **7.9**).
- On trial on indictment, where a racially or religiously aggravated form of this offence is charged and the jury find the defendant not guilty of that offence, they may find him/her guilty of the basic offence. But in a summary trial at magistrates' court there is no provision for such an alternative verdict, therefore also charge the defendant with the basic offence.

RRA **SSS** **E&S**

 Summary   6 months

 Summary: 6 months' imprisonment and/or a fine not exceeding level 5 on the standard scale.

Links to alternative subjects and offences

RRA Racially or religiously aggravated offence   **SSS** Stop, search and seize powers   **E&S** Entry and search powers

7.7 Intentional Harassment, Alarm, or Distress

7.8 Threatening/Abusive Words/Behaviour

Section 5 of the Public Order Act 1986 creates an offence of being threatening, abusive or insulting in a way which is likely to cause harassment, alarm, or distress.

> **Offence**
>
> A person is guilty of an offence if he—
> (a) uses threatening, abusive or insulting words or behaviour, or disorderly behaviour, or
> (b) displays any writing sign or other visible representation which is threatening, abusive or insulting,
>
> within the hearing or sight of a person likely to be caused harassment, alarm or distress thereby. **Public Order Act 1986 s 5(1)**

> **Points to prove**
> ✓ date and location
> ✓ used threatening/abusive/insulting words/behaviour or disorderly behaviour **or**
> ✓ displayed writing/sign/visible representation being
> ✓ threatening/abusive/insulting
> ✓ within hearing/sight of a person likely to be caused
> ✓ harassment/alarm/distress
> ✓ with the intention/an awareness
> ✓ that your conduct/actions
> ✓ would have that effect

Meanings

Threatening, abusive and insulting (see 7.6)

Harassment, alarm, and distress (see 7.7)

Disorderly behaviour

This is not defined, but the Oxford English Dictionary states: 'unruly, unrestrained, turbulent or riotous behaviour'.

Explanatory notes

- Distress should be taken into context of the term **likely to be caused**. What may distress an old woman of 75 years may not distress a young man of 20 years. The conduct has to be seen in its full context. However, you can feel for the safety of someone else, (particularly if you are a police officer), and it does not necessarily have to be for yourself (see *Lodge v DPP* The Times, 26 October 1988, QBD).

- A person is guilty of an offence under s 5 only if he intends his words or behaviour, or the writing, sign or other visible representation, to be threatening, abusive or insulting, or is aware that it may be threatening, abusive or insulting or (as the case may be) he intends his behaviour to be or is aware that it may be disorderly (s 6(4)).
- An offence under this section may be committed in a public or a private place except that no offence is committed when the words or behaviour are used, or the writing, sign or other visible representation is displayed, by a person inside a dwelling and the other person is also inside that or another dwelling.

Defences

It is a defence for the accused to prove—

(a) that he had no reason to believe that there was any person within hearing or sight who was likely to be caused harassment, alarm or distress; or

(b) that he was inside a dwelling and had no reason to believe that the words or behaviour used, or the writing, sign or other visible representation displayed, would be heard or seen by a person outside that or any other dwelling; or

(c) that his conduct was reasonable.   Public Order Act 1986, s 5(3)

Defence notes

The onus of proof is on the defendant, but like all defences need only be proved on the balance of probabilities. The points raised by the defence should be covered in interview or rebutted in other evidence.

Intoxication (see **Defence notes** in 7.4.1)

Related cases

Taylor v DPP [2006] EWHC 1202 (Admin) QBD The wording 'within the sight or hearing of a person' requires evidence that there was someone able to hear or see the conduct but the prosecution does not have to call evidence that the words were actually heard or behaviour seen.

Norwood v DPP [2003] EWHC 1564 (Admin), QBD Shortly after the '9/11' terrorist attack in New York the defendant displayed a poster in his flat window. The poster said, 'Islam out of Britain' and 'Protect the British People'. It bore a reproduction of one of the 'twin towers' in flames along with a Crescent and Star surrounded by a prohibition sign. All this was visible from the street.

Held that the poster was racially insulting to Muslims, and the circumstances of its location and display were capable of causing harassment, alarm or distress to any right-thinking member of society concerned with the preservation of peace and tolerance and the avoidance of religious and racial tension.

Whether or not the principles in Art 10 override the operation of a s 5 offence, the key issue is to consider whether the conduct was objectively reasonable having regard to all the circumstances. The rights of freedom of expression carry with them a duty to avoid unreasonable or disproportionate interference with the rights of others: if they do interfere, the state has a duty to intervene as in this case.

Vigon v DPP The Times, 9 December 1997 Using a concealed video camera to film customers undressing and trying on swimwear in a changing room was held to be insulting behaviour, likely to cause distress (s 5 offence). It is now a specific offence of voyeurism (see **6.10**).

Percy v DPP [2001] EWHC 1125 (Admin) P defaced an American flag (the defendant's own property) and stamped upon it outside an American airbase. It was basically a peaceful protest, albeit insulting to some American servicemen. It was held that a criminal prosecution was not a proportionate response and would breach an individual's right to freedom of expression as guaranteed by Art 10 of the European Convention on Human Rights (see **1.1**).

Director of Public Prosecutions v Hammond [2004] All ER (D) 50 (Jan) Displaying a sign with anti-homosexual remarks by a preacher was insulting behaviour.

Norwood v DPP [2003] EWHC 1564 (Admin), QBD Displaying a racially insulting poster (see **7.10.4** for details).

Chambers and Edwards v DPP [1995] Crim LR 896, QBD It is necessary to show that a person has been or is likely to be harassed **or** alarmed **or** distressed.

DPP v Orum [1988] 3 All ER 449 A police officer can only be subject to harassment, alarm, or distress where the actions or words amount to more than he would regularly see or hear in the course of his duty.

Lodge v DPP The Times, 26 October 1988, QBD Alarm can be experienced about the safety of an unrelated third party.

Practical considerations

- If this offence is racially or religiously aggravated (see **7.10**), the more serious offence under s 31(1)(c) of the Crime and Disorder Act 1998 should be considered. Also be aware that ss 17 to 23 of the Public Order Act 1986 relate to racial hatred offences (see **7.9**).
- This should be distinguished from the similar s 4A offence, which requires specific intent (see **7.7**)
- Words or behaviour are alternatives and one or other should be specified in the charge, and must be proved.
- Consider issuing a penalty notice for disorder for this offence (see **7.1**).
- It is not duplicitous if all three alternatives are charged, 'threatening, abusive or insulting', though all three need not be used.
- Also be aware of the Scottish case of *Kinnaird v Higson* 2001 SCCR 427 concerning the way in which the phrase, 'Fuck off', is used to police officers. This may be interpreted as the way in which a particular person usually speaks and/or common parlance in a specific locality. Therefore, what may constitute abusive language in one context or location may not amount to such in another.

7.8 Threatening/Abusive Words/Behaviour

• When investigating this offence consideration must be given to the CPS public order charging standards.

 Summary 6 months

A fine not exceeding level 3 on the standard scale.

Links to alternative subjects and offences

PND Penalty notice for disorder offences   **RRA** Racially or religiously aggravated offence   **CSO** Offences where CSO can use their powers

7.9 **Racial Hatred Offences**

Sections 17 to 23 of the Public Order Act 1986 relate to racial hatred offences. All references are to the 1986 Act unless otherwise stated.

7.9.1 **Meaning of racial hatred**

Racial hatred is defined by s 17 of the Public Order Act 1986.

Racial hatred

'Racial hatred' means hatred against a group of persons defined by reference to colour, race, nationality (including citizenship), or ethnic or national origins.

Explanatory notes

Racial hatred includes hatred manifested in Great Britain, but directed against a racial or religious group outside Great Britain.

7.9.2 **Use of words/behaviour or display of written material**

Section 18 creates the offence of using words or behaviour, or displaying written material, intending or likely to stir up racial hatred.

Offence

A person who uses threatening, abusive or insulting words or behaviour, or displays any written material which is threatening, abusive or insulting, is guilty of an offence if—
(a) he intends thereby to stir up racial hatred, or
(b) having regard to all the circumstances racial hatred is likely to be stirred up thereby.   Public Order Act 1986, s 18(1)

Points to prove

✓ used threatening/abusive/insulting words/behaviour or displayed threatening/abusive/insulting written material
✓ intended/likely to stir up
✓ racial hatred

Meanings

Threatening, abusive and insulting   (see 7.6)

7.9.2 Use of Words/Behaviour or Display of Written Material

Display   (see **7.6**)

Written material

Includes any sign or other visible representation.

Intention   (see **4.1**)

Racial hatred   (see **7.9.1**)

Explanatory notes

- Insulting does not mean behaviour which might give rise to irritation or resentment (eg running onto a tennis court at Wimbledon blowing a whistle and stopping the game).
- This offence may be committed in a public or private place, but no offence is committed where the words or behaviour are used, or the written material is displayed, by a person inside a dwelling and are not heard or seen except by persons in that or another dwelling.
- A person who is not shown to have intended to stir up racial hatred is not guilty of an offence under this section if he did not intend his words or behaviour, or the written material, to be, and was not aware that it might be, threatening, abusive or insulting. However, if having regard to all the circumstances racial hatred is likely to be stirred up then the case may be proved.

Defence

In proceedings for an offence under this section it is a defence for the accused to prove that he was inside a dwelling and had no reason to believe that the words or behaviour used, or the written material displayed, would be heard or seen by a person outside that or another dwelling.

Public Order Act 1986, s 18(4)

Defence notes

'Dwelling' means any structure or part of a structure occupied as a person's home or other living accommodation (whether the occupation is separate or shared with others) but does not include any part not so occupied, and for this purpose 'structure' includes a tent, caravan, vehicle, vessel or other temporary or movable structure.

Practical considerations

- This section does not apply to words or behaviour used, or written material displayed, solely for the purpose of being included in a programme service.
- A court by which a person is convicted of an offence under this section relating to the display of written material may order the forfeiture of the material to which the charge relates. This forfeiture applies to publishing or distributing written material (see **7.9.3**), distributing/showing/playing a recording, and possession of racially inflammatory material (see **7.9.4**).

- The following considerations apply to racially or religiously aggravated offences:
  - each of s 18 to s 23 creates one offence and one or more such offences may be charged in the same count or information;
  - where this offence is committed by a body corporate, if it is committed with the consent or connivance of a director, manager, secretary, or a person acting as such, s/he, as well as the company is guilty of the offence;
  - the consent of the Attorney-General/Solicitor-General is required for this offence.

E&S **RRA** **CSO**

 Either way

 None

Summary: 6 months' imprisonment and/or a fine not exceeding the statutory maximum.
Indictment: 7 years' imprisonment and/or a fine.

7.9.3 **Publishing/distributing written material**

Section 19 of the Public Order Act 1986 creates the offence of publishing or distributing written material intending or likely to stir up racial hatred.

Offences

A person who publishes or distributes written material which is threatening, abusive or insulting is guilty of an offence if:
(a) he intends thereby to stir up racial hatred, or
(b) having regard to all the circumstances racial hatred is likely to be stirred up thereby.

Public Order Act 1986, s 19(1)

Points to prove

✓ published/distributed
✓ threatening/abusive/insulting written material
✓ intended/likely
✓ to stir up racial hatred

Meanings

Publishes or distributes

Means its publication or distribution to the public or a section of the public.

7.9.4 Distributing, Showing, or Playing a Recording

Written material (see 7.9.2)

Threatening, abusive, or insulting (see 7.6)

Intends (see **4.1**)

Racial hatred (see 7.9.1)

Defence

In proceedings for an offence under this section it is a defence for an accused who is not shown to have intended to stir up racial hatred to prove that he was not aware of the content of the material and did not suspect, that it was threatening, abusive or insulting.   **Public Order Act 1986, s 19(2)**

Practical considerations (see 7.9.2)

  Either way   None

IIII **Summary:** 6 months' imprisonment and/or a fine not exceeding the statutory maximum.
Indictment: 7 years' imprisonment and/or a fine.

7.9.4 **Distributing, showing, or playing a recording**

Section 21 of the Public Order Act 1986 creates the offence of distributing, showing, or playing a recording of visual images or sounds which are threatening, abusive, or insulting intending or likely to stir up racial hatred.

Offences

A person who distributes, or shows or plays, a recording of visual images or sounds which are threatening, abusive or insulting is guilty of an offence if:
(a) he intends thereby to stir up racial hatred, or
(b) having regard to all the circumstances racial hatred is likely to be stirred up thereby.   **Public Order Act 1986, s 21(1)**

Points to prove

✓ distributed/showed/played
✓ recording of visual images/sounds
✓ which were threatening/abusive/insulting
✓ intended/likely
✓ to stir up racial hatred

Meanings

Distributes

Showing or playing to the public or a section of the public.

Recording

Means any record from which visual images and sounds may, by any means, be reproduced.

Explanatory notes

This section does not apply to the showing or playing of a recording solely to enable the recording to be included in a programme service.

Defence

In proceedings for an offence under this section it is a defence for an accused who is not shown to have intended to stir up racial hatred to prove that he was not aware of the content of the recording and did not suspect, and had no reason to suspect, that it was threatening, abusive or insulting.

Public Order Act 1986, s 21(3)

Practical considerations (see also 7.9.2)

- Section 23 creates the offence of possessing racially inflammatory material with intent or likely to stir up racial hatred, with a view to it being included in a programme service.
- Under s 24 a justice of the peace may issue a warrant on suspicion that an offence under s 23 is being committed. The warrant can authorize any constable to enter and search premises—being any place, and includes any vehicle, vessel, aircraft, hovercraft, offshore installations, and any tent or movable structure.

 Either way   None

 Summary: 6 months' imprisonment and/or a fine not exceeding the statutory maximum.
Indictment: 7 years' imprisonment and/or a fine.

Links to alternative subjects and offences

7.10 Racially/Religiously Aggravated Offences

Sections 28 to 32 of the Crime and Disorder Act 1998 relate to racially or religiously aggravated offences. All references are to the 1998 Act unless otherwise stated.

7.10.1 Meaning of 'racially or religiously aggravated'

Section 28 states when a specific offence is deemed 'racially or religiously aggravated' as follows.

Definition

An offence is racially or religiously aggravated for the purposes of ss 29 to 32 below if:

(a) at the time of committing the offence, or immediately before or after doing so, the offender demonstrates towards the victim of the offence hostility based on the victim's **membership** (or **presumed** membership) of a **racial or religious group**; or

(b) the offence is motivated (wholly or partly) by hostility towards members of a racial or religious group based on the membership of that group.   Crime and Disorder Act 1998, s 28(1)

Meanings

Membership

In relation to a racial or religious group, includes association with members of that group.

Presumed

Means presumed by the defendant (even if it is a mistaken presumption).

Racial group

Means a group of people defined by reference to race, colour, nationality (including citizenship), or ethnic or national origins.

Religious group

Means a group of people defined by religious belief or lack of religious belief.

Explanatory notes

It is immaterial for sub-s (1) whether or not the defendant's hostility is also based, to whatever extent, on any other factor not mentioned in the subsections.

Related cases

Taylor v DPP [2006] EWHC 1202 (Admin) QBD Guidance issued on racially aggravated offences.

R v Rogers [2005] EWCA Crim 2863, CA After an altercation called three Spanish women 'bloody foreigners' and told them to 'go back to their own country' before pursuing them in an aggressive manner. Held that hostility based on the fact that a person was 'foreign' could be just as objectionable as if it were based on a more specific racial characteristic. Convicted of using racially aggravated abusive or insulting words or behaviour under s 31(1)(a).

DPP v M [2004] EWHC 1453 (Admin) QBD Argument with a Turkish chef, where the defendant kept using the words 'bloody foreigners' before going outside and damaging the window of the kebab shop. The Court felt that the word 'foreignerss' did satisfy the meaning within s 28(3) and the word 'bloody' meant that the defendant had demonstrated some hostility towards a racial group.

Practical considerations

A police officer is just as entitled to protection under these provisions as anybody else (eg a person committing the offence of threatening behaviour by using racial taunts against the police could be prosecuted for the racially aggravated version of the offence).

7.10.2 **Racially or religiously aggravated assaults**

Section 29 relates to racially or religiously aggravated assaults.

Offence

A person is guilty of an offence under this section if he commits:
(a) an offence under s 20 of the Offences Against the Person Act 1861 [see **2.3.1**]; or
(b) an offence under s 47 of that Act [see **2.1.2**]; or
(c) a common assault [see **2.1.1**],
which is racially or religiously aggravated for the purposes of this section.

Crime and Disorder Act 1998, s 29(1)

Points to prove

✓ committed offence under s 20 or s 47 of OAPA 1861; or s 39 of CJA 1988
✓ such offence was racially/religiously aggravated

Meaning of racially or religiously aggravated (see 7.10.1)

Explanatory notes

If, on the trial on indictment of a person charged with this offence, the jury find the defendant not guilty of the offence charged, they may find him/her guilty of the relevant 'basic' offence (eg s 20 or s 47 of the OAPA 1861; or s 39 of CJA 1988).

Related cases

DPP v Woods [2002] EWHC 85 (Admin), QBD On being refused entry to licensed premises, the doorman was called a 'black bastard' and assaulted. Even though the offender used the words out of frustration, and the victim was unconcerned and did not consider the words racially offensive, the offence of racially aggravated common assault was still committed.

DPP v Pal [2000] Crim LR 256, QBD An Asian caretaker asked four youths, two Asian and two white, to leave the premises. One Asian youth refused, pushed the caretaker against a bin and accused him of being a white man's lackey and a brown Englishman. He then kicked the caretaker before leaving. He was charged with racially aggravated common assault. The caretaker was abused because of his job not his race. Therefore, this was **not** hostility based on the victim's membership of a racial group.

Practical considerations

Always charge the defendant with the relevant 'basic' offence, as there is no provision for an alternative verdict at a magistrates' court.

 Either way   None

 Offence under s 29(1)(a) or (b)
Summary: 6 months' imprisonment and/or a fine not exceeding the statutory maximum.
Indictment: 7 years' imprisonment and/or a fine.

Offence under s 29(1)(c)
Summary: 6 months' imprisonment and/or a fine not exceeding the statutory maximum.
Indictment: 2 years' imprisonment and/or a fine.

7.10.3 **Racially or religiously aggravated criminal damage**

Section 30 creates an offence of racially or religiously aggravated criminal damage.

Offence

A person is guilty of an offence under this section if he commits an offence under s 1(1) of the Criminal Damage Act 1971 (destroying/damaging property belonging to another) which is racially or religiously aggravated for the purposes of this section.   Crime and Disorder Act 1998, s 30(1)

Points to prove

✓ committed an offence under s 1(1) of the Criminal Damage Act 1971 (see **4.4**)
✓ such offence was racially/religiously aggravated

Meaning of racially or religiously aggravated (see 7.10.1)

Explanatory notes

- For the purposes of this section, s 28(1) (see **7.10.1**) has effect as if the person to whom the property belongs or is treated as belonging for the purposes of that Act was the victim of the offence.
- If, on the trial on indictment of a person charged with this offence, the jury find the defendant not guilty of the offence charged, they may find him/her guilty of the relevant 'basic' offence.

Practical considerations

- Where this offence is shown to be motivated by racial hostility under s 28(1)(b) (see **7.10.1**) there is no need to identify a specific victim (eg painting racist graffiti on a wall would be likely to constitute this offence).
- This offence is triable either way irrespective of the value of the damage caused (unlike the relevant 'basic' offence).

 Either way   None

Summary: 6 months' imprisonment and/or a fine not exceeding the statutory maximum.
Indictment: 14 years' imprisonment and/or a fine.

SSS Stop, search and seize powers   **E&S** Entry and search powers   **RRA** Racially or religiously aggravated offence

7.10.4 **Racially or religiously aggravated public order offences**

Section 31 relates to racially or religiously aggravated public order offences.

Offence

A person is guilty of an offence under this section if he commits:

(a) an offence under s 4 of the Public Order Act 1986 [fear/provocation of violence, see **7.6**]; or

(b) an offence under s 4A of that Act [intentional harassment, alarm, or distress, see **7.7**]; or

(c) an offence under s. 5 of that Act [harassment, alarm, distress, see **7.8**],

which is racially or religiously aggravated for the purposes of this section.

Crime and Disorder Act 1998, s 31(1)

Points to prove

✓ committed an offence

✓ under s 4 or s 4A or s 5 of the Public Order Act 1986

✓ such offence was racially/religiously aggravated

Explanatory notes

- If, on the trial on indictment of a person charged with an offence under s 31(1)(a) or (b), the jury find the defendant not guilty of the offence charged, they may find him/her guilty of the relevant 'basic' offence.

- For the purposes of s 31(1)(c), s 28(1) (see **7.10.1**) has effect as if the person likely to be caused harassment, alarm, or distress was the victim of the offence.

Related cases

DPP v McFarlane [2002] EWHC 485, DC During an argument over a disabled parking bay a white person referred to a black person as a 'jungle bunny', a 'black bastard' and a 'wog' and was charged with racially aggravated threatening behaviour. Anger about another's inconsiderate behaviour is not an excuse for racial comments.

Norwood v DPP [2003] EWHC 1564 (Admin), QBD Displaying a racially insulting poster in a window where it could be seen by the public can constitute an offence. Its location and contents were capable of causing harassment, alarm or distress to any right-minded member of society.

DPP v Ramos [2000] Crim LR 768, QBD Following a serious bomb attack, threatening letters were sent to an organization offering help and advice to the Asian community. It was held that it was the state of mind of the victim which was central, not the possible likelihood of violence happening shortly. Where the wording of the letter suggested immediate violence would occur, it was for the magistrates to decide whether the victim believed, or was likely to believe, that violence could occur at some time. The sender had established an intention to cause the victim to believe that violence could occur at any time.

DPP v Woods [2002] EWHC 85 (Admin), QBD When abuse is racially aggravated, it is important to prove racial hostility towards the victim or racial motivation.

Practical considerations

- If the defendant is found not guilty of the offence charged under s 31(1)(a) or (b) at magistrates' court there is no provision for an alternative verdict, therefore it is good practice to include the relevant 'basic' offence as an alternative charge.
- There is no longer a statutory requirement (under s 5(4)—now repealed) to warn an offender before arrest. However, such an arrest must always satisfy the 'necessity test' under s 24(5) PACE (see 12.2.1).

s 31(1)(a) or (b) offence

 Either way   None

 Summary: 6 months' imprisonment and/or a fine not exceeding the statutory maximum.
Indictment: 2 years' imprisonment and/or a fine.

s 31(1)(c) offence

 Summary   6 months

 A fine not exceeding level 4 on the standard scale.

7.10.5 **Racially or religiously aggravated harassment**

Section 32 creates the offence of racially or religiously aggravated harassment.

Offences

A person is guilty of an offence under this section if he commits:

(a) an offence under s 2 of the Protection from Harassment Act 1997; or

(b) an offence under s 4 of that Act,

which is racially or religiously aggravated for the purposes of this section.

Crime and Disorder Act 1998, s 32(1)

Points to prove

✓ committed an offence

✓ under s 2 or s 4 of the Protection from Harassment Act 1997

✓ such offence was racially/religiously aggravated

Explanatory notes

- If, on the trial on indictment of a person charged with an offence under s 32(1)(a), the jury find the defendant not guilty of the offence charged, they may find him/her guilty of the relevant basic offence.
- If, on the trial on indictment of a person charged with an offence under s 32(1)(b), the jury find the defendant not guilty of the offence charged, they may find him/her guilty of an offence under s 32(1)(a).
- Section 5 of the Protection from Harassment Act 1997 (restraining orders) has effect in relation to a person convicted of an offence under this section as if a reference to s 2 or s 4 included a reference to an offence under this section (see **7.11**).

Practical considerations

- If the defendant is found not guilty of the offence charged under s 32(1)(a) at magistrates' court there is no provision for an alternative verdict, therefore it is good practice to include the relevant basic offence as an alternative charge.
- Similarly there is no provision for an alternative verdict under s 32(1)(b) at magistrates' court, therefore it is good practice to include the offence under s (1)(a) as an alternative charge.

 Either way   None

   Offence under s 32(1)(a)

Summary: 6 months' imprisonment and/or a fine not exceeding the statutory maximum.

Indictment: 2 years' imprisonment and/or a fine.

Offence under s 32(1)(b)

Summary: 6 months' imprisonment and/or a fine not exceeding the statutory maximum.

Indictment: 7 years' imprisonment and/or a fine.

Links to alternative subjects and offences

7.11 **Harassment**

The Protection from Harassment Act 1997 provides criminal and civil remedies to restrain conduct amounting to harassment (stalking). Sections 42 and 42A of the Criminal Justice and Police Act 2001 concerns prevention of harassment of a person in his/her own home.

7.11.1 **Harassment—no violence**

Section 1(1) prohibits harassment, while s 2 creates the offence of harassment. All references within **7.11.1** to **7.11.4** (inclusive) are to the 1997 Act unless otherwise stated.

Offences

1(1) A person must not pursue a course of conduct:
- (a) which amounts to harassment of another, and
- (b) which he knows or ought to know amounts to harassment of the other.

1(1A) A person must not pursue a course of conduct:
- (a) which involves harassment of two or more persons, and
- (b) which he knows or ought to know amounts to harassment of those persons, and
- (c) by which he intends to persuade any person (whether or not one of those mentioned above):
  - (i) not to do something that he is entitled or required to do, or
  - (ii) to do something that he is not under any obligation to do.

2(1) A person who pursues a course of conduct in breach of s 1 is guilty of an offence.   Protection from Harassment Act 1997, ss 1(1), 1(1A), and 2(1)

Points to prove

✓ pursued a course of conduct
✓ on at least two occasions
✓ amounting to harassment
✓ which s/he knew/ought to have known amounted to harassment

Meanings

Course of conduct

- It must involve—
  - ♦ to a single person (s 1(1)), conduct on at least two occasions in relation to that person, or
  - ♦ to two or more persons (s 1(1A), conduct on at least one occasion in relation to each of those persons.
- Conduct includes speech.

Harassment

Includes causing the person(s) alarm or distress.

Explanatory notes

- If a reasonable person in possession of the same information as the defendant would think the course of conduct amounted to harassment, then the offender should have realized this as well.
- A person may be subjected to harassment by writing (eg emails or letters), orally (eg in person or by telephone) or by conduct (eg stalking).
- An offender does not have to act in a malicious, threatening, abusive, or insulting way. It could be that a 'stalker' may be infatuated by the victim and actually intends him/her no harm.
- In addition to any other punishment, the court can also impose a 'restraining order' (see **7.11.3**—restraining orders) on a defendant convicted of this offence.

Defences

Section 1(1) or (1A) does not apply to a course of conduct if the person who pursued it shows:

(a) that it was pursued for the prevention or detection of crime,

(b) that it was pursued under any enactment or rule of law or to comply with any condition or requirement imposed by any person under any enactment, or

(c) that in the particular circumstances the pursuit of the course of conduct was reasonable.   *Protection from Harassment Act 1997, s 1(3)*

Defence notes

- This defence may be available to police, customs, security services and similar bodies.
- A suspect suffering from some form of obsessive behaviour or schizophrenia cannot use their mental illness as a defence because of the 'reasonable person' test.

Related cases

Daniels v Metropolitan Police Commissioner [2006] EWHC 1622 QBD
In establishing vicarious liability for harassment there must be an established case of harassment by at least one employee/officer who is shown on at least two occasions to have pursued a course of conduct amounting to harassment, or by more than one employee/officer each acting on different occasions in furtherance of some joint design.

DPP v Baker [2004] EWHC 2782 (Admin), QBD Harassment may occur either continuously or intermittently over a period of time, in this case 2 years and 8 months. Providing at least one of the incidents that the prosecution wish to rely upon occurred within the six month limitation period then the provisions of s 127 of the MCA 1980 are not violated.

Kellett v DPP [2001] EWHC 107 (Admin), QBD Following several arguments a person telephoned the employer of another concerning the activities of the other in work's time. The other person was particularly upset by the calls. The caller knew, or ought to have known, that the calls to the other's employer amounted to harassment.

Pratt v DPP [2001] EWHC (Admin) 483, CA The fewer and wider apart the incidents were the more *unlikely* that harassment would be proved. In this case the second incident was sufficiently similar to the first incident to amount to a 'course of conduct'.

Lau v DPP [2000] All ER (D) 224, QBD Lau and his girlfriend had an argument during which he hit her across the face. Four months later he went to her house and threatened violence against her new boyfriend, who was also present. Held that Lau had not 'pursued a course of conduct' because of the time between the two incidents and, in the first incident, violence had been directed against the victim while in the second one it was against her new boyfriend.

Practical considerations

- Evidence of previous complaints of harassment to prove continuance of the harassment on at least two separate occasions.
- Two isolated incidents do not constitute a course of conduct.
- Have any previous warnings been given to the alleged offender?
- A campaign of collective harassment applies equally to two or more people as it does to one. Namely, conduct by one person shall also be taken, at the time it occurs, to be conduct by another if it is aided, abetted, counselled or procured by that other person.
- Consider racially or religiously aggravated harassment (see **7.10.5**).
- Obtain CJA witness statements.
- Consider other evidence (eg other witnesses, CCTV camera footage, detailed telephone bills, entries in domestic violence registers).
- Could the defences apply?
- If a restraining order is required to be imposed on the defendant, you must request the CPS to apply for one—they will not do so automatically

 RRA

 Summary 6 months

 6 months' imprisonment and/or a fine not exceeding level 5 on the standard scale.

7.11.2 **Harassment (fear of violence)**

Section 4 relates to a course of conduct, which, on at last two occasions, causes another to fear that violence will be used against him/her.

Offence

A person whose course of conduct causes another to fear, on at least two occasions, that violence will be used against him is guilty of an offence if he knows or ought to know that his course of conduct will cause the other so to fear on each of those occasions.   **Protection from Harassment Act 1997, s 4(1)**

Points to prove
✓ caused fear violence
✓ by a course of conduct on at last two occasions
✓ which you knew/ought to have known
✓ would cause fear of violence on each occasion

Meaning of course of conduct (see 7.11.1)

Explanatory notes
- The person whose course of conduct is in question ought to know that it will cause another to fear that violence will be used against him/her on any occasion if a reasonable person with the same information would think it would cause the other so to fear on that occasion (s 4(2)).
- A defendant found not guilty of this offence may be convicted of the lesser offence of harassment without violence (see **7.11.1**).
- In addition to any other punishment, the court can also impose a 'restraining order' (see **7.11.3**) on a defendant convicted of this offence.

Defences

It is a defence for a person charged with an offence under this section to show that:
(a) his course of conduct was pursued for the purpose of preventing or detecting crime,
(b) his course of conduct was pursued under any enactment or rule of law or to comply with any condition or requirement imposed by any person under any enactment, or
(c) the pursuit of his course of conduct was reasonable for the protection of himself or another or for the protection of his or another's property.
Protection from Harassment Act 1997, s 4(3)

Defence notes (see 7.11.1)

Related cases

Howard v DPP [2001] EWHC (Admin) 17, QBD A family suffered continual abuse from the defendant and their neighbours. One of the many threats made by the defendant was to kill their dog. Having regard to these threats and other ongoing circumstances, was sufficient grounds for the complainant/family to fear violence being used against them.

Caurti v DPP [2002] Crim LR 131, DC Conduct must be aimed against the same victim on at least two occasions. In this case there had been two occasions but aimed at two different victims, thus the s 4 offence had not been committed.

Practical considerations (see 7.11.1)

This offence is not limited to 'stalking', and could cover many long running problems where violence is a possibility against one of the parties.

 Either way   None

 Summary: 6 months' imprisonment and/or a fine not exceeding the statutory maximum.
Indictment: 5 years' imprisonment and/or a fine.

7.11.3 **Restraining orders**

Section 5 provides for the making of a restraining order against a person convicted under s 2 or s 4.

Offence

If without reasonable excuse the defendant does anything which he is prohibited from doing by an order under this section, he is guilty of an offence.   **Protection from Harassment Act 1997, s 5(5)**

Points to prove

✓ without reasonable excuse
✓ did something prohibited by a restraining order

Explanatory notes

- A court sentencing or otherwise dealing with a person ('the defendant') convicted of an offence under s 2 or s 4 may (as well as sentencing or dealing with him/her in any other way) make an order under this section.

7.11.4 Civil Remedies

- A restraining order may, to protect the victim of the offence or anybody else mentioned in it from further conduct amounting to harassment or that will cause fear of violence, prohibit the defendant from doing anything described in the order.
- The order may last for a specified period or until a further order is made.
- The prosecutor, defendant, or any person named therein may apply for it to be varied or discharged by a further order.

Related cases

R v Evans [2004] EWCA Crim 3102, CA In a restraining order the words 'should not be abusive by words or actions towards' were used. Held that the terms of an order must be precise and capable of being understood by the offender. In this case, the phrase 'abusive actions' was a question of fact, there was no need to give the phrase a specially narrow or wide interpretation.

Practical considerations

- Unlike the previous sections of this Act, one incident is sufficient to breach an order.
- These are criminal matters and should not be confused with civil injunctions.
- When an order is made it must identify the protected parties so ensure the details are available.
- Include a copy of the original order in the file for CPS attention.
- If you are dealing with an offence under this Act and require an order you must request CPS to obtain one—they will not automatically apply.

 E&S

 Either way   None

 Summary: 6 months' imprisonment and/or a fine not exceeding the statutory maximum.
Indictment: 5 years' imprisonment and/or a fine.

7.11.4 **Civil remedies**

Section 3 provides a civil remedy for harassment, allowing the victim to obtain damages and/or an injunction. Section 3A provides for injunctions to protect persons from harassment within s 1(1A).

Offence

Where:

(a) the High Court or a county court grants an injunction for the purpose mentioned in subsection (3)(a), and

(b) without reasonable excuse the defendant does anything which he is prohibited from doing by the injunction,

he is guilty of an offence.　　　　　**Protection from Harassment Act 1997, s 3(6)**

Points to prove

✓ without reasonable excuse

✓ pursued course of conduct prohibited by injunction

✓ granted by high/county court

Meanings

Injunction

An order or decree issued by a court for a person to do or not do that which is specified for a specified amount of time.

Subsection (3)(a)

In such proceedings the High Court or a county court grants an injunction for the purpose of restraining the defendant from pursuing any conduct which amounts to harassment

Reasonable excuse　(see 'Defence' below)

Explanatory notes

- An actual or perceived breach of s 1 may result in a claim in civil proceedings by the victim of the course of conduct in question.
- On such a claim, damages may be awarded for, among other things, any anxiety caused by, and financial loss resulting from, the harassment.
- Where, in such proceedings, the court grants an injunction restraining the defendant from pursuing any conduct amounting to harassment, and the plaintiff considers that the defendant has done anything contrary to that injunction, he may apply to have a warrant issued for the arrest of the defendant.
- The warrant application must be made to the court that issued the injunction.
- Any person who is or may be subject to a course of conduct under s 1(1A), may apply to the High Court/County court for an injunction restraining the relevant person from pursuing any course of conduct which harasses any person mentioned in the injunction.

Defence

The defence of reasonable excuse was meant for a life-saving situation such as a rescue from a burning house or something similar (*Huntingdon Life Sciences v Curtin* [1997] EWCA Civ 2486).

Related cases

Thomas v News Group Newspapers Ltd and another, The Times, 25 July 2001, CA A national newspaper and journalists were sued for harassment under s 3 after publishing an article about police discipline. The article gave the complainant's name and place of work (being a support staff member) and was described as 'a black clerk'. Held that it was not the conduct of the offender that created the offence or civil wrong of harassment, but the effect of that conduct.

DPP v Moseley, Woodling and Selvanayagam, The Times, 23 June 1999, QBD A High Court injunction had been granted to prevent harassment of a mink farmer. The defendant took part in a peaceful protest within the area covered by the injunction and was arrested, but claimed that this conduct was reasonable. Held that only in serious circumstances could it be reasonable to flout a High Court injunction.

Practical considerations

If a person is convicted of a breach of an injunction under this section, his/her conduct is not punishable as a contempt of court, or vice versa.

 Either way   None

 Summary: 6 months' imprisonment and/or a fine not exceeding the statutory maximum.
Indictment: 5 years' imprisonment and/or a fine.

7.11.5 Harassment of person in his/her home

Sections 42 and 42A of the Criminal Justice and Police Act 2001 provide a person in his/her home with protection from harassment. All references in the following are to the 2001 Act unless otherwise stated.

Offences

42(7) Any person who knowingly fails to comply with a requirement in a direction given to him under this section (other than a requirement under subsection (4)(b)) shall be guilty of an offence.

42(7A) Any person to whom a constable has given a direction including a requirement under subsection (4)(b) commits an offence if he:

    (a) returns to the vicinity of the premises in question within the period specified in the direction beginning with the date on which the direction is given; and

    (b) does so for the purpose described in subsection (1)(b).

42A(1) A person commits an offence if:

    (a) that person is outside or in the vicinity of any premises that are used by any individual ('the resident') as his dwelling;

    (b) that person is present there for the purpose (by his presence or otherwise) of representing to the resident or other individual (whether or not one who uses the premises as his dwelling), or of persuading the resident or such other individual:

        (i) that he should not do something that he is entitled or required to do; or

        (ii) that he should do something that he is not under any obligation to do;

    (c) that person:

        (i) intends his presence to amount to the harassment of, or to cause alarm or distress to, the resident, or

        (ii) knows or ought to know that his presence is likely to result in the harassment of, or to cause alarm or distress to, the resident; and

    (d) the presence of that person:

        (i) amounts to the harassment of, or causes alarm or distress to, any person falling within subsection (2); or

        (ii) is likely to result in the harassment of, or to cause alarm or distress to, any such person.

Criminal Justice and Police Act 2001, ss 42, 42A

Points to prove

s 42(7) offence

✓ outside/in vicinity of premises
✓ knowingly
✓ contravened the direction of a constable

s 42(7A) offence

✓ having been given a direction by a constable
✓ to leave the vicinity of premises
✓ not to return within a specified period
✓ returned there within that period
✓ to persuade the resident/another individual
✓ not to do something s/he is entitled to do/do something not obliged to do

7.11.5 Harassment of Person in his/her Home

> **s 42A(1) offence**
> ✓ present outside/in vicinity of a dwelling
> ✓ to persuade resident/other individual
> ✓ not to do something entitled/required to do/to do something not obliged to do
> ✓ intended to harass/cause alarm/distress to the resident
> ✓ knew/ought to have known such presence was likely to do so
> ✓ and their presence amounted to harassment/caused alarm/distress/likely to do so

Meanings

Directions

(1) Subject to the following provisions of this section, a constable who is at the scene may give a direction under this section to any person if—

    (a) that person is present outside or in the vicinity of any premises that are used by any individual ('the resident') as his dwelling;

    (b) that constable believes, on reasonable grounds, that that person is present there for the purpose (by his presence or otherwise) of representing to the resident or another individual (whether or not one who uses the premises as his dwelling), or of persuading the resident or such another individual—

        (i) that he should not do something that he is entitled or required to do; or

        (ii) that he should do something that he is not under any obligation to do; and

    (c) that constable also believes, on reasonable grounds, that the presence of that person (either alone or together with that of any other persons who are also present)—

        (i) amounts to, or is likely to result in, the harassment of the resident; or

        (ii) is likely to cause alarm or distress to the resident.

(2) A direction under this section is a direction requiring the person to whom it is given to do all such things as the constable giving it may specify as the things he considers necessary to prevent one or both of the following—

    (a) the harassment of the resident; or

    (b) the causing of any alarm or distress to the resident.

(3) A direction under this section may be given orally; and where a constable is entitled to give a direction under this section to each of several persons outside, or in the vicinity of, any premises, he may give that direction to those persons by notifying them of his requirements either individually or all together.

(4) The requirements that may be imposed by a direction under this section include—

    (a) a requirement to leave the vicinity of the premises in question, and

(b) a requirement to leave that vicinity and not to return to it within such period as the constable may specify, not being longer than 3 months; and (in either case) the requirement to leave the vicinity may be to do so immediately or after a specified period of time.

(5) A direction under this section may make exceptions to any requirement imposed by the direction, and may make any such exception subject to such conditions as the constable giving the direction thinks fit; and those conditions may include—

(a) conditions as to the distance from the premises in question at which, or otherwise as to the location where, persons who do not leave their vicinity must remain; and

(b) conditions as to the number or identity of the persons who are authorised by the exception to remain in the vicinity of those premises.

(6) The power of a constable to give a direction under this section shall not include—

(a) any power to give a direction at any time when there is a more senior ranking police officer at the scene; or

(b) any power to direct a person to refrain from conduct that is lawful under section 220 of the Trade Union and Labour Relations (Consolidation) Act 1992 (right peacefully to picket a work place); but it shall include power to vary or withdraw a direction previously given under this section.

Criminal Justice and Police Act 2001, ss 42(1)–(6)

Dwelling

Means any structure or part of a structure occupied as a person's home or as other living accommodation (whether the occupation is separate or shared with others) but does not include any part not so occupied, and for this purpose 'structure' includes a tent, caravan, vehicle, vessel, or other temporary or movable structure.

Harassment (see 7.11.1)

Explanatory notes

- A requirement under sub-s (4)(b) means to leave that vicinity immediately or after a specified period of time and not to return within a specified period (no more than 3 months).
- Under the s 42A(1)(d)(i) offence a person falls within sub-s (2) if he is the resident, a person in the resident's dwelling, or a person in another dwelling in the vicinity of the resident's dwelling.
- Under s 42 a constable in attendance may give a direction to any person if that person is outside or in the vicinity of premises used by a resident as his/her dwelling, having reasonable grounds to believe that the person's presence amounts to harassment of the resident or is likely to cause him/her alarm or distress.
- Such a direction requires the person to whom it is given to do everything specified by the constable as necessary to prevent the harassment of and/or the causing of alarm or distress to, the resident.
- A direction under s 42 may include a requirement to leave:

7.11.5 Harassment of Person in his/her Home

   (a) the vicinity of the premises in question, and
   (b) not return to it within such period as the constable may specify,
      not being longer than 3 months.

- The references in s 42A(1)(c) and (d) to a person's presence are references to his/her presence either alone or together with any other person(s) also present.
- For s 42A(1)(c) a person ought to know that his/her presence is likely to result in the harassment of, or cause alarm or distress to, a resident if a reasonable person possessing the same information would think that his/her presence would have that effect.

Practical considerations

- Any direction under this section may be given orally. It must be both heard and understood by the person.
- If a direction is given to more than one person the constable may give it to them either individually or all together.
- The power of a constable to give a direction under s 42 does not include where there is a more senior-ranking officer present or if the person(s) exercise their right to peacefully picket a work place.
- However, a constable may vary any direction previously given.

 Summary   6 months

 Offence under s 42(7)
3 months' imprisonment and/or a fine not exceeding level 4 on the standard scale.
Offence under s 42(7A) or s 42A
6 months' imprisonment and/or a fine not exceeding level 4 on the standard scale.

Links to alternative subjects and offences

7.12 Offensive/False Messages

The Malicious Communications Act 1988 makes provision concerning the sending and delivery of letters or other articles to cause distress or anxiety, while the Communications Act 2003 regulates all types of media and includes the sending of grossly offensive material via the public electronic communications network.

7.12.1 Send letters, etc. intending to cause distress/anxiety

Section 1 of the Malicious Communications Act 1988 creates offences in relation to the sending of indecent, offensive, or threatening letters, electronic communications, or articles with intent to cause distress or anxiety to the recipient. All references in the following are to the 1988 Act unless otherwise stated.

Offences

Any person who sends to another person:

(a) a letter, electronic communication or article of any description which conveys:
   (i)   a message which is indecent or grossly offensive;
   (ii) a threat; or
   (iii) information which is false and known or believed to be false by the sender; or
(b) any article or electronic communication which is, in whole or part, of an indecent or grossly offensive nature,

is guilty of an offence if his purpose, or one of his purposes, in sending it is that it should, so far as falling within paragraph (a) or (b) above, cause distress or anxiety to the recipient or to any other person to whom he intends that it or its contents or nature should be communicated.

Malicious Communications Act 1988, s 1(1)

Points to prove

s 1(1)(a) offence

✓ sent a letter/an electronic communication/an article
✓ which conveyed an indecent/grossly offensive message/a threat/false information which you knew/believed to be false
✓ for the purpose of causing distress/anxiety
✓ to the recipient/any other person
✓ to whom its contents/nature were intended to be communicated

---

---

s 1(1)(b) offence

✓ sent to another person
✓ an article/an electronic communication
✓ wholly/partly of an indecent/grossly offensive nature
✓ for the purpose of causing distress/anxiety
✓ to the recipient/any other person
✓ to whom its contents/nature were intended to be communicated

---

Meanings

Electronic communication

Includes:

(a) any oral or other communication by means of an electronic
    communications network; and
(b) any communication (however sent) that is in electronic form.

Electronic communications network

Means:

(a) a transmission system for the conveyance, by the use of electrical,
    magnetic or electro-magnetic energy, of signals of any
    description; and
(b) such of the following as are used, by the person providing the
    system and in association with it, for the conveyance of the
    signals—
    ♦ apparatus comprised in the system;
    ♦ apparatus used for the switching or routing of the signals; and
    ♦ software and stored data.

Grossly offensive

This has to be judged by the standards of an open and just multi-racial
society. Whether a message falls into this category depends not only on
its content but on the circumstances in which the message has been sent
(*DPP v Collins* [2005] EWHC 1308, HL).

Explanatory notes

• References to sending include references to delivering or transmitting
  and to causing to be sent, delivered, or transmitted and 'sender' will
  be construed accordingly.
• The offence only requires that the communication is sent—not that
  the intended victim actually received it.

Defence

A person is not guilty of an offence by virtue of sub-s (1)(a)(ii) above *(threat)*
if he shows:

(a) that the threat was used to reinforce a demand made by him on
    reasonable grounds; and

(b) that he believed, and had reasonable grounds for believing, that the use of the threat was a proper means of reinforcing the demand.

Malicious Communications Act 1988, s 1(2)

Practical considerations

- As well as letters and telephone systems this offence would include emails, fax, or text messages.
- What was the intended purpose of the defendant in sending the communication?
- If the intent is to cause the victim annoyance, inconvenience, or needless anxiety, also consider the offence under s 127 of the Communications Act 2003 (see **7.12.2**).
- An offence under this section could amount to an offence under s 2 of the Protection from Harassment Act 1997 (see **7.11.1**).
- If any threat used includes an unwarranted demand consider the more serious offence of blackmail (see **3.2.3**).
- Preserve the means or item that was used to deliver the message to the victim.
- The original message can be retrieved from phones or computers, the original letter or envelope can be fingerprinted or examined for DNA.

 Summary   6 months

 6 months' imprisonment and/or a fine not exceeding level 5 on the standard scale.

7.12.2 Improper use of electronic public communications network

Section 127 of the Communications Act 2003 creates offences regarding improper use of an electronic public communications network. All references in the following are to the 2003 Act unless otherwise stated.

Offences

(1) A person is guilty of an offence if he:
   (a) sends by means of a public electronic communications network a message or other matter that is grossly offensive or of an indecent, obscene or menacing character; or
   (b) causes any such message or matter to be so sent.
(2) A person is guilty of an offence if, for the purpose of causing annoyance, inconvenience or needless anxiety to another, he:

(a) sends by means of a public electronic communications network, a message that he knows to be false,

(b) causes such a message to be sent, or

(c) persistently makes use of a public electronic communications network.

Communications Act 2003, s 127(1), (2)

Points to prove

s 127(1) offence

✓ (a) sent

✓ by means of a public electronic communications network

✓ a message/other matter

✓ that was grossly offensive/of an indecent/obscene/menacing character;

or

✓ (b) caused such a message/matter to be so sent

s 127(2) offence

✓ to cause annoyance/inconvenience/needless anxiety to another

✓ (a) sent

✓ by means of a public electronic communications network

✓ a message he knew to be false

or

✓ (b) caused such a message to be sent

or

✓ (c) persistently made use

✓ of a public electronic communications network

Meanings

Public electronic communications network

Means an **electronic communications network** provided wholly or mainly for the purpose of making electronic communications services available for use by members of the public.

Electronic communications network (see 7.12.1)

Grossly offensive (see 7.12.1)

Menacing

Means a message which conveys a threat; which seeks to create a fear in or through the recipient that something unpleasant is going to happen. Here the intended or likely effect on the recipient must ordinarily be a central factor (*DPP v Collins* [2005] EWHC 1308, HL).

Persistently

Includes any case in which the misuse is repeated on a sufficient number of occasions for it to be clear that the misuse represents a pattern of behaviour or practice, or recklessness as to whether people suffer annoyance, inconvenience, or anxiety.

7.12.2 Improper use of Electronic Public Communications Network

Explanatory notes

- 'Electronic communications network' covers current and future developments in communication technologies (eg telephone, computers (internet), satellites, mobile terrestrial networks, emails, text messages, fax, and radio and television broadcasting including cable TV networks).
- These offences do not apply to anything done in the course of providing a broadcasting service, such as a television programme; public teletext; digital television; radio programme; or sound provided by the BBC.
- Sections 128 to 130 empower OFCOM (Office of Communications) to enforce this Act to stop a person persistently misusing a public electronic communications network or services.

Related cases

R v Johnson (Anthony Thomas) The Times, 22 May 1996, CA Making numerous obscene/offensive telephone calls can amount to a public nuisance (see **7.13.3**).

R v Ireland [1998] AC 147 HL & R v Burstow [1997] 4 All ER 225 HL The making of silent telephone calls which caused psychiatric injury to the victim was capable of amounting to an assault occasioning bodily harm (see **2.1**) or grievous bodily harm (see **2.3**) if they caused the victim to fear imminent violence on themselves. Expert evidence confirmed that the victims had suffered palpitations, breathing difficulties, cold sweats, anxiety, sleeplessness, dizziness, and stress.

Practical considerations

- These offences do not apply to a private/internal network. In these instances consider s 1 of the Malicious Communications Act 1988 (see **7.12.1**).
- Under sub-s (1) there is no requirement to show any specific purpose or intent by the defendant.
- Consider s 1 of the Malicious Communications Act 1988 (see **7.12.1**) if the offence involves intent to cause the victim distress or anxiety.
- Also consider an offence under the Protection from Harassment Act 1997 (see **7.11**).
- If the threats or information relate to bombs, noxious substances, or the placing of dangerous articles, consider the offences under the Anti-terrorism, Crime and Security Act 2001 and the Criminal Law Act 1977 (see **11.4.2**).
- Section 125 creates the offence of dishonestly obtaining an electronic communications service with intent to avoid the applicable payment.
- Possession or control of apparatus which may be used dishonestly to obtain an electronic communications service, or in connection with obtaining such a service is also an offence under s 126.
- A penalty notice for disorder may be issued by a police officer, community support officer or other accredited person for an offence under s 127(2) (see **7.1.1**).

Improper use of Electronic Public Communications Network 7.12.2

 Summary 6 months

 6 months' imprisonment and/or a fine not exceeding level 5 on the standard scale.

Links to alternative subjects and offences

7.13 **Anti-Social Behaviour**

Anti-social behaviour is provided for in various pieces of legislation including the Crime and Disorder Act 1998 (anti-social behaviour orders (ASBOs) and breaches thereof), the Police Reform Act 2002 (fail to give name and address) and also at common law (public nuisance).

7.13.1 **Anti-social behaviour orders—application/breach**

Section 1 of the Crime and Disorder Act 1998 empowers magistrates to make an ASBO against an individual whose conduct has caused harassment, alarm, or distress, and creates an offence for a breach of such an order.

Offence

If without reasonable excuse a person does anything which he is prohibited from doing by an anti-social behaviour order, he is guilty of an offence.

Crime and Disorder Act 1998, s 1(10)

Points to prove

✓ without reasonable excuse
✓ did an act
✓ prohibited from doing
✓ by anti-social behaviour order

Meanings

Anti-social behaviour order

(1) An application for an order under this section may be made by a **relevant authority** if it appears to the authority that the following conditions are fulfilled with respect to any person aged 10 or over, namely—
   (a) that the person has acted in an anti-social manner, that is to say, in a manner that caused or was likely to cause harassment, alarm or distress to one or more persons not of the same household as himself; AND
   (b) that such an order is necessary to protect relevant persons from further anti-social acts by him.
(3) Such an application shall be made by complaint to a magistrates' court.

(4) If, on such an application, it is proved that the conditions mentioned in subsection 1(1) above are fulfilled, the magistrates' court may make an order under this section (an 'anti-social behaviour order') which prohibits the defendant from doing anything described in the order.

Crime and Disorder Act 1998, s 1(1),(3)-(4)

Relevant authority

- Council for a **local government area** or County council (England);
- Chief constable of any police force maintained for a police area or of the BTP;
- Person(s) registered as a social landlord who provides/manages any houses/hostel in local government area or Housing action trust established by order.

Local government area

Means in England, a district or London borough, the City of London, the Isle of Wight, and the Isles of Scilly, and in Wales, a county or county borough.

Explanatory notes

- These are civil proceedings, but be aware that the standard of proof is the criminal standard of 'beyond reasonable doubt' and **not** the civil standard of 'balance of probabilities'. This is a safeguard owing to the serious consequences of the proceedings.
- The Human Rights Act does not prevent hearsay evidence being used in anti-social behaviour proceedings.
- Although the hearing at which such an order is granted is a civil matter, the breaching offence is dealt with as a criminal matter and is subject to the criminal rules of evidence.
- An application by a chief officer of police will only be made after consultation with the council in which the subject of the application resides or appears to reside. Similarly an application by a council will only be made after consultation with the chief officer of police for the police area within which the local authority lies.
- An ASBO prevents the person named in it from doing anything described in it.
- An ASBO is valid for the period of time stated in it (minimum 2 years) or until a further order is made.
- A warning letter will be served on the offender outlining the substance of any allegations and an application for an ASBO will only be made if the offending behaviour continues after the service of the letter.
- Where a person is convicted of an offence under this section the court cannot make an order for a conditional discharge.
- In criminal proceedings, under s 1C, if the offender is convicted of an offence and the court considers that s/he has acted in an anti-social manner and that an order under this section is necessary to protect other people in the area from further such behaviour, the court may issue an anti-social behaviour order against that individual. This order

may only be made in addition to the sentence imposed on the offence.

- An interim ASBO may be granted by a court pending the hearing of the main application. The interim ASBO will be for a fixed period, may be varied, renewed, or discharged and will, if it has not already done so, cease to have effect on determination of the main application.
- An ASBO may be varied or discharged on the application of the offender, the DPP, or a relevant authority. If the offender makes such application s/he must also send written notification of his/her application to the DPP.

Related cases

R v Stevens [2006] EWCA Crim 255 CA If the conduct which forms the breach of the order is also a distinct criminal offence with a maximum sentence threshold, then that should be remembered when sentencing on breach of the order in the interests of proportionality. The breach is a distinct offence on its own merit, with a maximum penalty of 5 years imprisonment, but that is not to say it should be used to circumvent maximum penalties considered as too lenient.

R v Nicholson [2006] EWCA Crim 1518 CA Ignorance, forgetfulness or misunderstanding may be capable of giving rise to a defence of reasonable excuse in cases involving the breach of an ASBO; but this is fact specific and the issues of fact and the judgment of those facts was matter for the court to decide.

R v Wadmore and Foreman [2006] EWCA Crim 686 CA Issued these guidelines when applying for an ASBO—

- Proceedings are civil, so hearsay is admissible, but the court must be satisfied to the criminal standard that the behaviour had been anti-social.
- The necessity of the order requires the exercise of judgement or evaluation.
- The findings of fact giving rise to the making of the order must be recorded.
- The terms of the order must be precise, capable of being understood and must be explained to the offender.
- The conditions must be enforceable, allowing any breach to be readily identified and capable of being proved.
- If an order is suspended until the offender has been released from custody (on licence subject to recall), the circumstances in which the necessity test can be met will be limited.
- An order must deal with the offender and be necessary to protect others from his/her anti-social behaviour.
- Not all conditions need to run for the full term of the order, provided the necessity test is met and restrictions are proportionate in the circumstances.
- The court should not impose an order prohibiting the commission of criminal offences if the sentence on conviction would be a sufficient deterrent.

- It is unlawful to impose an ASBO if it is a further sentence or punishment and must not be used to increase the sentence of imprisonment.

R (on the application of Chief Constable of West Mercia Police) v Boorman [2005] EWHC 2559 (Admin), QBD Stated that—

- The conduct and complaint must be within the 6 months limitation period, not the evidence. It is wrong to exclude evidence that was outside this period.
- ASBO is about preventive justice and is not part of criminal law, but Art 6 requires that reasons should be given about the making of an ASBO.
- Proof of mens rea on the part of the subject is not required, but the court (not the victim) decides whether the conduct was likely to cause harassment, alarm or distress.

R (Stanley & others) v Metropolitan Police Commissioner [2004] EWHC 2229 (Admin), DC Publicity was needed to inform and rein-force existing ASBOs; and to inhibit the behaviour of the offenders, or to deter others. It needed a photograph, name, and partial address so that people knew who the ASBOs referred to. The publishers must ensure there was no possibility of misidentification. No criminal convictions could be disclosed. Publicity may go beyond the excluded area, but it must be necessary and proportionate for protecting the rights of all con-cerned.

R (on the application of Kenny & M) v Leeds Magistrates Court [2003] EWHC (Admin) 2963, QBD After an area suffered large scale anti-social behaviour problems including drug dealing and associated crime, interim ASBOs without notice, were issued against 66 people. It was established that although Art 6(1) applied to ASBOs there was nothing unlawful in interim injunctions without notice and such power is only used to urgently protect the interests of other parties or to ensure the order of a court is effective.

Practical considerations

- An application for an ASBO is made by way of complaint to a magistrates' court, and is subject to the 6 months limitation period.
- Although the original order is issued as a result of civil proceedings the burden of proof of breach is 'beyond reasonable doubt' not the balance of probabilities.
- The application hearing is civil in nature but the hearing for a breach of the order is a criminal matter.
- In proceedings for an offence under this section a certified copy of the original ASBO is admissible as evidence of its issue and content.
- The police or local authority, in consultation with each other, can make an application for an ASBO against an individual or several individuals.
- No application for an ASBO is necessary in criminal proceedings.

Either way None

 Summary: 6 months' imprisonment and/or a fine not exceeding the statutory maximum.
Indictment: 5 years' imprisonment and/or a fine.

7.13.2 Act in anti-social manner—fail to give name/address

Section 50 of the Police Reform Act 2002 empowers a police officer to request the name and address of a person behaving in an anti-social manner, and creates an offence for failing to comply with that request.

Power to require name and address

If a constable in **uniform** has reason to believe that a person has been acting, or is acting, in an **anti-social manner** (within the meaning of s 1 of the Crime and Disorder Act 1998), he may require that person to give his name and address to the constable.

Police Reform Act 2002, s 50(1)

Meaning of anti-social manner

That is to say, in a manner that caused or was likely to cause harassment, alarm, or distress to one or more persons not of the same household as themselves (see **7.13.1**).

Offence

Any person who:
(a) fails to give his name and address when required to do so under subsection (1), or
(b) gives a false or inaccurate name or address in response to a requirement under that subsection,
is guilty of an offence.   Police Reform Act 2002, s 50(2)

Points to prove
- ✓ being a person whom a constable had reason to believe
- ✓ had been/was acting in anti-social manner
- ✓ failed or gave false/inaccurate details
- ✓ when required by the constable to provide their name and address

---

Explanatory notes

- If a constable in uniform has reason to believe that a person has been acting, or is acting, in an anti-social manner (within the meaning of s 1 of the Crime & Disorder Act 1998— see **7.13.1**), s/he may require that person to give their name and address.
- This power also applies to a community support officer.

Practical considerations

You must be in uniform to request the person's name and address.

 Summary 6 months

 A fine not exceeding level 3 on the standard scale.

7.13.3 **Public nuisance**

Public nuisance is an offence at common law.

> **Offences**
> A person is guilty of this offence if he:
> (a) does an act not warranted by law, or
> (b) omits to discharge a legal duty,
> if the effect of the act or omission is to endanger the life, health, property, morals or comfort of the public, or to obstruct the public in the exercise or enjoyment of rights common to everyone.   Common Law

---

Points to prove
✓ caused
✓ a public nuisance

Meanings

Act not warranted by law

Means illegal conduct.

Legal duty

Means a duty under any enactment, instrument or rule of law.

Explanatory notes

- This offence is described as 'a nuisance that is so wide spread in its range or so indiscriminate in its effect that it would not be reasonable to expect one person to take proceedings on his own responsibility to put a stop to it, but that it should be taken on the responsibility of the community at large'.
- The purpose that the defendant has in mind when s/he commits the act is immaterial if the probable result is to affect the public as described in the offence.
- Where some work is done by an employee in a manner that causes a nuisance it is no defence for the employer to claim that s/he did not personally supervise the work and had instructed that it be carried out in a different way.

Related cases

R v Rimmington; R v Goldstein [2005] UKHL 63 HL Where the ingredients of a statutory offence were made out, with possible defences, a prescribed mode of trial and maximum penalty it was only right that such conduct be prosecuted under the statutory offence and not a common law offence where the potential penalty was unlimited.

R v Shorrock [1993] 3 All ER 917, CA The defendant leased a field at his farm for a weekend and it was used for an acid house party/rave which caused a great deal of noise and disturbance. The defendant was away during event and stated that he did not have any knowledge that a public nuisance would be committed on his land. Held that the farmer was responsible for this nuisance which he knew or ought to have known about, because the means of knowledge were available, so would be the consequence of what he did or omitted to do.

R v Johnson (Anthony Thomas) [1996] 2 Cr App R 434, CA The defendant, over a number of years, used the public telephone system to cause nuisance annoyance, harassment, alarm, and distress to a number of women by making hundreds of obscene telephone calls. He was convicted of causing a public nuisance and appealed. It was held that the cumulative effect of all the calls was capable of being a nuisance, and the number of individuals affected was sufficient for his actions to be public. Therefore, the offence was complete.

Practical considerations

- The importance of this offence is its flexibility to cover circumstances not covered by specific legislation.
- For extreme acts of unpleasantness or lewdness consider an offence under the Sexual Offences Act 2003 (see **Chapter 6**) or the common law offence of outraging public decency (see **6.9**—indecent exposure).
- Conspiracy to commit this offence is contrary to s 1(1) of the Criminal Law Act 1977.

Either way None

 Summary: 6 months' imprisonment and/or a fine not exceeding the statutory maximum.
Indictment: Imprisonment and/or a fine.

Links to alternative subjects and offences

7.14 Vehicles Causing Annoyance

Section 59 of the Police Reform Act 2002 empowers police officers to seize motor vehicles used in such a way as to cause alarm, distress, or annoyance to members of the public. The Police (Retention and Disposal of Motor Vehicles) Regulations 2002 governs how such seized vehicles should be retained and disposed of.

7.14.1 Vehicles used in a manner causing alarm, distress, or annoyance

Section 59 of the Police Reform Act 2002 concerns the use of vehicles in a manner that causes alarm, distress, or annoyance to members of the public. All references in the following are to the 2002 Act unless otherwise stated.

Police powers

(1) Where a constable in uniform has reasonable grounds for believing that a **motor vehicle** is being used on any occasion in a manner which—
  (a) contravenes section 3 or 34 of the Road Traffic Act 1988 (careless and inconsiderate **driving** and prohibition of off-road driving), **and**
  (b) is causing, or is likely to cause, alarm, distress or annoyance to members of the public, he shall have the powers set out in subsection (3).
(2) A constable in uniform shall also have the powers set out in subsection (3) where he has reasonable grounds for believing that a motor vehicle has been used on any occasion in a manner falling within subsection (1).
(3) Those powers are—
  (a) the power, if the motor vehicle is moving, to order the person driving it to stop the vehicle;
  (b) the power to seize and remove the motor vehicle;
  (c) the power, for the purposes of exercising a power falling within paragraph (a) or (b), to enter any **premises** on which he has reasonable grounds for believing the motor vehicle to be;
  (d) the power to use reasonable force, if necessary, in the exercise of any power conferred by any of paragraphs (a) to (c).
(4) A constable shall not seize a motor vehicle in the exercise of the powers conferred on him by this section unless—
  (a) he has warned the person appearing to him to be the person whose use falls within subsection (1) that he will seize it, if that use continues or is repeated; and

(b) it appears to him that the use has continued or been repeated after the warning.

(5) Subsection (4) does not require a warning to be given by a constable on any occasion on which he would otherwise have the power to seize a motor vehicle under this section if—

(a) the circumstances make it impracticable for him to give the warning;

(b) the constable has already on that occasion given a warning under that subsection in respect of any use of that motor vehicle or of another motor vehicle by that person or any other person;

(c) the constable has reasonable grounds for believing that such a warning has been given on that occasion otherwise than by him; or

(d) the constable has reasonable grounds for believing that the person whose use of that motor vehicle on that occasion would justify the seizure is a person to whom a warning under that subsection has been given (whether or not by that constable or in respect of the same vehicle or the same or a similar use) on a previous occasion in the previous twelve months.

. . .

(7) Subsection (3)(c) does not authorise entry into a **private dwelling house**.   Police Reform Act 2002, s 59(1)–(5), (7)

Offence

A person who fails to comply with an order under subsection (3)(a) is guilty of an offence.   Police Reform Act 2002, s 59(6)

Points to prove

✓ failed to stop
✓ a moving vehicle
✓ on the order of a police constable in uniform
✓ s/he having reasonable grounds for believing
✓ that the vehicle was being used in a manner which
✓ contravened ss 3 or 34 of the Road Traffic Act 1988
and
✓ was causing/likely to cause alarm, distress, or annoyance to members of the public

---

Meanings

Motor vehicle (see **10.1**)

Driving (see **10.1.4**)

Private dwelling house

Does not include any garage or other structure occupied with the dwelling house, or any land appurtenant to the dwelling house.

7.14.1 Vehicles used in a Manner Causing Alarm

Explanatory notes

- A constable in uniform has the power to seize the vehicle but only after warning the person. If, after the warning has been given, the driving continues or is repeated then the vehicle can be seized.
- The requirement to give the warning does not apply where it is impracticable to do so or where it has been given on a previous occasion in that previous 12 months.
- The powers under this section cannot be exercised unless the driver is **both** using the vehicle anti-socially **and** is driving contrary to s 3 (careless and inconsiderate driving see **10.6**) or s 34 (prohibition of off-road driving see **10.23**) of the Road Traffic Act 1988.

Practical considerations

- The warning under sub-s (4) **must** be given and ignored before the vehicle can be seized (see **7.14.2**). Therefore it is important that the warning is both heard and understood.
- The warning does not have to be given if the circumstances make it impracticable, or if it has been given to that person within the last 12 months.
- A warning given within the last 12 months does not have to have been given in respect of the same vehicle.
- Where a motor vehicle is seized a seizure notice must be given to the person who appears to be the owner of the vehicle.
- A previous warning given on the same occasion need not have been given by the same constable nor does it have to have been given to the same person **or** in respect of the same vehicle. It could have been given to the same person using another vehicle or to different person using the same vehicle. This covers the situation where a number of people gathered together are using their vehicles anti-socially and swapping them around.
- Consider the powers given under the Anti-Social Behaviour Act 2003 as to dispersal of groups in a public place (see **7.15**) or the public nuisance offence might be more appropriate (see **7.13.3**).

 CSO

 Summary   6 months

 A fine not exceeding level 3 on the standard scale.

7.14.2 **Retention/disposal of seized motor vehicle**

The Police (Retention and Disposal of Motor Vehicles) Regulations 2002 relates to vehicles seized under s 59 of the Police Reform Act 2002 (see **7.14.1**). All references in the following are to the 2002 Regulations unless otherwise stated.

Power

(1) A relevant motor vehicle shall be passed into and remain in the custody of a constable or other person authorised under this regulation by the chief officer of the police force for the area in which the vehicle was seized ('the authority') until—
   (a) the authority permit it to be removed from their custody by a person appearing to them to be the owner of the vehicle; or
   (b) it has been disposed of under these Regulations.
(2) While the vehicle is in the custody of the authority, they shall be under a duty to take such steps as are reasonably necessary for its safekeeping.

Police (Retention and Disposal of Motor Vehicles)
Regulations 2002, reg 3(1), (2)

Meanings

Relevant motor vehicle

Means a motor vehicle that has been seized and removed under s 59(3)(b) of the Police Reform Act 2002 (see **7.14.1**).

The authority

Means a constable or other person authorized by the chief officer under reg 3(1).

Explanatory notes

- A relevant motor vehicle will pass into and remain in the custody of a constable or other person authorized under this regulation by the chief officer of police in the area in which it was seized until the authority permit a person appearing to them to be the owner of it to remove it, or it has been disposed of under these regulations.
- While the vehicle is in the custody of the authority, they must take any necessary steps for its safe keeping.
- As soon as possible after taking a vehicle into their custody the authority must take reasonable steps to serve a seizure notice on the person who is, or appears to be, the owner, except where the vehicle has been released from their custody.
- If a person satisfies the authority that s/he is the owner of the vehicle and pays the charges accrued concerning its removal and retention, the authority must allow him/her to remove it from their custody.
- A person otherwise liable to pay charges concerning the removal and retention of the vehicle will not be liable to pay them if s/he was not

the user when it was seized under s 59 of the Police Reform Act 2002 and s/he did not know of its use leading to the seizure, had not consented to such use and could not, by reasonable steps, have prevented such use.

- Where it has not been possible to serve a seizure notice on the relevant person, or such a notice has been served and the vehicle has not been released from their custody under these regulations, they may dispose of the vehicle in accordance with reg 7.
- The authority may not dispose of the vehicle under reg 7 within 3 months of its seizure or, if that date has already gone, before the 21 days after the seizure notice has been served or, during the 7 days following the date on which the vehicle is claimed under reg 5.
- Where the authority disposes of the vehicle by way of selling, it must pay the net proceeds of the sale to any person who, within a year of the sale, satisfies them that s/he was the vehicle owner at the time of the sale.

Practical considerations

- A seizure notice may be served by personal delivery to the person addressed in it, by leaving it at his/her usual or last known address or by registered delivery to his/her last known address.
- If the owner is a body corporate (eg a company) the notice must be served or sent to the company secretary or clerk at its registered office.
- The seizure notice must inform the owner that s/he has 21 days to collect the vehicle and that charges are payable.

Links to alternative subjects and offences

7.15 **Dispersal of Groups**

Sections 30 to 32 of the Anti-Social Behaviour Act 2003 provides, if the proper authority is in place, police powers to disperse groups of two or more people and return young persons under 16 years, who are unsupervised in a public place, to their residence. All references in the following are to the 2003 Act unless otherwise stated.

Authorisation

(1) This section applies where a **relevant officer** has reasonable grounds for believing—
   (a) that any members of the public have been intimidated, harassed, alarmed or distressed as a result of the presence or behaviour of groups of two or more persons in **public places** in any locality in his police area (the "**relevant locality**"), and
   (b) that **anti-social behaviour** is a significant and persistent problem in the relevant locality.
(2) The relevant officer may give an authorisation that the powers conferred on a constable in uniform by subsections (3) to (6) are to be exercisable for a period specified in the authorisation which does not exceed 6 months.

Directions

(3) Subsection (4) applies if a constable in uniform has reasonable grounds for believing that the presence or behaviour of a group of two or more persons in any public place in the relevant locality has resulted, or is likely to result, in any members of the public being intimidated, harassed, alarmed or distressed.
(4) The constable may give one or more of the following directions:
   (a) a direction requiring the persons in the group to disperse (either immediately or by such time as he may specify and in such way as he may specify),
   (b) a direction requiring any of those persons whose place of residence is not within the **relevant locality** to leave the relevant locality or any part of the relevant locality (either immediately or by such time as he may specify and in such way as he may specify), and
   (c) a direction prohibiting any of those persons whose place of residence is not within the relevant locality from returning to the relevant locality or any part of the relevant locality for such period (not exceeding 24 hours) from the giving of the direction as he may specify,
but this subsection is subject to subsection (5).

Anti-Social Behaviour Act 2003, s 30(1)–(4)

Offence

A person who knowingly contravenes a direction given to him under s 30(4) commits an offence.   Anti-Social Behaviour Act 2003, s 32(2)

Points to prove

✓ knowingly contravened a direction given by a constable/CSO
✓ under s 30(4) of the Anti-Social Behaviour Act 2003
✓ requiring you as part of a group
✓ to disperse immediately/by a specified time and in such way
✓ as was specified, **or**
✓ requiring you as a person not residing within the relevant locality
✓ to leave that locality or any part of it
✓ immediately/by a specified time and in such way
✓ as was specified, **or**
✓ prohibiting you as a person whose place of residence was not within the relevant locality
✓ from returning to the relevant locality or any part of it
✓ for such period (not exceeding 24 hours) from the giving of the direction
✓ as was specified

Meanings

Relevant locality

Means any locality in the **relevant officer's** police area.

Relevant officer

Means a police officer who has given the authorization being of or above the rank of superintendent.

Public place

Means any highway and any place to which at the material time the public or any section of the public has access, on payment or otherwise, as of right or by virtue of express or implied permission.

Anti-social behaviour

Means behaviour by a person which causes, or is likely to cause, harassment, alarm, or distress to one or more other persons not of the same household as the person.

Explanatory notes

• The power to disperse groups **or** to return people under 16 to their place of residence applies where a relevant officer has reasonable grounds for believing that any members of the public have been intimidated, harassed, alarmed, or distressed because of the presence or behaviour of two or more people in **public places** in the relevant locality and that **anti-social behaviour** is a significant and persistent problem in the relevant locality.

- Subsection (5) stipulates that a direction under s 30 may not be given to any person who is involved in an industrial dispute or a person taking part in a public procession in respect of which the appropriate notice, if required, has been given.
- The power to give directions must be for a specified period, as given in the authorization, but this cannot exceed 6 months.
- If, between the hours of 9 p.m. and 6 a.m., a constable in uniform finds a person in any public place in the relevant locality who s/he has reasonable grounds for believing is under the age of 16 years and is not under the effective control of a parent or responsible adult aged 18 years or older, s/he may remove them to the person's place of residence unless s/he has reasonable grounds for believing that the person would, if removed to that place, be likely to suffer significant harm (s 30(6)).
- An 'authorization notice' is a notice which states the authorization has been given, specifies the relevant locality, and specifies the period during which the relevant powers are exercisable (s 31(4)).
- The officer who gave it or another relevant officer whose police area includes the relevant locality who is of the same or higher rank than the officer who gave it may withdraw an authorization.
- Before withdrawal of an authorization, any local authority whose area includes the whole or part of the relevant locality must be consulted.
- The powers conferred on a constable in uniform by s 30(3) to (6) also apply to a designated community support officer.
- A community support officer is also empowered to require the name and address of any person who commits an offence under s 34(2) and may detain him/her/them for 30 minutes pending the arrival of a police constable.

Related cases

R (on the application of W) v Commissioner of the Metropolitan Police & Another [2006] EWCA Civ 458 CA Children, like adults, have a right to go as they wish in public but if they misbehave within a given dispersal area they are liable to a direction from the police as are adults. However, a child can be removed to a place of residence and should be protected as far as is possible. The removal power allows the use of reasonable force, is an express power which is coercive, but is not one of arrest. Section 30(6) does not have a curfew effect and does not provide an arbitrary power to remove any unaccompanied child within a designated dispersal area at night whatever the child was doing and whatever circumstances prevailing in the area. This power can only be used if in the light of its purpose it is reasonable to do so and the officer must have regard to the following: age of the child; time of night; is the child vulnerable or in distress and reason for being in the area/behaviour.

R (on the application of Singh & Another) v Chief Constable of West Midlands Police [2006] EWCA Civ 1118 CA Section 30 applies to protests. If the section had meant to exclude protests it would have made an express provision for such as it has done for industrial disputes or public processions in s 30(5).

7.15 Dispersal of Groups

Bucknell v DPP [2006] EWHC 1888 (Admin), QBD School pupils were simply going home from school by a reasonable route and behaving properly therefore the constable had no reasonable belief that the requirements were met. Section 30(3) is capable of operating by the presence alone of two or more persons, but great care should be taken if it is that alone that is relied upon. Unless there are exceptional circumstances a reasonable belief must normally depend, in part, on some behaviour by the group that can be construed as being possible of causing harassment, intimidation, alarm or distress to avoid the illegitimate intrusion into the rights of persons to go about their legitimate business.

Practical considerations

- The removal power allows the use of reasonable force, it is an express power which is coercive, but is not one of arrest.
- If the power to take a person under 16 to his/her residence is exercised any local authority whose area includes whole or part of the relevant locality must be informed (s 32(4)).
- A reference to the presence or behaviour of a group of people includes a reference to the presence or behaviour of any one or more of the people in the group (s 30(7)).
- An authorization must be in writing, must be signed by the relevant officer making it and must specify the relevant locality, the grounds on which it is given, and the period during which the powers are exercisable (s 31(1)).
- An authorization may not be given without the consent of the local authority or each local authority whose area includes the whole or part of the relevant locality (s 31(2)).
- Publishing an authorization notice in a newspaper circulated in the relevant locality and/or putting an authorization notice in a conspicuous place(s) in the relevant locality (s 31(3)) must announce the giving of an authorization.
- Section 31(3) must be complied with before the period mentioned in s 31(4)(c) commences.
- A direction under s 30(4) may be given orally, to an individual or to two or more persons together and may be withdrawn or varied by the person who gave it (s 32(1)).

 Summary

 6 months

 3 months' imprisonment and/or a fine not exceeding level 4 on the standard scale.

Links to alternative subjects and offences

7.16 Litter and Abandoned Vehicles

Litter is legislated for by the Environmental Protection Act 1990 and the Litter Act 1983. Whereas the Refuse Disposal (Amenity) Act 1978 concerns the removal and disposal of abandoned vehicles and other refuse.

7.16.1 Leaving litter

Section 87 of the Environmental Protection Act 1990 creates an offence of defacing a place by the leaving of litter.

Offence

A person is guilty of an offence if he throws down, drops or otherwise deposits any litter in any place to which this section applies, and leaves it.

Environmental Protection Act 1990, s 87(1)

Points to prove

✓ threw down/dropped/deposited litter
✓ in a place to which this section applies
✓ and left it there

Meanings

Deposits

Means no more than places or puts (*Felix v DPP* [1998] Crim LR 657).

Litter

Includes the discarded ends of cigarettes, cigars and like products, and discarded chewing gum and the discarded remains of other products designed for chewing.

Place

- Any place in the area of a principal litter authority that is open to the air. Land shall be treated as 'open to the air' notwithstanding that it is covered, providing it is open to the air on at least one side.
- This section does not apply to a place which is 'open to the air' if the public does not have access to it, with or without payment.

Explanatory notes

- It is immaterial for the purposes of this section whether the litter is deposited on land or in water, so the offence extends to dropping or depositing litter in bodies of water such as rivers and lakes.

- An authorized officer of a litter authority or a constable may, if s/he has reason to believe that a person has committed an offence under s 87, issue a fixed penalty notice to that person (s 88).

Defences

No offence is committed under subsection (1) above where the depositing of the litter is:

(a) authorised by law, or

(b) done with the consent of the owner, occupier or other person having control of the place where it is deposited.

Environmental Protection Act 1990, s 87(4A)

Defence notes

A person may only give consent under subsection (4A)(b) in relation to the depositing of litter in a lake or pond or watercourse if s/he is the owner, occupier, or other person having control of all the land adjoining that lake, pond, or watercourse and all the land through or into which water in that lake, pond, or watercourse directly or indirectly discharges, otherwise than by means of a public sewer.

Practical considerations

- The area of a local authority which is on the coast extends down to the low-water mark (s 72 of the Local Government Act 1972). Therefore, it becomes an offence to deposit litter on the beach.
- Consider penalty notice for disorder scheme (litter offence applies to constable only).
- If a **fixed penalty notice** is issued under s 88 by an authorized officer (suitably designated constable or community support officer) a copy of it must be sent to the relevant litter authority within 24 hours.

 Summary   6 months

 A fine not exceeding level 4 on the standard scale.

7.16.2 **Removal/interference with litter bins**

Section 5 of the Litter Act 1983 creates an offence in relation to the removal of, or interference with, litter bins.

7.16.2 Removal/Interference with Litter Bins

Offence

Any person who wilfully removes or otherwise interferes with any litter bin or notice board provided or erected under this section or section 185 of the Highways Act 1980 commits an offence.   Litter Act 1983, s 5(9)

Points to prove

✓ wilfully
✓ removed/otherwise interfered with
✓ litter bin/notice board
✓ provided under this section **or** s 185 of the Highways Act 1980

Meanings

Litter authority

In relation to England and Wales, means, except where otherwise provided:

(a) a county council;
(b) a district council;
(c) a London borough council;
(d) the Common Council of the City of London;
(e) a parish council;
(f) a community council;
(g) a joint body;
(h) the Sub-Treasurer of the Inner Temple, or
(i) the Under Treasurer of the Middle Temple.

Joint body

Means a joint body constituted solely of two or more such councils as are mentioned in paragraphs (a) to (f) of the definition of 'litter authority'.

Explanatory notes

- The litter authority in England and Wales may provide and maintain litter bins for refuse or litter in any street or public place.
- The duties of the litter authority includes emptying and cleaning the bins provided by them and they also have the power to empty and clean bins provided in any street or public place by any other person.
- The emptying must be sufficiently frequent to ensure no litter bin or its contents become a nuisance or gives reasonable cause for complaint.
- Where such litter bins are provided the authority may erect notices about the leaving of refuse or litter, and for this purpose may erect and maintain notice boards.
- No litter bin or notice board erected under this section on any land forming an open space provided by or under the management and control of another litter authority or parish meeting without the consent of that authority or meeting, or on land not forming part of a street without the consent of the owner and occupier of that land.

Practical considerations

- In addition to the penalty for this offence, the court may order a defendant to pay compensation to the litter authority concerned.
- This section also applies to receptacles provided under s 76 of the Public Health Act 1936 or s 51 of the Public Health Act 1961.
- If a bin is taken with a view to its never being recovered as opposed to a prank (eg moving round the corner) consider the offence of theft (see **3.1**).
- If appropriate, consider the offence of criminal damage (see **4.4**).

 Summary   6 months

 A fine not exceeding level 1 on the standard scale.

7.16.3 **Unauthorized dumping/abandoned vehicles**

Section 2 of the Refuse Disposal (Amenity) Act 1978 creates an offence of abandoning motor vehicles or any other thing on land in the open air.

Offences

Any person who, without lawful authority:

(a) abandons on any land in the open air, or on any other land forming part of a highway, a motor vehicle or any thing which formed part of a motor vehicle and was removed from it in the course of dismantling the vehicle on the land; or

(b) abandons on any such land any thing other than a motor vehicle, being a thing which he has brought to the land for the purpose of abandoning it there,

shall be guilty of an offence. Refuse Disposal (Amenity) Act 1978, s 2(1)

Points to prove

✓ without lawful authority
✓ abandoned on land
✓ in the open air/forming part of a highway
✓ a motor vehicle/part of a motor vehicle removed from it in the course of dismantling it on the land; **or**
✓ an item brought to the land
✓ for the purpose of abandoning it there

7.16.3 Unauthorized Dumping/Abandoned Vehicles

Meaning of motor vehicle

Means a mechanically propelled vehicle intended or adapted for use on roads, whether or not it is in a fit state for such use, and includes any trailer intended or adapted for use as an attachment to such a vehicle, any chassis or body, with or without wheels, appearing to have formed part of such a vehicle or trailer and anything attached to such a vehicle or trailer.

Explanatory notes

- A person who leaves any thing on any land in such circumstances or for so long that s/he can reasonably be assumed to have abandoned it or to have brought it to the land to abandon it there will be deemed to have abandoned it there or brought it there to be abandoned, unless the contrary is shown.
- In addition to any penalty, the court may order the defendant to pay any costs involved in the removal and disposal of the offending article.

Practical considerations

- The removal and disposal of items under this section is the responsibility of the local authority.
- If such articles are reported or found by you, report it to your local authority.
- Section 2A of the Refuse Disposal (Amenity) Act 1978 gives an authorized officer of a local authority the power to issue a fixed penalty in respect of the offence of abandoning a vehicle.
- Check any motor vehicles found thoroughly for other offences or involvement in crime.

 Summary   6 months

 3 months' imprisonment and/or a fine not exceeding level 4 on the standard scale.

Links to alternative subjects and offences

7.17 Trespassers Residing on Land/Failing to Leave

The Criminal Justice and Public Order Act 1994 empowers police officers to direct trespassers to leave land, seize and remove motor vehicles from land, including common land. All references are to the 1994 Act unless otherwise stated.

7.17.1 Power to remove trespassers from land

Section 61 empowers the senior police officer at the scene to direct two or more persons trespassing on land, intending to reside there for a period of time, to leave that land.

Directions

(1) If the senior police officer present at the scene reasonably believes that two or more persons are trespassing on land and are present there with the common purpose of residing there for any period, that reasonable steps have been taken by or on behalf of the occupier to ask them to leave and—

  (a) that any of those persons has caused damage to the land or to property on the land or used threatening, abusive or insulting words or behaviour towards the occupier, a member of his family or an employee or agent of his, OR

  (b) that those persons have between them six or more vehicles on the land,

he may direct those persons, or any of them, to leave the land and to remove any vehicles or other property they have with them on the land.

Offences

(4) If a person knowing that a direction under subsection (1) has been given which applies to him:

  (a) fails to leave the land as soon as is reasonably practicable, or

  (b) having left again enters the land as a trespasser within the period of 3 months beginning with the day on which the direction was given,

he commits an offence.

Criminal Justice and Public Order Act 1994, s 61(1) & (4)

Points to prove
✓ knowing a direction to leave land had been given which applied to you
✓ failed to leave the land as soon as reasonably practicable; **or**
✓ returned to the land as a trespasser within 3 months of day the direction was given.

Meanings

Land

Does not include buildings other than agricultural buildings or scheduled monuments. It does not include land forming part of a highway unless it is a footpath, bridleway, or byway open to all traffic or a road used as a public path, or is a restricted byway or a cycle track.

Trespass

Means (subject to the extensions effected by the references to common land), trespass as against the occupier of the land.

Property

In relation to damage to property on land, means property within the meaning of s 10(1) of the Criminal Damage Act 1971 (see **4.5**).

Damage

Means the deposit of any substance capable of polluting the land.

Vehicle

Means any vehicle whether or not it is in a fit state for use on roads, and includes any chassis or body, with or without wheels, appearing to have formed part of such a vehicle, and any load carried by, and anything attached to, such a vehicle. It includes a touring caravan, static caravan, or mobile home.

Explanatory notes

- Before giving the direction the senior officer must reasonably believe that two or more people are trespassing on land for the common purpose of residing there AND caused **damage** to the land/property OR used threatening, abusive, or insulting words or behaviour towards the occupier/family/employee/agent, OR that the trespassers have, between them, 6 or more vehicles on the land.
- The senior officer must also be satisfied that reasonable steps have been taken by or on behalf of the occupier of the land to ask them to leave.
- Once satisfied that the above criteria are met the senior officer may direct the trespassers to leave the land, together with their vehicles and any other property they have with them.
- If the senior police officer believes that the people in question were not originally trespassers but have since become trespassers, s/he must believe that the other criteria were met after they became trespassers before s/he gives the direction.

7.17.1 **Power to Remove Trespassers From Land**

- This section applies to common land as if references to trespassing and trespassers were references to acts or people doing acts constituting a trespass against the occupier or an infringement of the commoners' rights.
- References to 'the occupier' include any of the commoners or, where the public have access to common land, the local authority as well as a commoner.
- If there is more than one occupier a person will not trespass if s/he is permitted to be there by any one of the occupiers.
- 'Local authority', in relation to common land, means any local authority which has powers in relation to the land under s 9 of the Commons Registration Act 1965.
- 'Occupier' means the person entitled to possession of the land by virtue of an estate or interest held by him/her.
- Under s 62 a constable may seize and remove a vehicle if a direction has been given under s 61 and s/he reasonably suspects that a person to whom it applies has, without reasonable excuse, failed to remove a vehicle which appears to belong to him/her, or to be in his/her possession or under his/her control; or s/he has entered the land as a trespasser with a vehicle within 3 months of the direction being given.

Defences

In proceedings for an offence under this section it is a defence for the accused to show:
(a) that he was not trespassing on the land, or
(b) that he had a reasonable excuse for failing to leave the land as soon as reasonably practicable or, as the case may be, for again entering the land as a trespasser.　　Criminal Justice and Public Order Act 1994, s 61(6)

Practical considerations
- The direction must be given by the senior police officer present.
- Any constable at the scene may communicate the direction to the trespassers, and s/he does not need to be in uniform.
- There is no legal requirement to give the direction in writing, but it may negate arguments later.
- Check that reasonable steps have been taken by the occupier to ask the trespassers to leave.
- If the landlord has set a time limit for the offenders to leave do not give a direction under this section until that time has expired.
- For the purpose of this section a person may be regarded as having a purpose of residing in a place notwithstanding that he has a home elsewhere.
- If an alternative site is available then consider **7.17.2** (power to remove trespassers—alternative site available).
- The local authority have similar powers under s 77 where persons are for the time being residing in vehicle(s) within that authority's area

---

Power to Remove Trespassers—Alternative Site Available 7.17.2

on: land forming part of a highway; any other unoccupied land; or on any occupied land without the consent of the occupier. The authority may give them directions to leave the land and remove the vehicle(s) and any other property they have with them on the land.

 Summary 6 months

 3 months' imprisonment and/or a fine not exceeding level 4 on the standard scale.

7.17.2 Power to remove trespassers—alternative site available

Section 62A provides for the directing of trespassers to leave land when there is an alternative site available. Section 62B creates an offence of failing to leave the land as directed or re-entering it as a trespasser within 3 months and s 62C provides a power to seize any vehicle not so removed or taken back onto the land. Section 62D relates to common land.

Directions

(1) If the senior police officer present at a scene reasonably believes that the conditions in subsection (2) are satisfied in relation to a person and land, he may direct the person—
  (a) to leave the land;
  (b) to remove any vehicle and other property he has with him on the land.
(2) The conditions are—
  (a) that the person and one or more others (the trespassers) are trespassing on the land;
  (b) that the trespassers have between them at least one vehicle on the land;
  (c) that the trespassers are present on the land with the common purpose of residing there for any period;
  (d) if it appears to the officer that the person has one or more caravans (see subsection (6) below) in his possession or under his control on the land, that there is a suitable pitch on a **relevant caravan site** (see subsection (6) below) for that caravan or each of those caravans;
  (e) that the occupier of the land or a person acting on his behalf has asked the police to remove the trespassers from the land.
    Criminal Justice and Public Order Act 1994, s 62A(1) & (2)

357

Offences

A person commits an offence if he knows that a direction under s 62A(1) has been given which applies to him and:

(a) he fails to leave the relevant land as soon as reasonably practicable, or

(b) he enters any land in the area of the relevant local authority as a trespasser before the end of the relevant period with the intention of residing there.   Criminal Justice and Public Order Act 1994, s 62B(1)

Points to prove

✓ knowing that a direction under s 62A(1) had been given
✓ which applied to him/her
✓ failed to leave the land as soon as reasonably practicable, **or**
✓ entered any land
✓ in the area of the relevant local authority
✓ as a trespasser
✓ before the end of the relevant period
✓ with the intention of residing there

Meanings

Relevant period

Three months starting with the day on which the direction is given.

Vehicle (see 7.17.1)

Occupier (see 7.17.1)

Relevant caravan site

Means a caravan site that is situated in the area of a local authority within whose area the land is situated, and managed by a **relevant site manager**.

Relevant site manager

Means a local authority within whose area the land is situated or a **registered social landlord**.

Registered social landlord

Means a body registered as a social landlord under the Housing Act 1996.

Land

Does not include buildings other than agricultural buildings or scheduled monuments.

Local authority

Means:

- in Greater London, a London borough, or the Common Council of the City of London;
- in England outside Greater London, a county council, or the Council of the Isles of Scilly;
- in Wales, a county council or a county borough council.

The relevant land

Means the land in respect of which a direction under s 62A(1) is given.

The relevant local authority

Means:

(a) if the relevant land is situated in the area of more than one local authority (but is not in the Isles of Scilly), the district council, or county borough council within whose area the relevant land is situated;
(b) if the relevant land is situated on the Isles of Scilly, the Council of the Isles of Scilly;
(c) in any other case, the local authority within whose area the relevant land is situated.

Explanatory notes

- The senior officer present at the scene may, if s/he reasonably believes that certain conditions are satisfied concerning a person and land, give a direction to that person to leave the land and/or to remove any vehicle and other property s/he has with him/her on the land.
- The conditions that need to be satisfied are:
  - that one or more are trespassing on the land;
  - that they have between them at least one vehicle on the land;
  - that they have a common purpose of residing there for any period;
  - that there is a suitable pitch on a relevant caravan site for each caravan; and
  - that the land occupier/representative has asked the police to remove the trespassers from the land.
- Under s 62C a constable may seize and remove a vehicle if a direction has been given under s 62A(1) and s/he reasonably suspects that a person to whom it applies has, without reasonable excuse, failed to remove a vehicle which appears to belong to him/her, or to be in his/her possession or under his/her control; or s/he has entered the land of the relevant local authority as a trespasser with a vehicle before the end of the relevant period with the intention of residing there.
- Sections 62A to 62C apply to common land as if references to trespassing and trespassers were references to acts or persons doing acts constituting a trespass against the occupier or an infringement of the commoners' rights.
- References to 'the occupier' where the public has access to the land, include the local authority and any commoner or, in any other case, include the commoners or any of them.
- If there is more than one occupier a person will not trespass if s/he is permitted to be there by the other occupier.

Defences

In proceedings for an offence under this section it is a defence for the accused to show:

(a) that he was not trespassing on the land in respect of which he is alleged to have committed the offence, or

(b) that he had a reasonable excuse:
  (i) for failing to leave the relevant land as soon as reasonably practicable, or
  (ii) for entering land in the area of the relevant local authority as a trespasser with the intention of residing there, or

(c) that, at the time the direction was given, he was under the age of 18 years and was residing with his parent or guardian.

Criminal Justice and Public Order Act 1994, s 62B(5)

Practical considerations

- In practice liaison is made with the duty inspector and the 'relevant local authority' before any action is taken.
- A direction given may be communicated to the person to whom it applies by any constable at the scene, and s/he need not be in uniform.
- If it is intended to give a direction under this section and it appears that the person has one or more caravans in his/her possession or control on the land, every local authority within whose area the land is situated must be consulted about a suitable pitch for each caravan on a relevant caravan site situated in the local authority's area.

 Summary　　　　 6 months

 3 months' imprisonment and/or a fine not exceeding level 4 on the standard scale.

Links to alternative subjects and offences

7.18 Violent Entry to Premises/Squatters

Sections 6 and 7 of the Criminal Law Act 1977 relate to the use or threat of violence to secure entry into premises and unauthorized entry or remaining on premises in certain circumstances. All references are to the 1977 Act unless otherwise stated.

7.18.1 Violent entry to premises

Section 6 creates an offence of using or threatening violence to secure entry to premises.

> **Offence**
> Subject to the following provisions of this section, any person who, without lawful authority, uses or threatens violence for the purpose of securing entry into any premises for himself or for any other person is guilty of an offence, provided that:
> (a) there is someone present on those premises at the time who is opposed to the entry which the violence is intended to secure; and
> (b) the person using or threatening the violence knows that that is the case.
>
> Criminal Law Act 1977, s 6(1)

Points to prove
✓ without lawful authority
✓ used/threatened violence
✓ to secure entry to premises
✓ knowing someone who was present on the premises opposed that entry

---

Meanings

Premises

Means any building, any part of a building under separate occupation, any land ancillary to a building, and the site comprising any building(s) together with any land ancillary thereto.

Access

Means, in relation to any premises, any part of any site or building within which those premises are situated that constitutes an ordinary means of access to those premises (whether or not that is its sole or primary use).

Explanatory notes

- Section 6(1) does not apply to a **displaced residential occupier** or a protected intending occupier of the relevant premises or a person acting on behalf of such an occupier. If the defendant produces sufficient evidence that s/he was, or was acting on behalf of, such an occupier s/he will be presumed to be so unless the prosecution prove the contrary.
- '**Displaced residential occupier**' means, subject to the following exception, any person who was occupying any premises as a residence immediately before being excluded from occupation by anyone who entered those premises, or any access to those premises, as a **trespasser** is a displaced residential occupier of the premises so long as s/he continues to be excluded from occupation of the premises by the original trespasser or by any subsequent trespasser.
- The exception referred to above is that a person who was him/herself occupying the relevant premises as a trespasser immediately before being excluded from occupation shall not be a displaced residential occupier of the premises.
- '**Trespasser**' means someone who wrongfully enters onto someone else's premises.
- 'Protected intending occupier' is defined in s 12A.
- Anyone who enters, or is on or in occupation of, any premises under a title derived from a trespasser or by a licence or consent given by a trespasser or by a person deriving title from a trespasser will himself be treated as a trespasser (whether or not s/he would be a trespasser apart from this provision).
- The fact that a person has an interest in, or right to possession or occupation of, the premises does not, for s 6(1) constitute lawful authority for the use or threat of violence by him/her or anyone else to secure entry into those premises.

Practical considerations

- It is immaterial whether the violence is directed against a person or property and whether the violent entry is to acquire possession of the premises.
- A person who, by virtue of the definition of 'displaced residential occupier', is a displaced residential occupier of any premises is also deemed a displaced residential occupier of any access to those premises.
- A person on premises as a trespasser does not cease to be a trespasser under this legislation by being allowed time to leave there, nor does a person cease to be a displaced residential occupier of any premises because of any such allowance of time to a trespasser.
- A squatter is someone who possesses premises without the lawful consent of the owner.
- Proceed with care where squatting appears to have lasted for a long time. It is possible for a squatter to gain legal title if he/she has held the property for 12 years adversely but without disturbance or legal attempts to repossess it.

Summary 6 months

 6 months' imprisonment and/or a fine not exceeding level 5 on
the standard scale.

7.18.2 **Adverse occupation of residential premises**

Section 7 creates an offence of failing to leave residential premises once
the lawful occupiers have gained legitimate entry.

Offence

Subject to the provisions of this section and s 12A(9), any person who is on
any premises as a trespasser after having entered as such is guilty of an
offence if he fails to leave those premises on being required to do so by or
on behalf of:

(a) a displaced residential occupier of the premises; or
(b) an individual who is a protected intending occupier of the premises.

Criminal Law Act 1977, s 7(1)

Points to prove

✓ on premises
✓ as a trespasser
✓ having entered as such
✓ failed to leave when required
✓ by/on behalf of a displaced residential occupier/protected intending occupier.

Meanings

Premises (see **7.18.1**)

Trespasser (see **7.18.1**)

Explanatory notes

A reference to any premises includes a reference to any access to them,
whether or not the access itself constitutes premises.

Defences

7(2) It is a defence for the accused to prove that he believed that the person requiring him to leave the premises was not a displaced residential occupier or protected intending occupier of the premises or a person acting on their behalf.

7(3) In proceedings for an offence under this section it is a defence for the accused to prove that:

(a) the premises in question are, or form part of, premises used mainly for residential purposes; and

(b) he was not on any part of the premises used wholly or mainly for residential purposes.

...

12A(9) In proceedings for an offence under s 7 where the accused was requested to leave the premises by a person claiming to be or to act on behalf of a protected intending occupier of the premises:

(a) it shall be a defence for the accused to prove that, although asked to do so by the accused at the time the accused was requested to leave, that person failed at that time to produce to the accused such a statement as is referred to in s 12A(2)(d) or s 12A(4)(d) or such a certificate as is referred to in s 12A(6)(d); and

(b) any document purporting to be a document under 12A(6)(d) will be received in evidence and, unless the contrary is proved, will be determined to have been issued by or on behalf of the authority stated in the certificate.

Criminal Law Act 1977, ss 7(2), (3) and 12A(9)

Practical considerations

- Officers wishing to apply these provisions in an operational situation should make themselves conversant with the terms—displaced residential occupier, squatters and protected intending occupier.
- A leaseholder can go to a commissioner of oaths (usually a solicitor), with a written declaration which is then signed by the commissioner. The leaseholder can then use force (either personally or he can employ others on his behalf) to break into the premises to regain possession. Once the owner etc. has demanded that the premises be vacated, then s 7 makes it an offence (subject to any defences) for the squatters to remain.
- If the squatter is being evicted by a protected intending occupier (this does not apply to an eviction by a displaced residential occupier) then s/he is entitled to see a copy of the statement or certificate which must be held by the person making the eviction. S/he has a statutory defence if the certificate is not produced.
- If the squat appears to be long standing, see **7.18.1** (violent entry to premises).

7.18.2 Adverse Occupation of Residential Premises

 Summary   6 months

 6 months' imprisonment and/or a fine not exceeding level 5 on the standard scale.

Links to alternative subjects and offences

Chapter 8

Firearms, Fireworks, and Weapons

8.1 'Section 1 Firearms' Offences

The Firearms Act 1968 provides various offences connected with firearms, air weapons, shotguns, and associated ammunition.

8.1.1 Possessing s 1 firearm/ammunition without certificate

This offence involves being in possession of a firearm/ammunition without a valid firearm certificate. Any weapon or ammunition applicable to this section is commonly known as a 'section 1 firearm/ammunition'.

> **Offences**
>
> Subject to any **exemption** under this Act, it is an offence for a person—
> (a) to have in his **possession**, or to **purchase** or **acquire**, a **firearm** to which this section applies without holding a **firearm certificate** in force at the time, or otherwise than as authorised by the certificate;
> (b) to have in his possession, or to purchase or acquire, any **ammunition** to which this section applies without holding a firearm certificate in force at the time, or otherwise than as authorised by such certificate, or in quantities in excess of those so authorised. **Firearms Act 1968, s 1(1)**

Points to prove
- ✓ date and location
- ✓ possessed/purchased/acquired
- ✓ a s 1 firearm/ammunition
- ✓ without/not authorized by/in quantities exceeding those authorized by
- ✓ a firearms certificate

Meanings

Exemptions

This includes: antique firearms; rifles loaned on private land; carriers, auctioneers and warehousemen; crown servants; police; armed forces; athletics and other approved activities; museums; police permits; registered firearms dealers; rifle and pistol clubs; ship and aircraft equipment; licensed slaughterers; theatres and cinemas; Northern Ireland firearms certificate holder; visiting forces; visitors' permits.

Possession

This has a wide meaning. The term has two distinct elements:

- The mental element. Whereby the defendant must know of the existence of the firearm, but cannot claim ignorance that it was technically 'a firearm'.
- The practical element. As this term is broader than actual physical possession, a person can 'possess' a firearm in a house or premises under his/her control, even though he/she is not at the premises. Similarly, the same firearm could be 'possessed' by two people at the same time, such as the firearm's lawful owner and also its custodian who keeps the firearm at his home.

Purchase

This is not defined and should be given its natural meaning.

Acquire

Means to 'hire, accept as a gift or borrow'.

Firearm

Means a **lethal barrelled weapon** of any description from which any **shot, bullet or other missile** can be discharged and includes:

- any **prohibited weapon**, whether it is such a lethal weapon as aforesaid or not; **and**
- any **component part** of such a lethal or prohibited weapon; **and**
- any **accessory** to any such weapon designed or adapted to diminish the noise or flash caused by firing the weapon.

Lethal barrelled weapon

This is not defined although the courts have determined that the weapon must be capable of causing injury from which death may result. This also includes a weapon not designed to kill or inflict injury but capable of doing so if misused (such as a signal pistol or a flare launcher).

Shot, bullet, or other missile

These terms are not defined and should be given their natural meaning:

- 'Shot' usually means round pellets.
- 'Bullet' is normally discharged from a weapon with a rifled barrel.
- 'Missile' is a more general term—darts and pellets have been held to be missiles.

Prohibited weapons

Prohibited weapons are described in s 5. The list is quite lengthy but includes such items as rocket launchers, machine guns, CS spray, air weapons with self-contained gas cartridge system, and grenades. In order to trade in/manufacture these weapons you need written authority of the Defence Council. In order to possess them you need the authority of the Secretary of State.

Component part

Means any working part of the mechanism of a lethal weapon. This will include the trigger but not the trigger guard for example.

Accessory

This is given its natural meaning, and includes such accessories as a silencer or flash eliminator.

Section 1 firearm

Means any firearm to which s 1 applies, except:
• normal shotguns (see **8.2** for details);
• normal air weapons (see **8.7** for details);
• prohibited weapons.

Firearm certificate

Means a certificate granted by a chief officer of police in respect of any firearm or ammunition to which s 1 applies.

Ammunition

Means ammunition, being any shot, bullet, or other missile that can be used in a firearm. It includes grenades, bombs, and other like missiles, whether capable of use with a firearm or not; prohibited ammunition and blank cartridges.

Section 1 ammunition

Means any ammunition to which s 1 applies, except:
• cartridges containing 5 or more shots, none of which exceed. 36 inch in diameter;
• ammunition for an air gun, air rifle or air pistol;
• prohibited ammunition; or
• blank cartridges not more than one inch in diameter.

Explanatory notes

• This is an absolute offence so no intent is required, only knowledge of the existence of the item, as opposed to its nature.
• A telescopic laser/night sight is **not** a component part or accessory that requires a firearm certificate.
• Whether a silencer or flash eliminator can be an accessory will be a question of fact to be determined in all the circumstances. For instance, if they could be used with the particular firearm and whether the defendant had it with him/her for that purpose. It is the accessory that must be 'so designed or adapted' not the weapon.
• Blank cartridges are cases with primer (small explosive charge at the end of the cartridge) and gunpowder; or primed cartridges (as blank but without the gunpowder) both able to be used in a firearm and producing an explosive effect when fired.

8.1.1 Possessing s 1 Firearm/Ammunition without Certificate

- It is a summary offence under s 35 of the Violent Crime Reduction Act 2006 for a person to sell or purchase a cap-type primer designed for use in metallic ammunition for a firearm being either:
  - ♦ a primer to which this section applies,
  - ♦ an empty cartridge case incorporating such a primer; unless that person is a registered firearms dealer; it is their trade or business; produces a certificate authorizing possession; is in Her Majesty's Services entitled to do so; or shows that s/he is entitled by virtue of any enactment.
- Blank cartridges greater than one inch in diameter are s 1 ammunition.
- The diameter of a cartridge is obtained by measuring immediately in front of the cannelure or rim of its base.

Defence
There is no statutory defence as it is an absolute offence.

Related cases

Moore v Gooderham [1960] 3 All ER 575, QBD A lethal barrelled weapon must be capable of causing injury from which death may result.

Read v Donovan [1947] 1 All ER 37 A lethal barrelled weapon includes a weapon not designed to kill or inflict injury. It also includes one that is capable of doing so if misused (signal pistol).

R v Singh [1989] Crim LR 724 A lethal barrelled weapon can also include a flare launcher.

Grace v DPP The Times, 9 December 1988, QBD Evidence that the firearm can be fired is required from the prosecution to prove that it is a lethal barrelled weapon.

Price v DPP [1996] 7 CL 49 The defendant had someone else's rucksack containing s 1 ammunition. Although unaware of the contents of the rucksack, the offence was still committed.

Sullivan v Earl of Caithness [1976] 1 All ER 844, QBD Possession does not have to be physical possession.

R v Stubbings [1990] Crim LR 811, CA Primer cartridges are ammunition.

Watson v Herman [1952] 2 All ER 70 A telescopic laser/night sight is not a component part or accessory.

R v Buckfield [1998] Crim LR 673 The fact that a silencer may be designed for a different weapon does not prevent it from being an accessory to a firearm if it could be used as such and the defendant had it for that purpose.

Practical considerations

- This is an absolute offence so no *mens rea* ('intent') is required. The prosecution need only prove knowledge of the existence of the item, as opposed to its nature. Similarly, there is no onus to prove that the defendant knew that the article was a firearm.

- In practice, the Forensic Science Laboratory will examine weapons and say whether or not they are lethal. The main characteristic that is measured is the muzzle velocity (the speed at which the projectile leaves the barrel).
- Certain imitation or replica firearms now fall within the s 1 definition.
- A s 1 firearm can only be possessed by a firearms certificate holder or some other lawful authority such as a registered firearms dealer, member of the armed forces, or police officer.
- If someone had a silencer in their possession with no evidence linking it to a suitable weapon, possession alone is unlikely to be an offence.
- All repeating shotguns holding more than two cartridges (eg pump action and revolver shotguns) are 'section 1 firearms'.

 Either way None

 Summary: 6 months' imprisonment and/or a fine not exceeding the statutory maximum.
Indictment: 5 years' imprisonment and/or a fine.
Aggravated offence (see 8.1.2)

8.1.2 **Aggravated firearm offences**

The offences of possession of a s 1 firearm carry a greater punishment (7 years' imprisonment) if they are aggravated by the weapon being of a particular type which are:

- Any shotgun of which the barrel has been illegally shortened to less than 24 inches (making it into in a s 1 firearm).
- Anything having the appearance of a firearm which has been converted into a s 1 firearm.

Offence

It is an offence for a person other than a registered firearms dealer to convert into a firearm anything, which though having the appearance of being a firearm, is so constructed as to be incapable of discharging any missile through its barrel.   Firearms Act 1968, s 4(3)

> **Points to prove**
> ✓ date and location
> ✓ possessed/purchased/acquired
> ✓ a shortened shotgun/a thing converted into a firearm
> ✓ without holding/not authorized by
> ✓ a firearm certificate

Meaning of registered firearms dealer

Means a person who, by way of trade or business:
- manufactures, sells, transfers, repairs, tests or proves firearms or ammunition to which section 1 of this Act applies, or shot guns;
- sells or transfers air weapons.

Explanatory notes

This offence could apply to weapons such as starting pistols or imitation firearms which have been converted to s 1 firearms.

 Either way   None

 Summary: 6 months' imprisonment and/or a fine not exceeding the statutory maximum.
Indictment: 7 years' imprisonment and/or a fine.

8.1.3 Restrictions on s 1 firearms/ammunition to under 14 years

Sections 22(2) and 24(2) of the Firearms Act 1968 place tight restrictions on persons under the age of 14 years from possessing, receiving as gifts or on loan any s 1 firearms/ammunition.

> **Offences**
>
> *Possession by under 14*
>
> It is an offence for a person under the age of 14 to have in his **possession** any firearm or ammunition to which **section 1** of this Act or **section 15** of the Firearms (Amendment) Act 1988 applies, except where under subsections 11(1), (3) or (4) of this Act he is entitled to have possession of it without holding a firearm certificate.   **Firearms Act 1968, s 22(2)**

Make gift, lend, or part with possession to under 14

It is an offence—

(a) to make a gift of or lend any firearm or ammunition to which section 1 of this Act applies to a person under the age of 14; or

(b) to part with the possession of any such firearm or ammunition to a person under that age, except in circumstances where that person is entitled under section 11(1), (3) or (4) of this Act or section 15 of the Firearms (Amendment) Act 1988 to have possession thereof without holding a firearm certificate.   Firearms Act 1968, s 24(2)

Points to prove

Possess by under 14

✓ date and location
✓ being a person under the age of 14 years
✓ possessed
✓ any s 1 firearm or ammunition.

Make gift/lend/part possession to under 14

✓ date and location
✓ make a gift/lend/part with possession
✓ a s 1 firearm or ammunition
✓ to a person under the age of 14 years

Meanings

Possession

This has a wide meaning (see **8.1.1**).

Section 1 firearm or ammunition (see **8.1.1**)

Section 15

Section 15 of the Firearms (Amendment) Act provides the mechanism for the creation of approved rifle and **muzzle loading pistol** clubs where members can, if they wish, use such weapons without being the holder of a firearm certificate.

Muzzle loading pistol

Means a pistol designed to be loaded at the muzzle end of the barrel or chambered with a loose charge (such as gun powder) and a separate ball (or other missile).

Explanatory notes

• These restrictions are in addition to those imposed on persons under 17 years and under 15 years of age.
• Both offences can be committed anywhere and not just in a public place.
• The 1968 Act s **11 exceptions**, applicable to both offences are:

- ✦ carrying a firearm or ammunition belonging to a certificate holder under instructions from, and for the use of, that person for sporting purposes only;
- ✦ a member of a cadet corps (approved by Secretary of State) possessing a firearm/ammunition when engaged as a member of the corps in or in connection with drill or target shooting;
- ✦ a person conducting or carrying on a miniature rifle range (whether for a rifle club or otherwise) or shooting gallery at which no firearms are used other than air weapons or miniature rifles not exceeding .23 inch calibre, may possess, purchase, or acquire, such miniature rifles and ammunition suitable for that purpose; and
- ✦ any person using such rifles/ammunition at such a range or gallery.
- Any firearm or ammunition found on a person in these circumstances may be confiscated by the court.

Defences

Both offences—The section 11 exceptions (see 'Explanatory notes' above) may apply.

Section 24(2) offence—A statutory defence may be available (see **8.7.1**).

Related cases

Morton v Chaney [1960] 3 All ER 632 Shooting rats has been held not to be for sporting purposes.

 Summary

 48 months (Consent of DPP required after 6 months

 6 months' imprisonment and/or a fine not exceeding level 5 on the standard scale.

8.1.4 **Imitation/replica firearms**

Offence

Section 1 of the Firearms Act 1982 provides that this Act applies to an imitation firearm if it—
(a) has the appearance of being a firearm to which s 1 (firearms requiring a certificate) of the 1968 Act applies; and
(b) is so constructed or adapted as to be readily convertible into a firearm to which this section applies.

Points to prove
✓ date and location
✓ possessed/purchased/acquired
✓ an imitation firearm
✓ having the appearance of a section 1 firearm **and**
✓ is constructed/adapted so as to be readily converted into a s 1 firearm
✓ without holding
✓ a firearms certificate

Meanings

Firearm (see **8.1.1**)

Section 1 (see **8.1.1**)

Certificate (see **8.1.1**)

Explanatory notes
• Certain imitation firearms may be classed as s 1 firearms and as such will therefore require a firearms certificate. This is because some 'replica' weapons can be converted into a working firearm.
• Section 1(5) of the Firearms Act 1982 creates a defence for anyone charged with an offence under the 1968 Act as a result of a weapon being reclassified as a s 1 weapon from being an imitation.

Defence
If the accused can show that he did not know and had no reason to suspect that the imitation firearm was constructed or adapted as to be readily converted into a firearm to which s 1 of the 1968 Act applies.

Related cases

R v Howells [1977] 3 All ER 417, CA The defendant believed he had an antique gun (thereby falling within an agreed Home Office exemption) but it was in fact a replica—a s 1 firearm. The offence was still committed as it is one of strict liability.

Cafferata v Wilson [1936] 3 All ER 149, KBD A solid barrel that can be readily converted/adapted to fire missiles by boring the barrel may be a component part of a firearm.

 SSS **E&S**

 Either way ⏱ None

Summary: 6 months' imprisonment and/or a fine not exceeding the statutory maximum.
Indictment: 5 years' imprisonment and/or a fine.
Aggravated offence (see **8.1.2**): 7 years' imprisonment and/or a fine.

8.1.5 **Failing to comply with firearm certificate conditions**

Offences

It is an offence for a person to fail to comply with a condition subject to which a firearm certificate is held by him.   Firearms Act 1968, s 1(2)

Points to prove
✓ date and location
✓ failed to comply with condition
✓ subject to which firearm certificate is held

Meaning of firearm certificate (see 8.1.1)

Explanatory notes
- Section 27(2) of the 1968 Act stipulates that a firearm certificate shall be in the prescribed form and shall specify the conditions subject to which it is held. The general conditions which should be imposed are set out in the Firearms Rules 1998 (SI 1998/1941).
- A statutory condition under the Firearms (Amendment) Act 1988, s 14 also imposes a duty on auctioneers, carriers, or warehousemen to take reasonable care of the custody of firearms and/or ammunition in their possession and it is an offence for them either to fail to keep them in safe custody or to fail to notify any loss forthwith to the police.

Related cases
Hall v Cotton [1976] 3 WLR 681, QBD The owner/certificate holder is 'in possession' of the firearms even though they do not have physical control. Similarly, a custodial keeper of the guns has possession requiring a certificate.

R v Chelmsford Crown Court, ex parte Farrer [2000] 1 WLR 1468, CA Family members had knowledge of where the key to the gun cabinet was kept and so could gain access to the weapons. The Chief Constable was right to refuse renewal of shotgun and firearms certificates on the grounds of a breach of the condition to prevent, 'so far as is reasonably practicable', access to the guns by an unauthorized person.

Summary 48 months

 6 months' imprisonment and/or a fine not exceeding level 5 on the standard scale

Links to alternative subjects and offences

8.2 **Shotgun Offences**

The Firearms Act 1968 provides various offences connected with firearms, associated ammunition, air weapons, and shotguns.

8.2.1 **Shotgun without a certificate**

Section 2 of the Firearms Act 1968 creates the offence of possess, purchase, or acquire a shotgun when not being the holder of a relevant certificate.

Offence

Subject to any **exemption** under this Act, it is an offence for a person to have in his **possession** or to purchase or **acquire** a shotgun without holding a **certificate** under this Act authorising him to possess shotguns.

Firearms Act 1968, s 2(1)

Points to prove
- ✓ date and location
- ✓ possessed/purchased/acquired
- ✓ a shotgun
- ✓ without a certificate

Meanings

Exemptions   (see **8.1.1**)

Possession   (see **8.1.1**)

Purchase   (see **8.1.1**)

Acquire   (see **8.1.1**)

Shotgun

Means a smooth-bore gun (not being an air gun), which:
- has a barrel not less than 24 inches in length and does not have any barrel with a bore exceeding 2 inches in diameter;
- either has no magazine or has a non-detachable magazine incapable of holding more than 2 cartridges; **and**
- is not a revolver gun.

Shotgun certificate

Means a certificate granted by a chief officer of police under this Act authorizing a person to possess shot guns.

Explanatory notes

- The length of the barrel of a firearm is measured from the muzzle to the point at which the charge is exploded on firing and, in the case of a shotgun that length must not be less than 24 inches, otherwise it becomes a s 1 firearm.
- Some antique shotguns may be classed as an 'antique firearm' and thus be exempt from shotgun offences. However, if 'modern' cartridges can be bought and fired using an antique shotgun it cannot be exempt. This exemption does not cover a modern replica of an antique weapon.
- An auctioneer cannot sell shotguns without either being a registered firearms dealer or obtaining a police permit.
- A person may, without holding a shotgun certificate, borrow a shotgun from the occupier of private premises and use it on that land in the occupier's presence (s 11(5)).
- Similarly, (without holding a shotgun certificate) a person may use a shotgun at a time and place approved for shooting at artificial targets by the chief officer of police for the area in which the place is situated (s 11(6)).

Related cases

Watts v Seymour [1967] 1 All ER 1044, QBD The test as to when a purchase/sale was complete was if the purchaser could validly sell and transfer title to the weapon to another person.

R v Howells [1977] 3 All ER 417 A modern reproduction is not an antique.

Richards v Curwen [1977] 3 All ER 426, QBD Whether a firearm is an 'antique' is a matter of fact for justices to decide in each case.

Hall v Cotton [1976] 3 WLR 681, QBD The owner/certificate holder remained in possession of his shotguns despite having no physical control. Similarly, the custodial keeper of the shotguns also has possession and therefore requires a certificate.

Practical considerations

- All repeating shotguns holding more than two cartridges (eg pump action and revolver shotguns) are s 1 firearms.
- Any offence involving a shotgun that has an illegally shortened barrel (less than 24 inches) will be an 'aggravated offence' (see **8.2.2**) carrying a greater penalty. It will also make the shotgun a s 1 firearm.
- A shotgun is deemed to be loaded if there is a cartridge in the barrel or approved magazine that can feed the cartridge into the barrel by manual or automatic means.
- A shotgun adapted to have a magazine must bear a mark on the magazine showing approval by the Secretary of State.
- 'Shotgun' includes any component part of a shotgun and any accessory to a shotgun designed or adapted to diminish the noise or flash caused by firing the gun.

8.2.2 Aggravated Offences

 Either way   None

 Summary: 6 months' imprisonment and/or a fine not exceeding the statutory maximum.
Indictment: 5 years' imprisonment and/or a fine.

8.2.2 **Aggravated offences**

The offence of possession of a shotgun where the barrel has been illegally shortened to less than 24 inches, making it a s 1 firearm, will be classed as an aggravated offence and is punishable with a maximum of 7 years' imprisonment on indictment. It is an offence to shorten a shotgun barrel (creating a 'sawn off' shotgun).

Offence

Subject to this section it is an offence to shorten the barrel of a shotgun to a length less than 24 inches.   Firearms Act 1968, s 4(1)

Points to prove
✓ date and location
✓ shortened shotgun barrel(s)
✓ to length less than 60.96 cm/24ins

Meanings

Shotgun (see **8.2.1**)

Registered firearms dealer (see **8.1.2**)

Explanatory notes
The length of the barrel is determined by measuring from the muzzle to the point at which the charge is exploded on firing the cartridge.

Defence

It is not an offence under subsection 4(1) for a registered firearms dealer to shorten the barrel of a shotgun for the sole purpose of replacing a defective part of the barrel so as to produce a barrel not less than 24 inches in length.
                                                        Firearms Act 1968, s 4(2)

Either way None

 Summary: 6 months' imprisonment and/or a fine not exceeding the statutory maximum.
Indictment: 7 years' imprisonment and/or a fine.

8.2.3 **Shotgun restrictions to under 15 years**

Sections 22 and 24 of the Firearms Act 1968 imposes shotgun restrictions relating to persons under 15.

Offences

Possession by under 15

It is an offence for a person under the age of 15 to have with him an assembled shotgun, except while under the supervision of a person of or over the age of 21, or while the shot gun is so covered with a securely fastened gun cover that it cannot be fired.　　**Firearms Act 1968, s 22(3)**

Make gift to under 15

It is an offence to make a gift of a shot gun or ammunition for a shotgun to a person under the age of 15.　　**Firearms Act 1968, s 24(3)**

Points to prove

Possession by under 15

✓ date and location
✓ person under 15
✓ had with them
✓ assembled shotgun

Make gift to under 15

✓ date and location
✓ made a gift of
✓ shotgun/ammunition for a shotgun
✓ to a person under 15.

Meanings

With him

This phrase has a narrower meaning than 'possession' (see **8.3.6**).

Shotgun (see **8.2.1**)

8.2.4 **Fail to Comply with Shotgun Certificate Conditions**

> **Defence**
>
> A statutory defence is available, but only to the s 24 offence (see **8.7.1**).

Practical considerations

- These offences are in addition to those imposed on persons under 17 years.
- Both offences can be committed anywhere and not just in a public place.
- A court can order the destruction of any shotgun and ammunition to which this offence relates.
- Even tighter restrictions apply to persons under 14.

 Summary   6 months

 A fine not exceeding level 3 on the standard scale.

8.2.4 **Fail to comply with shotgun certificate conditions**

Section 2 of the Firearms Act 1968 creates an offence of failing to comply with a condition imposed by a shotgun certificate.

> **Offence**
>
> It is an offence for a person to fail to comply with a condition subject to which a shotgun certificate is held by him.   **Firearms Act 1968, s 2(2)**

Points to prove

✓ date and location
✓ failed to comply with condition
✓ subject to which shotgun certificate is held

Meaning of shotgun certificate (see 8.2.1)

Practical considerations

- Regarding public safety, the two main conditions applying to shotgun certificate holders are the failure to keep the shotgun(s)

---

and/or cartridges in safe custody or in failing to notify any loss forthwith to the police.

- A chief officer of police has to be satisfied that the applicant can be permitted to possess a shotgun without danger to the public safety or to the peace.
- No certificate shall be granted or renewed if the chief officer of police has reason to believe that the applicant is:
  (a) prohibited by this Act (eg ban on convicted persons) from possessing a shotgun; **or**
  (b) is satisfied that the applicant does not have a good reason for possessing, purchasing or acquiring one.

Firearms Act 1968, s 28(1A)

- There is a presumption in favour of granting unless the police can prove any of the exemptions.
- The certificate must contain a description of the weapon including any identity numbers.

 Summary   48 months

 6 months' imprisonment and/or a fine not exceeding level 5 on the standard scale.

Links to alternative subjects and offences

8.3 Criminal use of Firearms

There is a raft of legislation which has been put in place to try and curb possession of firearms by criminals: some of these measures are discussed below.

8.3.1 Ban on possession by convicted person

Section 21 of the Firearms Act 1968 creates an offence for the possession of any firearm or ammunition by convicted criminals. The section first provides three types of ban: total; 5 years from date of release; while under a licence, order, or binding over condition.

Lengths of ban

Total ban

Anyone sentenced to either preventive detention or a total of 3 years or more imprisonment or corrective training.   Firearms Act 1968, s 21(1)

5 years

Anyone who has been sentenced to either 3 months or more, but less than 3 years' imprisonment, youth custody/detention, or a secure training order. This ban applies from the **date of release**.

Firearms Act 1968, s 21(2)

Other bans

- s 21(2A) intermittent custody order—during any licence period (ban valid until date of final release).
- s 21(3) detention of young persons convicted of serious crime—while released on licence.
- s 21(3) condition (not possess, use or carry a firearm) of a binding over or recognizance—while still subject to that condition.

Offences

Possess whilst banned

It is an offence for a person to contravene any of the foregoing provisions of this section (ban on possession of firearm or ammunition, if subject to above types of ban).   Firearms Act 1968, s 21(4)

Sell/transfer/repair/test/prove for banned person

It is an offence for a person to sell or transfer a firearm or ammunition to, or to repair, test or prove a firearm or ammunition for, a person whom he knows or has reasonable ground for believing to be prohibited by this section from having a firearm or ammunition in his possession.

Firearms Act 1968, s 21(5)

Points to prove

Possess whilst banned

✓ date and location
✓ being person sentenced to
✓ imprisonment/youth custody/detention in YOI/detention in detention centre/subject to secure training order
✓ for a term of [period]
✓ possessed a firearm namely [description]
✓ while banned/before the expiration of ban

Sell/transfer/repair/test/prove for banned person

✓ date and location
✓ sell/transfer **or** repair/test/prove
✓ firearm or ammunition for
✓ a person
✓ prohibited by s 21 from possessing

Meanings

Date of release

This varies; the details are as follows:

• Normal sentence—the actual date a prisoner leaves prison.
• Part imprisonment and part suspended sentence—the date of release from prison.
• A 'secure training order' is whichever is the latest of the following:
  ♦ the actual date of release;
  ♦ the date the person was released from the order because of a breach;
  ♦ the date halfway through the total period of the order.

Possession (see 8.1.1)

Firearm or ammunition (see **8.1.1**)

Related cases

R v Fordham [1969] 3 All ER 532 A suspended sentence is not imprisonment for the purpose of this provision.

Practical considerations

• A suspended sentence is not imprisonment for the purpose of this section.
• Where there are several short sentences, it is the total sentence that counts.
• Anyone who is banned by these provisions can make application to the Crown Court for removal of the ban.
• Do not confuse the terms firearm or ammunition with s 1 firearms or ammunition. This section includes **all** firearms including air weapons and shotguns.
• An air weapon is not generally looked upon by the courts as a lethal barrelled weapon. Therefore, the prosecution must prove that the air

weapon can discharge a shot or missile and that it is capable of
causing injury from which death could result.

 Either way   ⏱ None

▦ **Summary:** 6 months' imprisonment and/or a fine not
exceeding the statutory maximum.
Indictment: 5 years' imprisonment and/or a fine.

8.3.2 **Possession with intent to endanger life**

Section 16 of the Firearms Act 1968 creates the offence of possession of
a firearm or ammunition with intent to endanger life.

Offence

It is an offence for a person to have in his **possession** any **firearm or
ammunition** with **intent** by means thereof to **endanger life** or to enable
another person by means thereof to endanger life, whether any injury has
been caused or not.   Firearms Act 1968, s 16

Points to prove
✓ date and location
✓ possessed firearm/ammunition
✓ with intent
✓ to endanger life/enable another to endanger life thereby

Meanings

Possession (see **8.1.1**)

Firearm or ammunition

Includes all firearms and ammunition (see **8.1.1**).

Intent (see **4.1**)

Endanger life

The key element is the intention that life be endangered, life need not
actually be endangered, although if there is danger to life this may assist
in proving intent. It is sufficient that life was endangered, there is no
need to prove harm or injury to any victim.

Explanatory notes

The intention to endanger life need not be immediate, but it must result from the firearm/ammunition (eg if the defendant possesses the firearm or ammunition but intends to endanger life some other way, say by arson, this offence is **not** committed).

Related cases

R v Bentham [1972] 3 All ER 271, CA Possession is a continuing state and the intention to endanger life might last as long as the possession. The intent may not be limited to an immediate intention.

R v El-hakkaoui [1975] 2 All ER 146, CA It is an offence for a person to have in his possession a firearm/ammunition with intent to endanger the life of people outside the UK.

R v Georgiades [1989] 1 WLR 759, CA Self-defence may be a defence here: it is a matter for the jury to decide.

R v Jones & Others The Times, 14 August 1996 Possession for another to endanger life requires the firearm to be held for that reason, not just for someone involved in crime.

Practical considerations

- Intention to endanger life in another country is also an offence under this section.
- The offence of possession for another to endanger life requires the firearm to be specifically held intending that the other should endanger life with it. If the firearm/ammunition is simply held for someone known to be involved in crime, that will be insufficient for this offence.
- Consider the alternative offences of:
  - ♦ possession with intent to cause fear of violence (which covers a wider set of circumstances) (see **8.3.3**).
  - ♦ committing/being arrested for a relevant offence and possessing a firearm at the time (see **8.3.5**).

 Indictable

 None

 Life imprisonment and/or a fine

8.3.3 **Possession with intent to cause fear of violence**

Section 16A of the Firearms Act 1968 creates an offence of possessing a firearm (or imitation firearm) with intent to cause others to fear unlawful violence being used against them.

Offence

It is an offence for a person to have in his **possession** any **firearm** or **imitation firearm** with intent—
(a) by means thereof to cause; or
(b) to enable another person by means thereof to cause
any person to believe that **unlawful violence** will be used against him or another person.   **Firearms Act 1968, s 16A**

Points to prove
✓ date and location
✓ had in your possession
✓ a firearm/imitation firearm
✓ with intent
✓ to cause/enable another to cause
✓ any person
✓ to believe unlawful violence will be used
✓ against him/her or another person

Meanings

Possession   (see **8.1.1**)

Firearm

Means all firearms, not just s 1 firearms (see **8.1.1**).

Imitation firearm

Means any thing that has the appearance of being a firearm (other than appearance of prohibited weapon for discharge of any noxious liquid, gas or other thing) whether or not it is capable of discharging any shot, bullet or other missile.

Intent   (see **4.1**)

Unlawful violence

Means the unlawful exercise of physical force so as to cause injury or damage to property.

Practical considerations
• The offence can be committed anywhere and does not require an intent to commit any specific criminal offence.

- It does not matter if the weapon is an imitation, inoperative or unloaded.

  Indictable   None

🏛 10 years' imprisonment and/or a fine.

8.3.4 Using a firearm to resist or prevent a lawful arrest

Section 17(1) of the Firearms Act 1968 creates the offence of using a firearm or imitation firearm to resist or prevent a lawful arrest.

> **Offence**
>
> It is an offence for a person to make or attempt to make any use whatsoever of a **firearm** or **imitation firearm** with **intent** to resist or prevent the lawful arrest of himself or another person.   **Firearms Act 1968, s 17(1)**

Points to prove
- ✓ date and location
- ✓ made/attempted to make use
- ✓ of a firearm/an imitation firearm
- ✓ with intent
- ✓ to resist/prevent lawful arrest/detention
- ✓ of self/another.

Meanings

Firearm   (see **8.3.3**)

Imitation firearm   (see **8.3.3**)

Intent   (see **4.1**)

Explanatory notes

In this section, 'firearm' means a complete weapon and does not include component parts and such items as silencers and flash eliminators.

Life imprisonment and/or a fine.

8.3.5 **Possession at time of committing/being arrested for specified offence**

Section 17(2) of the Firearms Act 1968 makes it an offence to be in possession of a firearm or imitation firearm at the time of arrest for certain specified offences.

> **Offence**
>
> If a person at the time of his committing or being arrested for an offence specified under **schedule 1** of this Act, has in his **possession** a **firearm** or **imitation firearm** he shall be guilty of an offence.   Firearms Act 1968, s 17(2)

Points to prove
- ✓ date and location
- ✓ at the time of
- ✓ being arrested for/committing
- ✓ a schedule 1 offence
- ✓ possessed firearm/imitation firearm

Meanings

Schedule 1 offences

- Criminal Damage Act 1971—damage; aggravated damage; arson
- Offences Against the Person Act 1861
  - ✦ unlawful & malicious wounding/GBH
  - ✦ garrotting
  - ✦ criminal use of stupefying drugs
  - ✦ laying explosive to building etc
  - ✦ endangering persons on the railway
  - ✦ assault with intent to resist lawful arrest
  - ✦ assault occasioning actual bodily harm
- Child Abduction Act 1984—abduction of children
- Theft Act 1968—theft; burglary; blackmail; robbery; taking of motor vehicles
- Police Act 1996—assaulting a police officer

- Criminal Justice Act 1991—assaulting a prisoner custody officer
- Criminal Justice & Public Order Act 1994—assaulting a secure training centre custody officer
- Immigration and Asylum Act 1999—assaulting a detainee custody officer
- Sexual Offences Act 2003
  + Rape
  + assault by penetration
  + cause person engage in sexual activity involving penetration
  + rape of a child under 13
  + assault of a child under 13 by penetration
  + cause/incite child under 13 to engage in sexual activity involving penetration
  + sexual activity with a mentally disordered person involving penetration
  + causing/inciting a person with mental disorder to engage in sexual activity involving penetration
- Aiding and abetting any of the above offences
- Attempting to commit any of the above offences.

Possession (see **8.1.1**)

Firearm (see **8.3.3**)

Imitation firearm (see **8.3.3**)

Defence
Possessing the firearm or imitation firearm for a lawful reason or purpose.

Explanatory notes
- In this section, 'firearm' means a complete weapon and does not include component parts and such items as silencers and flash eliminators.
- There is no need to prove any use or intended use of the firearm and the possession of it may be completely unconnected with the other offence committed by the person or for which they are arrested.

Related cases
R v Guy (1991) 93 Cr App R 108, CA Schedule 1 applies to any offence where theft is an element.

R v Nelson [2000] 2 Cr App R 160, CA When the defendant is arrested for a 'relevant' schedule 1 offence there is no need to prove the schedule 1 offence itself.

R v Bentham [2005] UKHL 18, HL Possession of an imitation firearm is not falsely pretending to have a firearm by putting your own fingers in a jacket you are wearing, but actually possessing an actual implement that is an imitation.

Indictable   None

Life imprisonment and/or a fine

8.3.6 Carrying firearm—criminal intent/resist arrest

Section 18 of the Firearms Act 1968 makes it an offence to carry a firearm or imitation firearm with criminal intent or resist/prevent arrest.

Offence

It is an offence for a person to **have with him** a **firearm** or **imitation firearm** with **intent** to commit an **indictable offence**, or to resist arrest or prevent the arrest of another, in either case while he has the firearm or imitation firearm with him.   **Firearms Act 1968, s 18**

Points to prove
✓ date and location
✓ had with him/her
✓ a firearm/imitation firearm
✓ with intent
✓ to commit an indictable offence/resist arrest/prevent the arrest of another

Meanings

Has with him

This is a narrower definition than 'possession'. Here there is a need to prove:
• a knowledge of the existence of the article;
• that the article was 'to hand and ready for use' (it may, for example, be hidden a few feet away, it does not have to be physically on the defendant's person).

Firearm (see 8.3.3)

Imitation firearm (see 8.3.3)

Intent (see 4.1)

Indictable offence

This includes either way offences.

Related cases

R v Duhaney, R v Stoddart The Times, 9 December 1997 CA Whether or not the firearm is used, or intended to be used, to further that particular offence, is irrelevant.

R v Pawlicki and Swindell [1992] 3 All ER 903, CA Accessibility, not distance, is the test for 'have with' him/her.

Practical considerations

- Proof that the defendant had a firearm or imitation firearm with him/her and intended to commit the further offence (or to resist or prevent arrest) is evidence that s/he intended to have it with him/her while doing so.
- Consider 'possess firearm with intent to cause the fear of unlawful violence' (see **8.3.3**) which has a much wider scope.

 SSS   E&S

 Indictable   None

 Life imprisonment and/or a fine

8.3.7 **Using person to mind a firearm/weapon**

Section 28 of the Violent Crime Reduction Act 2006 makes it an offence to use another person to look after, hide or transport a dangerous weapon, subject to an agreement that it would be available when required for an unlawful purpose.

Offences

(1) A person is guilty of an offence if—
  (a) he uses another to look after, hide or transport a **dangerous weapon** for him; and
  (b) he does so under arrangements or in circumstances that facilitate, or are intended to facilitate, the weapon's being **available** to him **for an unlawful purpose**.

Violent Crime Reduction Act 2006, s 28

8.3.7 Using Person to Mind a Firearm/Weapon

> **Points to prove**
> ✓ uses another person to
> ✓ look after/hide/transport
> ✓ dangerous weapon and
> ✓ under arrangements made or facilitation agreed/intended
> ✓ the weapon is made available
> ✓ for an unlawful purpose

Meanings

Dangerous weapon (s28(3))

In this section 'dangerous weapon' means—

(a) a firearm *[see 8.1.1]* **other than** an air weapon or a component part of, or accessory to, an air weapon *[see 8.7.2]*; or

(b) a weapon to which s 141 *[see 8.9.2]* or 141A *[see 8.10.2]* of the Criminal Justice Act 1988 applies (specified offensive weapons, knives and bladed weapons) (s 28(3)).

Available for an unlawful purpose (s28(2))

For the purposes of this section the cases in which a dangerous weapon is to be regarded as available to a person for an unlawful purpose include any case where—

(a) the weapon is available for him to take possession of it at a time and place; and

(b) his possession of the weapon at that time and place would constitute, or be likely to involve or to lead to, the commission by him of an offence.

 Indictable　　　 None

 Numerous penalties available 4–10 years imprisonment and/or fine. Type of penalty is subject to s 29 of the Violent Crime Reduction Act 2006 and depends on whether it is a prohibited firearm, firearm, s 141, s 141A and the age of the offender.

Links to alternative subjects and offences

8.4 Trespassing with Firearms

The Firearms Act 1968 provides various offences connected with firearms, air weapons, shotguns, and associated ammunition. Some such offences involve trespassing.

8.4.1 Trespass with any firearm in a building

Section 20 of the Firearms Act 1968 creates two offences of trespassing with firearms, one of which is concerned with trespass in buildings.

> **Offence**
>
> A person commits an offence if, while he has a **firearm** or **imitation firearm with him**, he enters or is in a building or part of a building as a trespasser and without reasonable excuse (the proof whereof lies on him).
>
> Firearms Act 1968, s 20(1)

Points to prove
- ✓ date and location
- ✓ had with him/her
- ✓ firearm/imitation firearm
- ✓ entered or was in
- ✓ building/part of building
- ✓ as a trespasser
- ✓ without reasonable excuse

Meanings

Firearm (see **8.3.3**)

Imitation firearm (see **8.3.3**)

Has with him (see **8.3.6**)

Explanatory notes
- A firearm in these circumstances means any firearm—shotgun, air weapon, prohibited weapon, and s 1 firearm.
- The terms 'enters', 'building', 'part of a building', and 'trespasser' should be interpreted as terms used in legislation/case law relating to burglary (see **3.3**).

Defence

Reasonable excuse (the burden of proof lies with the defendant). This defence could include saving life/property or self defence (eg the police carrying out a planned firearms operation). Whether an excuse is reasonable would be for the court to decide having considered all the circumstances.

Practical considerations

- It is important to note that although this is an either way offence, if the weapon is an air weapon or imitation firearm it is triable summarily only.
- If a defendant claims to have had a reasonable excuse, the burden of proof lies with him/her.
- Unless it is an imitation, there needs to be some evidence that the weapon is a firearm.

 Either way None

 Summary: 6 months' imprisonment and/or a fine not exceeding the statutory maximum.
Indictment: 7 years' imprisonment and/or a fine.

Air weapons/imitation firearms

 Summary 48 months

6 months' imprisonment and/or a fine not exceeding level 5.

8.4.2 Trespass with firearm on land

Section 20(2) of the Firearms Act 1968 creates an offence of trespass with a firearm on land.

Offence

A person commits an offence if, while he has a **firearm** or **imitation firearm with him**, he enters or is on any **land** as a **trespasser** and without reasonable excuse (the proof whereof lies on him). **Firearms Act 1968, s 20(2)**

8.4.2 Trespass with Firearm on Land

Points to prove
- ✓ date and location
- ✓ while having with him/her
- ✓ firearm/imitation firearm
- ✓ entered/was on land
- ✓ as a trespasser
- ✓ without reasonable excuse

Meanings

Firearm (see 8.3.3)

Imitation firearm (see 8.3.3)

Has with him (see 8.3.6)

Land

This includes land covered with water.

Trespass

Means 'to pass over a limit or boundary or to enter unlawfully upon another's land' (see 3.3).

Explanatory notes

A firearm in these circumstances means any firearm—shotgun, air weapon, prohibited weapon, and s 1 firearm.

Defence

Reasonable excuse (see 8.4.1).

Practical considerations

- In order to prove a trespass it must be shown that the defendant either knew that s/he was a trespasser or was reckless as to whether the facts existed which made him/her a trespasser.
- If a defence of reasonable excuse is claimed, the burden of proof lies with the defendant.
- Unless it is an imitation firearm, there needs to be some evidence that the weapon is 'a firearm'.

 Summary   48 months

 3 months' imprisonment and/or a fine not exceeding level four on the standard scale.

Links to alternative subjects and offences

8.5 Possessing Firearm or Imitation Firearm in a Public Place

The Firearms Act 1968 provides various offences connected with firearms, air weapons, shotguns, and associated ammunition. Some of these offences relate specifically to public places.

Section 19 of the Firearms Act 1968 provides various offences relating to the possession of shot guns, air weapons, firearms, and imitation firearms in a public place.

Offence

A person commits an offence if, without lawful authority or reasonable excuse (the proof whereof lies on him) he **has with him** in a **public place**:
(a) a **loaded shot gun**,
(b) an **air weapon** (whether loaded or not),
(c) any **other firearm** (whether loaded or not) together with ammunition suitable for use in that firearm, or
(d) an **imitation firearm**.   Firearms Act 1968, s 19

Points to prove

✓ date and location
✓ without lawful authority/reasonable excuse
✓ had with him/her in a public place a
✓ firearm (together with suitable ammunition) **or**
✓ loaded shotgun **or**
✓ loaded/unloaded air weapon **or**
✓ an imitation firearm

Meanings

Has with him   (see 8.3.6)

Public place

This includes any highway and any other premises or place to which at the material time the public have or are permitted access, whether on payment or otherwise.

Loaded

Means if there is a cartridge in the barrel or approved magazine that can feed the cartridge into the barrel by manual or automatic means.

Shotgun   (see 8.2.1)

Air weapon   (see 8.7.2)

Other firearm   (see 8.1.1)

Imitation firearm   (see 8.3.3)

Explanatory notes

In this offence the requirement for the weapons to be loaded or accompanied by ammunition varies:

- the requirement for a loaded weapon only applies to shotguns;
- for air weapons, simply having the air weapon is sufficient—there is no need to have ammunition with/for it;
- for other firearms, you must show that the defendant had ammunition suitable for use with that firearm.

Defence

Having lawful authority or reasonable excuse (the burden of proof lies with the defendant). This defence could include saving life/property or self defence (eg the police carrying out a planned firearms operation). Whether an excuse is reasonable would be for the court to decide having considered all the circumstances.

Related cases

R v Harrison [1996] Crim LR 200 During a robbery one of the robbers had a loaded sawn-off shot gun which the other knew nothing about. On the arrival of the police the other offender took possession of the gun. Even though he did not know it was loaded he still committed the offence.

Bates v DPP (1993) 157 JP 1004, QBD Inside a vehicle may be a public place.

Anderson v Miller [1976] Crim LR 743 The space behind a counter in a shop was held to be a public place.

Ross v Collins [1982] Crim LR 368, QBD A shotgun certificate gives no authority for a loaded shotgun in a public place.

R v Jones (Terence) [1995] 2 WLR 64, CA A firearms certificate does not give the holder a defence of 'lawful authority' against a charge under s 19. The certificate is granted for a specific purpose with conditions attached.

R v Morris & King (1984) 149 JP 60, 79 Cr App Rep 104, CA The test for an imitation firearm is whether the 'thing' looked like a firearm at the time when the accused actually had it with him.

Practical considerations

- If a defence of lawful authority or reasonable excuse is claimed, the burden of proof lies with the defendant.
- The 'guilty knowledge' that the prosecution must prove is knowledge of existence of the firearm, not the nature and quality of the weapon. An example would be: if an offender was given a holdall but was unaware that it contained a .38 revolver and suitable .38 ammunition, he would not commit this particular offence. However, if he knew that a revolver and ammunition were in the holdall, but not what type or that it was the correct ammunition, he would commit this offence.

8.5 Possessing Firearm or Imitation Firearm in a Public Place

- The prosecution must prove that the firearm is 'to hand and able to be used'.
- With an imitation firearm, the key word is 'appearance': whether the 'thing' looked like a firearm at the time of the offence. It is ultimately for the jury to decide although what a witness believed about the object, and/or any admissions made by defendant as to his/her reason for carrying the article will be directly relevant here.
- In *R v Bentham* [2005] UKHL 18, HL, the defendant carried out a robbery with his finger in his jacket pocket pointing towards the victim. The House of Lords decided that as the fingers were part of the person and not separate and distinct then they could never be possessed as a 'thing'.
- Offences involving imitation firearms are of having or possessing an imitation firearm not of falsely pretending to have one.
- Some 'replica'/imitation weapons can be converted into working firearms; as a result they will be classed as s 1 firearms requiring a firearms certificate (see **8.1.4**).
- Unless it is an imitation firearm, there needs to be some evidence that the weapon is a firearm.
- It is important to note that if the weapon is a shotgun or firearm then it is an either way offence. However, if the weapon is an air weapon or imitation firearm then it is summary trial only.

 SSS   E&S

 Either way   None

 Summary: 6 months' imprisonment and/or a fine not exceeding the statutory maximum.
Indictment: 7 years' imprisonment and/or a fine.

Air weapons/imitation firearms

 Summary   48 months

 6 months' imprisonment and/or a fine not exceeding level 5.

Links to alternative subjects and offences

8.6 Police Powers—Firearms

The Firearms Act 1968 provides various offences connected with firearms, air weapons, shotguns, and associated ammunition. Central to the practical effectiveness of that legislation, in policing terms, are the relevant powers that accompany these offences

8.6.1 Requirement to hand over firearm/ammunition

Section 47 of the Firearms Act 1968 deals with police powers to stop and search for firearms and provides an offence for failure to do so.

Police stop and search powers

A constable may require any person whom he has **reasonable cause to suspect**:
(a) of having a **firearm**, with or without **ammunition, with him** in a **public place**; or
(b) to be committing or about to commit, **elsewhere** than in a public place, an **offence relevant** for the purposes of this section,
to **hand** over the firearm or any ammunition for examination by the constable.

Firearms Act 1968, s 47(1)

Meanings

Reasonable cause to suspect

This concept is used in other legislation and depends very much on the circumstances in each case. There must be objective grounds for the suspicion based on facts, information or intelligence that are relevant to the likelihood of finding the article(s) (see **12.1**).

Firearm/ammunition (see **8.1.1**)

Has with him (see **8.3.6**)

Public place (see **8.5**)

Relevant offence

This refers to either a s 18 or a s 20 offence, being either having a firearm or imitation firearm:
• with intent to commit an indictable offence, or to resist arrest or prevent the arrest of another (see **8.3.6**);
• with him and enters either a building or part of a building **or** land as a trespasser (see **8.4**).

Offence

It is an offence for a person having a firearm or ammunition with him to fail to hand it over when required to do so by a constable under subsection (1) above.   Firearms Act 1968, s 47(2)

Points to prove

✓ date and location
✓ failed to hand over
✓ a firearm/ammunition for a firearm
✓ which defendant had with him/her
✓ when required to do so
✓ by a constable

Section 47 of the Firearms Act 1968 also provides qualified powers to search for firearms in respect of both people and vehicles and detain them for that purpose.

Police search and detain powers

Person

If a constable has reasonable cause to suspect a person of having a firearm with him in a public place, **or** to be committing or about to commit **elsewhere** than in a public place an offence relevant for the purposes of this section, the constable may search that person and may detain him for the purpose of doing so.   Firearms Act 1968, s 47(3)

Vehicle

If a constable has reasonable cause to suspect that there is a firearm in a vehicle in a public place, **or** that a vehicle is being or is about to be used in connection with the commission of an offence relevant for the purposes of this section elsewhere than in a public place, he may search the vehicle and for that purpose require the person driving or in control of it to stop it.
                                                    Firearms Act 1968, s 47(4)

Explanatory notes

• In exercising the above powers a constable may enter any place.
• The police also have the power to demand the production of shotgun or firearm certificates (see **8.6.2**).
• The power to stop the vehicle is not restricted to a constable in uniform.
• Officers should ensure that the stop and search procedures comply with PACE and the relevant Code of Practice (see **12.1.2**)
• With regard to premises a search warrant will have to be obtained under section 46 (see **8.6.3**).

Summary

 48 months

3 months' imprisonment and/or a fine not exceeding level 4 on the standard scale.

8.6.2 **Police powers—firearms/shotgun certificates**

Section 48 of the Firearms Act 1968 gives a constable power to demand from a person he believes to be in possession of s 1 firearm/ammunition or shotgun the production of a valid certificate or European pass or to show that s/he is exempt.

Production of certificate

A constable may **demand**, from any person whom he **believes** to be in possession of a **firearm** or **ammunition** to which the holding of a valid **firearm certificate** is necessary, or of a **shotgun**, the production of his firearm/ shotgun certificate.   Firearms Act 1968, s 48(1)

Meanings

Demand production

Where a person upon whom a demand has been made by a constable under subsection (1) and whom the constable believes to be in possession of a firearm fails—

(a) to produce a firearm/shotgun certificate;

(b) to show that he is a person who, by reason of his place of residence or any other circumstances, is not entitled to be issued with a document identifying that firearm under any of the provisions which in the other member States correspond to the provisions of this Act for the issue of European firearms passes; or

(c) to show that he is in possession of the firearm exclusively in connection with the carrying on of activities in respect of which, he or the person on whose behalf he has possession of the firearm, is recognised, for the purposes of the law of another member State relating to firearms, as a collector of firearms or a body concerned in the cultural or historical aspects of weapons,

the constable may demand from that person the production of a document which has been issued to that person in another member State under any such corresponding provisions, identifies that firearm as a firearm to which it relates and is for the time being valid.

Firearms Act 1968, s 48(1A)

Believes

This is a more stringent requirement than 'suspects' and requires stronger grounds.

Firearm/ammunition (see **8.1.1**)

Firearm certificate (see **8.1.1**)

Shotgun (see **8.2.1**)

Shotgun certificate (see **8.2.1**)

Offence

It is an offence for a person who is in possession of a firearm to fail to comply with a demand under subsection 48(1A) above.

Firearms Act 1968, s 48(4)

Points to prove

- ✓ date and location
- ✓ being in possession
- ✓ of a firearm
- ✓ failed
- ✓ to comply with a demand
- ✓ by constable
- ✓ to produce a valid certificate/document or show exemption

---

Seize/detain weapon and require details

If a person upon whom a demand is made fails to produce the certificate or document, **or** to permit the constable to read it, **or** to show that he is entitled by virtue of this Act to have the firearm, ammunition or shotgun in his possession without holding a certificate, the constable may seize and detain the firearm, ammunition or shotgun and may require the person to declare to him immediately his name and address. *Firearms Act 1968, s 48(2)*

Offence

If a person is required to declare to a constable his name and address, (requirement in subsection 48(2)—above) it is an offence for him to refuse to declare it or to fail to give his true name and address.

Firearms Act 1968, s 48(3)

8.6.3 Premises Search Warrant

Points to prove
- ✓ date and location
- ✓ having possession
- ✓ of a firearm/shotgun
- ✓ failed/refused
- ✓ to divulge
- ✓ when required by a constable
- ✓ their name and address

Explanatory notes

- A firearm certificate also includes a Northern Ireland Certificate.
- As the requirement is to declare 'immediately' his/her name and address, it is taken that the demand to produce a valid certificate/document or show exemption and (if applicable) the subsequent seizure of the firearm, ammunition or shotgun will also follow the same immediacy.

 Summary   6 months

 A fine not exceeding level 3 on the standard scale.

8.6.3 **Premises search warrant**

Section 46 of the Firearms Act 1968 deals with the issue of premises search warrants for firearms and authorities attached thereto.

Granting of warrant

If a justice of the peace is satisfied by information on oath that there are reasonable grounds for suspecting—

(a) that an **offence relevant** for the purposes of this section has been, is being, or is about to be committed; or

(b) that, in connection with a firearm or ammunition, there is a danger to the public safety or to the peace, he may grant a warrant for any of the **purposes** mentioned in subsection (2) below.

Firearms Act 1968, s 46(1)

Meanings

Relevant offences

All offences under the Firearms Act 1968 except an offence:
* under s 22(3) (unsupervised 15 year old possessing shotgun) (see **8.2.3**); or
* relating specifically to air weapons (see **8.7**).

Purposes of warrant

A warrant under this section may authorise a constable or civilian officer—

(a) to enter at any time any premises or place named in the warrant, if necessary by force, and to search the premises or place and every person found there;

(b) to seize and detain anything which he may find on the premises or place, or on any such person, in respect of which or in connection with which he has reasonable ground for suspecting—

   (i) that an offence **relevant** for the purposes of this section has been, is being or is about to be committed; or

   (ii) that in connection with a firearm, imitation firearm, or ammunition, there is a danger to the public safety or to the peace. Firearms Act 1968, s 46(2)

Offence

Intentionally to obstruct a constable/civilian officer in the exercise of their powers under section 46. Firearms Act 1968, s 46(5)

Points to prove

✓ date and location
✓ intentionally obstruct
✓ constable/civilian officer
✓ whilst exercising his/her powers under s 46

Meaning of civilian officer

Means a person employed by a police authority or the Corporation of the City of London who is under the direction and control of a chief officer of police.

Explanatory notes

* In some forces inspections of gun clubs and other routine firearms enquiries are performed by civilian staff rather than police officers.
* It is improbable that 'civilian officers' will ever be conducting enquiries into the more criminal aspects of firearms law (apart from areas such as forensic examination and testing).

8.6.3 Premises Search Warrant

 Summary 48 months

 6 months' imprisonment and/or a fine not exceeding level 5 on the standard scale.

Links to alternative subjects and offences

8.7 Air Weapons and Age Restrictions

The Firearms Act 1968 provides various offences connected with firearms, air weapons, shotguns, and associated ammunition. A number of important offences and restrictions relate to the age of the person involved.

8.7.1 Purchase/hire or supply air weapons, firearms or ammunition

Sections 22(1) and 24(1) of the Firearms Act 1968 prohibit purchase/hire or supply (sell or let on hire) any air weapon, firearm and ammunition by or to a person under 17/18 years of age.

Offences

Purchase/hire by under 17/18

(1) It is an offence—
    (a) for a person under the age of 18 to purchase or hire an air weapon or ammunition for an air weapon;
    (b) for a person under the age of 17 to purchase or hire any firearm or ammunition of any other description.

Firearms Act 1968, s 22(1)

Supplier (sell/hire) to under 17/18

(1) It is an offence—
    (a) to sell or let on hire an air weapon or ammunition for an air weapon to a person under the age of 18;
    (b) to sell or let on hire any firearm or ammunition of any other description to a person under the age of 17.

Firearms Act 1968, s 24(1)

Points to prove

Purchase/hire by under 17/18

✓ date and location
✓ purchased/hired, **either**
✓ by under 18 years—an air weapon/ammunition for an air weapon **OR**
✓ by under 17 years—firearm/ammunition of any other description

8.7.1 Purchase/hire or supply air weapons, firearms or ammunition

> ***Supplier (sell/hire) to under 17/18***
> ✓ date and location
> ✓ sold/let on hire, **either**
> ✓ air weapon/ammunition for an air weapon to under 18 **OR**
> ✓ firearm/ammunition of any other description to under 17

Meanings of firearm/ammunition
- Air weapons and air pellets/darts (see **8.7.2**);
- Shotguns and cartridges (see **8.2.1**);
- s 1/other firearms or ammunition (see **8.1.1**).

Defence
In proceedings for an offence under any provision of this section *[supplier]* it is a defence to prove that the person charged with the offence believed the other person to be of or over the age mentioned in that provision and had reasonable ground for that belief.   Firearms Act 1968, s 24(5)

Practical considerations
- Restrictions prevent people under 14 years of age from possessing, receiving as gifts or on loan any s 1 firearms or ammunition (see **8.1.3**).
- It is now an offence under s 24A for a person under 18 to purchase or to be sold an imitation firearm. The seller has a defence if they have reasonable grounds to believe that the buyer was 18 or over.
- Any firearm, air weapon, or ammunition seized by the police as a result of committing these offences may be confiscated by the court
- So far as shotguns are concerned, two specific offences (see **8.2.3**) apply to people under 15 years:
  - ✦ having an assembled shotgun without being supervised (by a person aged 21 years or over) or securely fastened in a gun cover;
  - ✦ making a gift of a shotgun or cartridges to such person.

SSS

 Summary   48 months

6 months' imprisonment and/or a fine not exceeding level 5 on the standard scale.

8.7.2 **Further offences/restrictions relating to air weapons**

The Firearms Act 1968 provides exceptions for young people to possess air weapons, but generally it is an offence for a person under 18 to have with them or be given an air weapon or ammunition for an air weapon. It is also an offence to fire missiles from an air weapon beyond premises, subject to a defence of consent from the other premises occupier.

Offence (by under 18)

Subject to **section 23**, it is an offence for a person under the age of 18 to **have with him** an air weapon or ammunition for an air weapon.

Firearms Act 1968, s 22(4)

Points to prove

✓ date and location
✓ being under 18 years of age
✓ had with him/her
✓ an air weapon or ammunition for an air weapon

Meanings

Section 23 (see Exceptions and offences below)

Has with him (see 8.3.6)

Air weapon

In reality, most air weapons are firearms, but not s 1 firearms (see **8.1.1**). Part of the definition of a s 1 firearm (s 1(3)(b) of the Firearms Act 1968) relates to every firearm, except air weapons: 'an air weapon that is to say, an air rifle, air gun or air pistol which does not fall within s 5(1) [being a prohibited weapon—having compressed gas cartridge system] and which is not of a type declared by rules [sets the power levels at which an air weapon becomes a s 1 firearm] made by the Secretary of State under s 53 of this Act to be specially dangerous.'

Exceptions and offences

(1) It is **not** an offence under Section 22(4) of this Act for a person to have with him an air weapon or ammunition while he is under the supervision of a person of or over the age of 21; **but** where a person has with him an air weapon on any premises in circumstances where he would be prohibited from having it with him but for this subsection, it is an **offence** for the person under whose supervision he is to allow him to use it for firing any missile beyond those premises.

(1A) In proceedings against a person for an offence under subsection (1) it shall be a defence for him to show that the only premises into or across which the missile was fired were premises the occupier of which had consented to the firing of the missile (whether specifically or by way of a general consent).

(2) It is **not** an offence under section 22(4) of this Act for a person to have with him an air weapon or ammunition at the time when:

   (a) being a member of a rifle club or miniature rifle club for the time being approved by the Secretary of State for the purposes of this section or section 15 of the Firearms (Amendment) Act 1988, he is engaged as such a member in or in connection with target shooting;

   (b) he is using the weapon or ammunition at a shooting gallery where the only firearms used are either air weapons or miniature rifles not exceeding .23 inch calibre.

(3) It is **not** an offence under section 22(4) of this Act for a person of or over the age of fourteen to have with him an air weapon or ammunition on private premises with the consent of the occupier.

Firearms Act 1968, s 23(1)–(3)

Points to prove

s 23(1) supervisor

✓ date and location
✓ being person of/over 21
✓ supervising person under 18 who had an air weapon
✓ on premises (**specify**)
✓ allowed him/her to fire a missile beyond those premises

Offence (make gift/part with possession to person under 18)

It is an offence—

(a) to make a gift of an air weapon or ammunition for an air weapon to a person under the age of 18; or

(b) to part with the possession of an air weapon or ammunition for an air weapon to a person under the age of 18 except where by virtue of section 23 *[above]* of this Act the person is not prohibited from having it with him.

Firearms Act 1968, s 24(4)

Points to prove

s 24(4)(a) make a gift to under 18

✓ date and location
✓ made a gift
✓ of an air weapon/ammunition for an air weapon
✓ to a person under the age of 18

s 24(4)(b) part possession to under 18 (not s 23 excepted)

✓ date and location
✓ parted with possession
✓ of an air weapon/ammunition for an air weapon
✓ to a person under the age of 18
✓ being prohibited from having possession

Defence (see 8.7.1).

Explanatory notes

- It is now an offence under s 21A of the Firearms Act 1968 for a person to have an air weapon on premises which is used to fire a missile beyond those premises. It is a defence if the occupier of the premises into or across which the missile was fired had consented.
- As 'air gun', 'air rifle' and 'air pistol' are not defined in the Firearms Act 1968, each case will have to be considered on its own facts and the article in question. Whether a weapon falls into these categories, the court will have to be aware of the following:
  - ♦ an 'air gun' is generally a weapon that has an unrifled barrel;
  - ♦ an 'air rifle' is a weapon that does have a rifled barrel; and
  - ♦ an 'air pistol' is a weapon designed to be fired by using one hand and having the appearance of a pistol.
- Air weapons using or designed/adapted for use with a self-contained compressed gas cartridge system will be a prohibited weapon (see 8.7.3).
- An air weapon is deemed to be loaded if there is ammunition in the chamber or barrel.

Related cases

Moore v Gooderham [1960] 3 All ER 575, QBD As an airgun is capable of causing injury from which death could result it is a lethal barrelled weapon.

Grace v DPP The Times, 9 December 1988, QBD Evidence that the weapon in question can be fired is required. The prosecution needs to prove that the rifle was a lethal barrelled weapon capable of discharging a shot or missile.

Practical considerations

- The prosecution have to prove that the air weapon was a lethal barrelled weapon capable of discharging a shot or missile.

8.7.3 Air weapons deemed prohibited weapons

- In practice, the Forensic Science Laboratory will examine weapons and say whether or not they are lethal. The main characteristic which is measured is the muzzle velocity (the speed at which the projectile leaves the barrel).
- An air weapon normally fires a projectile by compressed air/gases and is a firearm, namely 'a lethal barrelled weapon of any description from which any shot, bullet or other missile can be discharged' (do not confuse a 'firearm' with the narrower definition of a s 1 firearm).
- Certain air weapons can be subject to the prohibition under rules denoting them as especially dangerous.
- Air weapons using or designed/adapted for use with, a self-contained compressed gas cartridge system will be a prohibited weapon (8.7.3).
- Application may be made to the court for a confiscation order in relation to a seized air weapon or ammunition.
- Police powers relating to firearms/ammunition are discussed under 8.6.
- Normally it is an offence for a person under 18 years to have an air weapon and/or ammunition anywhere. However, a young person may possess one if accompanied by someone of or over 21 years of age.
- On premises the person under 18 years old is allowed to fire the weapon, but the missiles must not go beyond those premises—otherwise an offence is committed by the supervisor (subject to defence). Furthermore, the user (who must be at least 14 years old) may have with them an air weapon or ammunition on private premises with permission of the occupier.
- Consider the new offence under s 21A, which is for any person to have an air weapon on premises and it is used to fire a missile beyond those premises. Although it is a defence if the occupier of the premises into or across which the missile was fired had consented.

 Summary   6 months

Offences: s 22(4); s 24(4)(a); s 24(4)(b)

 6 months' imprisonment and/or a fine not exceeding level 3 on the standard scale.

Offences: s 23(1)(a); s 23(1)(b); s 23(4); s 21A

 A fine not exceeding level 3 on the standard scale.

8.7.3 Air weapons deemed prohibited weapons

Any person who has with him any air rifle, air gun, or air pistol that uses, or is designed or adapted for use with, a self-contained compressed gas cartridge system will be in possession of a prohibited weapon under s 5(1)(af) of the Firearms Act 1968 (see 8.1.1).

Explanatory Notes

- This ban does not apply to the CO_2 bulb system that gives a pressure less than 12 ft.lb. on air rifles or 6 ft.lb on air pistols. Over that pressure they become a s 1 firearm.
- If the air weapon contains a brass cartridge system and uses a self-contained gas cartridge system, that can be converted to fire conventional ammunition say, then this would make it a prohibited weapon under s 5(1)(af).
- If the weapon comes under s 5(1)(af), then it cannot be possessed, purchased, acquired, manufactured, sold or transferred without the authority of the Secretary of State.
- Under special arrangements, a person may have applied for and been granted permission to possess such a weapon under the terms of a firearms certificate.

8.7.4 'BB guns'

BB guns derived their name from guns that fire ball bearings by different methods such as compressed air or an electrical system: some even fire 4.5 mm lead shot. Such weapons would almost certainly be firearms for the purposes of s 1(3) (see **8.1.1**).

If the method of propulsion is a self-contained compressed gas cartridge, the BB gun will be a prohibited weapon (see **8.7.3**). However, most gas BB guns do not have cartridges: the built-in gas container is recharged by an external aerosol, which is not the same thing. A more common and readily available BB gun is designed to fire plastic or aluminium pellets which may be too powerful to be officially classed as a toy.

These are unlikely to be lethal barrelled weapons (see **8.1.1**) because they are usually too low powered to be 'lethal'.

This type of BB gun will normally have a power rating of about 0.06 ft. lbs.

Compare this to a BSA Airsporter .22 air rifle that has a power rating of 10.07 ft. lbs (150 times more powerful).

If required, the Forensic Science Laboratory can test the BB gun in order to ascertain its power rating, categorize the gun and say whether or not it is lethal.

As some BB guns closely resemble other firearms, if one is being used in a public place, consider the offence of possession of an imitation firearm in a public place (see **8.5.1**).

8.7.5 **Other firearms offences (in a highway/street)**

Highways Act

Section 161 of the Highways Act 1980 creates various offences relating to causing danger on the highway.

Offence

If a person without lawful authority or excuse:
(a) lights any fire on or over a highway which consists of or comprises a carriageway; or
(b) discharges any firearm or firework within 50 feet of the centre of such a highway,
and in consequence a user of the highway is injured, interrupted or endangered, that person is guilty of an offence.

Highways Act 1980, s 161(2)

Points to prove

✓ date and location
✓ without lawful authority/excuse
✓ discharged firearm within 50 ft centre of highway comprising a carriageway
✓ as a result
✓ user injured/interrupted/endangered

Meanings

Highway (see 8.8.6)

Carriageway (see 8.8.6)

 Summary   6 months

 A fine not exceeding level 3 on the standard scale.

Town Police Clauses Act

Section 28 of the Town Police Clauses Act 1847 creates numerous offences.

Offence

Every person who wantonly (recklessly, without regard for consequences) discharges a firearm in the street to the obstruction, annoyance, or danger of residents or passengers will commit an offence.

Town Police Clauses Act 1847, s 28

> ✓ being a person under the age of 18
> ✓ had in his/her possession
> ✓ in a public place
> ✓ an adult firework

Prohibition

Subject to **regulation 6** below, no person under the age of eighteen years shall possess an **adult firework** in a **public place**.

Fireworks Regulations 2004, reg 4(1)

Meanings

Regulation 6

- Regulations 4 and 5 shall not prohibit the possession of any firework by any person who is employed by/in trade or business as—
  - ✦ professional organizer or operator of firework displays;
  - ✦ manufacture of fireworks or assemblies;
  - ✦ supply of fireworks or assemblies,
  - ✦ local authority/Government department/establishment of the naval, military or air forces of the Crown for use at a firework display or national public celebration/commemorative event;
  - ✦ special effects in the theatre, on film or on television;
  - ✦ or acting on behalf of a local authority/enforcement authority/other body, for purposes of authority/body or exercising enforcement powers;
  - ✦ Government department use for research or investigations;
  - ✦ supplier of goods designed and intended for use in conjunction with fireworks or assemblies for testing and safety purposes; **and** who possesses the firework in question for the purposes of his trade, course of employment or business.
- Regulation 5 shall not prohibit the possession of any firework by any person who is employed in, or whose trade or business (or part of whose trade or business) is, the transport of fireworks and who possesses the firework in question for the purposes of his trade, employment or business.

Adult firework

Means any firework:
- that does not comply with the relevant requirements of Part 2 of BS 7114 when tested in accordance with the appropriate test method (if any) in Part 3 of BS 7114 (see **8.8.1**); or
- except Category 1 Indoor Fireworks, namely cap, cracker snap, novelty match, party popper, serpent, sparkler, or throwdown, which does comply with those requirements.

Public place

Includes any place to which at the material time the public have or are permitted access, whether on payment or otherwise.

8.8.3 Ban on Possession of Category 4 Fireworks

Explanatory notes

- This offence prohibits any person under the age of 18 years, from possessing any firework in a public place (except Category 1 Indoor Fireworks) (see **8.8.1**).
- Those people listed in reg 6 (above) are exempted from liability for this offence and are not prohibited from possession.

Practical considerations

- Any breach of the prohibitions in the Fireworks Regulations 2004 is a criminal offence under the Fireworks Act 2003, s 11(1).
- Consider issuing a penalty notice for disorder for this offence.
- There are powers to stop, search, and detain people or vehicles and to seize any found fireworks that a person possesses in contravention of a prohibition imposed by these Fireworks Regulations (see **12.1.1**).

 Summary 12 months

🏛️ 6 months' imprisonment and/or a fine not exceeding level 5 on the standard scale.

8.8.3 Ban on possession of Category 4 fireworks

Offence

Any person who contravenes a prohibition imposed by fireworks regulations is guilty of an offence.   **Fireworks Act 2003, s 11(1)**

Points to prove

✓ date and location
✓ breached a prohibition imposed by reg 5 of the Fireworks Regulations 2004, namely
✓ had in his/her possession
✓ a Category 4 firework
✓ when not exempt from such possession

Prohibition

Subject to **regulation 6** [see **8.8.2**], no person shall possess a **category 4 firework**.   **Fireworks Regulations 2004, reg 5**

Explanatory notes

- Those people listed in reg 6 (see **8.8.2**) are exempted from liability for this offence and are not prohibited from possession.
- Unless exempted by reg 6, this prohibits a person of any age from possessing **anywhere** a Category 4 firework and an offence will be committed by that person if they breach that regulation.

Practical considerations

- Any breach of the prohibitions in the Fireworks Regulations 2004 is a criminal offence under s 11(1) of the Fireworks Act 2003.
- Consider issuing a penalty notice for disorder for this offence.
- There are powers to stop, search, and detain people or vehicles and to seize any fireworks that a person possesses in contravention of a prohibition imposed by these Fireworks Regulations (see **12.1.1**).
- Category 4 fireworks are for specialist use only under reg 6 (see **8.8.1**).

  Summary   12 months

6 months' imprisonment and/or a fine not exceeding level 5 on the standard scale.

8.8.4 Use firework after 11 p.m.

Offence

Any person who contravenes a prohibition imposed by fireworks regulations is guilty of an offence.   Fireworks Act 2003, s 11(1)

Points to prove

- ✓ date and location
- ✓ breached a prohibition imposed by reg 7(1) of the Fireworks Regulations 2004, namely
- ✓ use an adult firework
- ✓ during night hours

Prohibition

Subject to paragraph (2) (*exception*) below, no person shall use an **adult firework** during **night hours**.

Fireworks Regulations 2004, reg 7(1)

8.8.4 Use Firework After 11 p.m.

Meanings

Exception

Regulation 7(2) states that reg 7(1) above shall not prohibit the use of a firework:

(a) during a **permitted fireworks night**; or

(b) by any person who is employed by a local authority and who uses the firework in question:

(i) for the purposes of putting on a firework display by that local authority; or

(ii) at a national public celebration or a national commemorative event.

Adult firework (see 8.8.2)

Night hours

Means the period beginning at 11 p.m. and ending at 7 a.m. the following day.

Permitted fireworks night

Means a period beginning at 11 p.m.:

- on the first day of the Chinese New Year and ending at 1 a.m. the following day;
- and ending at midnight on 5 November;
- on the day of Diwali and ending at 1 a.m. the following day;
- on 31 December and ending at 1 a.m. the following day.

Explanatory notes

- This prohibits the use of a firework (except category 1 'indoor fireworks') (see **8.8.1**) after 11 p.m. at night and an offence being committed by that person if they breach that regulation.
- Exceptions are New Year's Eve, Diwali, Chinese New Year (extended 11 p.m.–1 a.m.); Bonfire Night (extended 11 p.m.–midnight) or the local authority putting on a firework display.
- This offence is not restricted to a public place and will be committed if a person breaches this prohibition in their own private garden/land.

Practical considerations

- A breach of this prohibition is a criminal offence under s 11(1) of the Fireworks Act 2003.
- Consider issuing a penalty notice for disorder for this offence which applies to all offences under s 11(1) of the Fireworks Act 2003 (being a breach of the Fireworks Regulations 2004 prohibitions).
- Powers to stop, search, and detain people or vehicles and to seize any fireworks that a person possesses in contravention of a prohibition imposed by the Fireworks Regulations (see **12.1.1**).

Summary 12 months

 6 months' imprisonment and/or a fine not exceeding level 5 on the standard scale.

8.8.5 **Supply of fireworks to under 18**

Regulation 6 of the Fireworks (Safety) Regulations 1997 prohibits the supply of fireworks to people who are under the age of 18 years, making such supply an offence under s 12(1) of the Consumer Protection Act 1987.

Offence

Where safety regulations prohibit a person from supplying or offering or agreeing to supply any goods or from exposing or possessing any goods for supply, that person shall be guilty of an offence if he contravenes the prohibition.   Consumer Protection Act 1987, s 12(1)

Points to prove
- ✓ date and location
- ✓ breached a safety regulations prohibition imposed by reg 6(1) of the Fireworks Safety Regulations 1997, namely
- ✓ supply firework/assembly of fireworks
- ✓ to person apparently under 18 years

Prohibition
(1) Subject to regulation 6(2) below, no person shall **supply** any firework or any assembly to any person under the age of eighteen years.
(2) Regulation 6(1) above shall not prohibit the supply of any cap, cracker snap, novelty match, party popper, serpent or throwdown.
                    Fireworks (Safety) Regulations 1997, reg 6

Practical considerations
- A breach of this prohibition is a criminal offence under s 12(1) of the Consumer Protection Act 1987.
- Supply includes offering or agreeing to supply, and exposing or possessing for supply: it is not limited to sale.

- Prosecution will be more likely where fireworks have been supplied in the course of a business, rather than a 'casual supply' between friends or family.
- The offence includes all fireworks **except** innocuous 'indoor' ones listed in reg 6(2) of the Fireworks (Safety) Regulations 1997.
- Supply of the items listed in reg 6(2) may be an offence if the person is under 16.
- This offence **is not** an offence subject to the penalty notices for disorder procedure.

Defence

To show that s/he had no reason to suspect that the person to whom s/he supplied, offered to supply, or agreed to supply the fireworks was below the age specified in the regulations.

 Summary   12 months

 6 months' imprisonment and/or a fine not exceeding level 5 on the standard scale.

8.8.6 Other fireworks offences (in a highway/street)

Explosives Act

Section 80 of the Explosives Act 1875 creates various offences relating to throw, cast or fire any fireworks in the highway or public place.

Offence

It is an offence for any person to throw, cast, or fire any fireworks in or into any highway, street, thoroughfare, or public place.   Explosives Act 1875, s 80

Points to prove
✓ date and location
✓ throw/cast/fire
✓ a firework
✓ in/into a highway/street/thoroughfare/public place

Practical considerations

Consider issuing a penalty notice for disorder for this offence—
'Throwing fireworks in a thoroughfare' (see **7.1.1**).

SSS PND CSO

  Summary   🕐 6 months

▥ A fine not exceeding level 5 on the standard scale.

Highways Act

Section 161 of the Highways Act 1980 creates various offences relating
to causing danger on the highway.

> #### Offence
>
> If a person without lawful authority or excuse:
> (a) lights any fire on or over a highway which consists of or comprises a
>   carriageway; or
> (b) discharges any firearm or *firework* within 50 feet of the centre of such
>   a highway,
> and in consequence a user of the highway is injured, interrupted or
> endangered, that person is guilty of an offence.   Highways Act 1980, s 161(2)

Points to prove

✓ date and location
✓ without lawful authority/excuse
✓ discharged
✓ a firework
✓ within 50 ft centre of highway
✓ comprising a carriageway
✓ as a result
✓ user injured/interrupted/endangered

Meanings

Highway

Means all roads, bridges, **carriageways**, cartways, horseways, bridleways,
footways, causeways, churchways, and pavements.

Carriageway

Means a way constituting or comprised in a highway, being a way (other
than a cycle track) over which the public have a right of way of the
passage of vehicles.

8.8.6 Other Fireworks Offences (in a Highway/Street)

 Summary 6 months

A fine not exceeding level 3 on the standard scale.

Town Police Clauses Act

Section 28 of the Town Police Clauses Act 1847 creates numerous offences.

> **Offence**
>
> Every person who wantonly (without lawful motive and thoughtless as to possible consequences) throws or sets fire to a firework in the street to the obstruction, annoyance, or danger of residents or passengers will commit an offence. **Town Police Clauses Act 1847, s 28**

Points to prove
- ✓ date and location
- ✓ in street
- ✓ wantonly
- ✓ threw/set fire to a firework
- ✓ to the obstruction/annoyance/danger of residents/passengers

---

Meaning of street

Street includes any road, square, court, alley, thoroughfare, public passage, carriageway, and footways at the sides.

Explanatory notes

- None of the Town Police Clauses Act offences are complete unless it can be proved that they would obstruct, annoy, or cause danger to any residents or passengers.
- Note that this Act does not apply to the Metropolitan police district.

Related cases

Mantle v Jordan [1897] 1 QB 248 The Town Police Clauses Act offences can only be committed in the street, but the annoyance may be to 'residents', meaning the occupiers of houses in the street, although they may not be in the street at the time.

 Summary 6 months

 14 days' imprisonment or a fine not exceeding level 3 on the standard scale

---

Links to alternative subjects and offences

8.9 Offensive Weapons and Crossbows

Possession of offensive weapons in a public place, the manufacture and sale of offensive weapons, trespassing with a weapon of offence, and offences involving crossbows forms a key part of operational policing and will be dealt with in this section.

8.9.1 Offensive weapons—possession in a public place

The Prevention of Crime Act 1953 was introduced to prohibit the carrying of offensive weapons in public places without lawful authority or reasonable excuse. This legislation is important in understanding the way in which the courts have approached some cases.

> **Offence**
> Any person who without lawful authority or reasonable excuse, the proof of which shall lie on him, has with him in any public place any offensive weapon shall be guilty of an offence.   Prevention of Crime Act 1953, s 1(1)

> **Points to prove**
> ✓ date and location
> ✓ without lawful authority/reasonable excuse
> ✓ had with him/her
> ✓ in a public place
> ✓ an offensive weapon

Meanings

Has with him   (see 8.3.6)

Public place

Includes any highway and any other premises or place to which at the material time the public have or are permitted to have access, whether on payment or otherwise.

Offensive weapon

Means any article **made** or **adapted** for use for causing injury to the person, or **intended** by the person having it with him/her for such use by him/her, or by some other person.

Explanatory notes

- Within the meaning of offensive weapon particular terms were used and case law has provided meanings to those terms as follows:
  - ◆ **'made'** includes articles that have been specifically created for the purpose of causing injury, and includes knuckledusters, flick knives, butterfly knives, sword sticks, truncheons, daggers, bayonets, and rice flails. All of these items are generally classed as offensive weapons per se ('by themselves').
  - ◆ **'adapted'** consists of articles that have generally been altered in some way with the intention of causing injury, such as smashing a bottle to make the broken end into a weapon for causing injury.
  - ◆ **'intended'** these can be otherwise inoffensive articles that the defendant proposes to use to cause injury to a person, such as a bunch of keys held in the fist with the keys projecting through the fingers (making it an impromptu knuckleduster).
- However, it is important to note that the primary aim of the offence is the **carrying** of such weapons rather than their **use** in the heat of the moment.

Defence

Lawful authority

This extends to people such as an on duty police officer with a baton.

Reasonable excuse

Whether an excuse is reasonable is for the court to decide having heard all the circumstances. This could include:

- people carrying the tools of their trade (eg hammer/saw by a carpenter or filleting knife by a fishmonger),
- self-defence—if there is an imminent threat, this defence may be available.

Related cases

Evans v Hughes [1972] 3 All ER 412, QBD Before a defence of reasonable excuse can be successful, an imminent threat (in this instance self defence) has to be shown as to why the weapon was carried.

R v Cugullere [1961] 2 All ER 343, CA The accused must knowingly have article with him/her in a public place.

Davis v Alexander [1971] Crim LR 595, QBD No need for intention to use if offensive weapon per se.

Ohlson v Hylton [1975] 2 All ER 490, QBD and R v Veasey [1999] Crim LR 158, CA No offence committed if defendant seizes a weapon for 'instant use' on the victim or grabs something innocuous (like a hammer or snooker cue)—in the heat of the moment. In these cases the 'weapon' was not carried unlawfully with prior intent. The seizing and use of the weapon were all part of the assault.

R v Allamby and R v Medford [1974] 3 All ER 126, CA Kitchen knives were not offensive weapons per se and so intent to use must be proved.

Practical considerations

- Consider s 1 of the Police and Criminal Evidence Act 1984 where a constable can stop and search persons/vehicles relating to offensive weapons, bladed/pointed articles and to seize such weapons/articles (see **12.1.1**).
- Where an article is 'made' or 'adapted' to cause injury (offensive per se), the prosecution do not need to prove an intent to cause injury as merely having it with you is sufficient.
- The 'intended' use requires an element of intent to use the article to cause injury, which must be proved. An instant use of an innocent article will need proof of a prior intent otherwise no offence of carrying a weapon is committed.
- Upon conviction the court may make an order for the forfeiture or disposal of any weapon in respect of which the offence was committed.
- If appropriate, consider the offence of possession of a blade/pointed article in a public place (see **8.10**).
- There is a need to prove a knowledge of the existence of the article and that the article is 'to hand and ready for use' (it may, for example, be hidden a few feet away, it does not have to be physically on the defendant's person).
- The burden of proof for lawful authority or reasonable excuse lies with the accused.

 Either way   None

Summary: 6 months' imprisonment and/or a fine not exceeding the statutory maximum.
Indictment: 4 years' imprisonment and/or a fine.

8.9.2 **Offensive weapons— provide/trade/manufacture**

Transferring ownership, trading in, importing, or manufacturing certain offensive weapons is an offence.

> **Offence**
>
> Any person who manufactures, sells or hires or offers for sale or hire, exposes or has in his possession for the purpose of sale or hire, or lends or gives to any other person, a weapon to which this section applies.
>
> Criminal Justice Act 1988, s 141(1)

    SSS Stop, search and seize powers   **E&S** Entry and search powers

Points to prove

✓ date and location
✓ manufactured/sold/hired/lent/gave
✓ an offensive weapon

or

✓ date and location
✓ possess/exposed/offered
✓ for sale/hire
✓ an offensive weapon

Meaning of weapon

Weapons to which this section applies are dealt with in the Criminal Justice Act 1988 (Offensive Weapons) Order 1988 (see **8.9.3**).

Explanatory notes

- The importation of weapons to which this section applies is prohibited.
- Some will also fall into the category of being a blade/pointed article (see **8.10**).
- See also a warrant to search for and a power to stop/search/seize these weapons (see **8.11**).
- There are also separate restrictions on make/import/sale/hire of flick and gravity knives (see **8.10.3**).
- This section does not apply to any weapons subject to the Firearms Act 1968 (see **8.1**) or crossbows (see **8.9.5**).
- It is an offence under s 28 of the Violent Crime Reduction Act 2006 to use another person to look after, hide or transport a firearm, offensive/bladed weapon or knife, and that it would be available when required for an unlawful purpose (see **8.3.7**).

Defence

For any person charged in respect of any conduct of his relating to a weapon to which this section applies—

(a) with an offence under subsection 141(1) above; or

(b) with an offence under section 50(2) or (3) of the Customs and Excise Management Act 1979 [improper importation]

to prove that his conduct was only for the purpose of functions carried out on behalf of the Crown employees or of a visiting force.

Criminal Justice Act 1988, s 141(5)

Defence notes

- An antique weapon is exempt (more than 100 years old).
- Transfer of the weapon by giving/lending to a non-profit making museum or gallery; lending/hiring for artistic or cultural purposes by museums and galleries.

- Use is only for the purposes of functions carried out on behalf of the Crown or of a visiting force.

 Summary 6 months

6 months' imprisonment and/or a fine not exceeding level 5 on the standard scale.

8.9.3 **The Criminal Justice Act 1988 (Offensive Weapons) Order 1988**

This provides a list of weapons where their sale, hire, offering for sale/hire, exposing, or importation is prohibited.

This list only applies to s 141 offences (see **8.9.2**) and is not a list of all offensive weapons per se: knuckleduster; swordstick; butterfly knife; death star; belt buckle knife; hollow kubotan (cylinder holding sharp spikes); push dagger; kusari (rope, cord, wire or chain with hooked knife, sickle, hard weight or hand grip fastened at one end); foot or hand claw; blowpipe; telescopic truncheon; disguised knife; baton; stealth knife (non-metallic).

Explanatory notes

- There are exceptions even if the weapon is on this list.
- The list given above is not an exhaustive or descriptive list it just gives an idea of the type of weapons included in this order.
- Home Office Circular No 34 of 2004 draws attention to the provisions of this order, it states that:
  ◆ the Order does not create an offence of simple possession of a stealth knife or truncheon
  ◆ however, the design and construction of these items means that their possession in public may be an offence under:
    ▪ s 1(1) of the Prevention of Crime Act 1953 (**8.9.1**); or
    ▪ s 139(1) of the Criminal Justice Act 1988 (**8.10**).

8.9.4 **Trespassing with weapon of offence**

Section 8 of the Criminal Law Act 1977 creates the offence of 'trespassing with a weapon of offence'.

Offence

A person who is on any premises as a trespasser, after having entered as such, is guilty of an offence if, without lawful authority or reasonable excuse, he has with him on the premises any weapon of offence.

Criminal Law Act 1977, s 8(1)

Points to prove

✓ date and location
✓ on premises as trespasser
✓ having entered as such
✓ had weapon of offence
✓ without lawful authority or reasonable excuse

Meanings

Premises

'Premises' consist of:

- any building/part of a building (under separate occupation);
- any land adjacent to and used/intended for use in connection with a building;
- the site comprising any building(s) together with ancillary land;
- any fixed structure; and
- any moveable structure, vehicle, or vessel designed or adapted for residential purposes.

Trespasser (see **3.3**)

Has with him (see **3.4**)

Weapon of offence (see **3.4**)

Practical considerations

- This offence is worth bearing in mind if the carrying of offensive weapons in a public place/school premises or aggravated burglary does not apply.
- Consider s 1 of the Police and Criminal Evidence Act 1984 where a constable can stop and search persons/vehicles relating to offensive weapons, bladed/pointed articles and to seize such weapons/articles (see **12.1.1**).
- To commit this offence the entry must have been as a trespasser—it does not extend to a person who has entered lawfully and later becomes a trespasser (eg being asked to leave by the occupier).
- Although this offence was originally aimed at squatters, most of the definitions are the same as in the Theft Act 1968 (aggravated burglary).

Summary 6 months

 3 months' imprisonment and/or a fine not exceeding level 5 on the standard scale.

8.9.5 **Crossbows**

Crossbows are extremely accurate weapons and potentially as lethal as a firearm. This legislation creates offences in relation to persons under 18 years preventing them from possessing, hiring, or purchasing crossbows.

Sell or hire to under 18

Section 1 of the Crossbows Act 1987 creates the offence of selling or letting on hire such a weapon

> **Offence**
>
> A person who sells or lets on hire a crossbow to a person under the age of eighteen is guilty of an offence unless he believes him to be eighteen years of age or older and has reasonable grounds for that belief.
>
> Crossbows Act 1987, s 1

> **Points to prove**
> - ✓ date and location
> - ✓ sold/let on hire **or** sold/let on hire part(s) of
> - ✓ a crossbow
> - ✓ to person under 18 years of age

Meaning of crossbow

Section 5 of the Crossbows Act 1987 states that the Act does not apply to crossbows with a draw weight of less than 1.4 kilograms.

> **Defences**
> - Crossbows with a draw weight of less than 1.4 kilograms.
> - Having a belief, with reasonable grounds, that the person is 18 years or older

Practical considerations

Proof required of actual age (eg by means of birth certificate).

Summary   6 months

 6 months' imprisonment and/or a fine not exceeding level 5 on the standard scale.

Under 18—purchase/hire a crossbow

> **Offence**
>
> A person under the age of eighteen who buys or hires a crossbow or a part of a crossbow is guilty of an offence.   **Crossbows Act 1987, s 2**

Points to prove

✓ date and location
✓ person under 18 years of age
✓ hire/purchase **or** purchased/hired part(s) of
✓ a crossbow

Practical considerations

- Evidential proof required of the age of the person (eg by means of birth certificate).
- This Act only applies to crossbows, which are of a certain strength (called the draw weight).
- The draw weight limit is very low and can be determined by the Forensic Science Laboratory, only toys will be excluded by this definition.
- The Act allows a person of 18 or over to possess a crossbow in public in certain circumstances, but such possession may fall within the provisions of s 139 of the Criminal Justice Act 1988 (pointed article/blades) due to the crossbow bolts (**8.10**).

 Summary   6 months

 A fine not exceeding level 3 on the standard scale.

Under 18—possess a crossbow

> **Offences**
>
> A person under the age of eighteen who has with him—
> (a) a crossbow which is capable of discharging a missile, or

(b) parts of a crossbow which together (and without any other parts) can be assembled to form a crossbow capable of discharging a missile,

is guilty of an offence, unless he is under the supervision of a person who is twenty-one years of age or older. **Crossbows Act 1987, s 3**

Points to prove

✓ date and location
✓ being under the age of 18
✓ had with you
✓ a crossbow/crossbow parts (able to form a crossbow)
✓ capable of discharging a missile

Meanings

Has with him (see **8.3.6**)

Crossbow

This offence only applies to crossbows with a draw weight of more than 1.4 kilograms.

Explanatory notes

• This offence can be committed anywhere and not just in public.
• No offence will be committed if (under 18 year old) is under supervision of person age 21 or over.

Practical considerations

• Ages require actual proof (eg by means of birth certificate).
• This Act only applies to crossbows, which are of a certain strength (called the draw weight).
• The draw weight limit is very low and can be determined by the Forensic Science Laboratory, only toys will be excluded by this definition.
• The Act allows a person of 18 or over to possess a crossbow in public in certain circumstances, but such possession may fall within the provisions of s 139 of the Criminal Justice Act 1988 (pointed article/blades) due to the crossbow bolts (**8.10**).

SSS

 Summary   6 months

A fine not exceeding level 3 on the standard scale.

Crossbows—search and seizure powers

Section 4 of the Crossbows Act 1987 gives police officers quite wide powers of search, detain, seizure, and entry onto land; if a person under 18 years is unsupervised and is in possession of a crossbow/parts.

Powers

(1) If a constable suspects with reasonable cause that a person is committing or has committed an offence under section 3, the constable may—

    (a) search that person for a crossbow or part of a crossbow;

    (b) search any vehicle, or anything in or on a vehicle, in or on which the constable suspects with reasonable cause there is a crossbow, or part of a crossbow, connected with the offence.

(2) A constable may detain a person or vehicle for the purpose of a search under subsection (1).

(3) A constable may seize and retain for the purpose of proceedings for an offence under this Act anything discovered by him in the course of a search under subsection (1) which appears to him to be a crossbow or part of a crossbow.

(4) For the purpose of exercising the powers conferred by this section a constable may enter on any land other than a dwelling-house.

Crossbows Act 1987, s 4(1)–(4)

Explanatory notes

- A constable may detain a person or vehicle for the purpose of this search.
- A constable may seize and retain anything found in the course of this search which appears to be a crossbow or part of a crossbow.
- In exercising this power a constable may enter on any land **other than** a dwelling house.

Practical considerations

- If appropriate, consider powers under common law and s 1 PACE that could apply. Similarly compliance with PACE and Code of Practice procedures relating to stop and searches (see **12.1**)
- This Act only applies to crossbows, which are of a certain strength (called the draw weight).
- The draw weight limit is very low and can be determined by the Forensic Science Laboratory, only toys will be excluded by this definition.
- The Act allows a person of 18 or over to possess a crossbow in public in certain circumstances, but such possession may fall within the provisions of s 139 of the Criminal Justice Act 1988 (pointed article/blades) due to the crossbow bolts (**8.10**).

Links to alternative subjects and offences

8.10 Bladed Articles/Knives Offences

The main area of law that deals with knives/bladed articles is the Criminal Justice Act 1988, for having such articles in a public place or on school premises, and sale to a person under 18 years. The Restriction of Offensive Weapons Act 1959, however, deals with making/importing/selling/hiring a flick or gravity knife.

8.10.1 Possession of bladed/pointed article in public place

Section 139 of the Criminal Justice Act 1988 creates an offence of having a bladed or pointed article in a public place.

Offence

Subject to subsections (4) and (5) [defences] below, any person who has an article to which this section applies with him in a public place shall be guilty of an offence.   Criminal Justice Act 1988, s 139(1)

Points to prove

✓ date and location
✓ had with them
✓ without good reason/lawful authority
✓ an article being bladed/sharply pointed
✓ in a public place

Meanings

Article

This applies to any article that has a **blade** or is sharply pointed, except a folding pocket-knife where the cutting edge of the blade is 7.62 cm (three inches) long or less.

Blade

Examples of this will be the blade of a knife, sword.

Has with him   (see 8.3.6)

Public place

This includes any place to which the public have or are permitted access, whether on payment or otherwise.

8.10.1 Possession of Bladed/Pointed Article in Public Place

Explanatory notes

- A folding pocket-knife does not include a lock knife, regardless of the blade length.
- Possession of a multi-tool incorporating a prohibited blade/pointed article is capable of being an offence under this section, even if there are other tools on the instrument that may be of practical use (such as a bottle opener).
- The burden of proof has been placed on the defendant to show good reason or lawful authority for having the blade/pointed article with him/her.
- Possession of a lock knife for the purposes of persistent self-harm, may be a reason, but is not likely to be a good reason.
- Consider s 1 of the Police and Criminal Evidence Act 1984 where a constable can stop and search persons/vehicles relating to offensive weapons, bladed/pointed articles and to seize such weapons/articles (see **12.1.1**).
- Be aware of specific offences relating to possession of blade/pointed article and offensive weapons on school premises (see **8.10.4**).

Defences

(4) It shall be a defence for a person charged with an offence under this section to prove that he had good reason or lawful authority for having the article with him in a public place.

(5) Without prejudice to the generality of subsection (4) above, it shall be a defence for a person charged with an offence under this section to prove that he had the article with him—
  (a) for use at work;
  (b) for religious reasons; or
  (c) as part of any national costume.

Criminal Justice Act 1988, s 139(4), (5)

Defence notes

Examples of having the article with them could be:
- **for use at work**—fishmonger, carpet fitter, chef;
- **for religious reasons**—members of the Sikh religion having a *kirpan*;
- **as part of a national costume**—the *skean dhu* in Highland dress.

Related cases

R v Davis [1998] Crim LR 564, CA Ruled that a screwdriver was not a 'bladed article'. A blade needs to fall within the same category as a sharply pointed item or the blade on a folding pocket knife having a cutting edge.

Brooker v DPP [2005] EWHC 1132, QBD Stated that a butter knife was a bladed article—there is no rule that it only applies to sharp blades.

Harris v DPP [1993] 1 WLR 82, QBD A lock knife is not a folding pocket-knife, regardless of the blade length.

R v Daubney (2000) 164 JP 519, CA The prosecution must prove that the defendant had the article with him/her **and** his/her actual knowledge of the article.

R v Cheong Wang [2003] EWCA Crim 3228, CA A Buddhist practising the martial art of *Shaolin* had a sword and Gurkha-type knife with him in public, but had failed to provide sufficient religious reason for possession.

 Either way   6 months

Summary: 6 months' imprisonment and/or a fine not exceeding the statutory maximum.
Indictment: 4 years' imprisonment and/or a fine.

8.10.2 **Sale of knives/blades to persons under 18**

Section 141A of the Criminal Justice Act 1988 creates the offence of selling knives or certain articles with a blade or point to people under the age of 18.

Offence

An offence is committed by any person who sells to a person under the age of eighteen years an article to which this section applies.

Criminal Justice Act 1988, s 141A(1)

Points to prove
- ✓ date and location
- ✓ sold
- ✓ knife/axe/knife blade/razor blade **or**
- ✓ blade/sharply pointed article being made/adapted for use for causing injury
- ✓ to person under 18 years

Meaning of article

This applies to such articles as:
- any knife, knife blade, or razor blade,
- any axe,
- any other article that has a blade or is sharply pointed and is made or adapted for use for causing injury to the person.

Exemptions

- By virtue of the Criminal Justice Act 1988 (Offensive Weapons) (Exemption) Order 1996, this section does not apply to:
  - ♦ folding pocket-knives if the cutting edge of the blade does not exceed 7.62 centimetres (3 inches);
  - ♦ razor blades permanently enclosed in a cartridge or housing where less than 2 millimetres of any blade is protruding.
- Furthermore, this section does not apply to articles already covered by other legislation, for example:
  - ♦ s 1 of the Restriction of Offensive Weapons Act 1959: flick knives and gravity knives (see **8.10.3**); and
  - ♦ s 141(2) of the Criminal Justice Act 1988: knuckledusters, swordsticks, belt daggers (see **8.9.3**).

Defence

Proof that all reasonable precautions were taken and all due diligence was exercised to avoid the commission of the offence.

Defence notes

The seller's defence will be stronger if they have gone beyond judging by appearances or enquiring about the purchaser's age, by asking for proof (documentary evidence) as to age.

Practical Considerations

It is an offence under s 28 of the Violent Crime Reduction Act 2006 to use another person to look after, hide or transport a firearm, offensive/bladed weapon or knife, and that it would be available when required for an unlawful purpose (see **8.3.7**).

 Summary   6 months

 6 months' imprisonment and/or a fine not exceeding level 5 on the standard scale.

8.10.3 Make/import/sell/hire a flick or gravity knife

The Restriction of Offensive Weapons Act 1959 creates offences of trading in flick or gravity knives.

Offences

Any person who manufactures, sells or hires, or offers for sale or exposes or has in his possession for the purpose of sale or hire, or lends or gives to any other person—

(a) any knife which has a blade which opens automatically by hand pressure applied to a button, spring or other device in or attached to the handle of the knife, sometimes known as a flick knife or flick gun; or

(b) any knife which has a blade which is released from the handle or sheath thereof by the force of gravity or the application of centrifugal force and which, when released, is locked in place by means of a button, spring, lever, or other device, sometimes known as a gravity knife,

shall be guilty of an offence.

Restriction of Offensive Weapons Act 1959, s 1(1)

Points to prove

✓ date and location
✓ manufactured/sold/hired/offered for sale **or**
✓ exposed **or**
✓ had in his/her possession for the purpose of sale/hire **or**
✓ lent or gave
✓ to a person
✓ any flick knife/flick gun/gravity knife

Explanatory notes

- The importation of any flick knife, flick gun, or gravity knife is an offence under s 170 of the Customs and Excise Management Act 1979.
- A lock knife is not a gravity knife.

 Summary

 6 months

 6 months' imprisonment and/or a fine not exceeding level 4 on the standard scale.

8.10.4 **Possess weapon/blade/sharp point on school premises**

Section 139A of the Criminal Justice Act 1988 creates the offence of possessing an article with a blade or sharp point or an offensive weapon on school premises.

8.10.4 Possess Weapon/Blade/Sharp Point on School Premises

Offences

(1) An offence is committed by any person who has with him on school premises an article to which section 139 of the Criminal Justice Act 1988 applies.

(2) An offence is committed by any person who has with him on school premises an offensive weapon within the meaning of section 1 of the Prevention of Crime Act 1953.   **Criminal Justice Act 1988, s 139A(1), (2)**

Points to prove

✓ date and location
✓ without good reason/lawful authority
✓ had with him/her
✓ on school premises
✓ an offensive weapon/article being a blade/sharply pointed

Meanings

Has with him   (see 8.3.6)

School premises

Means land used for the purposes of a **school**.

School

Means an educational institution not within the further or higher education sector, which is an institution providing one or more of the following:
• primary education,
• full-time secondary education for pupils of compulsory school age (up to the age of 16) or
• full-time education for people over compulsory school age who have not attained the age of 19 years,

whether or not the institution also provides part-time education for junior pupils, further education, or other secondary education.

Article   (see 8.10.1)

Offensive weapon   (see 8.9.1)

Explanatory notes

• The premises can include open land, such as playing fields or schoolyards. However, dwellings occupied within the school premises by employees (such as caretakers or wardens houses) are outside the scope of this section.
• This definition seems to apply to both publicly maintained and independent schools.
• It is not necessary that the offence is committed during school hours; an offence can be committed at any time of the day or night, during term time or holidays.

- Many schools do not allow access to the general public outside or even during school hours, so these offences cover the situation where such weapons are carried on school premises that are not public places.
- Section 550A of the Education Act 1996, gives members of staff powers to restrain pupils to prevent the pupil from: committing a specific offence, causing personal injury/damage to property or engaging in any behaviour prejudicial to the maintenance of good order and discipline at the school.
- Section 550AA of the Education Act 1996, gives members of staff powers to search pupils for weapons namely a bladed article/knife (s 139—see **8.10.1**) or an offensive weapon (see **8.9.1**).
- Similar powers exist under the Further & Higher Education Act 1992—
  - Under s 85A a constable or authorized person can remove a person who is causing a nuisance or disturbance on higher educational premises from those premises.
  - Section 85B gives a member of staff in a further education institution power to search further education students and their possessions for a bladed article/knife (s 139—see **8.10.1**) or offensive weapon (see **8.9.1**).
- Consider the offence of causing/permitting a nuisance/disturbance on school premises (see **8.10.5**).
- There is a specific police power to enter and search school premises in connection with this offence (see **8.11.2**).
- Consider s 1 of the Police and Criminal Evidence Act 1984 where a constable can stop and search persons/vehicles relating to offensive weapons, bladed/pointed articles and to seize such weapons/articles (see **12.1.1**).

Defences

To prove, on the balance of probabilities, that the article or weapon that the defendant had with him/her was either:

- in his/her possession for a good reason or with lawful authority; or
- intended for use:
  - at work;
  - for educational purposes;
  - for religious reasons;
  - as part of any national costume.

 SSS   **E&S**

 Either way   🕐 None

Summary: 6 months' imprisonment and/or a fine not exceeding the statutory maximum.
Indictment: 4 years' imprisonment and/or a fine.

8.10.5 **Nuisance/disturbance on school premises**

Section 547 of the Education Act 1996 creates the offence of causing a nuisance or disturbance on school premises and gives the police power to remove people committing such an offence.

Offence

Any person who without lawful authority is present on premises to which this section applies and causes or permits nuisance or disturbance to the annoyance of persons who lawfully use those premises (whether or not any such persons are present at the time) is guilty of an offence.

Education Act 1996, s 547(1)

Points to prove

✓ date and location
✓ without lawful authority
✓ was present on
✓ premises of local authority maintained/grant-maintained school
✓ and permitted/caused
✓ a nuisance/disturbance
✓ to the annoyance of persons lawfully using those premises

Power to remove offenders

If a police constable, or an authorised person (of appropriate authority) has reasonable cause to suspect that any person is committing or has committed an offence under this section, he may remove him from the premises in question.

Education Act 1996, s 547(3)

Explanatory notes

- A power also exists to enter school premises and search persons on those premises on reasonable grounds for believing that offences are being or has been committed in relation to articles and weapons (see **8.10.4** and **8.11.2**).
- Similar powers exist with teachers at schools, and members of staff at higher education establishments (see **8.10.4**).

- This section applies to premises, including playgrounds, playing fields, and other premises for outdoor recreation of any:
  - ♦ school maintained by a local education authority,
  - ♦ special school not so maintained, and
  - ♦ independent school.
- It also applies to any premises that are provided by the local education authority for recreation, social, and physical training and used wholly or mainly in connection with instruction or leadership in sporting, recreational, or outdoor activities.
- Section 40 of the Local Government (Miscellaneous Provisions) Act 1982 deals with the same type of offence for local authority maintained colleges, providing further or higher education.

CSO

 Summary   6 months

A fine not exceeding level 2 on the standard scale.

Links to alternative subjects and offences

CSO Offences where CSO can use their powers

8.11 Powers—Knives and Offensive Weapons

The Criminal Justice Act 1988 deals with search warrants for premises, and also stop and search powers for school premises.

8.11.1 Search warrant for premises

Section 142 of the Criminal Justice Act 1988 creates a search power in respect of premises.

Grounds for issue of warrant

If on an application made by a constable a justice of the peace is satisfied that there are reasonable grounds for believing—

(a) that there are on premises specified in the application
  (i) knives such as are mentioned in section 1(1) of the Restriction of Offensive Weapons Act 1959; **or**
  (ii) weapons to which section 141 applies; **and**
(b) that an offence under section 1 of the Restriction of Offensive Weapons Act 1959 or section 141 above has been or is being committed in relation to them; **and**
(c) that any of the **conditions** specified in subsection (3) below applies, he may issue a warrant authorising a constable to enter and search the premises.   Criminal Justice Act 1988, s 142(1)

Meaning of conditions

The conditions referred to in (c) are any of the following:
- that it is not practicable to communicate with any person entitled to grant—entry to the premises or access to the knives or weapons to which the application relates;
- that entry to the premises will not be granted unless a warrant is produced;
- that the purpose of a search may be frustrated or seriously prejudiced unless a constable arriving at the premises can secure immediate entry to them.

Explanatory notes

- 'Knives' in the Restriction of Offensive Weapons Act 1959 refers to the offences relating to any flick knife, flick gun, or gravity knife (see **8.10.3**).
- Weapons under s 141 are listed in The Offensive Weapons Order 1988 (see **8.9.2** and **8.9.3**).
- A constable may seize and retain anything for which a search has been authorized under subsection (1) above.

8.11.2 Power for article/weapon on school premises

Section 139B of the Criminal Justice Act 1988 provides a power of entry to school premises to search for offensive weapons or articles with a blade or sharp point, and to seize/retain any weapon/article found.

Enter and search

A constable may enter school premises and search those premises and any person on those premises for—

(a) any article to which section 139 of the Criminal Justice Act 1988 applies, or

(b) any offensive weapon within the meaning of section 1 of the Prevention of Crime Act 1953,

if he has reasonable grounds for suspecting that an offence under section 139A of CJA 1988 is being, or has been, committed.

Criminal Justice Act 1988, s 139B(1)

Seize and retain

If, in the course of a search under this section, a constable discovers an article or weapon which he has reasonable grounds for suspecting to be an article or weapon of a kind described in subsection (1) above, he may seize and retain it. **Criminal Justice Act 1988, s 139B(2)**

Explanatory notes

- A constable may use reasonable force, if necessary, in the exercise of the power of entry conferred by this section.
- For the offence under s 139A of the CJA 1988 (see **8.10.4**).
- An article is a bladed/sharply pointed article (see **8.10.1**).
- For offensive weapon under the Prevention of Crime Act 1953, s 1 (see **8.9.1**).

Practical considerations

- Consider the Police and Criminal Evidence Act 1984, s 1 where a constable can stop and search persons/vehicles relating to offensive weapons, bladed/pointed articles and to seize such weapons/articles (see **12.1.1**).
- Powers under s 139B are additional to and overlap with the powers of entry and search in the Police and Criminal Evidence Act 1984, s 17 (see **12.3.2**).
- If a large number of people are involved, causing fear of a serious public order situation, then stop and search powers under the Criminal Justice and Public Order Act 1994, s 60, should be considered (see **8.11.3**).
- Consider the offence and power to remove a person who causes or permits a nuisance or disturbance on school premises (see **8.10.5**).

8.11.3 **Stop and search—serious violence/offensive weapon**

Section 60 of the Criminal Justice and Public Order Act 1994 allows senior police officers to authorize constables to stop and search people/vehicles in a specific area, either where a serious public order problem is likely to arise, or for offensive weapons or dangerous instruments. An offence will be committed if that person fails to comply.

Authorization

If a police officer of or above the rank of inspector reasonably believes—
(a) that incidents involving serious violence may take place in any locality in his police area, and that it is expedient to give an authorisation under this section to prevent their occurrence, or
(b) that persons are carrying dangerous instruments or offensive weapons in any locality in his police area without good reason,
he may give an authorisation that the powers conferred by this section are to be exercisable at **any place** within that locality for a specified period not exceeding 24 hours.

Criminal Justice and Public Order Act 1994, s 60(1)

Explanatory notes

- The inspector giving an authorization must, as soon as practicable, inform an officer of or above the rank of superintendent.
- If it appears to an officer of or above the rank of superintendent that it is expedient to do so, s/he may direct that the authorization shall continue in being for a further 24 hours.
- Any authorization shall be:
  - ✦ in writing;
  - ✦ signed by the officer giving it; and
  - ✦ must specify the locality and the period during which the powers are exercisable.

Power to stop and search pedestrian/vehicle

This section confers on any constable in uniform power—
(a) to stop any pedestrian and search him or anything carried by him for offensive weapons or **dangerous instruments**;
(b) to stop any vehicle and search the vehicle, its driver and any passenger for offensive weapons or dangerous instruments.

Criminal Justice and Public Order Act 1994, s 60(4)

Power to seize

If in the course of such a search under this section a constable discovers a dangerous instrument or an article which he has reasonable grounds for suspecting to be an offensive weapon, he may seize it.

Criminal Justice and Public Order Act 1994, s 60(6)

Meaning of dangerous instrument

Means any dangerous thing, which has a blade which can be used for performing an action or which is sharply pointed.

Offence

A person who fails to stop, or to stop a **vehicle**, when required to do so by a constable in the exercise of his powers under this section commits an offence.   Criminal Justice and Public Order Act 1994, s 60(8)

Points to prove

- ✓ date and location
- ✓ failed to stop (person) **or** vehicle
- ✓ when required to do so
- ✓ by a constable in uniform
- ✓ in exercising powers of stop/search

Meaning of vehicle

This is the natural meaning of vehicle and includes a caravan.

Explanatory notes

- Once written authority has been given for searches, it is **not** necessary for a constable to have 'reasonable grounds for suspicion' before stopping any person/vehicle or making a search of any person in that specific locality.
- Any persons searched under this section are entitled to a written statement stating that they were searched under these powers if they apply within 12 months.
- A person carries a dangerous instrument or an offensive weapon if s/he has it in their physical possession.

Related cases

R (on the application of Laporte) v Chief Constable of Gloucestershire [2006] UKHL 55, HL Three coaches stopped and searched under a s 60 authority on intelligence that occupants would cause disorder at RAF base and returned back to London. QBD determined that police actions were a reasonable and honest belief in preventing an apprehended breach of the peace. However, the HL ruled that the police had acted unlawfully because a breach of the peace was not 'imminent' at the time the coaches were stopped; thus the extent of interference with the protesters' rights under Art 10 and Art 11 was disproportionate.

Practical considerations

Where a s 60 authorization exists, a power under s 60AA can be brought into force so that any items or disguises which are used by the persons in order to conceal their identity can be removed. An offence is also

---

8.11.3 Stop and Search—Serious Violence/Offensive Weapon

committed if a person fails to remove an item worn by him/her when required to do so by a constable in the exercise of this power.

 Summary   6 months

1 month imprisonment and/or a fine not exceeding level 3 on the standard scale.

Links to alternative subjects and offences

Chapter 9
Licensing

9.1 Children and Alcohol

The sale and supply of alcohol is regulated by the Licensing Act 2003. This Act creates a number of offences, including offences relating to children, young people, alcohol, and offences concerning drunkenness and disorderly conduct.

The following offences will protect children both **on and off licensed premises**; some of them therefore apply anywhere and are not restricted to licensed premises.

9.1.1 Unaccompanied children prohibited from certain premises

It is an offence to admit children under 16 to certain categories of relevant premises if they are not accompanied by an adult or allow them to be on these premises between midnight and 5 a.m., and those premises are open for the supply of alcohol for consumption there. These two offences seek to protect unaccompanied children under the age of 16.

Offence

A person to whom **subsection (3) applies** commits an offence if—

(a) knowing that **relevant premises** are within subsection (4), he allows an unaccompanied **child** to be on the premises at a time when they are open for the purposes of being used for the supply of **alcohol** for consumption there, **or**

(b) he allows an **unaccompanied** child to be on relevant premises at a time between the hours of midnight and 5 am when the premises are open for the purposes of being used for the **supply of alcohol** for consumption there.   Licensing Act 2003, s 145(1)

9.1.1 Unaccompanied Children Prohibited from Certain Premises

---

Points to prove

✓ date and location
✓ being a person to whom sub-s (3) applies
✓ knowing they were relevant premises
✓ allowed an unaccompanied child
✓ to be on premises at a time/between midnight and 5 am
✓ when open for supplying alcohol for consumption therein

Meanings

Person to whom subsection (3) applies

Any person who—

- Works at the premises in a capacity, whether paid or unpaid, which authorizes him to request the unaccompanied child to leave the premises.
- In the case of licensed premises, to the holder of a premises licence in respect of the premises, and the designated premises supervisor (if any) under such a licence.
- In the case of premises in respect of which a club premises certificate has effect, to any member or officer of the club which holds the certificate who is present on the premises in a capacity which enables him to make such a request.
- In the case of premises which may be used for a permitted temporary activity by virtue of pt 5 of the Licensing Act 2003, to the premises user in relation to the temporary event notice in question (s 145(3)).

Relevant premises

- Relevant premises are **within this subsection** if—
  - (a) they are exclusively or primarily used for the supply of alcohol for consumption on the premises, **or**
  - (b) they are open for the purposes of being used for the supply of alcohol for consumption on the premises by virtue of Part 5 (permitted temporary activities) and, at the time the temporary event notice in question has effect, they are exclusively or primarily used for such supplies.   Licensing Act 2003, s 145(4)
- Relevant premises means—
  - ♦ licensed premises, or
  - ♦ premises in respect of which there is in force a club premises certificate, or
  - ♦ premises, which may be used for a permitted temporary activity by virtue of pt 5 of the Licensing Act 2003 (s 159).

Child

Means an individual aged under 16 (s 145(2)).

Alcohol

Means spirits, wine, beer, cider or any other fermented, distilled or spirituous liquor, but does **not** include—

(a) alcohol which is of a strength not exceeding 0.5 per cent at the time of the sale or supply in question,

---

(b) perfume,
(c) flavouring essences recognised by the Commissioners of Customs and Excise as not being intended for consumption as or with dutiable alcoholic liquor,
(d) the aromatic flavouring essence commonly known as Angostura bitters,
(e) alcohol which is, or is included in, a medicinal product,
(f) denatured alcohol,
(g) methyl alcohol,
(h) naphtha, or
(i) alcohol contained in liqueur confectionery.

Licensing Act 2003, s 191

Unaccompanied

Means not in the company of an individual aged 18 or over (s 145(2)).

Supply of alcohol

Means the sale by retail of alcohol, or the supply of alcohol by or on behalf of a club to, or to the order of, a member of the club (s 145(10)).

Explanatory notes

No offence is committed if the unaccompanied child is on the premises solely for the purpose of passing to or from some other place to or from which there is no other convenient means of access or exit (s 145(5)).

Defences
- That the conduct was by act or default of some other person and that the defendant exercised all **due diligence** to avoid committing it (s 145(8)).
- Where a person is charged with an offence under this section by reason of his own conduct it is a defence that:–
  (a) he **believed** that the unaccompanied child was **aged 16 or over** or that an individual accompanying the child was aged 18 or over, and
  (b) either—
      (i) he had taken **all reasonable steps** to establish the individual's age, or
      (ii) nobody could reasonably have suspected from the individual's appearance that he was aged under 16 or, as the case may be, under 18 (s 145(6)).

Defence notes
- For the purposes of subsection (6), a person is treated as having taken all reasonable steps to establish an individual's age if:
  (a) he asked the individual for evidence of his/her age, and
  (b) the evidence would have convinced a reasonable person (s 145(7)).
- This defence will fail if it is proved by the prosecution that the evidence of age was such that no reasonable person would have been convinced by it—for example, if the proof of age was either an obvious forgery or clearly belonged to another person.

• The defence also applies in situations where the child looks exceptionally old for his or her age.

Practical considerations

Age to be identified by use of birth certificate or similar document.

 Summary 12 months

 Fine not exceeding level 3

9.1.2 **Sale of alcohol to person under 18**

The sale of alcohol to a person under 18 **anywhere** is an offence.

Offence

A person commits an offence if he sells **alcohol** to an individual aged under 18.   Licensing Act 2003, s 146(1)

Points to prove
✓ date and location
✓ sold alcohol
✓ to person under the age of 18

Meaning of alcohol (see **9.1.1**).

Explanatory notes
• Similar offences apply to the supply of alcohol by or on behalf of a club (s 146(2), (3)).
• The sale of alcohol to children is not only an offence, if it occurs on relevant licensed premises, but **anywhere**.

Defences
• The defendant **believed** that the individual was **aged 18 or over**, and had either taken all **reasonable steps** to establish the individual's age, or nobody could reasonably have suspected from the individual's appearance that s/he was aged under 18.

- That the offence was committed by act or default of some other person and that the defendant exercised all **due diligence** to avoid committing it (s 146(6)).

Defence notes
- For the meaning of 'having taken all reasonable steps' (see **9.1.1** Defence notes).
- The statutory defence could apply, for example, where the actual sale was made by a barman and the manager had exercised all due diligence to avoid the offence being committed.

Practical considerations
- Age to be identified by use of birth certificate or similar document.
- This offence can be dealt with by way of a penalty notice for disorder (see **7.1.1**).

 Summary 12 months

 A fine not exceeding level 5

9.1.3 **Allowing the sale of alcohol to person under 18**

It is also an offence to allow alcohol to be sold to a person under 18.

Offence

A person to whom **subsection (2)** applies commits an offence if he knowingly allows the sale of **alcohol** on **relevant premises** to an individual aged under 18.   **Licensing Act 2003, s 147(1)**

Points to prove
- ✓ date and location
- ✓ being person to whom sub-s (2) applies
- ✓ on relevant premises
- ✓ knowingly allowed the sale of alcohol
- ✓ to a person under the age of 18

9.1.3 Allowing the Sale of Alcohol to Person Under 18

Meanings

Person to whom subsection (2) applies

Any person who works at the premises in a capacity, whether paid or unpaid, which authorizes him/her to prevent the sale (s 147(2)).

Alcohol (see 9.1.1)

Relevant premises (see 9.1.1)

Explanatory notes

- There are no statutory defences to this offence. The mental element 'knowingly' applies only to the allowing of the sale; it does not require knowledge that the individual was under 18. The prosecution need only prove that the individual was under 18 as a matter of fact.
- Similar offences apply to the supply of alcohol by or on behalf of a club (s 146(2), (3)).

Practical considerations

- Age to be identified by use of birth certificate or similar document.
- This offence can be dealt with by way of a penalty notice for disorder (see 7.1.1).
- An offence of **persistently selling alcohol to children (under 18)** will be committed under s 147A if on three or more different occasions, within a period of three consecutive months, alcohol is unlawfully sold on the same premises to an individual aged under 18.
- The following procedural requirements under s 147A also apply—
  - ◆ The premises must be either licensed premises or authorized premises for a permitted temporary activity by virtue of pt 5, and the offender must hold the premises licence or be the named premises user for a temporary event notice.
  - ◆ The same sale may not be counted as different offences for this purpose.
  - ◆ The following shall be admissible as evidence that there has been an unlawful sale of alcohol to an individual aged under 18 on any premises on any occasion—
    - a conviction for a s 146 offence in respect of a sale to that individual on those premises on that occasion;
    - a caution in respect of such an offence; or
    - payment of a penalty notice for disorder in respect of such a sale.
  - ◆ A sale of alcohol is not to count as an occasion if it took place before the commencement of s 147A (6 April 2007).
- Section 147B provides that if the holder of a premises licence is convicted of an offence under s 147A for sales on those premises, the court may order that the premises licence is suspended for a period not exceeding three months.
- A closure notice for persistently selling alcohol to children under 18 can be issued (see 9.3.4)

Summary 12 months

 A fine not exceeding level 5

9.1.4 **Purchase of alcohol by or on behalf of person under 18**

Offences are committed by a person under 18, or person on behalf of the under 18, who purchases or attempts to purchase alcohol anywhere. Similarly it is an offence for a person to buy or attempt to buy alcohol for consumption by a person who is under 18 on licensed premises.

Offence

(1) An individual aged under 18 commits an offence if he buys or attempts to buy **alcohol**.

(3) A person commits an offence if he buys or attempts to buy **alcohol** on behalf of an individual aged under 18.

(4) A person commits an offence if he buys or attempts to buy **alcohol** for consumption on **relevant premises** by an individual aged under 18.

Licensing Act 2003, s 149(1), (3), (4)

Points to prove

s 149(1) offence

✓ date and location
✓ being a person under the age of 18
✓ bought alcohol **or** attempted to buy alcohol

s 149(3) offence

✓ date and location
✓ bought alcohol **or** attempted to buy alcohol
✓ on behalf of individual under the age of 18

s 149(4) offence

✓ date and location
✓ bought alcohol **or** attempted to buy alcohol
✓ for consumption on relevant premises
✓ by an individual under the age of 18

9.1.4 Purchase of Alcohol by or on Behalf of Person Under 18

Meanings

Relevant premises (see 9.1.1)

Alcohol (see 9.1.1)

Explanatory notes

- Offences in s 149(1) and s 149(3) may be committed **anywhere**.
- 'On behalf of' does not mean that the purchase must be instigated by the child; the alcohol need only be bought for a child.
- An example of an offence under this section would be where a person under 18 gives money to an adult to buy alcohol in an off-licence for consumption by that child/young person.
- Similar offences under s 149 apply to the supply of alcohol at clubs under subsections (1)(b), (3)(b) and (4)(b) respectively.

Defences

Under s 149(1)

No offence is committed where the child buys or attempts to buy the alcohol at the request of a constable, or a weights and measures inspector who is acting in the course of his/her duty (s 149(2)).

Under s 149(3), (4)

The defendant had no reason to suspect that the individual was aged under 18 (s 149(6)).

Under s 149(4)

Subsection (4) does not apply where:

(a) the relevant person is aged 18 or over,

(b) the individual is aged 16 or 17,

(c) the alcohol is beer, wine or cider,

(d) its purchase or supply is for consumption at a **table meal** on relevant premises, and

(e) the individual is accompanied at the meal by an individual aged 18 or over (s 149(5)).

Defence notes

- **Under s 149(1)**—This allows test-purchasing operations to take place (see **9.3.1**)
- **Table meal**— Means a meal eaten by a person seated at a table, or at a counter or other structure which serves the purpose of a table and is not used for the service of refreshments for consumption by persons not seated at a table or structure serving the purpose of a table (s 159).
- Bar snacks do not amount to a table meal.

Related cases (see **9.3.1**)

Practical considerations

The s 149(4) offence of buy/attempt to buy for consumption on relevant premises can be dealt with by way of a penalty notice for disorder (see **7.1.1**).

 PND s 149(4) offence only

 CSO

 Summary

 12 months

| | s 149(1) offence
A fine not exceeding level 3.

s 149(3) and s 149(4) offences
A fine not exceeding level 5.

9.1.5 **Consumption of alcohol by person under 18**

Persons aged under 18 are not allowed to consume alcohol on relevant premises.

Offences

(1) A person under 18 commits an offence if he **knowingly consumes alcohol** on **relevant premises**.
(2) A **person to whom subsection (3) applies** commits an offence if he knowingly allows the consumption of alcohol on relevant premises by an individual aged under 18. *Licensing Act 2003, s 150(1), (2)*

Points to prove

s 150(1) offence

✓ date and location
✓ being a person under the age of 18
✓ consumed alcohol on relevant premises.

s 150(2) offence

✓ date and location
✓ being a person to whom sub-s (3) applies
✓ knowingly allowed
✓ an individual under the age of 18
✓ to consume alcohol on those premises

9.1.5 Consumption of Alcohol by Person Under 18

Meanings

Knowingly consumes

Means that the offence will not be committed if they inadvertently consume alcohol, for example if his/her drink is spiked.

Alcohol   (see 9.1.1)

Relevant premises   (see 9.1.1)

Person to whom subsection (3) applies

Any person who works at the premises in a capacity, whether paid or unpaid, which authorizes him/her to prevent the consumption (s 150(3)).

Explanatory notes

A similar offence applies to the supply of alcohol by clubs under s 150(3)(b) of the Act.

Defence (s 150(4))

Subsections (1) and (2) do not apply where:
- (a) the individual is aged 16 or 17,
- (b) the alcohol is beer, wine or cider,
- (c) its consumption is at a **table meal** on **relevant premises**, and
- (d) the individual is accompanied at the meal by an individual aged 18 or over.

Defence notes

Table meal   (see 'Defence notes' 9.1.4)

Practical considerations

- Age to be proved by use of birth certificate or similar documentation.
- This offence can be dealt with by way of a penalty notice for disorder (see **7.1.1**).

 Summary   12 months

 s 150(1) offence
A fine not exceeding level 3.
s 150(2) offence
A fine not exceeding level 5.

9.1.6 **Delivering alcohol to person under 18**

It is an offence for certain people to deliver or allow the delivery of alcohol to a person under 18.

Offences

(1) A person who works on **relevant premises** in any capacity, whether paid or unpaid, commits an offence if he knowingly delivers to an individual under 18 **alcohol** sold on the premises.

(2) A **person to whom subsection (3) applies** commits an offence if he knowingly allows anybody else to deliver to a person under 18 **alcohol** sold on **relevant premises**.   Licensing Act 2003, s 151(1), (2)

Points to prove

s 151(1) Offence

✓ date and location
✓ being a person who worked in a capacity, whether unpaid or paid
✓ on relevant premises
✓ knowingly delivered to an individual under the age of 18
✓ alcohol sold on those premises

s 151(2) Offence

✓ date and location
✓ being a person to whom subsection (3) applies
✓ on relevant premises
✓ knowingly allowed another person to deliver
✓ to an individual under the age of 18
✓ alcohol sold on those premises

Meanings

Relevant premises (see 9.1.1)

Alcohol (see 9.1.1)

Person to whom subsection (3) applies

Any person who works on the premises in a capacity, whether paid or unpaid, which authorizes him/her to prevent the delivery of the alcohol (s 151(3)).

Explanatory notes

- The offences in this section cover various situations, for example, where a child takes delivery of a consignment of alcohol bought by a parent from an off-licence, sub-s (1) (unless the defence applies); or where a person authorizes a delivery of that sort, sub-s (2).
- A similar offence applies to the supply of alcohol by clubs under s 151(4).

Defences s 151(6)

Subsections (1), (2) and (4) do not apply where:

(a) the alcohol is delivered at a place where the buyer or, as the case may be, person supplied lives or works, or

(b) the individual aged under 18 works on the relevant premises in a capacity, whether paid or unpaid, which involves the delivery of alcohol, or

(c) the alcohol is sold or supplied for consumption on the relevant premises.

Defence notes

This covers cases where, for example, a child answers the door and signs for the delivery of an order for the house, or where a 16-year-old office worker is sent to collect a delivery for their employer.

 Summary 12 months

 A fine not exceeding level 5

9.1.7 **Sending person under 18 to obtain alcohol**

A person under 18 must not be sent to obtain alcohol.

Offence

A person commits an offence if he knowingly sends an individual aged under 18 to obtain **alcohol** sold or to be sold on **relevant premises** for consumption off the premises.   Licensing Act 2003, s 152(1)

Points to prove

✓ date and location
✓ knowingly sent an individual under the age of 18
✓ to obtain alcohol
✓ sold or to be sold on relevant premises
✓ for consumption off those premises

Meanings

Alcohol (see **9.1.1**)

Relevant premises (see **9.1.1**)

Explanatory notes

- It is immaterial whether the individual aged under 18 is sent to obtain the alcohol from the relevant premises or from other premises from which it is delivered in pursuance of the sale or supply (s 152(2)).
- This offence covers, for example, circumstances where a parent sends their child to an off-licence to collect some alcohol, which had been bought over the telephone.
- The s 152(4) defence allows for test purchasing operations (see **9.3.1**).
- A similar offence applies to the supply of alcohol by clubs.

Defences

- No offence is committed where the individual aged under 18 works on the relevant premises in a capacity (whether paid or unpaid) that involves the delivery of alcohol (s 152(3)).
- No offence is committed where the individual aged under 18 is sent by a constable, or a weights and measures inspector, who is acting in the course of his duty (s 152(4)).

Related case

DPP v Marshall [1988] 3 All ER 683, QBD (See **9.3.1**).

Practical considerations

There are further offences concerning alcohol and children not dealt with in this book:

- sale of liqueur confectionery to children under 16 (Licensing Act 2003, s 148);
- prohibition of unsupervised sales by children (Licensing Act 2003, s 153).

 Summary 12 months

 A fine not exceeding level 5

Links to alternative subjects and offences

9.2 **Drunkenness on Licensed Premises**

The sale and supply of alcohol is regulated by the Licensing Act 2003. This Act creates a number of offences relating to alcohol and offences concerning drunkenness and disorderly conduct.

9.2.1 **Sale of alcohol to person who is drunk**

It is an offence to sell or attempt to sell alcohol to a person who is drunk, or to allow alcohol to be sold to such a person, on relevant premises.

Offence

A **person to whom subsection (2) applies** commits an offence if, on **relevant premises**, he knowingly sells or attempts to sell **alcohol** to a person who is **drunk**, or allows alcohol to be sold to such a person.

Licensing Act 2003, s 141(1)

Points to prove
✓ date and location
✓ person to whom sub-s (2) applies
✓ knowingly sold/attempted to sell/allowed the sale of alcohol
✓ on those premises to a person who was drunk

Meanings

Person to whom subsection (2) applies
- Any person who works at the premises in a capacity, whether paid or unpaid, which gives him authority to sell the alcohol concerned.
- In the case of licensed/permitted temporary activity premises and clubs, the same persons apply as given in s 145(3) (see **9.1.1**).

Relevant premises (see **9.1.1**)

Alcohol (see **9.1.1**)

Drunk

'Having drunk intoxicating liquor to an extent which affects steady self-control' (*Neale v RMJE (a minor)* (1985) 80 Cr App R 20).

Explanatory notes
- In each case, drunkenness will be a question of fact for the court to decide.

9.2.2 **Failure to Leave Licensed Premises**

• This offence applies in relation to the supply of alcohol by or on behalf of a club to or to the order of a member of the club as it applies in relation to the sale of alcohol, and also to premises which may be used for a permitted temporary activity (s 141(3)).

Related case

Neale v RMJE (a minor) (1985) 80 Cr App R 20 On the meaning of drunk (see above).

Practical considerations

• If the person is under 18 consider offences under s 145 (see **9.1.1**).
• The licence gives details of the holder and/or the designated premises supervisor, this should be clearly displayed in the premises.
• It is also an offence to obtain or attempt to obtain alcohol on relevant premises for consumption **on those premises** by a person who is drunk under s 142.

 Summary   12 months

 A fine not exceeding level 3 on the standard scale.

9.2.2 **Failure to leave licensed premises**

People who are drunk or disorderly may be requested to leave certain premises and commit an offence if they fail to do so.

> **Offences**
>
> A person who is **drunk** or **disorderly** commits an offence if, without reasonable excuse—
> (a) he fails to leave **relevant premises** when requested to do so by a constable or by a **person to whom subsection (2) applies**, or
> (b) he enters or attempts to enter relevant premises after a constable or a person to whom subsection (2) applies has requested him not to enter.
>
> Licensing Act 2003, s 143(1)

Points to prove

✓ date and location

✓ without reasonable excuse while drunk or disorderly

✓ failed to comply with request to leave **or not to** enter/attempt to enter relevant premises

✓ by a constable **or** a person to whom sub-s (2) applies

Meanings

Drunk (see 9.2.1)

Disorderly

Is not defined, but the dictionary meaning of 'disorderly behaviour' is 'unruly or offensive behaviour'.

Relevant premises (see 9.1.1)

Person to whom subsection (2) applies

- Any person who works at the premises in a capacity, whether paid or unpaid, which authorizes him/her to make such a request.
- In the case of licensed/permitted temporary activity premises and clubs, the same persons apply as given in s 145(3) (see **9.1.1**).

Explanatory notes

- No offence will be committed if the person has a reasonable excuse, for example, if they are physically prevented by disability or injury from leaving the premises.
- This offence also applies to clubs and to premises which may be used for a permitted temporary activity.
- In each case, whether a person is drunk and/or disorderly will be a question of fact for the court to decide.

Related cases

Neale v RMJE (a minor) (1985) 80 Cr App R 20 On the meaning of drunk (see 9.2.1).

Practical considerations

On being requested to do so by the appropriate person, under s 143(2), a constable must help to expel from relevant premises a person who is drunk or disorderly and/or help to prevent such a person from entering relevant premises.

 Summary 12 months

 A fine not exceeding level 1

9.2.3 **Allowing disorderly conduct on licensed premises**

It is also an offence to knowingly allow disorderly conduct on relevant premises.

Offence

A person to whom subsection (2) applies commits an offence if he knowingly allows disorderly conduct on relevant premises.

Licensing Act 2003, s 140(1)

Points to prove

✓ date and location
✓ being a person to whom sub-s (2) applies
✓ knowingly allowed disorderly conduct to take place on relevant premises

---

Meanings

Person to whom subsection (2) applies

- Any person who works at the premises in a capacity, whether paid or unpaid, which authorizes him/her to prevent the conduct.
- In the case of licensed/permitted temporary activity premises and clubs, the same persons apply as given in s 145(3) (see **9.1.1**).

Disorderly (see 9.2.2)

Relevant premises (see 9.1.1)

Explanatory notes

This offence also applies to clubs and to premises which may be used for a permitted temporary activity.

 Summary   12 months

 A fine not exceeding level 3 on the standard scale.

Links to alternative subjects and offences

9.3 Powers to Enter/Close Licensed Premises and Test Purchases

The sale and supply of alcohol is regulated by the Licensing Act 2003. Apart from the Act creating a variety of offences relating to alcohol, it also contains powers to enter/close licensed premises/clubs and allows test purchases.

9.3.1 Test purchases

The offence of 'purchase of alcohol by or on behalf of children' and the offence of 'sending a child to obtain alcohol' permit the police to conduct test purchases.

Authority

A constable may (in the course of their duty) request a child to buy or attempt to buy alcohol or send a child to obtain alcohol.

Licensing Act 2003, s 149(2)

Explanatory notes

This statutory authority allows test-purchasing operations to establish whether licensees and staff working in licensed premises are complying with the prohibition on underage sales.

Related cases

DPP v Marshall [1988] 3 All ER 683, QBD Police in plain clothes bought alcohol from a shop; it was argued that evidence should be excluded under s 78 of PACE, as the officers had not revealed the fact that they were policemen at the time of the purchase and this was unfair. On appeal it was held that evidence of police officers had been wrongly excluded; it had not been shown that the evidence would have had an adverse effect on the proceedings.

R v Loosely/Attorney-General's Reference No 3 of 2000 [2001] UKHL 53 This was a case on entrapment; police officers must not instigate the commission of an offence. But if police do what an ordinary customer would do, whether lawful or unlawful, this will not normally be regarded as objectionable.

Practical considerations

- Consider the protection of children engaged in such operations.
- Assess the reliability of their evidence.

9.3.2 **Police powers to enter licensed premises and clubs**

The Licensing Act 2003 contains provisions dealing with powers of entry to investigate licensable activities and offences, namely:

- A constable or an authorized person may enter premises, if s/he has reason to believe that they are being, or are about to be used for a licensable activity, in order to see whether the activity is being carried on in accordance with an authorization (s 179(1)).
  Note: This does not apply to clubs, unless there is other authorization apart from a club premises licence.
- A constable may enter and search any premises in respect of which s/he has reason to believe that an offence under the Licensing Act has been, is being or is about to be committed (s 180(1)).
- A constable may enter and search club premises where s/he has reasonable cause to believe that certain offences relating to the supply of drugs have been, are being or are about to be committed or that there is likely to be a breach of the peace (s 97(1)).

Explanatory notes

- In exercising these powers a constable may, if necessary, use reasonable force (s 180(2) and s 97(2)).
- It is not necessary to obtain a warrant.
- Police can require a person to produce a premises licence, club premises certificate, or temporary event notice (see Licensing Act 2003, ss 57, 94 and 109).
- The police may enter premises in order to inspect them before a licence or certificate is granted (see Licensing Act 2003, ss 59 and 96).

9.3.3 **Police powers—closure orders**

A police officer of, or above, the rank of inspector may close specific premises for up to 24 hours, if there is actual or imminent disorder on, or in the vicinity of and related to, the premises or if it is necessary to prevent a public nuisance caused by noise coming from the premises.

> **Offence**
>
> A person commits an offence if, without reasonable excuse, he permits **relevant premises** to be open in contravention of a closure order or any extension of it. *Licensing Act 2003, s 161(6)*

Points to prove
- ✓ date and location
- ✓ without reasonable excuse
- ✓ permitted relevant premises
- ✓ to be open in contravention of a closure order/extension to a closure order

Meanings

Relevant premises

Premises in respect of which a **premises licence** and/or a **temporary event notice** have effect.

Premises licence

Means a licence granted under the Licensing Act 2003, in respect of any premises, which authorizes the premises to be used for one or more licensable activities, namely:
- sale and/or supply of alcohol;
- provision of regulated entertainment;
- late night refreshments.

Temporary event notice

Used on premises where licensable activities are allowed to take place for not more than 96 hours.

Explanatory notes

- An inspector (or above) can make a closure order on reasonable belief that:
    - ♦ there is actual or likely imminent disorder and the closure of the premises is required in the interests of public safety; **or**
    - ♦ closure is necessary to prevent a public nuisance caused by excessive noise coming from the premises.
- This closure order cannot exceed 24 hours, after coming into force.
- If required the order can be extended (by inspector or above) for a further 24 hours if it is apparent that a magistrates court will not have had the opportunity to determine the matter.

Practical considerations

- A superintendent or above can make an application to a magistrates court for an order to close all licensed premises in an area experiencing disorder. If granted, it is an offence (under s 160) to knowingly allow/keep such premises open during the period of the order.
- Should a review of the licence be sought instead?
- Have other premises been closed/licence holders warned in the area?
- Has the licence holder been given any early reminders or warnings or the opportunity to close the premises voluntarily?
- The police have powers to close down premises, if there are reasonable grounds for believing that they are being used in

connection with the production, supply or use of Class A controlled drugs (see **5.3**).

 Summary   12 months

 3 months' imprisonment and/or a fine not exceeding £20,000.

9.3.4 **Police powers—closure notice**

Where an offence of persistently selling alcohol to children (under 18) has been committed under s 147A (see **9.1.3**) then a closure notice can be issued by a superintendent (or above) to close the premises for up to 48 hours.

Closure notice

A **relevant officer** may give a notice under this section (a 'closure notice') applying to any premises if—
(a) there is evidence that a person ('the offender') has committed an offence under section 147A in relation to those premises;
(b) the relevant officer considers that the evidence is such that, if the offender were prosecuted for the offence, there would be a realistic prospect of his being convicted; and
(c) the offender is still, at the time when the notice is given, the holder of a premises licence in respect of those premises, or one of the holders of such a licence.   Licensing Act 2003, s 169A(1)

Meaning of relevant officer

Means a police officer of the rank of superintendent or above; or an appointed inspector of weights and measures.

Explanatory notes

- The closure notice will:
  ♦ prohibit sales of alcohol on the premises, not exceeding 48 hours; and
  ♦ if accepted will discharge all criminal liability in respect of the s 147A offence (see **9.1.3**).
- A closure notice must:
  ♦ be in the form as prescribed by regulations;
  ♦ specify the premises and circumstances surrounding the offence;
  ♦ specify the period when sales of alcohol are prohibited;
  ♦ explaining the consequences/penalties of any sale of alcohol on the premises during that period; the rights of that person to be tried for that offence, and how that right may be exercised.

Practical considerations

- The period specified must be not more than 48 hours; and the time specifying when that period begins must be not less than 14 days after the date of the service of the closure notice.
- Service of the closure notice may be served on the premises by a constable or CSO to a person having control/responsibility for the premises; and only when licensable activities are being carried on there. A copy must be served on the licence holder of the premises.
- A closure notice must not be given more than 3 months after the s 147A offence.
- No more that one closure notice may be given in respect of offences relating to the same sales; nor may such a notice be given in respect of an offence in respect of which a prosecution has already been brought.
- Section 169B prescribes other matters when a closure notice has been issued:
  - ♦ No proceedings may be brought for the s 147A offence or any related offence at any time before the time when the prohibition proposed by the notice would take effect.
  - ♦ If the premises licence holder accepts the proposed prohibition in the manner specified in the notice then that prohibition takes effect (as specified) and no proceedings may brought against that person for the alleged offence or any related offence.
  - ♦ 'Related offence' means an offence under s 146 (see **9.1.2**) or s 147 (see **9.1.3**) in respect of any of the sales to which the alleged offence relates.

Links to alternative subjects and offences

9.4 Alcohol in Designated Places

Section 12 of the Criminal Justice and Police Act 2001 is intended to reduce the incidence of disorder and public nuisance arising from alcohol consumption in designated public places. A police officer can require a person to cease drinking alcohol in the designated public place, with powers to confiscate and dispose, and that failure to comply is an offence.

9.4.1 Power to require to cease drinking alcohol

Power

(1) Subsection (2) applies if a constable reasonably believes that a person is, or has been, consuming **alcohol** in a **designated public place** or intends to consume alcohol in such a place.

(2) The constable may require the person concerned—
   (a) not to consume in that place anything which is, or which the constable reasonably believes to be, alcohol;
   (b) to surrender anything in his possession which is, or which the constable reasonably believes to be, alcohol or a container for alcohol.

Criminal Justice and Police Act 2001, s 12(1), (2)

Meanings

Alcohol   (see **9.1.1**)

Designated public place

A designated public place is a place if it is a public place in the area of a local authority; and identified in an order made by that authority under sub-s 13(2) (s 13(1)).

Explanatory notes

- Local authorities may designate areas as public places for the purposes of this section. Once an order for has been made then police powers under s 12 automatically become available.
- The person must be informed that failure to comply with the police officer's request, without reasonable excuse, is an offence (see **9.4.2**).
- Section 14 of the Criminal Justice and Police Act 2001 denotes those areas that are not public places for the purposes of consuming alcohol in public places (eg consumption of alcohol in these places is allowed subject to regulation by other legislation):
- A place is not a designated public place or a part of such a place if it is:
   ♦ premises which have a premises licence or club premises certificate;

- ◆ a place within the cartilage of any premises which have a premises licence or club premises certificate;
- ◆ a place where the sale of alcohol is for the time being authorized by an occasional permission or was so authorized within the last 30 minutes;
- ◆ a place where facilities/activities relating to the sale/consumption of alcohol are permitted by a permission granted under s 115E of the Highways Act 1980.
- A constable may dispose of anything surrendered to him/her under sub-s (2) (above) in such manner as s/he considers appropriate (s 12(3)).
- There is also a power to confiscate alcohol from people under 18 years of age (see **9.5**).

9.4.2 **Failure to comply with alcohol requirements**

Offence

A person who fails without reasonable excuse to comply with a **requirement** imposed on him under subsection 12(2) [*see* **9.4.1**] commits an offence.

Criminal Justice and Police Act, s 12(4)

Points to prove

Surrender alcohol

✓ date and location
✓ without reasonable excuse
✓ failed to surrender
✓ something that was or that the constable reasonably believed to be
✓ alcohol or container for such
✓ in his/her possession
✓ in a designated public place
✓ when required by a constable

Consume alcohol

✓ date and location
✓ without reasonable excuse
✓ failed to comply with requirement
✓ imposed by constable
✓ not to consume in a designated public place
✓ something that was or that the constable reasonably believed to be
✓ alcohol

Example of constable's requirement:

'This is a designated public place in which I have reason to believe that you are/have been drinking alcohol. I require you to stop drinking and give me the container from which you are/have been drinking and any other containers (sealed or unsealed). I must inform you that failure to comply with my request, without reasonable excuse, is an offence for which you can be arrested.'

Practical considerations

- A constable who imposes a requirement on a person under sub-s (2) shall inform the person concerned that failing without reasonable excuse to comply with the requirement is an offence (s 12(5)).
- The seizure and disposal of alcohol in both sealed and unsealed containers is allowed.
- Officers should follow their own force orders in relation to disposal.
- Consider issuing a penalty notice for disorder (see **7.1**).

 PND   **CSO**

 Summary   6 months

 A fine not exceeding level 2 on the standard scale.

Links to alternative subjects and offences

9.5 Alcohol Confiscation/Offence Fail to Surrender

The Confiscation of Alcohol (Young Persons) Act 1997 was introduced to address the problem of young people drinking alcohol on the streets. The Act allows the police to confiscate alcohol from people under 18 years in certain public places.

9.5.1 Power to confiscate alcohol

Power

Where a constable reasonably suspects that a person in a **relevant place** is in **possession** of alcohol and that either—

(a) he is under the age of 18; or

(b) he intends that any of the alcohol should be consumed by a person under the age of 18 in that or any other relevant place; or

(c) a person under the age of 18 who is, or has **recently** been, with him has recently consumed alcohol in that or any other relevant place,

the constable may require him to surrender anything in his possession which is, or which the constable reasonably believes to be, alcohol or a container for such, and to state his name and address.

Confiscation of Alcohol (Young Persons) Act 1997, s 1(1)

Meanings

Relevant place

Means any **public place**, other than licensed premises; or any place, other than a public place, to which the person has unlawfully gained access; and for this purpose a place is a public place if at the material time the public or any section of the public has access to it, on payment or otherwise, as of right or by virtue of express or implied permission.

Possession

At common law possession is defined as: **actual** or **potential** physical control; and an intention to possess. In practice visible or external signs of possession, which can be demonstrated to a court, must support the two conditions above. (Source of definition: *Jowetts Dictionary of English Law*)

Recently

Is defined by *The Oxford English Dictionary* as 'lately' or 'comparatively near to the present time'. How the courts interpret this term remains to be seen.

Explanatory notes

- Officers can seize sealed and open containers, as well as the alcohol they hold, and dispose of both in an appropriate manner. However, a constable may not under sub-s (1) require a person to surrender any sealed containers unless s/he reasonably believes that the person is, or has been, consuming, or intends to consume alcohol in any relevant place. Where a young person has, for example, a sealed six-pack under his arm, officers should still consider who sold it, and whether there are any child welfare issues, and take action as appropriate (s 1(1)(A)).
- A constable may dispose of anything surrendered to him/her under sub-s (1) in such manner as he considers appropriate (s 1(2)).
- When imposing a requirement to surrender a constable must inform the person of the suspicion and that failing without reasonable excuse to comply with a requirement imposed under that subsection is an offence (s 1(4)).

Example of officer's requirement:

'I have reason to suspect that you are under 18 years of age. You are/have been drinking alcohol/beer/cider (or whatever). You must stop drinking immediately (if applicable). Please give me that can/bottle/plastic cup etc. What is your name and address? I must warn you that failure to comply with my request is an offence for which you can be arrested.'

Practical considerations

- Officers should follow their own force orders in relation to disposal.
- Suitably designated Community Support Officer (CSO), has the same powers as a police constable under this section (other than the arrest power).

9.5.2 Failing to surrender alcohol

Offence

A person who fails without reasonable excuse to comply with a requirement imposed on him under subsection (1) [see 9.5.1] commits an offence.

Confiscation of Alcohol (Young Persons) Act 1997, s 1(3)

Points to prove

- ✓ date and location
- ✓ without reasonable excuse
- ✓ failed to comply with requirement
- ✓ imposed by constable
- ✓ to surrender

9.5.2 Failing to Surrender Alcohol

> ✓ alcohol/suspected alcohol **or** a container for such
> ✓ in his/her possession
> ✓ and/or state his/her name and address

 6 months

 A fine not exceeding level 2 on the standard scale.

Links to alternative subjects and offences

Chapter 10

Road Traffic

10.1 Road Traffic: Meaning of Roads, Public Places, Vehicles, and Drives

10.1.1 Roads

The term 'road' has many meanings within various pieces of legislation.

Meaning of road

'Road' is defined in several Acts. The two most commonly used meanings of a road are:

- any highway and any other road to which the public has access, and includes bridges over which a road passes (Road Traffic Act 1988, s 192(1));
- any length of highway and any other road to which the public has access, and includes bridges over which a road passes (Road Traffic Regulation Act 1984, s 142(1).)

Explanatory notes

- 'Road' includes obvious public highways, footpaths and bridle ways maintained by government agencies or local authorities.
- The term 'public road' in the Vehicle Excise and Registration Act 1994 means a road repairable at public expense.
- The physical nature of a road provides a defined or definable route or way to which the general public has legal access, being a route allowing travel between two places.
- A field used for parking at an agricultural show was held not to be a road, as it had no definable way.
- Where there is no physical point at which a road ends reasonable judgment will need to be used to determine the road's end.
- A privately owned hotel forecourt used as a shortcut between two streets is a road.
- Walking or driving must take place on the road and such walking or driving must be lawful.

- Case decisions regarding roads need to be considered very carefully. As questions of 'fact', usually taken by lower courts, these decisions are heavily dependent on the individual circumstances of the case.

Related cases

Adams v Metropolitan Police [1980] RTR 289, QBD If the owner of a private road tolerates its use by the general public it may be a 'road to which the public have access'.

Cutter v Eagle Star Insurance Company Ltd [1998] 4 All ER 417, HL and Clarke v Kato and Others The Times, 23 October 1998, HL A part of a car park may be a road but the whole of the car park will not necessarily be (ie properly designated parking bays will not be a road, but a definable route (direction arrows, lane markings, etc) may make the rest of the car park a road under the Act).

Sadiku v DPP [2000] RTR 155, QBD A paved area used as a thoroughfare by pedestrians can be a road.

DPP v Coulman [1993] Crim LR 399, QBD A disembarkation lane at Eastern Docks, Dover is a public road.

Griffin v Squires [1958] 2 All ER 468, QBD Where the public used a car park, but only a certain sector of the public used it to gain access to private property, it was held not to have been a road.

Brewer v DPP The Times, 5 March 2004, QBD A railway station car park where the only people going through it are employees crossing to the staff car park is not a road.

McGurk and Another v Coster [1995] CLY 2912, Southport County Court Access to a temporary car park on a beach by driving over part of the beach between the sea and sand dunes was held not to be a road.

Practical considerations

- What are the physical characteristics, function, and public access of the place involved?
- Public access alone is not sufficient to make a place a road; similarly, some form of private use will not necessarily prevent it from being a road.
- Most important road traffic legislation relates to 'public places' as well—this is a wider and different definition that should be considered in each case (see 10.1.2).
- The footway, lay-by or verge is normally part of the road.
- The mode of transport is not relevant and such travellers may be on foot, riding on animals or in a vehicle.
- In instances of real doubt the courts have to decide on a case-by-case basis.
- It is not possible to trespass on a road.

10.1.2 **Public place**

Meaning of public place

The term 'public place' has, for the purposes of the Road Traffic Act 1988, been defined as: 'Any place to which the public have open access is a public place, even if payment must be made to gain entry.'

Explanatory notes

- Whether a place to which the public have limited or restricted access is a public place is a question of fact and degree in each case.
- The time at which the place was being used is important in dealing with 'public place' considerations. A car park of a public house may be a public place during licensing hours but may not be so outside those hours.
- An off-road parking bay adjacent to a highway with no physical impediment between the bay and the road is a public place.
- Lanes at a ferry port could be a public place as the public have access to them.

Related cases

DPP v Coulman [1993] Crim LR 399, QBD A hospital car park used by people visiting the hospital is a public place.

DPP v Neville (1996) 160 JP 758, CA Pier 7 of terminal 3 at Heathrow Airport has been held to be a public place.

R v Spence [1999] Crim LR 975, CA A company car park consisting of a small enclosed area in an industrial estate and used by employees, customers, and visitors on business was held not to be a public place.

Planton v DPP [2001] EWHC (Admin) 450, HC A man-made causeway between an island and the mainland, used only by residents and service industry workers, and having a sign stating 'Private Road—Residents and Authorized Vehicles only' at its entrance was held not to be a public place.

Practical considerations

- The test for whether somewhere that is not a public place is: 'do the people gaining access there have a special characteristic or personal reason which is not possessed by the general public?'
- Public use of the area must be shown evidentially.

10.1.3 **Vehicles**

Meaning of vehicles

General

The Oxford English Dictionary provides a general definition of 'vehicle' as a conveyance, usually with wheels, for transporting people, goods, etc; a car, cart, truck, carriage, sledge, etc; any means of carriage or transport; a receptacle in which something is placed in order to be moved.

For vehicle excise duty purposes

In the following provisions of this Act 'vehicle' means:

(a) a mechanically propelled vehicle, or

(b) any thing (whether or not it is a vehicle) that has been, but has ceased to be, a mechanically propelled vehicle.

Vehicle Excise and Registration Act 1994, s 1(1B)

Explanatory notes

- The above definitions of 'vehicle' should not be confused with the meaning of 'motor vehicle' or 'mechanically propelled vehicle'.
- 'Motor vehicle' means:
  - ◆ (subject to s 20 of the Chronically Sick and Disabled Persons Act 1970 which makes special provision about invalid carriages, within the meaning of that Act), a mechanically propelled vehicle intended or adapted for use on roads (Road Traffic Act 1988, s 185);
  - ◆ any mechanically propelled vehicle, whether or not it is intended for use on a road (Police Reform Act 2002, s 59);
  - ◆ any vehicle whose function is or was to be used on roads as a mechanically propelled vehicle (Vehicles (Crime) Act 2001, s 16).
- 'Adapted for use on a road' for the purposes of this definition means fit and apt for use on a road.
- A sidecar is part of a motor vehicle when attached to a motorbike and is not a trailer (Road Traffic Act 1988, s 186(1)).
- Conversely, a semi-trailer of an articulated vehicle is a trailer and not part of the towing vehicle (Road Traffic Act 1988, s 187(1)).
- An articulated bus ('bendy bus') should be treated as one vehicle (Road Traffic Act 1988, s 187(2)).
- A hovercraft is a motor vehicle (Road Traffic Act 1988, s 188).
- The term 'mechanically propelled vehicle' is not legally defined but, at its most basic, means a vehicle which can be propelled by mechanical means and would include electric or steam powered vehicles.
- Certain specialized vehicles may be used as invalid carriages on pavements without being classified as motor vehicles.

Related cases

Chief Constable of North Yorkshire Police v Saddington [2001] Crim LR 41, QBD A 'Go-Ped' (which resembles a child's scooter with an engine) has been held to be a motor vehicle. Despite a warning on it that it was not intended for use on a road, the correct test would be whether a reasonable person would say that one of its uses would be some general use on a road.

McEachran v Hurst [1978] RTR 462, QBD A moped being pedalled is still a mechanically propelled vehicle. Being constructed as such, it remains one until there was no possibility of it being mechanically mobile again, irrespective of the use to which it was being put.

Thomas v Hooper [1986] RTR 1, QBD A vehicle may no longer be a motor vehicle (under the Road Traffic Act 1988) if it has none of the normal vehicular controls operative.

Reader v Bunyard [1987] RTR 406, QBD A motor vehicle remains a mechanically propelled vehicle unless there was evidence that there was no likelihood of it being so used again. The onus was on the prosecution to prove its case.

Burns v Currell [1963] 2 All ER 297, QBD When deciding whether one of the uses of a vehicle would be on a road a 'reasonable person' test should be applied to the vehicle and not the intentions of the specific user at the time it was stopped.

Practical considerations

- What was the vehicle intended for and what use is it currently being put to?
- The onus of proving that a motor vehicle remained a mechanically propelled vehicle lies with the prosecution.
- Pedestrian controlled mowing machines, other pedestrian controlled vehicles and electrically assisted pedal cycles approved by the Secretary of State are **not** motor vehicles (Road Traffic Act 1988, s 189).
- It is a matter of fact and degree for the court to decide whether or not a vehicle is a motor vehicle/mechanically propelled vehicle at the time of a specific incident.
- In such cases, include evidence of the characteristics of the vehicle, which may be a photograph if appropriate.

10.1.4 **Drives/driving**

Meaning of drives/driving

- Whether or not someone is driving is predominantly a matter of fact and degree, and the court or jury will make the final decision in each individual case.
- Case law has laid down two tests:
  - ◆ 'the essence of driving is the use of the driver's controls for the purpose of directing the movement of the car however the movement is produced (*R v McDonagh* [1974] 2 All ER 257, CA);
  - ◆ whether or not a person was driving was ultimately a matter of fact for the court or jury to decide on the facts in the case (*Edkins v Knowles* [1973] 2 All ER 503, QBD).

Explanatory notes

- The vehicle does not have to be moving. A driver is still driving until he has completed the normal operations such as applying the handbrake, that occur at the end of a journey.
- A vehicle may halt temporarily such as at traffic lights. Each case will have to be looked at using three questions:

♦ What was the purpose of the stop?
♦ How long was the vehicle stopped?
♦ Did the driver get out of the vehicle?
• It is also possible for two people to be driving the same vehicle.

Related cases

Cawthorn v DPP The Times, 31 August 1999 Passenger releases brake when driver temporarily out of car. C was still in the course of his journey and he remained the driver until he finished that journey or someone else had taken over driving the vehicle. This intervening act did not make that person the driver, because the passenger never had sufficient control to fulfil the proper definition of driving. The question as to whether someone was a driver at any particular time was a question of fact.

DPP v Hastings (1993) 158 JP 118, QBD A passenger snatching the wheel momentarily is not a 'driver' because this action does not constitute the act of driving. In this instance H had interfered with the driving of the car, but was not the driver.

Burgoyne v Phillips [1982] RTR 49, QBD Since B had set the car in motion, was sitting in the driving seat and was trying to control the car, the fact that the steering was momentarily locked did not prevent B from 'driving' the car within the meaning of s 6 of the Road Traffic Act 1972. The question of whether or not a person was 'driving' was a matter of fact and degree.

Mcquaid v Anderton [1980] 3 All ER 540, QBD Steering a car being towed can be 'driving'. The essence of 'driving' was the use of the drivers controls in order to direct the movement of the car, the method of propulsion being irrelevant.

Tyler v Whatmore [1975] RTR 83, QBD Two people can be driving a vehicle at the same time. T was sitting in the front passenger seat and was leaning across steering the car, whilst the other driver manipulated the controls. In this case neither person had full control of both the brakes and the steering and although T could not control the propulsion, there was some control over the handbrake and ignition system. T was therefore driving the vehicle.

Practical considerations

• The law also recognizes that certain vehicles, such as steam rollers, may have a 'steersman' who steers and a driver who controls the propulsion. This is recognized by s 192 of the Road Traffic Act 1988, which provides: ' "driver", where a separate person acts as a steersman of a motor vehicle, includes (except for s 1 of this Act) that person as well as any other person engaged in the driving of the vehicle, and "drive" is to be interpreted accordingly.'
• If there is some doubt as to whether a person is driving or not, the circumstances must be looked at individually.

- As a general rule there are three elements to driving:
  - ✦ control of the steering; **and**
  - ✦ control of the propulsion; **and**
  - ✦ the actions of the person involved must fall within the normal everyday meaning of driving.

Links to alternative subjects and offences

10.2 Powers to Stop/Direct Vehicles and Pedestrians

The Road Traffic Act 1988 provides various powers to stop vehicles for different circumstances. These powers are given, in varying degrees, to police officers, traffic wardens, authorized vehicle examiners, and community support officers.

10.2.1 Drivers to comply with traffic directions

Section 35 of the Road Traffic Act 1988 provides for drivers who refuse or neglect to comply with traffic directions given by a police constable.

Offences

(1) Where a constable or traffic officer is for the time being engaged in the regulation of traffic in a road, a person driving or propelling a vehicle who neglects or refuses:

    (a) to stop the vehicle; or

    (b) to make it proceed in, or keep to, a particular line of traffic,

    when directed to do so by the constable in the exercise of his duty or the traffic officer (as the case may be) is guilty of an offence.

(2) Where:

    (a) a traffic survey of any description is being carried out on or in the vicinity of a road, and

    (b) a constable or traffic officer gives a person driving or propelling a vehicle a direction:

        (i) to stop the vehicle,

        (ii) to make it proceed in, or keep to, a particular line of traffic, or

        (iii) to proceed to a particular point on or near the road on which the vehicle is being driven or propelled,

    being a direction given for the purposes of the survey (but not a direction requiring any person to provide any information for the purposes of a traffic survey),

the person is guilty of an offence if he refuses or neglects to comply with the direction. **Road Traffic Act 1988, s 35(1), (2)**

Points to prove

s 35(1) offence

✓ constable/traffic warden/PCSO/traffic officer
✓ engaged in the regulation of traffic in a road
✓ driver/rider of vehicle neglected/refused
✓ to stop vehicle/make it proceed/keep to particular line of traffic
✓ as directed by constable/traffic officer in the execution of his/her duty

s 35(2) offence

✓ traffic survey being carried out in the vicinity of a road
✓ driver/rider of vehicle
✓ refused/failed/neglected to comply
✓ with directions given by constable/traffic warden/PCSO/traffic officer
✓ for the purposes of the survey

Meanings

Traffic officer

Means a person designated under s 2 of the Traffic Management Act 2004.

Road   (see **10.1.1**)

Driving   (see **10.1.4**)

Vehicle   (see **10.1.3**)

Explanatory notes

- The constable/traffic officer must be engaged in the regulation of traffic and acting in the execution of his/her duty.
- A constable may direct a person to disobey a traffic sign if it is reasonably necessary for the protection of life.
- The prosecution needs to show that the given signal was obvious and should have been evident to the motorist, not that the motorist saw it.
- Although a constable/traffic officer can direct a driver/rider to a specific point for a traffic survey, s/he cannot direct any person to supply information for the survey.
- Any direction in connection with a traffic survey must not cause undue delay to a person who indicates that s/he is unwilling to give information for the survey.
- Any reference to a constable includes a reference to a traffic warden.
- A suitably designated community support officer has the powers conferred on a constable under this section in any police area in England and Wales.
- NIP required (see **10.5**).

Practical considerations

- The offences under s 35 of the Road Traffic Act 1988 are not confined to mechanically propelled vehicles.
- Stop does not automatically mean the driver must remain stationary until signalled to proceed, unless the direction was to remain stationary.
- Notice of intended prosecution to be issued for offences under s 35.
- Consider using a traffic fixed penalty notice (see **10.4**).

 Summary   🕐 6 months

 A fine not exceeding level 3 on the standard scale.
Discretionary disqualification if committed in respect of a motor vehicle.
Obligatory endorsement—3 penalty points.

10.2.2 **Directions to pedestrians**

Section 37 of the Road Traffic Act 1988 empowers a constable in uniform or traffic officer engaged in the direction of vehicular traffic on a road, to also direct a pedestrian walking along or across the carriageway, to stop.

Offences

Where a constable in uniform or traffic officer is for the time being engaged in the regulation of vehicular traffic in a road, a person on foot who proceeds along or across the carriageway in contravention of a direction to stop given by the constable in the execution of his duty or traffic officer (as the case may be), either to persons on foot or to persons on foot and other traffic, is guilty of an offence.   **Road Traffic Act 1988, s 37**

Points to prove

✓ being a pedestrian proceeded along/across carriageway
✓ in contravention of direction of constable/traffic officer/PCSO/traffic warden
✓ engaged in direction of vehicular traffic on a road

Meanings

Traffic officer (see **10.2.1**)

Road (see **10.1**)

TFPN Traffic Fixed   **CSO** Offences where CSO
Penalty Notices   can use their powers

Explanatory notes

- Reference to a constable includes a reference to a traffic warden.
- A suitably designated community support officer has the powers conferred on a constable in uniform under this section in any police area in England and Wales.

Practical considerations

- A pedestrian offending against this section may be required to give his/her name and address.
- The constable must be in uniform but not necessarily on duty.
- Whether the constable was in uniform at the relevant time is a matter of fact—include details in evidence.

 Summary 6 months

 A fine not exceeding level 3 on the standard scale.

10.2.3 **Testing the condition of vehicles on a road**

Section 67 of the Road Traffic Act 1988 empowers authorized vehicle examiners to test motor vehicles on the road, but any vehicle stopped for a test must be stopped by a constable in uniform, a traffic warden or a suitably designated community support officer.

Offences

If a person obstructs an authorised examiner acting under this section, or fails to comply with a requirement of this section or Schedule 2 (deferred tests of conditions of vehicles) to this Act, he is guilty of an offence.

Road Traffic Act 1988, s 67(9)

Meanings

Authorized vehicle examiner

Includes a constable authorized so to act by or on behalf of the chief officer of police.

Test

Includes inspect or inspection.

Vehicle (see **10.1.3**)

It also includes a trailer drawn by it.

Explanatory notes

- Vehicle examiners may test all motor vehicles that are on the road.
- A vehicle shall not be required to stop for a test except by a constable in uniform.

Related cases

Sadiku v DPP [2000] RTR 155, QBD A constable requiring the test to be carried out may ask for the keys while awaiting the arrival of the examiner.

Practical considerations

- This section refers to the stopping of motor vehicles for test by authorized vehicle examiners.
- A constable who is not an authorized examiner cannot use this section to allow him/her to carry out the test him/herself.
- However, this does not prevent such a constable from enforcing the regulations concerning the construction and use of motor vehicles where the driver is cooperative.
- This section applies to vehicles registered outside Great Britain.

10.2.4 **Police powers to stop a vehicle on a road**

Section 163 of the Road Traffic Act 1988 empowers a police constable in uniform or a traffic officer to stop a mechanically propelled vehicle on a road.

Offences

(1) A person driving a mechanically propelled vehicle on a road must stop the vehicle on being required to do so by a constable in uniform or a traffic officer.

(2) A person riding a cycle on a road must stop the vehicle on being required to do so by a constable in uniform or a traffic officer.

(3) If a person fails to comply with this section he is guilty of an offence.

Road Traffic Act 1988, s 163(1)–(3)

Points to prove

✓ drove mechanically propelled vehicle/rode cycle
✓ on a road
✓ required by a constable in uniform/traffic warden/traffic officer/ designated CSO
✓ to stop the vehicle/cycle
✓ failed to do so

Meanings

Driving (see **10.1.4**)

Vehicle (see **10.1.3**)

D,Road (see **10.1.1**)

Traffic officer (see **10.2.1**)

Explanatory notes

- 'Mechanically propelled vehicle' is not defined in the Act and is a matter of fact and degree to be decided by the court.
- At its most basic 'mechanically propelled vehicle' means a vehicle, which can be propelled, by mechanical means, including both electric and steam powered vehicles.
- Unless the vehicle reaches the stage where there is no reasonable prospect of it being made mobile again it will still be a mechanically propelled vehicle.
- Whether an engine is fitted and in working order is important.
- Any reference to a constable in uniform includes a reference to a traffic warden.
- A suitably designated CSO, has the powers to stop a cycle, if that cycle is contravening s 72 of the Highways Act 1835 (riding on a footway).

Related cases

Reader v Bunyard [1987] RTR 406, QBD The onus is on the prosecution to prove that the vehicle is capable of being repaired, and not for the defence to prove it cannot be.

Thomas v Hooper [1986] RTR 1, QBD An abandoned vehicle hulk may cease to be a mechanically propelled vehicle.

McEachran v Hurst [1978] RTR 462, QBD A moped being pedalled on a road with no petrol in the machine and the engine not in working order is still a mechanically propelled vehicle.

Practical considerations

- Consider the issuing of a traffic fixed penalty notice.
- The condition and use of the vehicle at the time is important—can it be repaired? For what purpose was it being used?

 Summary

 6 months

 A fine not exceeding level 3 on the standard scale.

Links to alternative subjects and offences

10.3 Drivers—Failing to Comply with Traffic Sign

Section 36 of the Road Traffic Act 1988 creates an offence of failing to comply with certain traffic signs.

Offence

Where a traffic sign, being a sign:
(a) of the prescribed size, colour and type, or
(b) of another character authorised by the Secretary of State under the provisions in that behalf of the Road Traffic Regulation Act 1984,
has been lawfully placed on or near a road, a person driving or propelling a vehicle who fails to comply with the indication given by the sign is guilty of an offence.   Road Traffic Act 1988, s 36(1)

Points to prove

✓ traffic sign lawfully placed
✓ on or near a road
✓ driver/rider of vehicle on that road
✓ failed to comply with the direction of that sign

Meanings

Traffic sign

Means any object or device (whether fixed or portable) for indicating to traffic, or a specified class of traffic, on roads any warnings, information, requirements, restrictions, or prohibitions specified by regulations made by the Ministers acting jointly, or authorized by the Secretary of State, and any line or mark on a road for conveying such warnings, information, requirements, restrictions, or prohibitions (Road Traffic Regulation Act 1984, s 64).

Driving   (see 10.1.4)

Explanatory notes

- A sign will not be treated as having been lawfully placed unless it indicates a statutory prohibition, restriction or requirement or a provision of the Traffic Acts specifically states that it is a sign to which this section applies.
- Traffic signs are prescribed by regulations made under s 64 of the Road Traffic Regulation Act 1984.
- Some of the traffic signs to which this section applies are: double white line markings, box junction markings, traffic lights (including temporary traffic lights at road works), 'stop' sign (including manually operated at road works), flashing red 'stop' lights on

motorways or automatic tram/railway crossing, no entry sign, give way sign, directional arrow, keep left/right sign, bus/cycle/tramcar route sign, no U turn sign, weight/height restriction sign.

- A single dotted white line in the centre of the road separating two carriageways does not fall into this section.
- This section applies to a traffic survey sign which directs a vehicle to stop, proceed in, or keep to, a particular line of traffic, or proceed to a specific point on or near the road on which it is being driven or propelled for the purposes of the survey.
- A notice of intended prosecution must be served on the offending driver for contravention of certain traffic signs (see **10.5**).
- For contravention of a 'stop' sign it is necessary to prove that the vehicle did not stop before crossing the stop line or, if the stop line is not visible, before entering the major road.
- This section applies to emergency traffic signs put out by police (eg football matches, processions).
- Failure by the driver to see the traffic sign is not a defence (and will generally be evidence to support an offence of driving without due care and attention) (see **10.6**).
- A driver on a major road has a duty of care to a driver coming from a minor road even though the latter disregards a slow sign.
- 'Slow' means a reduction in speed so that a driver can stop quickly if a vehicle emerges from another road.
- A red traffic light signal is contravened if any part of a vehicle moves forward so that it crosses the stop line or, if there is no stop line, beyond the mounting of the primary signal.
- Emergency vehicles are exempted from the requirement to conform to a red traffic light, but must proceed so as not to cause danger to the driver of another vehicle or to cause such driver to change his/her speed or direction to avoid an accident, or cause danger to non-vehicular traffic.

Defences

This section creates absolute offences except for the possible defences of mechanical defect or automatism.

Defence notes

- 'Automatism' has been defined as 'the involuntary movement of a persons body or limbs'.
- The source or cause of the automatism must be something of which the driver was unaware or something that s/he could not reasonably be expected to foresee.
- Falling asleep whilst driving a vehicle does not amount to automatism.

Related cases

McKenzie v DPP The Times, 14 May 1996, QBD A vehicle can stop on a road where double white lines are present to drop/pick up passengers, load/unload goods, to carry out road/building work or to remove obstructions.

O'Halloran v DPP (1989) 154 JP 837, QBD Arrows warning drivers to pull back in as they are approaching solid white lines in the road are mandatory before every stretch of solid lines and not only at the beginning of a complete set of markings. If the arrow is missing it is not a legal traffic sign for this section.

Watmore v Jenkins [1961] 2 All ER 868, QBD A driver took the correct dosage of insulin prior to driving and drove normally most of the day. He was then seen to drive erratically for 5 miles before being stopped. He was dazed when stopped but recovered after treatment. He used the defence of automatism. The judges decided that there had been an element of conscious control in his driving and the defence of automatism was dismissed.

Attorney-General's Reference (No 2 of 1992) [1993] 4 All ER 683, CA Driving without awareness (such as falling asleep) is not a case where automatism could be used as a defence.

Practical considerations

- Traffic signs placed on or near a road are deemed to be of the correct specification and to have been lawfully placed there unless the contrary is proved.
- A stop sign at a junction indicates that a vehicle must momentarily stop at the stop line and not merely slow down.
- Consider issuing a traffic fixed penalty notice (see **10.4**).
- Is the relevant traffic sign one that is specified in relation to this section?
- Is the contravention evidence of a more serious offence (eg dangerous driving, driving without due care and attention?).
- If applicable, arrange for service of Notice of Intended Prosecution (see **10.5**).

 Summary   6 months

 A fine not exceeding level 3 on the standard scale.
If the offence is committed in respect of a motor vehicle contravening a specified sign discretionary disqualification, obligatory endorsement—3 penalty points.

Links to alternative subjects and offences

10.4 Traffic Fixed Penalty Notices

Traffic Fixed Penalty Notices (TFPNs) and procedures with regard to road traffic offences are covered by s 51 to s 90 of the Road Traffic Offenders Act 1988.

10.4.1 Traffic fixed penalty notices

Section 54 of the Act applies where, in England and Wales, a constable in uniform has reason to believe that a person s/he finds is committing or has on that occasion committed a traffic penalty offence. The constable may give them a TFPN in respect of that offence.

Offences

A person is guilty of an offence if he removes or interferes with any notice fixed to a vehicle under this section, unless he does so by or under the authority of the driver or person in charge of the vehicle or the person liable for the fixed penalty offence in question.

Road Traffic Offenders Act 1988, s 62(2)

A person who, in a response to a notice to owner, provides a statement which is false in a material particular and does so recklessly or knowing it to be false in that particular is guilty of that offence.

Road Traffic Offenders Act 1988, s 67

Points to prove

s 62(2) offence
- ✓ without the authority of the driver/person in charge of the vehicle/person liable for the fixed penalty
- ✓ removed/interfered with fixed penalty notice fixed to vehicle

s 67 offence
- ✓ in response to notice to owner
- ✓ provided false statement
- ✓ recklessly/knowing it to be false

Meaning of 'Traffic fixed penalty notice'

Means a notice offering the opportunity of the discharge of any liability to conviction of the offence to which the notice relates by payment of a fixed penalty in accordance with these sections of this Act.

Explanatory notes

- References to constable or constable in uniform include a reference to traffic warden.
- A traffic warden is not employed to enforce offences, which appear to him/her to involve obligatory endorsement unless it is committed in relation to a stationary vehicle.
- A suitably designated CSO may issue a fixed penalty notice for cycling on a footway.
- A TFPN must give sufficient details of the alleged offence, together with details of the suspended enforcement period, the penalty payable and how it should be paid.
- 'Suspended enforcement period' means the period following the date of the offence during which no proceedings will be brought against the offender.
- TFPNs apply where a constable in uniform believes that a person is committing or has, on that occasion, committed a relevant offence, and may be issued either at the time of the offence or at a police station.
- There is no obligation to issue a TFPN—it is at the constable's discretion.
- If the offence involves obligatory endorsement the constable may only issue a TFPN if the offender produces and surrenders their driving licence and counterpart to the constable and is not liable to disqualification under the 'totting up' procedure.
- Where the offender has no licence and counterpart with them, the constable may issue a notice requiring their production within 7 days at a specified police station and, if certain requirements are met, s/he will be issued with a TFPN there.
- If the offender complies with the above and surrenders their driving licence and counterpart, the person receiving them must issue a TFPN for the original offence.
- No proceedings will be brought against any person before the end of the suspended enforcement period.
- Where the penalty has not been paid or a hearing elected during the suspended enforcement period, the penalty plus 50 per cent may be registered against them.
- If the offence involves obligatory endorsement the surrendered licence and counterpart must be forwarded to the fixed-penalty clerk, who must endorse details on the counterpart then return both to the licence holder.
- The person receiving a surrendered licence and counterpart must issue a receipt, which will be valid for 1 month after issue. The fixed-penalty clerk, on application by the licence holder, may issue a new receipt expiring on a date specified therein.
- If the licence holder is liable to disqualification under the 'totting up' (see **10.13**) system, the fixed penalty clerk must not endorse the counterpart but forward it and the licence to the chief officer of police who may commence proceedings. Where such proceedings are

commenced any action already taken (eg registration as a fine) is void.

- A TFPN can be affixed to a vehicle for a non-endorsable fixed penalty offence. At the end of the suspended enforcement period, if the penalty has not been paid or a hearing requested by the driver at the relevant time, a notice to owner may be served on the owner.

- A notice to owner must include particulars of the alleged offence and TFPN concerned, the response time allowed (minimum 21 days) and the requirements on the recipient if the penalty is not paid before the end of that period.

- The notice to owner should also indicate that the recipient may, before the end of the response period allowed, request a hearing or, if s/he was not the driver and the actual driver wishes to request a hearing, provide a statutory statement of ownership together with the driver's statutory statement of facts.

- If the person on whom the notice to owner was served was not the owner of the vehicle at the time of the alleged offence and provides a statutory statement of ownership to that effect, s/he is not liable for the fine registered against them.

- If a notice to owner has been served, proceedings may not be brought against anybody else in relation to that offence unless s/he is identified as the driver at the relevant time in a statutory statement of facts.

- Proceedings for an offence to which a notice to owner relates may not be brought against the driver if the fixed penalty is paid before the end of the response period allowed.

- When a notice to owner is served on a vehicle-hire firm they must, within the suspended enforcement period, state that the vehicle was, at the relevant time, hired out and include a copy of the hiring agreement and statement of liability signed by the hirer.

- A vehicle owner is presumed to be the person by whom it is kept, and for proceedings the owner at any time is presumed to be the registered keeper at that time.

- Any document purportedly signed by the accused and produced by the prosecution in proceedings is presumed so signed unless the contrary is proved.

Relevant offences

The following are the offences relevant to the traffic fixed penalty notice scheme:

Greater London Council (General Powers) Act 1974

s 15—parking vehicles on footways, verges, and other related offences.

Highways Act 1835

s 72—driving/cycling on footway.

Highways Act 1980

s 137—obstruction of highway committed in respect of a vehicle.

Road Traffic Regulation Act 1984

s 5(1)—traffic regulation order outside Greater London.

10.4.1 Traffic fixed penalty notices

s 8(1)—traffic regulation order in Greater London.
s 11—experimental traffic order.
s 16(1)—temporary prohibition or restriction.
s 17(4)—wrongful use of special road.
s 18(3)—one-way traffic order on trunk road.
s 20(5)—prohibition/restriction of driving on certain classes of road.
s 25(5)—pedestrian crossing regulations.
s 29(3)—street playground order.
s 35A(1)—local authority parking place on a road.
s 47(1)—parking place designation order.
s 53(5)—parking place designation order under s 53(1)(a).
s 53(6)—designation order authorized parking on road without charge.
s 88(7)—minimum speed limit.
s 89(1)—speeding.

Road Traffic Act 1988

s 14—seat belt regulations.
s 15(2)—restriction re children in front of vehicles.
s 15(4)—restriction re children in rear of vehicles.
s 16—crash helmet regulations re motorcycle rider/passenger.
s 18(3)—breach use of eye protector regulations on motorcycles.
s 19—parking heavy commercial vehicle on verge/footway.
s 22—leave vehicle in dangerous position.
s 23—unlawfully carry passenger on motorcycle.
s 24—carry more than one person on pedal cycle.
s 34—drive mechanically propelled vehicle elsewhere than on road.
s 35—fail to comply with traffic directions.
s 36—fail to comply with prescribed traffic signs (see **10.3**).
s 40A—use vehicle where condition; purpose for which used; number of passengers/manner in which carried; weight/position/distribution of load, manner in which load is secured—is such that it involves a danger of injury to any person.
s 41A—breach of requirements re brakes, steering-gear or tyres.
s 41B—breach of weight requirement re goods and passenger vehicles.
s 41D—breach of requirements as to control of vehicle or full view of road or use hand-held mobile phone/similar devices.
s 42—breach of other construction and use regulations.
s 47—using vehicle without a test certificate.
s 87(1)—drive vehicle otherwise than in accordance with licence.
s 143—using a motor vehicle without insurance.
s 163—fail to stop vehicle when required by officer in uniform.
s 172—failure to notify police of information re driver of a motor vehicle.

Road Vehicles (Display of Registration Marks) Regulations 2001

Incorrect form of registration mark

Vehicle Excise and Registration Act 1994

s 33—use vehicle on public road without displaying vehicle licence.
s 42—driving/keeping vehicle without required registration mark.
s 43—drive/keep vehicle with registration mark obscured.
s 43C—offence of using an incorrectly registered vehicle.
s 59—fail to affix prescribed registration mark to vehicle.

Zebra, Pelican & Puffin Pedestrian Crossing Regulations 1997

reg 24—overtake moving/stationary vehicle in limits of crossing.

Practical considerations

- Consider the seriousness of the offence—there is no obligation to issue a TFPN.
- Is the fixed penalty scheme appropriate? Are there other reasons (eg National Intelligence Model) for conventional proceedings?
- Is the offence endorsable—if so, is the offender with the vehicle?
- Only a non-endorsable TFPN may be attached to a vehicle.
- Is the offender liable to disqualification under the totting up system?
- Using a mobile phone whilst driving on a road is a fixed penalty offence by virtue of s 41D of the Road Traffic Act 1988 (see **10.4.2**).

 Summary

 s 62 offence
A fine not exceeding level 2 on the standard scale.

s 67 offence
A fine not exceeding level 5 on the standard scale.

 If a statutory declaration is made stating that: a court hearing was elected before the end of the suspended enforcement period/in accordance with notice to owner; or no knowledge of the fixed penalty (until notice of registration received); or not the vehicle owner at the relevant time—then 6 months from the date of declaration (to a maximum of 12 months from the original offence).
In all other cases—6 months.

10.4.2 **Control of vehicle and use of hand-held mobile/communication device**

Offences

A person who contravenes or fails to comply with a **construction and use requirement**—

(a) as to not driving a motor vehicle in a position which does not give proper control or a full view of the road and traffic ahead, or not causing or

---

TFPN Traffic Fixed
Penalty Notices
    CSO Offences where CSO
can use their powers
    507

10.4.2 Control of Vehicle and use of Hand-Held Device

permitting the driving of a motor vehicle by another person in such a position, or

(b) as to not driving or supervising the driving of a motor vehicle while using a hand-held mobile telephone or other hand-held interactive communication device, or not causing or permitting the driving of a motor vehicle by another person using such a telephone or other device,

is guilty of an offence.   Road Traffic Act 1988 s 41D

Points to prove

s 41D(a) offence

- ✓ contravened/failed to comply with 'construction and use requirement'
- ✓ by driving a motor vehicle on a road
- ✓ without having proper control of the vehicle or full view of the road ahead **OR**
- ✓ caused/permitted the driver to commit above offences

s 41D(b) offence

- ✓ contravened/failed to comply with 'construction and use requirement'
- ✓ being the driver/driving supervisor
- ✓ of a motor vehicle on a road
- ✓ where driver used hand-held mobile/similar device **OR**
- ✓ caused/permitted the driver to commit above offence

Meaning of 'construction and use requirement'

Means a requirement imposed by a regulation made under s 41 of the Road Traffic Act 1988 (which is mainly the Road Vehicles (Construction and Use) Regulations 1986.

Explanatory notes

- Not being in a position to have proper control of the vehicle or a full view of the road and traffic ahead comes under reg 104 of the Road Vehicles (Construction and Use) Regulations 1986.
- Using a hand-held mobile telephone or similar device comes under reg 110 of the Road Vehicles (Construction and Use) Regulations 1986.

Practical considerations

- These offences provide for obligatory endorsement and disqualification (at the court's discretion).
- A two-way radio, which performs an interactive communication function by transmitting and receiving data is not a device under reg 110.

- Regulation 110(5) stipulates that a person does not contravene a provision of this regulation if, at the time of the alleged contravention—
  + s/he is using the telephone or other device to call the police, fire, ambulance or other emergency service on 112 or 999;
  + s/he is acting in response to a genuine emergency; and
  + it is unsafe or impracticable for him/her to cease driving in order to make the call, or in the case of a supervisor for the provisional licence holder to cease driving while the call was being made.
- A mobile telephone or other device is to be treated as hand-held if it is, or must be, held at some point during the course of making or receiving a call or performing any other interactive communication function.
- A person supervises the holder of a provisional licence if s/he does so pursuant to a condition imposed on that licence holder.

TFPN

 Summary   6 months

 Fine not exceeding Level 4 on the standard scale in respect of a goods vehicle or a vehicle adapted to carry more than eight passengers.
Fine not exceeding Level 3 on the standard scale in any other case.
Discretionary disqualification. Obligatory endorsement—3 penalty points.

Links to alternative subjects and offences

10.5 **Notice of Intended Prosecution**

Section 1 of the Road Traffic Offenders Act 1988 requires a notice of intended prosecution to be given to a defendant for certain offences.

Requirement

Subject to **section 2** of this Act, a person shall not be convicted of an offence to which this section applies unless:

(a) he was warned at this time the offence was committed that the question of prosecuting him for one or other of the offences to which this section applies would be taken into consideration, or

(b) within 14 days of the commission of the offence a summons for the offence was served on him, or

(c) within 14 days of the commission of the offence a notice of the intended prosecution specifying the nature of the alleged offence and the time and place where it is alleged to have been committed, was:

    (i) in the case of an offence under section 28 or 29 of the Road Traffic Act 1988 *[cycling offences]*, served on him, or

    (ii) in the case of any other offence, served on him or on the person, if any, registered as the keeper of the vehicle at the time of the commission of the offence.

Road Traffic Offenders Act 1988, s 1(1)

Meaning 'subject to s 2'

This section will not apply if:

- At the time of the offence or immediately after it, the vehicle concerned was involved in an accident.
  - However, the defendant must have been aware of the accident, otherwise a notice *is* necessary (*Bentley v Dickinson* [1983] RTR 356).
- A fixed penalty notice or a notice under the fixed penalty scheme requiring production of the defendant's licence and counterpart at a police station is issued (see **10.4**).

Explanatory notes

- A notice of intended prosecution may be served on a person by personal delivery to them, or by sending it by registered post, recorded delivery or first class post to their last known address.
- A notice of intended prosecution sent by registered post or recorded delivery is deemed served if addressed to them at their last known address even if it is returned undelivered or not received by them for some other reason.
- The requirements of this section are met unless the contrary is proved or if the defendant is charged and given a copy of the charge within 14 days of the commission of the offence.

- 'Within 14 days of the commission of the offence' means that the notice must be posted to reach the defendant within 14 days of the offence.
- A notice of intended prosecution posted the day after the offence, which failed to arrive within the 14 days, was good service; whereas one sent by recorded delivery on the 14th day was deemed not 'served'.
- Failure to comply with this section is not a bar to conviction if the court is satisfied that the name and address of the defendant or the registered keeper could not be ascertained with due diligence in time to comply, or that the accused's conduct contributed to the failure.
- If, in court proceedings, an alternative verdict is returned, the fact that the alternative offence requires a notice of intended prosecution is not a bar to conviction for that offence if the original offence did not require a notice of intended prosecution.

Related cases

Shield v Crighton [1974] Crim LR 605, DC 'At the time the offence was committed' is not limited to the exact time of the offence. It has to be construed sensibly, not literally.

Jollye v Dale [1960] 2 QB 258, QBD Within 2 hours of an offence occurring the driver was verbally warned that a prosecution for careless or dangerous driving was being considered. This was considered to be 'at the time the offence was committed'.

Relevant offences

Schedule 1 of the Road Traffic Offenders Act 1988 provides a list of offences for which a 'Notice of Intended Prosecution' is required under s 1 of the Act. They are:

Road Traffic Regulation Act 1984

s 16—contravene speed restriction at road works.
s 17(4)—contravene motorway speed limit.
s 88(7)—contravene minimum speed limit.
s 89(1)—exceeding speed limit.

Road Traffic Act 1988

s 2—dangerous driving.
s 3—careless, and inconsiderate, driving.
s 22—leaving vehicles in dangerous position.
s 28—dangerous cycling.
s 29—careless, and inconsiderate, cycling.
s 35—failing to comply with traffic directions.
s 36—failing to comply with traffic signs prescribed under s 36 (see **10.3**).

Practical considerations

- The offences to which this section applies are listed above.
- If the offence arises out of an accident of which the driver may not be aware a notice of intended prosecution should be sent.

10.5 Notice of Intended Prosecution

- No notice of intended prosecution is required if a fixed penalty notice (see **10.4**) is issued, or notice that one will be issued on production and surrender of driving licence and counterpart at a police station is issued.
- There is no need to quote Act and section of the alleged offence—keep it simple.

Links to alternative subjects and offences

10.6 Driving Without Due Care and Attention

Section 3 of the Road Traffic Act 1988 relates to the offence of driving without due care and attention or without reasonable consideration for other users of the road or public place. Whereas, s 168 requires a person alleged to have committed this offence to give their details to any person having reasonable grounds for obtaining them.

10.6.1 Driving without due care and attention

Offences

If a person **drives** a **mechanically propelled vehicle** on a **road** or other **public place** without due care and attention, or without reasonable consideration for other persons using the road or public place, he is guilty of an offence.   Road Traffic Act 1988, s 3

Points to prove
- ✓ drove a mechanically propelled vehicle
- ✓ on a road/other public place
- ✓ without due care and attention/reasonable consideration for others using the road/public place

Meanings

Drives (see **10.1.4**)

Mechanically propelled vehicle (see **10.1.3**)

Road

Defined by s 192 of the Road Traffic Act 1988 (see **10.1.1**).

Public place (see **10.1.2**)

Explanatory notes
- It is a question of fact to be decided by the court as to whether a standard of driving is careless or not.
- 'Without reasonable consideration for other road users' requires a subjective test and has to be decided by the court on the evidence placed before it.
- A defendant will have driven without due care and attention if their driving departs from the level of care and skill that would, in the circumstances of the case, have been exercised by a reasonable, prudent, and competent driver.

10.6.1 Driving without Due Care and Attention

- Breaching certain road traffic regulations—eg crossing central white lines without explanation—can be enough to prove this offence.
- Section 168 of the Road Traffic Act 1988 empowers the obtaining of the defendant's name and address (see **10.6.2**).
- Riding a pedal cycle without due care and attention is an offence under s 29 (see **10.12.2**).

Defences

The defences of automatism, unconsciousness and sudden illness, duress, sudden mechanical defect, assisting in the arrest of offenders and taking part in an authorized motoring event may be used.

Defence notes

- 'Automatism' means an affliction which overcomes the driver and causes them to lose control of the vehicle. It must be sudden and something that s/he was unaware of and could not reasonably be expected to foresee.
- 'Unconsciousness and sudden illness' applies if a driver is rendered unconscious and unable to control the vehicle. For example a blow to the head or sudden and unforeseen epileptic fit may cause this.
- The defence of duress may be split in to two parts—duress by threat or duress of necessity (of circumstances).
- For duress by threat to apply a person cannot deliberately put him/herself in a position where s/he is likely to be subject to threats and, if s/he can escape the duress by escaping the threats, s/he must do so.
- Sudden mechanical defect applies if a sudden and unexpected defect in the motor vehicle causes the driver to totally lose control. It does not apply to a defect which is already known to the driver or which could have been easily discovered with reasonable prudence.
- The defence of assisting in the arrest of offenders may be available to a driver if their driving, though careless or inconsiderate, amounted to reasonable force assisting in the arrest of an offender.
- A person will have a defence if they were driving a vehicle in a public place, other than a road, in an authorized motoring event.

Related cases

McCrone v Riding [1938] 1 All ER 157, KBD The standard of driving required from a driver is an objective one, fixed in relation to the safety of other users of the highway. It does not relate to the degree of proficiency or experience attained by the individual driver.

Kay v Butterworth (1945) 110 JP 75, CA If a driver allows him/herself to be overtaken by sleep whilst driving, s/he is guilty of at least driving without due care and attention.

Watts v Carter The Times, 22 October 1959, QBD A car leaving the road and mounting the footpath can be driving without due care and attention.

DPP v Harris [1995] August CL 537, QBD To justify a defence of 'necessity' it would be necessary to show that any actions were reasonable and proportionate in the light of a threat of death or serious injury.

Practical considerations

- This offence requires a notice of intended prosecution to be served (see **10.5**).
- There is no special standard for emergency vehicles.
- This section creates two offences and it is bad for duplicity to charge both of them as alternatives.
- Others persons may include other drivers, passengers in the vehicle, pedestrians, or cyclists.

 Summary   6 months

 A fine not exceeding level 4 on the standard scale.
Discretionary disqualification. Obligatory endorsement—3 to 9 penalty points.

10.6.2 **Request details after reckless, careless, or inconsiderate driving or cycling**

Offences

Any of the following persons:
(a) the driver of a mechanically propelled vehicle who is alleged to have committed an offence under section 2 or 3 of this Act, or
(b) the rider of a cycle who is alleged to have committed an offence under section 28 or 29 of this Act,
who refuses, on being so required by any person having reasonable ground for so requiring, to give his name and address, or gives a false name and address, is guilty of an offence. **Road Traffic Act 1988, s 168**

Points to prove

✓ being driver of mechanically propelled vehicle/rider of cycle
✓ alleged offence under ss 2/3 or 28/29 of RTA 1988
✓ when required to do so by person having reasonable grounds
✓ refused to give name and address/gave false name and address

Meanings

Mechanically propelled vehicle (see **10.1.3**)

Driver (see **10.1.4**)

10.6.2 Request Details

Explanatory notes

- Section 2 of the Road Traffic Act 1988 relates to dangerous driving (see **10.7**).
- Section 3 of the Road Traffic Act 1988 relates to driving without due care and attention/without reasonable consideration (see **10.6.1**).
- Sections 28 and 29 of the Road Traffic Act 1988 identical offences to riding pedal cycles (see **10.12**).

 Summary   6 months

 A fine not exceeding level 3 on the standard scale.

Links to alternative subjects and offences

10.7 Dangerous Driving

10.7.1 Dangerous driving

Section 2 of the Road Traffic Act 1988 relates to dangerous driving.

Offence

A person who drives a mechanically propelled vehicle dangerously on a road or other public place is guilty of an offence. **Road Traffic Act 1988, s 2**

Points to prove

✓ being the driver of a mechanically propelled vehicle
✓ drove dangerously
✓ on a road/other public place

Meanings

Drives (see **10.1.4**)

Mechanically propelled vehicle (see **10.1.3**)

Dangerously
- Means the way s/he drives falling far below what would be expected of a competent and careful driver, **and** it would be obvious to a competent and careful driver that driving in that way would be dangerous.
- If it would be obvious to a competent and careful driver that driving the vehicle in its current state would be dangerous.

Road (see **10.6.1**)

Public place (see **10.1.2**)

Explanatory notes
- In considering the state of the vehicle, anything attached to or carried in or on it, and the manner of it being so attached or carried is also relevant.
- In this section dangerous refers to either danger of injury to any person or serious damage to property.
- Consideration will be taken not only of the circumstances of which a competent and careful driver could be expected to be aware of, but also any circumstances shown to be within the defendant's knowledge.
- There is an offence of dangerous cycling under s 28 (see **10.12.1**).
- Section 168 of the Road Traffic Act 1988 empowers the obtaining of the defendant's name and address (see **10.6.2**).

Defence (see 10.6.1)

Defence notes (see 10.6.1)

Related cases

R v Spurge [1961] 2 All ER 688, CA A driver aware of a mechanical defect, which caused the vehicle to be dangerous, could not use the defence of mechanical defect.

R v Strong [1995] Crim LR 428, CA The danger is 'obvious' only if it can be seen or realized at first glance, or is evident to the competent or careful driver, or the defendant knew of it.

R v Roberts and George [1997] RTR 462, CA More may be expected from a professional driver than from an ordinary motorist (eg a police driver). Where the driver was an employee it was important to consider the instructions he had from his employer concerning checks to be made on the vehicle. Where they were apparently reasonable it would be wrong to expect him to do more than instructed.

R v Woodward [1995] 3 All ER 79, CA Evidence of consumption of alcohol is admissible only where it is to the effect that the defendant had drunk so much of it as would adversely affect a driver.

DPP v Milton [2006] EWHC 242 (Admin) QBD Excessive speed alone is not sufficient to establish dangerous driving; the driving has to be considered in the context of all the circumstances.

Practical considerations

- This offence requires a notice of intended prosecution to be served (see **10.5**).
- A court may convict them of an alternative offence under s 3 of the Road Traffic Act 1988 (see **10.6.1**).
- Consider any CCTV evidence if available.
- Forfeiture of the vehicle used may also be ordered.

 Either way   None

 Summary: 6 months' imprisonment and/or a fine not exceeding the statutory maximum.
Indictment: 2 years' imprisonment and/or a fine.
Obligatory disqualification until test passed.
Obligatory endorsement—3 to 11 penalty points (unless special reasons apply).

10.7.2 **Wanton or furious driving**

Section 35 of the Offences Against the Person Act 1861 provides for the offence of wanton or furious driving.

Offences

Whosoever, having the charge of any carriage or vehicle, shall by wanton or furious driving or racing, or other wilful misconduct, or by wilful neglect, do or cause to be done any bodily harm to any person whatsoever, shall be guilty of an offence. **Offences Against the Person Act 1861, s 35**

Points to prove

✓ had charge of a carriage/vehicle
✓ by wanton/furious driving/racing/other wilful misconduct/by wilful neglect
✓ did/caused bodily harm to be done to another

Meanings

Vehicle (see **10.1.3**)

Wanton

Means without any lawful motive and being thoughtless as to the possible consequences.

Driving (see **10.1.4**)

Bodily harm (see **2.1.2**)

Explanatory notes

A person riding a pedal cycle in a wanton or furious manner resulting in injuries to another person may be convicted under this section.

Practical considerations

• This offence can be committed anywhere.
• There is no power to disqualify an offender or endorse a licence for this offence.

 E&S

 Indictment None

 2 years' imprisonment

Links to alternative subjects and offences

10.8 Fatal Road Traffic Collision Incidents

A driver involved in a fatal road traffic incident has the same obligations as a driver involved in any other reportable road traffic collisions (see **10.9**). Each Police Force will have its own procedure for how these are dealt with and by whom.

The main legislation concerning fatalities resulting from road traffic incidents is found in s 1 (dangerous driving) and s 3A (causing death by careless driving when under the influence of drink or drugs) of the Road Traffic Act 1988.

10.8.1 Causing death by dangerous driving

Causing death by dangerous driving is an offence created by s 1 of the Road Traffic Act 1988.

Offence

A person who causes the death of **another person** by **driving** a **mechanically propelled vehicle dangerously** on a **road** or other **public place** is guilty of an offence.   Road Traffic Act 1988, s 1

Points to prove

✓ caused the death of another person
✓ by driving a mechanically propelled vehicle dangerously
✓ on a road/public place

Meanings

Another person

Means anybody, other than the defendant. It has been held to include a foetus *in utero* (still in the uterus) and subsequently born alive, but who later dies of their injuries.

Driving   (see **10.1.4**)

Mechanically propelled vehicle   (see **10.1.3**)

Dangerously   (see **10.7**)

Road   (see **10.6.1**)

Public place   (see **10.1.2**)

Explanatory notes

- The death of the person concerned must be shown to have been caused in some way by the incident to which the charge relates.
- The cause of death does not need to be a substantial cause, but neither should it be a slight or trifling link. It will suffice if the driving was a cause of the death even though it was not the sole or even a substantial cause.
- A person charged with this offence may be convicted of the alternative offences of dangerous driving (see **10.7**) or careless, and inconsiderate, driving (see **10.6**).

Defence (see 10.6.1)

Defence notes (see 10.6.1)

Related cases (see also 'Dangerous driving' cases 10.7.1)

R v Hennigan [1971] 3 All ER 133, CA A vehicle on the main road was travelling at an excessive speed, and collided with a vehicle emerging from the side road, killing the driver. The other driver was convicted of this offence on the basis that, even though the deceased was mainly to blame, the excessive speed and dangerous driving of the defendant was partly to blame.

R v Ash [1999] RTR 347, QBD Where only one blood sample is taken the result of the analysis can still be used under this section. The requirement to take two samples under s 15 of the Road Traffic Offenders Act 1988 does not apply to this section.

R v Buono [2005] EWCA Crim 1313, CA A fatal collision had been caused by the defendant taking a bend in the middle of the road at excessive speed. Similar fact evidence was admitted to show the manner in which the car had been driven earlier—swerving across the road and driving at excessive speed. Such evidence had considerable probative force, which undoubtedly outweighed any prejudice to the defendant.

Practical considerations

- This section applies to tramcars and trolley vehicles operating under a statutory power.
- Consider murder and manslaughter committed whilst driving (see **2.7**).
- Theoretically, two different drivers could cause the same death.
- *R v Beckford* (1994) 159 JP 305, CA (see **10.8.2**) also applies to this offence.
- When investigating this offence consideration must be given to the CPS driving offences charging standards.
- When dealing with the incident follow Force Policy but consider preserving the scene, involving CID and other agencies.
- Consider CCTV evidence if available.
- The vehicle may be forfeited.

Indictment None

14 years' imprisonment
Obligatory disqualification until extended test passed.
Obligatory endorsement—3 to 11 penalty points (only if special reasons apply).

10.8.2 Causing death by careless driving when under influence of drink/drugs

Section 3A of the Road Traffic Act 1988 provides an offence of causing the death of another by careless driving when under the influence of drink or drugs, or failing to provide a specimen.

Offences

If a person causes the death of **another person** by **driving a mechanically propelled vehicle** on a **road** or other **public place** without due care and attention, or without reasonable consideration for other persons using the road or public place, and:
(a) he is, at the time when he is driving, **unfit to drive** through drink or drugs, or
(b) he has consumed so much alcohol that the proportion of it in his breath, blood or urine at that time exceeds the prescribed limit, or
(c) he is, within 18 hours after that time, required to provide a specimen in pursuance of section 7 of this Act, but without reasonable excuse fails to provide it,
he is guilty of an offence. Road Traffic Act 1988, s 3A(1)

Points to prove
✓ caused the death of another person
✓ by driving a mechanically propelled vehicle which is a motor vehicle
✓ on a road/public place
✓ without due care and attention/without reasonable consideration for other users of that road/place **and**
✓ at the time of driving was unfit through drink/drugs **or**
✓ had consumed so much alcohol that the proportion of it in blood/breath/urine was over the prescribed limit **or**
✓ within 18 hours of the incident failed, without reasonable excuse, to provide a specimen when required

10.8.2 Causing Death by Careless Driving when Under Influence

Meanings

Another person (see 10.8.1)

Driving (see 10.1.4)

Mechanically propelled vehicle (see 10.1.3)

Road (see 10.6.1)

Public place (see 10.1.2)

Unfit to drive

In this section a person is unfit to drive at any time when his ability to drive properly is impaired.

Through drink or drugs (see 10.10)

Exceeds the prescribed limit (see 10.11)

Explanatory notes

- The careless or inconsiderate driving must be a cause of the death of another person (see 10.6).
- Sections 3A(1)(b) and (c) do not apply to a mechanically propelled vehicle. They only apply to a motor vehicle.
- It is not necessary for the intoxication to be a direct cause of the careless/inconsiderate driving.
- A person charged with this offence may be convicted of the alternative driving offences of careless, and inconsiderate (see **10.6**), unfit through drink/drugs (see **10.10**), excess alcohol in breath/blood/urine, or failing to provide a specimen (see **10.11**).

Defence (see 10.6.1)

Defence notes (see 10.6)

Related cases

R v Beckford (1994) 159 JP 305, CA Following a road traffic accident in which a passenger was killed, the vehicle was scrapped after a few weeks. The defendant relied upon the defence of 'mechanical defect' alleging that the steering had locked. This was not properly checked out before the vehicle was scrapped. The court made the point that 'procedures should be put in place to ensure that cars are not scrapped before express permission has been given by the police and that permission will never be given where serious criminal charges are to be brought which may involve the possibility of some mechanical defect in a car.'

Practical considerations

- When investigating this offence consideration must be given to the CPS driving offences charging standards.
- Cases where the actual standard of driving itself would not normally attract a prosecution, may merit proceedings for this offence.

Causing Death by Careless Driving when Under Influence 10.8.2

- As with all fatal road traffic collisions protect and prevent contamination of the scene.
- Ensure that cars are not scrapped, as serious criminal charges may be brought and the defence of a mechanical defect in the car maybe alleged. Consider seizing the vehicle as it may be forfeited.
- Consider CCTV evidence if available of both the collision and the manner of driving prior to the collision.

 Indictment   None

 14 years' imprisonment.
Obligatory disqualification. Obligatory endorsement—3 to 11 penalty points (only if special reasons apply).

Links to alternative subjects and offences

10.9 **Road Traffic Collisions**

Section 170 of the Road Traffic Act 1988 imposes duties on the driver of a mechanically propelled vehicle involved in certain road traffic collisions on a road or other public place.

10.9.1 **Incidents to which applicable**

Collisions which apply

If owing to the presence of a **mechanically propelled vehicle** on a **road** or other **public place**, an **accident** occurs whereby:

(a) personal **injury** is caused to a person other than the **driver** of that mechanically propelled vehicle, or

(b) damage is caused:

    (i) to a vehicle other than that mechanically propelled vehicle or a trailer drawn by that mechanically propelled vehicle, or

    (ii) to an **animal** other than an animal in or on that mechanically propelled vehicle or a trailer drawn by that mechanically propelled vehicle, or

    (iii) to any other property constructed on, fixed to, growing in or otherwise forming part of the land on which the road or place in question is situated or land adjacent to such land.

Road Traffic Act 1988, s 170(1)

Meanings

Mechanically propelled vehicle (see 10.1.3)

Road (see 10.6.1)

Public place (see 10.1.2)

Accident

This is an unintended occurrence having an adverse physical result.

Injury

Includes any actual bodily harm and may well include nervous shock.

Driver (see 10.1.4)

Animal

Means horse, cattle, ass, mule, sheep, pig, goat, or dog.

Related cases

Cawthorn v DPP [2000] RTR 45, QBD A driver left his vehicle for a few minutes in order to post a letter. He set the handbrake and switched on the hazard lights, but after interference from the passenger, the vehicle rolled down the hill and collided with a brick wall. Held that he remained the driver until the journey was complete or somebody else started to drive.

DPP v Hay [2005] EWHC 1395 (Admin), QBD H was driving a vehicle that was involved in an accident and was taken to hospital without exchanging details or reporting the accident to the police, and subsequently failed to report the accident after being discharged from hospital. Held that H had failed to comply with s 170, even though the police observed the accident and had made no request for information.

Practical considerations
- There must be some link between the presence of the vehicle and the occurrence of the accident.
- 'Vehicle', in respect of the other vehicle damaged, may include a pedal cycle.
- If attending a potential fatal collision preserve the scene and request assistance from specialist traffic officers, Scenes of Crime and CID (see 10.8).

10.9.2 **Duties of driver after accident**

Offences
(2) The driver of the mechanically propelled vehicle must stop and, if required to do so by any person having reasonable grounds for so requiring, give his name and address and also the name and address of the owner and the identification marks of the vehicle.

(3) If for any reason the driver of the mechanically propelled vehicle does not give his name and address under subsection (2) above, he must report the accident.

(4) A person who fails to comply with subsection (2) or (3) above is guilty of an offence.   Road Traffic Act 1988, s 170(2)– (4)

Points to prove
✓ being the driver of a mechanically propelled vehicle
✓ involved in a road traffic accident
✓ failed to stop **and**
✓ on being so requested by a person having reasonable for so doing
✓ failed to provide details, as required

Meanings
Driver (see 10.1.4)

Mechanically propelled vehicle (see 10.1.3)

Accident (see 10.9.1)

10.9.3 Duty of Driver to Report the Incident

Explanatory notes

- If the driver does not stop immediately s/he must do so as soon as it is safe and convenient to do so.
- The fact that the person requiring details from the driver knows them does not negate the obligation imposed on the driver.
- If personal injury is involved and the vehicle is a motor vehicle, and the driver does not, at the time of the collision, produce evidence of insurance to a constable or some person having reasonable grounds for requiring them to do so, s/he must report the collision and produce such evidence.
- After stopping the driver must remain there long enough to enable them, if required, to furnish the relevant information.

Related cases

DPP v McCarthy [1999] RTR 323, DC The requirement to give a name and address has a wider meaning than just the driver's home address. An address needs to be somewhere where a person can be contacted.

McDermott v DPP (1996) 161 JP 244, QBD The driver of a horsebox collided with the side of a car causing damage, and drove on to some stables 80 yards away. Although returning, the driver had left the scene, and could have stopped at the time of the accident

Practical considerations

- The driver does not commit this offence if s/he is unaware that an accident has happened.
- These two subsections create two separate offences (failing to stop and give information **and** failing to report). Therefore the driver may be charged with either one or both of them.
- The scene of the accident is the place in the road or public place where the collision occurs. Remember the vehicles themselves may also be 'scenes'.

 Summary   6 months

 6 months' imprisonment and/or a fine not exceeding level 5 on the standard scale.
Discretionary disqualification.
Obligatory endorsement—5 to 10 penalty points.

10.9.3 **Duty of driver to report the incident**

Section 170(5) and (7) of the Road Traffic Act 1988 provide for the obligation and a subsequent offence where a reportable accident occurs.

Offences

(5) If, in a case where this section applies by virtue of subsection (1)(a) above [injury, see **10.9.1**], the driver of a motor vehicle does not at the time of the accident produce such a certificate of insurance or security, or other evidence, as is mentioned in section 165(2)(a) of this Act:

(a) to a constable, or

(b) to some person who, having reasonable grounds for so doing, has required him to produce it,

the driver must report the accident and produce such a certificate or other evidence.

(7) A person who fails to comply with a duty under subsection (5) above is guilty of an offence.   Road Traffic Act 1988, s 170(5), (7)

Points to prove

✓ being the driver of a motor vehicle
✓ having been involved in a relevant road traffic accident
✓ did not at the time of the accident
✓ produce to a constable/person with grounds for requiring
✓ relevant evidence of insurance
✓ failed to report the accident and produce relevant insurance

---

Meanings

Driver (see **10.1.4**)

Motor vehicle (see **10.1.3**)

Accident (see **10.9.1**)

Explanatory notes

- To comply with the requirement to produce the relevant proof of insurance the driver must do so at a police station or to a constable, and must do so as soon as is reasonably practicable and, in any case, within 24 hours of it occurring.
- A person will not be convicted of this offence only because s/he failed to produce the relevant insurance document if, within 7 days following the accident it is produced at a police station specified by him/her at the time s/he reported the accident.
- The obligation to report the accident includes where there is nobody else about to whom the driver can give the details (eg damage to street furnishings).

Practical considerations

- Note that whereas s 170(2) and s 170(3) create offences in relation to a mechanically propelled vehicle, this offence is in relation to the use of a motor vehicle.
- This requirement does not apply to an invalid carriage.
- 'At a police station' means the motorist should report it in person at a police station or to a constable; a report by telephone will not suffice.

10.9.3 Duty of Driver to Report the Incident

 Summary   6 months

 6 months' imprisonment and/or a fine not exceeding level 5 on
the standard scale.
Discretionary disqualification.
Obligatory endorsement—5 to 10 penalty points.

Links to alternative subjects and offences

10.10 Drive/Attempt to Drive/in Charge of Vehicle Whilst Unfit Through Drink/Drugs

10.10.1 Drive/attempt to drive/in charge—whilst unfit drink/drugs

Section 4 of the Road Traffic Act 1988 provides for the offences of driving, attempting to drive, and being in charge of a mechanically propelled vehicle on a road or public place while unfit through drink or drugs.

Offences

(1) A person who, when driving or attempting to drive a mechanically propelled vehicle on a road or other public place, is unfit to drive through drink or drugs is guilty of an offence.

(2) Without prejudice to subsection (1) above, a person who, when in charge of a mechanically propelled vehicle which is on a road or other public place, is unfit to drive through drink or drugs is guilty of an offence.

Road Traffic Act 1988, s 4(1), (2)

Points to prove

s 4(1) offence

✓ drove/attempted to drive
✓ a mechanically propelled vehicle
✓ on a road/other public place
✓ when unfit to drive through drink/drugs

s 4(2) offence

✓ being a person in charge of a mechanically propelled vehicle
✓ which was on a road/public place
✓ was unfit to drive through drink/drugs

Meanings

Driving (see 10.1.4)

Mechanically propelled vehicle (see 10.1.3)

Road (see 10.6.1)

Public place (see 10.1.2)

Explanatory notes

• A person is unfit to drive properly if their ability is for the time being impaired.

- The evidence of a doctor who examines the defendant at the request of the police is admissible even if they had to persuade the defendant to allow the examination.
- If consent to the medical examination is given on the understanding that it is not part of the doctor's duty to determine whether the defendant is unfit to drive, the doctor's evidence of unfitness must be excluded.

Defence

For the purposes of subsection (2) above, a person shall be deemed not to have been in charge of a mechanically propelled vehicle if he proves that at the material time the circumstances were such that there was no likelihood of his driving it so long as he remained unfit to drive through drink or drugs.

Road Traffic Act 1988, s 4(3)

Defence notes

- In the case of *Sheldrake v DPP (Attorney-General's Reference No 4 of 2002)* [2005] 1 Cr App R 28 it was held that the burden of proof should remain on the defendant, to be decided on the balance of probabilities. This imposition did not contravene the presumption of innocence and was compatible with the European Convention on Human Rights.
- The court, in determining whether there was a likelihood of a person driving whilst still unfit through drink or drugs, should disregard any injury to them and any damage to the vehicle (ie it is not the practical possibility of the person being able to drive the vehicle that is relevant here, but rather the possibility of that person driving at all while still impaired).

Related cases

R v Ealing ex parte Woodman (1994) 158 JP 997, QBD If there was sufficient proof that s/he had taken more than their normal dose of insulin and failed to counterbalance it with food intake, insulin would be treated by the court as a drug under this section.

Smith v Mellors & Another [1987] RTR 210, QBD If the driver cannot be identified and each occupant of the car is over the prescribed limit, each one can be charged with the relevant drink driving offence and alternatively with aiding and abetting the other(s) to commit the drink driving offence. However, evidence of the aiding must be put to the court.

Practical considerations

- A charge under this section, which uses both the alternatives of 'drink or drugs', is not bad for duplicity.
- The CPS is unlikely to take the case forward unless there is evidence that the suspect was likely to drive while under the influence of drink/drugs.

- This section applies to trolley vehicles operated under statutory powers, but not to tramcars.
- The offence of driving or attempting to drive while under the influence of drink/drugs should not be tried with manslaughter, even with the agreement of the defence.
- An indictment containing a charge under s 1 of the Road Traffic Act 1988 (see **10.7**) should not include a charge under this section, as this section is triable summarily only.
- A non-expert witness may give evidence of the defendant's condition, but not of their fitness to drive.

 Summary 6 months

 s 4(1) offence
 6 months' imprisonment and/or a fine not exceeding level 5 on the standard scale.
 Obligatory disqualification for a minimum of 12 months.
 Obligatory endorsement—3 to 11 penalty points.

 s 4(2) offence
 3 months' imprisonment and/or a fine not exceeding level 4 on the standard scale.
 Discretionary disqualification.
 Obligatory endorsement—10 penalty points

10.10.2 **Preliminary test powers**

Section 6 of the Road Traffic Act 1988 provides for the requiring of preliminary tests for alcohol, impairment, or drugs to drivers of motor vehicles. Sections 6A to 6C relate to the specific tests, whilst s 6D provides a power of arrest and s 6E a power of entry.

Offence

A person commits an offence if without reasonable excuse he **fails** to co-operate with a **preliminary test** in pursuance of a **requirement** imposed under this section.   Road Traffic Act 1988, s 6(6)

Points to prove
 ✓ without reasonable excuse
 ✓ failed to cooperate with a preliminary test
 ✓ when required under this section

10.10.2 Preliminary Test Powers

Meanings

Fails

Fail includes refuse.

Preliminary test

Means a preliminary test—of breath/impairment or for drugs.

Requirements

- A constable may require a person to cooperate with any one or more preliminary tests administered to them by that constable or another constable, if the constable reasonably suspects that s/he:
  - ◆ is driving, attempting to drive, or is in charge of a motor vehicle on a road or other public place, and has alcohol or a drug in their body or is under the influence of a drug; **or**
  - ◆ has been driving, attempting, to drive or in charge of a motor vehicle on a road or other public place while having alcohol or a drug in their body or while unfit to drive because of a drug, and still has alcohol or a drug in their body or is still under the influence of a drug; **or**
  - ◆ is or has been driving, attempting to drive, or in charge of a motor vehicle on a road or other public place, and has committed a traffic offence while the vehicle was in motion.
- A constable may also require a person to cooperate as above if an accident occurs owing to the presence of a motor vehicle on a road or other public place, and a constable reasonably believes that the person was driving, attempting to drive, or in charge of the vehicle at the time of the accident.

Explanatory notes

- Only a constable in uniform may administer a preliminary test.
- 'Traffic offence' means an offence under pt II of the Public Passenger Vehicles Act 1981, a provision of the Road Traffic Regulation Act 1984, a provision of the Road Traffic Offenders Act 1988 (except pt III—fixed penalties), or a provision of this Act (except pt V—driving instruction).
- A preliminary breath test is a procedure by which the person taking the test provides a specimen of breath to ascertain, using a device approved by the Secretary of State, whether the proportion of alcohol in their breath or blood is likely to exceed the prescribed limit.
- For a preliminary impairment test the constable requesting it observes the person taking it performing tasks specified by the constable and makes any observations of the persons physical state as s/he thinks expedient.
- A code of practice issued by the Secretary of State will govern preliminary impairment tests.
- For a preliminary drug test a specimen of sweat or saliva is obtained (using a device approved by the Secretary of State) to ascertain whether the person tested has a drug in their body.
- A person will not be required at random to provide a specimen of breath for a breath test.

- An asthma sufferer who is incapable of providing a sample has a duty to inform the officer requiring it.
- A person who refuses (without good cause) to take a test is deemed to have failed to take it.
- Whilst in hospital, no person will be requested to supply a breath sample or laboratory specimen without the knowledge and permission of the doctor in charge of their case.
- Where specimens of breath have been provided under s 7 (see **10.11.2**) the powers of arrest above still have effect if the constable imposing the requirement has reasonable cause to believe that the approved device used for analysis did not produce a reliable result.

Power of arrest

(1) A constable may arrest a person without warrant if as a result of a preliminary breath test the constable reasonably suspects that the proportion of alcohol in that person's breath or blood exceeds the prescribed limit.

(2) A constable may arrest a person without warrant if:
  (a) the person fails to co-operate with a preliminary test in pursuance of a requirement imposed under s 6, and
  (b) the constable reasonably suspects that the person has alcohol or a drug in his body or is under the influence of a drug.

Road Traffic Act 1988, s 6D(1) and (2)

Power of entry

A constable may enter any place (using reasonable force if necessary) for the purpose of—

(a) imposing a requirement by virtue of section 6(5) *[preliminary test after accident]* following an accident in a case where the constable reasonably suspects that the accident involved injury of any person, or

(b) arresting a person under section 6D following an accident in a case where the constable reasonably suspects that the accident involved injury of any person.

Road Traffic Act 1988, s 6E(1)

Practical considerations

- A preliminary breath test requested because a constable suspects that a person has alcohol or a drug in their body or is under the influence of a drug may only be given at or near the place where it is requested.
- A preliminary breath test requested following an accident, preliminary impairment test or preliminary drugs test may be given at or near the place where it is requested or, if the constable requesting it thinks it expedient, at a police station specified by them.
- Only a constable approved by their chief officer may give a preliminary impairment test, which must satisfy the code of practice.
- A person arrested under the above powers may, instead of being taken to a police station, be detained at or near the place where the

preliminary test was, or would have been, administered, to impose a requirement there under s 7 on them (see **10.11.2**).

- A person may not be arrested under s 6D while at a hospital as a patient.
- A constable may enter (by reasonable force if necessary) to impose a requirement by virtue of an accident having occurred, or to arrest a person under s 6D following an accident, where s/he reasonably suspects that such accident involved injury to a person.
- If a motorist supplies enough breath for the device to give a reading they cannot be said to have failed to cooperate.

E&S

 Summary   6 months

 A fine not exceeding level 3 on the standard scale.
Discretionary disqualification.
Obligatory endorsement—4 penalty points.

Links to alternative subjects and offences

10.11 Drive/Attempt to Drive/in Charge Whilst over the Prescribed Limit

Section 5 of the Road Traffic Act 1988 provides the offences of driving, attempting to drive and being in charge of a motor vehicle on a road or public place while over the prescribed limit of alcohol in blood, breath or urine. Section 7 of the Act relates to the provision of specimens for analysis.

10.11.1 Drive/attempt to drive/in charge of motor vehicle while over the prescribed limit

Offences

If a person:
(a) drives or attempts to drive a motor vehicle on a road or other public place, or
(b) is in charge of a motor vehicle on a road or other public place,
after consuming so much alcohol that the proportion of it in his breath, blood or urine exceeds the prescribed limit he is guilty of an offence.

Road Traffic Act 1988, s 5(1)

Points to prove

✓ drove/attempted to drive/in charge of motor vehicle
✓ on a road/public place
✓ proportion of alcohol in blood/breath/urine exceeded prescribed limit

Meanings

Drive   (see 10.1.4)

Motor vehicle   (see 10.1.3)

Road   (see 10.6.1)

Public place   (see 10.1.2)

Consuming

This has a wide enough meaning to extend 'by mouth' and to include other means of ingesting it into the blood, breaths or urine.

10.11.1 Drive Motor Vehicle While Over the Prescribed Limit

Explanatory notes

- Be aware of the powers to administer a preliminary breath test (see **10.10.2**).
- Being so hopelessly drunk that s/he is incapable of driving a motor vehicle is not a defence to this offence.
- Evidence of the proportion of alcohol at the time of driving other than that provided by the specimen is admissible.
- Where it is established that the defendant was driving and has given a positive sample, it is assumed that the amount of alcohol at the time of the alleged offence is not less than the specimen provided.

Power of arrest (see 10.10.2)

Defence

It is a defence for a person charged with an offence of being in charge of a motor vehicle while over the prescribed limit to prove that there was no likelihood of them driving the vehicle while still in that condition.

Road Traffic Act 1988, s 5(2)

Defence notes

- The burden of proof is on the defendant and any such matters are to be determined on the balance of probability.
- In determining whether there was any likelihood of them driving, the court may ignore any injury to them or damage to the vehicle.

Related cases

DPP v Wilson [1991] Crim LR 441, QBD An officer is entitled to form an opinion that a driver has been drinking from information from an anonymous caller.

DPP v Johnson (1994) 158 JP 891, QBD The 'consumption' of alcohol may be by injection.

Sharpe v DPP (1994) JP 595, QBD If the officer is a trespasser at the time of the screening test it may invalidate the procedure but will not always do so.

Drake v DPP [1994] Crim LR 855, QBD The fact that a vehicle is wheel clamped may allow the defence to 'being in charge' to be used, but each case must be considered on its merits.

DPP v Jones and DPP v McKeown [1997] 2 Cr App R 155, HL If the Lion Intoximeter had an inaccurate clock this alone would not invalidate the accuracy of the relevant information on the printout. Similarly, this would not be a 'reasonable excuse' for failing to provide a specimen for analysis.

DPP v H [1997] 1 WLR 1406, QBD Insanity cannot be used as a defence against a charge under this section as there is no requirement for any intent; the offence is one of strict liability.

Lafferty v DPP [1995] Crim LR 430, QBD In considering a claim by the defence that the intoximeter reading was inaccurate the court may consider evidence of the roadside breath test.

Practical considerations

- The CPS is unlikely to take the case forward unless there is evidence of a likelihood of driving while under the influence of drink or drugs.
- A person acting as a supervisor of a provisional licence holder is 'in charge' of the vehicle and can commit that offence under this section.
- 'Lacing' a person's drink without their knowledge may constitute an offence of aiding and abetting the commission of an offence under this section, if there is proof that the intent was to bring about the offence.
- Be aware of the 'Hip Flask Defence' (where the suspect has claims to have had an alcoholic drink since driving but before providing a specimen). Ascertain amount drunk and inform the laboratory so the appropriate calculations can be made.
- A power of entry is available for the provision of a preliminary test in cases, which involve an injury accident. Reasonable force may be used to effect entry s 6E, carry out a preliminary test and arrest a person under s 6D (see **10.10.2**).
- Consider the indictable offence of riding a pedal cycle in a wanton or furious manner (see **10.7.2**).

 Summary   6 months

 s 5(1)(a) offence
6 months' imprisonment and/or a fine not exceeding level 5 on the standard scale.
Obligatory disqualification.
Obligatory endorsement—3 to 11 penalty points (if special reasons apply).

s 5(1)(b) offence
3 months' imprisonment and/or a fine not exceeding level 4 on the standard scale.
Discretionary disqualification.
Obligatory endorsement—10 penalty points.

10.11.2 Provision of specimens for analysis

Section 7(6) of the Road Traffic Act 1988 addresses the provision of specimens for analysis.

10.11.2 Provision of Specimens for Analysis

Offence

A person who, without reasonable excuse, fails to provide a specimen when required to do so in pursuance of this section is guilty of an offence.

Road Traffic Act 1988, s 7(6)

Points to prove

✓ without reasonable excuse
✓ failed/refused to provide specimen
✓ when lawfully required to do so

Meanings

Fails (see **10.10.2**)

Specimen

Specimens consist of two specimens of breath for analysis by an approved device or a specimen of blood or urine for laboratory analysis.

Explanatory notes

Specimens may be required from a person suspected of having committed an offence against s 3A (see **10.8.2**), s 4 (see **10.10.1**), or s 5 (see **10.11.1**).

Related cases

DPP v Smith (Alan) The Times, 1 June 1994, QBD The accused cannot insist that blood should be taken by their own GP.

Wade v DPP The Times, 14 February 1995, QBD A defendant on medication may have a medical reason for not providing a specimen of breath under this section.

DPP v Nesbitt and Duffy [1995] 1 Cr App R 38, QBD Where a request for blood or urine is made at a hospital the required warnings must explain the procedures in full, with reasons, and state the consequences of failing to comply.

DPP v Coyle [1995] 37 WLD 125, CA It is not necessary to wait for the intoximeter machine to 'time out' before a suspect's refusal or failure to give a sample of breath will be complete.

DPP v Garrett [1995] RTR 302, QBD Where the blood sample procedure was flawed, but the sample was not taken and used, it did not affect the request for a urine sample.

Hague v DPP The Times, 14 November 1995, QBD Breath samples were taken on an intoximeter machine. The officer believed the machine to be faulty and requested blood or urine, which was refused. The machine was examined and found to be working correctly. The readings were therefore admissible.

Francis v DPP The Times, 2 May 1996, QBD A request can be legitimately made of a mentally unstable person if s/he understands what is happening.

DPP v Wythe [1996] RTR 137, QBD If a medical reason is put forward by the suspect, the final decision as to whether or not blood can or should be taken is the doctor's.

DPP v Furby The Times, 23 March 2000, QBD A medical condition of which they are unaware, cannot later be used as an excuse for failing to provide the required sample.

Causey v DPP [2004] EWHC 3164 (Admin), QBD There is no general duty on the police to delay taking a specimen at the police station until the detainee has obtained legal advice.

DPP v Baldwin The Times, 17 May 2000, QBD The purpose of the requirement to provide a specimen of urine one hour after the first specimen is to give the motorist a finite time. If this period is extended, that extension does not make any findings inadmissible.

Practical considerations

- On requiring a person to provide a specimen under this section, a constable **must** warn them that failure to provide it may render them liable to prosecution.
- A requirement for a specimen of breath can only be made at a police station, a hospital, or at or near a place where a relevant breath test has been given to the person concerned or would have been so given but for their failure to cooperate.
- The constable requiring the breath sample must be in uniform, or have imposed a requirement on the defendant to cooperate with a breath test as a result of an accident.
- Where a requirement has been imposed for a person to co-operate with a relevant breath test at any place, the constable may remain at or near there to impose a requirement under this section.
- If a requirement is made for two samples of breath for analysis by an approved device at a place other than a police station, it may revert to being made at a police station if a device or reliable device is not available there or it is not practicable to use one there, or the constable making the previous requirement believes that the device has not produced a reliable result.
- Under this section, a requirement for a specimen of blood or urine can only be made at a police station or a hospital.
- A requirement for a sample of blood or urine can be made at a police station unless the constable requiring it believes that for medical reasons it cannot or should not be made, specimens of breath have not been provided elsewhere and an approved device is not available there, an approved device has been used but the constable believes the result to be unreliable, the constable believes, following a preliminary drugs test, that the defendant has a drug in their body or, if the offence is under s 3 or s 4 of the Act, the constable has been informed by a medical practitioner that the persons condition may be because of a drug.

10.11.2 Provision of Specimens for Analysis

- The above requirement may be made even if the defendant has been required to supply two specimens of breath.
- If a specimen other than breath is required, the question as to whether it is blood or urine (and, if it is blood, who will take it) will be decided by the constable making the requirement.
- If a medical practitioner or registered health care professional thinks that, for medical reasons, blood cannot or should not be taken the requirement will not be made. A urine sample may then be required instead.
- A specimen of urine must be provided within an hour of its being required and after the provision of a previous such specimen.

 Summary 6 months

 Driving or attempting to drive
6 months' imprisonment and/or a fine not exceeding level 5 on the standard scale.
Obligatory disqualification for 12 months.Obligatory endorsement—3 to 11 penalty points (if special conditions apply).

In all other cases
3 months' imprisonment and/or a fine not exceeding level 4 on the standard scale.
Discretionary disqualification.
Obligatory endorsement—10 penalty points.

Links to alternative subjects and offences

10.12 **Pedal Cycle Offences**

Sections 28, 29, and 30 of the Road Traffic Act 1988 provide similar offences for cyclists to those contained in ss 1, 2, and 3 for motorists. All references in the following are to the 1988 Act unless otherwise stated. Additionally, there is the offence of cycling on a footpath under s 72 of the Highways Act 1835.

10.12.1 **Dangerous cycling**

Section 28 creates an offence of dangerous cycling.

> **Offence**
> A person who rides a **cycle** on a **road dangerously** is guilty of an offence.
> Road Traffic Act 1988, s 28(1)

Points to prove
✓ rode a cycle
✓ on a road
✓ dangerously

Meanings

Cycle

Means a bicycle, a tricycle, or a cycle having four or more wheels, not being in any case a motor vehicle.

Road (see **10.6.1**)

Dangerously

A person is to be regarded as riding dangerously if and only if—

- the way that s/he rides falls far below what would be expected of a competent and careful cyclist; **and**
- it would be obvious to a competent and careful cyclist that riding in that way would be dangerous.

Explanatory notes

- The term 'danger' refers to danger either of injury to any person or of serious damage to property
- To determine what would be obvious to a competent and careful cyclist in a particular case consideration must be given to circumstances of which s/he could be expected to be aware and any shown to have been within their knowledge.

- A person may be convicted of the alternative offence of careless, and inconsiderate, cycling (see **10.12.2**).

Practical considerations

- A notice of intended prosecution is required (see **10.5**).
- This offence must be on a road—it does not extend to a public place.

 Summary 6 months

 A fine not exceeding level 4 on the standard scale.

10.12.2 **Careless, and inconsiderate, cycling**

Section 29 creates an offence of cycling without due care and attention or without reasonable consideration for other road users.

> **Offence**
>
> If a person rides a **cycle** on a **road** without due care and attention, or without reasonable consideration for other persons using the road, he is guilty of an offence.   Road Traffic Act 1988, s 29

> **Points to prove**
> - ✓ rode a cycle
> - ✓ on a road
> - ✓ without due care and attention/reasonable consideration for other road users

Meanings

Cycle (see **10.12.1**)

Road (see **10.6.1**)

Practical considerations

- A notice of intended prosecution is required (see **10.5**).
- This offence must be on a road—it does not extend to a public place.

 Summary 6 months

 A fine not exceeding level 3 on the standard scale.

10.12.3 **Cycling when under the influence of drink or drugs**

Section 30 creates an offence of cycling on a road or public place while unfit through drink or drugs.

Offences

A person who, when riding a cycle on a road or other public place, is unfit to ride through drink or drugs (that is to say, is under the influence of drink or a drug to such an extent as to be incapable of having proper control of the cycle) is guilty of an offence.   Road Traffic Act 1988, s 30(1)

Points to prove
- ✓ rode a cycle
- ✓ on a road/other public place
- ✓ while unfit to ride through drink/drugs

Meanings

Road   (see **10.6.1**)

Public place   (see **10.1.2**)

Practical considerations
- As there is no power to require a specimen of breath, blood, or urine, other methods of calculating the extent to which the defendant is under the influence of drink or drugs need to be used.
- This offence does not extend to being in charge of a cycle as it would with other forms of transport.
- A bicycle or tricycle is a carriage under the Licensing Act 1872. Therefore consider the offence of being in charge of a carriage under s 12 of that Act.

 Summary   6 months

 A fine not exceeding level 3 on the standard scale.

10.12.4 **Riding on the footpath**

Section 72 of the Highways Act 1835 creates an offence of riding on the footpath.

10.12.4 Riding on the Footpath

Offence

If any person shall wilfully ride upon any footpath or causeway by the side of any road, made or set apart for the use or accommodation of foot passengers ... he shall be guilty of an offence.　Highways Act 1835, s 72

Points to prove

✓ wilfully rode a pedal cycle
✓ upon a footpath/causeway
✓ by the side of a road
✓ made/set apart
✓ for the use/accommodation of foot passengers

Meanings

Wilfully

'Wilful' under this section means 'purposely'.

Footpath

A footpath is part of a highway, if it is beside a road.

Explanatory notes

• Proceedings may be instituted by anyone.
• Consider issuing a traffic fixed penalty notice (see **10.4**).

TFPN　CSO

 Summary　 6 months

 A fine not exceeding level 2 on the standard scale.

Links to alternative subjects and offences

10.13 **Driving While Disqualified**

Section 103 of the Road Traffic Act 1988 creates the offences of obtaining a driving licence while disqualified from driving and driving a motor vehicle on a road while so disqualified. All references in the following are to the 1988 Act unless otherwise stated.

Offences

A person is guilty of an offence if, while **disqualified** for holding or obtaining a licence, he:
(a) obtains a licence, or
(b) **drives a motor vehicle** on a road. Road Traffic Act 1988, s 103(1)

Points to prove

✓ while disqualified for holding/obtaining a licence
✓ obtained a licence/drove a motor vehicle on a road

Meanings

Disqualified

Means disqualified for holding or obtaining a licence and, where the disqualification relates only to vehicles of a particular class, a licence to drive vehicles of that particular class.

Drives   (see **10.1.4**)

Motor vehicle

This is defined by s 185 (see **10.1.3**).

Road   (see **10.6.1**)

Explanatory notes

- An underage driver (unless disqualified by the court) should be charged with the offence of 'driving otherwise than in accordance with a licence' (see **10.14**).
- Subsection (1)(b) does not apply to a person disqualified for obtaining a licence authorizing them to drive a motor vehicle of a specific class while s/he holds another licence to drive that class of vehicle.
- Such a person is disqualified for obtaining such a licence, even if the licence held is suspended (s 102).
- A person who is disqualified in England and Wales can not drive in Great Britain even if s/he holds a foreign or international driving licence or permit or a service driving licence.
- A driver disqualified in a foreign country would not be guilty of this offence, but may be guilty of driving without a licence.
- Disqualification by a court is usually for a specified period as punishment for a road traffic offence.

- If penalty points imposed by the court, together with any to be taken into account on that occasion, total 12 or more (the 'totting up' system) the court must, other than in exceptional circumstances, disqualify the defendant for at least a minimum period (Road Traffic Offenders Act 1988, s 35).
- The 'minimum period' referred to in s 35 of the Road Traffic Offenders Act 1988 is 6 months if no previous disqualification imposed on the defendant is to be taken into account, one year if one such period is to be taken into account and 2 years if two or more such periods are taken into account.
- A previous disqualification period is taken into account if it was fixed for a period of at least 56 days and was imposed within 3 years immediately prior to the commission of the latest offence for which penalty points are being imposed by the court.
- All penalty points imposed will be endorsed on the counterpart of the defendant's licence.
- Such endorsements generally remain effective if a disqualification order is made, for 4 years after the conviction, and, if no such order is made, for 4 years after the commission of the offence or until a disqualification order is made. However, where the offence was contrary to s 1 (see **10.8.1**) or s 2 (see **10.7.1**), the endorsement remains effective for 4 years from the conviction. If the offence was contrary to s 3A (see **10.8.2**), s 4(1) (see **10.10.1**), s 5(1)(a) (see **10.11.1**) or s 7(6) (see **10.11.2**) the endorsement remains effective for 11 years following conviction.
- The court may order a driver to be disqualified until s/he has passed a test. Such driver may not drive within the disqualification period and then only after obtaining a provisional licence.
- Failure of a person disqualified until passing a test to comply with the conditions of a provisional licence may result in a conviction for the above offence.

Related cases (see driving cases 10.1.4)

R v Derwentside Magistrates' Court ex parte Heaviside (1995) 160 JP 317, QBD Proper evidence that a driver was disqualified must be presented before the court—simply producing a court extract is not sufficient. Identification of the defendant as the person convicted in court may be established by admission, fingerprints, or by a person in court at the time of the conviction.

DPP v Barker [2004] EWHC 2502 (Admin), QBD If a person was disqualified until they had passed a driving test, the burden of proof was on the driver to show that s/he had a provisional license and was driving in accordance with the licence conditions.

Practical considerations

- A licence obtained by a disqualified person is not valid.
- Proof that the defendant knew of the disqualification is not necessary.
- A person is disqualified for holding or obtaining a licence to drive a certain class of motor vehicle if they are under the age stipulated for

that class (s 101), but the offence would be contrary to s 87(1) (see **10.14**).

• Minimum ages for driving specified classes of motor vehicles are shown in **10.14.2**.

 Summary

 Normally 6 months but, in any case, no prosecution may be brought more than 3 years after the commission of the offence.

 s 103(1)(a) offence
A fine not exceeding level 3 on the standard scale.

s 103(1)(b) offence
6 months' imprisonment and/or a fine not exceeding level 5 on the standard scale.
Discretionary disqualification.
Obligatory endorsement—6 penalty points.

Links to alternative subjects and offences

10.14 Driving not in Accordance with a Driving Licence

Section 87 of the Road Traffic Act 1988 require all people driving a motor vehicle on a road to hold a driving licence for that class of vehicle and to comply with any conditions attached to it. All references in the following are to the 1988 Act unless otherwise stated.

10.14.1 Drive motor vehicle of a class not authorized by driving licence

Offences

(1) It is an offence for a person to drive on a road a motor vehicle of any class otherwise than in accordance with a licence authorising him to drive a motor vehicle of that class.

(2) It is an offence for a person to cause or permit another person to drive on a road a motor vehicle of any class otherwise than in accordance with a licence authorising that other person to drive a motor vehicle of that class.

Road Traffic Act 1988, s 87(1), (2)

Points to prove

s 87(1) offence

✓ drove motor vehicle
✓ on a road
✓ otherwise than in accordance with licence
✓ authorizing the driving of that class of vehicle

s 87(2) offence

✓ caused/permitted
✓ another person to commit s 87(1) offence

Meanings

Drive (see **10.1.4**)

Road (see **10.6.1**)

Motor vehicle (see **10.13**)

Class (see **10.14.2 and Appendix 2**)

10.14.1 Drive Motor Vehicle of a Class not Authorized

Cause

Means involving some degree of control or dominance by or some express mandate from the causer. It also requires some positive action and knowledge by the defendant (*Price v Cromack* [1975] 1 WLR 988).

Permit

Is less direct or explicit than causing and involves leave or licence to do something. Permission can be express or inferred.

Licence

Means a licence to drive a motor vehicle under pt III of the Road Traffic Act 1988 or a **community licence**.

Community licence

Means a document issued by an EEA state (other than the UK) by authority of the EEA State authorizing the holder to drive a motor vehicle.

Full licence

Means a licence other than a **provisional licence**.

Provisional licence

Means a licence issued to enable an applicant to drive motor vehicles with a view to passing a test of competence to drive.

Explanatory notes

- The holder of a convention driving permit, a domestic driving permit issued by a country outside the UK, or a British Forces driving permit, who is resident outside the UK may drive any class of vehicle specified in the permit or licence for 12 months.
- People who become resident in Great Britain may drive on their domestic licence for 12 months.
- A person who is an EU citizen and holds a driving licence or permit issued in another EU country may drive on that licence or permit in this country in accordance with that licence or permit. S/he would not need to exchange the licence or permit for a UK licence no matter how long s/he stayed here.
- A person who has held a driver's licence, a community licence, a Northern Ireland licence, a British external licence, a British Forces licence, or an exchangeable licence may, in certain circumstances, still drive a relevant vehicle even if the licence and its counterpart have been surrendered or revoked. This includes where a qualifying application has been received at DVLA or their licence to drive that class of vehicle and its counterpart has been revoked or surrendered for renewal, it was granted in or contains an error, or for amendment of a requirement or the holder's name and address.

Practical considerations

- Where a person is charged with driving without a licence, the burden of proving that they have a licence is with that person (*John v Humphreys* [1955] 1 All ER 793, QBD).

- The police have powers to seize and remove a motor vehicle if the driver has no driving licence **or** there is no insurance in force for the vehicle (see **10.16.5**).
- It is an offence for a person not to produce his/her driving licence (see **10.16.3**).
- A traffic fixed penalty notice can be issued for the s 87(1) offence (see **10.4**).
- This offence includes circumstances where the driver is driving under age.
- The classes of vehicles which a licence holder is authorized by it to drive are stated on the licence itself.
- A licence is valid only when it is used in accordance with its conditions of use.

 Summary   6 months

 s 87(1) offence
A fine not exceeding level 3 on the standard scale.
If the licence could have been issued to them: Discretionary disqualification.
Obligatory endorsement—3 to 8 penalty points.

s 87(2) offence
A fine not exceeding level 3 on the standard scale.
Obligatory endorsement—minimum 3 penalty points.

10.14.2 Minimum ages for holding/obtaining driving licences

The minimum ages for holding or obtaining a licence to drive a specified class of vehicle is as follows:
- Invalid carriage—16 years.
- Moped—16 years.
- Motor bicycle—17 years.
- Where the motor bicycle is a large motor bicycle that age becomes 21 years, unless it is used for military purposes or has passed a test to drive large motor bicycles before 1 January 1997. Otherwise the person passed a test on or after 1 January 1997 to drive a motor vehicle category A (except subcategory 1A), and has held a full licence for 2 years.
- Agricultural or forestry tractor—17 years.
    - However, that age will be 16 years, if it is a wheeled tractor (not tracked) and is not more than 2.45 metres wide or has a trailer which is either 2-wheeled or close-coupled 4-wheeled (maximum

840 mm gap) and both have a maximum width of 2.45 metres **and** the person has passed, is going to, taking or returning from a test for a category F vehicle.

- Small vehicles—17 years. This age may become 16 years where the vehicle is driven without a trailer and the person is in receipt of the higher rate component of the disability living allowance.
- Medium-sized goods vehicles—18 years. Except:
  - ♦ where the vehicle is towing a trailer and the maximum authorized mass of the combination exceeds 7.5 tonnes that age will be 21 years; or
  - ♦ if the vehicle is being used for military purposes the minimum age will be 17 years.
- Other motor vehicles—21 years, but the age will be 18 years for:
  - ♦ a vehicle which carries over 8 passengers if the driver holds a full licence for that category **and** is carrying passengers on a regular 50 kilometre route **or** driving a vehicle in category D1;
  - ♦ a passenger carrying vehicle if the driver has a provisional licence for that category and there are no passengers;
  - ♦ a vehicle which is a category D1 vehicle AND is an ambulance;
  - ♦ a vehicle in category C1 + E with a maximum mass not exceeding 7.5 tonnes;
  - ♦ a person who is part of a training scheme for large goods vehicle drivers either with their employer or an authorized school.
- However, the age will be 17 years if the vehicle is being used for military purposes or the vehicle is a road roller propelled otherwise than by steam, has no wheel fitted with pneumatic, soft, or elastic tyres, does not exceed 11.69 tonnes unladen and only carries tools and equipment for its own use.

Explanatory notes

Appendix 2 contains two tables which provide further information such as:
- matching table, comparing old groups/class with new categories;
- vehicle categories and minimum driving age.

Links to alternative subjects and offences

10.15 **Drive with Defective Eyesight**

Section 96 of the Road Traffic Act 1988 creates an offence of driving with defective eyesight. All references in the following are to the 1988 Act unless otherwise stated.

Offences

Drive with uncorrected defective eyesight

(1) If a person drives a motor vehicle on a road while his eyesight is such (whether through a defect which cannot be or one which is not for the time being sufficiently corrected) that he cannot comply with any requirement as to eyesight prescribed under this Part of this Act for the purposes of tests of competence to drive, he is guilty of an offence.

Refuse to submit to eyesight test

(2) A constable having reason to suspect that a person driving a motor vehicle may be guilty of an offence under subsection (1) above may require him to submit to a test for the purpose of ascertaining whether, using no other means of correction than he used at the time of driving, he can comply with the requirement concerned.

(3) If that person refuses to submit to the test he is guilty of an offence.

Road Traffic Act 1988, s 96(1)–(3)

Points to prove

s 96(1) offence

✓ drove a motor vehicle
✓ on a road
✓ while unable to meet eyesight requirements

s 96(2) offence

✓ being the driver of a motor vehicle
✓ on a road
✓ and being required to take eyesight test
✓ by a constable
✓ refused to take such test

Meanings

Drives (see **10.1.4**)

Motor vehicle (see **10.13**)

Road (see **10.6.1**)

Explanatory notes

• This section creates two offences:
  ♦ driving with defective eyesight;

10.15 Drive with Defective Eyesight

          ♦ refusing to submit to an eyesight test.
- The prescribed 'requirement as to eyesight' can be found in the Motor Vehicles (Driving Licences) Regulations 1999.
- The prescribed requirement is for a person to be able to read, in good light (with visual aids if used) a number plate on a vehicle containing characters of the prescribed size.
  - ♦ 'Prescribed size' means characters which are 79.4 mm high and either 57 or 50 mm wide.
- The distance from which the number plate should be read is, for category K vehicles (eg mowing machines and pedestrian controlled vehicles), 12.3 metres or 12 metres respectively and, in any other case, 20.5 or 20 metres.
- Spectacles or contact lenses may be used for the test if s/he was wearing them while driving.
- For the purposes of this offence it does not matter whether the defect is one that can be corrected or not. The important matter is the state of their eyesight at the time they were driving.
- Knowledge of the defect by the defendant is not necessary, although this may be used in mitigation if the defendant has suffered a gradual and unnoticed deterioration in their eyesight.
- However, under s 92(1) any person holding or applying for a licence has a duty to inform the DVLA of any prescribed disability likely to cause the driving of a vehicle by him/her in accordance with the licence to be a source of danger to the public. This includes a 'prospective' disability such as a condition that does not at the time amount to a relevant disability, but which is likely to deteriorate to that level in the course of time.

Practical considerations
- The degree by which the defendant's eyesight fails to meet the requirement is particularly relevant as this will reflect the degree of risk taken or danger created by them.
- The more severe the defect the more difficult it will be for the defendant to mitigate the offence.
- An inability to read the characters in the test will amount to a prescribed disability and the person will have to inform the DVLA under s 92(1).

 Summary   6 months

 A fine not exceeding level 3 on the standard scale.
Discretionary disqualification.
Obligatory endorsement—3 penalty points.

Links to alternative subjects and offences

10.16 Vehicle document offences and Seizure of Vehicles

The requirement for a vehicle to be covered by third party insurance before it can be used on a road is provided by the Road Traffic Act 1988. All references in the following are to the 1988 Act unless otherwise stated.

10.16.1 No insurance

Section 143 requires the user of a motor vehicle to be insured or secured against third party risks.

Offences

(1) Subject to the provisions of this Part of this Act:
   (a) a person must not use a motor vehicle on a road or other public place unless there is in force in relation to the use of the vehicle by that person such a policy of insurance or such a security in respect of third party risks as complies with the requirements of this Part of this Act, and
   (b) a person must not cause or permit any other person to use a motor vehicle on a road or other public place unless there is in force in relation to the use of the vehicle by that other person such a policy of insurance or such a security in respect of third party risks as complies with the requirements of this Part of this Act.
(2) If a person acts in contravention of subsection (1) above he is guilty of an offence.   Road Traffic Act 1988, s 143(1), (2)

Points to prove
✓ used/caused/permitted another to use
✓ motor vehicle
✓ on a road/public place
✓ not covered by policy of insurance/security for third party risks

Meanings

Use

Means the driver of a vehicle, the driver's employer while it is being used for their business, the vehicle owner if s/he is in it while somebody else is driving it, or the steersman of a broken down vehicle which is being towed.

Motor vehicle (see **10.13**)

Road (see **10.6.1**)

Public place (see **10.1.2**)

Policy of insurance

This includes a cover note.

Cause (see **10.14.1**)

Permit (see **10.14.1**)

Explanatory notes

- This section does not apply to invalid carriages.
- This section does not apply to a person who keeps £500,000 deposited with the Accountant General of the Supreme Court while the vehicle is being driven under the owner's control.
- Section 144 states that s 143 does not apply to:
  - ♦ a vehicle owned by a county or county district council, City of London Common/Borough council, a National Park Authority, the Inner London Education Authority, the London Fire and Emergency Planning Authority, or a joint authority (except a police authority) established by pt IV of the Local Government Act 1985 or a joint board or committee which includes member representatives of such council, while the vehicle is being driven under the owner's control,
  - ♦ a police authority owned vehicle when it is being driven under the owner's control or a vehicle being driven for police purposes by or under the direction of a constable or a police authority employee,
  - ♦ a vehicle being driven to or from a place for the purposes of salvage under the Merchant Shipping Act 1995,
  - ♦ to the use of a vehicle as directed under s 166(2)(b) of the Army Act 1955 or the Air Force Act 1955,
  - ♦ a vehicle owned by a health service body, a Primary Care Trust or the Commission for Health Improvement when it is being driven under the owner's control,
  - ♦ an ambulance owned by a National Health Service Trust when it is being driven under the owner's control,
  - ♦ a vehicle made available by the Secretary of State to a person, body or local authority under s 23 or s 26 of the National Heath Service Act 1977 while it is being used in accordance with the terms under which it was made available.
- It would still be an offence (triable in UK) to use a vehicle exempted under the above in a member state of the European Community without insurance cover valid for that state.
- The exemption to insurance cover under s 143 applies to a constable's own car while it is being driven for police purposes (*Jones v Chief Constable of Bedfordshire* [1987] RTR 332).
- A visitor bringing a motor vehicle temporarily into this country, who holds an international motor insurance card, may register its particulars, and the card will then have effect as though it was an insurance policy under this Part of the Act.

- When an insurance company become aware that a policy is voidable (eg the policyholder has withheld information) it remains in force until they take steps to void it and the policyholder must be made aware of its being voided.

Defences

A person charged with using a motor vehicle in contravention of this section shall not be convicted if he proves:
(a) that the vehicle did not belong to him and was not in his possession under a contract of hiring or of loan,
(b) that he was using the vehicle in the course of his employment, and
(c) that he neither knew nor had reason to believe that there was not in force in relation to the vehicle such a policy of insurance or security as is mentioned in subsection (1) above.   Road Traffic Act 1988, s 143(3)

Related cases

Plumbien v Vines [1996] Crim LR 124, QBD A vehicle that has been left on a road for several months and its condition deteriorated so that it could not be moved is still at the disposal of the owner should he wish to use it. Such a vehicle is still required to be covered by insurance for its use.

Dodson v Peter H Dodson Insurance Services [2001] 1 WLR 1012, CA A motor vehicle owner obtained insurance for his vehicle, which also covered him to drive vehicles not belonging to him with the owner's permission. He then sold the vehicle but continued to drive other people's vehicles under the policy. In the absence of a condition in the policy of insurance making it clear that the policyholder would only be covered while he was the owner of the relevant vehicle, the policy is valid until the end of its term.

DPP v Hay [2005] EWHC 1395 (Admin), QBD After proving that the defendant used the motor vehicle on a road or public place, it is then for the defendant to show that there was in force an appropriate policy of insurance.

Practical considerations

- Read the conditions on the insurance very carefully. It does not follow that a person who is not a current driving licence holder does not have insurance. Similarly, it does not always follow that a valid insurance certificate covers the person for the particular vehicle being used for that particular purpose.
- A traffic fixed penalty notice for the s 143(1)(a) 'using' offence can be issued (see **10.4**).
- The policy must be issued by an authorized insurer (eg a member of the Motor Insurers Bureau).
- It is an offence to fail to produce insurance (see **10.16.4**).
- The motor vehicle can be seized if no insurance is in force for the vehicle (see **10.16.5**).

Summary

 Normally 6 months but, in certain circumstances, up to 3 years after sufficient knowledge of the offence.

 A fine not exceeding level 5 on the standard scale.
Discretionary disqualification.
Obligatory endorsement—6 to 8 penalty points

10.16.2 **No test certificate**

Section 47 creates an offence relating to motor vehicles over 3 years old being on a road without a valid test certificate in force, and s 53 creates a similar offences for goods vehicles over 12 months old.

Offences

Motor vehicle

A person who uses on a road at any time, or causes or permits to be so used, a motor vehicle to which this section applies, and as respects which no test certificate has been issued within the appropriate period before that time, is guilty of an offence. **Road Traffic Act 1988, s 47(1)**

Goods vehicle

If any person at any time on or after the relevant date:
(a) uses on a road a goods vehicle of a class required by regulations under s 49 to have been submitted for a goods vehicle test, or
(b) causes or permits to be used on a road a goods vehicle of such a class, and at the time there is no goods vehicle test certificate in force for the vehicle, he is guilty of an offence. **Road Traffic Act 1988, s 53(2)**

Points to prove
s 47(1) offence
- ✓ used/caused to use/permitted to use
- ✓ a motor vehicle
- ✓ on a road
- ✓ without a valid test certificate
- ✓ date of registration/manufacture of the motor vehicle

s 53(2) offence
- ✓ used/caused to use/permitted to use
- ✓ a goods vehicle
- ✓ on a road
- ✓ without a valid goods vehicle test certificate
- ✓ date of registration/manufacture of the goods vehicle

10.16.2 No Test Certificate

Meaning

Uses (see 10.16.1)

Road (see 10.1.1)

Causes (see 10.14.1)

Permits (see 10.14.1)

Motor vehicle (see 10.1.3)

Appropriate period

Means a period of 12 months or shorter as may be prescribed.

Related cases

Plumbien v Vines [1996] Crim LR 124, QBD A vehicle that has been left on a road for several months and its condition deteriorated so that it could not be moved is still at the disposal of the owner should he wish to use it. Such a vehicle still requires a test certificate for its use.

Explanatory notes

Motor vehicles

- **This section applies to** motor vehicles (not being goods vehicles) which have been registered under the Vehicles Excise and Registration Act 1994 for not less than three years or were manufactured at least three years ago and have been used on roads (whether in Great Britain or elsewhere) before being so registered.
- A motor vehicle used to carry passengers and having more than 8 seats excluding the driver's seat, a taxi licensed to ply for hire or an **ambulance**, is required to be submitted for an annual test from the first anniversary of its registration of manufacture.
- 'Ambulance' means a motor vehicle that is constructed or adapted, and primarily used, for the carriage of persons to a place where they will receive, or from a place where they have received, medical or dental treatment, and which, by reason of design, marking, or equipment is readily identifiable as a vehicle so constructed or adapted.

Goods vehicles

- Heavy motor cars, motor cars constructed or adapted to form part of an articulated vehicle, other heavy motor cars that exceed 3,500 kg design weight, semi-trailers, converter dollies manufactured on or after 1.1.1979 and trailers exceeding 1020 kg unladen weight **all require a goods vehicle test certificate**.
- All vehicles requiring a goods vehicle test certificate must be submitted for their first test, in the case of a motor vehicle, before the last day of the calendar month in which falls the first anniversary of its date of registration, and in relation to trailers, before the last day of the calendar month in which falls the first anniversary of the date on which it was first sold or supplied by retail.

Practical considerations

- It is an offence to fail to produce (if required) the test certificate, plating certificate, or goods vehicle test certificate (see **10.16.4**).
- Goods vehicles are required to be submitted for a goods vehicles test under s 49.
- The date of manufacture is taken to be the last day of the year in which its final assembly is completed.
- Consider issuing a traffic fixed penalty notice for a s 47 offence (see **10.4**).
- A traffic fixed penalty notice cannot be issued for a s 53 offence.
- It is an offence to fail to produce a test certificate (see **10.16.4**).

 Summary   6 months

  s 47(1) offence
A fine not exceeding level 3 on the standard scale.
Level 4 if vehicle adapted to carry more than 8 passengers.

s 53(2) offence
A fine not exceeding level 4 on the standard scale.

10.16.3 **Fail to produce driving licence, counterpart, motorcycle training certificate**

Section 164 empowers a constable or vehicle examiner to require production of a driving licence and its counterpart and a certificate of completion of a motorcycle course.

Offences

If a person **required** under the preceding provisions of this section **to produce** a licence and its counterpart or state his date of birth or to produce his certificate of completion of a training course for motorcyclists fails to do so he is, subject to subsections (7) to (8A) [*defences*], guilty of an offence.
Road Traffic Act 1988, s 164(6)

Points to prove
✓ when required by a constable/vehicle examiner under s 164
✓ failed to state date of birth or produce driving licence/ counterpart/motorcycle training certificate

10.16.3 Fail to Produce Driving Licence

Meanings

Required to produce [s 164(1)]

Any of the following persons:

(a) driving a motor vehicle on a road,

(b) whom a police constable or vehicle examiner has reasonable cause
    to believe to have been the driver of a motor vehicle at a time
    when an accident occurred owing to its presence on a road,

(c) whom a constable or vehicle examiner has reasonable cause to
    believe to have committed an offence in relation to the use of a
    motor vehicle on a road, or

(d) a person:

   (i) who supervises the holder of a provisional licence while the
       holder is driving a motor vehicle on a road, or

   (ii) whom a constable or vehicle examiner has reasonable cause to
        believe was supervising the holder of a provisional licence while
        driving, at a time when an accident occurred owing to the
        presence of the vehicle on a road or at a time when an offence
        is suspected of having been committed by the holder of the
        provisional licence in relation to the use of the vehicle on
        a road,

must, on being so required by a constable or vehicle examiner, produce
his licence and its counterpart for examination, so as to enable the
constable or vehicle examiner to ascertain the name and address of the
holder of the licence, the date of issue, and the authority by which
they were issued.

Required to state date of birth [s 164(2)]

• A person required by a constable under s 164(1) to produce their
  licence must in prescribed circumstances, on being required by the
  constable, state his date of birth.

• The circumstances in which a constable may require a persons date of
  birth are:

   ♦ the person fails to produce their licence for immediate
     examination;

   ♦ the person produces a licence which the constable had reason to
     suspect was not granted to that person, was granted to them in
     error or contains an alteration in particulars;

   ♦ the driver number has been altered, removed, or defaced; or

   ♦ the person is as specified in s 164(1)(d) and the constable suspects
     that s/he is under 21 years old.

Provisional licence (see **10.14**)

Explanatory notes

Other preceding provisions of the offence under s 164(6) in failing to
produce a driving licence, its counterpart or certificate of completion of
a training course for motorcyclists are:

• 164(3): Where a licence has been revoked by the Secretary of State, a
  constable may require its production, together with its counterpart,

and, if they are produced, may seize them and deliver them to the Secretary of State.

- 164(4): If a constable reasonably believes that a licence holder, or any other person, has knowingly made a false statement to obtain a licence s/he may require the holder to produce it and its counterpart to them.
- 164(4A): Where a provisional licence is produced by a motorcyclist and a constable reasonably believes that the holder was not riding it as part of an approved training course, the constable may require production of their certificate of completion of a training course for motorcyclists.
- 164(5): If a person has been required to produce their licence and its counterpart to a court and fails to do so, a constable may require them to produce them and, when they are produced, may seize them and deliver to the court.

Defences

(7) Subsection (6) *(offence)* does not apply where a person required on any occasion under the proceeding provisions of this section to produce a licence and its counterpart:

  (a) produces on that occasion a current receipt for the licence and its counterpart issued under s 56 of the Road Traffic Offenders Act 1988 and, if required to do so, produces the licence and its counterpart in person immediately on their return at a police station that was specified on that occasion, or

  (b) within 7 days after that occasion produces such a receipt in person at a police station that was specified by him on that occasion and, if required to do so, produces the licence and its counterpart in person immediately on their return at a police station.

(8) In proceedings against any person for the offence of failing to produce a licence and its counterpart it shall be a defence for him to show that:

  (a) within 7 days after the production of his licence and its counterpart was required he produced them in person at a police station that was specified by him at the time their production was required, or

  (b) he produced them in person there as soon as was reasonably practicable, or

  (c) it was not reasonably practicable for him to produce them there before the day on which the proceedings were commenced.

(8A) Subsection (8) above shall apply in relation to a certificate of completion of a training course for motorcyclists as it applies in relation to a licence.

Road Traffic Act 1988, s 164(7), (8), (8A)

Practical considerations

- A Photocard Driving Licence consists of a credit card style licence showing an image of the holder and their signature and issued with this licence is a paper Counterpart Driving Licence which gives details of the categories of vehicles a person can drive, their entitlement history and any endorsements together with name and address and image of signature. **BOTH** parts **must** be produced. It will be an offence under s 164(6) if only one part is produced.

• In certain circumstances a reference to a constable in s 164(1) and (2) includes a reference to a traffic warden.

 Summary   6 months

 A fine not exceeding level 3 on the standard scale.

10.16.4 Fail to produce insurance, test certificate, plating certificate, or goods vehicle test certificate

Section 165 empowers a constable or vehicle examiner to require production of insurance and vehicle test documents.

Requirements
Any of the following persons:
(a) driving a motor vehicle (other than an invalid carriage) on a road, or
(b) whom a constable or vehicle examiner has reasonable cause to believe to have been the driver of a motor vehicle (other than an invalid carriage) at a time when an accident occurred owing to its presence on a road or other public place, or
(c) whom a constable or vehicle examiner has reasonable cause to believe to have committed an offence in relation to the use on a road of a motor vehicle (other than an invalid carriage),

must, on being so required by a constable or vehicle examiner, give his name and address and the name and address of the **owner** of the vehicle and produce the following **documents** for examination.

Road Traffic Act 1988, s 165(1)

Offence
Subject to subsection (4) [defence], a person who fails to comply with a requirement under subsection (1) is guilty of an offence.

Road Traffic Act 1988, s 165(3)

Points to prove
✓ being a person falling under s 165(1)
✓ failed when required by a constable/vehicle examiner

> ✓ to give name and address or name and address of vehicle owner AND/OR
> ✓ produce for inspection a test certificate **or** goods vehicle test certificate **or** certificate of insurance **or** certificate of security

Meanings

Owner

In relation to a vehicle which is the subject of a hiring agreement this includes each party to the agreement.

Documents (s 165(2))

The documents specified in subsection (1) are:

- a relevant certificate of insurance or certificate of security;
- a test certificate where required by s 47; and
- a plating certificate or goods vehicle test certificate where required by s 53.

Explanatory notes

- Under s 165(5) a supervisor of a provisional licence holder must, on being required by a constable/vehicle examiner, give his/her name and address and the name and address of the owner of the vehicle.
- This supervisor's requirement applies when the provisional driver was driving a motor vehicle (except invalid carriage) on a road; or whom a constable/vehicle examiner believes was supervising when an accident occurred owing to presence of that vehicle on a road or suspecting that the provisional licence holder committed an offence by using the vehicle on a road.
- If the supervisor fails to comply with the name and address requirements, then under s 165(6) s/he will commit an offence.

Defences

A person shall not be convicted of an offence under subsection (3) by reason only of failure to produce any certificate or other evidence in proceedings against him for the offence if he shows that:

(a) within 7 days after the date on which the production of the certificate or other evidence was required it was produced at a police station that was specified by him at the time when its production was required, or

(b) it was produced there as soon as was reasonably practicable, or

(c) it was not reasonably practicable for it to be produced there before the day on which the proceedings were commenced,

and for the purposes of this subsection the laying of the information shall be treated as the commencement of the proceedings.

Road Traffic Act 1988, s 165(4)

Practical considerations

- In the above defence, the question of whether a defendant produced documents 'as soon as was reasonably practicable' will be a question of fact for the court to decide in each case.
- In this section a reference to a 'constable' includes, in certain circumstances, a traffic warden.

 Summary   6 months

 A fine not exceeding level 3 on the standard scale

10.16.5 **Seize and remove motor vehicle (no insurance/driving licence)**

Section 165A empowers a constable to seize and remove a motor vehicle, which s/he believes is being used without a driving licence or insurance.

Powers

Seizure

Under s 165A a constable may seize a motor vehicle under this section if when required under:

- s 164, by a constable in uniform to produce their licence and counterpart for examination (see **10.16.3**), a person fails to do so, and the constable reasonably believes that s/he is or was driving without a licence (see **10.14**);
- s 165, by a constable in uniform to produce evidence of insurance, a person fails to do so (see **10.16.4**), and the constable reasonably believes that the vehicle was being driven without such insurance (see **10.16.1**);
- s 163, by a constable in uniform to stop a vehicle, the driver fails to do so (see **10.2.4**), or fails to do so long enough for the constable to make appropriate enquiries, and the constable reasonably believes that s/he is or was driving without a licence or insurance.

Removal

Section 165B(1) allows the Secretary of State to make regulations as to:

- the removal and retention of motor vehicles seized under s 165A; and
- the release or disposal of such motor vehicles.

The Road Traffic Act 1988 (Retention and Disposal of Seized Motor Vehicles) Regulations 2005 specifically provides for the retention, safe keeping, and disposal by the police or persons authorized by them, of vehicles seized under s 165A.

Explanatory notes

- Before seizing the motor vehicle the driver or person appearing to be the driver must be warned of the consequences of failure to immediately produce their driving licence and its counterpart or provide evidence of insurance, whichever is relevant. But the constable is not required to give such a warning if the circumstances make it impracticable to do so.
- If the vehicle fails to stop or drives off and cannot be seized immediately, it may be seized at any time within 24 hours of the original incident.
- In order to seize the vehicle a constable may enter any premises (except a private dwelling house) on which he reasonably believes the vehicle to be. If necessary, reasonable force may be used in the exercise of this power.
- A dwelling house does not include a garage or other structure occupied with the dwelling house or land belonging to it.

Practical considerations

- In this section motor vehicle does not include an invalid carriage.
- A constable must be in uniform and may use reasonable force, if necessary, to exercise these powers.
- The police are under a duty to ensure the retention and safekeeping of a seized vehicle until it is released to the owner or otherwise disposed of under the 2005 Regulations (see 'Removal' above).
- Regulation 4 of the 2005 Regulations states that when the vehicle is seized, a seizure notice shall be given to the driver of the seized vehicle, unless the circumstances make it impracticable to do so. It also gives the procedure to follow in respect of seized vehicles.
- Where practicable a seizure notice must be given to the registered keeper and the owner.

Links to alternative subjects and offences

10.17 Seat Belts

Section 14 of the Road Traffic Act 1988 relates to the wearing of seat belts in motor vehicles by adults, s 15 concerns their use by children, and s 15A provides for safety equipment for children in motor vehicles. All references in the following are to the 1988 Act unless otherwise stated.

10.17.1 Seat belts—adults

Section 14 empowers the Secretary of State to make regulations concerning the wearing of seat belts in motor vehicles by adults, and creates an offence of failing to comply with such regulations.

> ### Offence
> A person who drives or rides in a motor vehicle in contravention of regulations under this section is guilty of an offence; but notwithstanding any enactment or rule of law, no person other than the person actually committing the contravention is guilty of an offence by reason of the contravention.   Road Traffic Act 1988, s 14(3)

Points to prove
- ✓ drove/rode in a motor vehicle
- ✓ contravened regulations made under this section

Meanings

Drives (see **10.1.4**)

Motor vehicle

This is defined by s 185 (see **10.1.3**), **but**, for the purposes of this section, **does not include** a motorcycle (with or without a sidecar).

Regulations

(1) Subject to the following provisions of these regulations, every person—
    (a) driving a motor vehicle; or
    (b) riding in a front or rear seat of a motor vehicle;
    shall wear an adult belt.
(2) Paragraph (1) does not apply to a person under the age of 14 years.
    Motor Vehicles (Wearing of Seat Belts) Regulations 1993, reg 5(1), (2)

Explanatory notes

- Regulation 6(1) gives exemptions to the requirements of reg 5:
    - ◆ a person holding a medical certificate;

- ✦ the driver/passenger in a motor vehicle constructed or adapted for carrying goods, while on a journey which does not exceed 50 metres being used for delivery or collection;
- ✦ the driver of a vehicle performing a manoeuvre including reversing;
- ✦ a qualified driver supervising a provisional licence holder who is performing a manoeuvre including reversing;
- ✦ a driving test examiner conducting a test of competence to drive and wearing a seat belt would endanger the examiner or any other person;
- ✦ a person driving or riding in a vehicle while it is being used for fire and rescue authority or police purposes or for carrying a person in lawful custody;
- ✦ a person driving or riding in a vehicle used for Serious Organised Crime Agency purposes;
- ✦ the driver of a licensed taxi used for seeking hire, or answering a call for hire, or carrying a passenger for hire, or driver of a private hire vehicle used to carry a passenger for hire;
- ✦ a person riding in a vehicle, used on trade plates to investigate or remedy a fault in the vehicle;
- ✦ a disabled person wearing a disabled person's belt; or
- ✦ a person riding in a vehicle taking part in a procession organised by or on behalf of the Crown.
- If the holder of a medical certificate is informed by a constable that s/he may be prosecuted for not wearing a seat belt s/he cannot rely on that exception unless s/he produces the certificate to the constable at the time s/he is so informed, or produces it within 7 days or as soon as practicable after being informed at a police station specified by them, or where it is not so produced it is not reasonably practicable to produce it there before the commencement of proceedings.

Practical considerations

- Consider issuing a traffic fixed penalty notice for this offence (see **10.4**).
- For regulations relating to people under the age of 14 years (see **10.17.2**).
- Regulation 5 above does not apply where there is no adult seat belt available in that part of the vehicle.
- Proceedings are commenced when the information is laid.

TFPN

 Summary   6 months

 A fine not exceeding level 2 on the standard scale.

10.17.2 **Seat belts—children**

Section 15 creates offences concerning the wearing of seat belts by children in motor vehicles.

Offences

(1) Except as provided by regulations, where a child under the age of 14 years is in the **front** of a **motor vehicle**, a person must not without reasonable excuse drive the vehicle on a **road** unless the child is wearing a **seat belt** in conformity with regulations.

(1A) Where—

    (a) a child is in the front of a motor vehicle other than a **bus**,

    (b) the child is in a rear-facing child restraining device, and

    (c) the passenger seat where the child is placed is protected by a front air bag,

a person must not without reasonable excuse drive the vehicle on a road unless the air bag is deactivated.

(2) It is an offence for a person to drive a motor vehicle in contravention of subsection (1) or (1A) above.

(3) Except as provided by regulations, where—

    (a) a child under the age of three years is in the rear of a motor vehicle, or

    (b) a child of or over that age but under the age of fourteen years is in the rear of a motor vehicle and any seat belt is fitted in the rear of that vehicle,

a person must not without reasonable excuse drive the vehicle on a road unless the child is wearing a seat belt in conformity with regulations.

(3A) Except as provided by **regulations**, where:

    (a) a child who is under the age of 12 years and less than 150 cms in height is in the rear of a passenger car,

    (b) no seat belt is fitted in the rear of the **passenger car**, and

    (c) a seat in the front of the passenger car is provided with a seat belt but is not occupied by any person,

a person must not without reasonable excuse drive the passenger car on a road.

(4) It is an offence for a person to drive a motor vehicle in contravention of subsection (3) or (3A) above.   Road Traffic Act 1988, s 15(1)–(4)

Points to prove

s 15(2) offence

✓ without reasonable excuse
✓ drove a motor vehicle
✓ on a road
✓ child under 14 years
✓ in the front of the vehicle

✓ not wearing a seat belt OR
✓ seated in a rear-facing restraining device protected by a front air bag not deactivated

s 15(4) offence

✓ per first four points of s 15(2)
✓ in the rear of the vehicle
✓ a child under the age of 3 years OR of or over the age of 3 years but under the age of 14 years
✓ not wearing a fitted seat belt

or

✓ motor vehicle was a passenger car
✓ child under 12 years and (per regulations) less than 135 cms tall
✓ with no rear seat belt fitted and
✓ a front seat (with belt) was available
✓ with no seat belt fitted in the rear of that vehicle
✓ when an unoccupied seat in the front of the vehicle had a seat belt

Meanings

Motor vehicle

This is defined by s 185 (see **10.1.3**), **but**, for the purposes of subsection (1), does not include a motorcycle (with or without a sidecar).

Road   (see **10.1.1**)

Seat belt

This includes any description of restraining device for a child.

Passenger car

Means a motor vehicle which:
• is constructed or adapted for use for the carriage of passengers and is not a goods vehicle,
• has no more than 8 seats in addition to the driver's seat,
• has four or more wheels,
• has a maximum design speed exceeding 25 kilometres per hour, and
• has a **maximum laden weight** not exceeding 3.5 tonnes.

Bus

Means a motor vehicle that:
• has at least four wheels,
• is constructed or adapted for the carriage of passengers,
• has more than eight seats in addition to the driver's seat, and
• has a maximum design speed exceeding 25 kilometres per hour.

Maximum laden weight

In relation to a vehicle or combination of vehicles means:
• in respect of which a gross weight not to be exceeded in Great Britain is specified in construction and use requirements, **that weight;**

- in respect of which **no such weight is specified** in construction and use requirements, the weight which the vehicle, or combination of vehicles, is designed or adapted not to exceed when in normal use and travelling on a road laden.

Regulations

Seated in front

The Motor Vehicles (Wearing of Seat Belts by Children in Front Seats) Regulations 1993 make provision for the wearing of seat belts and other restraints by children in the front of motor vehicles. Regulation 5 provides a description of belt or restraint to be worn.

Seated in rear

Motor Vehicles (Wearing of Seat Belts) Regulations 1993.

Small child

Is a child under the age of 12 years and under 135 cm in height.

Large child

Is a child who is not a small child.

Explanatory notes

- Subsection (3A)(a) stipulates that, 'Except as provided by regulations', a child is less than 150 cms in height. However, the regulations (see above) have reduced this height to 135 cms.
- The prohibitions in subsections (3), and (3A) of s 15 (rear seats) do not apply to:
  - ♦ a child for whom there is a medical certificate;
  - ♦ a small child aged under 3 years who is riding in a licensed taxi or licensed hire car, if no appropriate seat belt is available for him in the front or rear of the vehicle;
  - ♦ a small child aged 3 years or more who is riding in a licensed taxi, a licensed hire car or a small bus and wearing an adult belt if an appropriate seat belt is not available for him in the front or rear of the vehicle;
  - ♦ a small child aged 3 years or more who is wearing an adult belt and riding in a passenger car or light goods vehicle where the use of child restraints by the child occupants of two seats in the rear of the vehicle prevents the use of an appropriate seat belt for that child and no appropriate seat belt is available for him in the front of the vehicle;
  - ♦ a small child who is riding in a vehicle being used for the purposes of the police, security or emergency services to enable the proper performance of their duty;
  - ♦ a small child aged 3 years or more who is wearing an adult belt and who, because of an unexpected necessity, is travelling a short distance in a passenger car or light goods vehicle in which no appropriate seat belt is available for him; or
  - ♦ a disabled child who is wearing a disabled person's belt or whose disability makes it impracticable to wear a seat belt where a disabled person's belt is unavailable to him.

- The prohibitions in s 15(1) do not apply to:
  + a small child aged 3 years or more who is riding in a bus and is wearing an adult belt if an appropriate seat belt is not available for him in the front or rear of the vehicle;
  + a child for whom there is a medical certificate;
  + a disabled child who is wearing a disabled person's belt;
  + to a child riding in a bus which—is being used to provide a local service in a built-up area, or which is constructed/adapted for the carriage of standing passengers and on which the operator permits standing or
  + does not apply to a large child if no appropriate seat belt is available for him in the front of the vehicle.
- The prohibition in s 15(3A) does not apply to a child if no appropriate seat belt is available for them in the front of the vehicle.
- The driver of a motor vehicle has the same opportunity to produce a medical certificate relating to a child travelling in the vehicle without wearing a seat belt as an adult (see **10.17.1**).

Practical considerations

- Consider issuing a traffic fixed penalty notice for this offence (see **10.4**).
- The seat belt must be appropriate for a child of a particular weight and height travelling in a particular vehicle.
- A seat is regarded as provided with child restraint if the child restraint is:
  + fixed in such a position that it can be worn by an occupier of that seat, or
  + elsewhere in or on the vehicle but—could readily be fixed in such a position without the aid of tools, and is not being worn by a child for whom it is appropriate and who is occupying another seat.
- For the purposes of these regulations, a seat belt is considered appropriate:
  + in relation to a **small child**, if it is a child restraint of a description prescribed for a child of his height and weight by reg 5;
  + in relation to a large child, if it is a child restraint of a description prescribed for a child of his height and weight by reg 5 or an adult belt; or
  + in relation to a person aged 14 years or more, if it is an adult belt.
- In relation to ages and height, subject to exceptions/requirements:
  + Under 3 must travel in front or rear in an appropriate baby/child seat
    - EU approved and selected according to weight
    - Rear facing baby seats must not be used in front seat unless the air bag has been de-activated.
  + Aged 3—11 (and under 135 cms) in rear using appropriate child seat, booster seat or booster cushion
  + Aged 12—13 (over 135 cm) front or rear using adult seat belt
  + Aged 14 and over adult regulations apply (see **10.17.1**).

10.17.2 Seat Belts—Children

 Summary 6 months

s 15(2) offence
A fine not exceeding level 2 on the standard scale.

s 15(4) offence
A fine not exceeding level 1 on the standard scale.

Links to alternative subjects and offences

10.18 Motor Cycle—No Crash Helmet/Eye protectors

Section 16 of the Road Traffic Act 1988 empowers the Secretary of State to make regulations concerning the wearing of crash helmets by motorcyclists and creates an offence of contravening any such regulations. All references in the following are to the 1988 Act unless otherwise stated.

Offence

A person who drives or rides on a motor cycle in contravention of regulations under this section is guilty of an offence; but not withstanding any enactment or rule of law no person other than the person actually committing the contravention is guilty of an offence by reason of the contravention unless the person actually committing the contravention is a child under the age of 16 years.   Road Traffic Act 1988, s 16(4)

Points to prove

✓ drove/rode on motor cycle
✓ contravened regulations under s 16

Meanings

Drives (see **10.1.4**)

Motor cycle

Means a **mechanically propelled vehicle**, not being an invalid carriage, having less than 4 wheels and the weight of which unladen does not exceed 410 kg.

Mechanically propelled vehicle (see **10.1.3**)

Regulations

Every person driving or riding (otherwise than in a side-car) on a motor bicycle when on a **road** shall wear protective headgear (Motor Cycles (Protective Helmets) Regulations 1998, reg 4).

Road (see **10.1.1**)

Explanatory notes

- This section does not include people riding in a side-car or to the follower of the Sikh religion while he is wearing a turban.
- A British/EU standards mark must be on the helmet.
- Regulation 4 does not apply if the person is on a motor bicycle, which is a mowing machine or is being propelled by a person on foot (eg walking).

10.18 Motor Cycle—No Crash Helmet/Eye protectors

- If the vehicle is being propelled by 'scooter' style (eg the rider sat astride the machine and propelling it by pushing on the ground with his/her foot/feet) then a helmet should be worn.
- 'Motor bicycle' means a 2-wheeled motor cycle, whether or not having a side-car attached, and for the purposes of this definition where the distance measured between the centre of the area of contact with the road surface of any 2 wheels of a motor cycle is less than 460 millimetres, those wheels are counted as one wheel.
- *Eye Protectors offence*—Regulation 4 of the Motor Cycles (Eye Protectors) Regulations 1999 creates a further offence of not wearing approved eye protectors. It states that each person driving or riding (otherwise than in a side-car) on a motor bicycle is required to wear eye protectors of a prescribed type.

Related cases

DPP v Parker [2005] RTR 1616, QBD If a motor cycle is fitted with enhanced safety features (eg a roof) that does not negate the requirement to wear protective headgear.

Practical considerations

- Consider issuing a traffic fixed penalty notice for this offence (see **10.4**).
- Any helmet worn must be securely fastened using straps or other means of fastening provided.
- If the helmet has a chin cup it must have an additional strap to fit under the jaw.

 Summary

 6 months

A fine not exceeding level 2 on the standard scale.

Links to alternative subjects and offences

    (a) that each of the requirements of subsection (4) above had been complied with; or

    (b) that the commission of any offence under that subsection was due to the act or default of another person and that he took all reasonable precautions and exercised all due diligence to avoid the commission of such an offence by himself or any person under his control.

Highways Act 1980, s 139(6)— (9)

Practical considerations

- Where a person commits an offence under this section because of an act or default of another person, that other person is guilty of the offence, and may be charged with and convicted of the offence whether or not proceedings are taken against the first-mentioned person.
- The requirement for a skip to be moved must be made face to face (*R v Worthing Justices, ex parte Waste Management Ltd* (1988) 152 JP 362, DC).

CSO

 Summary   6 months

 A fine not exceeding level 3 on the standard scale.

10.22.4 Cause injury/danger/annoyance on the highway

Section 161 of the Highways Act 1980 creates various offences that relate to causing danger on a highway, including annoyance by playing games on the highway.

Offences

(1) If a person, without lawful authority or excuse, deposits any thing whatsoever on a highway in consequence of which a user of the highway is injured or endangered, that person is guilty of an offence.

(2) [See 8.7.5 and 8.8.6]

(3) If a person plays at football or any other game on a highway to the annoyance of a user of the highway he is guilty of an offence.

10.22.4 Cause Injury/Danger/Annoyance on the Highway

> (4) If a person, without lawful authority or excuse, allows any filth, dirt, lime or other offensive matter or thing to run or flow on to a highway from any adjoining premises, he is guilty of an offence.
>
> Highways Act 1980, s 161

Points to prove

s 161 (1) offence

- ✓ without lawful authority/excuse
- ✓ deposits any thing whatsoever on a highway
- ✓ thus injuring/endangering user of the highway

s 161 (3) offence

- ✓ played football/a game on a highway
- ✓ thus annoying a user of the highway

s 161 (4) offence

- ✓ without lawful authority/excuse
- ✓ allowed any filth, dirt, lime or other offensive matter or thing
- ✓ to run or flow on to a highway
- ✓ from any adjoining premises

Meanings (see 8.8.6)

Explanatory notes

- The s 161(2) offences relates to lighting any fire on/over a highway or discharging any firearm or firework within 50 feet of the centre of a highway and are dealt with in 8.7.5 and 8.8.6.
- Section 161A creates another offence of lighting a fire on any land (not part of a highway/carriageway) and as a result the user of any highway is injured, interrupted or endangered by smoke from that fire.
- If a any rope, wire or other apparatus is placed across a highway so as to cause danger to users of the highway, this is an offence under s 162, unless adequate warning has been given of this danger.
- The s 161(3) offence is very wide and covers all types of 'game'. For example, a mock hunt with a man dressed as a stag being chased by people in fancy dress and with trumpets has been held to be a game (*Pappin v Maynard* (1863) 27 JP 745).

 Summary   6 months

 s 161(1) offence
A fine not exceeding level 3 on the standard scale.

s 161(3) & (4) offences
A fine not exceeding level 1 on the standard scale.

   CSO   Offences where CSO can use their powers

10.22.5 **Unnecessary obstruction**

Regulation 103 of the Road Vehicles (Construction and Use) Regulations 1986 creates an offence of causing an unnecessary obstruction.

Offence

No person in charge of a motor vehicle or trailer shall cause or permit the vehicle to stand on a road so as to cause any unnecessary obstruction of the road.   Road Vehicles (Construction and Use) Regulations 1986, reg 103

Points to prove

✓ being a person in charge of a motor vehicle/trailer
✓ caused/permitted it
✓ to stand on a road
✓ so as to cause an unnecessary obstruction on that road

Meanings

Motor vehicle

Means a mechanically propelled vehicle intended or adapted for use on roads.

Trailer

Means a vehicle drawn by a motor vehicle, but does not apply to any part of an articulated bus.

Explanatory notes

- A motor vehicle left on a road for an unreasonable time may be unreasonable obstruction.
- An important factor for consideration is the use to which the highway was being put by the vehicle causing the obstruction. The highway is intended as a means of transit, not a store (*Nelmes v Rhys Howells Transport Ltd* [1977] RTR 266).
- It has been held that where a motorist parks his/her vehicle on one side of the road and the subsequent parking of vehicles on the opposite side of the road causes an obstruction, no offence under this regulation was committed by the parking of the original vehicle (*Langham v Crisp* [1975] Crim LR 652).

Related cases

Carey v Chief Constable of Avon and Somerset [1995] RTR 405, CA
The purpose of the Removal and Disposal of Vehicles Regulations 1986 is to clear the road of an 'obstruction' as a matter of urgency even if no-one is really at fault. They do not apply to s 137 of the Highways Act 1980 and reg 107 of the Road Vehicles (Construction and Use) Regulations 1986 which relates to obstruction of the highway without a lawful excuse and constitutes an unreasonable use of the highway.

10.22.5 Unnecessary Obstruction

Practical considerations
- Consider the fixed penalty scheme.
- 'Road' includes footpath.

 Summary ⏱ 6 months

🏛 A fine not exceeding level 4 on the standard scale if goods vehicle or a vehicle adapted to carry more than 8 passengers. A fine not exceeding level 3 on the standard scale in any other case.

Links to alternative subjects and offences

10.23 **Off-Road Driving**

Section 34 of the Road Traffic Act 1988 prohibits the driving of motor vehicles elsewhere than on a road. All references are to the Road Traffic Act 1988 unless otherwise stated.

Offences

Subject to the provisions of this section, if without lawful authority a person drives a mechanically propelled vehicle:

(a) on to or upon any common land, moorland or land of any other description, not being land forming part of a road, or

(b) on any road being a footpath, bridleway or restricted byway,

he is guilty of an offence.   Road Traffic Act 1988, s 34(1)

Points to prove

✓ without lawful authority
✓ drove a mechanically propelled vehicle
✓ on to/upon
✓ common land/moorland/land
✓ not being land forming part of a road

or

✓ without lawful authority
✓ drove a mechanically propelled vehicle
✓ on a road
✓ being a footpath/bridleway/restricted byway

Meanings

Mechanically propelled vehicle

Does not include a pedestrian controlled vehicle, a pedestrian controlled mowing machine or an electrically assisted pedal cycle.

Common land

Defined in s 22 of the Commons Registration Act 1965:

(a) land subject to '**rights of common**' whether those rights are exercisable at all times or only during limited periods; and

(b) waste land of a manor not subject to 'rights of common'.

Rights of common includes:

- rights of sole or several vesture or herbage (rights to take vegetation or flowers from the land);
- rights of sole or several pasture (allowing animals to be put out to pasture on the land);
- cattlegates and beastgates (a particular right, mainly existing in northern England, to graze an animal on common land).

They do not include rights held for a term of years or from year to year.

Driving/Road   (see 10.1.1)

Footpath

Means a highway over which the public have a right of way on foot only, not being a footway.

Bridleway

Means a way over which the public have the following, but no other, rights of way: a right of way on foot and a right of way on horseback or leading a horse, with or without a right to drive animals of any description along the way.

Restricted byway

Means a way over which the public have restricted byway rights within the meaning of pt II of the Countryside and Rights of Way Act 2000, with or without a right to drive animals of any description along the way, but no other rights of way.

Explanatory notes

- A way shown in a definitive map and statement as a footpath, bridleway, or restricted byway is to be taken to be a way of the kind shown, unless the contrary is shown.
- Nothing in this section affects the law of trespass to land or any right or remedy to which a person may be entitled by law in respect of such trespass.
- For police powers concerning the stopping, seizure, and removal of a motor vehicle that is used in contravention of s 34, which is causing, or is likely to cause, alarm, distress, or annoyance to members of the public see s 59 of the Police Reform Act 2000 (see **7.14**).

Defences

(3) It is not an offence under this section to drive a mechanically propelled vehicle on land within 15 yards of a road, being a road on which a motor vehicle may legally be driven, for the purpose only of parking the vehicle on that land.

(4) A person shall not be convicted of an offence under this section with respect to a vehicle if he proves to the satisfaction of the court that it was driven in contravention of this section for the purpose of saving life or extinguishing fire or meeting any other like emergency.

Road Traffic Act 1988, s 34(3), (4)

Practical considerations

- Consider issuing a traffic fixed penalty notice (see **10.4**).
- A power of entry to premises to exercise the powers of seizure and removal of the motor vehicle is granted by s 59 of the Police Reform Act 2000 (see **7.14**).
- Reasonable force may be used, if necessary, to stop, seize, or remove the motor vehicle, or of the power of entry under s 59 of the Police Reform Act 2000 (see **7.14**).

Summary   6 months

 A fine not exceeding level 3 on the standard scale.

Links to alternative subjects and offences

Chapter 11

General: Patrol

11.1 Community Support Officers (CSOs)

Section 38 of the Police Reform Act 2002 enables the chief officer of police to designate suitably skilled and trained civilians under his or her direction and control as community support officers and to exercise powers and undertake duties as described in Sch 4 to the Police Reform Act 2002.

In order to implement any of the powers, the CSO **must** be suitably designated with them by the chief officer. The chief officer can grant some or all of the powers described with certain limitations or restrictions. The powers may also be limited to a certain area or for a certain period. Many police forces now refer to CSOs as PCSOs (police community support officers), in compliance with ACPO guidelines.

11.1.1 General powers

Enter premises
- Where a power allows for the use of reasonable force when exercised by a constable, a CSO has the same entitlement to use reasonable force when exercising a designated power.
- If a CSO has been granted the power to force entry to premises, **it will be limited** to when he or she is both under the direct supervision of a constable and accompanied by them.
- The only exception to this requirement is when the purpose of forcing entry is to save life or limb or to prevent serious damage to premises.

Entry to save life or limb or prevent serious damage to property
A CSO will have the powers of a constable under the 1984 Police and Criminal Evidence Act, s 17 (see **12.3**), to enter and search any premises in the relevant police area for the purpose of saving life or limb or preventing serious damage to property.

Reasonable force

Where a CSO has a power to detain they can use reasonable force in respect of:

- relevant penalty notice offences;
- relevant licensing offences; (note the licensing exceptions to detention—see **11.1.2**)
- anti-social behaviour;
- searches for alcohol/tobacco;
- dispersal of groups;
- removal of child to their place of residence under s 15(3) Crime and Disorder Act 1998 (contravention of a curfew notice);
- preventing the person making off when subject to a requirement to provide name and address or accompanying CSO to the police station;
- power to remove truants and return them to school or designated premises.

Issue penalty notices

Fixed penalty notices

A CSO can issue **fixed penalty notices** for cycle riding on a footway, litter offences, failure to attend school, graffiti, fly-posting, and offences under dog control orders.

Penalty notices for disorder

In addition, **penalty notices for disorder** can be issued in respect of a range of anti-social behaviour and disorder offences under the Criminal Justice and Police Act 2001 (**except** the **theft and litter** listed offences). These offences are shown in the Penalty Notices for Disorder part of this book (see **7.1**).

Require name and address

- A CSO can be given this power without also being given the power to detain.
- A CSO can require the name and address of a person who has committed the following offence:
  - ✦ **relevant offence** in the relevant police area; or
  - ✦ **relevant licensing offence** within or outside of the **relevant police area**.
- A CSO may enforce a relevant by-law only within the place to which the by-law relates. Where a CSO has this power he or she also has the power of a constable under a relevant by-law to remove a person from a place.
- Failure to provide name and address is itself an offence.

Detain a person

- CSO can only be given the power to detain a person if they have also been given the power to request the person's name and address (but note the licensing exceptions to detention—see **11.1.2**)

- Where there is non-compliance with the request, or CSOs have reason to believe the information is false or inaccurate, they can require the other person to wait with them for up to 30 minutes, pending the arrival of constable.
- The individual may choose, if asked, to accompany the CSO to a police station rather than wait.
- A refusal of the requirement to wait or making off while subject to a requirement pending the arrival of a constable; or making off while accompanying the CSO to the police station, is an offence.
- See also **Reasonable force** (above).

Search, seize, and retain

- CSOs have a limited power to search a detained person for any item that could be used to injure themselves or others if the CSO believes the person could be dangerous.
- A CSO also has a power to search a detained person for anything that could be used to assist escape.
- The CSO must comply with the instructions of a constable about what to do with any seized item and inform the person from whom it has been seized about where s/he can make inquiries about it.

Meanings

Relevant offence

This means:

- a relevant fixed penalty offence (see **7.1**);
- contravention of a dispersal direction under the Anti-Social Behaviour Act 2003;
- an offence that appears to have caused alarm, injury, or distress to any other person or loss of or damage to any other person's property;
- an offence under the Parks Regulation Act 1872 (contravention of park regulations/assaulting park-keeper);
- begging (Vagrancy Act 1824, s 3);
- where a person has been convicted of begging and sleeps in certain unoccupied premises or in the open air without being able to give a valid reason for doing so;
- showing wounds or deformities to aid begging and to collect money for charitable purposes under false pretence (Vagrancy Act 1824, s 4);
- an offence under a relevant by-law.

Relevant licensing offences (see licensing **11.1.2**)

Relevant police area (see licensing **11.1.2**)

11.1.2 **Powers relating to licensing/alcohol**

Entry to investigate licensing offences

- CSOs have a limited power to enter and search licensed premises, other than clubs, under s 180 of the Licensing Act 2003 if they believe that one of the licensing offences has been, or is being committed. These are:

♦ the sale or attempted sale of alcohol to a person who is drunk;
♦ allowing alcohol to be sold to drunken person;
♦ obtaining alcohol for a person who is drunk;
♦ sale of alcohol to children (under 18);
♦ purchase or attempted purchase of alcohol by a child (under 18);
♦ purchase or attempted purchase of alcohol on behalf of an individual aged under 18;
♦ purchase or attempted of alcohol for consumption on relevant premises by an individual aged under 18;
♦ knowingly consuming alcohol on relevant premises by a person under 18;
♦ knowingly allowing the consumption of alcohol on relevant premises by an individual aged under 18;
♦ knowingly sending an individual aged under 18 to obtain alcohol.

• These licensing offences are all connected with the sale and consumption of alcohol by and to young people and persons who are already drunk.
• CSOs can enter any premises, other than clubs, for the purposes of investigating a relevant licensing offence with a constable.
• CSOs can only enter premises alone where they reasonably believe that a premises licence (a licence that permits premises to sell alcohol) authorizes the sale of alcohol for consumption off the premises.
• This limited power of entry and search adds to a CSO's powers to deal with alcohol-related anti-social behaviour and those that supply alcohol to young people.

Power to require name and address

• A CSO can require the name and address of a person who has committed a **relevant licensing offence** within or outside of the **relevant police area**.
• Failure to provide name and address is itself an offence.
• A CSO will have the power to require the person's name and address but the power to detain does **not** apply for the licensing offences in relation to the sale of alcohol to a drunk, sale to an under 18-year-old, and knowingly allowing the sale of alcohol to an under 18-year-old, if the offence is believed to have been committed on relevant licensed premises.
• CSOs may exercise their name and address powers in relation to a relevant licensing offence in any police area. Powers to enter and search premises in relation to a relevant licensing offence are restricted to the relevant police area in the company and under the supervision of a constable **unless** the CSO has reason to believe the premises are off licence premises.

Meanings

Relevant licensing offences

CSOs have limited power where they have reason to believe that a person on licensed premises has committed a ' **relevant licensing offence**' defined as follows:

- the sale or attempted sale of alcohol to a person who is drunk (see **9.2**);
- allowing alcohol to be sold to drunken person (see **9.2**);
- obtaining alcohol for a person who is drunk (see **9.2**);
- sale of alcohol to children (under 18) (see **9.1**);
- purchase or attempted purchase of alcohol by a child under 18 (see **9.1**);
- purchase or attempted purchase of alcohol on behalf of an individual aged under 18 (see **9.1**);
- purchase or attempted purchase of alcohol for consumption on relevant premises by an individual aged under 18 (see **9.1**);
- knowingly consuming alcohol on relevant premises by a person under 18 (see **9.1**);
- knowingly allowing the consumption of alcohol on relevant premises by an individual aged under 18 (see **9.1**);
- knowingly sending an individual aged under 18 to obtain alcohol sold or to be sold on relevant premises by children (under 18) (see **9.1**).

Relevant police area

This is the police area in which a CSO's powers apply.

Power to serve closure notice

Where the offence of persistently selling alcohol to children under 18 has been committed on licensed premises (see **9.1.3**) then a CSO can enter those premises to serve a closure notice on a responsible person during licensing hours (see **9.3.4**).

Alcohol consumption in designated public places

- A CSO has the powers of a constable under s 12 of the Criminal Justice and Police Act 2001 (see **9.4**) to:
    - ◆ require a person to cease drinking alcohol (or anything reasonably believed to be alcohol) in a designated public place, and
    - ◆ to confiscate and dispose of the alcohol and its container.
- Seizure can apply to both sealed and unsealed containers.
- The person **must** be informed that failure to comply with the CSO's request, without reasonable excuse, is an offence.

Confiscation of alcohol—young persons

- A CSO has the same powers (except for the arrest power) as a constable under s 1 of the Confiscation of Alcohol (Young Persons) Act 1997 (see **9.5**).
- A CSO can confiscate and dispose of the alcohol and its container.
- Seizure can apply to both sealed and unsealed containers.

- The person **must** be informed that failure to comply with the CSO's request, without reasonable excuse, is an offence.

Search and seizure powers—alcohol

- In association with the power to confiscate alcohol, CSOs have the power to search the person if they reasonably believe the person has either alcohol or its container in their possession.
- The search is limited to what is reasonably required for the purpose and does not authorize the CSO to require a person to remove any of their clothing in public other than an outer coat, jacket, or gloves.
- A person who refuses to be searched can be required to give their name and address.
- If a person refuses to give their name and address, or gives an answer that a CSO has reasonable grounds for suspecting to be false or inaccurate, CSOs can then invoke their detention powers.

11.1.3 **Powers relating to tobacco**

Confiscation of tobacco

- CSOs have the power of a constable or a uniformed park-keeper under s 7(3) of the Children and Young Persons Act 1933 to: 'seize tobacco or cigarette papers from any person who appears to be under 16 years old who they find smoking in any street or public place.'
- The CSO may then dispose of any seized material in such manner as the relevant police authority provides.

Search and seizure powers: tobacco

- In association with the power to confiscate tobacco, CSOs have the power to search the person if they reasonably believe the person has either tobacco or cigarette papers in their possession.
- The search is limited to what is reasonably required for the purpose and does not authorize the CSO to require a person to remove any of their clothing in public other than an outer coat, jacket, or gloves.
- A person who refuses to be searched can be required to give their name and address.
- If a person refuses to give their name and address, or gives an answer that a CSO has reasonable grounds for suspecting to be false or inaccurate, CSOs can then invoke their detention powers.

11.1.4 **Powers relating to drugs**

Seize and detain controlled drugs

- A CSO can seize and retain controlled drugs when found in a person's unlawful possession.

- A CSO must comply with a constable's instructions about what to do with any controlled drugs seized.
- If a person maintains that he or she is lawfully in possession of the controlled drug then the CSO must inform the person about where inquiries can be made about its recovery.
- If a CSO finds a controlled drug in a person's unlawful possession or reasonably believes that a person is in unlawful possession of a controlled drug then the CSO may require the person's name and address.
- If a person refuses to give their name and address, or gives an answer that a CSO has reasonable grounds for suspecting to be false or inaccurate, the CSO can then invoke their detention powers.

11.1.5 **Powers relating to truancy and curfews**

Children— curfew notices

- CSOs have the power of a constable where they have reasonable cause to believe that a child (under 16) is in contravention of a ban imposed by a curfew notice and they should, as soon as reasonably practicable, inform the local authority for the area that the child has contravened the ban.
- The CSO may remove the child to the child's place of residence unless they have reasonable cause to believe that the child would, if removed to that place, be likely to suffer significant harm.

Children/young persons—truancy

- CSOs have the power of a constable, to remove a child or young person to designated premises, or to the school from which they are absent, if they have reasonable cause to believe that the child or young person found by the CSO in a public place in a specified area during a specified period—
  + is of compulsory school age; AND
  + is absent from a school without lawful authority.
- 'Designated premises' are those premises notified to the police by the relevant Local Authority
- 'Specified area' and 'specified time' are to be determined by a police officer of at least the rank of superintendent.

11.1.6 **Powers relating to traffic matters**

Power to require name and address

- A CSO has powers to direct traffic and to require the name and address of a person who fails to comply with these directions.

- The powers are based on those of constables under ss 35 and 37 of the Road Traffic Act 1988 (see **10.2**) and allows CSOs to direct a person driving a vehicle to stop or follow a line of traffic and to direct pedestrians and traffic for the purposes of conducting a traffic survey.
- A CSO can require a driver or pedestrian to give their name and address for failure to follow the directions of a CSO or a police officer.
- If a person refuses to give their name and address, or gives an answer that a CSO has reasonable grounds for suspecting to be false or inaccurate, then CSOs can invoke their detention powers.
- CSOs can only exercise these traffic powers within their own police force area.

Vehicles causing obstruction/danger

A CSO has the same powers as a constable in uniform, within the relevant police area, under s 99 of the Road Traffic Regulation Act 1984— to require the removal of vehicles that are causing an obstruction or likely to cause a danger to other road users or are parked in contravention of a prohibition or restriction.

Power to stop vehicles for testing

- A CSO has the same powers of a constable in uniform, within the relevant police area, to stop a vehicle under s 67(3) of the Road Traffic Act 1988 (see **10.2**), for the purposes of a test under sub-s (1) of that section.
- These powers would enable CSOs to help agencies such as the Vehicle Inspectorate, the Vehicle and Operator Services Agency (VOSA), and local authorities to conduct roadworthiness and emissions tests and also to facilitate the escorting of abnormal loads.

Power to control traffic

- CSOs have the power to control traffic for the purposes of escorting a load of exceptional dimensions (either to or from the relevant police area).
- A CSO can also direct traffic in other situations, based on the powers constables have under s 35 and s 37 of the Road Traffic Act 1988 (see **10.2**).
- This will allow CSOs to direct a person driving a vehicle to stop or follow a line of traffic and to direct pedestrians.
- CSOs have the power to direct traffic for the purposes of conducting a traffic survey.
- A CSO can require a driver or pedestrian to give their name and address for failure to follow the directions of a CSO or a police officer.
- If a person refuses to give their name and address, or gives an answer that a CSO has reasonable grounds for suspecting to be false or inaccurate, then the CSOs can invoke their detention powers.
- CSOs can only exercise these traffic powers within their own police force area (except for escorting a load of exceptional dimensions).
- These powers will enable community support officers to assist with traffic management at public events, road traffic accidents, and other incidents where traffic diversions are necessary.

Power to stop cycles

CSOs have the power to stop cyclists riding on the pavement and to issue a fixed penalty notice. The power to issue a fixed penalty notice also applies where the CSO believes that the offence of riding on the pavement has been committed.

Carrying out of road checks

- A CSO has the power of a police officer to carry out an authorized road check under s 4 of PACE 1984 (see **10.2** for details). This enables a road check (authorized by a Police Superintendent or above) to be established for the purposes of ascertaining:
  - ◆ whether a vehicle is carrying a person who has committed an offence (other than a road traffic offence or a vehicle excise offence);
  - ◆ a person who is witness to such an offence;
  - ◆ a person intending to commit such an offence;
  - ◆ or a person who is unlawfully at large.
- It also includes the powers of a constable conferred under s 163 of the Road Traffic Act 1984 (see **10.2**) to enable him to require a vehicle to stop for the purpose of a road check.

Power to place traffic signs

- A CSO has the same power as a constable (under s 67 of the Road Traffic Regulation Act 1984) (see **10.3** for details) to place temporary traffic signs on a road in extraordinary circumstances.
- A driver who fails to comply with a traffic sign placed by a CSO commits an offence.
- This power helps CSO provide assistance with road traffic accidents and other road incidents.

Seizure of vehicles used to cause alarm

- A CSO has the powers of a constable under s 59 of the Police Reform Act 2002 (see **7.14**) regarding vehicles used in a manner causing alarm, distress, or annoyance.
- These include powers to stop and to seize and to remove motor vehicles where they are being driven:
  - ◆ off-road, contrary to s 34 of the Road Traffic Act 1988 (see **10.23**); or
  - ◆ on the public road or other public place without due care and attention or reasonable consideration for other road users, contrary to s 3 of the 1988 Act (see **10.6**)
- A police officer may enter premises, other than a private dwelling house, for the purpose of exercising these powers. However, the powers, in so far as they include power to enter premises, **are only exercisable by a CSO** when in the company of and under the supervision of a constable.
- It is an offence for a person to fail to stop a vehicle when required to do so by a police officer (or a CSO) acting in accordance with this section.

- The officer (or CSO) must warn the person before seizing the vehicle, to enable its anti-social use to be stopped. But the requirement to give prior warning does not apply where it is impracticable to do so or where a warning has previously been given.

11.1.7 **Power relating to anti-social behaviour**

Require name and address

- A CSO has the powers of a constable under s 50 of the Police Reform Act 2002 as to require the name and address of a person who is, or is believed to have been, acting in an anti-social manner (as defined in s 1 of the Crime and Disorder Act 1998), namely: 'in a manner that caused or was likely to cause harassment, alarm or distress to one or more persons not of the same household as himself.'
- A CSO can then invoke the power of detention in relation to a person who fails to comply with the requirement or appears to have given a false or inaccurate name or address.

11.1.8 **Power relating to terrorism**

Cordon areas

- A CSO has all the powers of a constable in uniform under s 36 of the Terrorism Act 2000, in respect of a cordoned areas established under the Act.
- This includes the power to give orders, make arrangements, or impose prohibitions or restrictions.

Stop and search vehicles in authorized areas

- A CSO has the powers of a constable under s 44 and s 45 of the Terrorism Act 2000 to:
  - ◆ stop and search vehicles;
  - ◆ search anything in or on a vehicle or carried by the driver or by any passenger in that vehicle;
  - ◆ search anything carried by a pedestrian;
  - ◆ seize and retain any article discovered in the course of a search by them or a constable under these provisions.
- **However**, the powers cannot be exercised by CSOs unless they are in the company of and under the supervision of a constable.

11.1.9 **Power relating to illegal trading**

Park trading offences

- Where a CSO reasonably suspects a person to have committed illegal trading in a Royal Park (or other specified place) and has required a person to await the arrival of a constable, the CSO may take possession of anything of a non-perishable nature that the person has under their control and the CSO reasonably believes to have been used in the commission of the offence.
- A CSO can retain the thing for a period not exceeding 30 minutes until able to transfer control of it to a constable.

11.1.10 **Power relating to photographing persons**

Persons arrested, detained, or given fixed penalty notices

A CSO has the power to photograph a person who has been arrested, detained, or given fixed penalty notices elsewhere than at a police station.

Links to alternative subjects and offences

11.2 Mentally Disordered People in Public Places

The Mental Health Act 1983 makes provisions in relation to people with a suspected mental disorder found in public places, in order to ensure their safety and that of the public.

Powers

(1) If a constable finds in a place to which the public have access a person who appears to him to be suffering from mental disorder and to be in immediate need of care or control, the constable may, if he thinks it necessary to do so in the interests of that person or for the protection of other persons, remove that person to a place of safety within the meaning of s 135.

(2) A person removed to a place of safety under this section may be detained there for a period not exceeding 72 hours for the purpose of enabling him to be examined by a registered medical practitioner and to be interviewed by an approved social worker and of making any necessary arrangements for his treatment or care.   Mental Health Act 1983, s 136

Meanings

Public place

This does not include a place adjacent to areas to which the public have access (*R v Roberts* [2003] EWCA Crim 2753, CA).

Mental disorder

Means **mental illness**, arrested or incomplete development of mind, **psychopathic disorder**, and any other disorder or disability of mind.

Severe mental impairment

Means a state of arrested or incomplete development of mind, which includes severe impairment of intelligence and social functioning and is associated with abnormally aggressive or seriously irresponsible conduct on the part of the person concerned.

Mental impairment

Means a state of arrested or incomplete development of mind (not amounting to severe mental impairment), which includes significant impairment of intelligence and social functioning and is associated with abnormally aggressive or seriously irresponsible conduct on the part of the person concerned.

Psychopathic disorder

Means a persistent disorder or disability of mind (whether or not including significant impairment of intelligence), which results in abnormally aggressive or seriously irresponsible conduct on the part of the person concerned.

Place of safety

Means residential accommodation provided by a local social services authority, a hospital as defined by this Act, a police station, an independent hospital or care home for mentally disordered persons or any other suitable place the occupier of which is willing temporarily to receive the patient.

Approved social worker

Means an officer of a local social services authority appointed to act as an approved social worker for the purposes of this Act.

Care home/Independent Hospital

Have the same meaning as in the Care Standards Act 2000.

Related cases

Francis v DPP [1997] RTR 113, QBD Police officers were not precluded from administering a breath test to a drink-drive suspect detained under s 136. Although they had formed an opinion about the suspect's mental state justifying detention under s 136, they could still conclude that the suspect understood both the request and knew what was happening. On that basis they had the right to breath test that person.

Practical considerations

- A suspected mentally ill person can only be taken from a place to which the public have access.
- A person cannot be deemed to be suffering from mental disorder by reason only of their promiscuity, immoral conduct, sexual deviancy, dependence on alcohol or drugs.
- The concept of **mental impairment** seeks to overcome the confusion that arises between two separate conditions (that of mental handicap, an unalterable condition usually acquired before birth) and mental illness (a potentially treatable condition that may be acquired at any age).
- If an offence has also been committed, the appropriate power of arrest could be considered.
- The power under s 136 is a **power of removal** for the purposes of getting the person out of a public place until they can be examined by a medical professional.
- Some practical difficulties arise because of differing interpretations (by the police, medical practitioners, psychiatrists, and social workers) on certain aspects of s 136, for example:
  - uncertainty as to the meaning of 'mental disorder' in this context;
  - how long may the police 'hold' such a mentally disordered person; and
  - whether a police station is an appropriate place for the prolonged detention of a person with such a disorder.
- Problems may arise where a person although 'confused' is assessed as not suitable for further compulsory detention under the Act. However, it is felt s/he requires 'treatment or care' and arrangements have to be made for that treatment or care.

- Some police areas have sought to avoid problems by forming inter-agency agreements with NHS agencies, this is encouraged by Home Office Circular 66/1990 and the DHSS Code of Practice on the Mental Health Act.
- The DHSS code suggests that the place of safety should be a hospital rather than a police station. It also suggests the attendance of an approved social worker; this is also required by the PACE Code of Practice C.
- Where possible, the detainee's general medical practitioner should be involved and should s/he not be available then the Force medical examiner should be present. Their role will be important in deciding whether or not there is to be a medical admission.
- Legality of detention issues:
  - ♦ People removed from public places under s 136 should be assessed as soon as possible. If that assessment is to take place in a police station, an approved social worker and registered medical practitioner **must** be called to carry out the interview and examination (PACE Code C 3.16). Once interviewed, examined, and suitable arrangements made for their treatment or care s/he can no longer be lawfully detained under s 136.
  - ♦ The person should not be released until s/he has been seen by an approved social worker and the registered medical practitioner.
  - ♦ If the decision has been made that the person is not 'mentally disordered', admittance for treatment must be done as a matter of consent.

Links to alternative subjects and offences

11.3 Illegal Entry into the United Kingdom

The legislation relating to immigration is vast. However, there are three major aspects that potentially affect everyday policing; these are dealt with below and include: illegal entry into the UK, illegal entry by deception, and assisting and harbouring an illegal immigrant.

11.3.1 Illegal entry into the UK

Section 24 of the Immigration Act 1971 creates offences in relation to illegal entry.

Offences

A person who is not a British citizen shall be guilty of an offence in any of the following cases:

(a) if contrary to this Act he knowingly enters the United Kingdom in breach of a deportation order or without leave;

(b) if, having only a limited leave to enter or remain in the United Kingdom, he knowingly either:
  (i) remains beyond the time limited by the leave; or
  (ii) fails to observe a condition of the leave;

(c) if, having lawfully entered the United Kingdom without leave by virtue of section 8(1), he remains without leave beyond the time allowed by section 8(1);

(d) if, without reasonable excuse, he fails to comply with any requirement imposed on him under Schedule 2 to this Act (report to a medical officer of health, or to attend, or submit to a test or examination, as required by such an officer);

(e) if, without reasonable excuse, he fails to observe any restriction imposed on him under Schedule 2 or 3 to this Act as to residence, as to his employment or occupation or as to reporting to the police to an immigration officer or to the Secretary of State;

(f) if he disembarks in the United Kingdom from a ship or aircraft after being placed on board under Schedule 2 or 3 to this Act with a view to his removal from the United Kingdom;

(g) if he embarks in contravention of a restriction imposed by or under an Order in Council under section 3(7) of this Act.

Immigration Act 1971, s 24(1)

Points to prove

✓ date and location
✓ not being a British Citizen committed one or more of the following acts:
  (a) knowingly entered the UK without leave/in breach of a deportation order, or
  (b) remained beyond the time limited by leave/failed to observe a condition of the leave, or
  (c) remained without leave beyond the time allowed, or
  (d) without reasonable excuse failed to comply with a requirement to report to a medical officer of health, or to attend, or submit to a test or examination or
  (e) without reasonable excuse failed to observe any restriction as to residence, employment or occupation, or reporting to the police/immigration officer or to the Secretary of State, or
  (f) disembarked in the UK from a ship or aircraft after being placed on board with a view to removal from the UK,
  (g) embarked in contravention of a restriction order.

Explanatory notes

- European Union nationals and those exercising EU rights do not need leave to enter or remain in the UK.
- A person commits an offence under s 24(1)(b)(i) on the day when s/he first knew that the time limited by the leave had expired and continues to commit it throughout any period during which s/he remains in the UK; but that person shall not be prosecuted more than once in respect of the same limited leave.

Related cases

R v Uxbridge Magistrates' Court ex parte Sorani, Adimi and Kaziu [1999] 4 All ER 529, Divisional Court Guidance on the prosecution of asylum seekers as illegal immigrants—see next paragraph.

Practical considerations

- Illegal entrants should not be prosecuted for offences of illegal entry or travelling on false documents if they are claiming political asylum, arriving directly from a place where they were in danger, present themselves immediately and show good reason for their entry. This is in line with the UN Convention relating to refugee status and was followed in the case of *R v Uxbridge Magistrates' Court ex parte Sorani, Adimi and Kaziu* [1999] 4 All ER 529. This only applies to offences relating to asylum seekers who face charges relating to the use of false documents for travel. Asylum seekers are subject to prosecution for other offences in the usual way.
- A constable may detain an aircraft, vehicle, or ship where someone has been arrested for assisting illegal entry.

Summary 36 months

 6 months' imprisonment and/or a fine not exceeding level 5 on the standard scale.

11.3.2 **Illegal entry by deception**

Offences

A person who is not a British citizen is guilty of an offence if, by means which include deception by him—
(a) he obtains or seeks to obtain leave to enter or remain in the United Kingdom; or
(b) he secures or seeks to secure the avoidance, postponement or revocation of enforcement action against him.   Immigration Act 1971, s 24A(1)

Points to prove

✓ date and location
✓ not British citizen obtain/seek to obtain leave to enter/ remain in UK
✓ by means including deception **or** in cases of avoiding enforcement:
✓ secured/sought to secure
✓ avoidance/postponement/revocation
✓ of enforcement action
✓ by means including deception

Meaning of enforcement action

Enforcement action in relation to a person, means:

- the giving of directions for removal from the UK;
- the making of a deportation order against him/her under s 5 ; or
- removal from the UK in consequence of directions or a deportation order.

 Either way None

 Summary: 6 months' imprisonment and/or a fine not exceeding the statutory maximum.
Indictment: 2 years' imprisonment and/or a fine.

11.3.3 **Assisting illegal entry**

Section 25 of the Immigration Act 1971 deals with assisting unlawful immigration to a member state.

Offence

A person commits an offence if he—

(a) does an act which facilitates the commission of a breach of immigration law by an individual who is not a citizen of the European Union,

(b) knows or has reasonable cause for believing that the act facilitates the commission of a breach of immigration law by the individual, and

(c) knows or has reasonable cause for believing that the individual is not a citizen of the European Union.   Immigration Act 1971, s 25(1)

Points to prove

✓ date and location
✓ did an act
✓ which facilitated the commission of a breach of immigration law
✓ by a person
✓ who was not a citizen of the European Union
✓ knowing/having reasonable cause for believing
✓ that the act facilitated the commission of a breach of immigration law
✓ by that person
✓ knowing/having reasonable cause for believing
✓ that person was not a citizen of the European Union

Meanings

Immigration law (s 25(2))

Means a law which has effect in a **member State** and which controls, in respect of some or all persons who are not nationals of the State, entitlement to:—

(a) enter the State,
(b) transit across the State, or
(c) be in the State.

Member state

Includes a reference to a state on a list prescribed for the purposes of this section by order of the Secretary of State (known as the 'Section 25 List of Schengen Acquis States').

Citizen of the European Union

Includes a reference to a person who is a national of a state on that list.

Practical considerations

- Section 25A of the Immigration Act 1971 creates an offence of knowingly and for gain facilitating the arrival into the UK of an individual, and knowing/having reasonable cause to believe that the individual is an asylum-seeker.
- Section 25D gives a power to seize the means of transport used: if a person has been arrested for an offence under this section, a senior officer or a constable may detain a relevant ship, aircraft, or vehicle until a decision is made whether to charge with offence; or if charged, until acquitted, charge dismissed, or case discontinued; or if convicted, until the court decides whether or not to order forfeiture of the ship, aircraft or vehicle.
- Section 25C provides power of court to order the forfeiture of the means of transportation.

 None

Either way

 Summary: 6 months' imprisonment and/or a fine not exceeding the statutory maximum.
Indictment: 14 years' imprisonment and/or a fine.

Links to alternative subjects and offences

11.4 Wasting Police Time

This section considers two aspects of taking up police resources on false pretences, that of wasting police time and of carrying out a bomb hoax.

11.4.1 Wasting police time

Section 5(2) of the Criminal Law Act 1967 creates the offence of the wasteful employment of the police by making false reports.

Offences

Where a person causes any wasteful employment of the police by knowingly making to any person a false report tending to show that an offence has been committed or to give rise to apprehension for the safety of any persons or property, or tending to show that he has information material to any police inquiry, commits an offence. Criminal Law Act 1967, s 5(2)

Points to prove
- ✓ date and location
- ✓ knowingly caused
- ✓ wasteful employment of police
- ✓ by false report
- ✓ that offence committed **or**
- ✓ giving rise to apprehension for safety of persons/property **or**
- ✓ had information material to police enquiry

Explanatory notes

Examples of 'giving rise to apprehension for the safety of any persons or property' could apply where:
- a mother falsely reports that her child is missing from home in an attempt to get her estranged husband back, or
- a person falsely reports a fire in one area of a town in order to commit a robbery in other area.

Practical considerations
- The consent of Director of Public Prosecutions is required before a prosecution may be commenced for this offence.
- However, if suitable, consider issuing a penalty notice for disorder (see **7.1.1**).
- Decisions to prosecute are often inconsistent and may bear no relation to the number of hours wasted on the investigation.

• Consider also other similar offences where such as: hoax bomb calls (see **11.4.2**) or false messages (see **7.12**).

 Summary 6 months

 6 months' imprisonment and/or a fine not exceeding level 4 on the standard scale.

11.4.2 **Bomb and terrorist type hoaxes**

Bomb hoaxes

Section 51 of the Criminal Law Act 1977 concerns bomb hoaxes.

Offences

(1) A person who—
  (a) places any article in any place whatever; or
  (b) dispatches any article by post, rail or any other means whatever of sending things from one place to another,
with the intention (in either case) of inducing in some other person a belief that it is likely to explode or ignite and thereby cause personal injury or damage to property is guilty of an offence.

(2) A person who communicates any information which he knows or believes to be false to another person with the intention of inducing in him or any other person a false belief that a bomb or other thing liable to explode or ignite is present in any place or location whatever is guilty of an offence. **Criminal Law Act 1977, s 51**

Points to prove

s 51(1) offence
✓ date and location
✓ place **or** dispatched by post/rail/other means
✓ an article
✓ with intent
✓ to induce in another the belief
✓ that the article
✓ was likely to explode/ignite
✓ and cause personal injury/damage to property

---

s 51(2) offence
- ✓ date and location
- ✓ communicated
- ✓ information
- ✓ you knew/believed to be false
- ✓ with intent
- ✓ of inducing a false belief in that person
- ✓ that bomb/thing liable to explode/ignite was present

Meanings

Article

Includes substance.

Intention (see **4.1**)

Person

It is not necessary for him/her to have any particular person in mind as the person in whom s/he intends to induce the belief in question.

Explanatory notes

- Subsection (1) concerns the placing or dispatching of articles with the intention that people believe that they are bombs or explosive devices, and sub-s (2) concerns people who communicate false information intending others to believe there is a bomb or explosive device likely to explode.
- This section does not require a specific place or location to be given.

Related cases

R v Webb [1995] 27 LS Gaz R 31, CA The hoax message does not have to give a location.

Terrorist-type hoaxes

Section 114 of the Anti-Terrorism, Crime and Security Act 2001 has created a similar offence for biological, chemical, and nuclear hoaxes. These include actions such as sending powders or liquids through the post and claiming that they are harmful.

Offences

(1) A person is guilty of an offence if he—
   (a) places any substance or other thing in any place whatever; or
   (b) sends any substance or other thing from one place to another (by post, rail or any other means whatever);
   with the intention of inducing in a person anywhere in the world a belief that it is likely to be (or contain) a noxious substance or other noxious

---

thing and thereby endanger human life or create a serious risk to human health.

(2) A person is guilty of an offence if he communicates any information which he knows or believes to be false with the intention of inducing in a person anywhere in the world a belief that a noxious substance or other noxious thing is likely to be present (whether at the time the information is communicated or later) in any place and thereby endanger human life or create a serious risk to human health.

Anti-Terrorism, Crime and Security Act 2001, s 114

Points to prove

s 114(1) offence

- ✓ date and location
- ✓ placed **or** sent
- ✓ a substance/thing
- ✓ intending
- ✓ to induce in a person
- ✓ a belief that it is likely to be/contain a noxious substance/thing
- ✓ and thereby endanger human life/create a serious risk to human health

s 114(2) offence

- ✓ date and location
- ✓ communicated information
- ✓ which you knew/believed to be false
- ✓ intending
- ✓ to induce in a person
- ✓ anywhere in the world
- ✓ a belief that a noxious substance/thing
- ✓ was likely to be present in any place
- ✓ thereby endanger human life/create a serious risk to human health

Meanings

Substance

Includes any biological agent and any other natural or artificial substance (whatever its form, origin, or method of production).

Intention (see 4.1)

Person (see 'Bomb hoaxes' 11.4.2)

Practical considerations

- A related offence is food contamination contrary to s 38 of the Public Order Act 1986. It is an offence under sub-s (1) to intend to cause alarm, injury, or loss by contamination or interference with goods or by making it appear that goods have been contaminated or interfered

11.4.2 Bomb and Terrorist Type Hoaxes

with in a place where goods of that description are consumed, used, sold, or otherwise supplied. It is also an offence to make threats or claims along these lines (s 38(2)) or to possess materials with a view to the commission of an offence (s 38(3)). Section 38 responded to a small number of well-publicized incidents of consumer terrorism, a minority of which involved animal rights activists.

- The court should be made aware of the disruptions and anxiety that was caused by the hoax
- How much time and expense was wasted by the hoax?

 Either way   None

 Summary: 6 months' imprisonment and/or a fine not exceeding the statutory maximum.
Indictment: 7 years' imprisonment.

Links to alternative subjects and offences

11.5 Supplying Intoxicating Substances

This subject is presented in two parts: first, the supplying of intoxicating substances and second, the supplying of butane lighter refills.

11.5.1 Supplying intoxicating substances

Section 1 of the Intoxicating Substances (Supply) Act 1985 creates offences, and a defence, in relation to the supply of 'inhalants' other than controlled drugs to people under 18 years of age.

Offences

It is an offence for a person to supply or offer to supply a substance other than a controlled drug—

(a) to a person under the age of eighteen whom he knows or has reasonable cause to believe, to be under that age; or

(b) to a person—

    (i) who is acting on behalf of a person under that age; and

    (ii) whom he knows or has reasonable cause to believe; to be so acting,

if he knows or has reasonable cause to believe that the substance is, or its fumes are, likely to be inhaled by the person under the age of eighteen for the purpose of causing intoxication.

Intoxicating Substances (Supply) Act 1985, s 1(1)

Points to prove

✓ date and location

✓ supplied/offer to supply a substance other than a controlled drug

s 1(1)(a) offence

✓ to a person under 18

✓ that you knew/had reasonable cause to believe was under that age

s 1(1)(b) offence

✓ person acting on behalf of person under 18 and

✓ whom you knew/had reasonable cause to believe was so acting

✓ knowing/having reasonable cause to believe substance/fumes were likely to be inhaled

✓ by person under 18 to cause intoxication

Meanings

Supply

In *The Oxford English Dictionary* it is defined as 'provide or make available (something needed or wanted); furnish for use or consumption'.

Controlled drug (see 5.1.1)

Explanatory notes

- This legislation was introduced to try and curb 'glue sniffing' or getting high on the fumes from solvents.
- The offence does not require that the substance must actually cause intoxication or even have the potential to do so; just that the under 18-year-old is likely to inhale it for that purpose.
- There may be a case against a shopkeeper who has the appropriate intentions and beliefs about the substance, believing that the person under 18 was going to be intoxicated on the substance supplied.

Defence

In proceedings against any person for an offence under subsection 1(1) it is a defence for them to show that at the time they made the supply or offer they were under the age of eighteen and was acting otherwise than in the course or furtherance of business.

Intoxicating Substances (Supply) Act 1985, s 1(2)

Practical considerations

- If you are unsure about a substance's likely effect, it may be possible to contact the manufacturers who may be willing to give expert advice.
- There is no definitive list of substances and more or less any chemical substance could be involved.
- The substance could even include products considered harmful such as aerosols for air fresheners, pain relief and anti-perspirants/deodorants. This is because it is the propellant and not the liquid in aerosols, which is inhaled, and the majority of aerosol products use butane as the main propellant.

 Summary 6 months

 6 months' imprisonment and/or a fine not exceeding level 5 on the standard scale.

11.5.2 Supplying butane lighter refills

The Cigarette Lighter Refill (Safety) Regulations 1999 (SI 1999/1844) make it an offence to supply butane lighter refills to people under 18.

Offences

No person shall supply any cigarette lighter refill canister containing butane or a substance with butane as a constituent part to any person under the age of eighteen years.   Cigarette Lighter Refill (Safety) Regulations 1999, reg 2

Points to prove

✓ date and location
✓ supplied
✓ cigarette lighter refill canister containing butane/substance with butane as constituent part
✓ to person aged under 18 years

Meaning of Supply (see 11.5.1)

Explanatory notes

- These Regulations prohibit the supply of cigarette lighter refill canisters containing butane to persons under the age of 18.
- Contravention of these Regulations is an offence under s 12 of the Consumer Protection Act 1987.

Defence

Under s 39 of the Consumer Protection Act 1987, it is a defence for a person to show that they took all reasonable steps and exercised all due diligence to avoid committing the offence.

 Summary   6 months

 6 months' imprisonment and/or a fine not exceeding level 5 on the standard scale.

Links to alternative subjects and offences

11.5.2 Supplying Butane Lighter Refills

11.6 Animal Welfare and Control of Dogs

The Animal Welfare Act 2006 is discussed in the first subject area, and the remaining topics deal with dogs that worry livestock; orders for their control; dangerous dogs; and guard dogs.

11.6.1 Animal welfare offences

The Animal Welfare Act 2006 has introduced a large number of offences that are intended to prevent harm and distress to animals. The offence of unnecessary suffering under s 4 is dealt with, but other offences within the Act are given in a bullet point/precis form so that the reader is at least aware of them.

Unnecessary suffering

Offences

(1) A person commits an offence if—
   (a) an act of his, or a failure of his to act, causes an animal to suffer,
   (b) he knew, or ought reasonably to have known, that the act, or failure to act, would have that effect or be likely to do so,
   (c) the animal is a protected animal, and
   (d) the suffering is unnecessary.
(2) A person commits an offence if—
   (a) he is responsible for an animal,
   (b) an act, or failure to act, of another person causes the animal to suffer,
   (c) he permitted that to happen or failed to take such steps (whether by way of supervising the other person or otherwise) as were reasonable in all the circumstances to prevent that happening, and
   (d) the suffering is unnecessary.   Animal Welfare Act 2006, s 4(1), (2)

Points to prove

s 4(1) offence

✓ did an act/failed to act
✓ that caused a protected animal to suffer
✓ knowing/ought to have known, that by this act/failure to act
✓ it caused/was likely to cause this suffering and
✓ the suffering is unnecessary

---

s 4(2) offence
- ✓ being responsible for an animal where
- ✓ another person did an act/failed to act
- ✓ that caused the animal to suffer
- ✓ permitted/failed to prevent this suffering happening
- ✓ it caused/was likely to cause this suffering and
- ✓ the suffering is unnecessary

Meanings

Animal

Means a vertebrate other than man. It does not apply to an animal while in a foetal or embryonic form.

Protected animal

Means that it is—

- of a kind which is commonly domesticated in the British Islands,
- under the control of man whether on a permanent or temporary basis, or
- not living in a wild state.

Responsible

A person is responsible for an animal—

- whether on a permanent or temporary basis
- when they are in charge of it
- when they own it
- when they have actual care and control of a person under the age of 16 who is responsible for it.

Explanatory notes

- Matters to consider whether suffering is unnecessary include—
  - ✦ Could it have been avoided or reduced?
  - ✦ Complying with legislation/licence/code of practice.
  - ✦ Was it for a legitimate purpose, such as benefiting the animal, or protecting a person, property or another animal?
  - ✦ Was it proportionate to the purpose of the conduct concerned?
  - ✦ Was the conduct that of a reasonably competent and humane person.
- This section does not apply to the destruction of an animal in an appropriate and humane manner.

 Summary

 A maximum of three years from the date of the offence, **but** six months from the date of having sufficient evidence to justify proceedings.

 6 months imprisonment and/or a fine not exceeding £20,000

Other Animal Welfare offences

Section 5—Mutilation

- It is an offence if a person carries out/causes to be carried out a prohibited procedure on a protected animal.
- Similarly the person responsible for the animal will commit an offence if they carry out the procedure or permit/fail to prevent this happening.
- The procedure involves interference with the sensitive tissues or bone structure of the animal, otherwise than for the purpose of its medical treatment.

Section 6–Docking of dogs' tails

- With certain exceptions it is an offence if a person removes/causes to be removed all/part of a dog's tail.
- Similarly the person responsible for the dog is liable if the dogs' tail is docked or permits/fails to prevent this happening.

Section 7–Administration of poisons or injurious drug/substance

- It is an offence if a person, without lawful authority or reasonable excuse administers or causes to be taken any poisonous or injurious drug or substance to/by a protected animal, knowing it to be poisonous or injurious.
- Similarly a person responsible for an animal, commits an offence if:
  - without lawful authority or reasonable excuse, another person administers a poisonous or injurious drug or substance to the animal or causes the animal to take such a drug or substance, **and**
  - s/he permitted that to happen or, knowing the drug or substance to be poisonous or injurious, s/he failed to take such steps (whether by way of supervising the other person or otherwise) as were reasonable in all the circumstances to prevent that happening.
- A poisonous or injurious drug or substance includes a drug or substance which, by virtue of the quantity or manner in which it is administered or taken, has the effect of a poisonous or injurious drug or substance.

Section 8—Offences involving animals fighting

- A person commits an offence if s/he—
  - causes an animal fight to take place, or attempts to do so;
  - knowingly receives money for admission to an animal fight;
  - knowingly publicizes a proposed animal fight;
  - provides information about an animal fight to another with the intention of enabling or encouraging attendance at the fight;
  - makes or accepts a bet on the outcome of an animal fight or on the likelihood of anything occurring or not occurring in the course of an animal fight;
  - takes part in an animal fight;
  - has in their possession anything designed or adapted for use in connection with an animal fight with the intention of its being so used;

- ♦ keeps or trains an animal for use for in connection with an animal fight;
- ♦ keeps any premises for use for an animal fight.
- A person commits an offence if, without lawful authority or reasonable excuse, s/he is present at an animal fight.
- A person commits an offence if, without lawful authority or reasonable excuse, s/he—
  - ♦ knowingly supplies a video recording of an animal fight,
  - ♦ knowingly publishes a video recording of an animal fight,
  - ♦ knowingly shows a video recording of an animal fight to another, or
  - ♦ possesses a video recording of an animal fight, knowing it to be such a recording, with the intention of supplying it.
- There are exceptions to the video recording offences involving an animal fight and they are that—
  - ♦ it took place outside Great Britain, or
  - ♦ it took place before 6 April 2007, or
  - ♦ it is for inclusion in a programme service.
- Interpretation of terms used in this section are given as—
  - ♦ *Animal fight*—means an occasion on which a protected animal is placed with an animal, or with a human, for the purpose of fighting, wrestling or baiting.
  - ♦ *Video recording*—means a recording, in any form, from which a moving image may by any means be reproduced and includes data stored on a computer disc or by other electronic means which is capable of conversion into a moving image.
  - ♦ *Supplying/publishing a video recording*—means supplying or publishing a video recording in any manner, including, in relation to a video recording in the form of data stored electronically, by means of transmitting such data.
  - ♦ *Showing a video recording*—includes showing a moving image reproduced from a video recording by any means.
- Section 22(1) gives a constable power to seize any animal that appears to have been involved in fighting, where the offences under s 8 (except video recording offences) has been committed.

Section 11—Transfer animals by sale/transaction/prize to under 16

- A person commits an offence if s/he sells an animal to a person having reasonable cause to believe to be under the age of 16 years.
  - ♦ Selling includes transferring ownership in consideration of entering into another transaction.
- It is an offence to enter into an arrangement with a person having reasonable cause to believe to be under the age of 16 years, where the 16 year old has the chance to win an animal as a prize, unless it is—
  - ♦ in the presence of and s/he is accompanied by a person over 16 years; or
  - ♦ in the belief that the person who has care and control has consented; or
  - ♦ arranged in a family environment.

Practical considerations

- Section 17 of PACE (see **12.3.2**) gives power to a constable to enter and search premises for purpose of arresting a person for offences under ss 4, 5, 6(1) and (2), 7 and 8(1) and (2) of this Act.
- The offences within the Act are all summary and carry a term of imprisonment not exceeding 6 months and/or fines either not exceeding £20,000 or level 4/5 on the standard scale.
- Time limits for prosecutions are a maximum of three years from the date of the offence, **but** six months from the date of having sufficient evidence to justify proceedings.

11.6.2 **Dogs worrying livestock**

The Dogs (Protection of Livestock) Act 1953 is intended to prevent dogs terrorizing and chasing farm animals.

> **Offence**
>
> Subject to the provisions of this section, if a dog **worries livestock** on any **agricultural land**, the owner of the dog, and, if it is in the charge of a person other than its owner, that person also, shall be guilty of an offence under this Act.   Dogs (Protection of Livestock) Act 1953, s 1(1)

Points to prove
- ✓ date and location
- ✓ owner/person in charge of dog
- ✓ worrying livestock
- ✓ on agricultural land

Meanings

Worrying

Under s 1(2) means—

(a) attacking livestock, **or**
(b) chasing **livestock** in such a way as may reasonably be expected to cause injury or suffering to the livestock or, in the case of females, abortion, or loss of or diminution in their produce, **or**
(c) being at large (that is to say not on a lead or otherwise under close control) in a field or enclosure in which there are sheep.

Livestock

Means cattle, sheep, goats, swine, horses, or poultry.

- 'Cattle' means bulls, cows, oxen, heifers, or calves.
- 'Horses' includes asses and mules.
- 'Poultry' means domestic fowls, turkeys, geese, or ducks.

11.6.2 Dogs Worrying Livestock

Agricultural land

Means meadow or grazing lands, or land used for crops, or for poultry or pig farming, or as market gardens, allotments, nursery grounds, or orchards.

Defences

(2A) Subsection (2)(c) of this section [*being at large*] shall not apply in relation to
   (a) a dog owned by, or in the charge of, the occupier of the field or enclosure or the owner of the sheep or a person authorized by either of those persons; or
   (b) a police dog, a guide dog, a trained sheep dog, a working gun dog or a pack of hounds.
(3) A person is not guilty of an offence under this Act for an act done by a dog, if the livestock are trespassing and the dog is owned by, or in the charge of, the occupier or a person authorized by them, except where the said person causes the dog to attack the livestock.
(4) A dog owner shall not be convicted of an offence under this Act for worrying livestock by the dog if he proves that someone whom he reasonably believed fit and proper to be so, was in charge of the dog when it worried the livestock.

Dogs (Protection of Livestock) Act 1953, s 1(2A), (3) (4)

Power of seizure

Where in the case of a dog found on any land:
(a) a police officer has reasonable cause to believe that the dog has been worrying livestock on that land, and the land appears to him to be agricultural land, and
(b) no person is present who admits to being the owner of the dog or in charge of it,
then for the purpose of ascertaining who is the owner of the dog the police officer may seize it and may detain it until the owner has claimed it and paid all expenses incurred by reason of its detention.

Dogs (Protection of Livestock) Act 1953, s 2(2)

Practical considerations

- Where a dog is proved to have injured cattle or poultry, or chased sheep, it may be dealt with as a dangerous dog (see **11.6.4**).
- The Animals Act 1971 concerns civil liability for damage done by animals and the protection of livestock. Section 9(1) provides a defence:
  - In civil proceedings for killing or causing injury to a dog, it is a defence for the defendant to prove that he:
    (a) acted to protect livestock and was entitled to do so; **and**
    (b) notified the officer in charge of a police station of the killing or injury within forty-eight hours.

- A person is entitled to protect livestock only if:
  - ♦ the land or livestock upon it belong to them or a person under whose express or implied authority they were acting; **and**
  - ♦ the circumstances are not such that liability for killing or causing injury to the livestock would be excluded by s 5(4) (that the dog either belonged to the occupier of the land or was authorized by them to be there).
- A person killing or causing injury to a dog shall be deemed to have acted for the protection of livestock only if either:
  - ♦ the dog was worrying or about to worry the livestock and there were no other means of preventing the worrying; **or**
  - ♦ the dog had been worrying livestock, had not left the vicinity, was not under the control of any person and there was no practicable way of ascertaining to whom it belonged.
- It is sufficient for the defence that the defendant believed that s/he had reasonable grounds for their action.

 Summary   6 months

A fine not exceeding level 3 on the standard scale.

11.6.3 **Dog control orders**

Section 2 of the Dogs Act 1871 allows magistrates' courts to make orders in respect of dangerous dogs.

Complaint

Any magistrates' court may hear a complaint that a dog is **dangerous** and not kept under **proper control**, and if satisfied that it is dangerous, may order that it be kept under proper control by the owner, or destroyed.

Meanings

Dangerous

Is not limited to meaning dangerous to people. It could include other animals.

Proper control

Is also a question of fact for the court. If a dog is kept under proper control, an order cannot be made in respect of it.

Explanatory notes

The expression '**dangerous**' will be a question of fact for the courts to determine, it includes:

- Being dangerous to livestock, birds and other dogs (*Briscoe v Shattock* The Times, 12 October 1998, QBD).
- However, a dog that killed two pet rabbits on only one occasion was held not to be dangerous, as it was in the nature of dogs to chase and kill other small animals.
- A dog could be dangerous on private property to which people have a right of access.

Practical considerations

- Where a court orders a dog to be destroyed, it may appoint a person to undertake the seizure and destruction, and require any person with custody to deliver it up, and in addition may disqualify the owner from having custody of a dog, under s 1 of the Dangerous Dogs Act 1989.
- In a statement of complaint, the victim must identify the dog. It is usually necessary for the victim to then identify the dog in the presence of the owner and the investigating officer. Any injuries should be examined by the officer and described in both their statement and that of the victim. This is a complaint rather than an offence, but it is advisable to interview the owner under the provisions of PACE.
- If there has been a genuine transfer of ownership of the dog, an order could only be made against the new owner.

11.6.4 **Dangerous dogs**

The Dangerous Dogs Act 1991 imposed restrictions on keeping dogs that are a danger to the public. Section 1 created offences relating to dogs bred for fighting.

Offences

(2) No person shall
  (a) breed, or breed from, a dog to which this section applies;
  (b) sell or exchange such a dog or offer, or expose such a dog for sale or exchange;
  (c) make or offer to make a gift of such a dog or expose such a dog as a gift;
  (d) allow such a dog of which he is the owner or for the time being in charge, to be in a public place without being muzzled and kept on a lead; or
  (e) abandon such a dog of which he is the owner or, being the owner or for the time being in charge of such a dog, allow it to stray.

(3) No person shall have any dog to which this section applies in his possession or custody except
  (a) in pursuance of the power of seizure; or

(b) in accordance with an order for its destruction under the subsequent provisions of this Act.

(7) Any person who contravenes this section is guilty of an offence.

Dangerous Dogs Act 1991, s 1(2), (3), (7)

Points to prove

s 1(2) offence

✓ date and location
✓ breed from/sell/exchange/make a gift of/allow in a public place without a muzzle and kept on a lead/abandon/allow to stray
✓ a fighting dog (as defined in s 1(1))

s 1(3) offence

✓ date and location
✓ had in possession/custody
✓ a fighting dog (as defined in s 1(1))

Meanings

Dog

- This section applies to any dog of:
  (a) the type known as the **Pit Bull Terrier**;
  (b) the type known as the **Japanese Tosa**; and
  (c) any dog of any type designated for the purposes of this section by an order of the Secretary of State, being a type appearing to him to be bred for fighting or to have the characteristics of a type bred for that purpose. *Dangerous Dogs Act, s 1(1)*
- An order has added another two dogs deemed dangerous—
  ✦ the type known as the **Dogo Argentino**; and
  ✦ the type known as the **Fila Braziliero**.

Public place

Means any street, road, or other place (whether or not it is enclosed) to which the public have or are permitted to have access, whether for payment or otherwise, including the common parts of a building containing two or more dwellings.

Defences

The above does not apply to dogs being used for lawful purposes by a constable or any other person in the service of the Crown, such as dogs being used by the Police, Prison Service, Military Police, and Customs & Excise.

Related cases

R v Haringey Magistrates' Court & Another ex parte Cragg The Times, 8 November 1996, QBD, and R v Trafford Magistrates' Court ex parte Riley (1996) 160 JP 418, QBD The offender may not be the owner, in which case the owner must be identified and be made party to, or informed of, a destruction hearing.

DPP v Kellet (1994) 158 JP 1138, Divisional Court Voluntary intoxication is not a defence. In this case, a dangerous dog wandered into a public place because the defendant was drunk and had left her front door open. She was convicted.

Bates v DPP (1993) 157 JP 1004, QBD A dog in a vehicle may be deemed to be in a public place if the vehicle itself is in a public place.

Cummings v DPP The Times, 26 March 1999, QBD Common areas located around council housing held to be a public place.

Practical considerations

- For further guidance on this Act see Home Office Circular 29/1997.
- The word 'type' has a wider meaning than 'breed' in that behavioural characteristics can also be taken into account: *Brock v DPP* [1993] 4 All ER 491, QBD.
- If it is alleged that a dog is of a type to which this section applies, it is presumed to be so until the owner proves to the contrary. If there is any doubt, the dog may be seized and taken to kennels where the owner may have it examined at his own expense.

 Summary   6 months

 6 months' imprisonment and/or a fine not exceeding level 5 on the standard scale.

11.6.5 **Guard dogs**

The Guard Dogs Act 1975 was introduced to regulate the use of guard dogs.

Offences

(1) A person shall not use or permit the use of a guard dog at any premises unless a 'handler' who is capable of controlling the dog is present, and the dog must always be under the control of the handler while being used, except while secured and not at liberty to wander the premises.

(2) The handler of a guard dog shall keep the dog under his control at all times while it is being used as a guard dog at any premises, except while

---

another handler has control of the dog or while the dog is secured and
not at liberty to wander the premises.
(3) A person shall not use or permit the use of a guard dog at any premises
unless a notice containing a warning that a guard dog is present is clearly
exhibited at each entrance to the premises.

Guard Dogs Act 1975, s 1(1)–(3)

Points to prove

s 1(1) offence

✓ date and location
✓ use/permit the use of
✓ a guard dog(s)
✓ on premises without a capable controller present
✓ and not under control
✓ of handler at all times

s 1(2) offence

✓ date and location
✓ handler of guard dogs(s)
✓ fail
✓ to keep dogs
✓ under control at all times
✓ on premises

s 1(3) offence

✓ date and location
✓ use/permit the use of
✓ a guard dog(s)
✓ on premises
✓ when warning notice(s) that a guard dog was present
✓ was/were not clearly exhibited at each entrance

Meanings

Guard dog

Means a dog which is being used to protect: premises; or property kept
on premises; or a person guarding premises or property on premises.

Premises

Means land **other than agricultural land** or land attached to and forming one enclosure with a dwelling-house; and buildings, including parts
of buildings, other than dwelling houses.

Agricultural land   (see 11.6.2)

Related cases

Hobson v Gledhill [1978] 1 WLR 215   The handler is not required to
be on the premises whilst the dog is properly secured.

11.6.5 **Guard Dogs**

 Summary 6 months

A fine not exceeding level 5 on the standard scale.

Links to alternative subjects and offences

Chapter 12

Powers and Procedures

12.1 Stop and Search Powers

The Police and Criminal Evidence Act 1984 creates the generic stop and search powers for a constable in places to which the public has access.

12.1.1 Search and detain

Section 1 of the Police and Criminal Evidence Act 1984 creates the power for a constable to stop and search people and vehicles for stolen property, offensive weapons, bladed/pointed articles, or prohibited fireworks.

> **Power—search and detain**
>
> (1) A constable may exercise any power conferred by this section—
>> (a) in any place to which at the time when he proposes to exercise the power the public or any section of the public has access, on payment or otherwise, as of right or by virtue of express or implied permission; **or**
>> (b) in any other place to which people have ready access at the time when he proposes to exercise the power but which is **not** a dwelling.
>
> (2) Subject to subsections 1(3) to (5), a constable—
>> (a) may **search**—
>>> (i) any person or **vehicle**;
>>> (ii) anything which is in or on a vehicle;
>>
>> for **stolen** or **prohibited** articles or any article to which subsection (**8A**) or any firework to which subsection (**8B**) applies; **and**
>> (b) may **detain** a person or vehicle for the purpose of such a search.
>>
>> Police and Criminal Evidence Act 1984, s 1(1), (2)

Meanings

Vehicle

This is not defined. In *the Oxford English Dictionary* it means 'a conveyance, usually with wheels, for transporting people, animals, goods or other objects and includes (amongst others) a car, cart, truck, bus, train carriage or sledge'. Although the Act stipulates that vessels (including any ship, boat, raft, or other apparatus constructed or adapted for floating on water), aircraft and hovercraft, also fall within the meaning of vehicles

Stolen article   (see **3.1**)

Prohibited articles

Prohibited articles means:
- an offensive weapon (see **8.9.1**) being any article:
  - ♦ made or adapted for use for causing injury to people;
  - ♦ intended by the person having it with him for causing injury to people, by him/her or by some other person;
- an article made or adapted for use in the course of or in connection with the following offences:
  - ♦ burglary (see **3.3**);
  - ♦ theft (see **3.1**);
  - ♦ taking a conveyance without consent (see **4.3**);
  - ♦ fraud (see **3.9**);
  - ♦ criminal damage (see **4.5**); **or** intended by the person having it with them for such use by him or by some other person.

Article (8A)

Pointed or bladed articles, where a person has committed, or is going to commit offence (see **8.10.1**).

Firework (8B)

Any firework, which a person possesses in contravention of a prohibition, imposed by the Fireworks Regulations 2004 (see **8.8**).

Reasonable grounds for suspicion

This section **does not** give a constable power to search a person or vehicle or anything in or on a vehicle **unless** he has **reasonable grounds for suspecting** that he will find stolen or prohibited articles, any article to which subsection (8A) applies or any firework to which subsection (8B) applies.   Police and Criminal Evidence Act 1984, s 1(3)

Meaning of reasonable grounds

Code of Practice A to the Police and Criminal Evidence Act 1984 governs the exercise by police officers of statutory powers of stop and search. Paragraphs 2.2 to 2.11 provide an explanation of what are considered to be reasonable grounds for suspicion when conducting a search.

PACE Code of practice A

Reasonable grounds for suspicion depend on the circumstances in each case, as follows:
- There must be an objective basis for that suspicion based on facts, information, and/or intelligence that are relevant to the likelihood of finding an article of a certain kind or, in the case of searches under the Terrorism Act 2000, s 43, to the likelihood that the person is a terrorist.

- Reasonable suspicion can never be supported on the basis of personal factors alone without reliable supporting intelligence or information or some specific behaviour by the person concerned. For example, a person's race, religion age, appearance, or the fact that the person is known to have a previous conviction, cannot be used alone or in combination with each other as the reason for searching that person.
- Reasonable suspicion cannot be based on generalizations or stereotypical images of certain groups or categories of people as more likely to be involved in criminal activity.

Further points contained within this code are:

- Reasonable suspicion can be on the basis of behaviour of a person (eg an officer encountering someone on the street at night who is obviously trying to hide something).
- On reliable information or intelligence that members of a group or gang habitually carry knives unlawfully or weapons or controlled drugs, and they wear a distinctive item of clothing or denote their membership by other means, if that distinctive means of identification is displayed that may provide the reasonable grounds to stop and search a person.
- An officer who has reasonable grounds for suspicion may detain the person concerned in order to carry out a search.
- Before carrying out a search the officer may ask questions relating to the circumstances which gave rise to the suspicion, as a result the grounds for suspicion may be confirmed or, because of a satisfactory explanation, be eliminated.
- Reasonable grounds for suspicion cannot be provided retrospectively by such questioning during a person's detention or by refusal to answer any questions put.
- Once reasonable grounds to suspect that an article is being carried ceases to exist, no search may take place. In the absence of any other lawful power to detain, the person is free to leave and must be so informed.
- There is no power to stop or detain a person in order to find grounds for a search.
- A brief introductory conversation or exchange is desirable, not only as a means of avoiding unsuccessful searches, but to explain the grounds for the stop/search, to gain cooperation and so reduce any possible tension.
- If a person is lawfully detained for the purpose of a search, but no search takes place, the detention will not subsequently be rendered unlawful.

Restrictions in a garden/yard

Subsections (4) and (5) of the 1984 Act stipulates that if a person/vehicle:

is in a garden or yard occupied with and used for the purposes of a dwelling or on other land so occupied and used a constable may not search that person/vehicle/anything in or on the vehicle in the exercise of the power conferred by this section, unless; the constable has reasonable grounds for believing:

(a) that the suspect/person in charge of the vehicle does not reside in the dwelling; **and**
(b) that the suspect/vehicle is not in the place in question with the express or implied permission of a person who resides in the dwelling.

Power to seize

If in the course of such a search a constable discovers an article which he has reasonable grounds for suspecting to be a stolen or prohibited article, an article to which subsection (8A) applies or a firework to which subsection (8B) applies, he may seize it.

Police and Criminal Evidence Act 1984, s 1(6)

12.1.2 **Conduct of a search**

Section 2 of the Police and Criminal Evidence Act 1984 provides safeguards for when a constable detains a person/ **vehicle** in the exercise of **any search powers prior to arrest**, they are:
- a search can be abandoned if it is no longer required or it is impracticable to conduct one;
- the time taken for conducting the search is such time as is reasonably required to permit the search to be carried out;
- a search and detain power does not authorize a constable to:
  - require a person to remove any of his clothing in public other than an outer coat, jacket, or gloves; or
  - stop a vehicle, if not in uniform;
- before commencing a search (except an unattended vehicle), the constable shall take reasonable steps to provide the following details to the detainee or person in charge of the vehicle:
  - name of constable and police station (where based), plus identification if the constable is not in uniform;
  - object of the search;
  - grounds for the search;
  - the entitlement to a copy of the written stop and search record, unless it appears to the constable that it will be practicable to make/provide the record at the time of the search (see **12.1.3**);
  - where an unattended vehicle is searched, a constable shall leave a notice inside the vehicle (unless it would damage the vehicle) stating: that he/she has searched it; name of the police station where based; that an application for compensation for any damage caused by the search may be made to that police station; the procedure as to the entitlement of a copy of the written stop and search record (see **12.1.3**).

Meaning of vehicle (see 12.1.1)

12.1.3 **Written records of stop and search**

Section 3 of the Police and Criminal Evidence Act 1984 details the procedures to be followed when making written records of stop searches carried out by a constable, while exercising **any of their stop and search powers**, relating to a person or **vehicle**. They are:

- a record shall be made in writing of the stop and search, unless it is not practicable to do so;
- if it is not practicable to make a record 'on the spot', s/he shall make it as soon as practicable after the completion of the search;
- a record of the search of a person shall include a note of their name (if known or ascertained), but a person may not be detained to find out these details. Otherwise a description of that person shall be entered in the record;
- similarly the record of the search of a vehicle shall include details describing that vehicle;
- a record of the search of a person or vehicle shall include:
  - ✦ the object of the search;
  - ✦ the grounds for making it;
  - ✦ the date and time made;
  - ✦ the place where it was made;
  - ✦ whether anything found, and if so what;
  - ✦ whether any injury to a person or damage to property was received as a result of the search, if so, details to be entered on the record;
  - ✦ details to identify the constable making it.
- a person searched or the owner/person in charge of a vehicle which has been searched, shall be entitled to a copy of the record, if s/he asks for one, before the end of the specified period (being 12 months, beginning with the date on which the search was made).

Meaning of vehicle (see 12.1.1)

Explanatory notes

- Fireworks possessed in contravention of any prohibitions imposed by the Fireworks Regulations 2004 would give grounds for invoking the 'stop and search' powers. Four specific categories of fireworks are given within British Standard 7114 (see **8.8.1** for details).
- Articles that are made, adapted, or intended for use for one of the listed offences could include:
  - ✦ crowbar/screwdriver (burglary),
  - ✦ car keys (for taking a vehicle without owner's consent),
  - ✦ stolen credit card (fraud), or
  - ✦ spray paint can/pens intending to cause graffiti (damage).
- This section does not give a constable power to search a person or vehicle or anything in or on a vehicle unless s/he has reasonable grounds for suspecting that s/he will find stolen property, prohibited articles or firework.

Related cases

R v Park (1994) 158 JP 144, CA Procedures laid down in the Police and Criminal Evidence Act 1984 and the Codes of Practice have to be followed as far as practicable. Any breach of these procedures could justify exclusion of evidence and render the search unlawful.

R v Fennelley [1989] Crim LR 142, CC The defendant had not been properly informed of the reasons for being subjected to a street search. It was held that the evidence obtained was unfair and excluded under s 78 of the Police and Criminal Evidence Act 1984.

O'Hara v Chief Constable of the RUC [1997] 1 All ER 129, HL Reasonable grounds for suspicion can arise from information/intelligence passed to an officer by a colleague, an informant, or anonymously.

Practical considerations

- All the Codes of Practice are legally binding—any failure by police officers to comply with them could result in the Crown Prosecution Service declining to institute or continue proceedings. Where the case results in a court hearing, it may be lost through evidence being disallowed and the police officer could be subject to severe penalties. Indeed, s 67(8) of the Police and Criminal Evidence Act 1984 specifically provides that failure to comply with these codes will make an officer liable to disciplinary proceedings.
- The Codes of Practice are not confined to police officers, they apply to all people who are involved in investigating offences and charging offenders including investigators from: HM Revenue & Customs, the DSS, private investigators, and security staff in industry.
- Code of Practice A provides assistance and guidance to police officers in the exercise of their powers to stop and search people and vehicles. It should always be read in conjunction with the law in this area.
- Searches based on up-to-date and accurate intelligence are most likely to be effective, lawful, and secure public confidence. Officers must ensure that all stop and search powers are used: objectively, fairly, and without any bias against ethnic or other groups within the community.
- Exercising these powers around criminal damage may bring officers into greater contact with juveniles. Officers must be fully aware of and ready to take account of the special needs of juveniles and other vulnerable groups.

Links to alternative subjects and offences

12.2 Powers of Arrest

Sections 24, 24A, and 28 to 31 (inclusive) of the Police and Criminal Evidence Act 1984 deal with arrest by a constable or other people and other related matters.

12.2.1 Arrest without warrant: constables

Arrest without warrant

Section 24 of the Police and Criminal Evidence Act 1984 provides the power of arrest for a constable without a warrant and the conditions that must apply before the arrest power can be used.

Powers

(1) A constable may arrest without a warrant—
  (a) anyone who is about to commit an offence;
  (b) anyone who is in the act of committing an offence;
  (c) anyone whom he has reasonable grounds for suspecting to be about to commit an offence;
  (d) anyone whom he has reasonable grounds for suspecting to be committing an offence.
(2) If a constable has reasonable grounds for suspecting that an offence has been committed, he may arrest without a warrant anyone whom he has reasonable grounds to suspect of being guilty of it.
(3) If an offence has been committed, a constable may arrest without a warrant:
  (a) anyone who is guilty of the offence;
  (b) anyone whom he has reasonable grounds for suspecting to be guilty of it.   Police and Criminal Evidence Act 1984, s 24(1)–(3)

Necessity criteria

But the power of summary arrest conferred by subsection (1), (2) or (3) is exercisable only if the constable has reasonable grounds for believing that for any of the **reasons** mentioned in subsection (5) it is **necessary** to arrest the person in question.

Police and Criminal Evidence Act 1984, s 24(4)

Reasons

(5) The **reasons** are—
  (a) to enable the name of the person in question to be ascertained (in the case where the constable does not know, and cannot readily ascertain, the person's name, or has reasonable grounds for doubting whether a name given by the person as his name is his real name);

(b) correspondingly as regards the person's address;

(c) to prevent the person in question—

    (i) causing physical injury to himself or any other person;

    (ii) suffering physical injury;

    (iii) causing loss of or damage to property;

    (iv) committing an offence against public decency (subject to subsection (6)); or

    (v) causing an unlawful obstruction of the highway;

(d) to protect a child or other vulnerable person from the person in question;

(e) to allow the prompt and effective investigation of the offence or of the conduct of the person in question;

(f) to prevent any prosecution for the offence from being hindered by the disappearance of the person in question.

(6) Subsection (5)(c)(iv) (**offence against public decency**) applies only where members of the public going about their normal business cannot reasonably be expected to avoid the person in question.

        Police and Criminal Evidence Act 1984, s 24(5), (6)

Explanatory notes

- The use of this arrest power is governed by Code G under the PACE Codes of Practice.
- An exception to using Code G would be an arrest under s 41 of the Terrorism Act 2000. In such a case Code H would apply.
- The Director General of SOCA may confer some or all of the s 24 powers on SOCA staff, and nominate them as 'designated persons' (role of constable, officer of Revenue and Customs or immigration officer).
- The above legislation means that a constable/designated person may only arrest a person without a warrant under this general power where:
  - ◆ s/he is about to commit/in the act of committing an offence;
  - ◆ there are reasonable grounds to suspect s/he is about to commit/to be committing an offence;
  - ◆ there are reasonable grounds to suspect that an offence has been committed, has reasonable grounds to suspect s/he is guilty of it;
  - ◆ an offence has been committed: s/he is guilty of the offence; reasonable grounds to suspect s/he is guilty of it; **and** the constable has reasonable grounds to believe (more than 'suspect') that it is **necessary** to arrest that person for any of the reasons listed.
- A lawful arrest requires both elements of:
  - ◆ a person's involvement or suspected involvement or attempted involvement in the commission of a criminal offence; **and**
  - ◆ reasonable grounds to believe that the arrest is necessary.
- The requirement for reasonable grounds makes this an **objective test**—that is, it requires some verifiable material fact other than the belief of the arresting officer.
- The exercise of these arrest powers will be subject to a test of necessity, based on the nature and circumstances of the offence and the interests of the criminal justice system.

12.2.1 **Arrest without Warrant: Constables**

- An arrest will only be justified if the constable believes it is necessary for any of the reasons set out, **and** s/he had reasonable grounds on which that belief was based.
- Criteria for what may constitute necessity remains an operational decision at the discretion of the arresting officer.
- Paragraph 4 of Code G deals with 'Records of Arrest' it stipulates that:
  - ◆ The arresting officer is required to record in his pocket book or other methods used for recording information:
    - ▪ the nature and circumstances of the offence leading to the arrest;
    - ▪ the reason or reasons why arrest was necessary;
    - ▪ the giving of the caution;
    - ▪ anything said by the person at the time of arrest (para 4.1).
  - ◆ Such a record should be made at the time of the arrest unless impracticable to do. If not made at that time, the record should then be, completed as soon as possible thereafter (para 4.2).
- Some of the reasons to consider under s 24(5)(e) maybe where there are reasonable grounds to believe that the person:
  - ◆ has made false statements;
  - ◆ has made statements which cannot be readily verified;
  - ◆ has presented false evidence;
  - ◆ may steal or destroy evidence;
  - ◆ may make contact with co-suspects or conspirators;
  - ◆ may intimidate or threaten or make contact with witnesses; or
  - ◆ where it is necessary to obtain evidence by questioning.
- If an arrest is made which is an indictable offence, there could be other reasons under s 24(5)(e) to consider such as a need to:
  - ◆ enter and search any premises occupied or controlled by a person;
  - ◆ search the person;
  - ◆ prevent contact with others; or
  - ◆ take fingerprints, footwear impressions, samples or photographs of the suspect.
- Another reason to consider under s 24(5)(e) could be to ensure compliance with statutory drug testing requirements.
- Apart from arrest, other options such as:
  - ◆ report for summons;
  - ◆ grant street bail;
  - ◆ issue a fixed penalty notice; or
  - ◆ other means of dealing with the offence will have to be considered and excluded before arrest is decided upon.
- This statutory power of arrest for a constable now applies to any offence. Note that offences under the Criminal Law Act 1967 of assisting offenders and concealing information on relevant offences (ss 4(1) and 5(1) respectively), still requires that the offences to which they relate carry a sentenced fixed by law or one in which a first time offender aged 18 or over could be sentenced to 5 years or more imprisonment.
- There are also some preserved powers of arrest under Sch 2 which have been retained.
- Arrest (without warrant) by other people is subject to s 24A of the Police and Criminal Evidence Act 1984 (see **12.2.4**).

• Use of reasonable force is dealt with in the 'Use of force resolution' subject (see **1.2**).

12.2.2 **Information to be given on arrest**

Cautions

Code of practice C deals with when a caution must be given.

Code of practice C

Police officers and other persons subject to observing PACE should be aware of the following paragraphs in this code of practice:

• A person whom there are grounds to suspect of an offence must be cautioned before any questions about an offence, or further questions (if the answers provide the grounds for suspicion) are put to them; if either the suspect's answers or silence, may be given in evidence to a court in a prosecution (see Code C para 10.1).

• A person need not be cautioned if questions are for other necessary purposes such as:
  ♦ solely to establish identity or ownership of vehicle;
  ♦ obtain information in order to comply with a statutory requirement;
  ♦ in order to conduct a proper and effective search;
  ♦ to seek clarification for a written record;
  ♦ when examining a person under statutory terrorism provisions.

• A person who is arrested or further arrested, must also be cautioned unless:
  ♦ it is impracticable to do so by reason of their condition or behaviour at the time;
  ♦ they have already been cautioned immediately prior to arrest (see Code C para 10.4).

• The **caution** that must be given on:
  ♦ arrest;
  ♦ all other occasions before a person is charged or informed they may be prosecuted,
  should (unless the restriction on drawing adverse inferences from silence applies) **be in the following terms**:
  'You do not have to say anything. But it may harm your defence if you do not mention when questioned something which you later rely on in Court. Anything you do say may be given in evidence.' (See Code C para 10.5).

Explanatory notes

• Whenever a person not under arrest is initially cautioned, or reminded they are under caution, that person must at the same time be told that they are not under arrest and are free to leave if they want to.

12.2.2 Information to be Given on Arrest

- Minor deviations from the words of any caution given in accordance with this Code do not constitute a breach of this Code, provided the sense of the relevant caution is preserved.
- After any break in questioning under caution the person being questioned must be made aware they remain under caution. If there is any doubt, the relevant caution shall be given again in full when the interview resumes.
- Failure to comply with cautioning procedures will allow the accused to claim a breach of this code at any subsequent court proceedings. By virtue of s 76 or s 78 of the Police and Criminal Evidence Act 1984 the court may then be obliged to exclude the evidence of confession so obtained.

Statutory requirements

Section 28 of the Police and Criminal Evidence Act 1984 determines the information that must be given to a person when they are told they are to be arrested.

Information to be given on arrest

(1) Subject to subsection (5) below, where a person is arrested, otherwise than by being informed that he is under arrest, the arrest is not lawful unless the person arrested is informed that he is under arrest as soon as is practicable after his arrest.

(2) Where a person is arrested by a constable, subsection (1) above applies regardless of whether the fact of the arrest is obvious.

(3) Subject to subsection (5) below, no arrest is lawful unless the person arrested is informed of the ground for the arrest at the time of, or as soon as practicable after, the arrest.

(4) Where a person is arrested by a constable, subsection (3) above applies regardless of whether the ground for the arrest is obvious.

(5) Nothing in this section is to be taken to require a person to be informed—
    (a) that he is under arrest; **or**
    (b) of the ground for the arrest,
    if it was not reasonably practicable for him to be so informed by reason of his having escaped from arrest before the information could be given.   Police and Criminal Evidence Act 1984, s 28(1)–(5)

Explanatory notes

- A person who is arrested, or further arrested, must be informed at the time, or as soon as practicable thereafter, that they are under arrest and the grounds for their arrest.
- When arresting using the power under s 24, the officer must tell the person, not only the offence/suspected offence involved, but also the reason why the officer believes that arrest is necessary. The necessity criteria must also be recorded by the officer.
- If it becomes apparent that a more serious offence may have been committed the suspect must be made aware of these facts immediately (eg originally arrested and interviewed for sexual assault, which now transpires is rape).

- It would be manifestly unfair if defendant did not know the true extent of the situation s/he was in and any interviews could be excluded at trial.

Related cases

Edwards v DPP (1993) 97 Cr App R 301, QBD When an arrest is made, reasonable grounds for suspicion and reason for the arrest must exist in the mind of the arresting officer at the time of arrest and be supported by objective evidence. The arresting officer should cite the offence and reasons for making the arrest.

Dhesi v CC West Midlands Police The Times, 9 May 2000, CA The officer informing the offender that s/he is under arrest and giving the grounds does **not** have to be the same officer as the one who is physically detaining that person.

R v Kirk [1999] 4 All ER 698, CA A suspect is entitled to know the nature of the offence(s) for which s/he is being arrested/interviewed, especially if it is/they are more serious than the offence for which he was originally arrested.

12.2.3 **Arrest procedures**

Arrest at police station—voluntary attendance

Where for the purpose of assisting with an investigation a person attends voluntarily at a police station or at any other place where a constable is present or accompanies a constable to a police station or any such other place without having been arrested—

(a) he shall be entitled to leave at will unless he is placed under arrest;

(b) he shall be informed at once that he is under arrest if a decision is taken by a constable to prevent him from leaving at will.

Police and Criminal Evidence Act, s 29

Arrest—not at a police station

Section 30 of the Police and Criminal Evidence Act 1984 provides the procedure to be applied when a constable either makes an arrest or takes a person into custody after arrest by a person other than a constable (at any place other than a police station), the relevant points are:

- The arrested person must be taken to a police station as soon as practicable after arrest.
- This must be a police station designated for dealing with 'PACE' prisoners, unless:
  - ◆ it is anticipated that the arrested person will be dealt with in less than six hours;
  - ◆ the arrest/taken into custody has been made without the assistance of any other constable(s) and none were available to assist;
  - ◆ it is considered that the arrested person cannot be conveyed to a designated police station without the arrested person injuring himself, the constable, or some other person.

12.2.4 **Arrest without Warrant: other Persons**

- If the first police station to which an arrested person is taken after their arrest is not a designated police station, he/she shall be taken to a designated police station not more than six hours after his arrival at the first police station unless he is released previously.
- Prior to arrival at the police station, the arrested person must be released without bail if the constable is satisfied that there are no longer grounds for keeping him under arrest or releasing him on bail; if this occurs the constable shall record the fact that he has done so and shall make the record as soon as practicable after release. This requirement should be read in conjunction with the necessity criteria as, once the relevant criterion making the arrest necessary has ceased, arguably the person should be released.
- A constable can delay taking a person to a police station or releasing him on bail, if the presence of the arrested person at a place (other than a police station) is necessary in order to carry out such investigations as it is reasonable to carry out immediately; if such delay occurs the reason(s) for the delay must be recorded when the person first arrives at a police station or (as the case may be) is released on bail.

Explanatory notes

The type of record that has to be made, if the arrested person is 'de-arrested' prior to arrival at the police station, is not specified, but could for example include completing a formal custody record, but is dependent on individual Force policies.

Arrest—for further offences

Where—
(a) a person—
   (i) has been arrested for an offence; and
   (ii) is at police station in consequence of that arrest; and
(b) it appears to a constable that, if he were released from that arrest, he would be liable to arrest for some other offence,
he shall be arrested for that other offence.

Police and Criminal Evidence Act 1984, s 31

Explanatory notes

The 'liability' to arrest referred to will have to take into account the necessity criteria under s 24 (see **12.2.1**).

12.2.4 **Arrest without warrant: other persons**

Section 24A of the Police and Criminal Evidence Act 1984 details the power of arrest (without warrant) which is available to other people.

Arrest power (other persons)

(1) A person **other than a constable** may arrest without a warrant—
   (a) anyone who is in the act of committing an **indictable offence**;
   (b) anyone whom he has reasonable grounds for suspecting to be committing an indictable offence.
(2) Where an indictable offence has been committed, a person other than a constable may arrest without a warrant—
   (a) anyone who is guilty of the offence;
   (b) anyone whom he has reasonable grounds for suspecting to be guilty of it.
(3) But the power of summary arrest conferred by subsection (1) or (2) is exercisable only if—
   (a) the person making the arrest has reasonable grounds for believing that for any of the **reasons** mentioned in subsection (4) it is necessary to arrest the person in question; and
   (b) it appears to the person making the arrest that it is not reasonably practicable for a constable to make it instead.
(4) The **reasons** are to prevent the person in question—
   (a) causing physical injury to himself or any other person;
   (b) suffering physical injury;
   (c) causing loss of or damage to property; or
   (d) making off before a constable can assume responsibility for him.

Police and Criminal Evidence Act 1984, s 24A(1)–(4)

Meaning of indictable offence

An indictable offence also includes triable 'either way offences'.

Explanatory notes

Therefore, a person (other than a constable) may only arrest a person without a warrant where:
- s/he is in the act of committing an indictable offence;
- there are reasonable grounds to suspect that s/he is committing an indictable offence;
- an indictable offence has been committed and:
   ♦ s/he is guilty of the offence; **or**
   ♦ there are reasonable grounds to suspect s/he is guilty of it.

However, this arrest power is only exercisable if the person making the arrest:
- has reasonable grounds to believe that it is **necessary** to arrest that person for any of the reasons listed in s24A(4); **and**
- decides that it is not reasonably practicable for a constable to make the arrest instead.

Practical considerations

- Searches, arrests, and any other statutory duties, including taking fingerprints and samples, are all subject to the use of reasonable force.

12.2.4 Arrest without Warrant: other Persons

- Consideration should be given to lawful authorities for using reasonable force and use of force resolution (see **1.2**).
- All the Codes of Practice are legally binding, failure to comply with them could result in evidence being disallowed and the police officer could be subject to disciplinary proceedings.
- Code C deals with the detention, treatment, and questioning of persons.
- Code G deals with the statutory power of arrest by police officers.
- Search upon arrest is subject to s 32 PACE (see **12.3**).
- Section 110(4) of the Serious Organised Crime and Police Act 2005 stipulates that s 24 and s 24A of the Police and Criminal Evidence Act 1984 are to have effect in relation to any offence whenever committed.

Links to alternative offences or subjects

12.3 Entry, Search, and Seizure Powers

Sections 32 and 17 to 22 (inclusive) of the Police and Criminal Evidence Act 1984 deal with matters relating to searching people/premises, seizure and retention of property plus entry and access for copying of seized items. These powers, without warrant, apply either upon or after arrest.

12.3.1 Search upon arrest

Section 32 of the Police and Criminal Evidence Act 1984 creates powers of search relating to arrested persons before they are conveyed to a police station. **The relevant points are:**

Person

A constable may search any person arrested at a place other than at a police station on reasonable grounds to believe that:
- the person may present a danger to themselves or others;
- concealed on the arrested person is anything which might be:
  - ♦ used to assist escape from lawful custody;
  - ♦ evidence relating to an offence.

Premises

- If a person is arrested for an **indictable offence**, at a place other than at a police station, a constable can enter and search any **premises** in which that person was:
  - ♦ when arrested;
  - ♦ immediately before they were arrested; for evidence relating to the indictable offence for which arrested, providing reasonable grounds exist to believe that the evidence is on the premises.
- If the premises consist of two or more separate dwellings, the power to search is limited to:
  - (a) any dwelling in which the arrest took place or in which the person arrested was immediately before their arrest; **and**
  - (b) any parts of the premises which the occupier of any such dwelling uses in common with the occupiers of any other dwellings comprised in the premises.

Seizure—person

A constable searching a person in the exercise of this power may seize and retain anything found on that person on reasonable grounds to believe that:
- the person might use it to cause physical injury to that person or to any other person;

12.3.1 Search upon Arrest

- the person might use it to assist him/her to escape from lawful custody (other than an item subject to **legal privilege**);
- it is evidence of an offence or has been obtained in consequence of the commission of an offence (other than an item subject to legal privilege).

Seizure—premises

Section 19 of the Police and Criminal Evidence Act 1984 applies (see **12.3.4**).

Meanings

Indictable offence

This includes triable 'either way offences'.

Premises

Premises includes any place, and in particular, includes:
(a) any vehicle, vessel, aircraft or hovercraft;
(b) any offshore installation;
(ba) any renewable energy installation; and
(c) a tent or movable structure.

Legal privilege

- Items subject to legal privilege relate to communications between the client and:
  - ♦ a professional legal adviser;
  - ♦ any person representing them;
  - ♦ between such adviser/representative and any other person.
  This communication was made in connection with the:
  - ♦ giving of legal advice;
  - ♦ contemplation of legal proceedings for such purpose.
- It also includes items enclosed with or referred to in such communications, when they are in the possession of a person who is entitled to them.
- Items held with the intention of furthering a criminal purpose are not items subject to legal privilege.

Explanatory notes

- This power to search a person does not authorize a constable to require a person to remove any items of clothing in public other than an outer coat, jacket, or gloves.
- It does authorize a search of a person's mouth.
- The power to search premises is only to the extent that is reasonably required for the purpose of discovering any such thing or any such evidence.
- Any search of premises must comply with Code of Practice B.
- Nothing in this section affects the power given by the Terrorism Act 2000, s 43.
- This power does not apply to an arrest which takes place at a police station.

- Unless an item is for furthering a criminal purpose, items held subject to legal privilege cannot be seized when discovered during a premises search or executing a search warrant for an indictable offence.
- Legal privilege does not extend to a conveyancing document, solicitor's time sheets, fee records, appointment books, and other similar documents.
- Generally, an expert working for the defence is covered by the same legal privilege as the rest of a defence team.
- For power to search other premises after arrest see **12.3.3** for details.
- For search warrants see **12.4** for details.

12.3.2 **Power of entry to arrest, save life, or prevent damage**

Power to enter premises

Section 17 of the Police and Criminal Evidence Act 1984 creates a power to enter premises to affect an arrest or to save life/prevent damage. **The relevant points are**:

Any constable may enter and search any premises for the purpose of:
- executing a:
  - ♦ warrant of arrest issued in connection with or arising out of criminal proceedings;
  - ♦ 'warrant of commitment';
- arresting a person for:
  - ♦ an **indictable offence**;
  - ♦ an offence:
    - of prohibition of uniforms in connection with political objects (Public Order Act 1936, s 1);
    - of fear or provocation of violence (Public Order Act 1986, s 4);
    - involving drink or drugs for staff on the transport system (Transport and Works Act 1992, s 27);
    - relating to control of rabies (Animal Health Act 1981, s 61);
    - any of sections 4, 5, 6(1) and (2), 7 and 8(1) and (2) of the Animal Welfare Act 2006 (offences relating to the prevention of harm to animals) (see **11.6.1**).
    - relating to squatting and unlawful eviction (Criminal Law Act 1977, ss 6, 7 8 or 10);
    - drive/attempt to drive/in charge vehicle whilst under influence of drink or drugs (Road Traffic Act 1988, s 4);
    - failure to stop when required to do so by a constable **in uniform** (Road Traffic Act 1988, s 163);
    - failure to comply with an interim possession order (Criminal Justice and Public Order Act 1994, s 76).
- arresting a child or young person who is absent being remanded or committed to local authority accommodation/place of safety (Children and Young Persons Act 1969, s 32(1A));

12.3.2 Power of Entry to Arrest, Save Life, or Prevent Damage

- recapturing any person who is unlawfully at large while liable to be detained:
  - in a prison, remand centre, young offenders institution, or secure training centre;
  - any other place (children and young persons guilty of grave crimes) (Powers of Criminal Courts Sentencing Act 2000, s 92);
- recapturing any person who is unlawfully at large, being a patient who has escaped from involuntary custody at a Mental Hospital and who is being **immediately** pursued by the constable;
- saving life or limb (human) or preventing serious damage to property.

Conditions

- Except for the purpose of saving life or limb (human) or preventing serious damage to property, these powers are only exercisable if the constable has reasonable grounds for believing that the person whom he/she is seeking is on the premises.
- In relation to premises consisting of two or more separate dwellings, these powers are limited to:
  - any parts of the premises which the occupiers of any dwelling comprised in the premises use in common with the occupiers of any other such dwelling; **and**
  - any such dwelling in which the constable has reasonable grounds for believing that the person whom s/he is seeking may be there.
- The power to search is only given to the extent that is reasonably required for the purpose for which the power of entry is exercised.

Explanatory notes

- Code of Practice B must be complied with when this power is exercised.
- A 'warrant of commitment' is a commitment warrant to prison issued under the Magistrates' Courts Act 1980, s 76 for failing to pay fines. It does not include 'default warrants' where an offender has defaulted on their payment of a fine.
- An **indictable offence** includes triable 'either way offences'.
- Saving animals could be preventing serious damage to property.
- A designated Community Support Officer has the same powers of a police constable to enter and search premises for the purpose of saving life or limb or preventing serious damage to property (see **11.1**).
- Nothing in this section affects any power of entry to deal with or prevent a breach of the peace, at common law (see **7.3**).

Related cases

Blench v DPP [2004] EWHC 2717, QBD A call was received from a female that a drunken man was taking her baby, she then told the police not to attend. Held that the police were allowed to enter the property as they had reason to believe that a child was at risk. Also there had been and was likely to be another breach of the peace. Therefore, their presence was lawful and they were not trespassers.

O'Loughlin v Chief Constable of Essex [1998] 1 WLR 374, CA When entry to premises is made in order to arrest a person for an offence, any occupier present should be informed of the reason for the entry, unless circumstances make it impossible, impracticable, or undesirable; otherwise the constable would not be acting lawfully.

R v D'Souza The Times, 16 October 1992, HL Forced entry was made to a dwelling by police officers in order to recapture a person who was unlawfully at large from a secure hospital (under the Mental Health Act). As the officers were not in 'immediate pursuit' they were acting unlawfully. **Note:** This 'immediate pursuit' requirement does not apply to people unlawfully at large from prison/custody/remand/serving a sentence.

12.3.3 **Searching of premises after arrest**

Section 18 of the Police and Criminal Evidence Act 1984, creates a power to enter and search premises after someone has been arrested for **an indictable offence** and provides a power to seize relevant items.

Power to enter/search after arrest

(1) Subject to the following provisions of this section, a constable may enter and search any premises **occupied** or **controlled** by a person who is under arrest for an **indictable** offence, if he has reasonable grounds for suspecting that there is on the premises evidence other than items subject to **legal privilege**, that relates—
  (a) to that offence; **or**
  (b) to some other indictable offence which is connected with or similar to that offence.
(2) A constable may seize and retain anything for which he may search under subsection (1) above.
(3) The power to search conferred by subsection (1) above is only a power to search to the extent that is reasonably required for the purpose of discovering such evidence.
(4) Subject to subsection (5) below, the powers conferred by this section may not be exercised unless an officer of the rank of inspector or above has authorised them in writing.
(5) A constable may conduct a search under subsection (1)—
  (a) before the person is taken to police station or released on bail under section 30A; **and**
  (b) without obtaining an authorisation under subsection (4), if the condition in subsection (5A) is satisfied.
(5A) The condition is that the presence of the person at a place (other than a police station) is necessary for the effective investigation of the offence.
(6) If a constable conducts a search by virtue of subsection (5) above, he shall inform an officer of the rank of inspector or above that he has made the search as soon as practicable after he has made it.

12.3.3 Searching of Premises after Arrest

(7) An officer who—
    (a) authorises a search; **or**
    (b) is informed of a search under subsection (6) above, shall make a
      record in writing—
        (i) of the grounds for the search; **and**
        (ii) of the nature of the evidence that was sought.

(8) If the person who was in occupation or control of the premises at the
    time of the search is in police detention at the time the record is to be
    made, the officer shall make the record as part of his custody record.

Police and Criminal Evidence Act 1984, s 18(1)–(8)

Meanings

Occupied

This is not defined, but refers to premises where the arrested person
resides or works and may include occupancy as an owner, tenant, or
'squatter'.

Controlled

This is not defined, but includes premises in which the arrested person
holds some interest, such as owning, renting, leasing, or has use of the
premises.

Indictable

An indictable offence includes triable 'either way offences'.

Legal privilege (see 12.3.1)

Explanatory notes

- A search should only be conducted if the officer has reasonable
  grounds for suspecting that evidence of that or another connected or
  similar indictable offence is on the premises.
- The search must be conducted in accordance with Code of Practice B.
- In addition to making the written authority, it is a matter of good
  practice for the inspector (or above), who authorizes the search, to
  endorse the custody record as well.
- Another power to search premises immediately after arrest is created
  by s 32 (see 12.3.1).
- A designated Community Support Officer has the same powers as a
  police constable to enter and search premises after arrest under this
  power.

Related cases

**R v Commissioner of the Metropolitan Police and the Home Secretary
ex parte Rottman** [2002] UKHL 20, HL Common law powers of seizure
still exist.

**Cowan v Commissioner of the Metropolitan Police [2000] 1 WLR 254,
CA** Where a constable may seize 'anything' which is on premises, there

is no reason why 'anything' could not mean 'everything' that was moveable and it was practicable to remove. It does not matter that property itself could be considered to be premises, so the removal of a vehicle (being premises) is lawful and can be seized if necessary.

12.3.4 **Powers of seizure from premises**

Section 19 of the Police and Criminal Evidence Act 1984 provides a constable who is lawfully on premises with a general power to seize property.

Power to seize

(1) The powers conferred by subsections (2), (3) and (4) below are exercisable by a constable **who is lawfully on any premises**.

(2) The constable may seize anything which is on the premises if he has reasonable grounds for believing—

    (a) that it has been obtained in consequence of the commission of an offence; **and**

    (b) that it is necessary to seize it in order to prevent it being concealed, lost, damaged, altered or destroyed.

(3) The constable may seize anything which is on the premises if he has reasonable grounds for believing—

    (a) that it is evidence in relation to an offence which he is investigating or any other offence; **and**

    (b) that it is necessary to seize it in order to prevent the evidence being concealed, lost, altered or destroyed.

(4) The constable may require any information which is stored in electronic form and is accessible from the premises to be produced in a form in which it can be taken away and in which it is visible and legible or from which it can readily be produced in a visible and legible form, if he has reasonable grounds for believing—

    (a) that—

        (i) it is evidence in relation to an offence which he is investigating or any other offence; **or**

        (ii) it has been obtained in consequence of the commission of an offence; **and**

    (b) that it is necessary to do so in order to prevent it being concealed, lost, tampered with or destroyed.

(5) The powers conferred by this section are in addition to any power otherwise conferred.

(6) No power of seizure conferred on a constable under any enactment (including an enactment contained in an Act passed after this Act) is to be taken to authorise the seizure of an item which the constable exercising the power has reasonable grounds for believing to be subject to **legal privilege**.

Police and Criminal Evidence Act 1984, s 19(1)–(6)

12.3.4 Powers of Seizure from Premises

Explanatory notes

- Officers using this power can (at all times they are on the premises lawfully) seize any evidence whether it is owned by the defendant or by someone else, provided the seizure of it is necessary for the purpose(s) described. However, this Act does not provide a specific power for seizure of an innocent person's property when it is in a public place.
- As vehicles are deemed to be 'premises' for the purposes of this Act, they can be seized under the same power (*Cowan v MPC* [2000] 1 WLR 254, CA).
- Motor vehicles, if owned by an innocent party and in a public place, may also be searched under authority of a s 8 warrant (see **12.4**) to search premises for evidence.
- A designated civilian investigating officer has the same seizure powers as a police constable.

Section 20 of the Police and Criminal Evidence Act 1984 relates to the seizure of computerized information from premises.

Seizure of computerized information

(1) Every power of seizure which is conferred by an enactment to which this section applies on a constable who has entered premises in the exercise of a power conferred by an enactment shall be construed as including a power to require any information stored in any electronic form and accessible from the premises to be produced in a form in which it can be taken away and in which it is visible and legible or from which it can readily be produced in a visible and legible form.

(2) This section applies—

    (a) to any enactment contained in an Act passed before this Act;

    (b) to sections 8 and 18 above;

    (c) to paragraph 13 of Schedule 1 to this Act; and

    (d) to any enactment contained in an Act passed after this Act.

Police and Criminal Evidence Act 1984, s 20(1), (2)

Seizure of bulk material

The Criminal Justice and Police Act 2001 allows seizure of bulk material in order to examine it elsewhere ('seize and sift').

Premises

Section 50 of the 2001 Act allows a person who is lawfully on premises to seize bulk material when using existing seizure powers, providing:

- there are reasonable grounds to believe that it is material which can be searched for and seized;
- in all the circumstances, it is not reasonably practicable for this to be ascertained whilst on the premises;
- it is necessary to remove it from the premises to enable this to be determined and the material to be separated;

- the existing seizure powers are listed in pt 1 of Sch 1 to the Act:
  - ◆ the Police and Criminal Evidence Act 1984 s 8 to s 33 (inclusive);
  - ◆ any of the other 65 named Acts with their respective sections.

Person

Section 51 of the 2001 Act gives the police additional powers of seizure of bulk material from the person, where there is an existing power to search as shown in pt 2 of Sch 1 of the Act:

- the Police and Criminal Evidence Act 1984 s 24 to s 33 (inclusive);
- any of the other seven Acts (with their respective sections) named in the 2001 Act.

Explanatory notes

- Powers given under s 50 also includes any other authorized people such as HM Revenue & Customs or designated investigating officers.
- What is reasonably practicable will differ in each case. Factors to consider include the time to examine and separate the material, and the type and number of people involved. In addition, the need to reduce the risk of accidentally altering or damaging any of the material may be relevant.
- Where legally privileged material forms part of the 'whole thing' then this can be seized in order to separate from the bulk of the material.
- Section 51 (seizure from person) could apply for example where the person has a hand held computer or computer disk which holds relevant electronic data; or a briefcase containing bulk correspondence which could not be examined in the street.
- Section 52 requires the occupier and/or some other person or persons from whom material has been seized to be given a notice specifying what has been seized and why, that they can apply to a judge for the return of the material or for access to and copying of the seized material.
- Section 21 of the Police and Criminal Evidence Act 1984 provides a person, from whom material has been lawfully seized by the police, with certain rights to access to and/or copies of it.
- Section 22 of the Police and Criminal Evidence Act 1984 provides directions and powers in relation to items that have been seized by the police.

Links to alternative subjects and offences

12.4 **Enter and Search Warrants**

Procedures for premises search warrants, the application and execution process for warrants and applying for access to excluded or special procedure materials are all controlled by the Police and Criminal Evidence Act 1984 (PACE).

There are, however, several warrants provided under specific pieces of legislation such as s 23 of the Misuse of Drugs Act 1971 and s 46 of the Firearms Act 1968. Although when executed these should be conducted in accordance with PACE and its Codes of Practice, they do retain individual powers peculiar to themselves.

12.4.1 **Premises search warrant**

Section 8 of the Police and Criminal Evidence Act 1984 provides the grounds and procedure to be followed when applying for a search warrant relating to an indictable offence. It also provides a power to seize certain incriminating items.

(1) If on an application made by a constable a justice of the peace is satisfied that there are reasonable grounds for believing—
    (a) that an **indictable offence** has been committed; **and**
    (b) that there is material on **premises** mentioned in subsection (1A) below which is likely to be of substantial value (whether by itself or together with other material) to the investigation of the offence; **and**
    (c) that the material is likely to be **relevant evidence; and**
    (d) that it does not consist of or include items subject to **legal privilege, excluded material** or **special procedure material;and**
    (e) that any of the following conditions specified in subsection (3) below applies in relation to each set of premises specified in the application,
    he may issue a warrant authorising a constable to enter and search the premises in relation to each set of premises specified in the application.
(1A) The premises referred to in subsection (1)(b) above are—
    (a) one or more sets of premises specified in the application (in which case the application is for a **'specific premises warrant'**); or
    (b) any premises occupied or controlled by a person specified in the application, including such sets of premises as are so specified (in which case the application is for an **'all premises warrant'**).
(1B) If the application is for an all premises warrant, the justice of the peace must also be satisfied—

    (a) that because of the particulars of the offence referred to in paragraph (a) of subsection (1) above, there are reasonable grounds for believing that it is necessary to search premises occupied or controlled by the person in question which are not specified in the application in order to find the material referred to in paragraph (b) of that subsection; and

    (b) that it is not reasonably practicable to specify in the application all the premises, which he occupies or controls and which might need to be searched.

(1C) The warrant may authorise entry to and search of premises on more than one occasion if, on the application, the justice of the peace is satisfied that it is necessary to authorise multiple entries in order to achieve the purpose for which he issues the warrant.

(1D) If it authorises multiple entries, the number of entries authorised may be unlimited, or limited to a maximum.

(2) A constable may seize and retain anything for which a search has been authorised under subsection (1) above.

(3) The **conditions** mentioned in subsection (1)(e) above are—

    (a) that it is not practicable to communicate with any person entitled to grant entry to the premises;

    (b) that it is practicable to communicate with a person entitled to grant entry to the premises but it is not practicable to communicate with any person entitled to grant access to the evidence;

    (c) that entry to the premises will not be granted unless a warrant is produced;

    (d) that the purpose of a search may be frustrated or seriously prejudiced unless a constable arriving at the premises can secure immediate entry to them.

(4) In this Act 'relevant evidence', in relation to an offence, means anything that would be admissible in evidence at a trial for the offence.

(5) The power to issue a warrant conferred by this section is in addition to any such power otherwise conferred.

(6) This section applies in relation to a relevant offence (as defined in section 28D(4) of the Immigration Act 1971) as it applies in relation to an indictable offence.

            Police and Criminal Evidence Act 1984, s 8(1)–(3)(5)–(6)

Meanings

Indictable offence

Includes triable 'either way offences'.

Premises   (see 12.3.1)

Relevant evidence

In relation to an offence, means anything that would be admissible in evidence at a trial for the offence (s 8(4)).

Legal privilege   (see 12.3.1)

Excluded material   (see 12.4.2)

Special procedure material   (see 12.4.2)

12.4.1 Premises Search Warrant

Specific premises warrant

This consists of one or more sets of premises named/specified in the application.

All premises warrant

Being all premises occupied or controlled by an individual.

Explanatory notes

- The effects on s 8 by the Serious Organised Crime and Police Act 2005 is to stipulate that warrants can only be applied for in relation to an indictable offence, that warrants can have a 'lifetime' of 3 months, and introducing two new type of warrants that allowed entry to:
  + named/specific premises—Specific premises warrant'; or
  + premises 'occupied or controlled by' and individual—All premises warrant.
- An 'all premises' warrant will apply when it is necessary to search all premises occupied or controlled by an individual, but it is not reasonably practicable to specify all such premises at the time of application. The warrant will allow access to all premises occupied or controlled by that person, both those which are specified on the application, and those which are not.
- Where items falling outside those which may be seized under s 8(2) are found on the premises, consider the seizure provided by s 19 PACE (see **12.3.4**).
- Whenever the application for and execution of warrants is under contemplation then s 15 and s 16 together with Code B should be the main basis of any strategy being considered in relation to necessary safeguards and its execution.
- In any application also consider the procedures for access to excluded material/special procedure material if relevant provided by s 9 PACE (see **12.4.4**).
- Failure to comply with these requirements will make the entry and subsequent seizure of property unlawful (*R v Chief Constable of Lancashire ex parte Parker* [1993] Crim LR 204 QBD).
- Officers should be aware of the extensive powers to search without a warrant on arrest under s 32 or after arrest under s 18.
- Home Office Circular 88/1985 states that the power to issue a warrant is in addition to existing powers to issue warrants.
- Warrants issued under the provision of s 8 do not normally authorize a constable to search people who are on the premises.
- Such people may only be searched if arrested, but there may be a specific power to search in the warrant (eg warrants issued under s 23 Misuse of Drugs Act 1971 and s 46 Firearms Act 1968).
- These persons should be moved to 'sterile' areas in the premises during the course of a search (eg drugs search) in order to facilitate the proper execution of the warrant and complete the search of the person out of public view.
- A designated investigating officer, can apply for this warrant for any premises in the relevant police area, as if s/he were a constable. Similarly s/he shall have the powers of seizure under s 8(2) above.

- In relation to seizure and examination of bulk material see **12.3.4** for details.

12.4.2 **Application procedures for a search warrant**

Section 15 of the Police and Criminal Evidence Act 1984 sets out the procedure to be followed when applying for a search warrant, the relevant points are:

Application procedure

- This section (and s 16) relates to the issue of warrants (**under any enactment**) for constables to enter and search premises.
- Entering or searching of premises under a warrant is unlawful unless it complies with this section and s 16 (see **12.4.3**).
- Where a constable applies for such warrant the following details must be given:
  - ✦ grounds on which application made;
  - ✦ enactment under which the warrant would be issued;
  - ✦ identify (as far as practicable) the articles or persons sought.
- Furthermore, if the application is for:
  - ✦ a warrant authorizing entry and search on more than one occasion:
    - ▪ ground on which application made;
    - ▪ whether unlimited number of entries is sought;
    - ▪ otherwise the maximum number of entries desired.
  - ✦ a specific premises warrant (see **12.4.1**):
    - ▪ each set of premises to be entered and searched.
  - ✦ an all premises warrant (see **12.4.1**):
    - ▪ specify (as far as reasonably practicable) the sets of premises to be entered and searched;
    - ▪ the person who is in occupation or control of those premises and any others which requires entering and searching;
    - ▪ why it is necessary to search more premises than those specified and why it is not reasonably practicable to specify all the premises to be entered and searched.
- Such a warrant shall specify:
  - ✦ the name of the person who applied for it;
  - ✦ the date on which it is issued;
  - ✦ the enactment under which it is issued;
  - ✦ the articles or persons to be sought (identified as far as is practicable);
  - ✦ each set of premises to be searched;
  - ✦ in the case of an all premises warrant:
    - ▪ the person who is in occupation or control of premises to be searched, together with any premises under his occupation or control which can be specified and which are to be searched.
- The following points also have to be complied with:

- ✦ Applications shall be supported by an information in writing and made ex parte (subject does not have to be present).
- ✦ The constable shall answer on oath any question that the justice of the peace or judge hearing the application asks him.
- ✦ A warrant shall authorize an entry on one occasion only—unless multiple entries are authorized, in which case it must specify whether the number of entries is unlimited, or limited to a specified maximum.
- ✦ Two copies shall be made of a specific premises warrant (specifying only one set of premises and not authorising multiple entries. Otherwise, as many copies as are reasonably required may be made of any other kind of warrant.
- ✦ Copies shall be clearly certified as copies.

Explanatory notes
- Advice and guidance are given in the Code of Practice B, under search warrants.
- Where premises are multiple occupancy (eg a single house converted into flats) the warrant must specify all the rooms required to be searched (including the common living areas), and not just give the main address.

Related cases
R v CC of Lancashire ex parte Parker and McGrath [1993] Crim LR 204, QBD The magistrate or judge who issues the warrant should make copies of the warrant and certify them with their signature.

12.4.3 **Execution of search warrants**

Section 16 of the Police and Criminal Evidence Act 1984 sets out the procedure to be followed when executing a search warrant, the relevant points are:

Execution procedure
A warrant to enter and search **premises**:
- may be executed by any constable;
- it may authorize persons to accompany any constable who is executing it;
  - ✦ such a person has the same powers as the constable, but only whilst in the company and under the supervision of a constable;
    - ▪ such a person will then be able to execute the warrant, and seize anything to which the warrant relates;
- must be executed within three months from the date of its issue;
- must be executed at a reasonable hour unless it appears that the purpose of a search may be frustrated on an entry at a reasonable hour;

- will only authorize a search to the extent required for the purpose for which the warrant was issued.

Specifically, no premises may be entered or searched unless an inspector (or above) authorizes entry for:

- an **all premises warrant**:
  + premises which are not specified;
- a **multiple entries warrant**:
  + for the second or subsequent entry and search;

Notification requirements exist, when a constable is seeking to execute a warrant to enter and search premises, the constable shall:

- where the occupier is present:
  + identify themselves to the occupier. If not in uniform documentary evidence produced to show that they are a constable;
  + produce the warrant and supply a copy of the warrant to the occupier;
- if the occupier is not present, but some other person is present who appears to the constable to be in charge of the premises:
  + the constable shall deal with that person as if they were the occupier and comply with the above requirements;
- if there is no person present (occupier or in charge):
  + the constable shall leave a copy of the warrant in a prominent place on the premises.

Where a constable has executed a warrant he/she shall:

- endorse the warrant stating whether:
  + the articles or persons sought were found;
  + any articles were seized, other than articles which were sought.
- unless the warrant is for one set of premises only:
  + separately endorse each set of premises entered and searched providing the above details.

A warrant shall be returned to the **appropriate person**:

- when it has been executed;
- in the case of:
  + a **specific premises warrant** (not been executed);
  + an all premises warrant;
  + any warrant authorising multiple entries;
  upon the expiry of the three month period or sooner.

Meanings

Premises   (see 12.3.1)

All premises warrant   (see 12.4.1)

Multiple entries warrant   (see 12.4.1)

Appropriate person

If the warrant was issued by:

- a justice of the peace:

- ✦ the appropriate person will be the designated officer for the local justice area in which the justice was acting when the warrant was issued;
- a judge:
  - ✦ the appropriate person will be the appropriate officer of the court from which the judge issued it.

Specific premises warrant (see **12.4.1**)

Explanatory notes

- A warrant returned to the appropriate person shall be retained by that person for 12 months from its return.
- An occupier of premises to which the warrant relates can inspect the warrant (and should be allowed to do so) during the 12 month retaining period.
- When executing a search warrant, advice and guidance should be obtained from the Code of Practice B, under search warrants.
- A person authorized in the warrant to accompany the constable may be an expert in computing or financial matters. Such an expert will then be able to take a more active role in the search and in seizing material, rather than merely being present in an advisory or clerical capacity.
- In practical terms the supervising constable must identify any accompanying persons to the occupier of premises prior to the start of any search and explain that person's role in the process. The constable in charge will have overall supervisory responsibility and will be accountable for any action taken.

12.4.4 Access to excluded and special procedure material

Section 9 of the Police and Criminal Evidence Act 1984 provides the procedures to be adopted in order to gain access to excluded material and special procedure material.

Access procedure

(1) A constable may obtain access to **excluded material** or **special procedure material** for the purposes of a criminal investigation by making an application under **Schedule 1** and in accordance with that Schedule.

(2) Any Act (including a local Act) passed before this Act under which a search of **premises** for the purposes of a criminal investigation could be authorised by the issue of a warrant to a constable shall cease to have effect so far as it relates to the authorisation of searches—
   (a) for items subject to **legal privilege; or**
   (b) for excluded material; **or**

(c) for special procedure material consisting of documents or records other than documents.

Police and Criminal Evidence Act 1984, s 9(1), (2)

Meanings

Excluded material

Means:

- **personal records** acquired or created in the course of any trade, business, profession, or other occupation or for the purposes of any paid or unpaid office;
- human tissue or tissue fluid taken for the purposes of diagnosis or medical treatment held in confidence;
- both sets of material held in confidence subject to:
  - ✦ an express or implied undertaking to do so;
  - ✦ a disclosure restriction or an obligation of secrecy contained in any legislation;

or

- **journalistic material** which consists of documents or records other than documents, being held or continuously held in confidence (by one or more persons), subject to an undertaking restriction or obligation of confidence since it was first acquired or created for the purposes of journalism.

Personal records

Means documentary and other records concerning an individual (whether living or dead) who can be identified from them and relates to:

- their physical or mental health;
- spiritual counselling or assistance given/to be given to them; or
- counselling or assistance given/to be given for their personal welfare, by any voluntary organization or individual who by reason of:
  - ✦ their office or occupation has responsibilities for this; or
  - ✦ an order a court has responsibilities for his supervision.

Journalistic material

- Is material acquired or created for the purposes of journalism?
- Providing it is in the possession of a person who acquired or created it for this purpose.
- It will be acquired if a person receives the material from someone who intends that the recipient uses it for that purpose.

Special procedure material

- Includes journalistic material, other than excluded material
- Includes material, other than items subject to legal privilege and excluded material, in the possession of a person who acquired or created it in the course of any trade, business, profession, or for the purpose of any paid or unpaid office; and holds it in confidence subject to:
  - ✦ an express or implied undertaking to do so;

12.4.4 **Access to Excluded and Special Procedure Material**

- ♦ a disclosure restriction or an obligation of secrecy contained in any legislation.
- Where material is acquired by:
  - ♦ an employee from their employer in their course of employment;
  - ♦ a company from an associated company;
  it is only special procedure material if it was special procedure material immediately before the acquisition.
- Where material is created by:
  - ♦ an employee in the course of their employment;
  - ♦ a company on behalf of an associated company;
  it is only special procedure material if it would have been special procedure material had the employer/associated company created it.

Schedule 1

Relates to Sch 1 of the Police and Criminal Evidence Act 1984 which gives full details of the procedure to be followed when making an application to a judge in order to gain access to excluded material or special procedure material.

Premises   (see **12.3.1**)

Legal privilege   (see **12.3.1**)

Explanatory notes

- Code of Practice B provides guidance regarding the conduct of searches and advice on Sch 1 searches.
- The Crown Prosecution Service makes Sch 1 applications and advice should be sought from them in any application.
- A designated investigation officer can obtain the same access to excluded and special procedure material as a police constable.
- Case law has established that:
  - ♦ police cannot see hospital records;
  - ♦ search warrant not lawful without the proper paperwork;
  - ♦ a Sch 1 notice should specify the documents being sought.
- In relation to seizure and examination of bulk material see **12.3.4** for details.
- Officers should be mindful of the powers to search (without a warrant) on arrest (see **12.3.1**) or after arrest (see **12.3.3**).
- Special procedure and excluded material can be searched for and seized under the Police and Criminal Evidence Act 1984, s 18 and s 32, provided:
  - ♦ lawful arrest is made, in good faith; **and**
  - ♦ the search is carried out strictly within the terms of those sections.

Related cases

R v Manchester CC ex parte Taylor [1988] 2 All ER 769, QBD It is sufficient to give verbal details of documents required to the recipient of a Sch 1 notice.

R v Maidstone CC ex parte Waitt [1988] Crim LR 384, QBD A hearing under Sch 1 should be with the knowledge and in the presence of both parties.

R v Leicester CC ex parte DPP [1987] 3 All ER 654, QBD Normally parties to an application are the police and those with custody of the documents being sought.

R v Bristol CC ex parte Bristol Press and Picture Agency (1986) 85 Cr App R 190, QBD Press photographs showing criminal acts. Access to them could identify the suspects. It was in the public interest to grant the order. Conditions were met.

Links to alternative subjects and offences

Chapter 13

Patrol Matters and Guidance

13.1 **Missing Persons**

These guidelines are based on established 'best practice' and are intended to provide guidance and assistance to police officers when taking a 'missing from home' report. However, individual force policies must always be complied with and acted upon.

A missing person can be defined as anyone whose whereabouts are unknown, whatever the circumstances of disappearance, who will be considered missing until located and their well being or otherwise established.

This is a wide definition and there will be times when a person is missing, but police intervention is not always appropriate (eg tracing a long lost relative).

Initial report

- An officer from the area from where the person has gone missing must attend the report.
- The officer must be aware that a missing person report could turn into the investigation of a serious crime. The officer must **investigate** why the person is missing, where they may have gone, and gather and preserve evidence. Remember it is not a 'paper exercise', just a matter of filling in a form: it should be treated with the seriousness that it deserves.
- The initiating officer taking the report must obtain the following:
  - ♦ name, address, date of birth, sex, skin and hair colour, details of any marks, scars, tattoos, or peculiarities (eg walks with a limp, stutters);
  - ♦ description of height, build, hair style/length, clothing (including shoes and outer clothing)
  - ♦ establish the circumstances of the disappearance—what was said, any clues as to where the missing person maybe/may intend to go (keep accurate records of what is said and by whom);
  - ♦ time and date last seen, where and by whom (obtain full details of the people who had last seen/spoken to the missing person—including contact details);
  - ♦ a recent photograph (obtain permission to release this photograph, if required, to the press/television);

- has the missing person left a note, taken any spare clothing, got a mobile phone (obtain number), passport, money, transport, access to savings/bank accounts, holder of credit/debit cards?
- full details (including contact numbers) of friends, relatives, work/school;
- if this person has gone missing before—details/circumstances, where were they found?
- suicidal, medical conditions, medication to be taken, details of doctor.

- Take details of the person reporting, relationship and contact details.Assess what, if any, level of support is required for the family/person reporting.
- Make a risk assessment (see below) concerning the missing person and record the reasons for your decision.
- Gather relevant evidence for the investigation to continue. The higher the risk the more detailed the information required.
- In a high-risk case notify a supervisor immediately. In a medium risk case, notify a supervisor without undue delay and in a low risk case notify a supervisor by the end of the tour of duty.
- Search the home and immediate vicinity. If appropriate, seize any items of investigatory/evidential value—diary, notes, correspondence, details of any medical treatment, and obtain a recent photograph.
- Carry out all relevant enquiries and make further searches to locate missing person.
- Circulate the person on PNC and any other relevant systems.

Making a risk assessment

When making such a risk assessment, all factors that lead to the decision must be fully recorded by the officer attending the report.

High risk

- Is in danger due to their own vulnerability.
- May have been the victim of a serious crime.
- There are substantial grounds for believing that the public is in danger.

Action

- Immediate deployment of appropriate resources.
- Notify supervision immediately for involvement in the investigation.
- Notify a member of the senior management team.
- If the victim of a serious crime an SIO should be appointed.
- A press/media strategy should be implemented.
- Establish and maintain close contact with other relevant agencies.

Medium risk

- The person is likely to be subject to danger and/or is a risk to themselves or others.

Action

- Notify supervision regarding the circumstances and concerns.
- Deployment of appropriate resources.

- Continue an active and measured response by police and other agencies.
- Involve the press/media.

Low risk

- No apparent threat of danger to themselves or the public.

Action

- Carry out appropriate enquiries to locate the missing person.
- Notify supervision by the end of the tour of duty.
- Keep the report under regular review.

Risk assessment factors

- Is the person vulnerable, due to age or infirmity or any other factor?
- Is this type of behaviour out of character?
- Is the person suspected of being the victim of a serious crime in progress (eg abduction?).
- Are there any indications that the person is likely to commit suicide?
- Is there a reason for the person to go missing?
- Are there any indications that the person made preparations for their absence?
- What was the person intending to do when they were last seen (ie go out to the shops, see a friend), and did they carry out that intention?
- Are there family and/or relationship problems or recent history of family conflict?
- Is the person a victim or perpetrator of domestic violence?
- Does the missing person have any physical illness, disability, or mental health problems?
- Are they on the Child Protection Register?
- Do they need essential medical treatment that is not likely to be available to them?
- Is there a belief that the person may not have the physical ability to interact safely with others or in an unknown environment?
- Are there any ongoing bullying or harassment, sexual, racial, or homophobic or any other cultural or community concerns?
- Were they involved in a violent and/or racist incident immediately prior to their disappearance?
- Are they (or a relative) a witness to an offence or otherwise involved in proceedings (eg a juror)?
- Have they previously been missing and been exposed to or suffered harm?
- Any problems with work, school, college, university, or money?
- Are they drug or alcohol dependent?
- Any other problem which may affect the risk assessment not mentioned here?

Subsequent investigation

- A detailed record must be kept of all enquiries carried out.
- Supervision must review the risk assessment and it should be reconsidered at every hand over.
- The report must be regularly reviewed.

- The point of contact for the police must be kept up to date with all the progress.
- The Police National Missing Persons Bureau should be notified within 14 days.
- Could the person be in hospital, prison or custody?
- Consider CCTV, taxi records, details of bank and phone records.
- There are different categories of missing persons, which could have an effect on the subsequent investigation:
  - ✦ lost person—a person who is temporarily disorientated such as a young child or elderly person;
  - ✦ missing person who has gone voluntarily—a person who has made a conscious decision to take this particular course of action;
  - ✦ missing person who is under the influence of a third party—a person who has gone missing against their will, ie abduction or kidnap.
- **It is always advisable to think the worst until the contrary is proved.**

Persons in care

People in care are mostly, by their very nature, vulnerable and special consideration should be given to any person who goes missing from care.

Children in care

- Children in local authority care, account for the largest number of missing person's reports.
- The categories of high, medium, and low risk still apply here but there is an additional category—unauthorized absence.
- Unauthorized absence is where the child has failed to return to the care home on time, is staying with a friend at a known location, or running away after a dispute with a member of staff.
- A risk assessment should be carried out as normal. The situation should be kept under review and if the child has not returned within a few hours, then the child should be reported missing.
- The children's home and foster carers are expected to act as any reasonable parent would and make the necessary enquiries into the whereabouts of the child, before making a report to the police.

Found safe and well

- When the missing person is located, if they are over 16 there is no obligation to inform the families of their whereabouts (only that they are safe and well), if it is against the person's wishes.
- If the missing person is under 16, then there **is** an obligation to return the child to their home or a **safe** location, if there are any doubts about the child's safety.
- The report must be completed with as much detail as possible as to the circumstances in which the person was found.
- All computer systems must be updated and relevant agencies informed of the return of the missing person.

Links to alternative subjects and offences

13.2 **Child Abuse**

Specialist departments will carry out most of the investigations into child abuse cases. However, patrol officers may well be the first point of contact with the victim and their families/carers and it is important to recognize child abuse and what action to take.

The following information is based on guidelines established as 'best practice'. However, Force policy must be adhered to and this section is intended as a guide to assist in following that policy.

Child abuse is:

- abuse involving any person under the age of 18;
- the abuse can be, physical, emotional, or sexual;
- the abuse can also take the form of neglect, a persistent failure to meet a child's basic physical or psychological needs which is likely to result in serious impairment of the child's development or health.

Taking the initial report

The following is a suggested checklist regarding the relevant information to obtain when taking the initial report. All reports should be treated as serious no matter how minor they appear to be.

Checklist

- Details of the reporting person and relationship to the child.
- Nature and location of the incident or concern.
- Details of the child.
- Current location and identity of any suspect including relationship to child.
- If name not known, then a detailed description of the suspect.
- Whether there are any injuries. If so, details of injuries and whether any medical assistance is required.
- Details of any other children present and whether they are safe.
- Details and locations of any witnesses.
- Whether weapons were used.
- Whether any person present has taken alcohol or drugs.
- Whether there is any history of involvement by social services. If so, details of the social worker.
- Whether there are any relevant court orders in place.
- Whether there are any details of any special needs.
- Details of the behaviour of all parties, reporting person, victim, and suspect.
- A verbatim account of the caller's story.
- Details of the child's school and doctor, if known.
- The Child Protection/Child Abuse Unit and a supervisor must be notified as soon as possible.
- Check all computer systems both national (PNC) and local, including the Child Protection Register. This can be done through the Child Protection Unit or through Social Services.

Welfare of the child

In child abuse cases, the welfare of the child is paramount. As patrol officers you have a responsibility to check the welfare of the child.

- There is no legal requirement for a parent or guardian to be present for an officer to speak to a child.
- If that person is suspected of being involved in the abuse then **every** attempt should be made to speak to the child separately.
- Care should be taken when speaking to the child, to limit the conversation to the welfare of the child and obtaining the minimum amount of information about the incident (offence, suspect, and location), for fear of prejudicing any subsequent prosecutions.
- Officers should take into account the physical appearance, condition, and behaviour of the child.
- Officers should be mindful of the reasons behind a parent/guardian's decision not to allow the police to assess the welfare of a child.
- Further enquiries should be made to establish the welfare of the child, if cooperation with the police is refused.
- Officers should make a record of reasons for refusal of cooperation.

Police powers

- Powers of entry (see **12.3** for details):
  - ♦ Under **s 17 PACE** a constable may enter premises for the purpose of arresting a person for an indictable offence.
  - ♦ Under **s 17 PACE** a constable may enter and search premises for the purpose of saving life or limb or preventing serious damage to property.
  - ♦ Under **common law** a constable has the power of entry to prevent a breach of the peace.
  - ♦ A warrant may be issued under **s 48 Children Act 1989** to search for children who may be in need of emergency protection.
- For offences involving child cruelty see **2.4.1** for further details.
- Taking a child into police protection (see **2.4.2** for further details):
  - ♦ The **Children Act 1989, s 46**, allows a constable to remove a child who s/he has reasonable cause to believe is at risk of **significant harm** or to keep the child at place of safety such as a hospital.
  - ♦ 'Harm' is defined as 'ill treatment or the impairment of health or development' and could include 'impairment suffered from seeing or hearing ill treatment of another'.
  - ♦ 'Significant' may be a traumatic event such as suffocating, poisoning, or other violence or a series of events, which together would constitute significant harm.
  - ♦ Before exercising this power advice should be sought from the Child Protection Unit where possible.
  - ♦ If this power is used the duty inspector must be informed as soon as possible.
  - ♦ The child can only be removed under this section for a maximum of 72 hours (although it is unlikely to be for this length of time).
  - ♦ This power should only be used in emergency situations. Wherever possible child protection orders should be granted by the courts.

♦ Where the power is exercised there will be an **investigating** officer (the officer who initially took the child into police protection) and a **designated** officer (an officer of at least the rank of inspector who is responsible for safeguarding and/or promoting the child's welfare).

♦ The child should **not** be taken to a police station (only in exceptional circumstances). Where possible, early liaison with the local authority should be undertaken to find the child suitable accommodation.

♦ Suitable accommodation would be a registered children's home, certified foster care, or where necessary with relatives or other suitable carers (appropriate checks must be carried out, PNC, sex offenders register, child protection register, and any relevant local systems). The investigating officer must ensure that placement with relatives does not place the child at further risk.

♦ If the local authority is not already aware of the situation, the investigating officer should inform them as soon as possible of the circumstances.

♦ The investigating officer should also keep the child informed, at all stages, of what has and is going to happen. If appropriate take into account and act upon their views and wishes.

Links to alternative subjects and offences

13.3 **Domestic Violence**

The below information is based on guidelines established as 'best practice'. However, Force policy must be adhered to and this section is intended as a guide to assist when acting in accordance with that policy.

Domestic violence can be defined as: 'Any incident of threatening behaviour, violence or abuse (psychological, physical, sexual, financial or emotional) between persons who are or have been intimate partners or family members regardless of gender.'

Parties involved

- It includes same sex partners and ex-partners irrespective of how long ago the relationship ended.
- Family members includes immediate family members (whether directly related or not), in-laws, and step relations.

Attending at the scene

- Prior to arrival at the scene, the officers **must** be in possession of any previous history of domestic violence.
- Officers must also be aware of any other relevant information, such as outstanding warrants, wanted markers, violence markers, child protection issues, and injunctions.
- The despatch/communications centre **must** ensure that all this information is passed to the officers prior to their arrival.
- The main duty of a police officer at a report of domestic violence is to **protect** the victims and children.

Initial report

- A further risk assessment should be carried out in line with force policy, paying particular attention to weapons.
- Check details of suspect.
- Check if the suspect is still present at the scene and if not where they are.
- Circulate full description if suspect has left the scene.
- **Always separate** the parties involved if suspect still at the scene.
- Check the welfare of any person in the house, especially children and assess any needs they may have, ie medical assistance.
- **Do not** ask the victim in front of the defendant for details of the incident, and particularly not if they want to pursue a complaint.
- **Positive action** must always be taken when dealing with cases of domestic violence.
- It is advisable to take the decision about arresting the suspect away from the victim and tell both parties that it is **your** decision to arrest.
- Be prepared to justify your decision where you decide not to arrest, just as much as when you arrest.
- Record everything said by everyone at the scene and their behaviour.
- Evidence should be gathered at the scene of domestic violence as it would at the scene of any other incident.

- A victim statement should be taken in **all** cases even if it looks like the victim will not support any prosecution.

Responsibilities with regards to children

- A child is any person under 18.
- Police officers have a duty to protect a child from harm.
- If no children are present, establish whether any children reside there and their current whereabouts.
- Check the premises to establish the presence of children.
- Obtain details of all children at the scene:
  ♦ name (all names presently or previously used);
  ♦ date of birth;
  ♦ sex;
  ♦ address;
  ♦ doctor;
  ♦ details of school;
  ♦ details of child's circumstances, clothing, behaviour, injuries, cleanliness;
  ♦ details of all children normally resident at the address.

Subsequent investigation

- Always bear in mind the safety of the victim and any children.
- When considering bail and bail conditions keep the victim informed at all times.
- Inform the victim about bail and what the conditions are prior to the release of the suspect.
- Give details of local and national support groups to the victim.
- Follow force policy with regard to notifying the Domestic Violence Unit.

Police powers for entry

- PACE, s 17—enter premises for the purpose of arresting a person for an indictable offence (see **12.3**).
- PACE, s 17—enter premises for the purpose of saving life or limb or preventing serious damage to property (see **12.3**).
- Breach of the peace—enter premises or prevent or deal with a breach of the peace (see **7.3**).

Counter allegations

- These are often made in domestic violence cases, some in self-defence and some false allegations.
- The primary aggressor needs to be identified, note this is not necessarily the first person to use violence.
- Officers should establish the following when investigating counter allegations:
  ♦ injuries of both parties need to be examined;
  ♦ examine the version provided by both parties, to see if self defence is a genuine issue for either party;
  ♦ any previous reports of domestic violence and counter allegations;
  ♦ any previous convictions/arrests for violence for either party.

Parental responsibility

- If the parents are married, both parents have parental responsibility.
- If the parents are not married the mother has parental responsibility but the father will only have it if he is named on the birth certificate or has obtained it through court proceedings.
- The police do not normally get involved in child custody disagreements unless there is a welfare concern for the child or the action constitutes a criminal offence (eg abduction).
- Any breach of a custody agreement is not a police matter and should be dealt with before a court.

Property

- The police will not get involved in the sharing of property between partners. If the parties involved cannot settle it between themselves then legal advice should be sought from a solicitor.
- If the parties are married all property is classed as joint regardless of whose name it is in or who bought it.
- Where the parties are unmarried it is more complicated and depends on who bought it and what contributions each party made.
- Each party has a right to collect property that belongs to them. The police will only get involved if there is a threat of violence to either party or a breach of the peace. The police will not get involved in resolving the property issues.

Civil action

- The victim should be made aware that they have certain rights enforceable in a civil court but should be advised of the consequences of pursuing these instead of involving police.
- Victims should be informed that civil action can be costly.
- Victims should be told that if they do obtain a civil injunction **with a power of arrest** details would be recorded on police computer systems.

Links to alternative subjects and offences

13.4 **Vulnerable Victim/Witness**

All victims are entitled under the Code of Practice for Victims of Crime to receive information about local support services. Services under the Code must be given to anybody who has made an allegation to the police, or on whose behalf an allegation has been made, that they have been directly subjected to criminal conduct under the National Crime Recording Standard.

The police must ensure that victims are provided with information and contact details and that the victim's contact details are referred to the appropriate Local Victim Support Group. Details are not routinely passed concerning the victims of certain minor offences (theft of or from a motor vehicle, minor criminal damage, and tampering with motor vehicles, unless there are aggravating factors) and only with the explicit consent of victims of sexual offences or domestic violence or the relatives of homicide victims.

The Code requires that special services are provided to vulnerable and intimidated witnesses.

Vulnerable victims

- Children under the age of 17 at the time of the offence (in all cases);
- If the police consider that the quality of the evidence given by the victim is likely to be diminished if the victim:
  - ♦ suffers from mental disorder within the meaning of the Mental Health Act 1983 (see **11.2**);
  - ♦ has a significant impairment of intelligence and social functioning; or
  - ♦ has a physical disability or are suffering from a physical disorder.

Intimidated victims

- Are those where the police are satisfied that the quality of evidence given by the victim is likely to be diminished by reason of fear or distress on the part of the victim in connection with testifying in the proceedings. The following must be taken into account:
  - ♦ the nature and alleged circumstances of the offence;
  - ♦ the age of the victim;
  - ♦ where relevant: social and cultural background and ethnic origins of the victim; the domestic and employment circumstances of the victim; any religious beliefs or political opinions of the victim.
  - ♦ any behaviour towards the victim on the part of the accused, members of the family, or associates of the accused, or any other person who is likely to be an accused or a witness in the proceedings.
- All reasonable steps must be taken to identify vulnerable or intimidated victims using the above criteria. Where such a victim may be called as a witness in criminal proceedings, special measures under the Youth Justice and Criminal Evidence Act 1999 must be

considered (see below). (See also **13.2** on Child Abuse, **13.7** on Dealing with People with Disabilities and **13.6** on Hate Incidents.)

- The police should consult the vulnerable victim/witness and those who know them best to seek advice on communicating with them.
- A 'supporter' should be present while a vulnerable witness is being interviewed.
- When deciding where interviews should take place, account should be taken of the needs and the wishes of the vulnerable witness.

Referrals to Victim Support

- If appropriate, a *Victims of Crime* leaflet should be handed to the victim. This explains that the victim's details will be passed to Victim Support unless the victim expresses a contrary wish (except in cases of domestic violence or sexual crime or bereaved relatives of victims of homicide where express consent is always required). This requirement could be met by officers using a standard form of words when recording details of the crime from the victim. This should be along the following lines: 'Victim Support is an independent charity which can offer you help. We recommend their services, and it is our (force) policy to refer your details to them unless you ask us not to.'
- If the victim then says that they do not want their details passing to Victim Support, the officer should record that fact in his/her notebook, or on the computer system, if recording the crime details over the phone, and ensure compliance. Unless such a response was formally recorded, it could be assumed that the victim was content for their details to be passed on. The Information Commissioner believes that where information systems are used to record the reporting of a crime, there is value in having a mechanism to record that the victim has received the notification. If a victim subsequently complained to the Commissioner that their details had been passed on to Victim Support without their knowledge, then any Chief Officer having such a record available would be well placed to rebut such an assertion.
- For further information see:
  - ♦ Home Office Circular 44/2001 Referral of victims' details to victim support/revised version of the 'Victims of Crime' leaflet;
  - ♦ ACPO—VICTIM SUPPORT Victim Referral Agreement (2003).

Special measures for vulnerable witnesses in court proceedings

Some witnesses are eligible for **special assistance** in criminal proceedings. The measures of the Youth Justice and Criminal Evidence Act 1999 are available:

- if the witness is under the age of 17 at the time of the hearing;
- if the quality of the evidence is likely to be diminished because the witness suffers from **mental disorder** or otherwise has significant impairment of intelligence and social functioning;
- the witness has a physical disability or is suffering from a physical disorder (Youth Justice and Criminal Evidence Act 1999, s 16);

- if the quality of evidence given by the witness is likely to be diminished by reason of fear or distress on the part of the witness in connection with testifying in the proceedings (Youth Justice and Criminal Evidence Act 1999, s 17).

Meanings

Mental disorder

- Means mental illness, arrested or incomplete development of mind, psychopathic disorder, and any other disorder or disability of mind and 'mentally disordered' is to be construed accordingly.
- There is no inherent reason why a person suffering from a mental condition would not make a reliable witness.

Special assistance

- The **special measures** include screening the witness from the accused, evidence by live-link, evidence given in private, removal of wigs and gowns, video-recorded evidence in chief and cross-/re-examination, examination through an intermediary, and aids to communication (Youth Justice and Criminal Evidence Act 1999, ss 23–30). Not all of these measures are currently available in both the Crown Court and the magistrates' court, some are being piloted. (For further information see Home Office Circular 59/2003):
- A video interview will not be needed in all cases. When dealing with a victim/witness who is a child or a vulnerable adult one should seek advice from the appropriate department regarding children and from a supervisory officer for vulnerable adults.

Video interview of evidence

To decide if video recording their evidence may benefit a vulnerable witness the following steps should be taken:

- identify vulnerable witness;
- decide on video interview or written statement;
- obtain authorization to video interview;
- witnesses under 17: record reasons for obtaining or for **not** obtaining video interview on the appropriate form;
- decide if any other special measures are applicable;
- on the appropriate forms: provide explanation on how the quality of the evidence (coherence, completeness, accuracy) would be improved by video interview. Include views of victim/witness;
- arrange for trained video interviewer to conduct interview;
- ensure that room is booked and witness is attending;
- complete short descriptive note of video interview on the appropriate forms.

Explanatory notes

- During the **investigation** the police must notify the victim of the progress of the case and its conclusion. In cases of serious crime, where no person has been charged, information must be given about the review procedure.

- A **Family Liaison Officer** must be assigned to relatives where a victim has died as result of (suspected) criminal conduct.
- Vulnerable and intimidated victims must be notified within one working day if a suspect is arrested/released/bailed and of bail conditions relating to the victim (all other victims within five working days). Victims must be informed in the same way about cautions, reprimands, final warnings, PNDs, or other non-court disposal methods. Where the offender is under the age of 18 the victim's contact details must be passed on to the Youth Offending Team unless the victim asks the police not to do so.
- For general advice on dealing with witnesses see: Criminal Justice System, The Code of Practice for Victims of Crime, October 2005.

Links to alternative subjects and offences

13.5 Forced Marriages

It is important that the difference between an arranged marriage and a forced marriage is recognized and understood.

An **arranged** marriage is **an agreement** between both parties (usually prompted by the parents) entered into freely and is a practice that has worked successfully in several cultures for many centuries.

A **forced** marriage is where one or both of the parties has **not agreed** to marry and has been forced to do so **against their own free will**. Although it is mostly women who are affected by this, there are cases of men who are also forced to marry and they should be treated in exactly the same way as a woman making the report.

The information contained within this chapter is based on official guidelines. However, Force policy must be adhered to and this section is intended as a basic guide to be acted on in accordance with that policy.

While there is currently no specific offence in England and Wales relating to forced marriages, there are criminal offences that can be committed by the family and (potential) husband/wife of the person when forcing someone into marriage. Possible criminal offences include assault, kidnap, sexual offences, and murder.

The initial report

The most important factors when dealing with cases of forced marriage are the safety of the person and confidentiality.

- The victim must be seen in a secure place and **on their own**.
- The nominated officer who has responsibility for such matters must be contacted as soon as possible, otherwise duty supervision must be notified.
- Reassure the victim about the confidentiality of police involvement.
- It is important to establish a safe and discreet means of contact with the victim in the future.
- Obtain full details to pass onto the nominated officer.
- Treat the victim in a respectful and sensitive manner and take into account their feelings and concerns.
- If the victim is under 18 then contact the Child Protection department.

If the nominated officer is not available to deal with the incident, then there are additional steps to take to ensure that information is gathered and the safety of the victim is ensured as far as possible.

- Ask the victim if they would prefer an officer of a certain gender, race, nationality or religion to deal with the report.
- Obtain **full** details of the victim, including National Insurance number and a copy of their passport.
- Make a record of any birthmarks distinguishing features.
- Obtain a recent photograph or take a photograph of the victim (with the victim's consent).

- Create a restricted entry on the local intelligence system.
- Make sure that the victim has the contact details for the nominated officer.
- Perform a risk assessment in every case.
- Identify any possible criminal offences and if appropriate submit a crime report.
- Secure any evidence in case of any future prosecutions.
- Keep a full record of all decisions made and the explanations for those decisions (including decisions not to take action).
- With the victim's consent refer them to local and national support groups.
- Tell them of their right to seek legal advice and representation.

As well as a list of steps to take, there are also things that should not be done:

Do not:

- Send the person away saying it is not a police matter.
- Send them back to the family home against their wishes.
- Approach the family without express consent of the victim.
- Inform anyone of the situation without express consent of the individual.
- Attempt to mediate and reconcile the family.

There are different types of situations where the issue of forced marriage can arise:

- Fear of being forced to marry in the UK or abroad.
- Already in a forced marriage.
- A third party report.
- A spouse brought from abroad.

It is likely that the nominated officer will take over enquiries, however, it is advisable to be aware of the necessary steps to take.

Fear of being forced to marry in the UK or abroad

Additional steps to be taken as well as those listed above are:

- Obtain as much detail as possible about the victim's family both here and abroad including the intended spouse's details.
- Discuss with the person if there is anyway of avoiding going abroad and if they did not go what difficulties that could cause.
- Obtain exact details of where the victim would be staying abroad.
- Ascertain if there is a family history of forced marriage.
- Report details of the case to the Forced Marriage Unit (FMU) at the Foreign and Commonwealth Office and pass on contact details (see **Appendix 1**) to the victim. The FMU provides advice and assistance to potential and actual victims of forced marriage. It works with partnership agencies both in the UK and abroad to assist those affected by forced marriage.

If the victim does travel abroad ensure the following:

- That they have details of their passport in a safe place.
- That they can learn at least one telephone number and email address of a trusted person.

- Ensure that they contact you on their return **without fail** and ask for an approximate return date.
- Decide on a code word so that if contact is made, verification of identity can be made.
- Advise they take emergency cash and details of a trusted person in that country.
- Ask the victim for details of a trusted person in the UK whom they will be keeping in touch with and who you can contact in case of problems, ie if they do not return on specified date. Contact that person prior to the departure of the victim and pass on yours or the nominated officers contact details.
- Ensure they have the details of the nearest Embassy/British High commission in the country they are visiting.

Already in a forced marriage

Additional steps to be taken as well as those listed above are:

- Obtain details of the marriage, where, when, who, etc.
- Ascertain if any other family members are at risk.
- Take a statement about adverse behaviour towards the victim, such as threats and harassment (if appropriate).
- Explain different courses of action to the victim.
- Refer the victim with their consent to local and national support groups.
- Establish a safe way to contact the victim and maintain contact with them.
- Refer the matter to the Forced Marriage Unit (see **Appendix 1** for contact details) if there are concerns about visa issues or one or both of the parties are from overseas.
- Make a referral to social services and Child Protection Department if the victim is, or has children under, 18.

A third party report

Additional steps to be taken as well as those listed above are:

- Obtain contact details of the informant and stay in contact with them and advise them against making their own enquiries as this may jeopardize the official investigation.
- Ascertain the relationship between the informant and the potential victim.
- Find out as much details as possible as where the victim is being held and in what circumstances and if there is any evidence available to corroborate the story.
- Check missing persons reports to see if the victim is reported missing.
- Obtain as much information as possible about the victim's family and the intended spouse's family and extended family in the UK and overseas.
- Obtain a recent photograph of the victim.
- Obtain some details (about the victim) that only the victim would know (an aid for verification of identity).

- Prior to contacting the police overseas it is essential to establish if any reliable links exist within that police force (this can be done through other police forces, Interpol and the Foreign and Commonwealth Office). **Do not** contact the force directly without making these enquiries.

A spouse brought from abroad

Additional steps to be taken as well as those listed above:

- Ensure that an independent authorized interpreter is available if required.
- Ensure the victim is put at ease as they may be very frightened, vulnerable, and isolated.
- Refer the victim with their consent to the relevant agencies and support groups, such as solicitors, immigration, and counselling.
- Notify domestic violence vulnerable witness coordinator if applicable.
- Refer to social services and Child Protection Department if the victim is, or has children under, 18.

Links to alternative subjects and offences

13.6 **Hate Incidents**

The information in this chapter is based on guidelines established as 'best practice'. However, Force policies and procedure must be adhered to and this section is intended to assist when these policies are being acted upon.

Hate crime/incidents

- A **hate incident** is any incident, which may or may not constitute a criminal offence, which is perceived by the victim or any other person, as being motivated by prejudice or hate.
- A **hate crime** is any hate incident, which constitutes a criminal offence, perceived by the victim or any other person, as being motivated by prejudice or hate.
- Hate crimes and hate incidents have to be distinguished. All hate crimes are hate incidents, but some hate incidents may not constitute a criminal offence and will not be recorded as hate crime. The police are responsible for data collection in relation to hate incidents and hate crimes.
- A hate crime/incident is determined by the **perception of the victim or any other person**. It is not relevant if there is no apparent motivation as the cause of an incident.
- The prejudice or hate perceived can be based on a number of factors: disability, age, religion, faith, sexual orientation, gender identity, race, etc. A victim of a hate incident does not have to be a member of a minority group or someone who is generally considered to be vulnerable. Anyone can be a victim of hate crime.
- For data recording purposes, the police have to specifically record hate incidents where the prejudice is based upon race, faith, sexual orientation, or disability.
- Romany Gypsies and Irish Travellers are specific ethnic groups. They are entitled to the full protection of the Race Relations Act 1976 and associated legislation outlawing racially aggravated conduct.
- Hate incidents may be related to **race, homophobia, faith/religion, disability.Homophobia** is an irrational fear and dislike for people who identify themselves as lesbian, gay, or bisexual.
- An incident where the effectiveness of the police response is likely to have a significant impact on the confidence of the victim, his/her family and/or their community is defined as a **critical incident**.
- The aim of a hate crime investigation is to identify and prosecute offenders to the satisfaction of the victim and the community and seek to reduce repeat victimization.

Legislation

- A witness statement may be admitted in evidence instead of the witness having to give oral evidence in certain circumstances, if the witness has made a written statement to a police officer (or similar investigator) and is prevented from testifying either in person or through fear (Criminal Justice Act 2003, s116).

- The Crime and Disorder Act 1998 creates **racially or religiously aggravated** provisions of the following offences: assault, criminal damage, public order offence, harassment (see **7.10**).
- Similarly s 17 to s 23 of the Public Order Act 1986 relate to racial hatred offences (see **7.9**)
- With other offences, the courts are required to consider racial or religious hostility as an aggravating factor when sentencing (Criminal Justice Act 2003, s 145).
- Hostility based on **disability or sexual orientation** must also be taken into account as an aggravating factor in sentencing (Criminal Justice Act 2003, s 146).

Reporting and recording of hate crime

- Ignorance, prejudice, and hostility are largely the basis for hate crime rather than personal gain.
- It is important that all police personnel, when dealing with hate crime victims, are aware of their unique needs and vulnerability.
- One should consider issues such as language, religion, and cultural/lifestyle backgrounds and should do the utmost to meet the diverse needs of each victim.
- It is essential to be aware that hate crime may escalate into a critical incident. Failure to provide an appropriate and professional response to such reports could cause irreparable damage to future community and confidence in the police service.
- An officer should attend the scene in response to any hate crime incident reported to provide reassurance and immediate support to the victim. It is vital that the level of support offered to the victim or witness is appropriate to his/her needs.
- Hate crime victims face the added trauma of knowing that the perpetrator's motivation may be an impersonal group hatred, relating to some feature that they will share with others.
- A crime that may normally have a minor impact becomes, with the hate element, a very intimate and hurtful attack that is likely to undermine the victim's quality of life.
- Understanding and respect must be shown to the victim.
- It should be explained to the victim that the details of the incident are likely to be shared with other agencies.
- The report of a hate crime should not be taken over the phone unless the victim expresses the wish to report it that way.
- A supervising officer has to be informed and should attend the scene.
- An officer of at least the rank of inspector has to be informed of any hate crime incident that may develop into a critical incident.
- Victims of possible homophobia should not be questioned regarding their sexuality. If they want to volunteer this information this should be recorded in the report. Where such information is provided it is vital that it remains confidential, otherwise disclosure could seriously erode his/her confidence in the police.

- Friends/family of the victim or witness may not have been told of their sexuality. (Inadvertent) disclosure could seriously erode his/her confidence in the police and that of the community he/she represents.
- Evidence of an offence is **not** required when **recording a hate incident**. There is no evidential test as to what is or is not a hate incident. All that is required is that the incident is perceived by the victim or another person as being motivated by prejudice or hate.
- If it is not immediately apparent that there is a hate element the person reporting should be asked the reasons for their belief. This should be recorded in order to assist identifying possible lines of enquiry. Incidents may be recorded as hate incidents at a later stage, if the victim discloses such a perception or the original perception changes.
- Even where the victim does not regard the incident as a hate incident police officers may identify it as such. This should be recorded in the appropriate manner. Victims may be unwilling to reveal that they are being targeted because of skin colour, religion, or lifestyle or may not be aware that they are a victim of hate crime even if this is apparent to other people.
- Where a hate incident is reported it **must be recorded** regardless of who reported it, whether a crime has been committed, and whether there is any evidence to identify the hate element.
- Individual forces use different hate incident report forms and the computerized Crime Reporting System.
- For further information see Home Office Police Standards Unit/ACPO, Hate Crime: Delivering a Quality Service, Good Practice and Tactical Guidance (2005).

Religious dates and events

Attached at **Appendix 4** is a list of the dates of religious events and celebrations of the main religions. There are other religions that have not been included in this list.

Links to alternative subjects and offences

13.7 **People with Disabilities**

Definition of disabled person

A person with 'a **physical** or, **mental impairment** which has a **substantial** and **long-term adverse effect** on his ability to carry out normal day-to-day activities'.   Disability Discrimination Act 1995, s 1

Meanings

Physical impairment

Means any impairment affecting the senses such as sight, hearing, or a weakening of part of the body, through illness, by accident or congenitally, such as paralysis of a leg or a heart disease.

Mental impairment

Means a form of diagnosed mental illnesses or condition.

Substantial adverse effect

Means that the effect of the physical or mental impairment on the ability to carry out normal day-to-day activities must be more than minor or trivial. It does not have to be a severe effect and the test of whether a person is so impaired must focus on the things they cannot do (or can do only with difficulty) rather than the range of things that they can do (see *Goodwin v Post Office* [1959] 2 Lloyd's Rep 495, QBD). The person must be affected in at least one of the following respects: mobility, manual dexterity, physical coordination, continence, ability to lift, carry or otherwise move everyday objects, speech, hearing, eyesight, memory or the ability to concentrate, learn or understand, or perception of risk or physical danger.

Long-term

Means that the effect has to have lasted, or be likely to last, overall for at least 12 months or for the rest of the life of the person affected.

Explanatory notes

* Under the Disability Discrimination Act 1995 it is unlawful for employers and providers of certain services (viz. public and transport authorities—including the police) to discriminate against people on the grounds of their disability.
* Many people have disabilities that are not visible. Many may not refer to themselves as disabled, but as having 'difficulty in hearing/walking', having 'sight-problems'. It is essential to screen callers in order to establish if the caller has any special requirements. This ensures that the officer can meet the caller prepared.
* If the person cannot read an ID card, a password may be agreed or simply the names of the officers provided.
* When dealing with disabled people certain words and phrases should be avoided as they may cause offence. Preferences vary and one should be prepared to ask the person. Terms such as 'the disabled', 'the blind' should be avoided, and expressions like 'disabled people'

or 'people with disabilities' used instead. Other terms to be used include 'mental health problems', 'learning difficulties', 'partially sighted', 'visually impaired', 'deaf and without speech', 'hard of hearing', 'a deaf person', 'short stature/restricted growth', 'a wheelchair user/physical disability'.

- One should not make assumptions about disabilities and never assume to know what assistance is required—one should always ask the individual and wait for any offer of assistance to be accepted before attempting to help.
- People with disabilities should be treated in the same manner and with the same respect and courtesy as anyone else, and appropriate physical contact should be used, such as a handshake.
- You should always speak directly to the disabled person, not through any companion, however severe the impairment may seem.

Visual impairments

- A white cane is often used by visually impaired people, a red and white one by deaf and blind people.
- When meeting visually impaired people you should introduce yourself clearly as well as other people present and indicate where they are located. The use of people's names makes clear who is being addressed.
- Use format as preferred by the disabled person, eg large print, Braille, audio cassettes. Typed or printed text is easier to read than handwritten.
- In unfamiliar areas you should describe the layout as well as any hazards. People should be guided to their seat and be told if one wants to offer assistance. Also, they should be told if someone leaves a room, or if they will be left on their own.
- During the search of premises the person should be told what is being done. All items should be returned to their original position.

Deaf or hard of hearing

There are various degrees of impairment of hearing. Therefore, communication has to be adapted to the wishes of the individual:

- Hearing loops or qualified British Sign Language interpreters may be used for interviews or meetings.
- Finger-spelling may be used as an alternative to sign-language.
- Many people use lip-reading to reinforce what they hear, some, who have no hearing at all, use this alone. This is a demanding and tiring skill. To assist keep background noise low; make sure the deaf person is looking at the speaker before he/she begins to speak; the speaker should look directly at the person and make sure the speaker's face is clearly visible; the speaker should stop talking if he/she must turn away, and not speak with his/her back to the light source. You should speak clearly and at an even pace, but not exaggerate lip movement or gestures or block the mouth with hands, food or cigarettes. Written notes can help to present complicated information. Check regularly that everything has been understood.

- Also consider using RNID (Royal National Institute for Deaf People) Typetalk a national telephone service, which enables deaf, deafblind, hard of hearing, or speech-impaired people to communicate with hearing people anywhere by telephone.

Speech impairment

- You should not assume that speech and language defects are caused by alcohol or drugs. Slow or impaired speech does not reflect a person's intelligence.
  - ♦ You should not correct or speak for other persons, but wait while they speak and let them finish their sentence.
  - ♦ It might help to break down questions, to deal with individual points, rather than with complex matters, so that short answers can be given.

Learning difficulties and disabilities

- People with such difficulties should be treated in a manner appropriate for their age.
  - ♦ You should make sure that everything has been understood.
  - ♦ It is helpful to repeat questions in plain, clear language if there are doubts.
  - ♦ PACE Codes of Practice must be complied with when dealing with people who have a learning difficulty or mental illness. For example Code of Practice C, s 3, paras 3.12 to 3.20 deal with special groups such as the deaf, juveniles, mentally disordered or otherwise mentally vulnerable when brought to a police station under arrest or if arrested at the police station (see **12.2.2**).

Wheelchair users

- You should use the term 'wheelchair user', not 'wheelchair bound'.
- When communicating with a wheelchair user, it is best to stand back far enough to maintain eye contact comfortably.
- Help with doors, steps and kerbs should be offered, but you should not attempt to push the wheelchair without asking if help is required.
- Leaning on a wheelchair is regarded as a major personal intrusion for most.

Links to alternative subjects and offences

13.8 **Contamination of Officers/Police Staff**

The information in this chapter is based on guidelines established as 'best practice'. However, force policies and procedure must be adhered to and this section is intended as a guide to be acted on in accordance with that policy.

Contamination is when any body fluid (blood, saliva, urine, vomit, etc) from a person or a dead body comes into contact with someone's mouth, eyes, ears, nose, or any open wound or if someone is bitten or someone's skin is broken.

Immediate action is necessary.

Eyes and **mouth** should be rinsed thoroughly with water only.

Wounds should be allowed to bleed shortly, then cleaned thoroughly with water and wiped with an antiseptic wipe.

A healthcare professional or police surgeon needs to take a **blood sample** from the contaminated person and (where possible) from the other person.

Appropriate forms must be used for samples. Blood samples are to be stored away from heat at room temperature, but not in a fridge or freezer.

The Occupational Health, Safety and Welfare Unit requires:

- name/rank/collar number;
- date of birth;
- division/department;
- extension number and home phone number;
- date of previous Hepatitis B vaccination;
- detainee's/donor's name;
- detainee's/donor's date of birth;
- (if known) drug user.

If the blood test suggests that extra protection is needed, Hepatitis B immunoglobin can be given to provide immediate protection.

Dealing with people suspected of contamination

When dealing with a person who is suspected of carrying HIV or Hepatitis B or any other contagious infection, a healthcare professional may be contacted for advice.

If staff have been in contact with a (suspected) contaminated person a note should be made, including:

- name, collar number, date of birth, date of Hepatitis B vaccination;
- whether they have any cuts, grazes, or other broken skin;
- how the contamination occurred;
- name and date of birth of contaminated person, whether drug user;
- what the contamination was suspected of being.

Dealing with property

Dealing with property presents a risk of infection. It can conceal items such as needles, knives. Contaminated property must be packaged appropriately and safely.

Cleaning of contamination

When dealing with a contaminated person or spillage appropriate protective equipment must be used.

All police vehicles contain first aid kits, resuscitation aids, vinyl gloves, antiseptic sprays/wipes, and sharp's bins. If surfaces like table tops or the interior of vehicles have been in contact with body substances, they should be cleaned with antiseptic wipes. Antiseptic wipes or sprays are effective against the HIV virus and the Hepatitis B virus. When cleaning spillage of blood, vomit etc appropriate protective equipment must be worn and antiseptic used. Contaminated items must be disposed of appropriately.

Forensic evidence

Items stained with body substances (blood, saliva, semen, urine, faeces, tissue) are potential sources of infection and must be handled with caution.

Items for scientific examination must be handled in accordance with Force policy.

- The handling of contaminated items or hypodermic needles should be restricted to a minimum. A high level of personal hygiene must be exercised.
- Samples from people known to be HIV or Hepatitis B positive must be handled with extreme care and advice should be sought from a healthcare professional/doctor/pathologist.
- Nobody who has a cut or open sore should handle samples of body substances (whether they are contaminated or not).
- Accidental injuries can always happen. Needles, staples, and other sharp objects must be avoided. Specimens should be carried in trays or boxes, not in hands. Specimen containers should be touched as little as possible.
- Everyone who is dealing with forensic samples (packaging, labelling, transport) must cover any cuts or grazes on hands with waterproof dressing. Gloves should be worn and hands washed immediately afterwards. Hands should be washed often, especially before meals and after dealing with samples.
- No smoking, drinking, or eating when carrying specimens or in labs.
- If specimens are transported, antiseptics should be carried in case of spillage/leaks.
- If specimens leak the laboratory must be contacted.
- Exhibits labelled 'Health Hazard' should only be opened in exceptional circumstances. If it is necessary to open such a bag the laboratory should be consulted about hazards and precautions for handling the item. Where possible the items should be destroyed by incineration in the sealed bag.

- In case of a cut or accident, however small, the supervisor must be informed and the facts recorded.
- If necessary ask for advice from the Occupational Health, Safety and Welfare Unit.

General advice

Advice about vaccinations can be obtained from the NHS, a GP, or the Occupational Health, Safety and Welfare Unit.

AIDS is caused by the Human Immunodeficiency Virus (HIV).

HIV is mainly acquired:

- by unprotected sex with an infected person;
- by inoculation of infected blood, eg by sharing drug injecting equipment;
- during pregnancy, childbirth, or breast feeding by the baby of an infected mother.

HIV is **not** transmitted by touching, coughing, or sneezing; sharing toilets, cutlery, or crockery; contact with saliva, tears, urine, or faeces; being bitten by insects or humans; being a blood donor.

Hepatitis is an inflammation of the liver. It has a number of causes, one is the Hepatitis B virus. Vaccination can effectively prevent Hepatitis B. Where a person has not been vaccinated, effective treatment can be given if administered within 72 hours.

Hepatitis B is spread by blood-to-blood contact with an infected person's blood or certain body fluids. Hepatitis B is **much more infectious and easily transmitted** than HIV and has been found in virtually all body secretions and excretions in significant quantities!

The main danger of becoming infected with contagious diseases are where blood or body fluids from an infected person come into contact with an open wound, rash, or sore, or if the skin is punctured by a contaminated needle or other sharp object or from a bite by a person. Such risk situations are searching, road traffic accidents, recovering a body, or handling a violent or disorderly person. All incidents involving spillage of blood and body fluids must be treated with special care.

While working in **risk situations**:

- **broken skin** must be properly dressed with waterproof dressing;
- **spillage** on the skin should be washed with soap and running water as soon as possible;
- **antiseptics** are active against HIV and the Hepatitis B virus;
- during **resuscitation** there is a very small risk of transmission of Hepatitis B, especially if there is blood present. A resuscitation aid should always be used, where possible;
- where an incident has occurred where infectious diseases could be present, **protective equipment** must be used.

If someone is ill, he/she should tell his/her doctor about the type of work done. It might be necessary to also contact and inform the laboratory.

Links to alternative subjects and offences

13.9 **First Aid**

This chapter covers some basic first aid skills. If, in any of the situations described below you are not sure or the injury ailment is serious, then you should **always** get professional help.

Treatment priorities

The first priority with any casualty is to make sure the airway is open, then to check that they are breathing normally. Once this has been established, the next priority is to treat any major bleeding or burns injuries. After this, the next stage, is to deal with any broken bones.

CPR (Cardiopulmonary Resuscitation)

The first issue to consider is safety. Always wear your gloves and use the resuscitation aid you have been issued with.

Prior to commencing this procedure you should check the following:

Response—Is the casualty conscious or unconscious? Are they responding to you? If they are not, then try to gently shake them to see if you can get some kind of response from them.

Airway—are there any signs of breathing? Watch the chest to see if it rises and falls, can you hear them breathing?

Breathing—If the person is breathing, them put them on their side into the recovery position. If there is any danger of an injury to the spine, then do not move the person.

If the person is not breathing, or you are not sure, then, before starting CPR, call for an ambulance.

CPR

Prior to commencing CPR official guidelines state that rescue breaths should be administered if the person is not breathing on their own or is making only the occasional gasp.

If rescue breaths are required:
- Get medical assistance prior to commencing this procedure.
- Place the victim on his back.
- Ensure there is no obstruction in the mouth.
- Tilt the head gently back to open the airway.
- Hold the nose and, using the resuscitation aid breathe into the person's mouth with two slow long breaths.
- Each breath should last about 2 seconds.
- Remove your mouth from the victims and wait for the chest to fall.
- Repeat the procedure.
- Check for signs of normal breathing, coughing, or other signs of movement by the person, do not take longer than 10 seconds to carry out these checks.

If there are signs of circulation, continue rescue breathing until the person starts to breathe on their own. If there are no signs or you are not certain then start CPR procedure.

The CPR procedure is in two parts chest compressions and breaths.

Chest compressions

- Ensure the person is lying on their back.
- Using your index and middle fingers find the lower edge of the rib nearest to you and slide them upwards to the point where the sternum joins the rib.
- Place your index finger on this point. Slide your other hand down the sternum until it reaches your fingers.
- Place your other hand on top and lace your fingers together to ensure a firm position.
- Place your self directly above the victim with your arms straight.
- Press the breastbone down and then release. Do this 15 times. You should do this at more than one depression per second.
- After 15 compressions give 2 breaths as described below.

Breaths

- Ensure there is no obstruction in the mouth. Tilt the head gently back to open the airway. Hold the nose and, using the resuscitation aid breathe into the person's mouth with two long breaths.
- Repeat the whole procedure and continue until help arrives.
- Only stop to check for signs of circulation if the person moves or takes an independent breath.

Chest compression only resuscitation

If you are unable (*or unwilling*) to give rescue breaths, then give 'chest compressions only' resuscitation, this will at least circulate any residual oxygen in the blood stream, and will be better than no CPR at all, also:

- If chest compressions only, give at a continual rate of 100 per minute.
- If breathing starts normally, stop to reassess the casualty—otherwise do not interrupt resuscitation.
- To prevent fatigue, change with another rescuer (if available) every two minutes, ensuring change over delay is kept to a minimum.

Small children (under 7)

- One hand for compressions.
- Gentle blow.
- Five compressions and one breath.

Babies

- Two fingers.
- A puff of air.
- Five compressions and one breath.

ABC procedure

Airway—establish an open airway by tipping the forehead gently back.

Breathing—check that the person is breathing, look for movement of the chest, listen for breath sounds, and feel if there is any air being expelled from nose/mouth.

Circulation—check for heartbeat/pulse. Look for signs of improved colour, eye movement, and coughing. Adverse signs are blueness around lips, cold and pale skin.

Bleeding

- Stop the bleeding straightaway using your hand (ensuring you **always** wear gloves) or the injured person's to apply pressure.
- Lay the person down (injuries permitting).
- If stabbed in arm or leg then attempt to raise the limb.
- If the person has been stabbed with an object and that object is still in situ, **do not** remove it but apply pressure around the object.
- If possible apply dressing making sure it is dressed firmly.

Broken bones

- Try and support the injured limb and prevent it from moving.
- **Do not** move the casualty unless they are in danger.

Burns

- Use cold water to try and relieve the pain, this should take at least 10 minutes (in the case of a chemical burn—20 minutes).
- Cover the area in sterile clean material (not cotton wool or similar, as it will stick to the skin). A polythene bag can be used if the burn is adequately cooled.
- If the burn is on the hand/arm if possible remove any jewellery they are wearing before swelling occurs.

Choking

- Encourage the person to cough.
- Lower the head, so that if the item is dislodged it will come out of the mouth and not go further down the airway.
- If the object is still stuck slap the person hard between the shoulder blades (up to five times), check whether the object has become dislodged between each slap.
- If the object is still lodged then stand behind the person, place your fist into the upper abdomen and hold onto your fist with your other hand. Pull sharply upward to expel the air. Repeat as necessary.
- If the person becomes unconscious, use the ABC procedure as above.

Diabetic emergency

These fall into two types, high blood sugar and low blood sugar.

- *High blood sugar*—this condition brings a slow change to the person; dry skin, possible unconsciousness, possible chemical smell on breath. This is **very similar to drunk and incapable.**
  Action: requires hospital treatment—insulin and monitoring.

- *Low blood sugar*—this condition brings on a quick change in the person; slurred speech, feeling weak and faint, shaking and trembling, being hungry, skin clammy and cold. Person can also become confused and angry. This is very **similar to drunk and disorderly**.
  Action: requires glucose—chocolate or sugary drink.

Drug/alcohol overdose

- **Alcohol**—the symptoms are, strong smell of alcohol, unconsciousness, the person will be flushed and their face damp, deep loud breathing.
  Action: protect from cold, as may develop hypothermia. Prevent from choking or inhaling vomit. See if casualty responds to calling their name and shaking shoulders. Call ambulance if necessary.
- **Drugs**—the symptoms are, unconsciousness, drug paraphernalia around the person, dilated pupils.
  Action: Get professional help and place in the recovery position (if safe to do so).

Fits

- Do not attempt to restrain the person as this could cause injury.
- Cushion the head to prevent injury.
- Only move if the person is in danger.
- Remove objects around the person to prevent injury.
- When the fit has stopped place the person in the recovery position.
- Check for medic-alert/indicators of epilepsy.

Heart attack

- Described as crushing pain in the chest (sometimes mistaken for indigestion).
- Can also spread to the rest of the body (or just affect throat, back, stomach, jaw).
- The person may also be weak, dizzy, breathless, pale, sweaty and feel cold.
  Action: Get professional help, tell the operator it is suspected heart attack. Sit the person up with knees bent up towards them, reassure the person. If the person becomes unconscious, follow ABC above.

Stroke

Symptoms are described as a sudden:

- numbness or weakness of the face, arm or leg, especially on one side of the body;
- confusion, trouble speaking or understanding;
- trouble seeing in one or both eyes;
- trouble walking, dizziness, loss of balance or coordination
- severe headache with no known cause.

Action: Stroke is a medical emergency, every second counts. It is imperative they reach hospital quickly and receive prompt treatment to prevent further brain damage. A *'FAST'* test is used by paramedics to diagnose stroke prior to reaching hospital:

Facial weakness—can the person smile? Has their mouth or eye drooped?

Arm weakness—can the person raise both arms?

Speech problems—can the person speak clearly and understand what you say?

Test all three symptoms.

Vomiting

- Ensure that the person does not choke or inhale any vomit.
- Keep the person warm (if necessary).

Links to alternative subjects and offences

Appendix 1

Useful Contacts

ACPO (Association of Chief Police Officers)
<http://www.acpo.police.uk>
Telephone: 020 7084 8950

ASBOs (Provides Home Office guidance and related links)
<http://www.crimereduction.gov.uk/asbos/asbos9.htm>

British Association of Women Police
<http://www.bawp.org>
Telephone: 07790 505204

CEHR (Commission for Equality and Human Rights) [Effective from October 2007]
<http://www.cehr.org.uk>
Telephone: 020 7215 8415

Citizens Advice Bureau (Provides local links)
<http://www.citizensadvice.org.uk>
Telephone: 020 7833 2181 (Admin office only)

Commission for Racial Equality (from October 2007 see **CEHR**)
<http://www.cre.gov.uk>
Telephone: 020 7939 0000

Consumer Advice (Provides local contact details)
<http://www.tradingstandards.gov.uk>

Copyright Protection (see **UK Intellectual Property Office**)

Courts Service (Her Majesty's Courts Service)
<http://www.hmcourts-service.gov.uk>
Telephone: 020 7189 2000 or 0845 456 8770

CPS (The Crown Prosecution Service)
<http://www.cps.gov.uk>
Telephone: 020 7796 8000

Crime Stoppers
<http://www.crimestoppers-uk.org>
Telephone: 0800 555 111

Appendix 1: Useful Contacts

Criminal Justice System
<http://www.cjsonline.gov.uk>
email: cjsonline@cjit.gsi.gov.uk>

DEFRA (Department for Environment Food and Rural Affairs)
<http://www.defra.gov.uk>
Telephone: 08459 33 55 77

Design Protection (see **UK Intellectual Property Office**)

Disability Rights Commission (from October 2007 see **CEHR**)
<http://www.drc-gb.org>
Telephone: Helpline 08457 622 633

Drugs (Government Drugs site)
<http://www.drugs.gov.uk>
Telephone: 0207 035 4848

DVLA (Driver and Vehicle Licensing Agency)
<http://www.dvla.gov.uk>
Provides links to service required

Equal Opportunities Commission (from October 2007 see **CEHR**)
<http://www.eoc.org.uk>
Telephone: 0845 601 5901

European Commission
<http://europa.eu.int/comm>
Telephone: 00800 67891011

Forced Marriage Unit
email: fmu@fco.gov.uk>
Telephone: 020 7008 0151 Outside office hours: 020 7008 1500

Foreign & Commonwealth Office
<http://www.fco.gov.uk>
Telephone: 020 7008 1500

Forensic Science Service
<http://www.forensic.gov.uk>
Telephone: 0121 607 6985

Gay Police Association
<http://www.gay.police.uk>
Telephone: 07092 700 000

GMB (Union)
<http://www.gmb.org.uk>
Telephone: 020 8947 3131

HMIC (HM Inspectorate of Constabulary)
<http://inspectorates.homeoffice.gov.uk/hmic>
Telephone: 020 7035 2004

HMRC (HM Revenue & Customs)
<http://www.hmrc.gov.uk>
Telephone: 0800 59 5000

Home Office (Police)
<http://police.homeoffice.gov.uk>
Telephone: 0207 035 4848

Identity and Passport Service
<http://www.passport.gov.uk>
Telephone: 0870 521 0410

Immigration (Immigration and Nationality Directorate)
<http://www.ind.homeoffice.gov.uk>

Information Commissioner (Oversees and enforces compliance with the Data Protection Act 1998 and the Freedom of Information Act 2000)
<http://www.ico.gov.uk>
Telephone: Helpline 01625 545 745

International Police Association
<http://www.ipa-uk.org>
Telephone: 0115 981 3638

International Association of Women Police
<http://www.iawp.org>

IPCC (Independent Police Complaints Commission)
<http://www.ipcc.gov.uk>

Law Society
<http://www.lawsociety.org.uk>
Telephone: 020 7242 1222

Legislation (Office of Public Sector Information)
<http://www.opsi.gov.uk/legislation>

Mental Illness advice: (SANELINE)
<http://www.sane.org.uk>
Telephone: 0845 767 8000

Ministry of Justice (formerly Department for Constitutional Affairs)
<http://www.justice.gov.uk> (formerly <http://www.dca.gov.uk>)
Telephone: 020 7210 8500

Appendix 1: Useful Contacts

Missing Persons (National Missing Persons Helpline)
<http://www.missingpeople.org.uk>
Telephone: 0500 700 700

National Black Police Association
<http://www.nationalbpa.com>
Telephone: 020 7259 1280

NPIA (National Policing Improvement Agency)
<http://www.npia.police.uk>
Telephone: 020 8358 5555

NSPCC (National Society for Prevention of Cruelty to Children)
<http://www.nspcc.org.uk>
Telephone: 0808 800 5000

Parliament
<http://www.parliament.uk>

Patent Protection (see **UK Intellectual Property Office**)

PNLD (Police National Legal Database)
<http://www.pnld.co.uk>
email: pnld@westyorkshire.pnn.police.uk
Telephone: 01924 208229

Police Federation (Police Federation)
<http://www.polfed.org>
Telephone: 020 8335 1000

Prison (HM Prison Office)
<http://www.hmprisonservice.gov.uk>
email: public.enquiries@hmps.gsi.gov.uk>

Probation (National Probation Service)
<http://www.probation.homeoffice.gov.uk>
Telephone: 020 7217 0659

Public services (Directgov—provides links)
<http://www.direct.gov.uk>

Rape (Rape counselling and advice service)
<http://www.rapecrisis.org.uk>
Provides local contact details

Revenue & Customs (see **HMRC**)

RSPB (Royal Society for the Protection of Birds)
<http://www.rspb.org.uk>
Telephone: 01767 693 690

RSPCA (Royal Society for the Protection of Cruelty to Animals)
<http://www.rspca.org.uk>
Telephone: 0870 55 55 999

Samaritans Organization:
<http://www.samaritans.org>
Telephone: 08457 90 90 90

Sentencing (Sentencing Guidelines Council/Sentencing Advisory Panel)
<http://www.sentencing-guidelines.gov.uk>
Telephone: 020 7084 8130

Superintendents Association (Superintendents Association)
<http://www.policesupers.com>
Telephone: 0118 984 4005

Trade Marks (see **UK Intellectual Property Office**)

Trading Standards (Provides local contact details)
<http://www.tradingstandards.gov.uk>

UK Intellectual Property Office
<http://www.ipo.gov.uk>
Telephone: 0845 9 500 505

Unison (Union)
<http://www.unison.org.uk>
Telephone: 0845 355 0845

Youth Justice Board
<http://www.yjb.gov.uk>
Telephone: 020 7271 3033

Traffic Data—Vehicle Categories and Groups

More information or exemptions could apply than is given in this Appendix. Therefore, this table is for guidance only. There will be some instances when a road traffic/policing officer should be consulted to confirm matters.

Descriptions of Vehicle Categories and Minimum Ages

Vehicle description	Category	Minimum age
Motorcycles[1] Motorcycles[2]	A1 A	17 21[a]
3 or 4 wheeled Light vehicles[3]	B1	17[b]
Cars[4] Automatic cars (with automatic transmission) Cars with trailers exceeding 750 kg[5]	B B Automatic B + E	17[c]
Medium-sized Goods vehicles[6] Medium-sized Goods vehicles[7]	C1 C1 + E	18[d]

[1] Light motorcycles not exceeding 125cc and power output not exceeding 11 kw. Motorcycles up to 25 kw. Power to weight ratio not exceeding 0.16 kw/kg.

[2] Any size motorcycle with/without sidecar.

[3] Motor tricycles or quadricycles with design speed exceeding 50 km/hr and up to 550 kg unladen.

[4] Motor vehicles up to 3500 kg/not more than 8 passenger seats/trailer up to 750 kg; or vehicle and trailer up to 3500 kg **and** the trailer does not exceed unladen weight of towing vehicle.

[5] Where the combination does not come within category B.

[6] Lorries 3500 kg—7500 kg, with a trailer **up to** 750 kg. Total weight up to 12000 kg.

[7] Trailer exceeds 750 kg. Total weight upto 12000 kg and trailer is less than weight of towing lorry.

[a] Or 2 years after passing test. If owned or driven by armed forces—17 years.

[b] 16 if receiving disability living allowance at higher rate, providing no trailer is drawn.

[c] 16 if receiving disability living allowance at higher rate.

[d] 21 if combination weight is over 7500 kg.

Appendix 2: Traffic Data—Vehicle Categories and Groups

Vehicle description	Category	Minimum age
Large Goods vehicles[8] Large Goods vehicles[9]	C1 C + E	21[e]
Minibuses[10] Minibuses[11]	D1 D1 + E	21[f]
Buses[12] Buses[13]	D D + E	21[g]
Agricultural tractors	F	17[h]
Mowing machines/pedestrian controlled vehicles	K	16
Mopeds	P	16

[8] Vehicles over 3500 kg, with trailer **up to** 750 kg.
[9] Vehicles over 3500 kg, with trailer **over** 750 kg.
[10] With 9–16 passenger seats, and trailer **up to** 750 kg.
[11] With 9–16 passenger seats, and trailer **over** 750 kg.
[12] More than 8 passenger seats, with trailer **up to** 750 kg.
[13] More than 8 passenger seats, with trailer **over** 750 kg.

[e] If trailer up to 750 kg—17 if member of armed forces or 18 if member of young drivers scheme.
[f] 17 if member of armed forces or 18 if member of young drivers scheme.
[g] If trailer up to 750 kg—17 if member of armed forces or 18 if member of young drivers scheme.
[h] 16 if tractor less than 2.45 m wide. Trailer less than 2.45 m (2 wheel) or 4 wheels if close coupled.

Exception

If the driver has held a car driving licence (category/group B) before 1 January 1997, then that person can (without taking separate tests) drive:

• a car and trailer exceeding 750 kg (B + E);
• motor vehicles 3500 kg–7500 kg, with trailers up to a combined weight of 8250 kg (C1 + E)
• passenger vehicles with 9–16 passenger seats, not used for hire or reward (D1 and D1 + E).

These entitlements last for the duration of the licence, without being required to undergo a medical.

However, when the licence expires or is no longer in force, then that person will be required to pass the relevant test and medical examination (as required by new licence holders).

Comparison Guide—Original Groups to Current Categories

More information or exemptions could apply than is given in this Appendix. Therefore, this table is for guidance only. There will be some instances when a road traffic/policing officer should be consulted to confirm matters.

Appendix 2: Traffic Data—Vehicle Categories and Groups

Vehicle description	Current category	Original group/class
Motorcycles & Scooters[14]	A	D
3 or 4 light wheeled vehicles[15]	B1	C
Invalid carriages	B1 Limited	J
Cars[16] Cars—with trailers over 750 kg Automatic cars	B B + E B Automatic	A A B
Medium-sized Goods vehicles[17] Medium-sized Goods vehicles[18]	C1 C1 + E	A A
Large Goods vehicles[19] Large Goods vehicles[20]	C C + E	HGV 2/3 HGV 2/3
Buses[21] Buses[22] Buses[23] Buses[24]	D1 D D Limited D Limited	A PSV 3 PSV 3 PSV 4

[14] With or without sidecar.
[15] Motor tricycles or quadricycles with design speed exceeding 50 km/hr and up to 550 kg unladen weight. If they exceed 550 kg they fall into a car category—B category.
[16] Includes cars or light vans up to 8 passenger seats and up to 3500 kg.
[17] Gross vehicle weight between 3500 kg–7500 kg, with trailer **up to** 750 kg. The combined weight not to exceed 8250 kg.
[18] Gross vehicle weight between 3500 kg–7500 kg, with trailer **over** 750 kg. The combined weight not to exceed 8250 kg.
[19] Gross weight of vehicle being over 3500 kg, with trailer **up to** 750 kg.
[20] Gross weight of vehicle being over 3500 kg, with trailer **over** 750 kg.
[21] Capacity between 9 and 16 passengers—**not** used for hire reward.
[22] Any bus with more than 8 passenger seats, with trailer up to 750 kg.
[23] Vehicles limited to 16 passenger seats.
[24] Vehicles with more than 8 passenger seats, but no longer than 5.5 m.

Firearms Offences Relating to Age

Under 18 offence

- Using a firearm for a purpose not authorized by the European weapons directive (despite lawful entitlement to possess—being the holder of a firearms/shotgun certificate).
- Purchase or hire an air weapon or ammunition for an air weapon (see **8.7.1**)
- Part with possession of an air weapon or ammunition for an air weapon **subject to exceptions below** (see **8.7.2**).
- Make a gift of an air weapon or ammunition for an air weapon (see **8.7.2**).
- Sell or let on hire or hire an air weapon or ammunition for an air weapon (see **8.7.1**)
- Purchase an imitation firearm (see **8.7.1**)
- Sell an imitation firearm (see **8.7.1**)
- Have an air weapon or ammunition for an air weapon (see **8.7.2**), except if:
  - ✦ that person is under the supervision of a person of or over the age of 21;
  - ✦ member of approved rifle clubs;
  - ✦ using at authorized shooting galleries (not exceeding .23 inch calibre);
  - ✦ that person has attained the age of 14 and is on private premises with the consent of the occupier, and is under the supervision of a person of or over the age of 21, but it is an offence for the superviser to allow him to fire any missiles beyond those premises (subject to defence—below).

Notes:

As from 1 October 2007, s 34 of the Violent Crime Reduction Act 2006 inserted s 21A into the Firearms Act 1968 which makes it an offence for anyone to fire a missile beyond premises—

(1) A person commits an offence if—
    (a) he has with him an air weapon on any premises; and
    (b) he uses it for firing a missile beyond those premises.

(2) In proceedings against a person for an offence under this section it shall be a defence for him to show that the only premises into or across which the missile was fired were premises the occupier of which had consented to the firing of the missile (whether specifically or by way of a general consent).

Appendix 3: Firearms Offences Relating to Age

Under 17 offences

- Purchase or hire **any** firearm or ammunition of any other description (see **8.7.1**).
- Sell or let on hire **any** firearm or ammunition of any other description (see **8.7.1**).

Under 15 offences

In addition to offences applicable to under 17 and 18:

- Have an assembled shotgun **except** while under the supervision of a person of or over the age of 21, **or** while the shot gun is so covered with a securely fastened gun cover that it cannot be fired (see **8.2.3**).
- Make a gift of a shot gun or ammunition for a shot gun to a person under the age of 15 (see **8.2.3**).

Under 14 offences

In addition to offences applicable to under 15, 17, and 18:

- Possess s 1 firearm or ammunition (see **8.1.3**), except for:
  - ✦ use of a certificate holder, being under their instructions and for sporting purposes only.
  - ✦ a member of an approved cadet corps when engaged as a member of the corps in or in connection with drill or target shooting;
  - ✦ a person conducting or carrying on a miniature rifle or shooting gallery for air weapons or miniature rifles not exceeding .23 inch calibre;
  - ✦ using such rifles/ammunition at such a range or gallery.
- Part with possession of a s 1 firearm or ammunition to a person under 14, **subject to above exceptions** (see **8.1.3**).
- Make a gift of or lend s 1 firearm or ammunition to a person under 14 (see **8.1.3**).

Religious Dates/Events

Advisory notes: These dates are provided for guidance purposes only. Some dates may vary as the festivals are guided by the lunar calendar and some local customs may also vary the date. The religions are listed alphabetically.

	2007	2008
Buddhist		
Mahayana Buddhist New Year		22–25 January 2008
Paranirvana Day		8 February 2008
Nirvana Day (alternative date)		15 February 2008
Magha Puja Day		21 March 2008
Therevadin Buddhist New Year		20–23 April 2008
Wesak (Buddha Day)		20 May 2008
Obon (Ulambana)		13–16 July 2008
Asalha Puja Day		18 July 2008
Bodhi Day (Rohatsu)	8 December 2007	8 December 2008
Catholic		
Mary Mother of God		1 January 2008
Feast of the Holy Family	30 December 2007	28 December 2008
Blessing of the Animals (Hispanic)		17 January 2008
Corpus Christi		25 May 2008
Sacred Heart of Jesus		23 June 2008
St Benedict Day		11 July 2008
Assumption of Blessed Virgin Mary		15 August 2008
St Francis Day	4 October 2007	4 October 2008
All Souls' Day	2 November 2007	3 November 2008
Immaculate Conception of Mary	8 December 2007	8 December 2008
Feast Day—Our Lady of Guadalupe	12 December 2007	12 December 2008
Chinese		
Lunar New Year		7 February 2008

Appendix 4: Religious Dates/Events

Christian

Twelfth Night		5 January 2008
Epiphany		6 January 2008
Shrove Tuesday		5 February 2008
Ash Wednesday (Lent begins)		6 February 2008
St David's Day		1 March 2008
St Patrick's Day		17 March 2008
Palm Sunday		16 March 2008
Maundy Thursday		20 March 2008
Good Friday		21 March 2008
Easter Day		23 March 2008
St George's Day		23 April 2008
Ascension Day		1 May 2008
Whit Sunday (Pentecost)		11 May 2008
Trinity Sunday		18 May 2008
Lammas		1 August 2008
All Hallows Eve	31 October 2007	31 October 2008
St Andrew's Day	30 November 2007	30 November 2008
Advent Sunday	2 December 2007	30 November 2008
Christmas Day	25 December 2007	25 December 2008

Hindu

Vasant Panchami (Saraswati's Day)		11 February 2008
Maha Shivaratri		6 March 2008
Holi		21 March 2008
New Year		6 April 2008
Ramayana Begins		6 April 2008
Ramanavami		14 April 2008
Hanuman Jayanti		19 April 2008
Guru Purnima		Observed on full moon day in the Hindu month of Ashad
Raksha Bandhan	28 August 2007	16 August 2008
Krishna Janmashtami	4 September 2007	24 August 2008
Ganesa Chaturthi	15 September 2007	3 September 2008
Navrati 1st Day	12 October 2007	30 September 2008
Navaratri Ends	20 October 2007	8 October 2008
Dasera	21 October 2007	9 October 2008
Diwali (Deepavali)	9 November 2007	28 October 2008

Islam

Waqf al Arafa (Hajj—Pilgrimage Day)	19 December 2007	8 December 2008
Eid-al-Addha (Day of Sacrifice)	20 December 2007	11 December 2008
Muharram (Islamic New Year)		10 January 2008
Day of Ashura		19 January 2008

Mawlid-al-Nabi (Birth of Prophet)		20 March 2008
Lailat Al-Isra wa Al-Miraj (Ascension to Heaven)		30 July 2008
Lailat al Bara'ah (Night of Emancipation)		16 August 2008
Commencement of Ramadhan (Fasting)	13 September 2007	2 September 2008
Laylat el qadr	9 October 2007	27 September 2008
Jummatul Wida		
Eid Al-Fitr (Completion of Fasting)	13 October 2007	1 October 2008

Jewish

Notes: All Jewish holidays commence/start on the evening before the actual date specified, as the Jewish day actually begins at sunset on the previous night.

Rosh Chodesh Sh'vat	8 January 2008
Tu B'Shvat	22 January 2008
Rosh Chodesh Adar	8 February 2008
Shabbat Shekalim	8 March 2008
Ta'anit Esther	20 March 2008
Shabbat Zachor	15 March 2008
Purim	21 March 2008
Shushan Purim	22 March 2008
Shabbat Parah	29 March 2008
Shabbat HaChodesh	4 April 2008
Rosh Chodesh Nisan	6 April 2008
Ta'anit Bechorot	17 April 2008
Shabbat HaGadol	19 April 2008
Pesach	20 April 2008
Yom HaShoah	2 May 2008
Rosh Chodesh Iyyar	5 May 2008
Yom HaAtzma'ut	8 May 2008
Yom HaZikaron	9 May 2008
Lag B'Omer	23 May 2008
Yom Yerushalayim	2 June 2008
Rosh Chodesh Sivan	4 June 2008
Shavuot	9 June 2008
Rosh Chodesh Tamuz	3 July 2008
Tzom Tammuz	20 July 2008
Rosh Chodesh Av	2 August 2008
Shabbat Hazon	9 August 2008
Tish'a B'Av	10 August 2008
Shabbat Nachamu	16 August 2008

Appendix 4: Religious Dates/Events

Rosh Chodesh Elul		31 August 2008
Rosh Hashana	13 September 2007	30 September 2008
Tzom Gedaliah	16 September 2007	2 October 2008
Shabbat Shuva	15 September 2007	4 October 2008
Yom Kippur	22 September 2007	9 October 2008
Sukkot	27 September 2007	14 October 2008
Shmini Atzeret	4 October 2007	21 October 2008
Simchat Torah	5 October 2007	21 October 2008
Rosh Chodesh Kislev	11 November 2007	28 November 2008
Rosh Chodesh Cheshvan	12 October 2007	29 October 2008
Chanukah	5 December 2007	22 December 2008

Sikh

Birthday of Guru Gobind Singh Ji		5 January 2008
Maghi		13/14 January 2008
Hola Mohalla		22 March 2008
Baisakhi (Vaisakhi)		13/14 April 2008
Martyrdom of Guru Arjan Dev Ji		16 June 2008
Installation of Scriptures as Guru Granth	20 October 2007	20 October 2008
Diwali (Deepavali)	9 November 2007	28 October 2008
Birthday of Guru Nanak Dev Ji	24 November 2007	13 November 2008
Martyrdom of Guru Tegh Bahadur Ji	24 November 2007	24 November 2008

Baha'l

World Religion Day		21 January 2008
Naw-Rúz (New Year)		21 March 2008
First Day of Ridvan		21 April 2008
Last Day of Ridvan		2 May 2008
Declaration of the Bab		23 May 2008
Ascension of Baha'u'llah		29 May 2008
Martyrdom of the Bab		9 July 2008
Birth of the B'ab	20 October 2007	20 October 2008
Birth of Baha'u'llah	12 November 2007	12 November 2008
Day of the Covenant	26 November 2007	26 November 2008
Ascension of 'Abdu'l-Baha	28 November 2007	28 November 2008

Jehovah's Witness

Lord's Evening Meal		22 March 2008

Index

Index

Index

Index

Index

Index

Index

Index

Index

Index

Index

Index

Index

Index

Index

Index

Index

Index

Index

Index